World History
in the Twentieth Century

R. D. Cornwell, M.A.

Headmaster,
Pilgrim School, Bedford

LONGMAN

LONGMAN GROUP LIMITED

Longman House, Burnt Mill, Harlow, Essex, UK

© *Longman Group Ltd (formerly Longmans, Green & Co. Ltd) 1969, 1980*

First published 1969
New edition 1980

Paper Edition: ISBN 0 582 33075.0
Cased edition: ISBN 0 582 33074.2

Printed in Great Britain by Spottiswoode Ballantyne Limited, Colchester

Acknowledgements

For permission to reproduce photographs we are grateful to the following: BBC Hulton
Picture Library, pages 17 *below*, 90 *below*, 406 *above left*, 517 *above left*; Camera Press,
pages 126 *above* (photo: Jevan Berrange), 289 *below* (photo: G. Perez), 406 *below* (photo:
Sarah Webb Barrell), 428 *below left* and *below right*, 441 (photo: Rory Dell); Imperial
War Museum, London, pages 17 *above*, 90 *above*; Keystone, pages 34 *above*, 34 *below
right*, 186 *above left*, 195 *above*, 239 *above*, 360 *above*, 374 *above right*, 374 *below*, 406 *above
right*, 471 *above*, 495 *below right*; Mansell Collection, pages 34 *below left*, 65 *below*, 139
above left; Popperfoto, pages, 65 *above*, 126 *below*, 139 *above right* and *below*, 186 *above
right* and *below*, 195 *below*, 239 *below*, 289 *above*, 325 *above* (UPI) and *below* (UPI), 360
below, 374 *above left*, 428 *above*, 495 *above* and *below left*, 517 *above right* and *below*; Sony,
page 471 *below*; United Nations, page 541 *above* and *below* (Y. Nagata).
Page 460 based on map from Williams: *World History Vol. 3*, Edward Arnold (Publishers)
Ltd; pages 26, 71, 460 based on maps from Gilbert: *Recent History Atlas*, Weidenfeld,
George & Nicholson Ltd.

Contents

4   Russia

5 United States of America

6 Great Britain

7   North Africa and the Middle East

8   Africa

9   The Indian Subcontinent

10   China

11 Japan

12 South-East Asia

13 Central and South America

14 World Organisations

List of Maps and Diagrams

Maps

Diagrams

I

Europe 1900 to 1919

Beginning of the Twentieth Century

The world of 1900 was dominated by the small continent of Europe. Scientific and industrial knowledge, combined with military and naval power, gave its 400 million people overwhelming political influence and a higher standard of living than most of the world's population.

Of the twenty independent states seven could claim the title of Great Power. These were: Russia, Germany, Austria-Hungary, Great Britain, France, Italy and the Turkish Empire. Germany and Italy were relatively new states, having been formed thirty years before, but Germany, because of her large population and her industrial and military might, was probably the strongest country on the Continent. Great Britain, however, was the most powerful country in the world, her strength being based on her Empire which included one quarter of the world's population and land area, her sea power—the British royal and merchant navies controlled the seas—and her industries.

Only two (France and Switzerland) of the twenty countries were republics; in the others monarchs ruled with varying degrees of power, ranging from the absolute dictatorships of the Tsar of Russia and the Sultan of Turkey to the dignified constitutional monarchy of Queen Victoria in Great Britain. Only Russia, Turkey and the tiny, mountainous state of Montenegro had no parliament.

The frontiers of European states were fixed with little regard for differences of race, language or religion, and consequently nationalism was proving one of the major problems. For example, Austria-Hungary contained Germans, Magyars, Czechs, Poles, Slovaks and Serbs; European Russia contained Finns, Estonians, Lithuanians, Poles and Romanians; and the Turks still ruled Albanians, Greeks, Serbs and Bulgars. Norwegian nationalism led to the separation of Norway from

Sweden in 1905, and Ireland was pressing for independence from Great Britain. Nationalism in south-east Europe was to prove highly dangerous to the peace of the continent.

The Great Powers 1900 to 1914[1]

Germany   The industrial achievements of Germany inevitably gave her a dominating position in Europe, and led to intense economic rivalry with Great Britain. This economic prosperity was largely the work of the German middle classes, who, having failed to secure any substantial political power, concentrated on industry and trade. The constitution gave vast authority to the Kaiser, and through him to the Chancellor and the Army. The Reichstag counted for little, partly because there were too many parties which were based on class interests rather than clear principles, but mainly because the government was not responsible to it.

The Chancellor was the head of the German government and was responsible only to the Emperor. From 1900 to 1909 von Bülow held the post. A man of conservative views, he believed that the German people were intellectually and temperamentally unfit for self-government and therefore needed the guidance of a strong executive. He was succeeded until 1914 by Bethmann-Hollweg, a well-meaning but plodding politician who did not have the strength of personality to control Kaiser William II (1888–1918).

William's character was complicated. Energetic and restless, erratic and impulsive, melodramatic and exhibitionist, he bewildered diplomats. His rash and boastful statements added considerably to the tension which built up in Europe before 1914. In 1900 he spoke favourably of the Huns and their reputation for terror, and said, 'In the future no great decisions in the world will be taken without Germany and the German Emperor.' In 1908 an interview with William II appeared in the London *Daily Telegraph*. Beginning with 'You English are mad, mad as March hares', it went on to offend Russia, France and Japan. Despite his many tactless statements, the Kaiser was in fact an intelligent man who meant well, and his second thoughts on subjects were usually sensible. But 'his impetuous interventions' into public affairs aroused resentment and tension.

France   In contrast to those of Germany, the governments of the Third French Republic were generally unstable. The constitution had made

[1] Russia and Great Britain are dealt with in chapters 4 and 6 respectively.

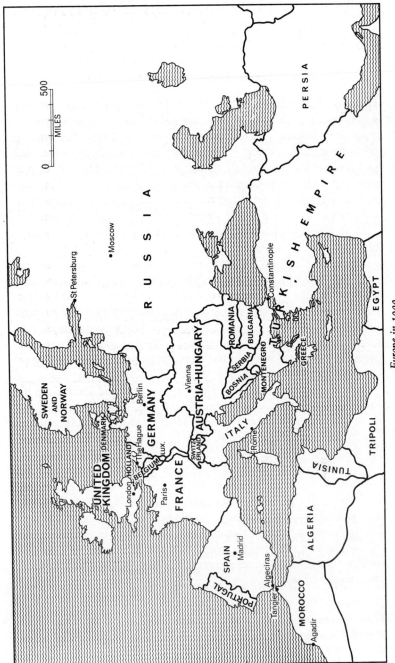

Europe in 1900

the executive weak and the legislature strong, and the latter contained too many parties which had sectional rather than national interests at heart. In general there was too much individualism in politics and too little willingness to compromise.

In addition a series of crises lowered the reputation of the republic. Boulanger, an army officer, had nearly become dictator in the 1880s, and this was followed by a major financial scandal involving the Panama Canal Company and several politicians. In 1900 France was just recovering from the shock of the melodramatic Dreyfus Affair. Dreyfus, a Jewish officer in the French Army, was wrongly sentenced by a military court to solitary confinement on Devil's Island. The exposure of this miscarriage of justice involved the honour of the army, which was supported by all conservative and monarchist groups in France, and opposed by republicans and radicals. Violent political feelings were aroused, and the whole episode dragged on for twelve years until 1906.

The Dreyfus Affair was followed by an outburst of anti-clericalism. In 1901 a law was passed which forced every religious order to apply for legal authorisation; later no member of a religious order was allowed to teach. The campaign against the Roman Catholic Church only died down after 1905 when the Church was disestablished.

The political crises and anti-clericalism so dominated politics that little social legislation was passed, and one consequence of this was an outbreak of strikes and violence after 1906. These were crushed ruthlessly, for on the whole France was a prosperous and largely conservative country. Socialist parties were weak and divided, and indeed after 1906 the nationalist right wing grew stronger. This did not, however, lead to an aggressive foreign policy. France was not warlike, and in 1913 it was only after a struggle that the government managed to increase military service from two to three years.

Austria-Hungary The Dual Monarchy of Austria and Hungary had been established in 1867. The two countries had separate governments, but under one Emperor had a common army, financial system and foreign policy. But there was continual pessimism regarding the future, for the Empire seemed always on the verge of dissolution. The Austrians and the Magyars (who often did not cooperate) ruled too many different races. Particularly, there was increasing pressure from the Slavs, either for the Empire to become a federal state or for them to leave, probably to join Serbia. As this Slav nationalism grew, and the government remained feeble and confused, so the problems and tensions in 'this ramshackle Empire' increased. It was generally believed that when the Emperor Francis Joseph (1848–1916) died, the Empire would collapse.

Italy Italy, like Germany, was one of the new states of Europe, but, unlike Germany, remained politically and economically weak with only pretensions to the status of a Great Power. Politically, Italy possessed few honest politicians and competent administrators and too many political parties; the result was unstable governments. Economically the country lacked material resources, and there was general poverty, especially in the south, which led to an outbreak of strikes and violence in the 1900s. In addition the Italian State and the Roman Catholic Church were at loggerheads.

Turkish Empire The Turkish Empire is partly dealt with in chapter 7 on the Middle East, where the Asiatic parts of the Empire and the growth of German influence are described. Turkey had for long been 'the sick man of Europe'. With the decline in law and order the Empire was crumbling, and its European parts in 1900 were reduced to Albania, Macedonia and Thrace, and, nominally, Bosnia and Bulgaria. Since 1876 Turkey had been ruled by Sultan Abdul Hamid II, an able, shrewd and powerful man whose government deteriorated into a regime of secrecy and terror. Living constantly in fear of assassination,[1] he was suspicious of everybody. After the massacres of Christian Armenians during the 1890s, Gladstone called him the 'Great Assassin' and Clemenceau referred to him as the 'Red Sultan'. 'He was responsible for murder and torture on a scale which, until the advent of Hitler, the world had not seen for centuries.'[2]

This harsh yet unsuccessful regime produced growing discontent, especially among young army officers, who supported the Young Turks organisation. This body wanted to end the humiliation of continual European intervention in Turkish affairs, and wished to set up a liberal constitution. In 1908 the Young Turks gained control of Constantinople, and Abdül Hamid became overnight a constitutional monarch. The change was too sudden, and in the following year the Sultan backed a counter-revolution. This failed and Abdul Hamid was deposed in favour of his brother. The Young Turks, however, proved no more successful than Abdul Hamid II in solving the problems of Turkey.

[1] 'It had needed all the ingenuity of a French electrical company to persuade Abdul Hamid that the dynamos were not connected with dynamite and that there was no risk of his being blown up at night if he had electricity installed in his palace.' J. Haslip, *The Sultan.*

[2] H. Nicolson, *The Observer,* 16 Nov. 1958.

International affairs 1900 to 1914

European alliances In 1900 five of the European Great Powers were divided into two armed camps. One camp consisted of the Central Powers, Germany, Austria-Hungary and Italy, who, under the guidance of Bismarck, had formed the Triple Alliance in 1882. The important point of this alliance was that Germany and Austria would help each other against a Russian attack on either of them. The other camp consisted of France and Russia whose alliance was made in 1894. These two countries promised mutual help in the event of a German attack on either of them. Of the other major powers, Great Britain was isolated, and the Turkish Empire was too feeble to have any coherent policy other than the traditional one of playing off one enemy against another.

By 1904, however, two developments had taken place: Italy had virtually left the Triple Alliance, and Great Britain had reached agreement with France on colonial issues. It was clearly in French interests for Italy to be separated from the Triple Alliance; Italy, on the other hand, wanted French support for an Italian occupation of Tripoli. In 1900, therefore, a secret agreement gave Italian approval for a French occupation of Morocco and French approval for an Italian conquest of Tripoli. Two years later Italy became an ineffective member of the Triple Alliance when she gave France a secret assurance that Italy would remain neutral if France was attacked.

The deliberate policy of Britain until about 1896 was one of 'splendid isolation'. Thereafter, for a variety of reasons, a sense of insecurity developed. Relations with France had become increasingly bitter because of colonial disputes in Siam (Thailand) and at Fashoda (see p. 265). British influence in the Middle East and the security of the Indian frontiers seemed to be threatened by Russian expansion in Persia and Afghanistan and the growing German interest in the Turkish Empire (see pp. 268-9). It appeared that Germany, hitherto a land power, was trying also to rival British naval power, for in 1898 and 1900 two Navy Laws provided for a large programme of shipbuilding. Events in South Africa only served to emphasise British isolation. In 1896, following the failure of the Jameson Raid (see p. 332) on the Transvaal, the Kaiser sent a telegram to Kruger congratulating him on the Boers' success. Later, when the Boer War broke out, British action was widely condemned by a hostile Europe.

Britain therefore decided to break her isolation and look for allies. Germany was approached twice, in 1898 and 1901, but public opinion in both countries was hostile, Germany's terms were too unrealistic, and negotiations petered out. This failure in negotiations with Germany, together with the rapidly developing strength of Japan, made an alliance with the latter attractive, and this was eventually concluded in 1902 (see p. 462). But since Japan was increasingly hostile towards Russia, and France was the ally of Russia, the Anglo-Japanese Alliance gave added incentive to Britain and France to reach an agreement. The right atmosphere for negotiations was provided by the visits of Edward VII to Paris and the French President to London. In 1904 agreement was reached on spheres of influence in Morocco and Egypt (see p. 267) and on other colonial disputes, and so began the Entente Cordiale and a long period of at least friendly relations if not always of cooperation.

By 1904, therefore, Germany's international position had seriously deteriorated. Italy was no longer a reliable ally, Austria-Hungary was facing serious internal difficulties, and Great Britain had reached a colonial agreement (although she had not made an alliance) with France.

In order to test the strength of this Anglo-French agreement, a most unwilling Kaiser was persuaded by Bülow to visit Tangier in 1905 (see p. 267). This first Moroccan crisis was deliberately provocative, but the results for Germany were unfavourable. At the Algeciras Conference in 1906, Germany was supported only by Austria, and Anglo-French relations were strengthened by an agreement that military and naval staff conversations should take place. In the following year, too, Britain reached agreement with Russia[1] over Persia, Afghanistan and Tibet (see p. 269).

Britain's agreements with France and Russia were far from being military alliances. But Germany's rapid naval building and aggressive diplomacy forced Britain into closer links with France. The Kaiser probably believed that a strong German navy would deter Britain from entering a continental war. He said publicly that a large navy was essential for the prestige of a Great Power and that the German navy had been created solely for that reason and not as a threat to British naval supremacy. Britain considered, however, that a German navy could only be directed against her, and therefore a naval building race was started which was not only expensive but served to heighten tension.

In 1911 the second Moroccan crisis erupted when the German gunboat *Panther* visited Agadir on the Atlantic Coast (see p. 267). The firm British attitude was of decisive importance, and again the solidarity of the British entente with France was shown.

The Balkans The division of Europe into two groups, the arms race between them and the crises in Morocco, all contributed to a situation capable of provoking a European war. The crisis which eventually

1 Thus was formed the Triple Entente of Britain, France and Russia.

caused the outbreak of war in 1914 was the culmination of a series of events in the Balkans.

South-east Europe had been a trouble spot throughout the nineteenth century because of the rivalry between Austria, Russia and the national-ist groups in the Balkans to take over the area from the weakening Turkish Empire. Between 1897 and 1908 Austria and Russia temporarily ceased their rivalry by agreeing to renounce any conquests should the Balkans be disturbed. But by 1908 both countries were again ready to pursue their ambitions in this part of Europe. As far as Russia was con-cerned, expansion in China had been stopped by the Japanese victories in 1904–5, and expansion into Persia and Afghanistan had been limited by agreement with Britain in 1907. There was also the need to divert attention from problems at home and to recover some of the prestige lost at the hands of Japan. In addition the supporters of Pan-Slavism (a vague term usually meaning the union of the Slavs of south-east Europe with those of Russia) were putting pressure on the government.

Austria, too, had decided by 1908 that action was required in the Balkans. Racial problems inside her empire were worsening. Serbia, a small, independent Slav state, was the centre of a strong Slav nationalist movement. Two alternative policies faced the Austrian government: either to allow the Slavs to leave the empire, or to expand Austrian frontiers to include Serbia and other troublesome Slav groups. The first alternative was rejected because it would mean the disintegration of the Habsburg empire, and therefore the second was adopted. This second policy would arouse the opposition of Russia, but Austria believed that if Germany supported her, there was the strong possibility that Russia would remain content with only verbal opposition.

The Young Turk Revolution of 1908 provided both Austria and Russia with the opportunity to resume their activities in the Balkans. The revolution meant the possibility of a strong and modern govern-ment in Turkey, and therefore, before it could become established, Austria and Russia met and agreed that Austria should annex Bosnia and Herzegovina,[1] while Russia should have freedom to move her warships through the Dardanelles and the Bosphorus to the Mediter-ranean. Soon after this Austria announced the annexation of the two provinces, while Bulgaria declared herself fully independent of Turkey, but Russia could get no international support, even from Britain and France, for her plan for the Straits.

Austria's action produced a ferment in the Balkans, and aroused intense opposition from a bitter Serbia and a frustrated Russia. But

[1] The two provinces had been administered by Austria since 1878, but they remained legally part of the Turkish Empire.

Germany gave Austria firm support, and this was decisive for Russia would not risk another war so soon after her defeat in the Far East. The whole episode had left Russia humiliated and Serbia (who had hoped to occupy Bosnia and Herzegovina herself) frustrated. But, even more important, Germany had encouraged Austria-Hungary to repeat her expansionist policy despite the provocation this would be to Russia and Serbia. In 1909 the Chief of the German General Staff went so far as to promise his opposite number in Austria that if Austria invaded Serbia and in consequence Russia helped Serbia, Germany would come to Austria's assistance.

For the next three years there was an uneasy peace in the Balkans. Then, prompted by the second Moroccan crisis, Italy invaded Tripoli in 1911. The Italian success in this last part of the Turkish Empire in North Africa encouraged the Balkan states to plan the partition of the remaining Turkish provinces in Europe, and in March 1912 the Balkan League was formed. This consisted at first of Serbia and Bulgaria who were soon joined by Greece and Montenegro. In October the League attacked and rapidly overwhelmed the Turks in the first Balkan War (1912–13).

The problem of the exact allocation of the newly conquered territories now arose. Serbia was supported by Russia in wanting to occupy Albania in order to have an Adriatic coastline. But Austria feared that this would make Serbia too strong, and insisted that Albania should become an independent state. Again, Germany supported Austria. In December 1912 Bethmann-Hollweg said, 'If Austria in the course of securing her vital interests . . . is attacked by Russia, Germany would fight.' Austria won her case. After the Conference of Ambassadors in London in May 1913 the Treaty of London was signed. Turkey in Europe was reduced to the area around Constantinople, the new state of Albania was formed, and the other Balkan states divided up Macedonia between them.

The division of Macedonia, however, did not satisfy Bulgaria, who suddenly attacked Serbia and Greece. But Bulgaria was herself attacked by Turkey and Romania, and was quickly defeated. The second Balkan War was ended by the Treaty of Bucharest in August 1913 by the terms of which Bulgaria lost territory to her neighbours.

The climax to these events in the Balkans occurred about a year later in the small mountain town of Sarajevo in Bosnia. On Sunday 28 June 1914 the Archduke Francis Ferdinand, nephew and heir to Francis Joseph, was assassinated by a Bosnian Serb named Princip. The murder was planned in Belgrade by the Black Hand, a secret society whose leader was also the head of military intelligence at the

Serbian war office. It has never been clear, however, whether the Serbian government knew of the plot.

South-east Europe after the Second Balkan War

The immediate Austrian reaction was to see in this event an opportunity to eliminate Serbia as an independent state. It was decided to partition Serbia between Bulgaria, Austria and Albania. But since Russia would probably support Serbia, it was first necessary to obtain an assurance of German backing. On 5 July the Austrian envoy was received by the Kaiser at Potsdam. William, who was angry at the death of his friend, the Archduke Francis Ferdinand, agreed to German support for Austria, the decision being made hurriedly, without any detailed discussion of the consequences. Bethmann-Hollweg was told of the Austrian request, and agreed to the Kaiser's reply, during a brief walk around the palace grounds. Other members of the German government and the heads of the armed services were not involved or consulted.

Austria then began to plan the ultimatum to Serbia. This was finally delivered on 23 July, and contained various harsh demands, including a request that Austrian officials should be allowed to enter Serbia to suppress the anti-Austrian agitation. Everybody believed that the demands were unacceptable, and Russia began to plan partial mobilisation. But the Serbian reply was conciliatory: some demands were accepted, and Serbia offered to submit the others to the International Court at The Hague.

Europe had generally believed that this Balkans crisis, like the previous ones, would be settled by a compromise, and that a European war could not come. This view now seemed confirmed. 'No reasons for going to war now exist,' wrote the Kaiser. Britain suggested a conference to negotiate a settlement. But Austria did not want a diplomatic solution, and, declaring the reply to her ultimatum unsatisfactory, she declared war on Serbia on 28 July 1914, and almost immediately began a bombardment of Belgrade.

The Russian attitude was now of decisive importance. Despite considerable misgivings, Russia felt that she had to support Serbia or else suffer further humiliation. Without Russian assistance not only would Serbia, a Slav nation, disappear, but the Central Powers would control the Straits since Romania, Bulgaria and Turkey supported Germany and Austria-Hungary. A French state visit to Russia had ended just before the Austrian ultimatum to Serbia, and French support for Russia seemed probable. Therefore, believing that German mobilisation was imminent, on 31 July the crucial decision ordering general mobilisation in Russia was made public.

It was not clear during these last few days of peace in Europe whether the Kaiser, the Chancellor or the army controlled German policy. Certainly there was a dangerous lack of coordination. It is probable that all were desperately worried about the situation and wanted to avoid war, but felt that if war had to come it was better in 1914 when Germany was strong than later. When the news of Russian mobilisation arrived, it was thought essential that Germany should strike first.

Accordingly, the German Army mobilised and on 1 August Germany declared war on Russia.

Germany had no quarrel with France, but because of the Franco-Russian Alliance, the German Army had for years planned a war against both France and Russia. Training and mobilisation were based on the Schlieffen Plan (drawn up in 1892) which envisaged a six-week offensive through Belgium to crush France before a general attack on Russia. There was no alternative plan, and therefore a quarrel with France was essential. The Germans first sent an ultimatum demanding French neutrality. When no direct reply came, Germany manufactured charges of French attacks on Germany, and on 3 August declared war on France.

During the summer of 1914 Britain was involved with the Irish crisis, and the Liberal Government and the country as a whole were not prepared for a European War. Opinion was divided on whether Britain should support France or not. The issue which united Britain against Germany was the German demand for free passage for their forces through Belgium, internationally acknowledged as a neutral country. The Belgians refused, and on 4 August Germany invaded Belgium. The British government then demanded a German withdrawal from Belgium before midnight. No answer was received, and therefore on 4 August Britain declared war on Germany.

Thus, after a period of general peace longer than any in its history, Europe was at war. 'The lamps are going out all over Europe,' said Sir Edward Grey, the British Foreign Secretary, 'we shall not see them lit again in our lifetime.'

First World War 1914 to 1918

The Contestants

The Central Powers consisted of Germany, Austria-Hungary, Turkey and Bulgaria. The last two countries entered the war in October 1914 and September 1915 respectively. German influence had been strong in the Turkish Empire since the beginning of the century, and, partly persuaded by the presence of a German battle cruiser opposite Constantinople, Turkey decided to join the Central Powers. Bulgaria joined in the hope of gaining the territory she had failed to win during the Balkan wars. Of the four states Germany was clearly the senior partner with an army of 5 million men, twice the size of that of Austria-Hungary.

The Central Powers were eventually opposed by nine states: Russia, France, Britain, Italy, the United States, Belgium, Serbia, Romania and Greece.[1] Italy was at first a neutral country, but decided to enter the war in the belief that this was an opportunity to gain territory in north-east Italy that was still ruled by Austria-Hungary. Therefore Britain, France and Italy signed in secret the Treaty of London in April 1915 by which

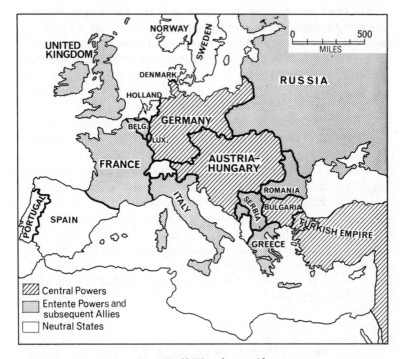

First World War: the two sides

Italy agreed to enter the war against the Central Powers in return for this territory after the war. In the following month Italy declared war. The attitude of the United States to events in Europe is given in more detail in chapter 5. Most Americans in 1914 wanted their country to remain neutral, and President Wilson saw himself as a peacemaker. For the next three years the United States gave increasing moral support and valuable material aid to Britain and France, and in April 1917 entered the war on their side.

[1] Romania and Greece, who declared war on the Central Powers in 1916 and 1917 respectively, played little part in events.

Russia had the largest but probably the worst trained and equipped army of all the countries involved in the First World War. France and her empire had in 1914 an army of 4 million men, while Britain's army was only a quarter of a million strong and half of these were overseas, leaving only 100,000 available for the defence of Belgium. The generals on both sides had seen little active service, and military strategy and tactics tended to be based on theory rather than practice. Both Britain and Germany had built up huge navies by 1914. The British navy was the stronger, having twenty dreadnoughts to Germany's thirteen, but it had more to defend: a world-wide empire and its connecting sea routes. The defeat of the British navy would have stopped the seaborne trade and this would almost certainly have led to a rapid British defeat. Air forces developed during the war. They were first used for reconnaissance and later for attacking enemy positions.

Initially the peoples of Europe showed a remarkable enthusiasm for this war. There were 3 million volunteers for the British army, and Rupert Brooke could exclaim: 'Now God be thanked who has matched us with His hour.' Amidst growing ignorance because of the censorship[1] of military news, the young men of Europe went to war almost cheerfully. They were soon to be disillusioned.

The Western Front

At the start of the First World War the German armies operated according to the Schlieffen Plan. Since the Franco-German frontier was heavily guarded, the strong right wing of the German army was to move through Belgium and to the west of Paris. It would then circle eastwards while small German armies attacked across the Rhine, so surrounding the French armies. This was the theory; in practice the plan did not succeed.

The German progress through Belgium, although fast, was nevertheless hindered by the stubborn Belgian defence and the destruction of railways which held up German reinforcements and supplies. This enabled the British Expeditionary Force (BEF) under Sir John French to take up its position at Mons on the left of the French line. German pressure pushed the French back, however, so the British also retreated in order to maintain contact with their allies, and the two armies took

---

[1] The result was that rumours flourished. 'A hundred thousand (or according to other accounts, a million) Russian troops were reported to have landed at Aberdeen, and passed through England on their way to the Western Front. Everyone knew some other person who had seen them; many claimed even to have seen the snow on their boots.' A. J. P. Taylor, *The First World War*.

up new positions north of Paris. The Germans then decided to attack Paris from the north, and early in September their armies crossed the Marne. The critical Battle of the Marne was then fought, the German advance was halted and the Germans withdrew to the River Aisne. Both sides then raced for the Channel coast in order to gain control of the ports, and there was fierce fighting around Ypres in Flanders.

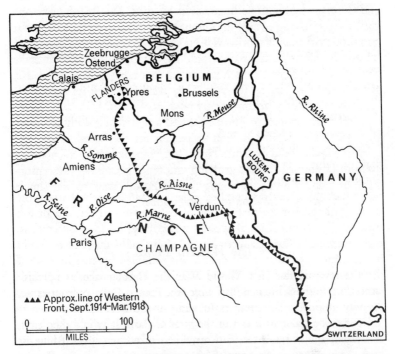

The Western Front, 1914–18

The end of 1914 found a continuous front from the sea just south of Ostend to the Alps. The war of movement ended and, with no flank to be turned, both sides dug an intricate system of trenches, so that a war of attrition became almost inevitable. Major operations were suspended during the winter while the armies recovered and developed their resources. The British, who held only thirty miles of the front, slowly organised for war, while the French, who were responsible for 400 miles of the front, took the burden of the allied effort. In 1915 the Germans decided to concentrate their efforts on attacking Russia in the east while defending the Western Front. Therefore, the year was largely taken up with French and British attacks on strong German defences in depth protected by barbed wire and machine gun posts. Some ground was gained, but there was never any likelihood of a breakthrough.[1] At the end of 1915 Sir Douglas Haig replaced French as the Commander of the British forces. Haig, an extremely competent and hard-working staff officer, was a soldier of great courage and self-confidence but lacked flexibility and original ideas.

Between February and July 1916 the Germans attacked Verdun, the famous fortress on a salient in the French line. Von Falkenhayn, the German Chief of Staff, probably intended to inflict heavy casualties on the French because there was no great value in taking Verdun itself. And heavy casualties there were. The French lost over 300,000, the Germans slightly fewer, in 'the mincing machine of Verdun'.[2] General Pétain promised the French people that 'they shall not pass' and, despite the horror and the slaughter, the German failure to capture the city almost seemed a French victory.

German pressure on Verdun, which was relaxing anyway, was sharply reduced in July by a major British offensive near the River Somme. This was preceded by the usual artillery bombardment which, while it could be heard a hundred miles away in Kent, took away the element of surprise, so that on the first day of the attack the British suffered 60,000 casualties of whom 20,000 were killed. Nevertheless, there were initial British successes and about eight miles of tactically insignificant ground was won. This was followed by two months of desperate, costly and inconclusive fighting. In September the British experimented with the tank but there were not enough to be effective. Heavy rain during the autumn stopped the offensive.

Over 1,600,000 casualties were suffered by both sides in the fighting at Verdun and the Somme, and the vision of corpses sprawled across barbed wire became the popular image of the Western Front. Robert Graves, the English poet, who fought in the war, later wrote:

From the winter of 1914 to the winter of 1918, the French and Flemish trenches were our homes, our prisons, our graveyards. And what were they like? Like air-raid shelters hastily dug in a muddy field, fenced by a tangle of barbed wire, surrounded by enormous craters; subjected not only to an incessant air-raid of varying intensity, but to constant surprise attacks by professional killers, and without any

---

[1] The British failure during the spring offensives was blamed on the shortage of shells. Therefore munition workers were encouraged to work harder and so public houses were shut during the afternoons, a restriction which still remains.
[2] A. J. P. Taylor, *The First World War*.

'The Menin Road' by Paul Nash, an official war artist who revealed to the British public the horror and desolation of the Western Front

The big three, Clemenceau, Wilson and Lloyd George, at the Paris Peace Conference, 1919

protection against flooding in times of heavy rain. No trees; no birds; no crops; no flowers, except an occasional rash of wild poppies; no wild animals except rats.[1]

The idealism present in 1914 had now become disillusionment.

During the last few weeks of 1916 there were changes in the leadership of Austria-Hungary and Britain. The death of Francis Joseph, the Austrian Emperor since 1848, occurred in November, and in the following month Asquith was replaced by the energetic Lloyd George as British Prime Minister (see chapter 6). Neither change had any immediate effect on the conduct of the war. In March 1917 the Germans withdrew to a carefully prepared line of defences known as the Hindenburg Line. During the rest of the year there were further British and French offensives. In April the British, in a highly successful surprise attack, captured the vital Vimy ridge near Arras. The French under Nivelle, a new and over-confident commander, attacked with disappointing results in Champagne. The French army, suffering from heavy casualties and poor arrangements for the wounded, lost faith in its leaders and mutinied. Fortunately for the Allies, the Germans did not realise the situation until after the mutiny ended. During the late summer of 1917 a British offensive in Flanders began with the dramatic mining of Messines Hill south of Ypres (the explosion was heard in No. 10 Downing Street) and ended in the usual clinging mud. The battle was popularly known as Passchendaele, the name of a village near Ypres.

In April 1917 the United States declaration of war on Germany greatly strengthened the morale of Britain and France. (The reasons for the American action are given in chapter 5.) By the end of the year, however, the American army was not yet trained and ready in effective numbers, while Britain and France had suffered heavy casualties. The collapse of Russia (see chapter 4) meant the transfer of German divisions from the Eastern to the Western Front. The Germans realised that this was their last chance. The British naval blockade of Germany was very effective and was causing grave shortages, while the German submarine campaign had failed. The Germans had to attack and win in the west while they had numerical superiority and before they were strangled economically by the blockade.

In March 1918 the German offensive began. Profiting by fog and the surprise caused by an attack which was not preceded by a preliminary bombardment, the Germans crushed the British resistance and gained forty miles of territory. In this critical situation, Foch, the French General, was appointed Commander-in-Chief of the Allied armies in

[1] Article in *The Observer*, 1958.

order to achieve coordination of effort. At the end of May the French were successfully attacked and the Germans were once more on the Marne. From seventy miles away an enormous German gun, 'Big Bertha', bombarded Paris.

The Allied armies, though pushed back, were not broken, however, and the Germans had lost irreplaceable men in this final effort. In mid-July Britain, France and the United States, now superior in numbers, counterattacked, and on 8 August there began a general offensive all along the front. This was 'the black day of the war' for the Germans who from this point onwards realised that they could not win. Early in October the British broke through the Hindenburg Line, and this convinced the German generals that the war was lost. Negotiations for an armistice were started through President Wilson of the United States. Finally at 11 a.m. on 11 November 1918, with the German army steadily retreating and with only a small area of France still in German hands, the guns of the First World War were silenced.

The Eastern Front

Fighting on the Eastern Front began with the Russian invasion of East Prussia and Austria. After initial Russian successes, German troops were hurried from the Western Front and successfully stopped the Russian 'steam-roller' at the Battles of Tannenberg and the Masurian Lakes. Thousands of Russian soldiers were drowned in the lakes and swamps of this part of East Prussia, and nearly 100,000 were taken prisoner. The Germans under Field Marshal von Hindenburg then invaded Russian Poland, and the Russian Army, whose training and equipment were totally inadequate, suffered colossal losses. Apart from some successes against the Austrians, the year 1915 was similarly a year of disaster for the Russians. Their soldiers, many of whom fought without rifles, lost ground the size of France. The Germans gained success after success and captured vast quantities of men and equipment. Warsaw was captured and the Russians were cleared from Poland and Lithuania.

Russia had equally vast reserves of men, however, and during the summer of 1916 began under General Brusilov an offensive against the Austrians which had dramatic success. The Germans again had to divert men from the west to maintain the Austrian army whose front had been smashed. The Russian advance was eventually halted, and in addition Romania, who had declared war on the Central Powers in 1916, was overrun by the Germans.

The events of 1917 in Russia are described in chapter 4. Despite the abdication of the Tsar in March and the confused situation at home, the

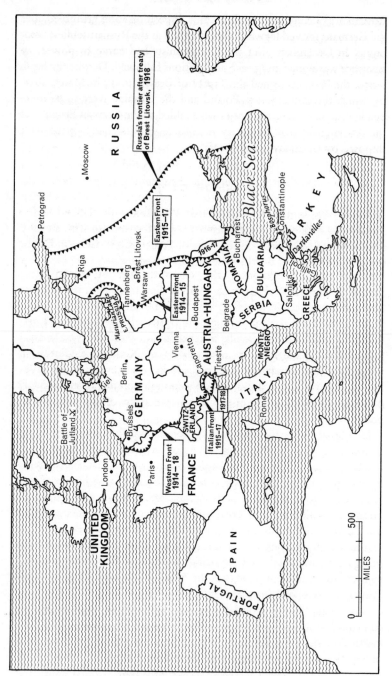

Europe during the First World War

Russian army continued to fight. But opposition soon crumbled, and the Germans moved forward almost at will as the Russian soldiers went home. In December, after the Communists had come to power, an armistice was signed and peace negotiations followed. Despite the harsh terms, the Russians signed the Treaty of Brest Litovsk in March 1918, by which the Baltic States, Poland and the Ukraine were to be independent. In fact, these territories were added to the German Empire for the few months that the treaty held force. Similar harsh terms were imposed by Germany on Romania.

South-east Europe

When the fighting in northern France reached deadlock at the end of 1914, some military strategists conceived the idea of turning the German flank by an attack in south-east Europe. This idea had three additional advantages to recommend it. A successful Allied attack in this region would at best knock Turkey out of the war and at least would cut off the Turkish armies in the Middle East from German supplies. More assistance could also be given to Serbia and possibly to Russia, particularly if free passage through the Dardanelles and the Bosphorus could be obtained. Churchill, Kitchener and Asquith were mainly responsible for the idea of an attack on the Gallipoli peninsula. If properly planned and executed, it could have achieved its objectives, but the British Cabinet did not give enough consideration to details of strategy, and the organisation and leadership of the attack were poor.

In February 1915 the British navy bombarded the outer forts of the Dardanelles. This removed the element of surprise so that a naval attack in March to force a passage through the narrow straits failed because of well-prepared Turkish defences in the form of mines and shore batteries. In April and August British, New Zealand and Australian troops landed on the Gallipoli peninsula. Their numbers were always inadequate, and the Turks held their dominating positions from which they could fire on the landing beaches. By the autumn it was clear that no progress was being made, and Kitchener, the British Minister of War, recommended an evacuation. In December 1915 the Allied troops were skilfully withdrawn, the one well-managed operation of the whole campaign.

'The Gallipoli expedition was a terrible example of an ingenious strategical idea carried through after inadequate preparation and with inadequate drive.'[1] 'We have always sent two-thirds of what was necessary a month too late,' said Churchill. The Allied troops from

[1] A. J. P. Taylor, *The First World War.*

Gallipoli were taken to Salonika, and for 2½ years half a million men remained there serving no useful purpose. Indeed the Germans called Salonika 'their largest internment camp'. Serbia, after repulsing two Austrian attempts to crush her, was finally overrun by a combined German, Austrian and Bulgarian attack in October 1915. In 1918 the Allied armies in Salonika moved north with considerable success, and had reached the Danube when the armistice was signed.

Italy

The Italian declaration of war on the Allied side diverted Austrian forces from the Russian front to north Italy. For two years the Austrians held the mountains and the Italians approaching from the plain made a series of fruitless attacks. In 1917, however, fighting on the Eastern Front ended with the collapse of Russia, and seven German divisions were transferred from Russia to northern Italy. In October the Italians were overwhelmed at the Battle of Caporetto, north of Trieste, and lost a quarter of a million men and large quantities of supplies. The British and French rushed in reinforcements and the Allied line was held north of Venice. Nevertheless, Italian morale was shaken, and disillusionment with the war set in to remain until after the war had ended.

The War at sea

In 1914 Britain had the strongest navy in the world. All German merchant and naval shipping was cleared from the seas (except the Baltic) during the first few weeks of the war, and the blockade of the German coast was begun. The number of engagements fought during the 4½ years of the war was few. In December 1914 a squadron of German ships was destroyed in the Falkland Islands, and in January 1915 the Germans narrowly escaped from superior forces on Dogger Bank. Otherwise the Germans stayed in port and concentrated on submarine warfare. The British liner, *Lusitania*, which was carrying some munitions, was sunk in May 1915, and about 1,000 people were drowned, including several Americans.

The one major sea battle of the war was fought in May 1916 off the Jutland peninsula. About 250 warships including fifty battleships were involved. The battle was inconclusive: British losses were heavier, but the German fleet returned to port never to emerge again for the rest of the war. Thus the strategical situation was unaltered with the British retaining control of the seas.

The real threat to Britain came in 1917. On 1 February Germany made the vital decision to resort to unrestricted submarine warfare. This meant that all ships in British waters, whether owned by countries involved in the war or not, would be targets for German submarines. United States ships were immediately sunk, and this, together with the Mexican incident (see p. 171), led to the United States' declaration of war on Germany in April. German submarines were extremely effective. During March and April 1917 600 merchant ships were sunk. To meet the threat Lloyd George instituted the convoy system which soon reduced the rate of loss from one in four to one in a hundred. The German hopes of starving Britain of essential supplies were dashed by the end of the year. In the spring of 1918, in a daring raid, block ships nearly closed up the harbours of Zeebrugge and Ostend, two German submarine bases.

So the British navy could justifiably claim to have won the war at sea, despite the lack of a decisive battle. The blockade of Germany was increasingly effective and the German submarine menace was ended. This control of the seas was rather undramatic but nevertheless highly important.

The armistice

The armistice took effect from 11 November 1918. The Germans were compelled by the military situation in France and the political situation at home—the Kaiser abdicated on 9 November—to accept harsh terms. The fleet and all war materials were to be handed over; all occupied territory was to be evacuated and there was to be an Allied occupation of the Rhineland; the treaties of Brest Litovsk and Bucharest with Russia and Romania respectively were to be annulled.

So ended the most destructive war ever fought up to this time. Eleven million people were killed; this indiscriminate human slaughter occurred mainly because the military leaders failed to discover any means of breaching the defences other than by direct frontal attack. The extent of the horror and the killing and the apparent uselessness of the sacrifice meant that a greater sense of waste and futility was bequeathed to posterity by the First World War than by the Second. In the 1939–45 war the aims of the two sides were comparatively clear; in the 1914–18 war it was difficult to elucidate the objectives of any country (except possibly Austria-Hungary). The sacrifice of lives without any clear objective contributed to the consequent pacifism in Britain in the 1920s and early 1930s.

The Peace Treaties

The Peace Conference in Paris

The Peace Conference opened in Paris in January 1919, two months after the signing of the armistice. Thirty-two nations, and three-quarters of the world's population, were represented, and there were a large number of unofficial delegations and pressure groups. Russia, the neutral powers and the defeated powers were not represented, but nevertheless this was the first great world peace conference.

At first the work was largely carried out by a Council of Ten which consisted of two representatives from the British Empire, France, the United States, Italy and Japan. Eventually these five countries were reduced to three, and the important decisions were taken by Clemenceau, prime minister of France, Lloyd George, prime minister of Britain, and President Wilson of the United States. These three men contrasted vividly with each other: Clemenceau, old, cynical and interested only in the security of France, Wilson, the stern idealist who was not really aware of the complexity of European problems, and Lloyd George, the energetic conciliator.

The Conference has been accused of slowness in that six months passed before a settlement was reached with Germany, and even longer before treaties were signed with the other defeated countries. But the issues were complex and were made more so by the social ferment caused by the Russian Revolution. The victorious powers had two basic aims. Firstly, they wished to form nation states in Europe from the ruins of the Russian, Turkish, Austro-Hungarian and German empires. In fact, the new states of eastern Europe came into existence as the war ended, but the Peace Conference had to decide the exact frontiers and attempt to make the states both economically viable and secure. The second aim was to weaken Germany and her allies and prevent a resurgence of German militarism. This was particularly the objective of France, who at one point wanted to create a buffer state in the Rhineland between the French and German frontiers. This idea was rejected by Britain and the United States however. In general Lloyd George moderated the terms as far as he could in view of the prevailing anti-German sentiment.[1]

The German government was eventually presented with terms which it regarded as unjustifiably severe. In October 1918, although their defeat was inevitable, the Germans had asked for an armistice in the

---

[1] During the British General Election in December 1918 slogans such as 'Hang the Kaiser' and 'Make Germany pay' were common.

belief that peace negotiations would be conducted on the basis of President Wilson's Fourteen Points. These were set out in a speech in January 1918, and proposed terms for a peace settlement to be based on national self-determination. However, faced with a threat of renewed war, the German government was forced to agree to the terms of the Paris Conference, and on 28 June 1919, exactly five years after the assassination at Sarajevo, the long peace treaty was signed in the Hall of Mirrors at Versailles.[1]

The terms

1. Northern Schleswig was given to Denmark and some small districts to Belgium.
2. Alsace-Lorraine was returned to France.
3. The Saar was to be administered by the League of Nations for fifteen years, and then a plebiscite would be held to decide its future. Meanwhile the coal mines were given to France.
4. The Rhineland was to be occupied by the Allies who would evacuate it in three stages; a 50 km. belt on the east bank of the Rhine was to be demilitarised.
5. The union of Austria and Germany (the Anschluss) was forbidden.
6. Poland was recreated with a corridor to the Baltic containing the German port of Danzig which was to be a free city under the auspices of the League of Nations.
7. A plebiscite was to determine the future of Upper Silesia (see chapter 14).
8. The former Russian territories of Finland, Estonia, Latvia and Lithuania were to be independent.
9. All German colonies became mandated territories under the League of Nations.
10. The German army was to be limited to 100,000 men. A small navy was allowed, but there were to be no submarines and no air force.
11. Germany was found guilty of starting the war, and therefore was to pay reparations as compensation for damage caused by the fighting. This was left to a Reparations Commission which in April 1921 decided on £6,600 million to be paid in instalments.
12. The Covenant of the League of Nations was included at the beginning of this and the other treaties forming the settlement after the First World War.

[1] In the same hall in January 1871 the German Empire had been created following the defeat of France in the Franco-Prussian War.

Legend:
- Former territory of Austria–Hungary
- Former territory of Russia
- Former territory of Germany

NORWAY

SWEDEN

FINLAND

Aaland Is.

Leningrad

ESTONIA

DENMARK

N.Schleswig

LATVIA

LITHUANIA

Polish Corridor

Danzig

EAST PRUSSIA

U. S. S. R.

HOLLAND

BELGIUM

Berlin

GERMANY

RHINELAND

Weimar

Upper Silesia

POLAND

Saar

Alsace

Lorraine

FRANCE

BAVARIA

Munich

CZECHOSLOVAKIA

Vienna

Geneva

SWITZ-ERLAND

AUSTRIA

HUNGARY

ROMANIA

TYROL

Trieste

Istria

YUGOSLAVIA

ITALY

Rome

ALBANIA

Corfu

GREECE

BULGARIA

Thrace

Constantinople

Ankara

Chanak

Smyrna

TURKEY

0   500
MILES

Central and Eastern Europe, 1923

Settlement in Eastern Europe

During the following year, 1919–20, treaties were signed with Austria, Hungary and Bulgaria. These provided for a major change in political geography, and it is most convenient to deal with them together.

1. Trieste, Istria and the south Tyrol in Austria were given to Italy.
2. Bohemia and Moravia in north Austria were to be the basis of the new state of Czechoslovakia.
3. South Hungary, Bosnia, Herzegovina, Montenegro and Serbia were to form the new state of Yugoslavia.
4. Eastern parts of Hungary joined Romania.
5. Some land was taken from Bulgaria and given to Romania and Greece.

In 1920 the Treaty of Sèvres was signed with the Sultan's government of Turkey. By this treaty the Turkish Empire in the Middle East became mandated territories of the League of Nations (see chapter 7), while Thrace and Smyrna were given to Greece. Turkish nationalists, led by Mustafa Kemal, who had conducted the defence of Gallipoli, were offended at this partition of Turkey itself. Consequently the Greeks were driven out of Smyrna, the Sultan was overthrown, and a new peace treaty was negotiated. By the Treaty of Lausanne in 1923 eastern Thrace and Smyrna were to remain Turkish, while the rest of the Treaty of Sèvres continued to operate.

Comment on the Versailles Settlement

The statesmen of Europe were faced with a huge task in framing a peace settlement after the First World War. They achieved 'the most complete reshaping of the political geography of Europe ever undertaken at one time'.[1] Inevitably such great changes aroused criticism, and six main faults have been found with the settlement and the way in which it was reached.

Firstly, the defeated powers were absent from negotiations. This was a Diktat or dictated peace, and therefore the Germans felt less obligation to keep to its terms since they had not been consulted in drawing them up. Secondly, self-determination was the principle applied to all the peoples except the Germans. The Germans who lived in the Polish corridor were sacrificed to Poland's economic need for a route to the Baltic; the Germans of the Sudetenland were included in Czechoslovakia for geographical and defence reasons; Austria, a German state, was not allowed to unite with Germany because the combination

[1] D. Thomson, *Europe since Napoleon.*

would be too powerful. Thus Germany was left with a sense of injustice which was heightened by imposition of reparations (the third fault). The sum of £6,600 million finally decided upon was well beyond Germany's capacity to pay. Not only did reparations create economic difficulties in the countries that received Germany's payments, but they also prolonged the bitterness of war. Keynes, the economist, was one of the first critics of reparations.

Fourthly, the settlement created a power vacuum in Europe. Germany was greatly weakened, politically and economically, but still possessed considerable potential strength. Instead of having the large Russian and Austro-Hungarian empires on her eastern frontier, however, she was now bordered by small, weak and new states. In addition two of the world's major powers had withdrawn from full participation in European affairs: Russia was now a Communist state and her relations with the rest of Europe consequently deteriorated, and in 1920 the United States retreated into isolation when the Senate refused to ratify the Treaty of Versailles. Only a greatly weakened France, with the half-hearted support of Britain, was left to balance Germany's potential strength.

Fifthly, it was said that the settlement did not pay enough attention to economic needs. Economic units like Upper Silesia were divided, while more countries and longer frontiers were created, which meant that tariffs, which increased prices and generally hindered the movement of trade, were more numerous. The final criticism was that the settlement created many national minorities within states. The population of Europe was so mixed that it was impossible to draw up tidy national frontiers with each country containing the people of one race only. Countries gave promises to respect the rights of minorities but often relations were bitter.

2

Europe 1919 to 1945

Introductory Survey

It has been estimated that £45,000 million was spent by the belligerents on the First World War, and this colossal sum does not include the value of ships sunk and property destroyed. While the economies of European states were geared to the war effort, countries outside Europe, especially the United States and Japan, benefited. Europe was, therefore, faced with the enormous task of recovering her relative prosperity and position in the world. Two factors hindered this recovery: European countries were too embittered to restart international trade quickly, and reparations and the repayment of war loans checked investment.

In 1921 the Reparations Commission set up by the Paris conference fixed the sum Germany was to pay to France, Belgium and Britain at £6,600 million. While Germany was paying out reparations, France was repaying loans to Britain, and Britain was repaying loans to the United States. Most of these debts were paid in gold which gradually accumulated in the United States. In 1923 Germany stopped paying reparations, and this was followed by the occupation of the Ruhr by French forces and the complete collapse of the German currency (see p. 43). After these disastrous years, Europe gradually recovered. The period from 1924 to 1929 was one of relative prosperity when the payment of reparations was continued under more reasonable terms while international trade expanded.

This recovery, however, was precarious and depended mainly on loans from the United States, and partly on the improved international atmosphere following the signing of the Locarno Treaties in 1925. Between 1929 and 1933 the economic recovery was wrecked by the world depression, and the international atmosphere was poisoned by events in Germany and the Far East. The United States had been experiencing an economic boom with huge speculation on the stock market, but in October 1929 there was a sudden collapse of confidence in American industry (see p. 175). There were two main results. Firstly, the United States stopped lending money abroad and demanded the repayment of loans; Germany and Austria were particularly affected by this. Secondly, agricultural prices in the United States fell rapidly with a consequent decline in the world prices of agricultural goods. The growers of these goods could not afford to buy other commodities, and therefore there was a general fall in the demand for manufactured goods throughout the world. The consequence was widespread unemployment which was accompanied by political troubles.

Immediately after the war democracy was the form of government in all European countries except Communist Russia. The dictatorships had been defeated by the democratic states and the prestige of democracy as a form of government was high. But, as David Thomson has said, events conspired to implant the belief that democracy was too feeble and ineffectual a form of government for dealing with the urgent postwar problems. One after another European countries adopted authoritarian governments: Hungary, Italy, Turkey, Spain, Albania, Portugal, Poland and Yugoslavia during the 1920s, and in the second half of the decade conservative governments came to power in Britain, France and Germany. There were various reasons for this trend. In Eastern Europe democracy was too difficult and novel a form of government, and the politicians in the Continent as a whole did not provide inspiring and effectual leadership. The main difficulty, however, was that economic and social conditions were too unsettled. 'It would be difficult to conceive a set of conditions less favourable to experiments in political self-government; and the speedy abandonment of so novel a form of government is hardly to be wondered at.'[1]

There seems to be a correlation between democracy and prosperity, for the economic slump of the 1930s increased the disillusionment with democracy, and nearly every European country experienced movements desiring authoritarian government. These were supported by army officers, Roman Catholic priests, landowners and big industrialists, as well as the unemployed working class. Democracy in Germany came to an abrupt end when Hitler came to power in 1933. Only in Britain and France among the major states did democracy continue to exist.

[1] D. Thomson, *Europe since Napoleon.*

The Spread of Dictatorships
Italy

The parliamentary system in Italy had been unstable since the formation of the country in 1870. After the war a succession of liberal Prime Ministers with small majorities proved unable to cope with the problems facing Italy. The economy was weak, there was a huge debt and industrial production was low. The country had suffered heavy losses in a war that was unpopular with both socialists and pro-Austrian Catholics, and the nationalists were disappointed with the gains in territory from the Treaty of Versailles. In 1919 a miniature Fascist state was set up in Fiume by the Italian poet D'Annunzio who conquered the city with a force of ex-soldiers. He was finally driven out by the Italian army. In addition there were strikes, lockouts and street warfare, the government tolerating this lawlessness in the hope that the violence would die down. This was the background to the rise of Fascism.

Benito Mussolini was born in 1883. His father was a blacksmith and a passionate socialist. Mussolini, a bad-tempered and moody boy, went to a succession of schools and finally qualified as an elementary school master. During the next few years he had a number of jobs—mason's mate, navvy, butcher's boy—and in the end became a journalist with socialist views. A forceful and authoritative speaker, he began to support the use of violence, and broke with the socialists when they opposed Italy's entry into the First World War. Mussolini was seriously wounded in 1917 and then returned to journalism. As the war ended, he pressed for a dictatorship.

In 1919 the Fascist Party was founded, and Mussolini immediately joined it. At first it had little support except from some ex-soldiers and conservatives. Its policy was not clear. It stood for authority, strength and discipline,[1] but 'no-one, not even Mussolini, knew what Fascism meant—beyond anti-leftish thuggery'.[2] By the end of 1920 the Fascists were vastly stronger. Support came from industrialists and landowners, nationalists and ex-soldiers, the middle classes and discontented youth. The Fascists used terrorism freely, and their opponents were attacked with knives, cudgels and guns.[3] In the 1921 elections they won thirty-five seats in Parliament, and membership of the party

---

[1] The fasces were a bundle of rods carried before the consuls in ancient Rome to symbolise their power to punish.

[2] E. Wiskemann, *Europe of the Dictators, 1919–45.*

[3] Forcing their enemies to drink castor oil and eat live toads were favourite methods.

grew fast. Other political parties were too divided to cooperate against this Fascist threat, and in fact there was a long ministerial crisis early in 1922. In October 1922 Mussolini organised the Fascist March on Rome. Four Fascist columns converged on the capital, and bowing before this show of force, the King invited Mussolini to form a government. The triumph of Fascism was due as much to the inability of the democratic party leaders to combine and act with resolution as it was to Mussolini's talents as a political tactician and a demagogue.

It was four years before Mussolini established his dictatorship. In the meantime the government was given full powers to restore order and carry out essential reforms. In the 1924 elections, after some intimidation of the electors, 65 per cent of the votes were cast for the Fascists. Matteotti, the socialist leader and an outspoken critic of Fascism, attacked the conduct of the elections. Soon afterwards he was murdered and it was clear that extreme Fascists were responsible. The opposition then withdrew from Parliament, but this had no effect on Mussolini's actions. The press was censored, free elections were ended, the opposition parties were dissolved and their leaders killed or imprisoned. Parliament was now only a rubber stamp for Mussolini's wishes. Assuming the title of Il Duce (the Leader), in 1926 he became a dictator with power to legislate by decree, and all power was now concentrated in his hands.

Mussolini was an unconventional prime minister. He did energetic physical exercises before breakfast, and would often attend royal receptions unshaven. Millions of Italians regarded him with idolatry—the glasses he drank from were prized as holy relics—and in some respects his government was beneficial to Italy.

In 1926 a law was passed organising unions and employers into corporations. These would settle wages and working conditions, any disputes being referred to tribunals. Strikes and lockouts were forbidden. The greater part of the population was grouped according to occupation into corporations. These were then organised into national federations, and the whole was supervised by the Minister of Corporations. Eventually in 1938 Parliament was abolished and was replaced by a body representing the Fascist Party and the corporations. It was a complicated system whose main purpose was probably to help the dictatorship to control the economy of the country. Effective power remained with Mussolini and the heads of the administration and the armed forces.

Mussolini realised the need to win the support of the Roman Catholic Church which was already sympathetic to Fascism. With this in mind, compulsory religious teaching in school was ordered. In 1929 the

Lateran Treaty was signed. This finally ended the breach between the Church and the Italian State which had existed since the unification of the country in the mid-nineteenth century. The Vatican City was recognised as an independent state, and in return the Church recognised the Kingdom of Italy. In addition the Roman Catholic faith was to be the religion of Italy. This treaty was Mussolini's most constructive and lasting achievement, and helped to give the Fascist Party respectability.

Fascism's economic achievements have been much publicised, particularly the public works which were its chief solution to unemployment. New bridges, roads and canals, railway stations, hospitals and schools were constructed. Land, especially the Pontine Marshes around Rome, was reclaimed by draining and afforestation. There were big increases in the production of artificial silk, hydroelectric power, iron and steel and wheat. But despite these real achievements, standards of living hardly improved. During the years of depression in the early 1930s the high numbers of unemployed were hardly affected by the public works. In fact, the popular discontent with Fascism had reached such a pitch by 1935 that it provided two reasons for the invasion of Ethiopia: this military operation diverted attention away from the economic troubles and provided employment.

Mussolini conducted a strong, nationalist foreign policy in which the general object was to raise Italy's prestige in Europe. For example, in 1923, when four Italians were killed during a frontier dispute between Greece and Albania, Mussolini, who regarded himself as the protector of the Albanians, demanded an apology and an indemnity from the Greeks. When this was refused, he bombarded and occupied the Greek island of Corfu. Intervention by the League of Nations and the ambassadors of the great powers eventually led to a settlement: the Greeks paid the indemnity and the Italians evacuated Corfu. In 1924 agreement was reached with the new state of Yugoslavia over Fiume. The city became part of Italy while the Slav lands around it were incorporated into Yugoslavia.

Two of the motives for the invasion of Ethiopia have been given above. In addition Mussolini wanted to avenge the Italian defeat at the hands of the Ethiopians at Adowa in 1896, and also to complete Italy's East African Empire by occupying Ethiopia and so linking Eritrea with Italian Somaliland. In December 1934 there was a border clash between Italian and Ethiopian troops in which about thirty Italians were killed. Italy demanded compensation and Ethiopia appealed to the League of Nations. While a settlement was being negotiated, Italian troop movements continued, and in October 1935 Mussolini suddenly attacked Ethiopia in force.

Neville Chamberlain appears to be reasoning with an obstinate and aggressive looking Mussolini

General Franco during the Spanish Civil War

Adolf Hitler

Within a week the League of Nations declared Italy the aggressor and agreed to impose economic sanctions against her. However, Britain and France did not wish to offend Mussolini too much for fear that Italy would draw closer to Nazi Germany. Therefore, coal and oil were not included in the sanctions, and the Suez Canal was not closed to Italian shipping. In addition, Hoare, the British Foreign Secretary, and Laval, the French Premier, agreed to a plan in December 1935 by which about two-thirds of Ethiopia would go to Italy in return for a small strip of territory that would link the rest of Ethiopia with the Red Sea. When this plan was made public, Hoare was forced to resign and was replaced by Eden. This made little difference to policy, however, and the export of oil to Italy continued.

Meanwhile, with the assistance of aircraft and mustard gas, the Italian armies were conquering Ethiopia, and in May 1936 the capital, Addis Ababa, was occupied. In July sanctions were ended. The result of the affair was to strain relations between Italy and Britain and France, and so lead to closer relations between Italy and Germany.

The policy of Mussolini regarding the Spanish Civil War, the actions of Hitler, Albania and the Second World War are dealt with later in this chapter. Until 1940 Mussolini was successful in his conduct of foreign affairs. He 'gave Italy the appearance, though not the equipment, of a Great Power'.[1] He tended, however, to miscalculate Italy's strength and that of other countries, and the last years of his regime saw Italy increasingly enslaved to the humiliating overlordship of the Germans.

Turkey

The First World War ended with Turkey defeated, her Empire occupied, and an Allied military administration in Constantinople. It was clear that any peace treaty would provide for the separation of the Arab provinces of the empire. In 1919, however, it appeared that the partition of Turkey itself was possible, for a Greek army landed at Smyrna, and in the following year the Sultan's government agreed to the Treaty of Sèvres which provided for a Greek administration in Smyrna for five years.

The Allied governments, however, were now faced with Turkish nationalist resistance. The one undefeated Turkish general of the war, Mustafa Kemal, the hero of the defence of Gallipoli, organised resistance to the Greeks in Anatolia. Kemal established his headquarters at the small town of Ankara, and from this base conducted a victorious

[1] A. J. P. Taylor. Review article in *The Observer*, 14 June 1964.

campaign against the Greeks who were finally driven out of Smyrna. Fresh negotiations were then conducted with the Allies, and the Turks won better terms in 1923 in the Treaty of Lausanne (see p. 27). In 1922 Kemal abolished the Sultanate,[1] and in the following year Turkey was declared a republic with Kemal as president. Ankara, little more than a large village, without electricity and other comforts of civilisation, became the new capital.

Kemal, who later took the title of Atatürk, meaning 'Father of the Turks', was one of the true revolutionaries of history. His aim was to transform Turkey from an Asiatic into a European country. This meant a fundamental revolution in the habits and outlook of a conservative people. Kemal organised his supporters into the Republican People's Party, and at first introduced a constitution which provided for universal suffrage and an assembly which elected the president who then chose the government. However, opposition from those who disapproved of Kemal's other changes and a rebellion among the Kurds led to the suppression of opposition parties and the establishment of a one-party dictatorship in 1925. Thereafter Kemal did not again really attempt government through a parliamentary system. His was orderly and progressive government but not democratic.

The strict Islamic religion was opposed to the westernising reforms that Kemal intended to introduce. Therefore, he first had to weaken Islam. The Ministry of Religious Affairs and the Caliphate, the religious head of Islam, were abolished. Muslim schools were closed and secular education was started. Religious brotherhoods were suppressed, and sacred tombs were closed as places of worship. Religious law courts were abolished, and new legal codes based on European examples replaced Muslim law. In 1928 Turkey was declared a secular state, so that Islam was no longer the state religion. One of the best-known reforms was making the wearing of the fez, a symbol of Islamic orthodoxy, a criminal offence. Kemal attempted to emancipate women: greater mixing with men was encouraged—in 1925 Kemal danced with a woman in public, the first time this sort of thing had ever happened in Turkey; women became eligible to vote in parliamentary elections and could become MPs; polygamy was abolished and the wearing of veils was discouraged. The Latin alphabet replaced the Arabic, and Kemal even composed an Alphabet March for the people to sing and so learn their letters more quickly. All of this amounted to a great social revolution and was not done without considerable religious opposition.

The poverty of Turkey was made worse by the devastation of the

[1] The Sultan and his wives and followers were smuggled out of his palace in two British army ambulances, and were then taken in a British battleship into exile.

war which ended in 1923 and by the departure of Greek businessmen. Asiatic Turkey is a high barren plateau with an arid soil, so agriculture is limited. Nevertheless, three-quarters of the population were engaged in agriculture, and Kemal made a start to land reform by dividing up the big estates. There was extensive railway construction, and some industrial and mining development, and money was spent on industry rather than agriculture. Kemal was no economist, however, and there was no major economic development.

Kemal's foreign policy was one of peaceful and friendly relationships with neighbouring countries. After an exchange of Turks living in Greece with Greeks living in Turkey, good relations were maintained with Greece. In 1934 Turkey, Greece, Romania and Yugoslavia guaranteed each other's frontiers, and drew closer as the Fascist threat increased.

Kemal Atatürk died in 1938. His achievement was great, although possibly less than his legend suggests, for there was still much to do to make Turkey a modern state. Ismet Inönü became the new president, and he managed to keep Turkey out of the Second World War.

Spain

Spain was economically a poor country with inadequate industry and backward agriculture giving rise to social discontent in the provinces. Before 1923 parliamentary government failed to work well for various reasons: regional loyalties were strong, especially in Catalonia; extremists, such as Communists and anarchists, were active; the Church and the army were both very powerful—the former controlled education and was very conservative, and the latter believed it had the right to step in and change the government in every crisis. Politics were discredited and few men of real ability and leadership emerged with the result that governments were weak and shortlived.

As a result of this situation, Primo de Rivera, captain-general of Catalonia, overthrew the government in 1923 and set up a military dictatorship. The King, the army, industrialists and landowners all gave their support, and opposition came only from the socialists. Civilian government had clearly broken down, however, and the desire for law and order brought general support for the new regime. Seven years of tough, but quite popular, military dictatorship followed. Order was restored in Spanish Morocco where rebellious tribesmen had helped to precipitate the coup. An economic boom in Europe during this period helped the government which in addition organised public works to reduce unemployment. The politicians and the left wing continued to oppose, however, and in 1929 Primo de Rivera lost the support of the army. Next year, tired and disillusioned, he left Spain and died in Paris six weeks later. The municipal elections in 1931 revealed a huge pro-Republican vote in the cities, and the King, Alfonso XIII, also went into exile.

In 1931 Spain became a republic with a single-chamber Parliament elected by universal suffrage. However the constitution contained a number of anti-clerical clauses—the Church was disestablished, the Jesuits were expelled, and divorce by consent was recognised—and these automatically aroused the hostility of the right-wing groups, especially since the constitution was accompanied by a wave of anti-clerical violence, such as the burning of churches. Parliament, a majority of whose members wanted a social revolution, passed an Agrarian Law in 1932. This was intended to nationalise unworked land in certain areas and give it to landless peasants, but the law was implemented half-heartedly so that the initiative in the countryside passed to extremists. Then the law which deterred public criticism of the armed forces was abolished, and this exposed the army to hostile press attacks.

In 1933 elections produced a huge swing to the right, and for the next three years right-wing Republicans ruled Spain. But discontent grew. There were frequent changes of government, and in 1934 a general strike leading to a revolt in Catalonia and the Asturias was harshly suppressed by the army under General Franco. In February 1936 the elections were won by a Popular Front of republicans, socialists and communists. The new government was strongly opposed by the right wing which was now represented by the Falange, the Spanish Fascist party, founded by the son of the late dictator, Primo de Rivera. Gradually the country relapsed into chaos and violence. Strikes, the burning of churches, political assassinations, and the seizure of land by the peasants in the south, all indicated that the government had lost control of the country.

In July 1936 the efficient and ruthless General Franco, a soldier of considerable military ability, started an army revolt in the Spanish zone of Morocco. He crossed to Spain, and the towns in the extreme south fell into rebel hands, but the rest of the country resisted. The army had expected little opposition except from the politicians, and the resistance of the mass of the people made civil war inevitable.

The rebels, referred to as the Nationalists, were supported by the western part of the country, whereas the east, north and centre of Spain supported the Republican side. The Republicans were stronger economically, being in control of most of the cities, and had greater popular support. The anarchist, socialist and communist militia were the basis of their armies. The Nationalist armies had more weapons and men and greater military skill. Unfortunately for Spain, however, each side attracted foreign support. Italy provided 60,000 troops and Germany sent key technical advisers and units of dive bombers to support Franco. (The Germans regarded Spain as a training ground for tactics and weapons.) The Republicans received valuable but limited aid from Russia and from large numbers of volunteers[1] from many countries. It was the policy of Britain and France to stop foreign intervention in order to prevent the conflict becoming international, but this merely meant that the Republicans did not receive as much foreign help as the Nationalists. The extent of foreign assistance was probably the decisive factor in the war.

The war was fought with ferocious brutality. Behind the front lines, each side killed its prisoners, and the capture of every town was followed by executions. There was enormous destruction; for example, the town of Guernica in northern Spain was virtually flattened by a sudden German air raid[2] with very great loss of life.

The Republic was on the defensive throughout, and despite determined fighting, gradually lost territory. By the spring of 1938 the Nationalists had reached the Mediterranean between Barcelona and Valencia, and their opponents were then divided. A year later both cities fell, and the resistance in Madrid then ended. The war caused massive destruction—probably over half a million people died—and the Second World War added to the economic difficulties of recovery. General Franco continued to rule Spain until his death in 1975.

Portugal

Portugal before 1910 suffered from the same problems as Spain: political instability, weak finances and strong left-wing movements. In 1910 there was a republican revolution which received general popular support including that of the army. But the situation did not improve: there were frequent changes in government and the economy virtually collapsed.

In 1926 the army intervened and established a military dictatorship. Two years later Salazar, a professor of economics, was brought into the

[1] Josip Broz, the future Marshal Tito of Yugoslavia, organised the flow of recruits through France from a small left bank hotel in Paris. Some 'sheer adventurers in search of excitement joined—such as Nick Gillian, the Belgian, who gave his reason as "spirit of adventure, lassitude, and this rainy autumn of 1936" '. H. Thomas, *The Spanish Civil War*.
[2] This is commemorated in a famous painting by Picasso.

government as Minister of Finance. In 1932 he became Prime Minister and ruled Portugal until 1968.

Countries of Eastern Europe

Hungary   In the general disorder at the end of the First World War, a communist government was set up in Hungary. However, the western powers blockaded the country, the Romanians invaded, and by the end of 1919 Admiral Horthy assumed power. A semi-Fascist dictatorship was then established with the support of conservative elements, and this remained in being until the Soviet occupation in 1944.

Poland   In 1919 the republic of Poland was created, with Pilsudski as head of state. The Poles decided upon a highly democratic constitution, but soon discovered that the lack of political experience made this form of government too difficult to work efficiently. In 1926 Pilsudski, who had earlier retired into private life, seized power with the support of the army. There was now stronger, though far from despotic government, and the country made more rapid economic progress.

Albania   The leader of a Muslim clan, Ahmed Bey Zogu, became the virtual dictator of Albania after the war. In 1928 he made himself King Zog and ruled until the occupation of his country by Italy in 1939.

Yugoslavia and Romania   Parliamentary government broke down in Yugoslavia in 1929 and in Romania in 1938. In both countries royal dictatorships were established.

Austria   After the Versailles Settlement, Austria became a small land-locked state whose two main parties both wanted union with Germany. The constitution provided for parliamentary government, but after the Catholic priest, Seipel, became Chancellor, the country moved towards authoritarianism. During the three years after Seipel's resignation in 1929, a succession of short-lived governments failed to prevent the economy from collapsing. Finally, Dollfuss (a little man under five feet tall who was known as Millimetternich or Mickey Mouse) became Chancellor and set up a virtual dictatorship.

Democracy in France

Nearly two million French soldiers and civilians were killed during the First World War, the north of France was devastated and an enormous national debt accumulated. In the elections of 1919 the conservatives were given a large majority, and this was regarded as a vote for peace and order and for maintaining the military strength of France. In the following year the prime minister, Clemenceau, too authoritarian and now too old, retired into private life, and for the next decade French politics were dominated by Poincaré and Briand. For two years, 1924–26, a left-wing government was in office, but it was too divided to rule effectively, and in 1926 Poincaré again took office at the head of a coalition government composed of all the leading politicians. The government was given power to deal with the economic problems by issuing decrees, and there followed three years of relative calm and prosperity, with international tensions relaxed and a considerable improvement in the economy. In 1929, however, Poincare retired and Briand, the foreign minister, was ageing. No leaders with their ability emerged during the 1930s.

France, with her economy well balanced between industry and agriculture, was for a long while less affected by the world economic crisis than other countries, but by 1933 she had well over one million unemployed. Parliament, with its many parties, could not agree on the policy to deal with the situation, and, with the formation of a succession of cabinets, French politics reached a deadlock. Then, during the autumn of 1933, a major political crisis was created by the Stavisky affair. The death in suspicious circumstances of Stavisky, a Russian-Jewish financier with friends in important positions in Parliament, the police and the judiciary, helped to create in the public mind the impression that Parliament was corrupt.

A few months later, in February 1934, an attempted right-wing coup produced a day of bitter street fighting in Paris. Although the coup was crushed, extreme right-wing groups grew steadily more powerful in France during the next two years. In view of this Fascist threat, the Communists, under orders from Moscow, began to collaborate with the Socialists, and after the 1936 elections a Popular Front government was set up under the leadership of Blum. It lasted a year before economic problems and internal divisions led to Blum's resignation. A succession of weak governments held office until 1940.

There were a number of reasons for the weakness of France between the two world wars. The economy was backward: there was little mass production, farming was inefficient, and the falling birthrate caused serious concern. Politics were unstable: the executive was weak and no really great men emerged to dominate affairs, while Parliament contained too many mediocre members organised into too many parties. Reform was often blocked by the conservative outlook of the deputies. Throughout the period there was constant propaganda from right-wing journalists hostile to the Republic. Nevertheless, democracy survived in France despite economic and political difficulties. It was foreign invasion which finally ended the Third Republic in 1940.

Germany

The Weimar Republic 1919 to 1933

In November 1918 Germany was clearly defeated militarily and the army's authoritarian influence in politics was consequently weakened. A weary and disillusioned people revolted against the form of government which had brought Germany to defeat. There were disturbances in Berlin and Munich and in the fleet at Kiel, and soviets were formed in these cities. The Kaiser abdicated, a republic was declared, and a new government was set up under Ebert, a right-wing socialist. In January 1919 there were elections for a National Assembly to work out a constitution. In the following month the Assembly met temporarily in the small town of Weimar because of disturbances in Berlin.

The National Assembly drew up 'one of the most completely democratic paper constitutions ever written'.[1] Germany remained a federation with power divided between the central government in Berlin and the provincial governments. The Reichstag was to be elected by universal suffrage and proportional representation, and the government was made responsible to it. The president was to be directly elected by the people as in the United States, and he was given wide emergency powers. Ebert became the first president. Thus for the first time Germany had a genuinely democratic constitution. The national and international climate needed to be very favourable for such a constitution to work in a country with no experience of democracy. Unfortunately, the Weimar Republic, born of defeat and with little positive support from the people, could hardly have had a more stormy beginning.

In January 1919 there was a communist rebellion in Berlin which is known as the Spartacist rising. Led by Karl Liebknecht and Rosa Luxemburg, a brilliant Polish Jewess, it was soon crushed by irregular

[1] D. Thomson, *Europe since Napoleon*.

right-wing forces officered by professionals from the dissolved army. During most of 1919 there was sporadic rioting in Munich, and this too was eventually ended by right-wing forces. In June the Weimar government was compelled to sign the Treaty of Versailles. To most Germans the terms appeared extremely harsh and unjust, and the politicians who agreed to the treaty were highly unpopular—many, indeed, were murdered by right-wing extremists. In 1920 the right wing attempted a *coup d'état* in Berlin. An obscure provincial official named Dr Kapp proclaimed a new regime, but a general strike of Berlin workers soon ended the putsch.

In 1921 the commission appointed by the Paris Conference to calculate the amount of reparations to be paid by Germany decided on the sum of £6,600 million. Germany made regular payments for two years. During this time the mark, which had declined in value during the war because of the huge increases in paper money, dropped in value still further. Foreign loans to Germany were therefore stopped, and in 1923 the German government said that it could no longer pay reparations. French forces immediately occupied the Ruhr, and, despite a general strike, they got production going and cut off the Ruhr from the rest of Germany by a customs barrier. This caused the currency to collapse, as illustrated in the following table:

Exchange value of £1. .

1914	—	15 Marks
1922	—	760 Marks
Jan. 1923	—	72,000 Marks
Nov. 1923	—	16,000 million Marks

A vast amount of paper currency was printed, since huge quantities of bank notes were required to buy even a cup of coffee. Those who owed money benefited, and those who owned property prospered. But the value of savings, paper investments and pensions was completely wiped out, and the purchasing power of wages was almost nil. All who suffered in this way were embittered, and consequently were potential supporters of Hitler.

In September 1923 the French withdrew on the understanding that the German government, now led by Gustav Stresemann, would restart the reparation payments. A swift improvement in Germany's economy followed.

Hitler and the Nazi Party Two months after the French withdrawal Hitler failed in his first attempt to take over the German government. Adolf Hitler was born in 1889 in a small Austrian town on the German frontier. His father was a customs official. At the age of eighteen, Hitler went to Vienna to study art, but after two attempts failed to gain entrance to the Vienna Academy of Fine Arts. He then spent four unhappy, lonely and frustrating years in which he held a succession of jobs—labouring work, painting postcards of views of Vienna, and painting posters and advertisements. During these years his opinions were formed: he became a passionate German nationalist, regarding the Slavs as an inferior race, and he developed an hysterical hatred of the Jews whom he denounced as being responsible for almost everything he disliked. He had no use for democracy.

In 1913 Hitler moved to Munich and when the First World War started, he immediately volunteered for service. For the greater part of four years he was in or near the front line. He became a corporal and was a conscientious and brave soldier for he was awarded the Iron Cross. Temporarily blinded in the autumn of 1918, he was in hospital when the war ended. Soon after he returned to Munich.

In 1919 Hitler joined the very small and insignificant National Socialist German Workers' Party (later shortened to Nazis). He soon became leader and built up a mass following in Munich. The policy of the party was vague, but was basically a mixture of nationalism and socialism, a blend which proved to be popular. In practice, all who were aggrieved in any way were allowed to join. Hitler, 'the greatest demagogue in history',[1] possessed a remarkable gift for oratory. This, together with the uniforms, the swastika flag, the marching songs and the use of violence, attracted support. Roehm, Hess and Goering, all ex-officers, joined; Streicher, a school-teacher, whose opinion of the Jews was even worse than Hitler's, ran a party newspaper.

Hitler believed that the crisis of 1923 was his opportunity to capture power in Bavaria and possibly in Berlin. In November he dramatically announced the 'National Revolution' at a meeting in a beer hall on the outskirts of Munich. But the next day a long column of Nazis led by Hitler and ex-Field Marshal von Ludendorff, whom Hitler had persuaded to join, was routed by the police. Hitler was tried and sentenced to five years' imprisonment.

Only nine months of his sentence were served before Hitler was released. But during this time he worked on *Mein Kampf* ('My Struggle'), a semi-autobiographical book containing his political ideas. For example, he considered that the Germans were the master race and that they needed *Lebensraum* (living space); therefore eastern Europe must be conquered to provide this land.

1924 to 1929   Stresemann was the Chancellor of Germany in the latter

[1] A. Bullock, *Hitler: A Study in Tyranny*.

part of 1923, and then continued as Foreign Minister until his death in 1929. A practical statesman, he guided the Weimar Republic in its one short period of apparent prosperity. The old worthless currency was recalled, and a new currency which secured public confidence was issued. Large American loans became the basis of a rebuilt and modernised German industry, and Germany soon began to dominate Europe economically. That this economic improvement was precarious was only seen later.

In 1924 the Dawes Plan (called after the American chairman) made a new arrangement for the payment of reparations. Germany was to pay 2,500 million marks per year, to pay more if she became more prosperous, while the total amount of reparations was left undetermined. The Young Plan of 1929 finally decided on annual payments of reparations over a period of fifty-nine years.

This relative prosperity had the effect of reducing the appeal of the political extremists, the nationalists and the communists. In the 1924 elections the moderates had a working majority as long as they kept together, and in 1928 the Nazis only managed to win twelve seats. President Ebert died in 1925, and Field Marshal von Hindenburg, a soldier who knew nothing about politics and who was seventy-seven years old, was elected in his place. Hindenburg was naturally sympathetic towards the right wing, but this did at least have the result that the nationalist opposition to the republic lessened.

International tension died down during the second half of the 1920s. In 1925 the Locarno Treaties were signed. These provided firstly, a British and Italian guarantee of the permanence of the German frontier with Belgium and France, and secondly, a French guarantee of Germany's undertaking that she would not seek to change her eastern frontiers other than by peaceful means. Locarno did contribute to the general pacification of Europe, but it also had two adverse effects: it implied that the Treaty of Versailles was invalid unless the clauses were individually ratified by Germany, and it made Germany's eastern frontier uncertain. However, the following year Germany joined the League of Nations. Two years later, in 1928, the Kellogg Pact was arranged. Sixty-five states signed a pact renouncing war as a means of settling disputes. This easing of international tension was largely due to the frequent meetings between Stresemann, Briand and Austen Chamberlain.

Meanwhile, the Nazi Party had been refounded, but recruitment was slow. One valuable recruit, however, was Josef Goebbels, a highly intelligent journalist, who had a real flair for propaganda.[1] The army of

---

[1] He once said, 'Any lie frequently repeated will ultimately gain belief.'

brown-shirted and jack-booted storm-troopers (the SA) was expanded, and within the SA was formed the SS, a select bodyguard for Hitler. The Hitler Youth was created, the Labour Front set up, and the annual Party rally, always an occasion for huge emotional displays, was started at Nuremberg in 1927. But, despite these new developments, the Nazis did badly politically. The world economic crisis was required to increase their fortunes.

The economic crisis and the Nazi Party. The reasons for the world economic slump which began in the United States in the autumn of 1929 are given in chapter 5. No country was more susceptible than Germany to this depression, since American loans to and investment in Germany immediately ceased, and the demand for German goods dropped sharply. The figures for unemployment rose from 1·3 million in September 1929 to over 6 million in January 1933. This latter figure represented one-third of the adult male population.

Early in 1930 the government attempted to economise by reducing expenditure on social services. The Reichstag opposed, but President von Hindenburg enforced this policy of deflation by using his emergency powers. Both the policy and the method of enforcing it were unpopular, and the Nazis, with the financial support of the leaders of big industry, conducted a bitter propaganda campaign against it. In the elections of September 1930 they polled 6 million votes and won 107 seats. The Communists won seventy-seven seats so that the strength of the extremists in the Reichstag was now much greater. The combination of high unemployment and extremist strength led to general lawlessness with street battles between the Nazis and the Communists.

In April 1932 Hitler stood for the presidency against the 84-year-old Hindenburg. The President was re-elected with 19 million votes, but 13 million Germans supported Hitler. In the following July fresh elections gave the Nazis 230 seats. They were now the largest party but did not have an overall majority. Von Papen, the recently appointed right-wing Chancellor, now invited Hitler to join the government as Vice-Chancellor, believing that the Nazis could be tamed by giving them office. Hitler aimed at the highest position, however, and refused the offer. In November the Nazis lost 2 million votes in the new election and the number of seats they held fell to 196. It seemed that a reaction against their violence had set in, and this encouraged those politicians who could never believe that Hitler was really dangerous. In January 1933 negotiations were conducted between the Nationalists under von Papen and the Nazis under Hitler to form a coalition government. On 30 January 1933 Hitler became Chancellor of

Germany with von Papen as Vice-Chancellor.

It was now only a matter of time for the Weimar Republic as a democratic state to come to an end. Hitler wanted a majority in the Reichstag, and persuaded Hindenburg to call yet another election. The Nazis now controlled the radio, the press, and government funds, and conducted a massive propaganda campaign. At the end of February, a week before the elections were to be held, the Reichstag building in Berlin was destroyed by fire. Though it is probable that the Nazis were responsible, the fire was blamed on the Communists. This was the excuse for a week of unrestrained Nazi violence against the Communists and all other opponents. An emergency decree suspended the guarantees of individual liberty contained in the Weimar constitution.

Despite all this, the elections in March gave the Nazis only 43 per cent of the vote. However, the Communist Party was suppressed and the Nazis, with the support of the Nationalists and the Roman Catholic Centre Party, gained the two-thirds majority necessary to pass the Enabling Law. This conferred dictatorial powers on the Chancellor for four years. Hitler could now issue whatever decrees he chose, and Germany's brief experiment with democracy was at an end.

The Weimar Republic had been faced with too many problems in too short a time. It had lost popularity almost at the start by having to accept the Treaty of Versailles, and the two major economic crises of 1923 and 1929–33 reduced its support even more. The short-lived coalition governments did not possess the economic knowledge or the political stability to deal with the issue of unemployment. The Republic was always politically weak. There were too many parties and, with the exception of Stresemann, the leaders were of limited ability. Stresemann was a great minister, but other politicians derided and attacked him. It has been said that the Germans were not by nature democratic. 'Men of truly democratic heart were rare in the German Republic.'[1] The Germans were certainly inexperienced in the workings of democratic government. It was partly for this reason that Hitler, a politician of very great ability, was able to win such widespread support.

Germany under Hitler 1933 to 1945

Domestic policy Nazi control of all aspects of the life of Germany was obtained in a variety of ways. All other political parties were outlawed. Trade Unions were abolished, their leaders were arrested and all workers were compelled to join the German Labour Front. Strikes

[1] E. Eyck, *A History of the Weimar Republic*.

were made illegal, wages were fixed by the government, and the Labour Front was used by the Nazis to control industry. The state governments and parliaments were abolished, and Germany ceased to be a federation. The civil service and judiciary were brought under Nazi control, so that there was no protection for anybody that the Nazis wished to terrorise.

The Nazi Party organisation was powerful and far reaching. A hierarchy of officials stretched from Hitler at the top to the wardens of every block of tenement flats at the bottom. Propaganda was controlled by Goebbels who, like Hitler, had an uncanny understanding of German psychology. At Nazi rallies enormous crowds repeated the phrase 'ein Volk, ein Reich, ein Führer' ('one People, one Empire, one Leader'). Considerable pressure was put on young people to join the Hitler Youth where the emphasis was placed on obedience to the Führer. The press, radio and all forms of art and literature were subjected to a deadening censorship. Education was controlled and textbooks were rewritten.

The Gestapo or Secret State Police was formed and run by Himmler, a former chicken farmer, who also controlled the SS and who was the most powerful man in Germany after Hitler. Himmler's second-in-command was Heydrich, who was responsible for the concentration camps. These were barracks surrounded by electrified fences and watch towers. In them several hundreds of thousands of Germans, and later millions of Jews, suffered barbaric punishments and death. The German people knew of the existence of these camps as their main purpose was to act as a deterrent to any form of opposition to Hitler. From the Jews the most abject submission was required, and eventually even this was not sufficient. When the Nazis came to power, many German Jews went into voluntary exile. Those that remained were forbidden to hold positions of any importance. In 1935 the Nuremberg Laws on race deprived the Jews of citizenship rights and forbade any marriages between Jews and non-Jews. In November 1938 a Jewish refugee killed a German embassy official in Paris. This produced organised anti-Jewish rioting in Germany and a fine of over £80 million on the Jewish community.

One possible source of opposition to the Nazis was the SA. This was one of the earliest Nazi organisations, and was now over 2 million strong. Its members were mainly working class and put more emphasis on the socialism of 'National Socialism' than Hitler liked. Its leader, Roehm, had hoped to become Defence Minister and wanted to unite the SA with the regular army. Both the Nazi government and the army disliked such a strong and independent body. Hitler, therefore, gained the support of the army in an attempt to reduce the importance of the SA, and in return the army agreed to Hitler becoming president on the death of Hindenburg. Before dawn on 30 June 1934 Roehm and other SA leaders were arrested and executed by the SS. The opportunity was taken to remove any other people who had at any time opposed Hitler. At least 150 people lost their lives in the 'Night of the Long Knives', and the figure is probably much larger. The result was a shift in power from the semi-civilian SA to the highly efficient and ruthless SS and the Gestapo. The SS increased in size and importance, with its own courts and its separate military branch called the Waffen SS. All members had to prove that they were of 'pure' German and Aryan descent, and it was intended eventually that the SS would breed 'pure' children who would rule other Germans.

In August 1934 Hindenburg died and Hitler, in addition to being Chancellor, became both President and Commander-in-Chief of the armed forces. Meanwhile the number of unemployed was being reduced. This was caused partly by the natural recovery of the economy as the depression ended, and partly by the actions of the government. Public works in the form of housing programmes, road construction and land reclamation, helped considerably, and rearmament employed a growing number of people. Thus, the German people supported a regime which had ended disorder, removed unemployment, and through its foreign policy brought back national prestige.

Foreign policy Historians are not agreed on the aims of Hitler's foreign policy. Some believe that Hitler was an improviser who reacted to events, while others believe that he had a number of more or less precise objectives and had a planned timetable for achieving them. However, most historians are agreed that he had at least four general aims that he hoped to achieve: he wished to restore the armed strength of Germany and then annul those parts of the Versailles Settlement which he disliked. In addition he wished to extend the Reich to include all Germans who would then look to eastern and south-eastern Europe for *Lebensraum*.

When Hitler came to power in 1933, a Disarmament Conference organised by the League of Nations was being held at Geneva. The basic problem was the relative size of French and German strength in the future. The French refused to agree to German rearmament and equality with France, although Britain was willing to grant arms parity to Germany after four years. Hitler's reaction to this was German withdrawal both from the Disarmament Conference and from the League of Nations. A plebiscite in Germany showed an enormous majority in

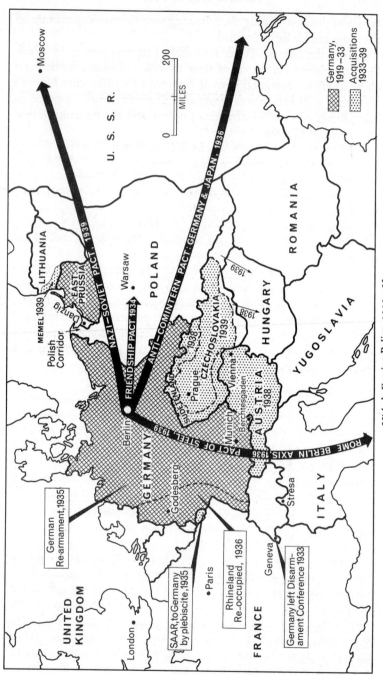

Hitler's Foreign Policy, 1933–39

Germany, 1919–33

Acquisitions 1933–39

UNITED KINGDOM

London•

FRANCE

Paris•

Geneva

Stresa

ITALY

German Re-armament,1935

SAAR, to Germany by plebiscite,1935

Rhineland Re-occupied, 1936

Germany left Disarmament Conference 1933

Godesberg

Berlin○

GERMANY

FRIENDSHIP PACT 1934

ANTI-COMINTERN PACT : GERMANY & JAPAN, 1936

NAZI–SOVIET PACT, 1939

Polish Corridor

Danzig

MEMEL 1939

LITHUANIA

EAST PRUSSIA

POLAND

Warsaw•

U. S. S. R.

Moscow•

0   200

MILES

SUDETENLAND 1938

CZECHOSLOVAKIA 1939

Prague•

Munich•

Berchtesgaden•

Vienna•

AUSTRIA 1938

1938

1939

HUNGARY

ROMANIA

YUGOSLAVIA

ROME BERLIN AXIS 1936   PACT OF STEEL 1939

favour of this step. During the following year German expenditure on the army and air force doubled.

In 1934 the German-Polish Friendship Pact was signed, by which Germany renounced the use of force to settle differences for the next ten years. This was a good piece of diplomacy by Hitler since Poland's friendship with France was weakened. Thereafter France worked to bring Russia into the French alliance system, and in 1934 Russia joined the League of Nations.

In July 1934 the Nazis attempted a coup in Vienna. Austria, suffering from economic and political weaknesses similar to those of the Weimar Republic, had a powerful Nazi Party which decided to end the authoritarian government of Dollfuss. However, although Dollfuss was murdered, the army and the remaining Austrian ministers, led by Dr Schuschnigg, put down the revolt with the support of Mussolini. Von Papen was sent as German Ambassador to Austria to restore good relations.

Under the terms of the Treaty of Versailles, a plebiscite was to be held in the Saar in January 1935. The population was to decide whether they wished to join Germany or France, or remain under League of Nations' rule. Ninety per cent voted for a return to Germany rather than union with France, and in March 1935 the Saar was incorporated into Germany. This was a big boost for Hitler's prestige since it occurred after two years of Nazi rule by which time the character of Nazism was becoming apparent.

Early in 1935 Britain and France announced increases in expenditure on armaments. With this as a partial excuse, the German government in March 1935 announced the intention of building up her army by conscription to over half a million men. This was the first breach of the Treaty of Versailles, and in April a Three Power Conference of Britain, France and Italy met at Stresa while the League Assembly met at Geneva. Both meetings condemned the German action but took no further steps. Instead alliances were negotiated between France and Russia and between Czechoslovakia and Russia, while in June 1935 direct negotiations between Britain and Germany produced a naval agreement. This said that Germany could build up to 35 per cent of British naval strength and that there should be equality in submarine strength. Britain's action broke the Stresa front by implying that Germany had the right to rearm.

The British and French attitude to Mussolini's invasion of Ethiopia helped Hitler. It led to a breach between Italy and the two democracies and consequently better relations between Italy and Germany. This was the beginning of the Rome-Berlin Axis.

The last Allied troops left the Rhineland in 1930. Thereafter it was to be demilitarised. In March 1936 Hitler decided to send a token force to occupy the area, despite the fears of the German army commanders who knew that their military strength was still relatively weak. It is now known that if the French had resisted, the Germans would have withdrawn. But the gamble succeeded. There were protests, but these were half-hearted and ineffectual. In Britain it was widely held that Germany had the right to occupy her own country, and also that it was less important to limit Germany's army than her navy and air force. The French army was stronger than the German, but economic weakness and political divisions made France unwilling to resist by force this further breach of the Treaty of Versailles. Thus the German army was now on the French frontier and there was armed protection for the Ruhr.

The beginning of the Spanish Civil War in 1936 not only diverted attention from events in central Europe but led to closer relations between Hitler and Mussolini because of German and Italian aid for Franco. In October 1936 the Rome–Berlin Axis, a rather imprecise alliance, came into being, and soon after the Anti-Comintern (Communist International) Pact was signed with Japan. The events of 1936 in the Rhineland, Ethiopia and Spain formed a watershed in international relations in the 1930s. Thereafter Europe was on the downward slope towards war. In 1937 Britain and France began effective rearmament, the French emphasis being on defence. France's allies in eastern Europe knew, after the building of the purely defensive Maginot Line (see p. 57), that they would be unwise to count on French help.

Hitler, an Austrian by birth, had always wanted Austria and its German people to be brought into some sort of unity with Germany. In February 1938 Schuschnigg, the Austrian Chancellor, was invited to Berchtesgaden in the Bavarian Alps to meet Hitler. Here Schuschnigg was presented with two alternatives: either to legalise the Austrian Nazi Party, appoint its leader as Minister of the Interior (and therefore in charge of the country's police), and integrate Austria's economy with that of Germany, or to refuse these terms and provoke an overwhelming German invasion. Austria had lost her protector in Mussolini when the Rome–Berlin Axis was formed, so Schuschnigg inevitably chose the first alternative.

Hitler now believed that the Austrian Nazis would gradually take over the country, but Schuschnigg decided on a plebiscite. The Austrians were to declare whether they wished to be independent or united with Germany. Sunday 13 March was fixed as polling day, and the vote was expected to go against Germany. But on 11 March the German army took up positions along the frontier. Schuschnigg agreed to cancel the plebiscite, and then resigned, saying, 'We are resolved that on no account . . . shall German blood be spilled.' A Nazi government was formed, and this then invited German troops to 'restore order' in the country. On 12 March the German army entered Vienna, and the Austrian government announced Austria's membership of the German Reich. After a triumphal drive 'in Vienna, Hitler addressed a gigantic audience from the balcony of the palace where the Habsburgs had resided while he slept in doss-houses'.[1]

The plebiscite was then allowed to take place, and 99·75 per cent of the voters approved of Austria's new status as part of a large state again. Though the figures were probably exaggerated, the change was genuinely popular amongst many Austrians. The British government adopted the attitude that, like the Rhineland, this was German territory and the Austrian people apparently approved. The French government had just resigned. So the Anschluss, condemned at Versailles, came about. Germany now controlled the communications of the middle Danube region, Hitler's prestige was high, and the lack of resistance encouraged him to seek further gains, this time in Czechoslovakia.

Czechoslovakia was a new multinational state formed in 1919. It had an efficient and well-equipped army, strong fortifications and defence agreements with France and Russia. Moreover, it had enjoyed good and democratic government under Masaryk, president until his retirement in 1935, and then under Beneš. However, there was constant trouble from the foreign minorities, especially the 3 million Sudeten Germans who wanted self-government. Hitler encouraged their demands, for he was determined to occupy this democratic Slav state created by the hated Versailles Treaty. In June 1938 he therefore sent a secret directive to the German army: 'It is my unalterable decision to smash Czechoslovakia by military action in the near future.'

This was followed by an increase in Nazi violence in the Sudetenland, and a stream of Nazi propaganda about the Czechs' harsh treatment of their German subjects. In August Neville Chamberlain, the British Prime Minister, sent Lord Runciman to Prague to investigate the situation, and on 15 September Chamberlain himself went to Germany for the first of three conferences with Hitler. At the Berchtesgaden meeting, Hitler demanded the cession of the Sudetenland and threatened war if this was not agreed to. While the Führer continued his military preparations, Chamberlain discussed the matter with the French, and the Czechs, who felt betrayed and deserted, eventually agreed to cede to Germany all territories where more than half the inhabitants were

[1] R. Grunberger, *Germany, 1918–45.*

German.

A week later, at Godesberg on the Rhine, Chamberlain informed Hitler of this decision. The Führer, however, did not want and did not expect this appeasement. He hoped for an excuse to invade Czechoslovakia, and now demanded that his army should occupy the Sudetenland by 1 October before any plebiscite could be held. Opinion began to harden in London and there was an atmosphere of impending war. But Britain, still less France, was not yet prepared for war, and Chamberlain believed that the British people wanted peace at any price. So the third conference was held at Munich, and there the British, French, German and Italian premiers agreed that the German army should occupy the Sudetenland on 1 October, and that parts of Czechoslovakia should go to Poland and Hungary.

The following day Chamberlain told cheering crowds in London that the Munich Agreement was symbolic of the desire of the British and German peoples 'never to go to war with one another again'. The majority of the British public supported this policy of appeasement. They said that it gained time for Britain to grow stronger, that Germany had been harshly treated in 1919 and would behave better if concessions were made to her, and that everything possible should be done to avert another major war. On the other hand Germany had gained in territory, population, resources and prestige, and the policy had encouraged aggression and only postponed war. Czechoslovakia had been deserted despite the guarantees, and the democracies had lost a small but powerful ally. The opponents of appeasement believed that a stand should have been made against the dictator before he became too powerful.

The new frontiers of Czechoslovakia were guaranteed by the four Powers at the Munich Conference. In March 1939, however, disorders between the Slovaks and the Czechs provided the excuse for a German occupation. This was an act of naked aggression, and Chamberlain's policy of appeasement now came to an abrupt end: British public opinion now forced their leaders to stand firm against any further aggression.

Hitler's attention now moved to Poland and the Baltic coast. In March the small area of Memel was ceded to Germany by Lithuania, but German propaganda was centred on Danzig and the Polish corridor, and it was clear that Hitler's intention was to link East Prussia with Germany. At the end of March, however, the British and French governments gave Poland full support in rejecting any demands for territory. Similarly, when in April Mussolini invaded Albania, Britain and France gave guarantees to Greece, Romania and Turkey. This firm attitude on the part of the democracies persuaded Germany and Italy to sign the Pact of Steel, a stronger military alliance.

It was now clear that Communist Russia held the balance of power in Europe. The guarantees that Britain and France had given Poland were militarily weak because of Poland's geographical position. It was therefore necessary to secure Russian help. During the early summer of 1939, Britain and France negotiated with Russia, but little progress was made, partly because of mutual distrust and partly because Russia was not yet prepared for a war against Germany. Since the Russians wanted both territory and peace, and Germany could offer both, talks began between these two countries, and on 24 August the Nazi-Soviet Pact was signed in the Kremlin. The secret clauses were the important part: Eastern Europe was clearly demarcated into German and Russian spheres of influence, and Poland particularly was to be divided.

The balance of power was now in Germany's favour, and early on 1 September the German army and air force attacked Poland. On Sunday, 3 September came the British ultimatum: unless German troops were withdrawn from Poland Britain and Germany would be at war. The ultimatum was ignored, and the Second World War began.

Historians differ in their interpretations of the causes of the war. Some trace the basic cause to the Treaty of Versailles at the end of the First World War, in that the German wish to change the terms of the treaty was justifiable. Others blame the policy of appeasement followed by the British and French governments in the 1930s. The war arose, so it is said, because the British and French refused to stand up to the dictators while they were still weak. There should have been a Franco-British invasion of Germany in 1936 when Germany invaded the Rhineland. But during the early years of Hitler's rule the overwhelming majority of the British public was totally unwilling to wage war—only Churchill amongst leading British politicians proposed that Britain and France should move against Hitler as soon as he broke an international agreement. It was only by the beginning of 1939 that the feeling grew that Hitler could only be stopped by force or the threat of force.

The British historian, A. J. P. Taylor, has argued that Hitler's aims were moderate and justifiable. 'In principle and doctrine, Hitler was no more wicked and unscrupulous than many other contemporary statesmen . . . Danzig was the most justified of German grievances.'[1] He has criticised British policy for not appeasing Hitler more, and has seemed to absolve the Nazi dictator from sole responsibility for the war.

Other historians lay emphasis on the failure of Britain and France to

[1] A. J. P. Taylor, *Origins of the Second World War*.

reach agreement with Russia. They not only distrusted Russia but feared Communism, and made little response to the Russian proposals for collective security put forward from 1934 onwards. In addition, it seems clear that the Nazi-Soviet Pact of August 1939 precipitated the war.

Most historians, however, emphasise the responsibility of Hitler. 'The Second World War was Hitler's war. He planned it, began it, and ultimately lost it.'[1] It was his unscrupulous, ruthless and aggressive policies which plunged the world into six years of devastating warfare.

Second World War 1939 to 1945

September 1939 to September 1940

Fifty-six German divisions attacked Poland, the German air force controlled the skies, and there was never any doubt about the result. The Germans conducted the campaign at lightning speed against a weak Polish army whose only serious resistance was around Warsaw. Fighting ceased at the end of September, exactly four weeks after the invasion, and Poland was then partitioned between Russia and Germany. Russia had invaded Eastern Poland halfway through September, her armies had taken part in none of the fighting, and now the three Baltic states and half of Poland fell to her. The remainder of Poland was occupied by Germany.

Meanwhile, the Poles hoped unsuccessfully for an Anglo-French attack in the west. Indeed, the Allies missed a golden opportunity in that the Siegfried Line, the German defence system of her western frontier, was relatively weak. The French generals, however, never seriously considered an offensive, and the British army was too small at this stage to be really effective. Instead, both sides contented themselves with patrols, occasional skirmishes and some artillery fire. It was Hitler's intention to attack France in November, but this was postponed until the spring. Thus, for eight months there was a 'phoney war' on the western front which resulted in a false sense of security in London and Paris and some relaxation of effort.

At the end of November 1939 the Russian army invaded Finland with the intention of extending Russian territory to the north-west of Leningrad. Despite the size of the Russian army, the Finns, who were better equipped and trained for winter warfare, put up an heroic and skilful resistance until March 1940. Meanwhile, Britain and France negotiated with Sweden with the object of sending troops to help Finland. After the defeat of Finland, Hitler believed that there was a

[1] E. L. Woodward, *The Listener*, 3 Sept. 1964.

danger that the Allies might occupy Norway in order to control the Swedish iron ore which was exported through Narvik. Therefore, on 9 April German forces occupied Denmark and the strategic ports of Norway. Resistance in the rest of Norway was soon ended, and the Germans installed a Norwegian Nazi named Quisling as ruler. Narvik was recaptured by the British but was evacuated in June.

At dawn on 10 May Hitler struck in the west. Holland, Belgium and Luxemburg had hoped to remain neutral in the war, but the presence of the extremely strong Maginot Line on the Franco-German frontier meant that the German attack on France had to pass through the Low Countries. Dutch resistance collapsed after four days of fighting which included the heavy bombing of Rotterdam. The French, British and Belgians attempted to form a front between the west end of the Maginot Line and Antwerp, but the German armies, taking an unexpected route through the Ardennes, broke through the French lines at Sedan. The result was that the British, Belgians and some French were cut off from the main French armies. The Germans did not aim for Paris as in 1914 but for the mouth of the River Somme, which they reached on 20 May. They then moved north and forced the British back towards Calais and Dunkirk. Between 27 May and 4 June nearly 340,000 British, French and Belgian trops were evacuated from a narrow and shrinking strip of coast near Dunkirk. They were helped by a three-day pause in the German advance, by calm weather in the Channel, and by the hundreds of boats of all sizes from warships to small private yachts which brought the shattered armies back to England. Morale was high and the evacuation was almost regarded as a famous victory. In fact, Dunkirk was a staggering defeat: the British armies had lost nearly all their equipment and their French allies were left to bear the brunt of the German attack.

On 5 June the German attack on France recommenced. Within a few days Paris was occupied and soon after German panzers crossed the River Loire. Reynaud, the Prime Minister, resigned, and the new French government headed by the 85-year-old Marshal Pétain asked for an armistice. This was dictated by Hitler on 22 June in the same railway carriage in which the Germans signed the armistice of November 1918. In view of his devastating victory, Hitler's terms were relatively moderate. Northern France, including Paris, and the Atlantic coast were to be occupied by Germany, the French paying the costs of the occupation. The rest of France, with its capital at Vichy, was to be administered by the French and not occupied by the Germans. French prisoners-of-war remained in German hands as hostages. On 10 June Mussolini, having decided who was winning the war, invaded France in the Alps. After a fortnight's inconclusive fighting an armistice was signed between Italy and the Vichy government.

The German victory was a triumph for advanced strategy, brilliant organisation and superior equipment. The Germans concentrated their forces while the French armies were dispersed; the Germans were aggressive while the French were defensive; the Germans had meticulously planned their attack while the French were unprepared and poorly led. In addition, French politicians and the country generally were divided and defeatist. This collapse of morale was an important factor in the fall of France.

On 10 May Winston Churchill replaced Neville Chamberlain as Prime Minister of Britain (see chapter 6). The task facing him was daunting. Following the surrender of France, only the Channel prevented a German invasion of Britain, but the Channel was controlled by the British navy. Early in July the French navy at Oran in North Africa was destroyed by the British: the French had refused to sail to an allied or neutral port and if used by the Germans, the French fleet would have tilted the balance of naval power in Germany's favour. In view of British superiority at sea, it was vitally necessary for Germany to gain control of the air if an invasion across the Channel was to take place. If the Luftwaffe could gain air superiority not only could it cover an invasion, but it could possibly force Britain to make peace.

The 'Battle of Britain' lasted from July to September. Germany had about 2,600 aircraft, more than twice the number of planes available to the Royal Air Force. During July the Germans raided Channel shipping and ports, but in mid-August the Luftwaffe turned its attention to airfields and London. It inflicted great damage, but in so doing suffered too greatly itself for the raids to continue, and in early September it switched to night attacks on London and the big cities. But again the Germans suffered heavily from the attacks of British fighter planes (Spitfires and Hurricanes): during August and September the Luftwaffe lost 1,244 planes. In mid-September Hitler postponed the invasion of Britain, and soon after this intensive bombing by the Germans ended. The Battle of Britain was of vital importance. Speaking of the few hundred fighter pilots who, with the assistance of radar communications, ended the German threat, Churchill said: 'Never in the field of human conflict was so much owed by so many to so few.'

September 1940 to October 1942

In the summer of 1940, following the defeat of France, Hitler began to prepare for the invasion of Russia. The defeat of Russia would remove a potential ally of Britain and would also strengthen the position of Japan, Germany's ally, in the Far East. Hitler had always opposed Communism and hoped to destroy the only Communist government then in existence. It is probable, however, that his primary motive was the expansion of German power into eastern Europe. Not only did Germany require supplies, food and oil particularly, but Hitler could not contemplate the presence of a rival military force on the continent of Europe. 'There must never be a military power other than Germany west of the Urals.'

However, Hitler was forced to modify his plans because Mussolini's independent foreign policy widened the area of conflict. In September and October 1940 Italy invaded Egypt and Greece respectively. However, the Italian forces, like the French, were obsolescent and soon defeated by the British and the Greeks. In these circumstances Hitler felt compelled to come to his ally's help. Hungary and Romania had already been occupied by Germany and Nazi regimes established, and in March 1941 Germany occupied Bulgaria. The government of Yugoslavia agreed to join Germany in return for Greek territory, but there was popular opposition to this and the government was overthrown. Hitler then decided to postpone the start of his invasion of Russia in order to crush Yugoslavia. Early in April 17,000 people were killed in a sudden German divebomber attack on Belgrade. In two weeks Yugoslav resistance was ended, and the Germans began an invasion of Greece. The British rushed reinforcements to Greece from Egypt, but these were soon forced to retreat to the island of Crete. After a week's fighting at the end of May 1941, Crete fell to the Germans. Thus all of south-east Europe was under German control.

Meanwhile, Hitler sent German forces under Rommel to North Africa to help the Italians. The British, weakened by the assistance given to the Greeks, were driven back to the Egyptian frontier. From the British point of view, the only success at this time was their occupation of Italian East Africa, although in addition their resistance in Greece and Crete had delayed the German attack on Russia.

On 22 June 1941, exactly a year after the French armistice, 160 German divisions invaded Russia: Operation Barbarossa had begun. The Russian army consisted of about 200 divisions but these were very badly led and inadequately equipped. In consequence three German armies penetrated deeply and quickly into Russia in the direction of Leningrad, Moscow and Kiev. Against the advice of his generals who wanted a strong thrust against Moscow, Hitler insisted that the three armies remain roughly the same size. He intended that the two armies heading for Leningrad and the Ukraine should, having achieved their

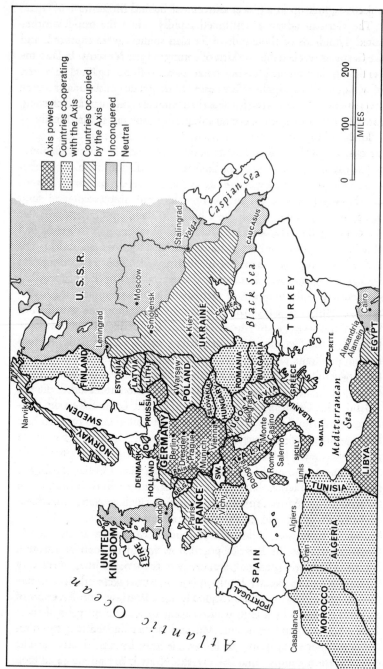

Legend:
- Axis powers
- Countries co-operating with the Axis
- Countries occupied by the Axis
- Unconquered
- Neutral

0 100 200 MILES

Europe at the height of Hitler's power, September 1942

objectives, link up in a pincer movement behind Moscow.

The German advance continued rapidly while the good weather lasted. Hundreds of thousands of Russian soldiers were captured, and the Germans reached the outskirts of Leningrad and Moscow. In December the Russians under Zhukhov counterattacked and regained land west of Moscow. Campaigning then ceased in the arctic conditions of a very severe winter. Whereas the Russians had suitable equipment and clothing for these conditions, the German soldiers had not and suffered badly.

In the spring of 1942 Hitler insisted on concentrating the German attacks on southern Russia. Again the Germans had spectacular victories, capturing the Crimea and driving towards the Caucasus Mountains. In September they began the attack on the big city of Stalingrad on the River Volga, an important industrial and communications centre whose capture would be a blow to Stalin's prestige. Instead of surrounding the city, the Germans under von Paulus made a frontal attack. Every street and every house was bitterly defended until at the end of October the Germans had an army of a quarter of a million besieging about 60,000 Russians in the central part of Stalingrad.

Meanwhile in other parts of the world Germany and her ally, Japan, were successful. In Egypt the British were forced to retreat to El Alamein, about seventy miles from Alexandria, and there was a real possibility that the Germans in North Africa and southern Russia would link up in a huge pincer movement in the Middle East. In the Far East the Japanese victories were as spectacular as those of the Germans (see chapter 11), and British power in India seemed threatened. In the Atlantic the German U-Boat threat to Allied communications was extremely serious. Nine hundred ships were sunk during 1942; in July twenty-three out of thirty-four ships on convoy to Archangel in Russia were sunk by fast and powerful German submarines.

In Germany and occupied Europe the Nazis began to put their racial theories into practice. The population of eastern Europe was to be reduced in order to provide space for German settlers. Therefore, educated Poles were to be exterminated while the remainder were to become a slave class. All available food in Russia was to be sent to Germany so that the Russian population would be reduced through famine. The Nazis intended particularly to remove the Jews, eventually by extermination. Nearly 2 million Jews in Russia were killed by extermination squads. In 1940 the 400,000 Jews of Warsaw were herded into a ghetto enclosed by a high wall. During 1942 three-quarters of these were taken away to be exterminated, and the remainder after a stubborn resistance were killed in the following year by an SS attack. The extermination camps organised by the Nazis killed about 4½ million

Jews. The largest of these camps was at Auschwitz in Poland where eventually Zyklon B. gas was used and the bodies were burnt.[1] In addition, about 5 million slave workers, often prisoners-of-war, toiled in appalling conditions in German industry.

September 1942 marked the height of Hitler's power. The territory under this one man's control stretched from the Spanish frontier to Moscow, and from the northern tip of Norway to Egypt. However, British and Russian industry was now geared to the production of weapons of the same quality or better than those of the Germans. In addition, the Japanese by attacking Pearl Harbour in December 1941 had brought the United States into the war. The combined strength of America, Russia and Britain meant that German defeat was ultimately almost inevitable.

October 1942 to June 1944

The Battle of Stalingrad was fought between September 1942 and January 1943. Until mid-November the Germans had the initiative, but after this point the besiegers became the besieged. The Russians moved in to the west of Stalingrad and cut off the Germans fighting in the city from the main German armies. Hitler refused to contemplate a retreat and at the end of January von Paulus surrendered. It was a crushing defeat for the Germans, who during 1943 were gradually pushed back by a general Russian advance. By the winter of 1943 Smolensk, Kiev and the Crimea had been recaptured. Early in 1944 the Russians, now superior in numbers and equipment, entered Poland.

When the German pressure on Russia was at its greatest during 1942, Stalin wanted Britain and the United States to open a second front in Western Europe. Initially the Americans acquiesced to this proposal, but eventually they agreed with the British that the preparations needed for a major invasion were too great for it to be accomplished in 1942. Therefore the two Allies decided to concentrate their forces in North Africa.

At the beginning of September 1942 the Germans under Rommel, the 'Desert Fox', attacked the British 8th Army under Montgomery at El Alamein. The British held their ground and Montgomery, an imaginative and careful general who could inspire the soldiers under him, pre-

---

[1] 'It now only took from three to fifteen minutes to kill the people in chambers, according to climatic conditions. We knew when the people were dead because their screaming stopped. . . . After the bodies were removed our special commandos (i.e. special squads of Jewish inmates) took off the rings and extracted the gold from the teeth of the corpses.' (Rudolf Hoess, commandant of Auschwitz.) Quoted by W. Shirer, *Rise and Fall of the Third Reich*.

pared his counterattack. The decisive Battle of El Alamein was fought at the end of October, and by the end of it the Germans were in full retreat. By January 1943 the British had reached the German defence line on the Tunisian border. Meanwhile, in November 1942 the Americans had landed at Casablanca, Oran and Algiers. Morocco and Algeria, who had supported the Vichy government in France, were quickly occupied. Hitler sent large reinforcements to Tunisia which delayed the outcome, but in May 1943 the German armies, numbering 160,000 men, surrendered. This was a major German defeat and exposed the southern flank of the Axis empire—'the soft under-belly' in Churchill's phrase—to attack.

The delay in defeating the Germans in North Africa meant that the attack on France had to be postponed until 1944. Therefore it was decided to invade Italy with the object of removing Italy from the war and then possibly striking eastwards to the Balkans. In July 1943 the Allies landed in Sicily. About three weeks later Mussolini was deposed,[1] and the new government sued for peace at the beginning of September. At the same time, Sicily having been occupied, the Allies landed at Salerno and in southern Italy. However, although Italy had surrendered, the growing number of German troops put up a strong resistance and slowed down the Allied advance. The first few months of 1944 saw very heavy fighting around the Benedictine monastery of Monte Cassino. In June Rome was captured.

During 1943 there were two top level conferences between the Allies. In January Churchill and Roosevelt met at Casablanca. Here they made two decisions: to postpone the invasion of France until the following year, and to accept only the unconditional surrender of Germany. The second conference was at Teheran in Persia, and was held in November. Stalin was also present on this occasion. The conference was largely concerned with strategy. Stalin and Roosevelt pressed for a cross-channel assault on France, while Churchill tended to favour an attack directed at central Europe. The British premier feared that it would be difficult to dislodge the Russians from eastern Europe if they were allowed to occupy it. The Americans, however, believed that an attack on France was wisest on military grounds; political motives, for them, were less important.

June 1944 to May 1945

The preparations for the Anglo-American invasion of France continued for many months before 6 June 1944, which was eventually fixed as

[1] In April 1945 Mussolini was killed by Italian resistance fighters.

D-Day. The Supreme Commander for the invasion was the American, General Eisenhower, while Montgomery commanded the actual landings and the first campaigns. The Germans had sixty divisions in France, but did not know at which point on the coast the Allies would land. Heavy bombing of the coastal areas north of the mouth of the Seine, and particularly around Calais, led the Germans to expect an attack there. Throughout France the railway system was bombed into paralysis, and the small German air force was driven from the skies.

On 6 June 130,000 Allied troops were landed on the Normandy coast east of the Cherbourg peninsula, while parachute troops secured bridges and other strategic points at both ends of the landing area. There was no serious resistance, and within a month one million troops were brought to Normandy. An artificial harbour was towed across the Channel, and this helped in the landing of vast quantities of weapons and supplies. Pluto—pipe line under the ocean—brought fuel from England to the Allied forces. Montgomery's plan was for the British to draw the German forces to them around Caen, while the Americans gained control of the Cherbourg peninsula and then struck south. In July 100,000 German troops were surrounded at Falaise, and their defeat[1] there destroyed German military power in France. By mid-August Normandy was cleared of German forces, and on 25 August Paris was liberated.

By the beginning of September, helped by an American landing in the south of France, the Allies had gained control of the whole of the country, and began the occupation of Belgium. At this point German resistance stiffened, and the Allied advance was also hindered by their long lines of communications. In mid-September the Allies attempted to secure a bridgehead over the Rhine at Arnhem by landing three airborne divisions by parachute. However, bad weather and the presence of two SS Panzer divisions ended any hope of success. For the next three months the front line changed little, although Aachen was captured, the first German city to fall into Allied hands. In December Hitler made a last desperate attack in the Ardennes, but after ten days the German advance was stopped.

During this period Allied bombing of Germany became more destructive. There was precision bombing of communication centres, rocket sites, submarine pens, factories and other similarly important

[1] 'The battlefield at Falaise was unquestionably one of the greatest "killing grounds" of any of the war areas. Roads, highways and fields were so choked with destroyed equipment and with dead men and animals that passage through the area was extremely difficult. . . . It was literally possible to walk for hundreds of yards at a time stepping on nothing but dead and decaying flesh.' (D. Eisenhower.) Quoted by R. C. Mowat, *Ruin and Resurgence, 1939–65.*

D–Day: troops coming ashore from landing craft, 6 June 1944

A concentration camp near Munich, 1945. American troops force German civilians to dig graves for the half–burnt, emaciated bodies of 4,000 Jews

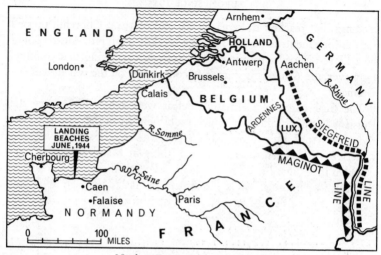

Northern France and the Low Countries

objectives, and also area bombing in which large sections of cities were destroyed. The results of bombing as far as production was concerned were disappointing for the Allies: in fact, German war production increased until the middle of 1944. The object of area bombing was partly to break civilian morale. Altogether 600,000 German citizens were killed as a result of bombing raids (cf. 60,000 in Britain). In February 1945 135,000 civilians and 1,600 acres of city were destroyed in a single enormous raid on Dresden[1] (cf. 71,000 killed at Hiroshima, and 600 acres of London destroyed during the whole war). However, these raids probably had little effect in hastening the end of the war.

Meanwhile the Russian advance continued in the east. During 1944 Russian armies occupied Romania, Bulgaria and Hungary, and passed through the northern part of Yugoslavia. In August the Polish Resistance organised a rising in Warsaw against the Germans. It was hoped that the Russians, who were rapidly approaching the capital, would help, but the Russian army halted some distance from Warsaw and then moved forward very slowly. After desperate fighting, the Germans crushed the rising. Two reasons are given for the Russian failure to render any assistance: firstly, the German resistance was strong, and secondly, the Russians hoped that the leaders of the rising who supported the Polish government-in-exile in London would be removed to clear the way for a rival Polish government-in-exile in Russia.

The Allied armies in Italy were rather neglected after the Normandy

[1] A discussion in *The Times* of this raid suggested that reports of civilian casualties may have been greatly exaggerated.

landings, but reached Bologna by the end of 1944. Churchill pressed for reinforcements to be sent so that a breakthrough into Austria could be achieved in order to prevent the Russians occupying that country. However, the Americans wanted to concentrate on the war in western Germany.

The final stages of Germany's defeat were rapid. In January the Russians began an offensive which took them from the Vistula to the Oder. In April they occupied Vienna. Meanwhile the British and Americans succeeded in crossing the Rhine in March and soon surrounded the Ruhr. British forces then moved north-east to the foot of the Jutland peninsula, while the Americans headed for Dresden and Leipzig. On 25 April the Russian and American armies met on the Elbe. German resistance in North Italy collapsed, and early in May 1945 Germany surrendered.

Since January Hitler had been living in the concrete bunker in the gardens of the Chancellery in Berlin. He was now 'a stooped figure with a pale and puffy face, hunched in his chair, his hands trembling, his left arm subject to a violent twitching which he did his best to conceal. A sick man. . . . When he walked he dragged one leg behind him.'[1] Now totally unrealistic, he still controlled the strategy of the German armies. He refused to give up voluntarily any territory conquered by Germany, with the result that large German forces remained in Denmark and Norway and in northern Italy and Austria when they could have been withdrawn for the defence of Germany. But with the Russians fighting in the outskirts of Berlin, the downfall of the Third Reich was inevitable. On 29 April Hitler appointed Admiral Dönitz as his successor. He then married his mistress, Eva Braun. About thirty-six hours after the wedding Hitler and his new wife committed suicide. This was on the afternoon of Monday, 30 April 1945. On Hitler's instructions, his body was then burned. He was 56 years old.

The war of 1939–45 was much more of a world war than that of 1914–18. This was partly because the movement of armies was more extensive, and partly because of the part played by Japan.[2] In consequence the loss of life, the damage to property and the cost of the war were vastly greater than during the First World War. It has been calculated that up to 40 million people died because of the Third Reich. The loss of life due to the Far East war added enormously to this figure. Europe was now much weaker, and it was clear that the two dominating powers in the world were the United States and Russia. Soon Europe was to be divided between them.

[1] Manteuffel. Quoted in W. Shirer, *The Rise and Fall of the Third Reich*. Hitler was wounded in an attempt on his life in July, 1944.

[2] The war in the Far East is described in chapter 11.

3

Europe since 1945

The End of Wartime Unity 1945

In February 1945 the three Allied war leaders, Roosevelt, Churchill and Stalin, met in conference at Yalta in the Crimea. Here they discussed and reached agreement on some of the postwar problems facing Europe and the world. It was arranged that a conference should meet in April at San Francisco to draft the Charter of the United Nations Organisation. Agreement was reached on Russian representation at the United Nations and on the form of voting in the Security Council. It was then decided that Russia should enter the war against Japan not later than three months after the defeat of Germany. Agreement was also reached on the problem of zones of occupation of Germany. It had originally been decided to have three zones—British, American and Russian—but it was now agreed that a fourth French zone should be formed. In addition, although Berlin was to be in the Russian zone, it was to be divided likewise into four parts, with a Joint Control Commission to coordinate the government. The three Powers agreed, in a Declaration on Liberated Europe, that there should be representative governments and free elections in Eastern Europe.

The main point of disagreement at the Yalta Conference concerned Poland. Britain had entered the war in 1939 in order to protect the liberties of Poland, and after the Russo-German occupation and partition of the country, a Polish government-in-exile came to London. After the German attack on Russia in 1941, Russia formed a rival Communist government-in-exile in Moscow. This Communist government was put in power in Poland by the Russians when the Red Army had swept the Germans out of the country. At Yalta Britain and the United States agreed with Russia on two points: firstly, that the Curzon Line should be Poland's eastern frontier so that Russia could keep that part of Poland which had fallen to her in 1939; secondly, that if some non-Communists, including the head of the London Polish government, were included in the Communist government imposed by Russia on Poland, this provisional government would be recognised by Britain and the United States. On a third point no agreement was reached: Stalin wanted German territory east of the Rivers Oder and Neisse to be given to Poland as compensation for her losses to Russia. Britain and the United States would not agree to this, and said that the final fixing of Poland's western frontier should await the Peace Conference.

Between February and July 1945 British and American disagreement with Russian policy grew. Churchill had long feared Russian intentions, and was now very pessimistic for the future as the Red Army forced its way into central Europe. Roosevelt became disillusioned, but was also a tired and sick man. He died on 12 April, and was succeeded as president by Harry S. Truman.

The West's fears for the future of Eastern Europe seemed to be justified. In Poland the non-Communist political leaders were imprisoned. In Hungary the Russians imposed very heavy reparations on a devastated country, and in March enforced a hasty and unfair land reform. In 1944 there were only about 900 Communists in Romania, yet in March 1945 the Russians forced the appointment of a Communist as Prime Minister. In Bulgaria the Communists seized power when the Russians arrived and all opponents were suppressed. In Czechoslovakia a coalition government was set up in which the key positions were held by Communists. In Yugoslavia the resistance movement against the Germans during the war was led by Communists under Tito, who arranged with Stalin that the Yugoslavs rather than the Russians should set up a government after the Germans were defeated. Therefore, in March 1945 a coalition government, largely composed of Communists, was set up by the Yugoslavs. In Albania Communist guerrillas took over the country and declared a republic. In addition eastern Germany and eastern Austria were occupied by the Russians. Therefore, when the next conference of the three wartime Allies was held in July, the Communists, backed by Russian power, held all the important positions in the governments of eastern European countries.

In July 1945 the three victorious countries in the Second World War met at Potsdam near Berlin. Russia was represented by Stalin and his foreign minister Molotov, the United States by Truman and Byrnes, and Britain by Churchill and Eden. Halfway through the Conference, Churchill was defeated in the British General Election (see p. 229) and thereafter the British representatives at Potsdam were Attlee and Bevin.

The main subject of the Conference was the future organisation of defeated Germany. Germany and Berlin were to be divided into four zones as agreed at Yalta, with a Joint Control Commission in Berlin. Germany was to be disarmed and the Nazi Party destroyed. There was to be no central government in Germany 'for the time being', but Germany was to be treated as one economic unit. It was agreed that the foreign ministers should prepare peace treaties with Italy, Bulgaria, Romania, Hungary and Finland. On two subjects, however, no agreement was reached. The German lands east of the Oder-Neisse line were now under Polish administration, but while Russia considered this as a *fait accompli*, Britain and the United States regarded it as a provisional arrangement only. In addition Russia wished to impose huge reparations on Germany, but Britain and the United States, after the experience of reparations in the 1920s, opposed this, and the matter was left undecided. 'Potsdam marked the real end of wartime unity.'[1] The conference had revealed the fundamental cleavages between the United States and Britain on the one side and Russia on the other, and the meeting broke up in an atmosphere of mutual accusation which augured ill for the future.

The Rift Widens 1945 to 1947

During the two years after the Potsdam Conference, Communism strengthened its grip on eastern Europe. There were some non-Communists in the Polish government, but by censorship and terrorism non-Communist political strength was reduced. Rigged elections early in 1947 gave the Communists 400 out of 450 seats. In Hungary the Russians allowed free elections in November 1945 and a majority of seats was won by the Small Farmers Party. The Communists led by Rakosi won 17 per cent of the votes. Nevertheless, Communists held the key positions in the government, and the power of the non-Communist ministers was gradually reduced.

In Romania the Russian-imposed Communist government held elections in November 1946. These resulted in a big majority for the government. Similarly in Bulgaria, non-Communist leaders were killed or imprisoned, and elections in October 1946 produced a large majority for the Communist government. In November 1945 elections were held in Yugoslavia. Ninety-six per cent of the electorate supported Tito's People's Front, and thereafter Yugoslavia became a republic and a fully Communist state. The one exception in Russian-controlled

[1] W. Hayter, review article in *The Observer*.

Central and Eastern Europe in 1945: territorial changes and zones of occupation

eastern Europe was Czechoslovakia. In May 1946 democratic elections were held resulting in a coalition government in which the Communists remained in a minority.

In Greece during the German occupation the Communists were the main resistance group. On Stalin's instructions they cooperated with the non-Communist government which was formed after the Germans left. In December 1944, however, the Communists attempted to take over the government and, while this was prevented by British troops, they still controlled large areas of Greece. Elections in 1946 resulted in a majority for the right-wing royalists and a plebiscite showed that 70 per cent of the population favoured a monarchy. This was the signal for a renewed Communist revolt which lasted three years from 1946 to 1949. The Communists received supplies from Albania, Yugoslavia and Bulgaria, and only British and American help for the government prevented a Communist victory in this devastated country.

The dispute between Russia and the West in Persia is dealt with in chapter 7. Stalin's attempt to obtain bases in Turkey helped to arouse Western suspicions. There was also a dispute over the control of Trieste, the port at the northern end of the Adriatic. In 1945 part of the city and the surrounding area was occupied by the Yugoslavs and part by the British and Americans. Neither side would transfer its zone to the other.

In Germany there were disagreements about reparations. There was no economic coordination between the four zones, as the French refused to cooperate. (The Russians would probably have refused anyway.) Therefore, no central economic agencies for the whole of Germany were set up. However, in March 1946, agreement was reached on a permitted level of industry for Germany; the proportion of industrial plant above this level was available to Russia as reparations, and it was expected that the Russians would allow food from their zone to enter the three Western zones. The Russians, though, took the machinery but provided no food in return, and in consequence in May 1946 the West stopped the payment of reparations. In March 1947 the Russians suggested a provisional government including some Communists for the whole of Germany. This government would then pay ten billion dollars in reparations. This idea was rejected by the West.

The only successful negotiations during this period were concerned with the peace treaties with Italy, Hungary, Romania, Bulgaria and Finland. These were signed in February 1947 in Paris. Russia gained land from Romania and Finland, and Italy lost her colonial empire. There were other transfers of territory but these were of little significance.

During the war quite strong sympathies for the Russian people had developed in Britain and the United States. This was based on their struggle against a common enemy. The change from alliance to bitter and frustrated opposition in the immediate postwar years was very sudden, and even governments, who were aware of the difficulties in the alliance during the war, found difficulty in adapting themselves to a new situation, one in which the Soviet Union rather than Germany was the enemy. A divided Europe and mutual hostility between East and West reluctantly came to be accepted. In 1946 Churchill said at Fulton in the United States: 'From Stettin in the Baltic to Trieste in the Adriatic an Iron Curtain has descended across the continent.' Gradually the point of view developed that, as Truman put it, 'unless Russia is faced with an iron fist and strong language, another war is in the making'.

Three main reasons have been suggested to explain Russia's policy. The occupation of eastern Europe would provide security for Russia in the event of an attack by the Western Powers. The West's hostility towards Communism was shown by its intervention in the Russian Civil War (see pp. 143–5), and in the 1930s Stalin feared that the West would reach agreement with Hitler to allow a German attack on Russia. Stalin was suspicious of the apparent slowness of Britain and America in opening up a second front in France against Germany. In addition, the two Western Powers did not inform Russia about the development of the atomic bomb until the war against Germany was over. Thus Stalin regarded the Communist states of eastern Europe as a buffer between Russia and a hostile West which might include a future German aggressor.

It is believed by some historians that the occupation of eastern Europe was a continuation of Russia's traditional policy of imperialist expansion. Russia's satellites would assist with her economic recovery, and would enable her to rival the strength of the United States and the British Empire. Other writers on this period stress Russia's wish to increase the areas of the world under Communist domination. They believe that the Communist takeover of eastern Europe was part of revolutionary Marxist policy aiming at world domination, and point out that the Rusians emphasised the imminent collapse of capitalism. It is by no means clear which of these three motives was the most important for Stalin.

The Cold War 1947 to 1953

Truman Doctrine

During the winter of 1946–47 the British government decided to reduce its foreign commitments. The cost of keeping troops in Germany,

Austria, Trieste and Greece, as well as other parts of the world, was proving too heavy, and in February 1947 Britain told the United States that she could not continue to give aid to Greece after the end of March. Truman's response was immediate. Without Western aid Greece would be added to the list of Soviet satellites. Therefore, in an address to Congress, he said, 'It must be the policy of the United States of America to support free peoples who are resisting attempted subjugation by armed minorities, or by outside pressure.' Truman asked for and received $400 million as aid to Greece and Turkey. This Truman Doctrine of the containment of Communism by direct American aid to countries threatened with Communism, became accepted US policy, and marked a radical departure from precedent.

Marshall Plan

In 1943 the United Nations Relief and Rehabilitation Administration (UNRRA) was set up. Its function was to provide relief in countries liberated from Germany until, and after, national governments could assume responsibility. It existed from 1944 to 1947, and during this time it provided clothing, food and medical supplies, and helped in the rehabilitation of agriculture and industry in Greece, Yugoslavia, Czechoslovakia, Austria, Italy and Poland. Sixty-five per cent of its funds came from the United States.

By 1947 it was clear that much greater aid was required to restore the economy of Europe. Therefore, in June 1947, Marshall, the new American Secretary of State, offered United States aid to the states of Europe on condition that they produced a joint, coordinated plan for its use. Spain was excluded from this offer, but Russia, who thought that this was a method of spreading American influence, also refused and prevented the Soviet satellites from taking part in the plan. The result was that in 1948 sixteen European states and the three Western zones of Germany set up the Organisation for European Economic Cooperation (OEEC). This body administered the funds received from the United States. Marshall Aid lasted for four years (1948–52). This generous aid had two results: it speeded up the economic recovery of western Europe, and, through the frequent meetings of OEEC, it helped to develop the idea of Western European cooperation.

Communist coup in Czechoslovakia 1948

During the autumn of 1947 anti-Communist feeling was growing in Czechoslovakia. This was due to the activities of the Communist-controlled secret police, and to resentment at being excluded by Russia from Marshall Aid. The Communist Party therefore began preparations to end democracy and establish a full Communist regime. In February 1948 the Red Army in Austria moved units to the Czech frontier. In Prague non-Communist police commanders were dismissed and non-Communist ministers in the government resigned. Organised demonstrations in the streets supported the coup, and any opposition was stifled by a rigorous censorship. In May elections were held with a single list of Communist candidates. Another country was added to the Soviet bloc.

Yugoslavia's quarrel with Russia

In September 1947 the Cominform was established. Directed from Moscow, it consisted of the Communist Parties of France, Italy and the countries of eastern Europe, and its function was to coordinate their work. In the Soviet bloc this was the start of a new phase marked by very much tighter Russian control of her satellites. It was assumed that the Russian road to socialism was the only one possible, and therefore heavy industry, collectivisation of agriculture, rigid centralisation and the total exclusion of non-Communists from the work of government were imposed. Life was regimented, trade and other contacts with non-Communist countries were sharply reduced, and trade between Russia and her satellites was increased. In 1949 Comecon was founded as Russia's reply to OEEC in western Europe. This was intended to co-ordinate the economies of the satellites.

In 1948, however, the uniformity of Communism in eastern Europe received a sharp blow from Marshal Tito of Yugoslavia. Albania and Yugoslavia were probably the only two Communist states in Europe where the majority of the people supported the Communist Party. Tito was a nationalist as well as a Communist. Secretary-General of the Yugoslav Communist Party since 1937, he considered that the Yugoslavs, not the Russians, had liberated Yugoslavia from the Germans. He therefore objected to Stalin's attempt to interfere in Yugoslavia's affairs. He disliked Russian spies in Yugoslavia, Russia's veto of closer links between Yugoslavia, Bulgaria and Romania, and Russia's criticism of his agricultural policy. Stalin, on the other hand, objected to Tito's independent mind, and in June 1948 expelled Yugoslavia from the Cominform and stopped economic and other aid.

The basic cause of the quarrel was whether Stalin or Tito was the ultimate ruler of Yugoslavia. Stalin had little doubt that Tito would be brought to heel, but this did not happen. The importance of the quarrel was that Yugoslavia now provided an alternative brand of Communism, for although not in the Soviet bloc, Yugoslavia remained a Communist state. In order to prevent a repetition of this independence, Stalin made quite sure that all potential 'Titos' in the other Communist states were removed from power.

Berlin blockade 1948 to 1949

The two years immediately after the war were particularly bad for the German people. Large numbers of refugees and returned prisoners-of-war were homeless and unemployed; there were shortages of food, fuel and housing and in consequence prices rocketed and the black market flourished. In January 1947 the British and American zones were linked economically, and early in 1948 the French zone also joined to form one large economic unit. At the same time German local government was revived. In February 1948 a conference in London of the United States, Britain, France and the Benelux[1] countries decided to proceed with the economic and political recovery of the three western zones, and, in the absence of agreement from Russia, to plan a constitution for Western Germany only. In June 1948 a new currency was introduced in the three western zones, and controls on prices and rationing were removed except on essential goods. This produced a rapid improvement in the economy with more goods available and higher production. The contrast between the improving standard of living in Western Germany and the continued poverty in Eastern Germany was growing more marked, and this was particularly so between the three western zones of Berlin and the area around them.

Russia's response to this situation was to put pressure on communications between West Berlin and West Germany. In March 1948 new regulations provided for the inspection of traffic along these lines of communication. Then passenger trains were not allowed to leave West Berlin for the western zones, and in June the Russians stopped all road and rail traffic between West Berlin and West Germany. There was an immediate crisis. The Western Powers had three alternative courses of action. Firstly, they could evacuate Berlin, but this was rejected because, as the US Commander in Germany said, 'When Berlin falls, Western Germany will be next. If we mean . . . to hold Germany against Communism, we must not budge.' Secondly, they could use force to reach Berlin, but this was rejected because the risk of a full-scale war between Russia and the West would have been too great. Thirdly, they could maintain contact with West Berlin by air, and this was the alternative that was adopted. For nearly eleven months West

---

[1] Belgium, the Netherlands and Luxembourg.

Berlin was supplied by air, and vast quantities of supplies were flown in at immense cost. In May 1949 the Russians ended their ban on land traffic and the crisis ended.

The Berlin blockade and the Communist *coup d'état* in Czechoslovakia had three consequences. They accelerated the creation of the state of Western Germany and the formation of a western defence system, and they made relations between Russia and the West even worse.

North Atlantic Treaty Organisation 1949

In the immediate postwar years Western European countries, despite the friendship of the United States, felt dangerously insecure. Russia had been very successful in imposing Communism on eastern Europe, her latest conquest being Czechoslovakia in February 1948. Russia confidently predicted the victory of Communism, and possessed an army of 4 million to give weight to her claim. Moreover, Russia said that she had the knowledge to make nuclear weapons, and in September 1949 she exploded her first atomic bomb. Then the Berlin blockade raised tension. As a result of this apparent threat, Britain, France and the Benelux countries met in Brussels in March 1948, and there signed a treaty which provided for military, political, economic and cultural collaboration. The five Brussels Treaty Powers then set up a joint military staff with headquarters at Fontainebleau near Paris.

It was clear, however, that the Brussels Pact was not strong enough for the defence of Western Europe, and that the US must be brought in. Discussions were therefore held during 1948, and in April 1949 the North Atlantic Treaty was signed. The North Atlantic Treaty Organisation (NATO) originally consisted of twelve countries: the United States, Britain, France, Belgium, Holland, Luxembourg, Canada, Portugal, Denmark, Iceland, Italy and Norway. Greece and Turkey joined in 1952 and West Germany in 1955. The key article of the treaty said that 'an armed attack against one or more (of the member states) shall be considered an attack against them all'. Members handed over control of their defence forces to a NATO Command Organisation which consisted of the North Atlantic Council of political members, the Military Committee of Chiefs of Staff and an elaborate system of military commands.

NATO's military forces were gradually built up so that eventually the Supreme Commander in Europe had a permanent force of about 25 divisions at his disposal. This compared with the Soviet bloc's 240 divisions, so that NATO depended ultimately on the nuclear deterrent provided by the United States and, to a much lesser extent, Britain.

The inclusion of the US in a peacetime alliance marked America's final break with her traditional isolation. This major change was caused, not only by her hostility to communism, but by the realisation that with the development of long-range bombers and, later, intercontinental missiles, she would be in the front line in a future war and not protected as earlier by two wide oceans. The creation of NATO brought an immediate increase in tension because there was now a return to balance of power diplomacy with all the danger that a relatively minor incident involving one country from each side would produce a major war. The start of the Korean War in 1950 was such an incident. This escalated into a major war but, fortunately, it was contained within the borders of Korea.

Creation of two German states 1949

The Berlin blockade did not prevent the three Western Powers from continuing with the political and economic unification of their zones of Germany. Early in 1948 they decided to create a federal government for West Germany. The Germans and the three occupying Powers then worked out a new constitution for the German Federal Republic. This was less democratic than the Weimar constitution, and the federal government was less powerful in that the states were given considerable rights. In August 1949 elections were held for the first Bundestag, the Lower House of the Federal Parliament, and Dr Konrad Adenauer became Federal Chancellor.

In October 1949 Russia responded to these moves in the West by creating the German Democratic Republic in the Soviet zone. The partition of Germany was now apparent.

German rearmament and Western European union

The creation of West Germany and the continued weakness of NATO's conventional forces in face of Communist strength, led to the view that West Germany should contribute to Europe's defence. In view of Germany's history, however, it was felt that her rearmament must be strictly controlled. Since the final control of forces in NATO remained with the national governments, it was felt that direct German membership of NATO leading to the creation of a German armed force over which Germany herself had ultimate control involved too much risk.

In 1950 the French, therefore, suggested the creation of a European Defence Community (EDC). This would be a supranational organisation similar to the European Coal and Steel Community (see p. 122),

Its members would hand over their defence forces to be integrated in a European army (with its own uniform) which would be under the complete control of the Council of Europe (see p. 122). Thus the German army would not be under the control of Germany. The Benelux countries supported the proposal. France, however, would only join if Britain did, for then Britain and France would dominate Germany. If Britain did not join, Germany would dominate France, especially with most of the French army fighting in Indo-China. But Britain refused to join for three reasons: she believed that a closely integrated European army would be inefficient, that her overseas responsibilities were too great, and that anything to do with European federation should be avoided by Britain. In view of Britain's refusal, France rejected the EDC in 1954.

Britain then suggested a new way of bringing Germany into a European defence system. The Brussels Treaty (1948) had become largely redundant since the creation of NATO in 1949. Britain now proposed a European army, integrated as far as possible, and directed, not by the Council of Europe but by the Brussels Treaty Organisation which would be extended to include West Germany and Italy. This proposal was accepted, and the seven states signed and ratified the Western European Union Treaty in 1955.

The Western European Union (WEU) forces were not supranationally controlled but were so integrated that they could not operate effectively as separate units. They formed part of NATO forces and West Germany, now given the status of a sovereign state, became a member of NATO. The treaty also said that West Germany was not to change her frontiers by force or to manufacture atomic weapons or long-range missiles. In addition, the small territory of the Saar, German in culture and ruled by France since 1945, was to be 'Europeanised'. However, this proposal was rejected by the Saarlanders, and in 1957 the Saar was incorporated into Germany.

Thaw in the Cold War 1953 to 1959

Relations between East and West were particularly bad when it was announced in Russia in March 1953 that Stalin had died. The new Russian ministers, especially Malenkov and Khrushchev, wished to relax international tension and the Russians showed a more conciliatory attitude in world affairs. In July 1953 the prolonged negotiations for an armistice in Korea were finally concluded, and early in 1954 the foreign ministers of the great powers met for the first time for five years. In 1954 a settlement of the war in Indo-China was reached at the Geneva Conference (see p. 494), and in the following year a summit conference at Geneva was mainly concerned with the problems of German unity and disarmament. In May 1955 a peace treaty was finally signed with Austria which provided for the neutralisation of the country. In the same month Khrushchev visited Yugoslavia, and publicly supported the view that each Communist country could choose its own road to socialism. Less than a year later, in February 1956, Khrushchev made the famous speech in which he not only denounced Stalin but said that peaceful coexistence with the West was possible.

The Anglo-French invasion of Egypt (see p. 304) and Russia's harsh treatment of the Hungarian rebels (see p. 89) in the autumn of 1956 temporarily ended the thaw in international relations. Khrushchev, however, continued to preach peaceful coexistence. During 1959 there was a foreign ministers' meeting at Geneva, and in September Khrushchev visited the United States. He had a number of meetings with President Eisenhower at Camp David near Gettysburg, and on the whole received a friendly welcome. In the following year the Soviet leader said: 'In our time the capitalist and socialist countries must co-exist in order to prevent war, so that all disputes are settled peacefully, through discussion and not through war.' Khrushchev still believed that the Communist conquest of the world would come, but it would be as a result of the superior economic policies of Russia rather than through war.

Meanwhile Russia continued to demonstrate her military strength. In 1953 she announced her possession of hydrogen bombs. She then began to concentrate on the development of rockets, and in October 1957 she astonished the world by launching the first sputnik (artificial satellite). This was followed by a big series of nuclear tests. In April 1961 Russia's progress was such that the Russian cosmonaut, Gagarin, became the first man to circle the earth in space. In addition, Russia increased her apparent strength by forming the Warsaw Pact in 1955. This was the Soviet reply to West Germany's membership of NATO and gave Russia the legal right to keep troops in eastern Europe. The way in which Russia crushed the risings in East Germany in 1953 and in Hungary in 1956 showed that her grip on her satellites had not relaxed.

There were two particular questions, however, which hindered any major reduction in tension, those of German reunification and disarmament. There were two problems connected with German reunification: firstly, how should it be achieved, and secondly, which side, if any, should a united Germany support in the Cold War? The first could not be decided until the second was settled. At a number of meetings on the subject the West proposed that reunification should be based on free elections which should be internationally supervised. This would mean that the 18 million East Germans would be merged with the 48 million West Germans, and consequently Communism would be eliminated. This was naturally rejected by Russia who instead proposed that the two parts of Germany should be given equal status in a reunited Germany. This proposal was rejected by the West.

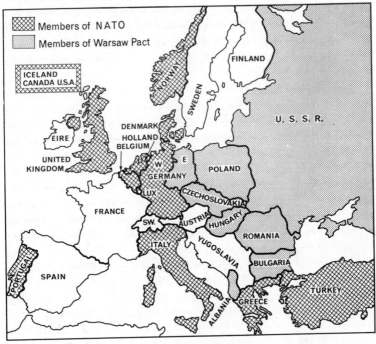

Division of Europe

Clearly there was a need for a compromise solution. Russia suggested that after Germany had been reunited, it should be given a status similar to that of Austria which had become a reunited and neutral country in 1955. The West, however, considered that they would be giving up more than Russia: 48 million to 18 million people, and a large to a small territory. Moreover, NATO's defence system would be very much weakened. At the Geneva Conference in 1955 Eden, the British Prime Minister, proposed a partially demilitarised zone down the centre of Europe between NATO and the Warsaw Pact Powers. This would allow German reunification and also encourage disarmament. This proposal, or variants of it, has also been put forward by others (for example, Rapacki, the Polish foreign minister) after 1955, but has not been accepted. So Germany remains disunited and a potential source of instability in central Europe.

Stockpiling of more and more devastating weapons by the two sides in the Cold War was a basic cause of international tension. After 1953 both sides possessed H-bombs, the devastation caused by one of which would be vastly greater than that resulting from the Hiroshima atomic bomb. The development of long-range bombers and later of intercontinental missiles meant that these weapons could be delivered anywhere in the world. It was becoming clear that a full-scale nuclear war, with the devastation caused by explosion together with the spread of radioactive materials, would probably be tantamount to world suicide.

The problem of disarmament lies in creating an atmosphere of mutual trust, and in trying to secure this by devising a method of inspection to find out whether each side is carrying out its promises to disarm. The United States wanted international inspection, but this was rejected by Russia. In 1955 Eisenhower made his 'open skies' proposal at the Geneva Conference. This involved allowing each side to fly over and photograph the other's country, but discussion on this idea ended inconclusively. Russia has suggested the positioning of inspectors at ports, railway junctions and other important communications centres to report excessive military movement. This, however, has been rejected by the West as inadequate. Eden's proposal for a partially demilitarised zone in central Europe has already been mentioned. The problem was complicated by the fact that, whereas Russia and the West by the mid-1950s were of approximately equal strength in nuclear weapons, Russia was far superior to the West in conventional forces.

1960 to 1978

Crisis in East–West relations 1960 to 1962

During the spring of 1960 preparations were made for a Summit Conference to be held in Paris in May. However, hopes of any positive results soon began to decline. A long conference on disarmament achieved nothing, the French began a series of nuclear tests, and Khrushchev visited Indo-China indicating that Russia wished to maintain her influence in neutral countries. Then on 1 May an American U2 reconnaissance plane was shot down over Russia. Eisenhower admitted that he knew of these flights over Russia, and Khrushchev was furious. A fortnight later the Russian and American leaders, together with

Macmillan of Britain and de Gaulle of France assembled in Paris for the Summit Conference. Khrushchev refused to begin the Conference, however, until Eisenhower agreed to cancel the U2 flights and to apologise to Russia for them. Eisenhower refused and Khrushchev returned to Moscow after an angry scene, and withdrew the invitation to Eisenhower to visit Russia.

The motives for Khrushchev's attitude are not yet clear: he could have been genuinely angry at American spying, or he could have been trying to appease those Russian and Chinese critics of his policy of peaceful coexistence. The meeting of the United Nations Assembly in September 1960 was attended by most of the world's leaders, but an attempt by the neutralists to arrange a meeting between Eisenhower and Khrushchev failed. Russia attacked both Hammarskjöld, secretary-general of the United Nations, and the office itself, wanting instead a commission of three, representing the Communists, the West and the Neutralists. This would have made the United Nations even less effective than it already was, and the idea was disliked by the neutral states as well as by the West. Khrushchev spent much of his time in the UN Assembly heckling and interrupting, and on one occasion banged his desk with his shoe.

In June 1961 there were inconclusive discussions between Khrushchev and President Kennedy in Vienna. Two months later the Berlin Wall was built. The movement of refugees from East Germany into West Berlin had totalled about 3 million since the end of the war, and the Russians now decided to seal off West Berlin. A series of very large Soviet nuclear tests was held in the autumn of 1961.

In 1958, Fidel Castro, a left-wing nationalist, came to power in Cuba. A series of radical measures led to opponents of his regime going to the US. In April 1961 these Cuban refugees invaded Cuba with the open moral support of Kennedy's government, and were completely defeated in the Bay of Pigs. Thereafter Castro declared himself a Communist and received considerable military and economic aid from the Communist bloc. In 1962 the US discovered and photographed a number of offensive surface-to-surface missile bases in Cuba. These Communist missile bases, less than 200 miles from the Florida coast, represented a major threat to American security. Kennedy, therefore, ordered an American naval blockade of Cuba to stop all ships carrying missile equipment, and threatened an American invasion of Cuba unless the missiles were removed. For a few days the world seemed on the verge of a major nuclear war. But Khrushchev gave way: he agreed to the withdrawal of the missiles and the dismantling of the bases, and the Americans agreed not to invade Cuba.

Easing of tension 1963 to 1968

The Cuban crisis had a considerable psychological effect on American and Russian thinking. It was realised that the world had been on the brink of a nuclear catastrophe, and that this must not be repeated. It was appreciated in Russia that in a future war the Communist as well as the non-Communist world would suffer dreadfully, and that peaceful competitive coexistence was a better alternative. Khrushchev said that Lenin's view that war between the imperialists and the Communists was inevitable and would lead to a Communist victory, was out of date—circumstances had changed.

In June 1963 a 'hot-line' was installed between the White House in Washington and the Kremlin in Moscow. This allowed direct radio-telephonic communication between the two capitals which could be used in a crisis (for example, if one side mistakenly thought it was being attacked and was about to take counter measures). In August 1963 the Partial Test Ban Treaty was signed by the US, Russia and Britain. In order to prevent radioactive pollution of the atmosphere, these countries agreed not to test nuclear devices above the ground. Four years later a treaty prohibited the placing of nuclear weapons in outer space, and in 1968 the Treaty on the Non-Proliferation of Nuclear Weapons was signed. At this point the nuclear powers were the United States, Russia, Britain, France and China. The first three of these countries undertook not to transfer the technology involved to other states. Eventually about a hundred states signed the treaty and thus agreed not to develop nuclear weapons. Nevertheless, India became the sixth nuclear power in 1974.

The rise of nationalism within East and West Europe apparently weakened both the Warsaw Pact and NATO. Romania (see p. 91) wished to develop an independent foreign policy, while France under President de Gaulle (see p. 99) left the military side of NATO and developed contacts with eastern Europe. The Russian leadership remained moderate. Khrushchev resigned in 1964, but Brezhnev and Kosygin continued his foreign policy in broad outline; they were cautious and careful, although conservative and unchanging in their general attitude to the West. Many people during this period held the view that industrial society in both East and West had become very similar and would eventually converge.

The areas of tension were mainly outside Europe. The United States was increasingly involved in Vietnam (see pp. 493–501). Relations between the United States and China were hostile and, therefore, Russia, conducting its own quarrel with its Communist rival, could not afford to be seen as friendly towards the United States. The Big Powers took opposite sides in the Arab–Israeli dispute: the United States supported Israel politically and militarily, while Russia supported the Arabs. There was the constant danger that this dispute would involve the two countries in conflict. Another unstable and unpredictable element was China in the throes of the Cultural Revolution (see pp. 440–3).

Thus the detente marked time. The fear of hostilities in Europe dwindled, but tension increased elsewhere. Consequently there was no disarmament. In 1967 Soviet-American talks to prevent the construction by both sides of anti-ballistic missile defence systems failed. In the following year America said that in 1967 Russia had doubled its force of intercontinental missiles, and that nuclear stalemate had now been reached, that is each side had the same capacity to destroy the other.

1968 to 1978

In 1968 the focus of concern was again Europe. East Germany restricted access to West Berlin, and there was a Russian campaign against the resurgence of a neo-Nazi party in West Germany. The West had assumed during the previous five years that the division of Europe into two camps, each united and hostile to the other, was ending. This view received a sharp jolt in August 1968, when the Russians invaded Czechoslovakia. The West did not intervene because the United States considered that the maintenance of good relations with Russia should have priority. The Russian invasion, however, brought more Soviet troops up to the front line in Europe, thus affecting the military balance. The West was concerned, too, that NATO was dependent on the American nuclear deterrent to prevent an all-out Russian attack.

However, the shock to public opinion in the West of events in Czechoslovakia did not last. During the next ten years it was widely held that Russia had no conceivable motive for starting a war, that Russia was too concerned about her east European empire and the hostility of China to wish to extend her empire westwards. Above all, it was considered that no country, including Russia, would risk a nuclear war. Consequently, the conventional weapons strength of NATO did not keep pace with that of the Warsaw Pact, and the military balance in Europe shifted in favour of the east: American forces decreased, Russian forces increased. By 1971 the Warsaw Pact had three times more tanks than NATO had. In the past the numerical superiority of the Warsaw Pact had been offset by the qualitative superiority of NATO's weapons and equipment. By 1977 this was no longer so. The Communists were modernising faster and expanding in size as well. The Institute of Strategic Studies, in its report for 1977–78, said: 'In general the pattern is one of military balance moving steadily against the West'.

Meanwhile there was continued hostility between East and West in three areas: the Middle East; Vietnam until fighting ended in 1975; and Africa, both southern and eastern. After 1975 the United States reacted to events in Vietnam by showing great reluctance to further involvement in similar disputes. However, the period 1969 to 1972 was one in which East–West relations became more fluid. While relations between Russia and China worsened (see p. 456), those between the United States and China improved (see p. 457). The friendship between Russia and Egypt, the leading Arab state, ended in 1972. France and Romania continued their independent line. A major change in policy was the *Ostpolitik* of Brandt, the West German Chancellor (see p. 108). Thus there was some movement and change in international affairs.

However, the development of weapons of mass destruction continued on a terrifying scale. In 1977 £200,000 million was spent on military forces and their equipment by the world; that is the equivalent of £550 m. each day. Twenty million men and women are permanently under arms around the globe. In 1977 'the world's armed forces have at their disposal explosives equivalent to 15 tons of TNT for every man, woman and child in the world'.[1] In the late 1970s the United States was developing the neutron bomb, an enhanced radiation weapon, which kills but causes relatively little material damage. It is meant for use on the battlefield and could blur the distinction between nuclear and conventional weapons.

The continued growth of armaments gave a new urgency to attempts to limit such growth. In 1969 the Strategic Arms Limitation Talks (SALT) began between Russia and the United States. The aim of the discussions was a mutual reduction in strategic weapons, that is long-range aircraft and missiles. The strategists considered that war was prevented by a situation of mutual deterrence: each side was deterred from attacking the other because of fear of unacceptable damage that would result from the victim retaliating. It was crucially important, therefore, for there to be parity of weapons. The development of new weapons or defensive systems could change the balance: for example, the manufacture of a missile with a number of warheads, each capable of being targeted independently; the development of the American cruise missile which follows the contours of the earth at a

[1] B. Hembry, *Let Civilisation Begin*, p. 1, United Nations Association of Great Britain and Northern Ireland, 1977.

hundred feet and thus avoids an enemy radar screen; anti-ballistic missiles which intercept enemy missiles and destroy them in space: these developments could for a time alter the balance of mutual deterrence.

The Salt talks proved difficult. However, an interim agreement was signed in Moscow in 1972. This limited the number of defensive and offensive missiles each country could possess. A further agreement was made at Vladivostok in 1974. However, trust between the two sides was lacking, and progress was slow. Technological developments made agreements quickly out of date; it became, for example, increasingly difficult to distinguish between tactical and strategic weapons. This applies also to talks on mutual force reductions which started in 1973 between NATO and the Warsaw Pact. Progress has been negligible for two reasons: firstly, there is the problem of verification; secondly, the Warsaw Pact, which had larger forces, wanted each side to reduce by the same number, while the West wanted each side to reduce by the same percentage.

At intervals from 1972 to 1975 thirty-five countries, including the United States and Russia, took part in talks on European Security and Cooperation. The discussions ranged over security in Europe, cooperation in the fields of science and technology, cooperation in humanitarian areas, issues concerning the freer movement of people and information, and whether existing frontiers could be changed. The object of the tough negotiations was detente, and finally the Helsinki Agreement was signed in 1975. This set out ways of improving economic and technological cooperation between East and West, it renounced the use of force or threat of force in relations between states and said that frontiers could only be changed peacefully. It also said that friendly relations and cooperation depend on governments respecting human rights. The Western powers thus indicated that they considered future detente with Russia to be dependent on respect for human rights in Eastern Europe. During the next two years preparations were made for a follow-up conference to review the implementation of the Helsinki Agreement and to discuss new proposals. The Belgrade Conference met from October 1977 to March 1978, but no new agreement was made.

Eastern Europe since 1953

1953 to 1956

Following the death of Stalin and the struggle for power inside the Soviet Union, Moscow's control of her satellites was less firm. The peoples of Eastern Europe were generally discontented, partly because of the low standards of living and partly because of national dislike of Russian control. On 16 June 1953 the workers of East Berlin revolted, and this was followed by risings all over East Germany. Portraits of Stalin and of Ulbricht, the fanatical and humourless Communist leader, were burned, and workers seized control of factories. On the following day Russia ordered the army to crush the revolt, and in the process many hundreds of people were killed or injured. Thereafter Russia endeavoured to raise the standard of living in East Germany. For example, reparation payments were ended and there was less investment in heavy industry.

In the same month there were similar risings, but on a smaller scale, in Czechoslovakia. In Hungary, where the economy was in a state of collapse, the new Russian leaders replaced the detested premier Rakosi by Imre Nagy, who believed in a gentler economic policy with greater emphasis on raising living standards.

In May 1955 Khrushchev visited Belgrade and reached an agreement with Tito which referred to 'different forms of socialist development'. During the next twelve months Russia asked her satellites to apologise to Yugoslavia, and the Cominform (see p. 75), which had frequently attacked Tito, was dissolved. In February 1956 Khrushchev gave his famous speech criticising Stalin to the Twentieth Congress; the weakness of Stalin in his treatment of Tito was revealed: ' "I will shake my little finger," said Stalin, "and there will be no more Tito. He will fall." This did not happen to Tito. No matter how much or how little Stalin shook, not only his little finger but everything else that he could shake, Tito did not fall.' Russia now offered financial and technical aid to Yugoslavia and Tito was welcomed in Moscow.

All this was very disturbing to the people of the satellites. Coming on top of the discontent with the standard of living and with the power of the Russian-backed security police, they now saw the Russians themselves criticising Stalin, the man who had enforced Communism in eastern Europe. Moreover the Russians were now helping Tito, the one east European who had dared to oppose Russia. In the summer and autumn of 1956 the resentment exploded into open revolt in Poland and Hungary.

The Polish rising 1956

Following Khrushchev's speech on Stalin there was increasing opposition to Stalin's Communist ministers in Poland, and workers began to demand higher wages and better conditions. In June there were strikes and demonstrations on a wide scale. Order was soon restored, but the demonstrations and criticism continued. The Communists were themselves divided between those who wished to follow the orthodox Stalinist line, and those who wished to develop an independent Polish approach to Communism. The latter were led by Gomulka. In October Khrushchev and other Russian leaders visited Warsaw and as a result of stubborn Polish resistance, an agreement was reached whereby Poland would remain a Communist state and would follow Russia's foreign policy, but would have freedom to conduct her internal affairs as she wished. This was largely the work of Gomulka, a loyal Communist and a loyal Pole, who became First Secretary of the Polish Communist Party.

The Hungarian rising 1956

Rakosi, dismissed as premier in 1953, had continued to control the Communist Party, and two years later he secured Nagy's dismissal as premier. Nagy, who was not a good leader, had poor support from his own government and from the Russians. During the next twelve months Hungary returned to a traditional Stalinist economic policy, and discontent mounted. Writers and other intellectuals led the opposition to the regime, demanding the resignation of Rakosi and freedom for the press. Although Rakosi was dismissed by the Russians in July 1956, the opposition still continued.

Finally, on 23 October Budapest erupted in rebellion. The revolt began as a peaceful demonstration organised by a few intellectuals, but during the next twenty-four hours it became a national rising against a foreign oppressor and the Hungarian henchmen of that oppressor. Arms were distributed, the radio building besieged, and a huge metal statue of Stalin was broken up. On 26 October the Russians agreed to Imre Nagy becoming premier again. During the next few days Nagy introduced a multiparty system, set up a coalition government, released Cardinal Mindszenty who had been imprisoned since 1948 for his uncompromising attitude to Communism, and then decided to withdraw Hungary from the Warsaw Pact and to proclaim her neutrality.

This was too much for the Russians and many Hungarian Communists. Moscow was prepared to accept the Polish revolution because

The Yalta Conference, 1945. Seated are Churchill, Roosevelt and Stalin, and standing directly behind are their foreign ministers, Eden, Stettinius and Molotov

Hungarian Rising, 1956. A Russian colonel tries to stop photographs being taken by Western journalists

it remained under Communist control, but the Hungarian revolution was becoming non-Communist. On 4 November the Russian army was brought into Hungary in overwhelming force, and within a few days the revolt was crushed. Three thousand people were killed and many buildings destroyed.

Russia was obliged to intervene if she was to maintain her influence in eastern Europe. The Hungarian rising occurred simultaneously with the Anglo-French-Israeli attack on Egypt. However, even if the western powers had not been preoccupied with Suez, there was never any chance of them intervening in Hungary. On the other hand, it is possible that there was no direct Russian participation in the Suez affair because of events in Hungary.

Thereafter the new Russian nominee, Kadar, restored order. In 1958 Nagy was executed, but in general the powers of the secret police were sharply reduced, and there has been more freedom and an improved standard of living. This has been the experience, too, of the other satellites.

1956 to 1968

The twelve years after 1956 saw a further weakening of the strict Russian control of eastern Europe. In 1961 the Sino-Soviet dispute came into the open, and both sides began to canvas for support. This was the opportunity for the satellites to win much more national independence from Russia. The one east European country to give open support to China was tiny Albania, ruled since 1945 by Enver Hoxha. The other countries, relieved by Soviet preoccupation with her eastern frontier, supported Russia hoping that the reward would be greater national freedom.

Comecon had been established in 1949 (see p. 75). In 1962 Khrushchev tried to use it as the means of forcing economic integration on the countries of eastern Europe with the idea that each country, except the USSR, should specialise in certain products. Thus, for example, Romania would be a source of raw materials while Czechoslovakia would concentrate on heavy industry. This pressure was resisted, particularly by Romania who wanted to develop a more balanced economy in its own national interest. Comecon, Romania said, should coordinate but not integrate economies. As a result Romania in the 1960s launched a drive for industrialisation. At the same time, however, she adopted a series of postures in defiance of the Soviet Union. Anti-Russian measures were passed—for example, the abolition of Russian as a compulsory school subject—and an increasingly neutralist foreign policy was followed. Although a member of the Warsaw Pact, Romania refused to have Russian troops on her soil, and seemed increasingly friendly towards both China and the Western powers. Economic and commercial agreements were made with West Germany, France, Britain and Yugoslavia.

Other east European states followed Romania's example, although less ostentatiously. Rigid centralised economic planning gave way to a much freer decentralised system. More attention was paid to market forces, the profit motive and individual enterprise. Popular discontent was removed with more consumer goods. In 1968 Hungary introduced economic reforms known as the New Economic Mechanism. Managers were to have greater freedom and were told to make profits instead of merely fulfilling production targets. Kadar remained the ruler of Hungary, and became a popular national leader. The 1960s saw an immense growth of individual wealth under Kadar's enlightened, efficient and benevolent dictatorship.

In all these countries, however, the relaxation was purely in the economic and cultural spheres. In military and political matters there were no changes. Romania's independent foreign policy was tolerated by Russia only because there were no indications of internal democracy. In Czechoslovakia in 1968 things were quite different.

Czechoslovakia 1968[1]

In 1953 Novotny became Secretary of the Communist Party and in 1957 President of Czechoslovakia. Until the early 1960s he had ruled as a typical Stalinist dictator with rigid central control and no freedom of assembly, speech or movement. During the 1960s popular discontent grew. Czechoslovakia had once been the most advanced communist nation, but the economy was now ailing and progressive economists were frustrated by half-measures and political interference with reforms. In addition, there was an acute housing shortage and the transport system was in chaos. An influential group of intellectuals disliked the attempts to curb their freedom of speech, while ordinary people wanted an end to government dishonesty, muddle, clumsy planning and the muzzling of opinion. During 1967 the opposition to government policies deepened. When student demonstrations in Prague were brutally suppressed by the police, there was wide sympathy for the protest movement. This protest coincided with a

[1] Prague, the capital of Czechoslovakia, has been the scene of three major crises in the twentieth century, each of which has been a turning point in Europe's history—1939, 1948 and 1968.

crisis within the party leadership. Progressives, who were opposed to the Novotny faction, had a small majority in the central committee. Matters came to a head in January 1968 when Novotny and the conservatives were replaced by Dubcek and the progressives.

Events then moved rapidly during what became known as the Prague Spring. The whole system of government in Czechoslovakia was subjected to a frank and public examination. In an unprecedented step for any communist regime, censorship was ended. The new leaders, with widespread popular support, aimed at democracy and freedom in public life. The National Assembly, for long just a rubber stamp, was to be revived and given real powers and responsibilities. The idea of opposition parties was discussed. The internal security apparatus was gradually dismantled. In March Novotny resigned the presidency and was succeeded by Svoboda. Dubcek, the leader of the Communist Party, Cernik, the Prime Minister, and President Svoboda were responsible for this sudden freedom of debate. They enjoyed remarkable popular support.

From the start the Russians, and the leaders of East Germany and Poland particularly, regarded this domestic liberalisation with concern. Dubcek emphasised many times that Czechoslovakia had no intention of leaving the Warsaw Pact or Comecon, and that the reformers wanted no more than political freedom and economic efficiency. In the view of Brezhnev, however, such a liberalising programme would allow 'reactionaries' freedom in the present and power in the future. Czechoslovakia could well be lost to communism. In addition, the infection of such political freedom would spread to the other satellites, and Russia's control of eastern Europe would disintegrate. Therefore pressure was put on the Czech government to reverse the reforms. In May there were Russian troop movements in Poland near the Czech frontier. During June and July there were Warsaw Pact exercises in Czechoslovakia. At the same time the propaganda campaign against the Czechoslovak reform policies was intensified. In mid-July the leaders of Russia, East Germany, Poland, Hungary and Bulgaria met in Warsaw, and issued a menacing demand to Dubcek to conform. At the end of July the Czech and Russian leaders met at Cierna, a village in Czechoslovakia near the Russian frontier. At the beginning of August the leaders of the countries that had met in Warsaw came together again at Bratislava in southern Czechoslovakia. The Bratislava meeting was apparently a success. Dubcek agreed to keep Czechoslovakia within the communist camp, but Brezhnev conceded the Czechoslovak government's right to pursue its own domestic policies. It seemed the risk of conflict was reduced. In mid-August President

Tito of Yugoslavia and President Ceausescu of Romania visited, and gave their support to Dubcek.

But Russia's fears remained. Consequently on 21 August the Russian army invaded in overwhelming strength. Dubcek and Cernik were arrested and taken to Moscow. With half a million Soviet troops in occupation, and the Czech people's passive resistance gradually turning to active shooting and sabotage, President Svoboda went to Moscow. The three leaders returned to Prague on 28 August having accepted the Soviet ultimatum: Russian troops were to be stationed indefinitely in Czechoslovakia, censorship was to be restored and new political groupings not allowed. In practice the Russians controlled the country, although the Czech National Assembly condemned the Soviet occupation as illegal. The Russian action was condemned by the Western Powers, and by China, Albania and Yugoslavia. Romania said it was a 'flagrant violation of the national sovereignty of a socialist country.' The Soviet government defended its action in what became known amongst the Western Powers as the Brezhnev Doctrine: this states the right of the communist countries as a whole to intervene in the territory of any one of them if there is the danger of that country turning from communism to capitalism.

The invasion of Czechoslovakia had important consequences for international affairs (see p. 85), but in eastern Europe it restored Russian control and showed clearly the limits of Russian tolerance in the face of the popular wish for national independence and freedom. As far as Czechoslovakia was concerned, the previous form of government was gradually restored. In 1969 Dubcek was replaced by Husak, the liberal reforms were stopped, and party control on lines approved by the Kremlin was reimposed. During the early 1970s there was a purge of all those connected with the changes in 1968.[1]

Poland 1970

Gomulka ruled Poland from 1956 to 1970. By the mid-1960s he was increasingly set in his ways and out of touch with realities. During these years industry, most of it nationalised, expanded greatly, and most of the excess rural population was drawn off to the new industrial cities. Agriculture needed modernisation, but 85 per cent of the land was in private peasant hands, and production could not be

---

[1] Civilised countries in weak, exposed positions, alongside powerful neighbours, are often prone to introversion and irony: the novel *The Good Soldier Svejk* by Jaroslav Hasek, a Czech who died in 1923, describes the subterfuges, dumb insolence and life of resignation of a private soldier in the face of a great power.

controlled. This, combined with two bad harvests in the previous years, resulted in a food shortage in 1970. A week before Christmas the government announced huge increases in food and fuel prices. There were protests and demonstrations, the militia over-reacted, and about 300 people were killed. The crisis forced the resignation of Gomulka. His successor in December 1970 was Gierek, no friend of liberal democracy and loyal to the Soviet alliance, but an energetic, practical and determined technocrat.

1968 to 1977

During the three years after 1968 the trend of Soviet policy was towards firmer control of Eastern Europe, and closer integration of national economies. At the same time greater priority was given to consumer goods, housing, real wages and trade openings to the West. Chancellor Brandt's *Ostpolitik* (see p. 108) and the improvement in relations between West Germany and Russia stimulated the liberalising trends, at least in economic matters. The period 1971–75 was one of relative peace: there was considerable Western investment in Eastern Europe, incomes rose, and when the international oil crisis of 1973–74 resulted in inflation and recession in the West, prices remained stable in the East because Soviet oil remained cheap.

After 1975, however, the Communist regimes faced a number of difficulties. Soviet oil prices increased simultaneously with the price of essential Western imports. Exports to Western Europe decreased because of the economic recession in the West. These economic problems coincided with frustrated political expectations. The Helsinki Conference (see p. 87) raised hopes of liberalisation which were not satisfied. Conditions varied in each country. In East Germany Ulbricht had been replaced by Honecker as party leader in 1971. Trade with West Germany was encouraged, and the country enjoyed reasonable prosperity. Similarly in Hungary Kadar's government has been successful. No political opposition is allowed and there is total loyalty to Russia in foreign affairs. In return Hungary has been allowed to develop its own brand of communism in which the profit motive is an important factor. On the other hand, Gierek's regime in Poland, after initial successes, has been faced with renewed riots when it has been compelled to raise prices. Romania had the lowest living standards among the Comecon countries. The policy of rapid industrial growth meant long hours of work, inadequate housing and shortages of consumer goods in order to raise the necessary capital from a backward agricultural country.

France

Vichy Regime 1940 to 1944

In a 'state of numbed confusion',[1] the Third Republic came to an end in June 1940. The area of France unoccupied by the Germans and administered by France was ruled from the health resort of Vichy by Pétain, the 84-year-old hero of the defence of Verdun. Pétain was an honest and dignified man, very right wing in his views, and of no great ability, but he at least provided leadership for France at a time of crisis and helped to restore French morale. His government was divided between those who wished to be neutral in the continuing war, and those who wanted full collaboration with the Germans. Laval led the latter group —in a broadcast in 1942 he said that he wanted victory for Germany. In November 1942, however, Vichy France was occupied by the Germans following the American invasion of North Africa. Vichy then continued as a puppet regime until the liberation in August 1944.

Meanwhile French opposition to Germany was increasingly centred around General Charles de Gaulle. Born in 1890, he fought in the First World War and in the 1930s was one of the few French officers to see the advantages of mobility in attack. Just before the armistice he flew to London and broadcast over the BBC: 'I, General de Gaulle, now in London, call on all French soldiers and men who are at present on British soil . . . to get in touch with me.' The response was very poor, and the relations of the proud de Gaulle with the British government were difficult. But gradually his position as the chief representative of France was recognised. After the liberation of North Africa in 1943, de Gaulle set up a French Committee for National Liberation. He had strong links with the Maquis, as the French resistance was called, and when the German occupation of France was ended in August 1944 de Gaulle was given an enthusiastic welcome by the French people.

Government of de Gaulle 1944 to 1946

De Gaulle's immediate job was to set up an administration behind the Allied lines, and this was done quickly and efficiently. In September he chose his Cabinet and established an independent government. This ensured food supplies and maintained law and order, although it is prob-

[1] A. Cobban, *History of Modern France*, Vol. 3, 1871–1962.

able that in the immediate aftermath of liberation some 30,000 collaborators[1] were lynched. Despite his exclusion from the Yalta and Potsdam conferences, de Gaulle pressed for French equality with the other three Great Powers, and France was given a zone of Germany to administer.

By an overwhelming majority the French people decided against continuing the Third Republic, and in October 1945 a Constituent Assembly was elected to decide on a constitution for the Fourth Republic. The elections gave about 150 seats to each of three main parties, the Communists, the Socialists and a new progressive Catholic party called the MRP (Christian Democrats in other countries). De Gaulle, who now became head of a democratic government, formed a left-wing coalition. In January 1946, however, he resigned. He found it difficult to work with the politicians, and particularly with the Communists, and the Assembly had rejected his view that the new constitution should provide for a very much more powerful President.

The Fourth Republic 1946 to 1958

The constitution of the Fourth Republic was eventually accepted by a referendum in October 1946. The voting was 9·3 million in favour, 8·1 million against, while 8·5 million abstained. Therefore, only about 36 per cent of the population showed their support for a constitution which was very similar to that of the Third Republic. The Presidency remained weak while the Assembly remained strong. Like the Third Republic, too, the Assembly contained several parties and the result was coalition government. Between de Gaulle's resignation and the collapse of the Fourth Republic, a period of twelve years, there were fourteen prime ministers. The result was government which was often indecisive and was sometimes paralysed.

From January 1946 to May 1947 the coalition governments were composed of the Communists, the Socialists and the MRP. However, the development of the Cold War, combined with a series of bitter industrial disputes, led to the dismissal of the Communists who opposed all future governments. In 1947 de Gaulle founded the Rally of the French People (RPF), a right-wing movement aiming at a strong executive. In the 1951 elections the RPF captured 21 per cent of the votes. From 1947 onwards, then, the centre parties who formed the governments of these years were challenged by strong left- and right-wing parties.

1 Pétain and Laval were tried after the war. Pétain was imprisoned for life and Laval was executed.

The effect of government instability can be exaggerated. Prime Ministers fell but other ministers remained, and the efficient civil service provided continuity. Nevertheless, in 1957 there was no government for five weeks, and in April 1958 there was no government for four weeks. Such a situation could not fail to be dangerous.

While politically weak, the Fourth Republic was remarkably successful in economic affairs. In 1946 Jean Monnet produced his plan for modernising French industry. This concentrated on steel, cement, transport and fuel. With the help of domestic investment, Marshall Aid and French participation in the European Coal and Steel Community, industrial production doubled between 1947 and 1958. The two major economic weaknesses were inflation and the problem of markets for agricultural produce.

Events in Algeria (see p. 320) finally brought the Fourth Republic to an end. In May 1958 the French army and the Europeans in Algeria revolted against a prime minister who appeared to favour negotiations with the Algerian rebels. After a fortnight's stalemate during which neither the French army in Algeria nor the French government in Paris could impose its authority on the other, President Coty appointed General de Gaulle as prime minister. De Gaulle, who had been living in semi-retirement at his country home, was accepted by the Assembly in June, and was given powers of decree for six months. He then drew up a new constitution which was approved by a large majority in a referendum, and in December 1958 he was elected President of the Fifth Republic.

The Fifth Republic 1958 to the present

President de Gaulle 1958 to 1969 The new French constitution provides for presidential government on the American model. It was first arranged that the president should be chosen for a seven-year term of office by an electoral college, but this was changed in 1962 so that the president is now directly elected by a referendum. There is an Assembly and a Senate which both have to agree to laws before they can be passed. The executive, however, is very much stronger than it was during the Fourth Republic. The President chooses the prime minister, and the ministers of the government are not in the parliament. In addition the President can dissolve the Assembly, and in certain circumstances can take over full powers.

General de Gaulle was re-elected President in 1965, winning 54 per cent of the votes. When he came to power he formed a new political party, the Gaullist Party, which had a large majority in the 1958 and

1962 elections. The Gaullists only just managed to retain control in the Assembly in 1967, but then had a huge majority—358 seats out of 485—in the June 1968 election.

De Gaulle came to power as a result of the Algerian problem, and this continued to dominate events during the first four years of his government. Although the French Algerians had hoped that the authoritarian and patriotic de Gaulle of all people would never allow majority rule and independence for Algeria, the President believed that this was the only realistic policy. Algeria was given her independence in 1962 (see chapter 7). Between 1958 and 1960 de Gaulle also allowed the French colonies in West and Equatorial Africa to become independent (see chapter 8). It has been pointed out that a man who seemed obsessed with France's greatness obliterated the French empire.

In foreign affairs de Gaulle's consistent object was Great Power status for France, and he asserted the interests and enhanced the prestige of France with very considerable success. He displayed suspicion of, and opposition to, what he considered to be an Anglo-Saxon domination of the western alliance, and he particularly showed an anti-Americanism which took apparent delight in annoying the United States. De Gaulle signed economic agreements with Russia and China, and gave diplomatic recognition to Peking. He said on many occasions that he favoured the unification and neutralisation of North and South Vietnam. In 1967, during the Middle East crisis (see p. 287), de Gaulle declared that Israel was the aggressor: an unpopular view in France, but it won for de Gaulle the support of Arabs. Later in 1967 he visited Expo 67 in Canada, and gave Quebec separatism his backing to the intense objection of English-speaking Canadians. De Gaulle gave lukewarm support to NATO, refusing to allow American nuclear stockpiles on French territory, withdrawing the French Mediterranean fleet from NATO Command, and finally in 1966 requesting all NATO forces to leave France and withdrawing all remaining French forces from NATO. France affirmed that she had no intention of withdrawing from the Atlantic Alliance, only from NATO, the military organisation of the alliance. In addition, de Gaulle refused to sign the Test Ban Treaty of 1963, and speeded up the manufacture and testing of France's own nuclear weapons.

The Common Market was formed in 1957, before de Gaulle came to power. While accepting its economic benefits, the President was unenthusiastic about the supranational element in the European Economic Community. He preferred a loose union of sovereign states in which governments rather than European organisations take the major decisions. In 1963 de Gaulle exercised his right to veto the British application to join EEC. Almost immediately afterwards de Gaulle and Adenauer signed the Franco-German Treaty of cooperation. There was a storm of opposition to the French veto of British membership in 1963, but in 1967 this action was repeated. The prevailing view within the European Movement then was that it was urgent to strengthen the political ties within Europe. The EEC Commission reported in favour of enlarging the Community and re-opening negotiations with Britain. De Gaulle took the opposite view, saying that he considered British membership would lead to the break up of the EEC. France was again faced with deeply disgruntled partners.

Although possessing a cold and aloof personality, de Gaulle had a romantic vision of France. He identified himself with that mythical being, La France. Until 1966 his policies caused resentment amongst the allies of France, but also produced respect. After 1967, however, irritation and frustration became the prevailing attitude to de Gaulle's policies, which were thought to be arbitrary, improvised and contradictory. However, there is no doubt that he restored the prestige and popularity of France, especially in Africa, Asia and the Arab world.

Foreign affairs dominated de Gaulle's thinking. Domestic events tended to take second place unless they pushed themselves to the fore, as in 1968. In February and March of 1968 student demonstrations began, caused by discontent over inadequate premises and staffing and poor administration. They became violent and widespread, and the general sympathy of the public with the students was increased by a certain measure of police brutality. The students were supported by industrial workers, who had their own grievances over wages, so that in May, with factories occupied and 9 million people on strike, there was mounting economic chaos, while the continuing demonstrations and street fighting in Paris were a major threat to law and order. The aim of the students' leaders had proceeded well beyond the original educational reforms, and was now the destruction of the existing organisation of society. Left-wing students had exploited the real grievances of students and industrial workers for their own ends. President de Gaulle was slow to exert his authority. He returned from a state visit to Romania, and his first proposals for greater worker participation in management were ineffective. As the situation worsened, there was talk of the possibility of de Gaulle's resignation, and an indication of the seriousness of events was his visit to Baden Baden to consult the general commanding French forces in Germany. However, on the following day, 30 May, the situation suddenly improved. In a broadcast de Gaulle called for the return of order and he announced a general election. Pro-Gaullist demonstrations followed, the number of clashes between students and police declined, and there was a gradual resumption of work. In the election campaign that followed, de Gaulle not only appealed for law and order, but also said he wanted a society which was neither capitalist nor communist. The election produced a huge Gaullist majority, and was followed by a series of educational and industrial reforms.

The French economy at the end of the 1950s faced a number of problems. Farming was relatively uncompetitive and needed modernisation. In addition, considerable resources were tied up in small-scale industry and commerce. There was generally inadequate investment and consequent unemployment. The government was faced with the familiar problem of how to obtain growth, which would increase production and reduce unemployment, without also causing inflation. There was also the attendant problem of balance of payments deficits. After the rise in wages in 1968 there was a rapid rise in consumption and therefore increase in imports which almost produced a big devaluation of the franc in the autumn of that year. Despite these problems the 1960s was a period of economic transformation. Political stability, membership of the EEC and good leadership led to a major expansion of the economy.

Early in 1969 de Gaulle decided on a measure of decentralisation. The government wished to establish regional assemblies and to reconstitute the Senate and change its functions. In April a referendum was held on this proposal, and de Gaulle also made it a vote of confidence in himself. On previous occasions the electorate was faced with the choice of 'de Gaulle or chaos'. On this occasion, however, Pompidou, the Prime Minister from 1962 to 1968, announced that if there was an election for the presidency, he would be a candidate. The government proposals were defeated by 53 per cent to 47 per cent. De Gaulle promptly resigned, and retired to his country home at Colombey-les-deux-Eglises in eastern France. He died in November, 1970.

For eleven years de Gaulle gave France firm and stable government. By his assiduous provincial tours, by his reputation as a political wizard, and by the success of his colonial and foreign policies, he maintained his personal authority. Confident of his ability to dominate events, he was at the same time sensitive to realities and ready to profit from experience. A stubborn and proud man with great character and courage, he was a rare combination in politics of intellectual, romantic and tough military leader.

President Pompidou 1969 to 1974 Pompidou campaigned energetically and effectively for the presidency, and won on the second ballot with

58 per cent of the votes. The left wing was divided, but this result exceeded de Gaulle's 1965 performance. The regime was consolidated by the smoothness of Pompidou's election and assumption of power. He was an experienced politician with a reputation for shrewdness and skill in negotiation. A man of the moderate right, he was more cautiously pragmatic and flexible than his predecessor.

Although there was a basic continuity of foreign policy, the government's emphasis was now on domestic affairs. Chaban-Delmas was prime minister from 1969 to 1972 and Messmer from 1972 to 1974. It was clear, however, that the President intended to control policy and the composition of the government. The Gaullists remained the largest party, but after the 1973 election they no longer had an overall majority. They were originally a conglomerate of many political views, welded together by devotion to de Gaulle, but under Pompidou the Gaullists emerged as a moderate Centre Party. This was part of a general move to the left in French politics. The Socialist Party was rejuvenated under the leadership of Mitterand, and in 1972 formed an alliance with the Communists and adopted a common programme. A built-in weakness of the constitution was the possibility of a clash between the president and the majority in parliament, and there was considerable debate during the 1973 election campaign as to whether Pompidou, a Gaullist president, would accept a left-wing government if the Gaullists lost the election. Pompidou interpreted the political mood of the country as indicating that while the electors rejected communism they did expect social progress.

During the decade up to 1974 France enjoyed a period of unprecedented economic prosperity. The economic growth rate was exceeded only by Japan among the highly industrialised countries. National income trebled, industry became highly competitive and agriculture much more efficient. Although one Frenchman in six lived in Paris or its surroundings, there was spectacular growth of regional centres like Lyons, Marseilles and Toulouse. Huge housing complexes were built, and industry spread into the countryside. Large-scale French agriculture, modern and highly mechanised, could compare with the most efficient in any country. The small traditional, family-type farm was fast declining—indeed, the exodus from the land was causing some concern. Agriculture particularly, but all sections of the economy, benefited enormously from the existence of the EEC. The confidence resulting from political stability and continuity of policy was the other major factor behind this economic leap forward. Most sections of society benefited from the prosperity, wage increases keeping ahead of price rises.

The main features of de Gaulle's foreign policy—national independence, hostility to power blocs, development of French nuclear weapons—were all continued by Pompidou. In the Middle East the French official line was 'pro-Arab neutrality'. Nevertheless, France became a major arms supplier: the sale of Mirage jets to Libya is an example. France continued to be no more receptive to ideas of integrated defence or a European deterrent. Foreign policy, however, became more realistic and more conventional under Pompidou. The good relationship with Russia was maintained, but relations with Britain and the United States were greatly improved. In 1971 Heath, the British Prime Minister, visited Paris, and Pompidou indicated that France would no longer oppose British membership of the Common Market.

During 1973 there was a general feeling in France that the government was drifting, that there was a lack of decisiveness at the top. It was later known that Pompidou was suffering from ill-health. Nevertheless, his sudden death in April 1974 was quite unexpected. Pompidou had the difficult task of succeeding de Gaulle. Despite the predictions of catastrophe, he successfully steered the difficult course between continuity and change, and the Fifth Republic not merely survived but prospered.

President Giscard d'Estaing 1974 to the present   The increasing popularity of the left wing in France was reflected in the election for president. In the first ballot, Mitterand, the Socialist leader, gained 43 per cent of the votes and was well ahead of Giscard d'Estaing, the leader of the small Independent Republican Party, who gained 32 per cent. The Gaullist candidate polled only 15 per cent. In the second ballot, however, the centre and right wing vote combined to give Giscard the narrowest of victories over Mitterand: 50.8 to 49.1 per cent. Thus the youngest French president since Louis Napoleon in 1848 assumed office.[1] Elegant, talented and ambitious, Giscard d'Estaing had as Finance Minister guided the French economy during the years of growth and expansion. He considered that in addition to this economic prosperity, France now wanted more equality, less bureaucracy and centralisation, quicker and more effective justice, and in general a more liberal approach to social problems. 'You will be surprised', he said on the night of his election, 'by the scope and speed of the change we shall introduce in France.'

[1] Giscard not only simplified presidential protocol, but dined out with ordinary French families and invited dustmen to breakfast at the Elysée.

Giscard appointed Jacques Chirac as Prime Minister, the youngest that France has ever had. During its first year in office, the government introduced a whole series of reforms: voting rights at 18, the liberalisation of divorce laws, increase in unemployment benefits to 90 per cent of wages, penal reform, extra benefits for pensioners, families, the handicapped, the lowest paid workers, and reform of the law on abortion. Unfortunately for a reforming president, Giscard came to power at a time of very difficult economic circumstances. The energy crisis and the world recession that followed resulted in unemployment, inflation and a fall in industrial production. France had come to take relatively rapid growth and rising real wages as a norm. The mounting economic problems therefore came as a shock. In addition, the government had uncertain political support. The Gaullists were the largest party in the Assembly but were a minority in the cabinet. For the first time since 1958 they no longer controlled the government, and their support for Giscard was grudging. Despite the reform and the wooing of the left-of-centre voters, there was a steady advance in the popularity of the left wing. Chirac resigned in 1976 and was succeeded as prime minister by Barre, but the impression in 1977 was of indecision and ineffectiveness at the top. In the 1978 elections France showed itself to be split almost equally between the parties of the Left (Communists, Socialists and Radicals) and those of the Centre-Right (Giscardians and Gaullists). However, in terms of seats in the National Assembly the Left only obtained 200 while the Gaullists (153) and Giscardians (137) together had 290.

Foreign policy was more successful. Previous policy was upheld, but there was rather more emphasis on removing tension, and on dialogue and cooperation. By 1977 France had succeeded in maintaining its independence in world affairs, but without the prickly hauteur and jealous nationalism of de Gaulle.

West Germany
1949 to the present

Adenauer (Christian Democrat) 1949 to 1963 In September 1949 Dr Konrad Adenauer was elected as the first Chancellor of the German Federal Republic. He was aged seventy-three, and was beginning his career in national politics. His experience until this point had been in local government: he had been chief burgomaster of Cologne from 1917 to 1933 when he was dismissed by the Nazis. Adenauer proved himself to be a statesman of great shrewdness and resourcefulness. He was naturally authoritarian and paternal, with supreme confidence in his own judgment, but he now showed respect for the new German constitution and nursed the rebirth of German democracy.

Adenauer remained Chancellor from 1949 to October 1963. For most of this period government was by a coalition dominated by the Christian Democrats, the party led by Adenauer. The Socialist Party was the chief rival of the Christian Democrats, while the number of small parties was greatly reduced as a result of the law passed in 1953 which said that a party had to receive 5 per cent of the national vote in order to be represented in the Bundestag. After the disasters of the Weimar Republic, the German reintroduction to democracy was successful, and this was largely due to Adenauer.

Another important reason for political stability was the economic prosperity that West Germany enjoyed in the 1950s. Professor Erhard, the Minister of Economics, was given credit for the 'economic miracle' of Germany's recovery from the misery and confusion of the immediate postwar years. In 1950 there were 15 million unemployed, while in 1960 there was a labour shortage, despite the large influx of refugees from East Germany. American aid and the currency reform of 1948 helped considerably. The damage suffered by industry in the war was less than at first appeared. Erhard, a confident advocate of free competition, encouraged a high rate of investment, which was helped by the small expenditure on defence. (German armed forces were not reintroduced until 1956.) Prices were kept steady, and the German people worked hard and skilfully. Unemployment imposed a rigid industrial discipline, but the reorganisation of the trade union movement into sixteen industry-wide trade unions, together with a measure of industrial democracy, produced good industrial relations. Eventually the movement of refugees into West Germany postponed a labour shortage and the dangers of inflation. In addition, West Germany's membership of the European Coal and Steel Community and later of the European Economic Community helped her recovery. The consequence was that real wages rose rapidly during the 1950s and this economic prosperity was one reason for the return of the Christian Democrats with an absolute majority in the 1957 elections.

Adenauer had four main aims in foreign policy: he wished to end the occupation and restore the sovereignty of Germany, to integrate Germany into the new European organisations that were formed in the 1950s, to reconcile Germany and France, and to reunite Germany. The occupation of West Germany ended in 1952 and in 1954 the treaty was signed by which Germany acquired full sovereignty and a national army within the framework of the Western European Union. In 1955 West Germany became a member of NATO. Adenauer was a firm supporter from the beginning of the 'European Movement'. He eagerly joined Schuman's European Coal and Steel Community in 1951 and the Common Market in 1957, and was bitterly disappointed at the French decision in 1954 not to go ahead with the European Defence Community. Adenauer wished to reunite the two parts of Germany, but after the failure of his visit to Moscow in 1955 he refused to consider any reconciliation with Communist opinion. His government claimed to speak for the whole of Germany and regarded the recognition of East Germany by other countries as an unfriendly act.[1]

Throughout his period of office Adenauer aimed to reconcile France and Germany so that there would be no repetition of the wars fought between the two countries during the previous century. In the late 1950s he developed increasingly close relations with France at the expense of those with Britain. In January 1963 the Franco-German treaty of cooperation was signed, and this was regarded by the Chancellor as the climax of his life's work.

During his last three years in office Adenauer's popularity declined. The economic boom ended in the early 1960s, there were undignified party squabbles, and the government was universally condemned for arresting the editor and occupying the offices of the magazine *Der Spiegel*, which had criticised the German Army. Adenauer seemed to be inflexible and autocratic, with little faith in the maturity of judgment of the German people in general. In the 1961 elections the Christian Democrats lost their absolute majority. The Free Democrats, a small liberal party, entered a coalition with them, but wanted Erhard to replace Adenauer as Chancellor. Finally, in October 1963 he was persuaded to resign. He was then aged eighty-seven, and was succeeded by Erhard. Adenauer was a great leader who gave Germany self-respect and stability at a time when it was most needed. He died in April 1967.

Erhard (Christian Democrat) 1963 to 1966   The Christian and Free Democrat coalition continued with Erhard as Chancellor. The 1965 elections produced little change. Erhard, however, though popular as a person, was not a success as Chancellor. The *laissez-faire* attitude which had produced economic success in the 1950s was inadequate for dealing with the domestic and foreign problems of the mid-1960s. Economic growth was limited by a shortage of labour: the 1.2 million

[1] Hallstein Doctrine—Professor Hallstein, then an official in the West German Foreign Ministry, formulated this policy.

foreign workers in Germany in 1965 were insufficient. Relations between Bonn and Paris did not live up to the expectations of the 1963 treaty. West Germany found it very difficult to reconcile friendship with the United States (and therefore the need to support American policy towards Russia, China and Vietnam) and friendship with a France led by the anti-American de Gaulle. In November 1966 the mounting dissatisfaction with the leadership of Erhard came to a head over a dispute with the Free Democrats about the budget. The Free Democrats left the coalition and Erhard resigned.

Kiesinger (Christian Democrat) 1966 to 1969 A 'big coalition' of the two large parties, the Christian and Social Democrats, ruled West Germany during these three years. The small Free Democrats formed the Opposition. Kiesinger, a Christian Democrat, was Chancellor, while Brandt, the leader of the Social Democrats or socialist party, was in charge of foreign affairs.

For the first year of the Kiesinger government there was an economic recession and unemployment was relatively high. The Deutsche Mark, however, was by now the world's most stable currency, and by 1968 the economy had recovered. Indeed, the country's huge trade surplus helped to cause international monetary problems, and there was talk of a new economic miracle. Despite this renewed economic prosperity, the second half of the 1960s was marked by the growth of political extremism, both of the left and right. A neo-Nazi Party, the National Democrats, led by von Thadden, received growing support in state elections. One consequence was discussion within the coalition about a proposal to change the electoral system to one of majority voting on the British pattern with the aim of reducing the number of small parties. There were also fears that Russia might use the excuse of the National Democrats' influence to intervene in West German affairs. At the other extreme, militant left-wing students campaigned for university reform. Large and sometimes violent student demonstrations in 1968 demanded not merely reform of educational institutions but of society generally, parliament to be replaced by soviets of workers and intellectuals.

Kiesinger and Brandt aimed to improve relations with France and with East European countries. The priority given to maintaining the 'special relationship' with France was shown when West Germany reluctantly supported France in again opposing British entry into the EEC. No progress was made in improving relations with East Germany. Ulbricht, the East German Communist leader, said no progress would be made until Bonn surrendered its claim to represent all Germans.

The Hallstein Doctrine said that Bonn would not recognise those countries which had diplomatic relations with East Germany. This was modified in 1967 when diplomatic relations were established with Romania. Russia would have allowed her satellites a further exchange of diplomatic representatives only if West Germany recognised East Germany. Following the Soviet invasion of Czechoslovakia in 1968, the United States, Britain and France reiterated their guarantees for the security of West Berlin and West Germany. The visit of President Nixon to West Berlin early in 1969 was important in this respect.

Brandt (Social Democrat) 1969 to 1974   The federal elections in September 1969 resulted in the Christian Democrats gaining 46 per cent of the votes and 242 seats. However, the Social Democrats (224) and Free Democrats (30) formed a new coalition government with Brandt as Chancellor. For the first time since the Federal Republic was formed, the Christian Democrats found themselves in Opposition. The new Chancellor was to become a highly respected figure in international politics. The Social Democratic Party preached a very moderate brand of socialism, and Brandt, a strong leader backed by effective colleagues, occupied the centre of politics and gradually broadened the basis of his support. The 1972 election saw the height of Brandt's popularity: the Social Democrats became the largest party, but still without an overall majority and depending on the support of the Free Democrats.

Brandt wished to improve relations with the Communist countries of Eastern Europe, especially East Germany and Poland. He considered that the reunification of Germany was not attainable in the foreseeable future but should remain an ultimate aim, and that in the meantime it would be realistic to accept that there were 'two German states within one German nation', as he put it. At the same time Brandt emphasised that West Germany must remain firmly within the Western Alliance. In 1969 West Germany signed the nuclear non-proliferation treaty which reassured the eastern bloc. In 1970 Brandt visited East Germany and met the East German Prime Minister. Talks continued between officials during the year. In August 1970 West Germany signed treaties with Russia and Poland. By these treaties West Germany accepted the Oder-Neisse Line (see p. 69) as the western frontier of Poland, thus renouncing claims to one third of the territory of pre-war Germany. West Germany said the treaty meant that the frontiers of Europe could be changed by mutual agreement but not by force. Neither treaty could be ratified until there was a satisfactory conclusion to the Four Power negotiations on Berlin. In 1971 a Berlin Agreement was signed. In return for a reduction in the power of the Federal Government in West Berlin, the Russians promised not to impede communications between West Germany and West Berlin, renounced their claim to the right to intervene in West German affairs, and agreed to an extension of visits by West Germans to East Germany. Consequently in 1972 the 1970 Treaties with Russia and Poland were ratified, and the Basic Treaty governing relations between the two German states was signed. In the same year Brandt visited Brezhnev in Russia, and the Russian leader went to Bonn in 1973. In that year diplomatic relations were established with Czechoslovakia, Hungary and Bulgaria.

West Germany's *Ostpolitik,* as her policy towards Eastern Europe is known, was successful and popular at home and abroad. Some West German politicians and some foreign countries, especially France, considered that Brandt was losing interest in Western Europe and West Germany was veering towards neutrality. The Chancellor considered, however, that his policy of detente with the East did not harm West Germany's position in the EEC and in the Western Alliance. Brandt's reputation was based on the success of his policy of reducing tension in central Europe. In 1971 he was awarded the Nobel Peace Prize. In addition, the economic boom continued, real wages increased, job vacancies far exceeded unemployment. By the end of the 1960s West Germany was the strongest country in Europe, self-confident, relaxed and with strong and sensible leadership. Under Brandt for the first time since the war she showed this self-confidence in international affairs.

When the Social Democrats came to power in 1969 Brandt spoke of the need for domestic reforms to create a more equal and just society. Again after 1972 Brandt talked of improving the quality of life. Little was done, however, to fulfil these promises and by 1974 there was widespread criticism of Brandt's leadership. The immediate reason for his resignation in May 1974 was the discovery that a Chancellery aide had been spying for East Germany. Although the security service were later blamed for grave mistakes, Brandt admitted political responsibility for negligence.

Schmidt (Social Democrat) 1974 to the present   The Economics Minister, Schmidt, succeeded Brandt as Chancellor, and the coalition government of Social and Free Democrats remained in office. In the 1976 election both parties lost seats but retained a narrow majority. At the age of 55 Schmidt was to be widely regarded as Europe's most gifted political leader, cool, dynamic and decisive. There were no important changes of policy, and West Germany remained a country admired for its economic strength, democracy, prosperity, social security and orderliness. Nevertheless, West Germany in the mid-1970s had its problems. Brandt's successful Ostpolitik aroused expectations which were not fulfilled. The world economic recession resulted in unemployment of over 1 million, while inflation reached 7 per cent.[1] The expression of social concern and criticism was much less inhibited, and a number of civic action groups opposed, amongst many other things, to nuclear power stations, were formed. The extreme right-wing neo-Nazi party had become insignificant, but an apparent threat to society came from the terrorist activities of a group of urban guerrillas known as the Baader-Meinhoff group. They were responsible for a series of politically motivated crimes—murder, bank robbery, arson, forgery and kidnapping. In 1975 six of these terrorists seized the West German embassy in Stockholm, and demanded the release of 26 prisoners. When they were refused, the terrorists blew up the embassy. In 1977 the group kidnapped and eventually killed a leading industrialist named Schleyer.

Italy

In 1943 Italy was both defeated and humiliated. During the next two years there was heavy fighting over much of the country resulting in immense destruction of property. When the Second World War ended, therefore, Italy was in a disastrous economic condition which seemed likely to strengthen an already large Communist Party. However, the twenty years after 1945 saw steady economic progress and during the first half of the period political stability.

In the immediate post-war period Italy received valuable help from UNRRA and Marshall Aid. During the 1950s she joined the ECSC and the EEC, and Italian industry benefited from the wider market. A high proportion of industrial and other installations were new and up to date, labour costs were low, industrialists were confident and eager to expand, while the government's handling of the economy was skilful. The result was remarkable industrial growth in the 1950s and 1960s, almost an industrial revolution. Productivity was high,

---

[1] After the bewildering experience of very great inflation after two World Wars, German politicians were insistent that price rises were kept to a minimum. The following is a comparison of British and German annual inflation rates (%):—

	1967	1968	1969	1970	1971	1972	1973	1974	1975	1976	1977	1978
WG:	1·4	2·6	1·9	3·4	5·3	5·5	6·9	7·0	6·0	4·5	3·9	2·0
UK:	2·5	4·7	5·4	6·4	9·4	7·1	9·2	15·9	24·2	15·8	16·0	9·0

Figures derived from *Main Economic Indicators*, OECD 1976, 1979.

particularly in the north of the country. However, the decade 1968-78 was less happy. In 1968-69 there were widespread strikes to obtain higher wages. These raised industrial costs and reduced production. Inflation during the 1970s, partly caused by the energy crisis of 1974, reduced internal demand. In consequence the economy began to flounder and unemployment rose steeply. Small and medium-sized industries were particularly hit.

In 1945 de Gasperi formed the Christian Democratic Party, which immediately became the largest group in Parliament. From 1948 to 1953 it had an absolute majority, and this produced political stability. The leader of the Christian Democrats and the dominating politician in Italy until his death in 1954 was de Gasperi himself. 'In eight successive coalitions this great statesman showed himself to be the most astute and courageous leader since Cavour himself, and one of the most high-principled.'[1]

After 1953, however, parliamentary democracy weakened. There were four main political groups: from 'left' to 'right', the Communists, Socialists, Christian Democrats and the right-wing parties. There were several socialist and right-wing parties, and the Communists and Christian Democrats never had an absolute majority. Consequently, Italy was ruled by the Christian Democratic Party, either in precarious coalition with other groups of the Left or Right, or occasionally alone and therefore liable to fall if the other parties combined to vote together. When a government fell, it would often take several weeks of political bargaining before the next one could be formed. For example, in 1974 there was no government for 50 days. In 1970, when the fourth administration since the general elections of two years before was defeated, the prime minister said that in his view the country was approaching ungovernability.[2] The method of election, proportional representation, allowed society's divisions to be reflected in parliament. Apart from the great number of parties, they each contained a variety of views. The Christian Democrats, the largest party, had within it a kaleidoscope of opinions. There was not much ideological content to weld together each party. The Communist Party, which became the largest in the western world, steadily grew until in 1974 it had the support of 34 per cent of the electorate. Until quite recently, however, it was assumed that Communists could not be trusted with government, and a large section of the Italian people were consequently prevented from participation in national govern-

[1] Mack Smith, *Italy*.

[2] Mussolini once said that governing Italy was not impossible but pointless, meaning that the Italians could manage perfectly well by themselves.

ment. However, the apparent independence of the Italian Communist Party from Russian control—in 1968 it criticised Russian action over Czechoslovakia—led to the situation in 1976 in which a minority Christian Democrat government ruled with the tacit support and close collaboration of the Communists. In the following year, left-wing students showed their dislike of the Communist Party playing, as they saw it, conventional politics with the bourgeois system.

The 1970s have for Italy been a period of growing economic, political and social anarchy. The striking economic development of the previous twenty years had seen a move of population from the south to the north, and from the country to the towns. This produced a variety of social problems: schools, health services, housing were inadequate. There were other problems: the judicial system was slow and cumbersome, the civil service was ridden with bureaucracy, and the universities had grown enormously (one million students, with 170,000 at the University of Rome alone) while curricula and methods of teaching and administration were antiquated. The old problem of the division between north and south remained and in some ways was accentuated by economic growth. All these social resentments produced violence. Political violence by extremist groups, kidnappings,[1] sporadic rioting, all contributed to the growing turbulence of public life. Attempts at reform met with obstruction—there were too many vested interests who wished to keep the status quo—and the feeling grew that politicians were more intent on keeping power than dealing with national problems and that the pressing business of political manoeuvring was more important than dealing with the economy or the problems of a changing society. One important administrative problem was dealt with: in 1972 central government transferred certain of its powers to the regions—public health, education, housing, agriculture, tourism. Generally, however, the political will for change seemed lacking, and in many ways Italian politics had much in common with the politics of the Fourth Republic in France. There was a mood of scepticism and aimlessness and a general wish for stronger government.

Spain

For twenty years after the end of the Civil War in 1939 General Franco was mainly concerned with establishing an effective administra-

---

[1] In 1978 Moro, leader of the Christian Democrat Party, was kidnapped and killed by the Red Brigade.

tion and preventing the emergence of democracy. A Fascist government was set up, and Spain became a highly centralised and authoritarian one-party state. The National Movement (the Falange) was the
only legitimate party in the country. There were no elections, and the
regime was based on the army, the Roman Catholic Church and the
syndicates, which were government-controlled unions of employers
and employees. Regionalism, Protestantism and Socialism were
crushed by a government whose main popular support was based on
the fear of another civil war.

In the late 1950s a new group of politicians entered the administration. They were members of a powerful secular Catholic organisation
called Opus Dei. Authoritarian and elitist in politics, they had liberal
and progressive attitudes in economic matters and in their approach to
European affairs. These technocrats or Europeans gave impetus to
industrial development. Economic progress had been slow up to this
point, but during the 1960s Spain began to catch up with the rest of
Europe. As a result of modernisation of the administration, finance
and industry, the economy at last 'took off', and living standards rose
remarkably. In 1960 Spain joined OECD, commercial links with
Europe grew, and Spain's interest in the EEC could have been treated
sympathetically if her political system had been more acceptable. The
tourist industry boomed: in 1972, for example, 33 million foreigners
visited Spain, while 9 million Spaniards travelled abroad. This contact
with the rest of Europe, and the increased prosperity, produced social
changes and forces which could not be adequately contained in the
political structures of fascist Spain.

Until the mid-1950s Spain was largely isolated in the world.
Franco's decision in 1940 to keep out of the war was of great help to
the Allied cause. Nevertheless, Spain was debarred from membership
of the United Nations and generally the world was hostile to the
fascist government, a factor which, incidentally, helped to rally Spanish
opinion behind Franco. During the 1950s, by patience and skilful
planning, Franco gradually widened Spain's contacts. Although the
United States was reluctant to be associated with Franco, she needed
strategic bases, and in 1953 made an agreement by which American
aid was given in exchange for military bases. In 1959 President
Eisenhower visited Spain. In 1955 Spain became a member of the UN.
Relations with the Arab world, especially Morocco and Algeria, were
carefully cultivated, although Rio de Oro with its huge phosphate
deposits was kept by Spain despite Arab threats. During the 1960s
Spain put pressure on Britain for the return of Gibraltar to Spain.

Gibraltar, 2¼ square miles with 25,000 people, had internal self-rule, and had been British since 1713. It was no longer strategically important to Britain, and the United Nations called upon Britain to leave. But the people of Gibraltar, as they showed in a referendum in 1967, were nearly unanimous in wishing to maintain their links with Britain. Nevertheless, by the end of the 1960s Spain had succeeded in projecting abroad an image of a more moderate and progressive country.

Between about 1968 and 1972 a number of groups began to demand political and social changes. Students wanted an enquiry into the alleged torture of political prisoners and called for the abolition of the Special Tribunals. The Roman Catholic Church, once a pillar of the regime but now affected by the reforming spirit of the Vatican Council, demanded faster social progress. The protest movement which gained most attention was the group of Basque separatists who were prepared to use violence to achieve their ends. The Basque provinces in north Spain were a wealthy area. The Basque Nationalists with considerable popular backing wanted at least autonomy and at most complete independence from Spain. In 1970 the military trial opened of sixteen Basque activists accused of sedition. Progressive opinion in Spain and abroad, although unsympathetic to Basque nationalism, was critical of military judges trying political cases. Franco eventually commuted the death sentences that were imposed to life imprisonment. The restrictions on political liberty were increasingly resented.

In his later years Franco became preoccupied with the form government should take in Spain after he died. In 1947 Spain was declared a kingdom. Many years of speculation as to which member of the Spanish royal family would be the heir ended in 1969 when Prince Juan Carlos, the grandson of Alfonso XIII, was named as the future king. In 1973 Admiral Carrero Blanco, long one of Franco's closest political associates, became Prime Minister, while Franco continued as Head of State. Six months later Carrero Blanco was killed by Basque separatists. He was succeeded by Carlos Arias Navarro. During the next two years acts of terrorism by political extremists undermined further attempts to introduce liberal reforms.

In November 1975 General Franco died at the age of 82. He had ruled Spain for 36 years. Following the civil war his government aroused strong feelings both in Spain and abroad. It is undoubtedly true, however, that he gave his country a long period of peace, order and political stability. There had been no precedent for this in Spain since the eighteenth century, and it was no mean achievement.

On the death of Franco, Prince Juan Carlos became King. Arias remained as Prime Minister until July 1976 when the King appointed in his place an able young lawyer, Suarez, who had risen through the Falangist Party. During the next twelve months a series of remarkable changes took place. An amnesty allowed the release of hundreds of political prisoners. In November 1976 Suarez persuaded the very conservative parliament to agree to the election of a parliament by universal suffrage. This was confirmed in December when the Spanish people voted overwhelmingly in a referendum for the government's proposals. Early in 1977 political parties, including the Communist Party, were made legal. Finally in June 1977 a General Election was held in which Suarez's Democratic Centre Union won 166 seats and 47 per cent of the votes, and the Socialists 118 seats. The Communists and neo-Francoists won 20 and 17 seats respectively. Thus a parliament was elected in which the centre right and the centre left parties had 81 per cent of the seats, with the extremists very much in the minority. King Juan Carlos and his prime minister, Suarez, showed both sincerity and political skill, and the Army remained loyal and politically neutral. In view of some violence by small groups of terrorists and a worsening economic situation, to move from dictatorship to free elections in eighteen months without serious upheavals was a remarkable achievement.

Portugal

The authoritarian government of Salazar continued in Portugal until 1968. He was Prime Minister for 36 years, and, like Franco in Spain, could justly claim to have replaced chaos with order. His government relied heavily on the secret police. Domestic criticism of the regime was easily crushed, but international opposition mounted during the 1960s as a result of Portuguese policy towards their African possessions. Salazar was a gifted administrator and a cold intellectual. Political and economic life remained stagnant during his long government, which ended when he suffered a stroke in 1968.[1] He died in 1970.

From 1968 to 1974 Portugal was ruled by Dr Caetano. The new Prime Minister permitted little change, but there was some relaxation of the control over free speech with the result that various politicians called for reforms. The war in Angola and Mozambique (see p. 354) was the factor which caused most concern, and eventually brought down the government. Following the criticism by General Spinola of

---

[1] The deck-chair which collapsed beneath Dr Salazar, causing a stroke which eventually proved fatal, was British made.

the continued military involvement in Africa, there was a military *coup d'etat* in April 1974. This revolution was followed by two years of disorder and violence. A coalition government representing several political groups was formed at first, but the pendulum swung steadily to the left. Although elections held in April 1975 showed the electorate to favour the liberal and socialist parties, the Communists, with only 12 per cent of the votes, ignored the results and at the end of the year tried to take over the government by force. After the failure of this left-wing coup, the pendulum swung back to the centre. In June 1976 General Eanes was elected President and Dr Soares, the Socialist Leader, became Prime Minister. The government now had the enormous task, not only of developing democratic institutions, but of building up a demoralised, run-down and out-of-date economy in this, the poorest country in western Europe. Soares's minority administration was defeated in December 1977, but early in 1978 he formed a new coalition government.

Greece

Although the word democracy originated in ancient Greece, only rarely in twentieth-century Greece has the practice of it worked effectively. From 1924 to 1935 the Greek republic experienced several military coups. In 1935 the monarchy was restored, but soon after General Metaxas began his four-year dictatorship. The German occupation of Greece during the Second World War was followed by a civil war in which the Greek Communists attempted to take over the government. By 1945 the country was devastated.

The elections of 1946 produced a right-wing government and a plebiscite showed that a large majority of the population favoured a return of the monarchy. This was the signal for a renewed Communist revolt. The second phase of the civil war lasted from 1946 to 1949: half a million people died during the revolt, and the economy only survived as a result of Marshall Aid from the United States. Following the end of the civil war a moderate conservative government under Papagos ruled until 1955. This was followed by a similar government under Karamanlis. The period from 1949 to 1963 was one of relative political stability.

In 1963, however, a left-wing prime minister, Papandreou, took office, and a few months later the young King Constantine came to the throne. Papandreou wished both to purge the right-wing elements in the army and to reduce the powers of the monarch. Papandreou resigned in 1965, and his government was followed by a succession of weak administrations during which political disorder and irresponsibility increased. The army feared that Papandreou and the left wing would win fresh elections and in order to forestall such a victory decided to intervene. In April 1967 a small group of senior officers overthrew the government. The leader of the new military junta was Colonel Papadopoulos. In December events in Cyprus (see p. 120) lowered the junta's prestige and persuaded King Constantine to attempt a counter-coup. Amateurish in its planning, this failed, and King Constantine went into exile.

The military junta ruled Greece from 1967 to 1974. During these seven years there was a totalitarian dictatorship with all the normal apparatus of a police state. Foreign criticism was widespread, but there was no large-scale manifestation of domestic opposition until 1973. An abortive naval mutiny earlier in the year was followed by student riots in November. Papadopoulos promised elections and was promptly deposed by other army officers. The opposition continued, however, and matters came to a head in July 1974 when it became clear that the coup against Archbishop Makarios in Cyprus (see p. 121) had been master-minded from Athens. The unity of the army government suddenly collapsed, and an invitation was sent to Karamanlis, Prime Minister from 1955 to 1963, to return from Paris and form a civilian government.

Karamanlis, who had the stature of a statesman and national leader, restored democracy and civilian government. His New Democracy Party had a landslide victory in elections in 1974 and he was able to form a strong government. A referendum decisively rejected a restoration of the monarchy, and a new constitution in 1975 increased the powers of the executive. In the 1977 elections Karamanlis kept a comfortable, though reduced, majority.

Turkey

In 1945 Ismet Inönü, President of Turkey and leader of its only political party, the Republican People's Party, decided to introduce western-style democracy to Turkey. For the next five years the Republican People's Party continued to rule. It had the support of the army and the educated classes, and wanted a continuation of the modernising and westernising reforms first introduced by Kemal Atatürk in the 1920s and 1930s. In 1950, however, the new Democrat Party led by Menderes, won the election, and ruled for the next decade. The

Democrats were a conservative party, based on the support of the peasant majority in Turkey, and were more traditional and pro-Islamic in their attitude. Meanwhile the economy gradually developed, helped by Western aid particularly from the United States. In 1952 Turkey became a member of NATO.

Atatürk had striven to inculcate into the officer corps of the army the idea that they, together with other educated people, were responsible for defending his westernising reforms. Consequently during the 1950s the army was alarmed at the strength and views of the Democrat Party. In 1960 the Democrats, who had achieved power democratically, seemed to be heading for a one-party dictatorship, with the result that the army intervened and arrested and executed the Prime Minister, Menderes. It then restored democracy but under a new constitution with many checks and balances, and proportional representation which was designed to encourage small parties and thus divide the peasant majority. Despite proportional representation, the Justice Party, the successor of the Democrats, came to power with an absolute majority in 1965, and its moderate leader, Demirel, became Prime Minister. Although there were increasingly close ties with Russia and eastern Europe, Turkey remained pro-Western and in favour of free enterprise. The Justice Party continued to be opposed by the left-of-centre Republican People's Party led, until 1972, by Inönü.

At the end of the 1960s Turkey experienced the student disorders that were part of a general European university turmoil. In Turkey a small radical movement conducted a campaign of urban terrorism. The army, discontented at what it considered to be the inadequacy of the government's social reforms, considered that the Justice Party was weak in its efforts to repress these left-wing extremists. Consequently, in March 1971 it again intervened and Demirel was removed from office. For two years, 1971 to 1973, non-party governments ruled with military support, Marxist movements were ruthlessly suppressed, but parliament, which was allowed to continue, blocked reforms. In 1973 a General Election was held but no party emerged with an overall parliamentary majority. The result was that largely ineffectual coalitions ruled for the next four years. There was no firm government, decisions on important policies were continually deferred, and after 1975 there was a disturbing growth of political violence by extremists of both left and right. A small and extreme religious party, determined that economic and social progress should not be at the cost of the traditional values of Islam, held the balance of power. The General Election of 1977 did not alter this situation. In January 1978 Ecevit, the leader of the Republican People's Party, Turkey's largest party, formed a new government. However, problems of internal security, inflation and unemployment, and issues of foreign affairs, including the Cyprus problem and relatons with Greece, were not solved, and Demirel returned to office in October 1979.

Cyprus

Cyprus had been British territory since 1878, before which it had been part of the Turkish Empire. Cyprus contains two ethnic groups: about 80 per cent of the present-day population of 600,000 are Greek-speaking and Orthodox in religion, while the remaining 20 per cent are Turkish-speaking and Muslim. The Greek Cypriots had long wanted *enosis,* or union with Greece, but the demand was not pressed seriously until 1954. In that year Britain issued a new constitution for Cyprus which gave little power to Cypriots because it was intended that the island would remain a British military base in the eastern Mediterranean. The Greek Cypriots, influenced by the nationalism of the nearby Arab states, then pressed for union with Greece.

The Greek government eventually supported the demand for *enosis.* The Turkish government, however, supported the Turkish Cypriots who refused to be ruled by the Greek majority. In addition Turkey objected to the idea of an island so close to her southern ports coming under the rule of Greece. In 1955 the Greek Cypriots began demonstrations in support of their claim. These soon escalated into rioting, bomb throwing and shooting, much of it organised by a guerrilla organisation named Eoka, led by General Grivas. The British administration took repressive measures and eventually had 35,000 troops on the island. In 1956 the Greek Cypriot leader, Archbishop Makarios, was deported to the Seychelles for a year. However, the violence continued, and led to increasingly bitter relations between Turkey and Greece, both members of NATO.

It appeared that there were three solutions to the problem: union with Greece, partition, or independence for Cyprus. Partition would have involved a substantial transfer of population as the two communities were scattered about the island. In 1959 the decision in favour of independence was reached. Conferences were held at Zurich and London and a compromise constitution was drawn up. Seventy per cent of the members of parliament were to be Greek-speaking and the remaining 30 per cent were to be Turkish. Each community had the right to veto legislation. The cabinet, civil service and police were to be formed in the same ratio. The president of the new republic of Cyprus was to be Greek-speaking and the vice-president Turkish-speaking. Britain was to retain sovereignty over two small areas. The partition of the country and *enosis* were forbidden, and the independence of Cyprus was guaranteed by Britain, Turkey and Greece.

In 1960 Cyprus became an independent republic within the Commonwealth with Archbishop Makarios as its first President, and Dr Kuchuk, the leader of the Turkish community, as its Vice-President. The constitution, however, was found to be unworkable by the Greeks and inadequate by the Turks it was intended to protect. After three years the settlement broke down through lack of trust between the two communities. Makarios wished to revise the constitution to end some of the Turkish safeguards which he believed were hampering the government. In December 1963 fighting broke out between the Greek and Turkish communities, and early in 1964 the United Nations sent in troops to restore order. For the next four years there were intermittent skirmishes which occasionally flared up into open battles. The Turkish Cypriots were largely concentrated in enclaves whose economic life was very restricted by a blockade imposed by the Greek Cypriots. The governments of Greece and Turkey were increasingly involved and increasingly tempted to intervene in the dispute. Since Cyprus occupied an important strategic position in the east Mediterranean, and because both Greece and Turkey were members of NATO, there was a danger of a chain reaction involving outside powers and weakening the southern flank of NATO. The United Nations troops had a very limited mandate. They could use force only in self-defence and although they were invaluable in containing the fighting and preventing minor incidents from escalating, the UN had not the authority to resolve the dispute.

A crisis was reached in November 1967 when serious fighting broke out between the two communities. The Turkish government threatened to invade Cyprus and a powerful invasion force was built up in southern Turkey. The situation was defused in December when the 12,000 Greek troops left Cyprus. The significance of this move is that the Greek government, together with its supporters in Cyprus, appeared to abandon the policy of *enosis*. During 1968 tension was reduced and the first steps towards a return to normality were taken. The Greek Cypriot government lifted economic restrictions against the Turkish minority and removed road blocks. Talks started between Clerides and Denktash on behalf of the Greek and Turkish communities respectively. These intercommunal talks were to continue for the next six years with the object of finding a *modus vivendi* for the two peoples of Cyprus. Little progress was made. Meanwhile Makarios remained President and exercised a benevolent and paternalistic dictatorship which the large majority of Greek Cypriots willingly accepted. Life on the island returned to relative peace. Since independence in 1960 and despite years of discord and strife, the island's economy made steady progress, helped considerably by a UN development programme.

In 1974 this peace and progress were shattered. During the previous four years militant supporters of *enosis,* both in Cyprus and Greece, renewed their activities. In 1970 they attempted to assassinate Makarios who they considered had betrayed the *enosis* cause. Relations between Nicosia and Athens deteriorated. In July 1974 matters came to a head when the Cypriot National Guard under new Greek officers attacked the presidential palace and appointed a former Eoka gunman as president. Makarios, however, escaped and was flown to Britain. A few days later Clerides assumed the presidency. Meanwhile the Turkish government had sent its forces to invade the north coast of Cyprus. The Turks demanded a federal solution to the problem of Cyprus. When this was refused, they proceeded to occupy about two-fifths of the island (in the north and east). 200,000 Greek Cypriots were displaced from the occupied areas. During 1975, despite the return of Makarios, attitudes hardened, and the transfer of populations was virtually completed with Turks in the north and Greeks in the south. The northern part was declared a Turkish Cypriot state, and Turks from the mainland began to settle there. The remainder of the island was left to solve enormous problems of resettlement and readjustment. In August 1977, when Makarios died, a Cyprus settlement had still not been made, and the situation remained deadlocked.

The European Movement

Common Market

One of the most revolutionary movements in postwar Europe has been the progress made in integrating the states of Western Europe. The ultimate object of those in favour of this movement, the Europeans as they are called, is a united European state. They have four basic motives. Firstly, they wish to prevent further European wars by ending the sovereign independence of national states, and they particularly wish to end the rivalry of France and Germany. Secondly, a united Europe would be in a much stronger position to resist the threat from Soviet Russia. Thirdly, the creation of a third force in the world would counterbalance the strength of the United States and Russia. Fourthly, full use could be made of the economic and military resources of Europe by organising them on a continental rather than a national scale.

In 1944 the three Benelux countries agreed to form a customs union. This began to operate in 1948 and was the forerunner of much bigger schemes. The Europeans were also encouraged by the support of Churchill who, in a speech at Zurich, said, 'We must build a kind of United States of Europe.' The movement was given impetus by the Communist threat revealed by the *coup d'état* in Czechoslovakia and the Berlin blockade. In 1948 the Organisation for European Economic Cooperation was formed following American insistence that Marshall Aid would only be given if the states of Europe cooperated in its administration.

In 1948 at The Hague a conference of 700 prominent Europeans exerted pressure on governments to form a European Parliament. The result was that in May 1949 in London ten countries signed the Statute of the Council of Europe. These ten were France, Britain, Belgium, Holland, Luxembourg, Denmark, Ireland, Italy, Norway and Sweden. Nine more countries joined by 1978—Greece, Turkey, Iceland, West Germany, Austria, Cyprus, Switzerland, Malta and Portugal. The Council of Europe, whose headquarters is at Strasbourg, has a Secretariat and two main organs, a Committee of Ministers and a Consultative Assembly. The former consists of the Foreign Ministers of the member countries, or their deputies, and their decisions are recommended to member governments. In 1978 the Assembly consisted of 154 representatives drawn from the parliaments of the nineteen members. It was hoped originally that there would be direct elections by the people of Europe to this assembly, but Britain opposed this. The Council of Europe has no real power, and has been described as a mere debating forum.

European Coal and Steel Community 1951 + (6 yr)

Since the Europeans believed that the power of the Council of Europe was too limited, they aimed at setting up European organisations for particular functions. Their hope was that these functional organisations, while beneficial in themselves, would help to create the essential feeling of working together in a community which was necessary for political unity. In 1950 two such organisations were proposed: the European Defence Community and the European Coal and Steel Community. Both of these were opposed by Britain, and in 1954 the EDC was finally rejected by France (see p. 79). However, despite

British refusal to take part, the ECSC was founded in 1951.

The originator of the Coal and Steel Community was the French Foreign Minister, Robert Schuman (1886–1963). He had spent most of his early life in Lorraine, which was then in Germany, and he was an officer in the German army in the First World War. After 1919 he became a member of the French Parliament. One motive behind the Schuman Plan on coal and steel was to improve Franco-German relations, but he also regarded his plan as 'a first step in the direction of European federation'. The Schuman Plan, which was accepted in the French cabinet in May 1950, provided for a supranational authority which could enforce a common market with no trade restrictions of any sort in the two basic industries of coal and steel. The object was to increase efficiency and therefore productivity in these two industries.

Both the Labour and Conservative parties in Britain disliked the scheme. They regarded the British coal and steel industries as too important to be taken from the control of the British government. Six countries, however, approved of the scheme: France, West Germany, Italy, Belgium, Holland and Luxembourg. In 1951 a treaty setting up the ECSC was signed in Paris, and in August 1952 it began functioning from its headquarters in Luxembourg. The executive of the ECSC, the High Authority, had nine members, and it was controlled by an Assembly of 78 delegates from the member countries. The President of the High Authority until 1954 was Jean Monnet.

Common Market

European Economic Community 1957

The Coal and Steel Community was very successful. Production increased and trade within the Community rose particularly fast. It was, therefore, felt desirable to expand it to include free competition in all industries in order to achieve comprehensive economic integration. It was also felt that further progress towards European unification should be made. In 1954 the Assembly of the ECSC urged the Community to widen its activities, and in June 1955 the foreign ministers of the six member countries met at Messina in Sicily. A committee under Spaak, foreign minister of Belgium, was set up to plan further economic integration. The committee reported in the following year, and in March 1957 the six countries that belonged to the ECSC signed the Treaty of Rome which established the European Economic Community (EEC, or the Common Market). In addition the European Atomic Energy Community (Euratom) was set up. Both treaties were ratified by the member countries before the end of the year and came into effect in January 1958.

France, Italy, West Germany and the three Benelux countries agreed that trade barriers in the form of customs and quotas should gradually be removed. During the transitional period of twelve to fifteen years starting in 1958 a common market would be established between the six countries who would at the same time develop a common external tariff against non-members. At the end of the transitional period, there would be completely free movement of persons, goods, services and capital between member countries. Overseas territories of the six could be included in the Market. In the preamble to the Treaty of Rome the members declared themselves 'determined to establish the foundations of an ever closer union among the European peoples'. They believed that the habit of working together would grow over the years, and that eventually economic unity would lead to political unity so that a United States of Europe would in time be set up.

The constitution of the European Economic Community provided for five main bodies. There was an Executive Commission of nine members which managed the Community. The members were appointed by unanimous agreement of the governments, but the Commission acted independently and was answerable only to the Assembly. The Commission's headquarters was in Brussels, and its first President was Professor Hallstein. Each government appointed one member to the Council of Ministers. This took decisions on proposals of the Commission, and unanimity was required in voting on important items, particularly the new membership of other countries. The Assembly contained 142 delegates from the parliaments of the Six. It had advisory powers only, except that it could dismiss the Commission by passing a vote of censure by a two-thirds majority. The first President of the Assembly was Robert Schuman. In addition there was a Court of Justice and a Secretariat. Euratom aimed at the pooling of financial and research resources to develop a nuclear industry.

European Free Trade Association 1959

Britain had the opportunity to become a member of the European Economic Community and took part in the original meetings to set it up. However, she decided not to join for a variety of reasons (see chapter 6), but particularly because of her dislike of a supranational authority which would mean a decline in Britain's sovereignty. Yet Britain feared the high tariffs which would be erected against her exports by the six countries of the Common Market. In 1956, therefore, she proposed a Free Trade Area to cover all the countries of the OEEC (see p. 74). Over a period of twelve to fifteen years these

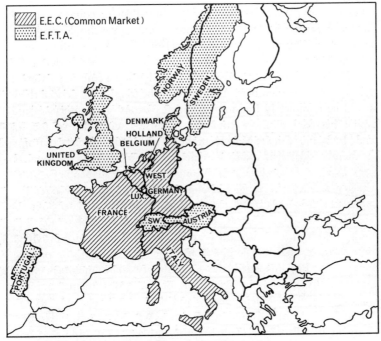

E.E.C. (Common Market)
E.F.T.A.

European Economic Blocs in 1960

countries would gradually remove the tariffs against each other's goods, but, unlike the EEC which has a common external tariff, the members of the Free Trade Area would be free to maintain what tariffs they liked against outside countries. This would allow Britain to keep commonwealth preferences.

The scheme, however, was rejected by the Six. Britain, therefore, decided to form a European Free Trade Association among countries which came to be known as the Outer Seven—Britain, Portugal, Denmark, Austria, Norway, Sweden and Switzerland. EFTA was formed in 1959 and began functioning in May 1960. Its headquarters are in Geneva.

Progress of the European communities

In the period from 1958 to 1963 the total value of trade within the European Economic Community increased by 130 per cent. Between 1958 and 1972 the Six increased trade with each other eightfold. External trade also rose considerably. This remarkable progress resulted both in an influx of foreign capital attracted by the growth prospects

Prague, 21 August 1968. Young Czechs, some with shopping baskets, mill about as Soviet tanks are held up by blazing improvised barricades

Anti-Common Market rally in Trafalgar Square, London, in October 1971

of the EEC and in a rapid rise in the standard of living.[1] The Commission under Professor Hallstein gave good leadership, and there was steady progress in the reduction of trade barriers. A major advance in the early 1960s was agreement on a Common Agricultural Policy (CAP). The aim of this policy was to increase productivity, to provide stable markets and therefore a fair living for farmers, and to fix reasonable prices for consumers. Each country pays into a common agricultural fund. Levies are placed on imported food if its price is lower than that in the Community. In addition, the Community will buy and remove from the market goods when prices fall; this reduces the supply to the market and prices then stabilise. The Community also promotes the modernisation of farming.

There were two main areas of progress in the years 1965 to 1969. In 1967 the three communities—the EEC, Euratom and the Coal and Steel Community—were merged, and a single new Commission took office. The French refused to accept Hallstein as President of the new Commission and Rey, a former Belgian Minister of Economic Affairs, became President. The rest of the year was spent on reorganising the structure into a single administration. 1968 saw the completion of full free trade for industrial products, two years ahead of the date laid down in the Treaty of Rome ten years before. A common market for 180 million people was thus in force, with no internal customs barriers and with a common external tariff.

Nevertheless, these were years of comparative stagnation, largely resulting from the influence of President de Gaulle of France. De Gaulle had had no part in creating the EEC. It was formed shortly before he came to power, and he never liked it. However, he realised the opportunities, both economic and political, which its restricted membership offered to France, and he exploited them to the full. French farmers were probably the most backward of the Six and stood most to gain from the CAP. In addition, de Gaulle regarded the EEC as a means of freeing Western Europe from dependence on the United States. But he disliked the independent authority and supranationalism of its institutions, especially the 'Eurocrats' of the Commission, whose members are appointed by national governments but who are sworn to be independent of any national interests. De Gaulle opposed proposals which would provide the Commission with its own financial resources, and in the second half of 1965 France boycotted all Community meetings.

[1] Rise in real wages, 1958–68: Belgium 47%, France 41%, West Germany 66%, Italy 55%, Luxembourg 46%, Netherlands 75%, United Kingdom 20%. (Derived from figures published by the European Movement in *The Times*, 23 March 1971).

De Gaulle's influence was felt most obviously over the question of Britain's wish to join the Community. The British government, after long debate, decided in 1961 to apply for membership. Negotiations continued throughout 1962, but in January 1963 the application was vetoed by France. In 1967 the British reapplied. Five of the Six supported Britain, but France did not, and at the end of the year de Gaulle for the second time vetoed the British application. There were several reasons for his action: to have new members would reduce the influence of any one of the existing members; new members would increase the problems of organisation and communication and generally change the nature of the Community; Britain, he said, was not a convinced European country—it was too insular, it had its Commonwealth and its 'special relationship' with the United States, and sterling was a world currency; in addition, until Britain's economy improved, she would be a liability to the Community.

There were other problems, too, during these years. The large surpluses and high costs of the CAP were criticised. Although free trade in industrial goods was achieved by 1968, many controls remained in force on the frontiers. There were differing conceptions of the future of the Community. The general feeling was one of stagnation and disillusionment: men who had begun to think of themselves as Europeans were once again talking as Germans, Frenchmen or Belgians.

In April 1969 de Gaulle resigned (see p. 101), and was succeeded by Pompidou who was more favourably disposed to the development of the Community. During the next four years there was progress. In December 1969 there was a Summit Meeting at The Hague. This, together with meetings held immediately afterwards, took a number of important decisions: talks were to start with countries applying for membership, Euratom, which had done little for several years, was revived and the Euratom Research Centre was given a new direction, more closely linked with industry; the levies on farm imports would now go direct to the central Community budget and thus the Community would have its own direct revenues, not contributed from national budgets. The Hague meeting was dominated by Brandt, the West German Chancellor. He spoke of the need for West Germany to be closely involved in the process of European integration, and for Britain to join the Community.

During 1970 and 1971 negotiations continued between the Community and four would-be members: Britain, Ireland, Denmark and Norway. The applicants had to accept not just the Treaty of Rome but also the various agreements that had been made between 1958 and

1971. The issue in negotiations was how they were to adapt to all this during a transitional period, and particularly their contribution to the size of the Community budget which in practice meant the CAP. At a meeting in Paris in 1971 between Pompidou and Heath, the British Prime Minister, more fundamental French doubts about Britain's attitude to Europe were removed, and thereafter there was rapid progress. In January 1972, at an impressive ceremony in Brussels, the four applicant countries signed documents which committed them to becoming full members of the European Community on 1 January 1973. Referenda in Ireland and Denmark, and a vote in parliament in Britain, ratified these decisions. The Norwegian referendum, however, showed a majority against membership, and Norway did not therefore join the Community.

In January 1973 the Six became the Nine. At that point the total population of the European Community was 255 million, made up as follows:[1]

France	52 m.	Netherlands	13 m.
West Germany	62 m.	Belgium	10 m.
Italy	54 m.	Denmark	5 m.
Britain	56 m.	Ireland	3 m.
		Luxembourg	0.3 m.

How the Nine in 1971 compared in certain respects with the United States, Russia and Japan is shown below:[2]

	European Community	USA	USSR	Japan
Population (m.)	253	204	243	103
Gross National Product (m. dollars)	637,850	975,240	434,870	198,840
Steel output (m. tons)	139	122	120	93
Annual car production (m.)	9·7	6·6	0·4	3·7
Telephones per 1,000 population	203	567	50	194
TV sets per 1,000 population	230	399	127	214
Regular armed forces (m.)	2	2·4	3·7	0·3
Average growth rate (%) per head (1960–70)	3·6	3·2	5·8	9·6

[1] Compiled from the *Monthly Bulletin of Statistics,* United Nations.

[2] Figures derived from an article published in *The Times,* 3 Jan. 1973.

In July 1972, an agreement to have full free trade in industrial goods was reached between the European Community and six other countries (Austria, Sweden, Switzerland, Finland, Iceland, Portugal), who wanted some links but not full membership. In October 1972 a Summit Meeting of the Nine in Paris decided to proceed with a further stage of economic and monetary union. Two other important decisions were reached: to put a new emphasis on social progress as a goal of equal importance with economic expansion, and to create a fund which would help the more backward regions of the Community.

Progress continued in some respects during the years from 1973 to 1977. In 1975 a five-year agreement was signed covering trade and economic aid between the Community and 46 developing nations: this is known at the Lomé Convention. In the same year the Regional Development Fund was set up. An important development was the plans for direct elections to the European Parliament. The Parliament had so far been almost exclusively advisory in its function, and had often been totally disregarded. It was widely felt, however, that the Community lacked democratic political institutions, and that Parliament should have greater powers over finance and legislation. If Parliament were directly elected, the peoples of Europe would feel more loyalty towards the Community, and this would be a spur to more rapid progress in unification. Consequently, in 1975 the existing European Parliament voted by an overwhelming majority in favour of direct elections. These were eventually held in June, 1979.

However, progress during these years was limited by a number of problems. The energy crisis which erupted with the sudden quadrupling of oil prices in October 1973 produced world economic recession. The rapid growth of previous years was not maintained. There were doubts over the British commitment to Europe. The British Labour Party had opposed British membership in 1972. During 1973 there was widespread disillusionment in Britain about the Community which was used as a scapegoat for many problems, especially inflation. When the Labour Party was returned to power in 1974 it decided to renegotiate the previous entry terms. Some relatively minor changes in Community policies followed, and a referendum was then held which showed a decisive majority (67 to 33%) in favour of continued British membership. Many members of the Community remained critical of the Common Agricultural Policy. Agricultural production in Europe had risen spectacularly. The CAP had been successful in replacing smaller, less efficient farms by larger units, and had been instrumental in bringing about a steady migration from countryside to towns to reduce the surplus rural population. But the financial costs were high.

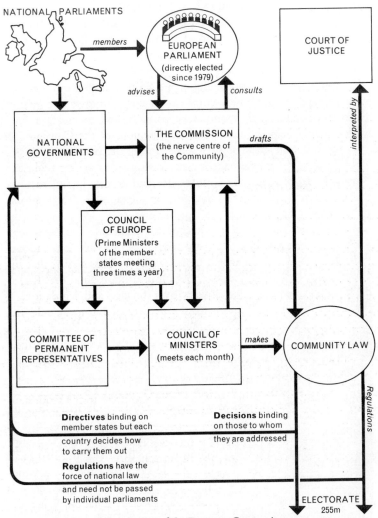

The structure of the European Community

The system was accused of keeping prices artificially high in the interests of farmers, and of creating food 'mountains'. Finally, it was widely felt that a more efficient and streamlined organisation was required. Nine was more cumbersome than Six. Greece, Portugal and Spain wished to join the Community, and Twelve would be even more complicated. It was also suggested that the number of official languages (six) should be reduced, and the power of veto by individual states should be replaced by majority voting.

4

Russia

Beginning of the Twentieth Century

Politics

In 1900 Imperial Russia covered over eight million square miles, that is about one-sixth of the land area of the world, and contained 130 million people. Like Turkey, the Russian Empire was both European and Asiatic; about eighty different nationalities lived within it, and less than half the population was Russian. This vast area was ruled by 'the world's most inefficient, petrifying, abusive, corrupt, clumsy and unenterprising bureaucracy'.[1] The hub of this bureaucracy was Tsar Nicholas II (1894–1917). Nicholas was a well-meaning ruler and devoted to his family, but he lacked self-confidence and was too easily influenced by characters stronger than his own, and was also blind to the seriousness of the political and economic problems facing Russia. 'Nicholas was incapable,' says Charques, 'except in the perverse obstinacy of the weak, of a mind or will of his own.'[2] It was unfortunate, too, that Nicholas was married to a strong-willed but politically foolish wife.[3]

The government was an inefficient dictatorship. The State Council advised the Tsar, but the latter had complete power, and his first principle was that he must preserve this centuries-old autocracy, and in this he was supported by the nobility and the Orthodox Church. The press was censored, education and the judiciary were controlled by the state, and all radical movements were repressed. The Minister of the Interior who controlled the police and collected taxes was the most influential minister. There was one group of councils which did involve some democracy, the *zemstvos*. These were rural elected councils and were

---

[1] J. N. Westwood, *Russia, 1917–1964.*

[2] R. Charques, *Short History of Russia.*

[3] Nicholas and his wife have often been compared with Charles I and Henrietta Maria and with Louis XVI and Marie Antoinette.

first started in 1864. Their activities were purely local—repair of roads, poor relief, health, schools—but their powers had been gradually reduced and they now consisted mainly of representatives of the gentry.

Economic affairs

Russia was a mainly agricultural country and two-thirds of the population were peasants. Life for most of these was bleak and hopeless. After the abolition of serfdom in 1861, land was sold, not to individual peasants, but to the village commune. The peasants in the commune continued to make heavy payments to the government for the land, but the commune itself actually owned the land. The commune's agreement was necessary if a peasant wanted to leave his village, but this was difficult to obtain because the remaining peasants would have to make proportionately higher payments. The medieval strip system still operated, and the strips were periodically redistributed amongst the peasants. The growth in population meant that the average size of holdings shrank. A particular grievance of the peasantry was the power of the Land Captains. These were officials responsible to the Minister of the Interior, and their arbitrary authority over the peasants was bitterly resented. The organisation of agriculture and the poverty of the peasants meant that techniques remained backward and production was so low that in the early 1900s famine conditions developed.

This agricultural stagnation was in sharp contrast with the remarkable industrial activity, and for the latter Sergius Witte (1849–1915) was largely responsible. From small beginnings he rose to become minister in charge of transport and then finance. Under his vigorous direction the Trans-Siberian railway was started in 1891 and opened ten years later, so that it was now possible to reach the Pacific from Moscow in eight days. Witte encouraged the development of heavy industry—iron, coal, oil, shipbuilding, chemicals, metal-working. Half of the capital for this investment was foreign (mainly French and Belgian); other money came from peasant taxes and from loans, and all was invested directly by the state.

Russian industry, though still far behind the leading Western countries, greatly improved. One consequence was the strengthening of the urban working class: in 1900 this numbered 10–15 million of whom over 2 million were factory workers. These industrial workers lived in overcrowded and unhygienic houses, and suffered from the usual evils of rapid and unplanned industrialisation—payment of wages often in kind, long hours and the employment of women and young children.

Political Parties

The political and economic conditions in Russia gave rise to a number of political groups outside the ranks of the conservatives. Many members of the zemstvos were liberals and wanted reforms, and there was a whole range of revolutionary groups of the left of which two stand out: the Social Revolutionaries and the Social Democrats.

During the 1870s small groups of intellectuals in Russia began to study the writings of Karl Marx. Their numbers gradually grew, and many were exiled and settled particularly in Switzerland where their most influential leader was Plekhanov. The view developed that revolutionary changes in Russia would only come with the support of the industrial workers, not the peasants, and through political action, not by terrorist methods. Therefore the Social Democratic Party was formally founded at Minsk in 1898. Eight of the nine delegates were immediately arrested by the police, but the party continued to exist abroad among exiles and in Russia as an underground organisation. It was soon clear that its most strong-willed and single-minded member was Vladimir Ulyanov who adopted the pseudonym, Lenin.

Lenin was born near the Middle Volga in 1870. His parents were educated, his father becoming a school-inspector. When Lenin was seventeen his eldest brother was hanged for terrorist activities. 'I'll make them pay for this. I swear it,' said Lenin, and he joined revolutionary groups. Qualifying as a lawyer from St Petersburg University, and already bald and with a scanty reddish beard, Lenin began instructing Marxist study groups of factory workers in St Petersburg, until he was arrested in 1895. He spent the next few years in Siberia, but in 1900 was released, and for the next seventeen years he and his wife moved from one boarding house to another in the big cities of Europe.

In 1903 a congress of forty-three delegates of the Social Democratic Party met in a disused flour warehouse in Brussels. To escape the Belgian police, they moved to London, and here the congress split on an issue of organisation and strategy. Lenin wished to restrict the membership of the party to disciplined, professional and militant revolutionaries. 'We must train people,' he said, 'who will dedicate to the revolution, not a spare evening, but the whole of their lives.' Many of the delegates, however, and these included Plekhanov and Trotsky, wanted a mass party containing as many well-wishers as possible. Lenin gained a small majority (bolshinstvo) for his view, and in future he led the Bolshevik Party. His opponents, in a minority (menshinstvo), were called Mensheviks. In fact there were always fewer Bolsheviks than Mensheviks before about 1920.

The Social Revolutionary Party was the chief party of the left, being far superior in numbers to the Social Democrats. Apart from the demand for the nationalisation of land, it had no clear policy, and included a number of radical groups. Its support came mainly from the towns, especially from students, and it concentrated upon mass propaganda and terrorist attacks on tsarist officials.

The 1905 Revolution

Living and working conditions soon produced riots and terrorism in the countryside and strikes and demonstrations in the towns. The answer of Plehve, the Minister of the Interior, was the usual policy of arresting and deporting the peasants' and workers' leaders. In 1904, however, he, like so many of his predecessors in this ministry, was assassinated, and in the same year Russia blundered into war against Japan (see p. 462). This proved a humiliating disaster as successive Russian defeats lowered the prestige and morale of the Tsar's government. In November 1904 a meeting of zemstvo leaders demanded agrarian and industrial reforms and a national assembly elected by universal suffrage.

It was clear that discontent with the government was widespread, but it only became really dangerous after Sunday, 22 January 1905. On this day Father Gapon, a priest and police agent, organised five long columns of men, women and children who marched on the Tsar's Winter Palace in St Petersburg. The processions were peaceful and unarmed, and intended to present a petition asking for a national assembly and the removal of grievances. But police and soldiers fired on the processions as they approached the centre of the city; probably a thousand were killed and many thousands wounded.

Passions then flared up in the violent atmosphere created by the events of this day (known as Bloody Sunday) and by riots, strikes and terrorism. The governor-general of Moscow, an uncle of the Tsar, was killed by a bomb, and mutinies spread in the armed forces.[1] In August the Tsar announced his proposals for a duma or parliament, but its function would only be to give advice—it would have no power. This was no longer satisfactory and the anarchy continued. In the autumn peasant violence reached new heights. Private estates were seized and plundered, and their owners murdered. In October a general strike in St Petersburg developed into a nationwide stoppage which involved most groups from railwaymen to ballet dancers. Urban life in Russia

[1] The mutiny of the crew of the battleship *Potemkin* has been made famous by Eisenstein's film.

came to a complete halt. A soviet (council) of workers' delegates was formed in St Petersburg on the initiative of the left-wing parties and was led by Trotsky. Similar soviets were set up in other cities. Clearly the survival of the Tsar's government was now at stake and there had to be concessions.

On 30 October Witte persuaded Nicholas to issue the Imperial Manifesto. This proclaimed the summoning of a Duma, with legislative powers, elected by popular franchise. The government's change of policy immediately won the support of the moderates, and the alliance between liberals and revolutionaries was broken. The left wing continued their opposition, peasant disorders remained as savage as before, and another general strike was planned. But the government was now in control of the situation. The members of the St Petersburg soviet were arrested, and law and order were gradually restored with harsh effectiveness in town and country.[1]

1906 to 1914

Early in 1906 the elections for the promised Duma were held. The result was a massive victory for the liberals and other parties opposed to the Tsar's policies. But when the Duma met in May it found that its powers had been much reduced. Laws had to have the agreement of both the Duma and the government-dominated State Council, and the government could legislate by decree when the Duma was not sitting. In practice the Tsar remained an autocrat. In addition a huge French loan had just been negotiated by Witte, so the Tsar was in a strong position financially. In frustration the Duma demanded a whole series of reforms, all of which were rejected. After ten weeks it was dissolved.

The second Duma met in March 1907. Although the government had greatly interfered with the elections, the large majority of deputies were again opposed to the government. The result was further deadlock, and after three months it, too, was dissolved. The electoral law was then thoroughly revised with the result that the rural gentry dominated the lists of candidates; half the electors were landowners and less than a quarter were peasants. When further elections were held the left-wing parties were nearly extinguished, and a conservative assembly was elected. The third Duma met late in 1907 and lasted its full term of five years. Its function was to act as a rubber stamp for decisions taken by the government.

Meanwhile important changes were taking place in the countryside.

[1] Although the Bolsheviks played a very small part in the 1905 Revolution Lenin regarded 1905 as a dress rehearsal for 1917.

From 1906 to 1911 the chief minister in the government was Stolypin. A strong and ruthless personality, he acted quickly and sternly to bring to an end the remaining terrorism in town and country. But he also realised that if the peasants' grievances were met, particularly their wish to own their own land, much of the disorder would automatically disappear. In November 1905 the outstanding payments to the government for land given to the commune back in 1861 were cancelled. In 1906 Stolypin took power away from the hated Land Captains, and peasants also were able to leave their commune at will. If two-thirds of the village agreed, peasants could consolidate their scattered strips into small farms which would then become their personal property.

So in Russia after 1906 there was gradually created a property-owning peasant class which used more modern methods of farming. But the process was too slow and only affected a small minority of peasants. With huge amounts of land still owned by the gentry, there was not enough land for the peasants. Nevertheless, the changes were too great for the conservatives who surrounded the Tsar. Probably with Nicholas's connivance, Stolypin was assassinated at a theatre in Kiev in 1911. Thereafter the Tsar's ministers were mediocrities. Elections were held for the fourth Duma in 1912, and these resulted in a further swing to the right. The fourth Duma ended with the revolution of 1917.

The period from 1906 to 1914 was one of relatively significant achievement. The Dumas had not received the power that was expected after the Imperial Manifesto, but they had provided experience in the function and running of parliament. Despite their grievances, the peasantry were more satisfied than they had been for many years. There had been considerable industrial development and by 1913 Russia was the fifth largest industrial nation in the world. Education had progressed, and some social legislation, such as health and accident insurance laws, had been passed. These achievements, together with the general reaction against revolutionary upheaval after 1905, sharply reduced the support for the left-wing groups. Their leaders were in exile in Europe, and in Russia the prospect of revolution seemed small. However, all this was changed by the First World War.

First World War 1914 to 1917

An outline of the military events of the war is contained in chapter 1. Here we are dealing with the effect of the war upon Russia. During the first few weeks there was a show of enthusiastic patriotism, and St Petersburg, which sounded German, was renamed Petrograd. But this enthusiasm was superficial and soon disappeared, particularly as news from the front came in.

The Russian army was completely unprepared for a modern war against a major Power. Everything was defective: the leadership was incompetent, communications were unorganised, medical and other services were inadequate, and there was a desperate shortage of munitions, soldiers often being expected to arm themselves with the weapons of the dead and wounded. Only manpower was not lacking: by the beginning of 1917 an army of 15 million was in the field. Casualties were enormous. 'Sometimes in our battles with the Russians,' said Hindenburg, 'we had to remove mounds of enemy corpses from before our trenches in order to get a clear field of fire against fresh assaulting waves.' The Russians had in all 8 million casualties, of whom 2½ million were dead. By the end of 1916 the army had, not surprisingly, lost its capacity to fight.

In 1915 Nicholas made himself Commander-in-Chief of the Russian armies. This had little effect on the conduct of the war, but it did have two important results. Firstly, the Tsar became responsible in the eyes of the people for Russian defeats, and secondly, since the Tsar was with his armies, he lost touch with the government in Petrograd. As one member of the Duma put it, 'Russia was an autocracy without an autocrat'. Government fell more and more into the hands of the highly religious and superstitious Empress[1] who was by now completely under the domination of Rasputin.

Rasputin (the word means 'dissolute') was a coarse and illiterate holy man from Siberia. A man of violent lusts and peasant cunning, he was often drunk and frequently blasphemous, but he became friendly with Nicholas and his wife in 1906 when it appeared that he was able to stop the bleeding of their son who suffered from haemophilia. Soon the Empress fell under Rasputin's spell. To her he was 'a man of God', and any criticism of his behaviour exasperated her. During 1915 and 1916 he was largely responsible for the appointment of ministers. The aristocracy both hated and feared Rasputin, but one night late in December 1916 some of their number, after considerable difficulty,[2] murdered him.

Military defeats and anarchy in the government combined with mounting economic strain. The disruption of communications and the

---

[1] 'Be more autocratic', was the Empress's advice to Nicholas. He replied and signed himself, 'Your poor little weak-willed hubby.'

[2] Rasputin first ate cakes injected with cyanide of potassium and drank poisoned wine to no effect. He was then shot several times with a revolver, yet climbed a flight of stairs and ran into a courtyard. Shot twice again and kicked viciously, his body was then thrown into the icy River Neva, and even then there was evidence that he was not dead.

Tsar Nicholas II guarded by Communist troops a few months before his execution in 1918

Lenin addressing a meeting in Moscow in 1917

A Bolshevist crowd demonstrating in the square before the Winter Palace, Petrograd, 1917

German blockade meant shortages and therefore inflation. The distribution of food was particularly affected, and in Petrograd and other big cities during the autumn and winter of 1916 the cold and hungry workers queued for food. While hostility to the government was growing, the machinery of administration was beginning to disintegrate. Revolutionary propaganda spread in factories and barracks, and there was increasing desertion from the front. Despite all this the Tsar, who did not appear to realise the seriousness of the position, refused to take any action. Outwardly Petrograd remained much as usual, but the first mutterings of revolution were being heard. In an atmosphere of foreboding, the police expected an imminent upheaval.

The 1917 Revolution

The long-expected revolution finally began in Petrograd on 8 March[1] 1917, when people queueing for food attacked the houses of suspected hoarders. Immediately strikes broke out, and demonstrations and processions were held. The crowds were joined by soldiers, weapons were distributed to the people, and authority quickly collapsed. On 12 March two organisations were formed. Ten members of the Duma formed an Emergency Committee which, two days later, became a Provisional Government, and secondly, a Soviet of workers' and soldiers' deputies was created. On 15 March, one week after the revolution started, Nicholas II abdicated.

From March to November 1917 the Provisional Government of ex-Duma members ruled in theory, pending the election of a constituent assembly. Certainly this body conducted government business and took policy decisions, but real power lay with the Petrograd Soviet. This first supported the Provisional Government, but undermined its strength by issuing Order No. 1 that Petrograd soldiers were to obey no order from the Provisional Government that the Soviet opposed. The Soviet was dominated by Mensheviks and Social Revolutionaries; the handful of Bolsheviks were timid and undecided, and most were in favour of working with the Provisional Government. The latter was headed by the well-meaning Prince Lvov, but the one man of action was Kerensky, the Minister of Justice, a confident and fiery orator, who was a member of both the Government and the Soviet.

The situation was transformed by the arrival of Lenin. The Bolshevik leader was in Switzerland when the revolution broke out. The Germans

[1] The Russian calendar was thirteen days behind that used in Western Europe. Here Western European dates are used.

who, throughout the war, had encouraged left-wing groups in Russia in order to undermine the government, now allowed Lenin to travel back to Russia. On 16 April he arrived at the Finland Station in Petrograd. Huge crowds greeted him, but his message was not at first to their liking. Lenin wanted continued revolution. Power should be taken from the bourgeois Provisional Government and given to the proletarian Soviet, and within that to the Bolsheviks. Capitalism should be overthrown and a socialist state set up. These proposals sounded reckless, but the slogan of 'All power to the Soviets' soon won over the workers' leaders, while the masses were attracted by the slogan of 'Bread, Peace and Land'.

During the summer of 1917 the Provisional Government made two crucial mistakes. Firstly, it was too slow in dealing with the peasants' demand for the redistribution of land still under private ownership. A decision on this was postponed until the Constituent Assembly met, but meanwhile peasants began to take possession of private land. When news of this reached the army, peasant soldiers deserted to join in the land grabbing. Secondly, despite the general opposition to the war and the difficulty of restoring order in a war situation, the Government decided to continue fighting. The main reason was the fear of harsh peace terms and even a German occupation. A fresh Russian offensive in Galicia in July soon turned into a disastrous rout, however. This provoked a further rising in Petrograd which was eventually led by the Bolsheviks. But after four days the rising petered out, and public opinion turned against the Bolsheviks. The rumour spread that Lenin was a German spy and, disguised as a train driver, he went into hiding in Finland. Trotsky (who had now left the Mensheviks) and other Bolsheviks were arrested, and *Pravda* was banned.

Kerensky now became Prime Minister at the head of a new coalition of liberals and moderate Socialists. But having successfully resisted an attack from the extreme left wing, Kerensky was now faced by an attempted *coup d'état* by the right wing. General Kornilov, the tough but politically naïve commander-in-chief of the Russian army, tried in September to dismiss both the Government and the Soviet. The attempt was crushed by the Soviet and particularly by the Bolsheviks who consequently returned to popularity.

It was now clear that Kerensky and the Provisional Government only existed with the permission of the Soviet, which was now completely dominated by the Bolsheviks. Late in October Lenin persuaded the Bolshevik Central Committee to decide on immediate revolution, and the detailed plans were made by Trotsky. On 7 November the key buildings in Petrograd were seized by armed factory workers and revolutionary troops. The Winter Palace, Kerensky's headquarters, was besieged for one day, but there was remarkably little fighting.[1] In Moscow there was more opposition to the Bolsheviks, but this too was soon ended. On 8 November 1917 a new Communist government was in office in Russia, and at its head was Lenin.

1917 to 1921

Bolsheviks consolidate their power

In November 1917 the Bolsheviks controlled little more than the big cities of European Russia. Other socialist parties had far greater support. From the start, however, Lenin opposed a coalition government, and the Bolsheviks' immediate problem was to assert their authority. The administration was organised,[2] and the key positions in the public life of Russia were filled by Communists. At the end of November 1917 the freest elections in Russian history were held for a constituent assembly. The Bolsheviks received about 10 million votes out of the 42 million cast, and over half the seats went to the Social Revolutionaries. Russia thus voted for moderate socialism rather than Communism, but less than twenty-four hours after the assembly met in January 1918, Lenin and the Soviet government dissolved it. In July 1918 a new constitution provided for a hierarchy of soviets. Only the Bolsheviks (officially called the Communist Party in 1918) were allowed to function.

Within a month of coming to power the Communists formed the Cheka. This was the powerful political police who organised mass terror against all enemies of the regime. Its activities really started after Lenin was seriously wounded in an assassination attempt in the summer of 1918. Five hundred people in Petrograd were shot for this attack on Lenin, and all over Russia the Cheka executed those suspected of opposing the Communist government. In July 1918 ex-Tsar Nicholas II and his family were shot and their remains were burnt and strewn in a swamp. 'Do you really think that we shall be victorious without using the most cruel terror?' asked Lenin. A. J. P. Taylor has stated that Lenin 'never doubted that dictatorship and tyranny were necessary and never ceased to deplore them'.[3]

---

[1] In the fighting in the palace 'neither side seems to have been very certain of itself: at one stage a Red Guard suddenly found himself confronted with the reflection of a painting of a horseman in a huge mirror, and with a horrified cry of "the Cavalry" he turned and bolted with his men.' A. Moorehead, *The Russian Revolution.*

[2] The original Soviet treasury consisted of a clothes box protected by a semicircle of chairs and a sentry.   [3] *The Observer,* 17 Jan. 1965.

In two particular ways the Communists won considerable popular favour. Firstly, they gained the support of the peasants by a decree abolishing and dividing up the private estates. The result was the creation of about 25 million smallholders. Secondly, the Communists ended Russian participation in the First World War.

It was clear that the task of the Communist government would be made infinitely more difficult if war continued against the Germans. The Provisional Government's failure to make peace was probably the most important factor in its fall. Therefore Lenin immediately appealed for peace, and in December an armistice was signed. In the negotiations that followed the Central Powers demanded very harsh terms: Poland and the Baltic States were to go to Germany and Austria-Hungary, and the Ukraine was to be independent. One-quarter of European Russia and three-quarters of her iron and coal resources would be lost. Trotsky, who was in charge of negotiations, rejected these terms, and in desperation tried a policy of neither peace nor war, with the result that the Germans penetrated deep into Russia. Lenin, who wanted peace on any terms and who regarded any settlement as temporary, then persuaded those ministers who doubted to agree to the German demands. In March 1918 the Treaty of Brest Litovsk was signed. Fortunately for the Communists, Germany was defeated a few months later by the imperialist powers.

The Civil War 1918 to 1920

The Civil War between the Communists known as the Reds, and their opponents, the Whites, began in the early summer of 1918. The first six months of Communist government had aroused great opposition. The signing of the peace treaty and the murder of the royal family had incensed the Tsarist officers, while the liberals, Social Revolutionaries and Mensheviks suffered from the dissolution of the constituent assembly and the Cheka terror. In addition, Britain, France and the United States disliked the ending of the eastern front, and landed troops during the summer of 1918 at Murmansk and Archangel and at Vladivostok on the Pacific coast. The initial purpose was to help the Whites to continue the war against the Central Powers, but after November 1918, when the First World War ended, allied intervention was intended to assist in the crushing of the Communist government while it was still weak. Not only was Communist ideology hated in the ruling circles of Western Europe and America, but the Soviet government had renounced all Russian debts, had nationalised foreign-owned industry without compensation, and was supporting revolutionary activity in Europe.

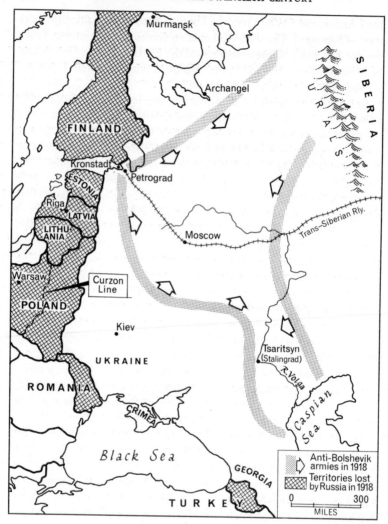

Russia during the Civil War, 1918–20

When the war started a small but well-equipped White army controlled the area north of the Crimea and was besieging Tsaritsyn.[1] There were also White forces under Admiral Kolchak along the Trans-Siberian railway, and these included a 40,000 strong Czech army which during the First World War had deserted to Russia and now opposed the Communists. By 1919 the French were supporting nationalists in

[1] Renamed Stalingrad in 1925 and later Volgograd.

the Ukraine, and a White army had been formed in the Baltic provinces west of Petrograd. The threat to Lenin's government was intense. From the east Kolchak's White army crossed the Urals and moved north-east of Moscow. From the south, the Whites, having captured Tsaritsyn, arrived within 200 miles of Moscow.

But the threat petered out. Revolts in the rear of Kolchak's army forced him to retreat and his army was defeated. The White army in the south was gradually compelled to retreat back to the Crimea. Soviet forces occupied the Ukraine, and the White attack from Estonia on Petrograd failed. By the end of 1920 the war had virtually ended. The Communists won for a number of reasons. They had the advantage of interior lines of communication, and Trotsky organised and controlled the Red Army with energy and ability. The Whites were divided into too many political groups, while Western help for them was half-hearted and soon withdrawn, but did have the effect, however, of giving the Communists the advantage of Russian nationalist support. The peasants who had little enthusiasm for either side, were less opposed to the Communists who had at least given them land while the Whites said they would restore the landlords.

The main interest of most people during the war was survival.[1] There were acute shortages of food and fuel, and disease, especially typhus, spread. Atrocities were committed by both sides; after battles the captured officers were always shot and prisoners were often mutilated; looting was common. One historian has spoken of 'unspeakable horror . . . a chaos of competitive savagery'.[2] Fourteen million people died during the civil war and 2 million emigrated.

An additional strain upon the Communists was the attack in 1920 by the Poles who wished to move their frontier east of the Curzon Line (a boundary fixed by the Allies in December 1919). The Polish army was driven back and the Russians even captured Warsaw, but in its turn the Red Army was forced to retreat by a second Polish advance. Finally Poland gained a considerable belt of territory east of the Curzon Line by the Treaty of Riga in 1921.

The economy

When the Communist government came to power, industrial production stood at three-quarters of that for 1913, the cultivated area was smaller, the railway system was chaotic, and prices were rising fast. At first Lenin's policy was to change gradually from a capitalist to a

---

[1] A brilliant description of life in Russia during the war is given by Pasternak in his novel *Doctor Zhivago*. [2] R. Charques, *Short History of Russia*.

socialist economic system, and therefore there was some official national-isation—armament factories, banks and some trade. But circumstances forced a more extreme approach. Unofficial nationalisation by the workers themselves, the continued shortage of food in the towns and the outbreak of the civil war made greater state control over the economy necessary. Therefore in June 1918 all firms were nationalised, the requisitioning of grain from the peasants was started, private trade was banned and labour was directed by the state.

This War Communism, as it was called, was, according to Lenin, 'dictated not by economic but by military needs'. Certainly the econo-mic results were disastrous. The central body that was supposed to control the economy did not have enough factual knowledge, was too bureaucratic and gave impractical orders. Manufactured goods were scarce because the disruption in communications meant that raw materials were not available and markets had shrunk. In 1921 industry produced only 15 per cent of its total for 1913. In addition food was scarce. This was partly because of the breakdown in communications, and partly because the peasants so objected to the forced requisitioning of food that they only produced enough to feed themselves. By 1921 grain production was only half that of 1913, and there was a similar reduction in livestock. In 1920–21 a drought in the Volga region resulted in 5 million deaths.[1] Workers in the towns went to the countryside to look for food, and at one point even privileged workers were only issued with one ounce of food per day. The shortages inevitably caused inflation. In the three years after November 1917 prices rose a hundred times. Paper money became almost valueless and exchange was by barter.

By 1921 Russia was on the verge of economic collapse, and discon-tent in the towns and countryside was at a dangerous level. There were a number of peasant riots, and in March 1921 the sailors at Kronstadt revolted. After savage fighting the revolt was crushed. But clearly a change in economic policy was required.

1921 to 1928

New Economic Policy

In March 1921 Lenin introduced his New Economic Policy (NEP). This involved the partial restoration of capitalism in which only the larger, basic industries remained nationalised. All firms with less than

[1] The number would have been greater but for American food and medicines sent by Hoover following Nansen's appeal to the League of Nations.

twenty employees were returned to their former owners, and the administration of the remaining state-owned firms was decentralised so that they could make their own arrangements for obtaining materials and selling goods. By 1923 nearly 90 per cent of firms were controlled by private individuals, but nevertheless the remaining 10 per cent that were state-owned employed over 80 per cent of all workers. The requisitioning of grain from the peasants was replaced by a fixed tax, first in kind and later in money. Vigorous attempts were made to increase fuel supplies, and in 1923 a new currency was issued which ended the inflation. Gradually the economic position improved. By 1926 industry was back to its prewar level, private trade had revived and harvests had much improved.

Foreign policy

The primary aim of Soviet foreign policy was to defend the revolution. During the first three years when civil war was raging in Russia, the government attempted to organise revolution in Europe. By 1920, however, it was clear that the prospect of European revolution was declining, and that Russia's own revolution would be better defended by improving relations with capitalist states. There was the need, too, for trade with the West.

The first moves in improving relations came in 1921 when trade agreements with Britain and Germany were signed. During the following year Germany and Russia, both the 'pariah nations' (Lloyd George) of Europe, moved closer together. Arrangements were made for the Germans to train the Red Army, and German factories were set up in Russia for the production of munitions. In 1922 the two countries signed the Treaty of Rapallo by which Germany gave diplomatic recognition to the Russian government, and economic agreements were made. This Russo-German friendship continued until the advent of Hitler in 1933. Meanwhile in 1924 other countries, including Britain, granted diplomatic recognition to the Communist government.

Formation of the USSR

In 1924 Russia's new constitution, the work of Stalin, came into effect. Russia became a federation called the Union of Soviet Socialist Republics (USSR). In each republic there was a soviet elected by a hierarchy of soviets below it. All adults could vote for the local soviets. The soviets in each republic elected the 2,000 members of the federal Congress of Soviets, later called the Supreme Soviet. This unwieldy body which only met for one week each year elected a 300 strong Central Executive Committee which in its turn elected a small presidium or executive of ten members. At every level in this hierarchy of government was a parallel Communist Party organisation. The equivalent of the Congress of Soviets was the Party Congress, which elected the Central Committee which in turn elected the Politburo. The membership of the Presidium and the Politburo overlapped. In 1936 an amended version of this constitution was issued.

The death of Lenin 1924

Between 1917 and 1922 Lenin was undisputed leader of the Communist Party and therefore of Russia. But in May 1922 he had a heart attack, and thereafter his participation in government grew less and less. Two other attacks followed, and on 21 January 1924 Lenin died at the age of fifty-three. His body, which was embalmed and placed in the mausoleum in Red Square in front of the Kremlin, soon became an object of pilgrimage.

By any standards Lenin's achievement was a great one. A man of acute political sense, he had modified Marx's teachings to suit Russian conditions, and by his ruthlessness and strong will had created Communist Russia. 'Among the Bolshevik leaders he was the only one who combined the honesty to admit his mistakes, the courage to change course accordingly, and the authority to ensure full support for such changes.'[1] And in the words of an American journalist, John Reed: 'A strange popular leader—a leader purely by virtue of intellect; colourless, humourless, uncompromising and detached, without picturesque idiosyncrasies—but with the power of explaining profound ideas in simple terms, of analysing a concrete situation.'[2]

The struggle for leadership

From 1922 until 1929 a ruthless struggle for the leadership of Russia was fought out in the Politburo. A triumvirate of Zinoviev, Kamenev and Stalin ruled until 1926. All three were opposed to Trotsky, but the basic struggle in these years was between Stalin and Trotsky.

Stalin, whose original name was Joseph Djugashvili, was born in 1879, the son of a poverty-stricken shoemaker in Georgia. He was the one important leader among the early Bolsheviks who came from the peasant class. Stalin was educated at a church school and then trained for the priesthood at a theological seminary until he was expelled for

[1] J. N. Westwood, *Russia, 1917–1964.*   [2] J. Reed, *Ten Days that Shook the World.*

his political activities. He then became a fulltime revolutionary, organising street demonstrations and secret meetings, and spreading propaganda, with the result that of the ten years before 1917 he spent seven in prison. However, he soon reached the top ranks of the Bolshevik Party, and during 1917 he edited *Pravda*, the party newspaper. When the Communists came to power, he first became Commissar of Nationalities and then Commissar of the Workers' and Peasants' Inspectorate. In the first post he gained experience in dealing with the non-Russian peoples of the country, and in the second he created a civil service and appointed his own supporters to key posts. In 1922, just before Lenin's first illness, Stalin became Party Secretary, and his Secretariat, as the body which carried out the wishes of the executive, became gradually more important.

So, in these rather unexciting posts, Stalin quietly gathered supporters. Trotsky described Stalin as 'the Party's most eminent mediocrity', and Deutscher, Stalin's biographer, has said, 'What was striking in the General Secretary was that there was nothing striking about him.'[1] But this 'mediocrity' could be quite ruthless. In December 1922 Lenin wrote of Stalin: 'I am not sure that he always knows how to use . . . power with sufficient caution.' In 1923 Lenin recommended Stalin's dismissal.

Trotsky was a completely different character. The son of a wealthy Jewish farmer, he was a man of enormous energy and tremendous intellectual power. In both 1905 and 1917 he took a prominent part in events, and during the civil war he was Minister of War. But his popularity, and control of the Red Army, were balanced by the fact that he had supported the Mensheviks before 1917, by his arrogant individuality, and by his weakness as regards political tactics compared with Stalin's shrewd political sense.

The struggle for leadership developed during Lenin's illness and intensified after his death. It was caused mainly by personal ambition, and only partly by differences over policies.[2] Stalin held that Communism should concentrate on building up Russia rather than attempt world revolution at this point. Trotsky opposed 'socialism in one country' and wanted instead 'permanent revolution' throughout the world, a view which many at the time deemed to be impractical.

Stalin, however, had a majority in the Politburo, and in 1925 Trotsky was dismissed from his post as Commissar of War, and in 1926 both he and Kamenev were expelled from the Politburo and Zinoviev was

---

[1] I. Deutscher, *Stalin*.

[2] 'Stalin won because he was a far astuter politician and abler organiser than his rivals, not because his policies differed from theirs.' E. H. Carr, *The Listener*, 30 May 1963.

dismissed from the leadership of the Communist International (the body which organised revolutionary activity outside Russia). In 1927 Trotsky was expelled from the Communist Party and soon after he was sent to Central Asia. After 1929 he lived in exile and was assassinated in Mexico in 1940. In 1929, too, the moderates were removed from the Politburo, so that when the year ended the struggle for power was over. Stalin's fiftieth birthday was celebrated throughout Russia; statues and huge portraits appeared in public places: the new dictator had emerged.

1928 to 1941

The Five Year Plans and collectivisation

By 1926 industry and agriculture had reached their prewar rate of production. Any further economic progress with existing plant would be slow, and if the standard of living was to be raised and Russia was to be stronger economically, it was clear that new plant and the expansion and modernisation of industry and agriculture were necessary. Further, if Russia was to be stronger militarily, the country would have to make economic progress. 'We are fifty or a hundred years behind the advanced countries,' said Stalin in 1931. 'We must make good this lag in ten years. Either we do this or they crush us.'

Stalin therefore aimed at very rapid industrialisation, and he intended to achieve this with the help of agriculture. He reasoned that, in order to buy the necessary foreign machinery, agricultural exports must be increased. This would be done by reorganising the 25 million independent peasant households so that very large farms were formed. These would help mechanisation, would make grain collection easier, and would reduce the amount of labour needed so that excess labour would move to the towns. These new farms would therefore be more efficient and produce more goods more cheaply. Cheaper agricultural produce would mean firstly that urban wages could be reduced so that manufacturing costs would go down, and secondly, that exports would increase so that there could be more imports of capital goods. Stalin also believed that this revolution in the economy would be good in two other ways: it would be sound ideologically in that it implied much greater state control and fewer class divisions in society, and secondly, it would require force to carry it through and therefore the strong leadership which Stalin could provide was essential.

The revolution in farming began in 1928 and reached its height in 1930. Large collective farms were formed by amalgamating groups of about twenty small farms. Land, except for small private plots, was taken from private ownership, and the peasants who worked the collective farm owned it in common. Wages were paid according to the time spent working on the collective farm. Most of the produce, which was mainly grain, had to be sold to the state at low prices.

Even the poorer peasants did not like collectivisation, but the richer peasants, who were known as kulaks, violently opposed the loss of their land. Stalin's answer was to 'liquidate the kulaks as a class'. Red Army units rounded up the kulaks and killed them or deported them to labour camps. The kulaks in retaliation killed their cattle, destroyed machinery and burned their crops. 'Collectivisation degenerated into a military operation, a cruel civil war. Rebellious villages were surrounded by machine guns and forced to surrender. Great numbers of kulaks were deported to remote unpopulated lands in Siberia. Their houses, barns and farm implements were turned over to the collective farms.'[1]

Between 1930 and 1934 Stalin slowed down the process of collectivisation, but nevertheless by 1937 99 per cent of farmland was collective. The result was, on the whole, disastrous. The immediate chaos led to poor harvests and a famine in which over 10 million people died (and during which Russia continued to export grain). The best farmers had been liquidated, the peasants were depressed and resentful, the numbers of livestock were halved, the younger and more energetic peasants had left for the towns, and, moreover, the new collective farms proved less productive than the small ones they had replaced.

Meanwhile industrialisation was proceeding apace. The first Five Year Plan was started in 1928 and was declared completed after four years. The emphasis was on heavy industry—coal, iron, steel, oil, electricity, machine-building. For economic and strategic reasons, the new industries were mainly sited away from the western frontiers: for example, a new iron and steel industry was started in the Urals. The second Five Year Plan (1932–37) again concentrated on heavy industry. There was more technical assistance from abroad and, although the plan was mainly underfulfilled and the quality of goods remained poor, there was still a great increase in production. The third Five Year Plan (1937–41) put more emphasis on consumer goods, but the dangerous foreign situation soon led to a switch to arms production.

The State Planning Commission was responsible for all the plans. It collected statistics and decided on targets for each industry and each individual firm within an industry. Since a failure to reach the target could lead to imprisonment, figures for production were often exaggerated by managers. In general, too, the plans were too inflexible and failed to make the best use of resources: oil production was slowed

[1] I. Deutscher, *Stalin*.

down in favour of coal; too many canals were built rather than roads and railways. And the cost in human suffering was great (compare the English industrial revolution of the nineteenth century); the standard of living fell continually.[1]

Nevertheless industrial production made huge strides forward. Russia was transformed from an agrarian into an industrial country. Also, there is evidence that many workers responded to the propaganda for increased production. Distinctions such as 'Hero of Socialist Labour' were soon augmented by wages based on piece rates and other financial inducements which reversed the trend towards equality of incomes.

The purges

Before 1934 Stalin's treatment of political opponents had been ruthless but relatively limited in scope. Opponents in the Politburo and elsewhere were dismissed from their posts and discredited, but so far Stalin had opposed the use of terror against Communists. But in 1934 policy changed, and during the next four years a purge was made of all possible anti-Stalinists, a purge greater by far than the persecutions of Ivan the Terrible or Robespierre.

In 1934 Kirov, the handsome and popular head of the Leningrad Party organisation, was assassinated, possibly with Stalin's agreement. The murder was the excuse for mass terror in which first non-Communists and then Communists were arrested and either shot or sent to Siberia (where prison life was made particularly unpleasant[2]). In a spectacular series of public trials during 1936–38 Kamenev, Zinoviev and other leading members of the Communist Party were tried for, and usually confessed to, the most serious crimes against Stalin and the Soviet state. Vyshinsky, the vicious Chief Prosecutor, usually ended his speeches with the words: 'I demand the shooting of all these mad dogs.' All the members of Lenin's Politburo, except Stalin and Trotsky, were shot. Of the 139 members of the Communist Central Committee elected in 1934, over 90 were arrested and most of these were shot. The army was not exempt. Thirty-five thousand army officers, including thirteen of the fifteen generals, were arrested. Millions of Russian citizens just disappeared, most died, many were sent to Siberia. Many both inside and outside Russia believed the trials to be fair and the accusations to be true, particularly in view of the confessions. But it is

---

[1] Some Russians posed the riddle: Why were Adam and Eve like Soviet citizens? Answer: because they lived in Paradise and had nothing to wear.

[2] See *One Day in the Life of Ivan Denisovich* by Solzhenitsyn for life in a Siberian labour camp under Stalin.

now clear that techniques of physical and mental torture produced these confessions, and that the victims were largely innocent.[1]

There is no certainty about Stalin's motives. It is clear that the economic revolution had produced widespread discontent, and it is possible that the purges started with the aim of removing any potential opponents of Stalin. With the threat of war growing stronger, Stalin would have regarded the removal of these opponents as essential to maintain internal peace. Alternatively, or in addition, the motives may have been sheer cruelty and the lust for absolute power.

By 1938 it was clear that the purges were weakening the USSR both economically and militarily, and with the final purge of the purgers, the terror gradually declined.

Foreign policy

Before 1933 Russia's relations with Germany had been friendly and those with France and Britain had been cool. After the Nazis came to power, however, this position was reversed. Hitler had always hated Communists and Slavs, and maintained that German expansion would be to the east. Russia, fearing another war against Germany, now adopted a friendlier attitude towards Britain and France. In 1934 the USSR entered the League of Nations. In 1935 a pact of mutual assistance was made with France, and Russia agreed to help Czechoslovakia if the latter was attacked provided France also came to Czechoslovakia's aid.

But this policy of collective security had little success. The Anglo-French policy of appeasement in the face of Fascist aggression on the part of Hitler, Franco, Mussolini and the Japanese, persuaded Stalin that Britain and France were not reliable allies. In 1936 the Anti-Comintern Pact between Germany and Japan opened up the strong possibility that Russia would be faced with a war on two fronts.

Therefore, in order to postpone what he regarded as the inevitable war against Germany, Stalin began to seek better relations with the Nazi government.

In 1939 Molotov replaced Litvinov who favoured agreement with Britain and France, and in August the Soviet-Nazi Pact was signed. It was agreed that East Poland, Finland, Estonia and Latvia were to go to Russia, while West Poland and Lithuania went to Germany. For Hitler the treaty kept Russia friendly while he dealt with France and Britain; for Stalin the treaty postponed the German invasion of Russia. But the postponement was for less than two years. The war in the West was

[1] Arthur Koestler's brilliant novel *Darkness at Noon* describes the fate of one such victim.

much shorter than Stalin had hoped, and on 22 June 1941 the German invasion of Russia commenced.

Russia at War 1941 to 1945

In the Second as in the First World War, the Russian army contained greater numbers of men than the German, but badly led mass attacks led to enormous casualties. The Russian soldier fought bravely. Indeed, he had no option, for the Germans would work him to death if he was captured, while the political police would shoot him if he retreated. Officers had suffered from the political purges of the 1930s, and those who survived were militarily unimaginative, many of them being replaced on military grounds in 1942.

The Russian people suffered not only from bad working and living conditions—malnutrition and long hours—but also from ill-treatment at German hands in the occupied areas. Probably there were about 15 million civilian deaths during the war, and about 10 million members of the armed forces were killed, so that over one-tenth of Russia's population died altogether. Yet the people remained loyal to the government despite Hitler's hopes of an anti-Stalin revolution. This was partly because of anti-German propaganda, partly because of police control and partly because of patriotism. The Russian people were genuinely grateful for Stalin's conduct of the war. He was regarded as 'a prodigy of patience, tenacity and vigilance, almost omnipresent, almost omniscient'.[1] On a vast number of issues of all kinds Stalin took the final decision.

The Last Years of Stalin 1945 to 1953[2]

Industry and agriculture

Both industry and agriculture were in a terrible state when the war ended. Most of the towns and countryside of Western Russia had been devastated. Although there was some new industry east of the Urals, elsewhere factories had been destroyed, machinery was worn out, mines were flooded, and the labour force was weary and depleted. Stalin's policy for reconstruction was to restore the aims and methods of the 1930s. The emphasis again was on producer rather than consumer goods, and heavy rather than light industry. The targets in the fourth Five Year Plan (1946–50) were achieved well within the allotted period.

[1] I. Deutscher, *Stalin.*

[2] Foreign Affairs are mainly dealt with in chapter 3.

There were two main reasons for this: firstly, there were advantageous trade agreements with eastern Europe which was now controlled from Moscow, and secondly, directed by the state, the Russian people worked extremely hard for low wages so that the increased profits could be used for new investment. Living standards declined. Russia grew richer and richer while the people grew poorer and poorer. The condition of agriculture in 1945 was probably worse than that of industry. Cattle had been slaughtered, stocks of seed and fertilisers depleted, the labour force reduced, the organisation of collective farms had deteriorated, and horses and tractors were in such short supply in some places that women were harnessed to ploughs. Improvement was very slow. Between 1948 and 1952 the grain harvest averaged 80 million tons[1] annually, and half the population were required to produce this inadequate amount. In 1950 Khrushchev was put in charge of agriculture, a subject in which he showed great interest. He decided to amalgamate the 250,000 collective farms into 95,000 larger farms, partly because larger farms could make better use of mechanical aids and experts, and partly because it would be easier to achieve party control. Khrushchev wanted to create even bigger units called agro-towns, but this idea was shelved.

Government

Stalin continued to be an all-powerful and awe-inspiring figure. Although he rarely appeared in public or made public pronouncements, he was given an almost god-like status. Praised for all the Russian successes in war and peace, statues of him appeared all over Russia, cities were called after him, and on his seventieth birthday in 1949 the Museum of Revolution in Moscow staged an exhibition of his birthday gifts. He was undisputed leader. There was no question of independence or criticism. All forms of art and literature were censored, and all contacts with the West were forbidden. He suffered from chronic suspicion. Khrushchev said that Stalin was 'a profoundly sick man who suffered from suspiciousness and persecution mania'. According to Khrushchev, Bulganin once said: 'It happens sometimes that a man goes to Stalin, invited as a friend; and when he sits with Stalin he does not know where he will be sent next, home or to jail.' During these years the relative influence of the Communist Party declined because its organs were bypassed by Stalin. For example, no party congress met between 1939 and 1952.

Below Stalin the rivals for his favour competed. First Malenkov, the

[1] In 1913 the total was 86 million tons and in 1940 95 million tons.

young, middle-class ex-head of the Moscow Party organisation seemed on top. Then the tough, dogmatic Zhdanov became Stalin's closest adviser until his death in 1948. In the following year Khrushchev came to Moscow from the Ukraine to head the Party organisation, and he soon became the chief rival of Malenkov.

Late in 1952 it seemed likely that another purge was coming. Nine Kremlin doctors were accused of, and under torture confessed to, various unlikely crimes. Many thought that the accusations were a cover for a further purge, particularly when Stalin began to attack a number of eminent Communist leaders. But this was not to be, for in March 1953 Stalin died. His body was embalmed and was placed next to Lenin's in the mausoleum in Red Square. There is no doubt of the magnitude of his achievement and the ruthlessness of his methods. His biographer, Deutscher, says that he 'found Russia working with a wooden plough and left her equipped with atomic piles'.[1] Djilas, a Yugoslavian, considered that Stalin was 'one of the cruellest and most despotic figures in history'.[2] And according to Khrushchev, 'like Peter the Great, Stalin fought barbarism with barbarism, but he was a great man'.

The Decade of Khrushchev 1953 to 1964

Struggle for power 1953 to 1958

On the day following the official announcement of the death of Stalin, Malenkov became both Prime Minister (that is, Chairman of the Council of Ministers) and Secretary of the Party's Central Committee. A week later, however, Khrushchev became Party Secretary, and so power was divided: Malenkov was head of the government while Khrushchev, who was still regarded at this point as not really important, was head of the Party. For two years this partnership continued. But Khrushchev wished to dominate. His supporters were appointed to important posts and Malenkov, who lacked Khrushchev's keen political sense, was gradually weakened. In February 1955 he resigned to be succeeded by Bulganin, one of Khrushchev's supporters.

For the next three years, from 1955 to 1958, 'B and K' as they were known in the West, were theoretically joint leaders. Together they went to the Geneva Conference, to Yugoslavia, India and Britain. But in fact Khrushchev was the senior partner. His policies and flamboyant character were not popular amongst the old Stalinists in the government and while he and Bulganin were visiting Finland in June 1957 his opponents planned his dismissal. But the majority of the Central

[1] I. Deutscher, *Stalin*.   [2] M. Djilas, *Conversations with Stalin*.

Committee, with the backing of the army, supported Khrushchev, and his critics, who included Malenkov and Molotov, were dismissed to minor posts far from Moscow. In 1958 Bulganin resigned and went into obscurity. He was replaced by Khrushchev himself who was now head of both the government and the Party.

Nikita Khrushchev was born in south Russia in 1894. The son of a peasant, he worked first as a herdsboy until the age of ten when he went to school for two years. In 1908 his family moved to a coalmining area, and Khrushchev became an apprentice fitter at an engineering works and then a mechanic in a mine. In 1918 he joined the Communist Party, and after three years' study at a technical college, he gradually worked his way up the hierarchy of the Party in the Ukraine. He then moved to Moscow where in 1934 he became leader of the local Party organisation. Four years later he was made First Secretary of the Ukrainian Communist Party, whose members he purged with Stalinist ruthlessness. He remained in the Ukraine during the war and the period of reconstruction after the Germans were driven out. In 1949 he returned to Moscow and he remained at the centre of power thereafter.

Khrushchev was a jovial, quick-witted and garrulous man whose unaffected behaviour was in many ways appealing. While he was impatient and impulsive and did not think sufficiently of the consequences of his actions, he was at the same time tough, adaptable and shrewd with enough ability and common sense to abandon an unsuccessful or dangerous policy. His power was never as great as Stalin's and he reasserted the control of the Communist Party over policy. Nevertheless it was he who ultimately controlled that policy and the strategic positions in the state were filled by his own nominees. His rule was flexible and he was willing to adapt. Efficiency rather than ideological purity was the criterion of success.'[1]

Destalinisation

The years from 1953 to 1956 saw the steady reversal of Stalin's policies. The use of persecution and terror was ended. The arrested doctors were released: Beria, the minister in charge of the powerful political police, was shot at the end of a cabinet meeting,[2] and the power of the political police was curtailed; many of the labour camps were dissolved and conditions in the remaining ones were improved. The control over intellectuals (for example, novelists) was relaxed. Russian leaders made

[1] J. Lively, in *Since 1945: Aspects of Contemporary World History*, ed. J. L. Henderson.
[2] Subscribers to the Great Soviet Encyclopedia were asked to replace his entry with another on the Bering Straits.

visits abroad, and foreign tourists were allowed to visit Russia. There was more emphasis on the production of consumer goods and on financial incentives for farmers.

The more drastic changes, however, followed the Twentieth Congress of the Russian Communist Party in February 1956. Before an audience of 1,400 delegates and foreign representatives, the Russian leaders gave a series of speeches attacking Stalin's character and policies. Khrushchev gave the most sensational speech. He did not condemn anything Stalin had done before 1934, including the forced collectivisation of agriculture, but bitterly criticised three major aspects of Stalin's policy after that date. Firstly, in connection with the purges of the 1930s, he questioned the necessity for the execution of Stalin's early rivals, he believed the murder of Kirov had probably been arranged by Stalin, he revealed that the confessions were the result of torture, and said that thousands of innocent Communists had been murdered. Secondly, he criticised the leadership of Stalin during the war. Thirdly, he condemned Stalin's personal dictatorship as 'self-deification' and 'flagrant misuse of power'; any who opposed Stalin were doomed to 'moral and physical annihilation'. More positively Khrushchev said that peaceful coexistence with the West was possible and that there were different ways by which a country could achieve socialism.

'In three hours Khrushchev turned Stalin from the benevolent leader of genius, in whom every Soviet child was brought up to believe, into a sinister despot, proper heir to the Tsars who had terrified and tormented Russia in her dark past.'[1] The speech had a shattering effect, both in Russia and in other Communist countries. Stalin's economic policy was criticised much less than his purges and his dictatorship, but in subsequent years all of Stalin's policies were changed enormously. In addition, statues of the late dictator were removed, Stalingrad was renamed Volgograd, and Stalin's body was removed from the mausoleum to an obscure position inside the Kremlin wall.

Thereafter Russia very slowly became a freer country. The terror was ended and the tension relaxed. Whereas in the past rebels would be shot or sent to Siberia, now they would be sent to a psychiatric hospital. After the bitter cold of Stalin's regime, a thaw set in, and the Soviet people began to breathe more easily.

Industry and agriculture

Industry continued to be centrally planned through Five Year Plans, but after 1957 Moscow's control was less rigorous than it had been.

[1] M. Frankland, *Khrushchev*.

Khrushchev believed that over-centralisation had produced inefficiency and therefore in 1957 he divided Russia into about a hundred regions, each of which had the power to plan and organise its own industry under the general oversight of Moscow. In 1962 the number of regions was halved. Khrushchev was keen that the standard of living in Russia should rise, and therefore more resources were devoted to light industry and the production of consumer goods, although this was at first difficult because of the opposition of local administrators and the need for agricultural machinery. However, production figures for most types of industry reached high levels; for example, in 1963 80 million tons of steel were produced (compared with 4 million tons in 1928). Another indication of the changes in Russia after Stalin was the support in the early 1960s for the view that profit should be the gauge of a factory's efficiency, and that output should be planned on the basis of consumer demand.

Khrushchev played a leading role in formulating agricultural policy because of his genuine interest in farming and because agriculture remained the weakest and most sluggish sector of the economy. In various ways he tried to increase production. Fairer prices were paid by the state for goods; more power was given to each collective farm to act on its own initiative; more machinery and chemical fertilisers were produced, and the use of the services of agricultural specialists was encouraged; in 1954 the 'virgin lands' in southern Siberia, an area equal in size to the entire cultivated area of Canada, were ploughed up. The result was certainly an increase in grain production, which rose from 82 million tons in 1953 to 147 million tons in 1962. But this was mainly because of the cultivation of land which many believed was capable of growing crops for a short time only. The 'virgin lands' project suffered from mismanagement, insufficient use of fertilisers and eventually diminishing returns. Because of exhausted land and bad weather the 1963 harvest was reduced to 110 million tons, and Russia was forced to buy grain from North America. Despite Khrushchev's reforms, Russian farming remained inefficient. With five times the labour force, the Russians produced less than three-quarters of American output, and the privately-owned plots of land produced far greater yields than the state-owned land.[1]

Downfall of Khrushchev 1964

After about 1961 opposition to Khrushchev within the top ranks of the Party began to increase. The reasons are not yet clear, but it is probable

[1] Khrushchev complained in 1958 that private cows multiplied while socialist cows did not.

that a number of different factors were involved. Khrushchev had staked his reputation on economic success, yet after about 1961 the production of consumer goods began to decline, prices rose and harvests had declined. In addition there seemed to be too many changes in organisation. In foreign affairs[1] the improvement in relations with the United States up to 1960 had been followed by the U2 affair and the Paris summit meeting, and the Cuba missile crisis of 1962 in which Khrushchev lost face. His colleagues may have come to fear his flamboyant diplomacy, his undignified behaviour (for example, the dramatic shoe-banging performance at the United Nations) and his dangerous off-the-cuff remarks. Almost certainly another factor was the growing quarrel with China, and to a lesser extent with Romania. This had developed into a personal vendetta between Mao Tse-tung and the Russian leader who seemed determined to force a showdown.

It is probable that by 1964 Khrushchev was becoming increasingly difficult to work with. His methods were too autocratic, and the other leading Russians disliked this one-man rule. For example, he made President Nasser of Egypt a Hero of the Soviet Union and promised him a £100 million loan without consulting his fellow ministers in Moscow. In addition, the appointment of his son-in-law as Editor of *Pravda* was not popular.

In October 1964 Khrushchev was on holiday by the Black Sea when he was summoned before the Central Committee. To his surprise and anger, he was openly criticised and the vote went against him. In practice he was dismissed, but officially he was granted his 'request that he be relieved of his duties in view of advanced age and deterioration of health'. He was succeeded as Prime Minister by Kosygin and as Party Secretary by Brezhnev.

Khrushchev was a great personality, a man who both clowned and bullied, who was proud and yet humble, who was indiscreet and yet statesmanlike. 'He went not because he was reactionary, and not because he was liberal, but because he was erratic, unpredictable, unmanageable, now increasingly dictatorial.'[2] He was important, not only because of his realisation of the dangers of nuclear war, but because of his political and economic reforms at home and in the east European satellites. It has been correctly said of him that 'he left his country a better place than he found it, both in the eyes of the majority of his own people, and of the world'.[3] Khrushchev lived in retirement until his death in 1971.

---

[1] The foreign policy of Khrushchev is dealt with elsewhere. See the sections on Europe, the Middle East and China.

[2] E. Crankshaw, *Khrushchev*.

[3] M. Frankland, *Khrushchev*.

Brezhnev 1964 to mid-1970s

Government

Khrushchev was succeeded as Prime Minister by Kosygin and as Party Secretary by Brezhnev. In contrast to the period of Khrushchev, government was now characterised by orthodoxy, conservatism and stability. For the first six years there was collective leadership with Brezhnev *primus inter pares*. But in about 1971 Brezhnev increasingly came into the limelight. He played a more dominant role in foreign policy and the propaganda machine gave him much greater prominence. In 1977, when a new constitution replaced that of Stalin, first issued in 1936, Brezhnev became President as well as leader of the Communist Party. Although he gradually emerged as unchallenged leader and principal policy maker, nevertheless he remained chairman of a coalition rather than a new dictator.

Brezhnev was born in the Ukraine. He was 18 when Lenin died in 1924. Working first in agriculture, he then graduated as an engineer, and in 1931 joined the Communist Party and began to work his way up the provincial party machine. He did political work in the army during the war and in 1952 he became a member of the Presidium. He was appointed by Khrushchev in 1954 to administer the great Virgin Lands plan. A more cautious and less colourful man than Khrushchev, an unsensational, undramatic manager, Brezhnev was none the less a shrewd manipulator of the party machine. There were to be no great reversals of policy; rather there should be a generally middle-of-the-way approach with a tendency towards conservatism and normality.

Economy

The Soviet economy during this period showed a growth rate which most Western countries would have considered very satisfactory. The excessive inflation and the expansion and contraction of the trade cycle hardly affected Russia. In total output the Russian economy ranked second to the American. But this apparent success hid important weaknesses. The root problem was low productivity. The 1973 Russian economic year-book rated Soviet industry as just about half as efficient as American, the construction industry about two-thirds as efficient and agriculture about one-quarter. In per capita output Russia was about 25th in the world in the early 1970s. Heavy industry continued to have priority. Although in the 1971–75 Five Year Plan there should have been more light industry producing consumer goods, by 1975 heavy industry still took up about 70 per cent of resources.

There appear to be three main factors accounting for the low productivity of Russian industry. Firstly, the economy is too centralised. It is often said that centralised planning is suited to the time when the economy must be built up rapidly from small beginnings, but is less suitable for the expansion and development of an already sophisticated and complex economy. In this situation individual managers should be free to conclude their own supply and marketing contracts. Secondly, there is not enough good modern technology. Instead there is over-manning to avoid unemployment, and a general suspicion of new inventions, products and ideas. Thirdly, a number of social factors: too little connexion between efficiency and reward, too much bureau-cracy, waste and petty corruption. These factors are recognised in Russia, and are indeed discussed in their press. Up to 1968 there were moves to loosen the central controls over factories and to use the profit motive as an incentive for greater efficiency. However, the atmosphere following the Russian invasion of Czechoslovakia killed economic decentralisation. Since then there have been campaigns to reduce the number of managerial staff and to discipline workers who do their work badly. Nevertheless, the basic problems remain.

Agriculture presents similar difficulties. Grain production fluctuated enormously. In the second half of the 1960s it was usually about 160–170 m. tons annually; in 1973 it reached a record 220, while in 1975 it dropped to a mere 140 m. tons. Targets were usually underful-filled, and grain had to be imported. In contrast to the big state and collective farms, the intensively farmed private plots of the peasants were most successful producing high value crops (for example onions or fruit), and their products were essential. Twenty-seven per cent of the total value of farming products in 1974 came from private plots that occupied about 3 per cent of the agricultural land.[1]

On some occasions the weather had near disastrous effects on farming. For example, in 1972 frosts, the worst drought of the century, forest fires and then rain at the time of harvest, would have spoiled the crops of the most efficient farmers. But Soviet agriculture suffers from under-mechanisation, too few incentives to improve produc-tivity, and a high turnover of skilled workers. The most able and energetic move to the towns in search of higher living standards, leaving the less able and elderly to run the farms. The government has not neglected agriculture. There has been immense investment: mechanisation, irrigation, chemical fertilisers and industrial farming techniques are expanding. But still there is backwardness and too much

[1] See A. Nove, *The Soviet Economic System*, Allen & Unwin, 1977.

work is done by hand.

An important reason for the relative lack of success of industry and agriculture is that spending on the defence and space programmes has been enormous. These have been given national priority, and here there is much greater efficiency and concentration on quality. The period of Brezhnev's government has seen a great expansion of the armed forces, especially the navy. In space the Russians have matched the achievements of the Americans. In 1969 two manned spacecraft were joined in flight, and there was a landing on Venus. In 1970 an 8-wheeled vehicle was landed on the moon's surface.

Society

In the early 1970s the population of the USSR reached 250 million. Clearly a society as large as this is varied and complex, but there are broadly three classes: the political elite, the professional classes and leaders in areas of life other than politics, and the workers. The first group, the political elite, number several million. They are the more important members of the Communist Party, and are recruited from the discreet, conformist and loyal. They have both status and power, live a relatively stable, secure and privileged life, and are better clothed, fed, housed and medically cared for. The real policy makers, who possibly number a few thousand, live very comfortable lives.

The second group are given a certain degree of private freedom and material privilege. The great majority of the intelligentsia are awed by the threat of police methods and toe the party line. For example, historians will manipulate the past to justify the current Communist Party viewpoint, and film producers will glamorise the lives of manual workers. The workers, who are the vast majority, have a generally low standard of living compared with that of Western Europe. 'Despite the impressive gains, the level of living of the Soviet people in 1970 was merely one-third of that in the United States, about one-half of that in England, France and West Germany, perhaps a little below that even in Italy and Japan, and well below that in the East European Communist countries of East Germany and Czechoslovakia.'[1] The indications of this lower standard of living were the low wages, the shortage of housing, the poor quality and inefficient distribution of all sorts of consumer goods[2] with consequent shortages. There are all

[1] G. Schroeder, quoted in H. Smith, *The Russians*, p. 80, Sphere Books, 1976.

[2] Sometimes the anomalies are baffling. Leningrad can be overstocked with cross-country skis and yet go several months without soap for washing dishes.' Smith, p. 82. *The Russians.*

sorts of examples: matches are in short supply because Russia is short of timber and the needs of the building and paper industries must come first. In the countryside standards are lower than in the towns.

The basic reason for this situation is that consumers have low priority. Planning is from above rather than in response to consumer demand from below. Defence, investment in heavy industry and agriculture, and overseas aid have a higher priority. There are compensations: rents are very low and public transport is cheap; medical care is good and free. In the 1970s, too, there were improvements. But while there is economic advance, expectations are rising even faster.

Political freedom

One of the features of the period from 1968 to the mid-1970s was the expression of opposition to the government by a number of intellectuals. There were never more than a thousand dissidents, and they were not united in their views. Generally, however, they wanted greater political and intellectual freedom, decentralisation and less administrative rigidity, and the end to censorship. Their views about how they would reform Russia were circulated, to some extent, in Russia, but mainly were sent to the West who transmitted them by radio back to the Soviet Union.

Three men particularly led this movement: Medvedev, an historian, Sakharov, a nuclear physicist of world reputation and one of the designers of the Soviet hydrogen bomb, and Solzhenitsyn, the novelist. In January 1945 Solzhenitsyn, who was then in the army, wrote a letter criticising Stalin's conduct of the war. As a result he was sentenced without a trial to eight years' imprisonment in Siberia. Then between 1953 and 1957 he was exiled to a village in Soviet Central Asia, and part of the time was treated for cancer in a hospital in Tashkent. In 1957 Solzhenitsyn was formally rehabilitated and obtained a teaching post in Moscow. Between 1962 and 1968 he published three novels for which he became world famous. *One Day in the Life of Ivan Denisovich* is an account of life in a Siberian labour camp. *Cancer Ward* describes human behaviour in the shadow of death, while *The First Circle* is a novel about prison life. In 1970 he was awarded the Nobel Prize for Literature.

The dissidents—historians, poets, scientists, novelists, scholars—were mainly eminent people. The official Soviet reaction was hostile. The big names managed to survive, but the less well-known suffered for daring to speak their views. Some were dismissed from their jobs, their writings were not published, they were expelled from the Union

of Writers, and not allowed to live in or near Moscow. Many others
were confined to mental hospitals where life was brutal, or sentenced to
periods in labour camps. Although Sakharov was awarded the Nobel
Peace Prize in 1975, by that point it appeared that the Russian civil
rights movement was weakening. In the previous year Solzhenitsyn
was expelled from Russia, and a sense of futility and disenchantment
reduced support. Indeed, some Russians considered that the effect of
the protest movement was to delay rather than encourage reforms.

There was one other source of political opposition to the Russian
government. Rising nationalism among minority national groups—
Ukrainians, Lithuanians, Latvians and others—led to protests and
consequent arrests. One aspect of life which the authorities were unable
to undermine was religion. Despite argument, propaganda and persecution, Christians, Muslims, Jews and Buddhists not only kept their
religion but in some areas support for religion was increased.

Russia in the mid-1970s

In November 1977 Russia celebrated the sixtieth anniversary of the
Communist Revolution. During the years since 1917 the power of
Russia has grown enormously. In military strength Russia is the equal
of the United States and has regained her national self-respect. The
government is secure and, despite the dissident movement, very
probably has massive popular support. Both industry and agriculture
have developed greatly. It is likely, however, that the capacity for rapid
growth is now over. Russia in the mid-1970s is run by 'an autocracy
of elderly and cautious conservatives'[1]. The test for the future will be
the extent to which the Communist government can adapt to new
conditions, both at home and abroad.

[1] The Times, 7 November, 1977.

5

United States of America

Beginning of the Twentieth Century

The population of the United States in 1900 was 75 million, bigger than that of any European state other than Russia. Between 1820 and 1930 38 million people emigrated to the United States, nearly all from Europe; a third of this number arrived during the first fourteen years of the century. Most of the newcomers lived in slums, in conditions far from those of the American dream that had attracted them. The steady stream of immigrants meant that manpower was always available for industry. Between 1860 and 1900 the value of manufactures increased seven-fold, and by 1900 the United States was the foremost producer of iron, steel and coal in the world. Very big firms or trusts were built up which controlled wages, prices and markets, and gradually removed the small firms. In consequence some men became very wealthy, and in 1900 there were 5,000 millionaires in the United States. Two of these were Carnegie and Rockefeller. Andrew Carnegie, who came to America as a penniless boy of twelve, eventually received an annual income of $23 million from his steel firm. John D. Rockefeller (1839–1937) built up the Standard Oil Trust and probably became the richest man in the world. One historian, in writing about these massive industrial combines, has called the second half of the nineteenth century the 'Age of the Dinosaurs'. In 1890 an act was passed to prevent the creation of big trusts, but this was not effectively applied. Politicians believed that rather than interfere in business they should protect it with tariffs against foreign competition.

Despite the success of industry, two-thirds of the population lived in

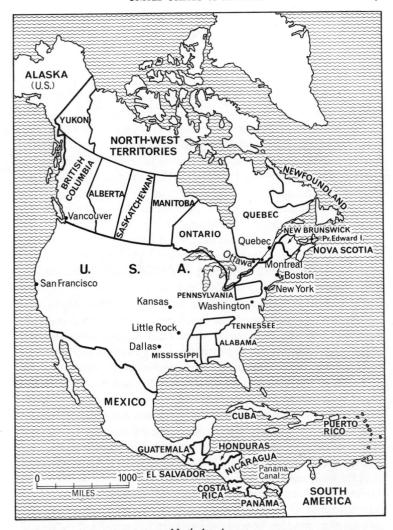

North America

the countryside. Here there had been equally important advances. During the twenty-five years between the end of the Civil War and 1890, the far west was explored, settled and farmed, and by 1900 the United States was the world's leading producer of wheat and other foodstuffs.

The United States has a federal constitution with power divided between the state governments and the federal government in Washington. In the latter power is shared between the Executive, the Legislature and the Judiciary. The head of the Executive is the President who is elected for four years by an electoral college which is directly elected by the people. The President appoints the members of the administration who cannot be members of Congress; he cannot initiate legislation but can recommend Bills to Congress and he can veto Bills although his veto can be overruled by a two-thirds majority in both Houses of Congress. Congress consists of the House of Representatives and the Senate. The House of Representatives is elected every two years by over 400 constituencies each of approximately the same size in population. The Senate consists of two members from each state, and one-third of the Senators are elected every two years. All legislation must pass both Houses. The Supreme Court contains nine judges appointed by the President. Its principal function is to interpret the constitution and it has the power to rule legislation unconstitutional.

There are two main parties in the United States, the Republicans and the Democrats. There are no pronounced ideological differences between them: in fact divisions are often greater within parties than between them. While each party is divided between liberals and conservatives, the Republican Party tends to contain more conservatives who support big business and resist the extension of federal power. The liberal element, which is stronger in the Democratic Party, would like the power of the federal government to be extended. In 1900 it wished to use this power to introduce a number of reforms, such as the regulation of trusts, public health programmes and tax reforms. After about 1890 criticism of big business and the methods of the 'Robber Barons' grew. Many writers spurred the politicians on to reform, and a party known as the Populists, drawing most of its support from the poor in town and countryside, began to agitate for an improvement in conditions.

In the decade before 1900 the United States came to the forefront of world powers, and began to follow an aggressive imperialist policy. The far west had been occupied by 1890 and expansion within North America came to an end. Conscious of her power and wealth and influenced by the current wave of European imperialism in Africa and the Far East, the United States began to assert herself. In 1898 the Spanish were defeated and Cuba, Puerto Rico and the Philippines were occupied, and the United States began to rival Britain's influence in Latin America. This imperialism was not unopposed in the United States, but on the whole the public who, in Theodore Roosevelt's words, wanted to 'Americanise the world', favoured a policy which brought not only prestige but also naval bases and foreign markets.

US administrations 1901 to 1977

President Theodore Roosevelt 1901 to 1909

In 1900 President McKinley (Republican) was elected for a second term. Six months after his inauguration, however, he was assassinated by an anarchist, and the 43-year-old Vice-President, Theodore Roosevelt, succeeded to the presidency.

Roosevelt, a Harvard graduate, came from a prosperous family of Dutch descent. Politician, cowboy, police commissioner, Assistant Secretary of the Navy, organiser of the Rough Riders regiment in the Cuban War, his career, like the man himself, was picturesque and striking. A man of wide interests, with great personal charm and dynamic energy, Roosevelt was at the same time a good administrator and a cautious political realist. He claimed that he wanted to give ordinary men and women 'a square deal', but while he was certainly a liberal Republican, his programme was not especially radical.

In domestic affairs Roosevelt distinguished between good and bad trusts, and he prosecuted those large business corporations that he regarded as harmful. He was very interested in the prevention of reckless exploitation of natural resources, especially forests, and he fostered public interest in the conservation, reclamation and irrigation of land. There was not much social legislation. Roosevelt's attitude was revealed when he intervened in the Pennsylvania coal strike on the side of the miners, but no important reforms were made. The army was modernised and the navy particularly became a powerful force.

Roosevelt conducted an aggressive foreign policy. The opposition of Colombia was overcome so that the United States could build a canal at Panama (see p. 523), and Roosevelt's attitude to Latin America was summed up in his statement, 'Speak softly and carry a big stick.' Europe now clearly recognised the United States as a major power. In 1905 Roosevelt acted as mediator to end the war between Russia and Japan (see p. 462), and in 1906 American support was valued by Britain and France at the Algeciras Conference (see p. 267).

Roosevelt was elected as president in his own right in 1904, but decided not to stand again in 1908. During his period of office he made no great changes. One historian has said that he was more of a politician than a reformer, in that he preferred to avoid the really controversial issues rather than split the Republican Party. Nevertheless, Roosevelt publicised the problems that needed attention and showed that he favoured strong federal action to solve them.

President Taft 1909 to 1913

Roosevelt's successor as president was Taft, his Secretary of War. A large friendly man and a good administrator, he carried on his predecessor's rather cautious policy but without Roosevelt's flair. Taft seemed lethargic at a time when the country needed strong leadership. The Republican Party soon became disunited, the conservatives being satisfied with Taft's policies, while the liberals wanted radical changes.

Roosevelt, meanwhile, was energetically shooting lions[1] in Africa, giving lectures at Oxford, visiting kings and even receiving the Nobel Prize for peace. He was also growing more and more sympathetic towards the radical view that the federal government should intervene far more to reconstruct society. At the next presidential election in 1912, however, the conservatives of the Republican Party chose Taft as their candidate. Roosevelt immediately founded the Progressive Party and also stood for president. Thus the Republicans were divided, and the Democratic candidate, Woodrow Wilson, was elected by a large majority.

President Woodrow Wilson 1913 to 1921

Wilson was born in 1856, the son of a Presbyterian minister. Following an academic career, he became Professor of Political Science and then a reforming president of Princeton University. In 1910 he was elected Governor of New Jersey, and this was his only experience of politics until his election as Democratic President of the United States. Although cold, austere, aloof and rather arrogant as a man, Wilson possessed a penetrating intelligence and considerable political skill. He clearly belonged to the liberal wing of the Democratic Party, believing in greater federal authority to protect the small man against big concentrations of power. In view of his large majority Wilson further believed that the electorate had given him a mandate for 'the New Freedom', and during his first term of office he proceeded to carry out a notable programme of reform.

Tariffs were reduced in order to encourage trade competition and to lower the cost of living. The loss of revenue was made good by a small federal income tax. The law against the formation of trusts was strengthened. 'I am for big business and I am against trusts,' said Wilson who was more concerned with unfair monopoly than with the size of

[1] Roosevelt was also famous as a bear-stalker. The 'teddy bear' is called after him.

firms. The banking system was reformed, federal reserve banks being created to provide security for small banks. Farming was assisted by making it easier for farmers to borrow money to improve their lands. The hours worked by some groups of workers were reduced, and working conditions improved.

When the First World War started in Europe in 1914, Wilson, with the support of the vast majority of Americans, maintained a judicious and profitable neutrality. Industry and agriculture expanded enormously as Britain and France sold their assets in the United States and then received American loans in order to buy American goods. In 1915 the liner *Lusitania* was sunk with the loss of 128 American lives. Yet despite the threat from German submarines and the invaluable economic help given to Britain and France, Wilson managed to maintain American neutrality.

In 1916, with growing prosperity at home and a foreign policy based on the slogan 'He kept us out of the war', Wilson was re-elected president, but this time with only a small majority. He attempted to mediate between the two sides in Europe and failed. During February and March 1917 eight American ships were sunk by German submarines. Evidence came to light that Germany had promised support to Mexico[1] in any war against the United States. Public opinion was changing to support American intervention in Europe, and in April 1917 the United States declared war on Germany. 'The world must be made safe for democracy,' said Wilson. The 'New Freedom' was now neglected and the government devoted itself to war.

The war was run with great efficiency. Five million men had been called up by November 1918, and one million of these were in France when the war ended. The Americans suffered 125,000 casualties, including 53,000 killed. Federal power grew enormously: communications, prices, industry, agriculture and many other aspects of life were controlled by the government. All expression of opposition was repressed by the Espionage Acts which many believed were a serious danger to civil liberties. Throughout the twenty months of the war the Republicans enthusiastically supported the Democratic government's war effort, but none was brought into the administration so giving the impression that United States' participation in the war was purely the responsibility of the Democrats.

In November 1918 when the Congressional elections were held, the national unity of wartime immediately gave way to bitter party

[1] Following the Mexican revolution of 1910 the large American economic interests were threatened, and in 1916 Wilson finally sent American troops to intervene (see chapter 13).

rivalry. Despite Wilson's 'New Freedom' reforms and his efficient running of the war effort, his policies had aroused opposition. German- and Irish-Americans disapproved of the support given to Britain, the wartime controls were disliked, and there was a general wish for a return to the old policy of federal inactivity in the running of the country. In addition many eminent Republicans personally disliked Wilson. The elections resulted in small Republican majorities in both Houses of Congress. Wilson, a Democratic President, was now faced with a Republican Congress.

Wilson decided to attend the Paris Peace Conference himself. After six months of negotiations the peace treaty was signed at Versailles (see chapter 1), and in July 1919 was presented to the Senate for ratification. But there was opposition from three groups: from German-, Irish-, and Italian-Americans, from the few liberals who saw the defects in the treaty, and from those Americans who had become disillusioned both with the war and America's involvement in European problems and who felt that ratification of the treaty (and therefore United States' participation in the League of Nations) would perpetuate this unnecessary involvement. The Senate Foreign Relations Committee particularly opposed the powers given to the Council of the League of Nations (see chapter 14).

Wilson, tired and already disillusioned from his experiences in Paris, began a speaking tour to try to convert the American people to the support of the League. After a hundred speeches in less than a month, his campaign was cut short in September 1919 when he collapsed from a paralytic stroke. For the remainder of his term of office, Wilson was an invalid. Nevertheless, he refused to consider any compromise with the Senate over the League of Nations, and in 1920 the Treaty of Versailles failed to gain the necessary two-thirds majority in the Senate. It was, therefore, not ratified.

A sharp economic recession in 1920 heightened the opposition to Wilson's policies and in the presidential election of November 1920 Harding, the undistinguished Republican candidate, was elected with a large majority. Woodrow Wilson lived until 1924. Faulkner has written of his achievements: 'they show statesmanship of a high order in the reform legislation of his first administration, pre-eminent energy and organisation as a war leader, and superb vision in helping plan a new world organisation.'[1]

---

[1] H. Faulkner, *From Versailles to the New Deal.*

Presidents Harding, Coolidge and Hoover 1921 to 1933

The Progressive or liberal era which had begun with the presidency of Theodore Roosevelt in 1901 ended with the Republican victory in the elections of 1918. Though Wilson remained president until March 1921 he was powerless to effect any further reforms. The Progressive era gave way to the 'Age of Normalcy', a phrase coined by President Harding. Americans, he believed wanted a return to 'normalcy', a return to the safe and stable times when the federal government was as inactive as possible and when the United States ignored the problems of the outside world. So during the 1920s three successive Republican presidents, Harding (1921–23), Coolidge (1923–29) and Hoover (1929–1933) followed a policy of *laissez-faire*, of reducing the government's interference in the affairs of the country.

The three presidents provide a considerable contrast. Harding, a well-liked and sincere Ohio senator, possessed few talents, little executive experience and no real understanding of the problems facing his country. 'A small man in a big job',[1] he appointed to his cabinet men who later were found guilty of corruption. Harding died while in office and his Vice-President, Calvin Coolidge, succeeded to the presidency, being elected in his own right in the elections of 1924. Coolidge was a cautious, puritanical Yankee lawyer. An experienced administrator and a clever politician, he cleared up the corruption left by Harding and provided a reassuring air of stability to an America undergoing great social changes.

In March 1929 the third successive Republican president took office with a large majority supporting him. Hoover (1874–1964) was in early life a brilliant mining engineer. Because of his extremely capable work as Chairman of the Belgian Relief Commission and as United States Food Administrator in Europe during and after the war, he was an international figure. He had been Secretary for Commerce for eight years, and was the symbol of the successful businessman. It was believed that 'Hoover efficiency' would safeguard 'Coolidge prosperity'. Yet within a few months of his inauguration as president, Hoover was faced with the most serious economic slump in the world's history, and his methods for dealing with a disastrous situation proved inadequate.

The 1920s were a period of great contrasts. Industry flourished as never before while farmers remained in a state of depression; the

---

[1] H. Faulkner, *From Versailles to the New Deal.*

manufacture and sale of alcohol was forbidden and religious fundamentalism had a powerful influence,[1] while moral standards changed in the direction of sophisticated emancipation and crime became big business. The Roaring Twenties saw a revolution in ways of living. The building of skyscrapers, the greater use of electricity, the introduction of hire-purchase, the popularity of the cinema, the emancipation of women—these new features of American life were interwoven with much that was old and traditional.

The decade began with two years of economic depression, but this was followed until 1929 by tremendous business activity. Some industries—coalmining, shipbuilding, textiles—did badly; but on the whole the business world was prosperous. 'This increased productivity was made possible by the application of science to technology and management.'[2] Nowhere was this better seen than in the great mass-production car industry. In 1913 Henry Ford introduced the assembly line system with a consequent huge reduction in price. In 1919 there were 6 million motor vehicles in the United States; in 1929 there were 29 million.

Agriculture, on the other hand, was in a depressed state. Huge war-time demands from Europe for agricultural goods had led to an increase in prices and production. But after the war demand was much reduced. There were three main reasons for this. Firstly, normal peace-time farming had restarted in Europe; secondly, high American tariffs prevented Europe selling manufactured goods to the United States in exchange for American agricultural goods; thirdly, competition from Canada, Australia and Argentina had greatly increased. Despite this reduction in demand, farm production in America increased during the 1920s. In consequence prices dropped and farm income was greatly reduced. Those farmers who had borrowed heavily to buy land when the price was high now found themselves in desperate plight.

One of the subjects which aroused most passion in the 1920s was the federal prohibition in 1919 of the manufacture and sale (but not consumption) of alcoholic drink. This was the work of a strong pressure group which wanted to end drunkenness, and gained most of its support from the countryside and the small towns. Rural, Protestant America, it has been said, was taking its last major stand against the immigrant urban masses. But the attempt at prohibition failed. Drink was smuggled into the country by gangs who soon became rich and powerful.[3] Millions broke a law which proved impossible to enforce, and in 1933 prohibition was ended.

---

[1] Many states made the teaching in schools of Darwin's theory of evolution illegal.

[2] H. Faulkner, *From Versailles to the New Deal.*

[3] For example, Al Capone's gang in Chicago.

One sinister feature of the 1920s was the revival of the Ku Klux Klan. This was an old organisation refounded in 1915 that had reached a membership of about 4 million ten years later. Its members had to be white, Gentile and Protestant. Using violent and terrifying methods, it encouraged racial and religious intolerance.

United States foreign policy has been dealt with elsewhere. Public opinion was almost equally divided between those who wished to follow an isolationist policy and those who wished to involve the United States in world problems. Harding's attitude represented the former view: 'We seek no part in directing the destinies of the Old World. We do not mean to be entangled.' But circumstances modified this view. The problem of naval power in the Pacific was solved by the Treaty of Washington (1922). The vast problem of German reparations was temporarily settled by the plans of two Americans, Dawes and Young. Coolidge, his Secretary of State, Kellogg, and Hoover attempted to achieve disarmament, and the United States was represented at many non-political League of Nations meetings.

The general prosperity of the 1920s ended with a crash in October 1929. Businessmen had believed that prosperity was permanent, and their confidence affected all classes of society. The result was that huge amounts were spent on shares by millions of Americans who before this decade would never have dreamed of owning them. The big profits that were made by the rapid rise in share prices led to frenzied speculation. It was clear that share prices were far above their true value, and that a fall would eventually come. Both industry and agriculture had over-expanded. Their international markets were limited by tariffs which hindered trade and the uneven distribution of wealth in the United States reduced the size of the potential home market.

In the summer of 1929 profits began to fall. During October share prices slowly fell on Wall Street, the New York stock exchange. On 24 October panic struck and 16 million shares were sold in one day. In an atmosphere of hysteria the recession spread and the value of shares slumped. By early 1932 stock prices had fallen by over 80 per cent. This lack of confidence in industry was increased as the slump became worldwide and foreign markets were reduced. The consequence was large-scale unemployment.

At the height of the depression over 15 million were unemployed, and the wages of those who did have work were much reduced. So purchasing power was lowered still further. There was no unemployment insurance, and those without work depended largely on the help of charity.[1]

[1] Bing Crosby made famous the song, 'Buddy—can you spare a dime?'

President Hoover believed that the federal government should intervene as little as possible in this crisis. Thinking the depression to be less serious than it really was, he tried to create confidence in industry, but the measures taken by the government at first only worsened the position. For example, in 1930 the tariff was raised still further in order to correct the balance of payments deficit. This not only meant that foreign countries raised their tariffs too, but imports were reduced so that less money was available for foreigners to buy American exports. Hoover was too orthodox and lacked the capacity for really bold imaginative thinking. When the economy failed to recover, Hoover eventually took federal action. Taxes were reduced to increase purchasing power, and in 1932 the Emergency Relief and Reconstruction Act provided loans to the states and employment of men on federal public works. But this action was not sufficiently drastic, and at the beginning of 1933 the banking system of the United States virtually collapsed.

At this point Franklin Roosevelt became president. It was clear in the presidential election of November 1932 that Roosevelt, the Democratic candidate, would be elected. Hoover said that the nation must choose between individualism and regimentation, between liberty and federal bureaucracy. But the traditional opposition in America to increased federal power had been greatly weakened by the depression, and Roosevelt was elected by a large majority.

President Franklin Roosevelt 1933 to 1945

Franklin Delano Roosevelt, a distant relation of Theodore Roosevelt, was born of wealthy parents in New York in 1882. Educated at Harvard, he became a lawyer, and in 1910 began his political career with election to the New York State Senate as a Democrat. When Wilson became president, Roosevelt was made Assistant Secretary of the Navy, and was the vice-presidential candidate in the 1920 elections. In 1921 he was suddenly struck down with poliomyelitis and was paralysed from the waist down. 'I spent two years lying in bed trying to move my big toe,' he said. Although his legs remained paralysed, he gradually returned to public life, and in 1928 was elected Governor of New York. His term of office coincided approximately with the depression, and by using the state government to help the unemployed he demonstrated the policy that he was later to follow as President. Despite his physical disabilities Roosevelt and his team of advisers travelled 20,000 miles on the election campaign. He was a man of enormous energy, of infectious courage and great self-confidence and determination. In addition he possessed an intuitive understanding of the people. 'This nation asks for action, and action now,' he said in his inaugural address, and earlier he had pledged himself 'to a new deal for the American people'.

All of Roosevelt's energy and political ability were required in March 1933 when he became president. The banking system had collapsed, and Roosevelt's first action was to close all the banks and to forbid the withdrawal of gold and silver. The federal reserve banks were reopened first and then private banks that were solvent. A few months later an act was passed by which the federal government guaranteed deposits. The vigorous way in which the banking system was dealt with helped to restore confidence, and Roosevelt realised the need for this. 'The only thing we have to fear is fear itself,' he said.

Many of the policies that made up the New Deal were implemented during the first 'Hundred Days' of furious activity up to June 1933. In that month the National Industrial Recovery Act was passed. The general aim of the act was to stabilise production, maintain or increase the level of wages and so create purchasing power, and in this it was successful. It set up two particular bodies, a Public Works Administration which concentrated on heavy construction projects, and a National Recovery Administration which aimed to end cut-throat competition, firms which cooperated being given a 'Blue Eagle' badge. The NRA failed, partly because of too much red tape, and partly because the codes governing fair competition were not enforced. In 1935 the whole act was declared illegal by the Supreme Court.

Agriculture was in a desperate plight in 1933. On top of the depression and loss of markets came drought and dust storms. The Roosevelt Administration's policy was to limit production in order to raise prices. Those farmers who agreed to limit their production received government aid. Although this deliberate destruction of wealth was unpopular—for example, cotton plants were ploughed up and young pigs killed—nevertheless, it had the desired effect of raising prices. The government also gave aid to improve land and encourage mechanisation. One particular project of the government deserves special mention. The land of the Tennessee Valley had become exhausted by intensive farming and by 1933 was eroded and barren. Two months after coming into office, Roosevelt set up the Tennessee Valley Authority, a corporation organised and financed by the federal government. The Authority built a series of dams on the river for hydroelectric power and the prevention of flooding. The electricity resulted in new industries, some of which produced cheap fertilisers. New farming methods were encouraged, with the result that the area became a government show piece.

The effect of Roosevelt's actions was immediate. Prices were increased and business improved with a consequent drop in unemployment. Nevertheless, the number of unemployed remained large, and various bodies were established to create work. These were largely public works such as forest improvement and the building of schools, roads and bridges. Two other pieces of legislation should be mentioned. In 1934 an Act was passed to regulate the stock market, and in 1935 the Social Security Act became law. The latter has been described as the most far-reaching piece of social legislation in American history. It co-ordinated federal and state action for the relief of unemployed people, old people, children, widows and the blind. This was a striking innovation in American legislation for never before had the state helped the poor.

The distinguishing feature of the legislation which made up the New Deal was greatly increased federal power, and despite its success in restoring the American economy, many conservatives within the Republican and Democratic parties were opposed to this change. In the 1936 elections, however, Roosevelt was re-elected by a popular majority of 9 million, and 523 electoral votes to eight. Roosevelt interpreted this massive victory as a mandate to carry on the New Deal, but his first attempt to clear the way for this to be done failed.

One function of the nine judges of the Supreme Court is to decide whether laws passed by Congress are in harmony with the constitution. If they believe that any law is contrary to the constitution, they have the right to veto it. This gives the Court an extraordinary political power which Roosevelt believed was being used to prevent social progress. 'In the last four years', said Roosevelt, 'the Court has been acting . . . as a policy-making body.' The Court had declared illegal two important laws concerned with industry and agriculture passed in 1933 as well as other New Deal legislation. In 1937 none of the judges had been appointed by Roosevelt, and he now introduced a Bill which would allow the president to replace judges over the age of seventy who had served ten years in the Court. If passed, six of the nine judges could have been replaced.

But Roosevelt ran into unexpected opposition. The Bill was opposed, not only by conservatives, but also by liberals of both parties. Congress feared that the President was trying to gain too much power for himself, and that the old constitution was in danger. The Bill was, therefore, defeated. But Roosevelt nevertheless gained his objective, for the Supreme Court suddenly ended[1] its opposition to social legislation.

[1] 'A switch in time that saved nine,' someone said.

For example, an act was confirmed which supported trade unions. Several of the judges retired voluntarily during the next few years, and Roosevelt was able to replace them with his own nominees. Many federal laws were passed that would probably have been vetoed before 1937.

The New Deal was over by 1938. Thereafter legislation was concerned with the threat of war and with the war itself. What had the New Deal achieved? The depression had been ended and prosperity restored; the poorer classes of the community who could not help themselves had been given aid by the government; and in general Americans' dislike of federal interference in the life of the country had been partly overcome.

The remaining years of Roosevelt's life were devoted to foreign affairs. Since 1933 he had followed a 'good neighbour' policy in Latin America. The United States relinquished its long-held right to intervene in this area, and instead concentrated more on economic power to maintain American influence. The Philippines moved towards self-government. Towards Europe American public opinion was isolationist. Disillusionment with the First World War and its aftermath was heightened by the ending of the payment of war debts to the United States in the early 1930s. As a result Congress passed legislation which prevented trade in arms and the extension of credit to belligerents and any countries who had defaulted in payment of war debts to the United States.

In opposing this trend, Roosevelt was fighting a losing battle before 1939. In 1935 he said, 'We cannot build walls around us and hide our heads in the sand.' But most Americans did not think that Germany, Italy and Japan threatened American security. In November 1939, however, Roosevelt was able to persuade Congress to allow belligerents to buy war materials on a cash and carry basis. By 1940 the United States was growing alarmed at the German and Japanese success, and opinion was openly sympathetic to the Allies. It was realised after the surrender of France that Germany and Italy controlled Europe and Japan controlled Asia, and that only Britain and her empire stood between America and a Fascist world.

American aid to Britain began to cross the Atlantic in large quantities. In September 1940 the United States introduced conscription, the first occasion this had happened in peacetime. In November Roosevelt was re-elected as president for a third term,[1] and even his Republican opponent agreed with his foreign policy of assistance for Britain. In March 1941 the system of Lend-Lease provided Britain and later

[1] Franklin Roosevelt has been the only president to serve more than two terms.

Russia with American supplies. Four motives for this assistance were given by Roosevelt: to support freedom of speech, freedom of religion, freedom from want and freedom from fear. In August 1941 Roosevelt and Churchill signed the Atlantic Charter which contained a statement of war aims. Some American-German naval fighting took place in the Atlantic, and it was clearly only a matter of time before the United States and Germany would be at war. Then on 7 December 1941 the Japanese struck at Pearl Harbour. The following day the United States declared war on Japan and on 11 December Germany and Italy declared war on the United States.

An account of America's part in the war and her relations with her Allies is given in chapters 2 and 11. The power of the federal government grew more than it did during the First World War. Prices were fixed, public transport controlled, and industry was quickly and efficiently reorganised for war production. There was general prosperity: farmers' income increased fourfold during the war, and unemployment, still 9 million in 1939, had disappeared by 1943.

Roosevelt was reluctant to stand as a candidate in the 1944 elections, but he was persuaded to do so and was re-elected, with Senator Harry S. Truman as Vice-President. It was clear that his health was declining fast, and on 12 April 1945 he died. By all counts Franklin Roosevelt was one of the greatest of American Presidents. One historian has said that there were two great innovations in his presidency: 'progressive social policies strongly spiced with Keynesian economic measures, and the irrevocable commitment of American men, money and prestige to the international community of which the United States was a part'.[1]

President Truman 1945 to 1953

Harry S. Truman was born in 1884, the son of a horsetrader. After serving as an artillery officer in the First World War, he held a succession of jobs—bank clerk, farmer, the manager of a men's clothes shop—before entering politics in Kansas. Before the age of fifty he was largely unknown outside his own state, but from 1934 until Roosevelt's death he was a member of the Senate where he gained the favourable attention of the public. Inconspicuous, humble, very ordinary in appearance and background, Truman was initially bewildered and shocked at becoming president.

However, Truman grew in stature in his new post, and he made good appointments both in the cabinet and in the diplomatic service. His

[1] D. Snowman, *Since 1945, Aspects of Contemporary World History*, ed. J. L. Henderson.

first problem was whether to use the newly-developed atomic bomb on Japan or to continue the war by conventional means. It was thought that the second alternative would mean a heavier loss of life, and Truman made the decision which led to Hiroshima and Nagasaki and the surrender of Japan (see chapter 11).

Truman described his legislative programme as the 'Fair Deal'. He wished to expand social security, raise minimum wages, clear the slums, protect natural resources and maintain full employment. This meant a great extension of federal authority and was a more radical policy than Roosevelt's 'New Deal'. But much of this was frustrated by Congress which was very conservative on the question of domestic legislation. In addition, while the country was generally prosperous, the first year of peace brought a number of problems. As a result of the huge domestic and foreign demand, all goods were in short supply. Therefore when price controls were lifted, the cost of living went up sharply. This contributed to labour difficulties. There were strikes for higher wages in a variety of industries but especially in coalmining and steel. Public resentment against the unions helped Truman in taking a strong line against the workers. In addition there was great pressure on Truman to 'Bring the boys home', with the result that demobilisation was carried out too fast and the armed forces were left in a comparatively weak state.

Inflation, strikes, the growth of federal power and divisions within the cabinet made Truman unpopular, and in the 1946 mid-term elections the Republicans won control of both Houses of Congress. During the next two years the Democratic President and Republican Congress were at war. Congress refused to pass Truman's Bills, and Truman vetoed Congress's Bills. In two cases Congress, by a two-thirds majority, overcame Truman's veto. Firstly, it passed a Labour law which severely restricted the power of the unions, and secondly, it passed an act sharply reducing taxes on the rich.

But while Congress was very conservative on domestic issues, it accepted Truman's internationalist foreign policy (see chapter 3). In 1945 the United States supported the formation of the United Nations Organisation. Nearly 70 per cent of the cost of UNRRA's relief programme in Europe was borne by the United States, and in 1947 the Secretary of State, Marshall, drew up the plan for aid to Europe which is called after him. In the same year Truman described his policy for the containment of Communist expansion, and this had the general support of Congress.

In 1948 Truman was rather unenthusiastically nominated as Democratic candidate, but it was assumed from the start of the election campaign that he would lose. Not only were his 'Fair Deal' policies unpopular in the country as a whole, but he had split his own party. His support for a Civil Rights programme to improve the status of blacks had led to a split among the Democrats, the so-called Dixiecrats from the right wing forming their own party. Then the liberals from the left wing of the Democrats formed a separate party because they believed Truman's domestic policies to be inadequate and his foreign policy to be too anti-Russian. Thus the Democrats were divided, the press was anti-Truman and the opinion polls indicated a Republican victory.

But Truman's campaign was energetic and aggressive. He attacked the 'do-nothing' Congress rather than his opponent. He won the support of the farmers and the blacks, of the trade unions (because of Congress's Labour Act), and of all those who wanted more welfare legislation. In consequence Truman was re-elected with a large majority of the electoral votes, and the Democrats regained their majority in both Houses of Congress.

However, Truman did not really control Congress. Although there was more support for farmers, and an act was passed to improve housing conditions, many southern Democrats opposed his legislation, and the 'Fair Deal' was not accomplished. In fact relations between the President and Congress deteriorated. Three factors account for this: some evidence of bribery and corruption in government circles, Communist successes abroad and the fear of Communism at home.

In 1949 the American policy of support for Chiang Kai-shek in his war against the Communists ended in failure as the Nationalists were driven from the mainland of China to the island of Formosa. In the same year the Russians exploded their atomic bomb. Then in 1950 Communist North Korea attacked South Korea. The American forces of the United Nations were at first hard pressed, but when they had driven the Communists back to the Chinese frontier, Truman dismissed the autocratic General MacArthur for expressing views contrary to his government's Korean policy. MacArthur was very popular and there were wildly enthusiastic scenes on his return to the United States. Events in China and Korea helped to weaken Truman's position at home especially in view of the apparent success of Communist subversion in the United States itself.

During the Second World War the public began to fear the danger of Communist subversion, and in 1946 the hunt for Communists in government service began. In 1950 three cases seemed to confirm these fears: Hiss, a high-ranking official of the State Department, was found guilty of having passed American secrets to the Russians in the 1930s, and it was discovered that Julius and Ethel Rosenberg in the United States and Fuchs in Britain had betrayed atomic secrets to the Russians. In consequence the Communist Party, which was regarded as a conspiracy rather than a party, was outlawed in many states. Congress also passed the Internal Security Act which put restrictions on Communists. This was passed despite the veto of Truman who said, 'In a free country, we punish men for the crimes they commit but never for the opinions they have.'

This atmosphere of suspicion explains the success of Senator McCarthy. In 1950 he gained an audience by accusing State Department officials of knowingly harbouring eighty-one Communists. He failed to substantiate these and other wild accusations, but nevertheless gained support in the country. McCarthy was a gifted demagogue, tough and ruthless, with a great talent for abuse, and he soon became the mouthpiece of the right wing who opposed such policies as the New and Fair Deal at home and internationalism abroad.

In 1951 an amendment to the constitution prevented a presidential third term, and the Democratic candidate in the 1952 election was Adlai Stevenson, a liberal intellectual with constructive ideas. The Republicans, however, had the extremely popular General Eisenhower as their candidate. After the war, when he had been Allied Commander in Europe, Eisenhower had become President of Columbia University and then NATO Supreme Commander. The campaign was fought on the issues of Korea, Communism and corruption, and such was the state of public opinion that Eisenhower won with a large majority. He became President in January 1953 at the age of sixty-two.

President Eisenhower 1953 to 1961

Eisenhower was honest, amiable and a confident soldier, simple and straightforward, with no intellectual distinctions. His government was a businessmen's administration,[1] and was organised like a military staff. But Eisenhower, who spent an unusual amount of time playing golf, failed to provide positive leadership and did not seem to do enough work on problems himself. His speeches were disappointing—journalists used to say, 'Now he's crossing the 38th platitude again.' Nevertheless, he was utterly in tune with the people who regarded him as a model American, and throughout his presidency he maintained his popularity.

The economic policy of Eisenhower's government was to reduce

[1] At first the cabinet consisted of 'eight millionaires and a plumber', and the plumber soon resigned.

federal expenditure where possible. It was friendly towards private enterprise, and believed that federal power should be used only when private resources were inadequate. Farmers tended to suffer from over-production, and the government helped by making payments for taking land out of cultivation. In 1953–54 and again in 1958 the economy was in a depression, and the government acted by increasing the amount of money in circulation. In general, however, the 1950s were a period of prosperity for most workers. In 1956, for example, 96 per cent of American families owned a refrigerator, 80 per cent had television, and 75 per cent owned at least one car.

After Eisenhower's election as president, McCarthy became chairman of the Senate Committee on Government Operations. For nearly two years he concentrated on his self-appointed task of hunting for Communists in important positions in American life. General Marshall, the ex-Secretary of State, Oppenheimer, the director of the laboratory that made the first atomic bomb, army generals and government officials, were accused relentlessly and recklessly. During the summer of 1954 investigations into the army were given nationwide television coverage. But this marked the beginning of McCarthy's downfall for his charges and insinuations became confused and ridiculous, and his bullying techniques alienated support. 'As the public watched, McCarthy seemed to change from a national hero into something of a villain, then into a low buffoon.'[1] At the end of the year the Senate voted a resolution condemning his activities. Three years later he died. The McCarthy affair showed in an unpleasant way how mass hysteria could grip a nation.

Eisenhower left most of the conduct of foreign affairs to his Secretary of State, Foster Dulles, a man he greatly admired. Dulles, a cold and severe character, had had long experience of foreign affairs, and believed that tough, unrelenting policies were required to prevent the spread of Communism. The details of these policies are given elsewhere.

In September 1955 Eisenhower had a heart attack. Although he recovered, he was ill again in the following year and underwent a serious operation. Nevertheless, he was renominated as the Republican candidate in the 1956 elections, again with Stevenson as his opponent. The result was a landslide victory for Eisenhower. His second term was marked by three main features: firstly, the launching in 1957 of the first Soviet artificial satellite, Sputnik I, which provoked a speeding up of the American space programme and the production of missiles; secondly, foreign affairs; thirdly, the Civil Rights campaign to improve the status of the 18 million American blacks.

[1] F. Freidel, *America in the Twentieth Century*.

The status of blacks, which had improved after the abolition of slavery in 1865, had deteriorated again during the 1890s. Blacks were disfranchised by the imposition of a poll tax and literacy and property qualifications, and the Supreme Court upheld the principle of 'separate but equal' facilities for blacks. Facilities were certainly separate but were not equal, and until after the Second World War blacks remained both underprivileged and largely resigned to their inferior status.[1] In the southern states blacks were disfranchised, went to inferior schools and were excluded from jury service. In the northern states the black suffered economically rather than politically or legally. Here the principle of integration in schools was accepted, and considerable progress had been made in prohibiting discrimination in employment and in public places. Nevertheless, segregation was very obvious in the north, where the centres of cities were black and the suburbs white. The move to the north of blacks seeking better wages and living conditions only enlarged the shabby black areas of cities.

But from 1954 onwards there was a marked improvement in the legal position of blacks. There were three reasons for this: firstly, federal intervention in the affairs of those states who practised segregation; secondly, a determined campaign by blacks and white liberal sympathisers; thirdly, the influence of independent Asian and African states who could not be indifferent to the status of coloured people in the United States.

In 1954 the United States Supreme Court decided that 'in the field of public education the doctrine of "separate but equal" has no place. Separate educational facilities are inherently unequal.' The Court instructed the seventeen states who had no integrated educational system (education is a state, not a federal, concern) to implement the decision 'with all deliberate speed'. But the states used various legal devices to prevent integration, and a crisis was eventually reached at Little Rock in Arkansas. Here the Governor refused to allow seventeen black students into a white school until Eisenhower put the Arkansas National Guard under his own command, and sent 1,000 crack paratroopers into Little Rock to enforce the law.

Meanwhile, segregation on public buses was ended in Alabama following the success of a black bus boycott organised by the Reverend Martin Luther King, a black leader who believed in Gandhian methods of non-violence to achieve civil rights. In 1957 Congress passed a law to remove some of the obstacles imposed by states on the black right to

[1] The autobiography of Malcolm X, a leader in the early 1960s of a militant Negro organisation called the Black Muslims, vividly describes the life of a poor Negro and the motives for his anti-white attitude.

Franklin Roosevelt   *Kennedy*

American marines shelter behind a tank during heavy street fighting in Hué, South Vietnam

vote. (In 1955 only one per cent of blacks in Mississippi had voted.) In 1960 black leaders organised café sit-ins—blacks entered cafés previously restricted to whites only—and integration was gradually spreading when the Eisenhower era ended.

President Kennedy 1961 to 1963

In the 1960 election the Republican candidate, Nixon, who had been vice-president under Eisenhower, was opposed by Senator Kennedy, a Democrat. Kennedy was elected by a very small majority of 100,000 votes, after a campaign which included four debates on television between the two candidates. The Democrats also won control of Congress.

Kennedy was the first Roman Catholic and also the youngest elected president in American history. Born in Boston in 1917, his great grandparents had emigrated from Ireland in the mid-nineteenth century, and his father, later a controversial American ambassador to Britain, became a multimillionaire. During the Second World War Kennedy commanded a motor-torpedo boat in the Pacific until one night in 1943 it was cut in half by a Japanese destroyer.[1] After the war he was elected to Congress and in 1952 he entered the Senate. Kennedy was forty-three when he was inaugurated president in January 1961. His youth, his idealism, his enormous driving energy and the presence of a wife with charm, culture and good looks brought a sense of excitement and anticipation to Washington.

Dean Rusk became the new Secretary of State, but Kennedy kept a strong personal control over foreign policy. In 1961 he was faced with crises in Laos, Berlin and Cuba. The Bay of Pigs fiasco in Cuba was mishandled partly because of ignorance of the real situation on the island, and it made Kennedy conscious of the complexities of political decisions and the possible consequences of failure. The Cuba affair and the abortive meeting with Kennedy in Vienna may have convinced Khrushchev that he was dealing with an inadequate adversary, and this may have encouraged the buildup of Soviet missiles in Cuba. The Cuba missile crisis in October 1962, which brought the world to the brink of nuclear war, was handled by Kennedy with cool and ruthless judgement. Thereafter relations with Russia improved greatly, and in 1963 the Partial Test Ban Treaty was signed. Meanwhile, Kennedy gave unwilling support to the Diem regime in South Vietnam; relations with

[1] Five days of dangerous adventure followed, which included towing a badly burned man on a three-mile swim to a neighbouring island with his teeth in the other's life jacket.

Latin America improved; but, while Anglo-American relations were good, the Atlantic alliance as a whole was in poor shape.

Kennedy called his domestic policy the 'New Frontier', and he hoped to recreate the spirit of Roosevelt's Hundred Days. But foreign affairs tended to dominate events, and Kennedy found that Congress, despite tactful and tireless propaganda and prodding, was unwilling to pass many of his Bills. There was a rise in minimum wages and federal aid for housing increased, but the Bills to provide medical care for the aged and federal help for education were defeated. Kennedy often began his sentences in speeches with 'I am not satisfied . . .' and he urged Congress to act, but he could not communicate his own sense of urgency. One important Bill was passed by Congress, the Trade Expansion Act. This gave the President the power to negotiate mutual tariff cuts, and so began the so-called Kennedy Round of Tariff reductions.

In 1961 the Peace Corps was founded. This was composed of young specialists who worked for two years in undeveloped areas of the world. The Civil Rights movement continued, and integration gradually spread. The segregation of black and white people on interstate buses was ended, and in 1962 the University of Mississippi was forced to admit a black student. By mid-1963 only the state of Alabama had no integrated schools. In August 1963 an enormous rally met at the Lincoln Memorial in Washington in support of Kennedy's Civil Rights Bill which aimed at strengthening earlier legislation against racial discrimination.

On 22 November 1963 President Kennedy was assassinated while visiting Dallas in Texas. The motive is not known, and the suspected assassin was himself murdered before his trial. So ended in tragedy a presidency of three brief years.

President Johnson 1963 to 1969

Kennedy was succeeded by Lyndon B. Johnson, the Vice-President. Johnson was a southerner from Texas, a fact which was both his weakness and his strength. To make progress in politics in the southern United States requires toughness, shrewdness, staying power and an understanding of how politics works. Johnson was a master of the system, and became Senate Majority leader. His earthiness and drawl were attractive to many Americans; his political skill and experience were invaluable, and his liberal views and ideals resulted in important social legislation. On the other hand, his background was a disadvantage. The American Establishment, men who had attended eastern private schools and universities, were suspicious of him, and he of them. Although as Vice-President he had spoken out passionately against racial discrimination, the liberals and the blacks were uncertain of his intentions. The dignity and culture which the Kennedys had brought to the White House were now discarded. Johnson's background, character and manner meant that, even at the height of his popularity, he never really had the affection and trust of Americans. He was thought to be too devious and secretive, and was never confident of his position.

Johnson's first important duty, in the aftermath of Kennedy's assassination, was to achieve national unity and demonstrate the continuity of presidential government. The cabinet agreed to remain, and during the next year several of Kennedy's New Frontier measures were passed by Congress, partly because of the emotional reaction following Kennedy's death, and partly because of Johnson's political skill in achieving a better relationship between the executive and legislative branches of government. The Civil Rights Bill and a bill which allocated federal grants to local authorities to combat poverty were passed.

In the presidential election of 1964 Johnson was opposed by an extreme right-wing Republican candidate, Goldwater. The latter, who declared, 'Extremism in the defence of liberty is no vice. . . . Moderation in the pursuit of justice is no virtue', opposed federal intervention in domestic affairs and wanted a more nationalist foreign policy. Goldwater was overwhelmingly defeated. Johnson was now President in his own right, and the Democrats had large majorities in both Houses of Congress.

Important social legislation was passed during Johnson's presidency: federal hospital insurance for people over the age of 65, federal aid for schools and teacher training, revision of the immigration laws in order to abolish the quota system which had imposed limitations on the number of people of any one nationality entering the country, a big housing programme, federal aid for the arts, and attempts to prevent air and water pollution. During 1965 alone over 300 measures concerning social legislation were passed, together with the Civil Rights legislation described below. However, in the second half of Johnson's presidency little progress was made in social reforms. The programme to fight crime failed to pass Congress which also refused to increase taxation to pay for further federal reforms and the Vietnam war as well. In addition, bureaucratic muddle dissipated some of the effectiveness of the measures already passed.

The period from 1961 to 1970 was one of uninterrupted growth in the economy. The mood was optimistic and the economy boomed in almost every area. Government spending increased to finance the Vietnam war and the increased social legislation. Industrial production reached record levels: for example, in 1965 11 million motor vehicles were produced. There were problems: a deepening deficit on the balance of payments; very large budget deficits, bigger than any recorded since the end of the Second World War; the growth of the money supply and a shortage of labour. Some were concerned that economic expansion was too rapid, and that there would be inflation and a sudden recession. Nevertheless, their fears were not realised.

One area of major success for the Johnson Administration was the space programme. From 1957 to 1963 Russia had remained in the lead in space exploration. In 1959 Lunik 3 sent back to earth pictures of the far side of the Moon; in 1960 the USSR launched two dogs into space and recovered them alive and well after eighteen orbits of the earth; in 1961 Yuri Gagarin became the first man to circle the earth in space, and in 1963 Valentina Tereshkova became the first woman cosmonaut. Meanwhile, the Americans were devoting more money and manpower to catching up with the Russians, and in 1962 John Glenn became the first American to circle the earth in space. Between 1963 and 1968 American progress was more rapid: a moon probe sent back many thousands of close-up TV pictures of the moon; the first close-up pictures of Mars were sent back to earth; two spacecraft launched from Cape Kennedy achieved the first rendezvous in space, six feet apart, flying at 17,000 m.p.h. and 185 miles above the earth. Finally in 1968 three American astronauts took three days to travel to the moon, made ten orbits and sent back to earth spectacular close-up photographs of the moon's surface.

Johnson, a southerner, was opposed to racial discrimination. The process of ending discrimination continued and earlier legislation was given some teeth by the 1964 Civil Rights Act which, for example, banned discrimination in any institution receiving financial assistance from the federal government. However, the process was very slow. Integration of schools proceeded at a negligible rate until 1964, and not much faster thereafter. In 1965 6 per cent of the total enrolment of 3 million black pupils in eleven southern states were in schools with white pupils. The figure had risen to 18 per cent by 1968. The South had abandoned legal segregation but, as the experience of the North had shown, this did not necessarily produce a true racial mix. There was a great deal of opposition from both whites and blacks to the use of buses to integrate schools, and when black pupils did join white schools they were often not treated equally. In addition, a large number of white pupils left the public (state) school system in favour of private schooling.

A further factor that achieved prominence in the mid-1960s was the poverty and lack of opportunity of those blacks who lived in the centre of the big cities. The slowness in dealing with this and other problems involving white–black relations, together with a restlessness and atmosphere of protest caused by the anti-Vietnam war demonstrations, resulted in the leadership of the Civil Rights Movement gradually moving from moderates to militants. The ideal of integration and non-violence was abandoned by many in favour of separation and force.

The first problem facing Johnson early in 1965 was how to secure the blacks' right to vote in southern states. In one area of Alabama, for example, only 900 out of 87,000 resident blacks were registered voters. Attempts by blacks to be placed on the voters' register were subjected to delays and harassment. Black demonstrations were broken up by the police with an apparent excessive use of force, and in March a white woman working for civil rights was shot by four members of the Ku Klux Klan. Johnson introduced new legislation which provided federal intervention to ensure that black voters were registered. In his speech on this occasion he used effectively the title of the Civil Rights Movement song of protest 'We Shall Overcome'.

In August 1965 there occurred probably the worst riots in the United States this century. For four days uncontrolled mobs, consisting mainly of blacks, burnt and looted buildings and shot at police and civilians in the Watts district of Los Angeles. Troops were sent in and gradually imposed order. Thirty-four people were killed, 800 seriously injured and $100 million of damage caused. A commission of inquiry attributed the cause to black unemployment, and recommended job training, improved public transport to reduce the isolation of citizens of central areas of cities, and better education.

During the next two summers there was similar violence. In 1967 riots affected seventy cities with many people killed and injured. Black feeling was indicated at a conference held in 1967 when a resolution was passed calling for the splitting of the United States into two nations, one white and one black. One delegate said, 'Black people do not want to be absorbed into the white community'. A report by the National Advisory Committee on Civil Disorders concluded that of all the causes of the 1967 disturbances 'the most fundamental is the racial attitude and behaviour of white Americans towards black Americans'. In 1967, too, there was little progress with social reforms, and a new Civil Rights Bill failed to get through Congress.

In April 1968 Dr Martin Luther King, the black civil rights leader, was murdered.[1] He was in Memphis, Tennessee, organising support for dustmen on strike, when he was shot dead while standing on the balcony of his hotel. Since organising the bus boycott in Alabama, King had become a civil rights leader of international repute, and in 1964 he was awarded the Nobel Peace Prize. But he was opposed, not only by white diehards, but increasingly by black militants who thought his principles of non-violence to be ineffective. The assassination led to a wave of riots, looting and arson throughout the United States.

One reason both for the slowness in dealing with civil rights and the violence of that movement, was Vietnam. It is probable that Kennedy never gave his full attention to Vietnam, and similarly in 1964 and 1965 Johnson mainly concentrated on civil rights and the anti-poverty programme. However, Americans found themselves more and more involved in Vietnam, and the issue dominated American political life in the second half of the 1960s. Johnson's policies (see pp. 497–9) were at first supported by the vast majority, and perhaps throughout had the backing of most Americans as he attempted to steer a middle road between the hawks, who wanted a full-scale invasion of North Vietnam, and the doves who wanted American withdrawal from South Vietnam. However, the opposition grew, mainly based in the universities. In 1967 4,000 university teachers signed an advertisement in the *New York Times* headed 'Mr President, Stop the Bombing'. Leading Democrats, including Senator Robert Kennedy, the brother of the late President, publicly urged Johnson to stop the bombing of North Vietnam. Anti-war demonstrations increased in size and significance; on one occasion demonstrators occupied the corridors of the Pentagon, the headquarters of the American Armed Forces, and many young Americans sought to avoid being drafted into the armed forces.[2]

Johnson gradually lost his earlier popularity and seemed to become isolated and out of touch with Americans. In March 1968 he decided not to stand as a candidate for a second term of office. A struggle then followed for the Democratic nomination, a struggle tragically ended by the second assassination of 1968: in June, Robert Kennedy was shot by a Jordanian Arab while speaking to a crowd of supporters at a hotel

---

[1] Dr King's mother was shot dead in 1974 while playing the organ in a church in Georgia.

[2] The most well-known of these was Cassius Clay, or Mohammed Ali, as he was later known, world heavy-weight boxing champion, who was sentenced to five years' imprisonment.

in Los Angeles. His elder brother had been killed at Dallas five years before. A chaotic Democratic Party Convention was held in Chicago. Outside large crowds of anti-Vietnam demonstrators were involved in violent clashes with an apparently over-aggressive police force. The Vice-President, Humphrey, emerged as the Democratic candidate.

The Republicans chose Richard Nixon. The result was close, each candidate gaining 43 per cent of the popular vote. In the electoral college, however, Nixon had a clear majority.

President Nixon 1969 to 1974

Nixon was aged 56 when he became President. He had had long and successful experience of politics. Qualifying and then practising as a lawyer in California, he served in the navy during the war. In 1946 he was elected to the House of Representatives where he helped to draft the Taft-Hartley Act which reduced the power of trade unions, and played an important part in the hunt for Communists in government service. In 1950 he was elected to the Senate and three years later became Vice-President. In this office he travelled extensively and because of Eisenhower's ill-health, undertook more important duties than are usual for a Vice-President. Narrowly defeated by Kennedy in the 1960 presidential election, he then resigned his law practice, again travelling widely and working vigorously for the Republican Party. Nixon was a man of conservative views: he disliked federal intervention, wanted active involvement by the United States in world affairs, and put emphasis on law and order rather than civil rights. In character he was a somewhat enigmatic and lonely introvert, and was never popular.

During Nixon's Administration there were important developments in foreign policy: the reversal of US policy towards China, the loosening of ties with Japan, the detente with Russia, developments in Vietnam and the Middle East. These are dealt with elsewhere. Dr Henry Kissinger was of particular importance in foreign affairs. He was Nixon's assistant for national security affairs, but largely overshadowed Rogers, the Secretary of State.

Vietnam continued to dominate American politics. In 1970 four students were shot dead by police during a demonstration at Kent State University, Ohio, against US involvement in Vietnam and Cambodia. In April 1971 200,000 people marched on Washington in a demonstration against the Vietnam war. In the same month the sentence of life imprisonment imposed on an American serviceman, Lt Calley, for the massacre of Vietnamese civilians at a village called

My Lai, exposed the pressures under which American soldiers served. In June 1971 the Pentagon Papers, a summary of some documents officially classified as top secret, were published in the *New York Times*. It was alleged that they had been given to the newspaper by Dr Daniel Ellsberg, a former official of the State Department. Despite opposition from the government, the Supreme Court said that publication was legal. The documents were a study of American policy towards Indo-China, and were commissioned in 1967 by Robert McNamara, then Secretary for Defence. The articles shocked and surprised Americans because of the discrepancy they revealed between what actually happened and what the public was told happened. It was clear, for example, that concern for the Vietnamese people had had low priority among the reasons for continuing America's involvement in Vietnam.

As the Nixon Administration began, there were signs that the period of expansion of the economy was coming to an end. In 1969 inflation was 6 per cent and industrial production decreased. Nixon had the difficult job of trying to reduce inflation while avoiding too sudden a slowdown in demand. 1970 was a dismal year for the economy with no real growth and both inflation and unemployment reaching 6 per cent. There were many strikes and some major businesses collapsed. Early in 1971 the bankruptcy of the famous British firm Rolls Royce threatened to bankrupt also the American Lockheed Aircraft Corporation whose airbus programme was dependent on the Rolls Royce RB211 engine. Consequently in 1971 there was a sudden and dramatic reversal of economic policy: amongst a packet of economic measures was a 10 per cent surcharge on imports, and a 90-day freeze on wages and prices. In 1972 the economic position improved when both inflation and unemployment were reduced, and industrial production and investment increased.

The achievement in space continued. In July 1969 the moon trip of the previous December was repeated, but this time Neil Armstrong and Edwin Aldrin landed on the surface of the moon. At 3.56 (British Standard Time) on 21 July, Armstrong stepped down from the lunar module on to the moon. Six hundred million people watching on television heard him say, 'I'm going to step off the LM now. That's one small step for a man, one giant leap for mankind.' The two men collected rock samples and carried out a number of experiments. There was a further moon landing later that year. Twelve astronauts, all American, have so far walked on the moon's surface.

The Americans had been brilliantly successful. President Kennedy had launched the Apollo programme as an answer to Russia's successes.

President Nixon (right) and Brezhnev, the Soviet leader, during part of the SALT negotiations in 1973.

Buzz Aldrin on the moon, 1969

He wanted to galvanise American science and engineering and raise American prestige, but also saw the programme as an adventure and challenge, and as a peaceful and constructive form of international competition. The result was a remarkable achievement in applied science and organisation. Furthermore, man had also looked at the earth from outside its orbit, and this had given him a new perspective. However, the programme was extremely expensive: it had diverted resources and expertise away from the problems of the earth and had brought no immediate benefits—for example, no mineral resources worth mining were found on the moon. After 1972 the programme continued with orbiting space laboratories.

There was little domestic legislation during Nixon's Administration. The President was by nature unsympathetic to social legislation, and he concentrated mainly on economic and foreign policy and, after 1972, on Watergate. In addition, existing large government deficits meant there was little money for social measures, and large Democratic majorities in both Houses of Congress were unsympathetic to much that a Republication President presented to them. The Civil Rights Movement became much less prominent.

In the 1972 election campaign Nixon was opposed by McGovern. Nixon appeared moderate and statesmanlike, and there was a reaction against demonstrators and those who disturbed law and order. Consequently, the political centre supported Nixon who was re-elected with a much increased majority.

The period from November 1972 to August 1974 was completely dominated by the Watergate Affair. In June 1972 five men were caught red-handed, with cameras and electronic bugging gear for tapping telephones, in the Watergate office building in Washington, head-quarters of the Democratic Party. This was at the height of the presidential election campaign. Two months later these five, and two others from the Committee for the Re-election of the President (CREEP) were charged with conspiracy to bug telephones. At the time the matter aroused relatively little interest and certainly had no effect on Nixon's election campaign.

In January 1973 the trial of the seven men was held in Washington before Judge Sirica. Two of the men were former White House officials and one, McCord, was a member of CREEP and also an official in the Central Intelligence Agency. All seven were found guilty, but Judge Sirica said he had found difficulty in elucidating the facts and wanted further investigations. Therefore, he would not for the time being sentence the men, but the severity of the eventual sentences would depend on their cooperation. Next month the Senate decided to hold its own investigation, and a small committee was established under the chairmanship of Senator Ervin. In March McCord told both Judge Sirica and the Senate Committee that there was political pressure on the seven men to remain silent. He also said that Mitchell, the Attorney General from 1969 to 1972 and then Nixon's election campaign manager, had personally approved the bugging plans, and that a number of the President's closest aides had prior knowledge of the plot, including Haldeman, Nixon's chief of staff, and Dean, the President's chief legal counsel.

Nixon's response to these allegations was to say that 'no one presently employed' in his administration was involved, but he refused to allow his staff to appear before the Senate Committee and the allegations continued amidst growing criticism of Nixon. In April 1973 Mitchell admitted he was aware of the Watergate bugging but had opposed it. Nixon now said there was evidence of a cover-up. At the end of the month Haldeman resigned and Dean was dismissed. The Attorney-General was given authority by Nixon to appoint a special prosecutor (Professor Cox of Harvard University) to investigate the whole matter. The President said he had known nothing of the cover-up until the previous month (March 1973). This statement was repeated several times in succeeding weeks.

In May 1973 the Senate Committee began public hearings (known popularly as 'The Sam Ervin Show'), and in June Dean testified before it. He alleged that on several occasions before March 1973 he had had conversations with Nixon about concealing the White House involvement in the Watergate break-in. Dean referred in detail to conversations in which money was offered in return for silence. This was denied by the White House: Mitchell and Haldeman both said that Nixon was ignorant of the cover-up. Up to this point there was no evidence to prove or substantiate any of the accusations made. It seemed clear that there had been a conspiracy, but it was not clear whether the President had been involved in it.

Then in July 1973 it became known that Nixon had tape-recorded his conversations with every visitor to the White House, as well as all telephone calls. It seemed that these vital tapes would provide the corroborative evidence, and all three investigators—the Senate Committee, Professor Cox and Judge Sirica—asked to hear the part of the tapes relevant to their enquiries. But Nixon refused: the tapes were confidential, and anyway would not settle matters. The matter eventually went to the Federal Appeal Court who in October ruled against Nixon and ordered him to hand over the tapes. Nixon dismissed Professor Cox, who had refused to accept a summary of the tapes. However, the public outcry was so great that the President gave in. Nixon agreed to hand over to Judge Sirica the nine tapes that had been requested. A month later seven tapes[1] were handed over. The remaining two did not exist because, Nixon said, they had never been made.

During 1973 three other events served to increase the criticism of the President. Firstly, at the trial of Dr Ellsberg, who was charged with stealing the Pentagon Papers and giving them to the *New York Times,* a former assistant to John Ehrlichman, one of Nixon's closest advisers, admitted breaking into the office of Ellsberg's psychiatrist hoping to use mental health records against Ellsberg. Secondly, after allegations that businessmen had made secret contributions to Nixon's election campaign fund, a joint committee of Congress decided to examine all aspects of Nixon's tax affairs. Thirdly, in August 1973 Vice-President Spiro Agnew was accused of bribery and tax fraud during the 1960s. After being fined and placed on probation in October, Agnew resigned. He was replaced by Mr Gerald Ford, the Republican leader in the House of Representatives.

Despite Nixon's efforts to divert public attention to other issues, the pressure from the legal system on the President to hand over all the remaining tapes was maintained in 1974. In April Nixon issued his own transcript of the tapes, but some tapes remained 'missing', the transcripts raised more questions than they answered, and in addition they aroused serious doubts about the manner and style of the deliberations of the nation's leaders. Nixon continued to maintain that he had no knowledge of the Watergate break-in before it occurred, and had no knowledge of the cover-up until March 1973.

In July 1974 matters came to a head. The House of Representatives issued its own transcript of the White House tapes, and its version showed damaging variations on Nixon's own edition. Then the Supreme Court unanimously voted to order the President to surrender all missing tapes and papers to the Special Prosecutor. Nixon complied with this. Finally the Judiciary Committee of the House of Representatives voted to recommend that President Nixon be impeached for obstructing justice. On 5 August Nixon for the first time admitted that he had held back information about Watergate, and said that he knew about the cover-up five days after the break-in. In the face of otherwise certain impeachment, President Nixon resigned on 9 August 1974.

While it lasted the Watergate affair was clearly of major importance.

[1] One of the seven was inaudible for 18 minutes because of a mistake made by the President's secretary.

It is too early to estimate its longer-term significance. The affair completely dominated politics for 18 months and led to the resignation of an American President half way through his period of office. It damaged the political and moral authority of the presidency, and created an impression of general ruthlessness in the pursuit of political aims. But more especially Watergate triggered off an explosion of disillusionment with American government, already under attack for its Vietnam policies and the way these had been conducted. In addition, Watergate was an indication of the power of the press, since a major part in uncovering the affair was played by two reporters of the *Washington Post*, Carl Bernstein and Bob Woodward.[1]

President Ford 1974 to 1977

Nixon was succeeded by the man he had appointed as Vice-President only nine months before. Gerald Ford thus became President of the United States without being elected either to that office or the vice-presidency. Rockefeller, the millionaire, became the new Vice-President, Dr Kissinger remained as Secretary of State, and by the end of 1974 new appointments had been made to all the major positions on the White House staff. After the crisis of Watergate, it was an orderly succession and confirmed the basic strength of American institutions.

In September 1974 President Ford granted his predecessor a full pardon for all offences he may have committed in office. Despite the inevitable protests at this decision, it was taken with the object of ending the Watergate affair as quickly as possible: a trial of an ex-president of the United States would have distracted attention from other more important issues. The economy was suffering from worldwide recession. Unemployment was high despite huge budget deficits and serious inflation. There were major problems in foreign affairs: in 1975 a Communist offensive led to the collapse of South Vietnam and the end of the war; the consequent strength of isolationism in the United States contributed to the neglect of events in southern Africa; despite Dr Kissinger's efforts stalemate seemed to have been reached once again in the Middle East. In addition the publication in 1975 of a report that the American CIA (Central Intelligence Agency) had plotted to kill foreign leaders (for example, Lumumba of Congo and Castro of Cuba) was described by Kissinger as a foreign policy disaster. Allegations of bribery by American firms seeking foreign business,

[1] The uncovering of Watergate has been made into a popular film entitled *All the President's Men*.

and the near bankruptcy of New York, added to the general feeling of disillusionment and lack of confidence.

Ford's achievement during this period was to provide honest and respectable government after the Nixon regime. He was a safe and reassuring figure, an embodiment of all the decent virtues and therefore respected. However, he was a Republican President and was opposed on most important issues by a Congress which had large Democratic majorities in both Houses. Basic distrust and differences over policy threatened to paralyse the government's capacity for action. In addition 1976 was election year, not a good time for major initiatives by government. Ford stood as the Republican candidate, but, perhaps inevitably after all that had happened under a Republican administration, was defeated in November by Jimmy Carter, the Governor of Georgia, who became the next Democratic President in January 1977. When Ford went out of office, Dr Henry Kissinger, the Secretary of State, went with him. He had managed American foreign policy for eight years, and had preserved the government's authority abroad after its loss at home. Kissinger was almost alone in being a point of stability in American affairs. His achievements were considerable.

6

Great Britain

Beginning of the Twentieth Century

The population of Great Britain (that is, England, Wales and Scotland) in 1900 was 37 million. Ireland, the whole of which was then ruled from London, contained a further $4\frac{1}{2}$ million. Despite the slums and poverty[1] which were common in town and country, no nation in the world enjoyed a higher standard of living. The lives of the upper and middle classes were leisurely and secure, and the growing number of skilled workers were relatively prosperous. Education was compulsory up to the age of twelve. This was provided by School Boards and voluntary bodies, while the best secondary education was given by the public schools. Technical and university education was expanding.

The high standard of living was based on Britain's long pre-eminence in industrial production. For a century Britain had been the 'workshop of the world', exporting large quantities of cotton goods, woollens, worsteds, linen, machinery, coal, iron and steel. In 1900, however, there were significant signs of decline. During the last quarter of the nineteenth century the United States and Germany first equalled and then shot ahead of Britain in steel production. The industry of these two countries was more up to date and efficient both in techniques and organisation. Hostile foreign tariffs were limiting sales of some British goods abroad, while the increase in exports of ships and machinery only meant that foreigners would ultimately need fewer British goods and services. The most important technological inventions were coming from abroad. For example, Europe led Britain in motor-car engineering and in the electrical industry. In addition, British agriculture was suffering from the competition of cheap prairie wheat. These points demon-

[1] In 1899 Rowntree found that 28 per cent of the population of York earned less than the amount necessary to satisfy essential needs.

strate the relative decline of Britain. In absolute terms she had never been more prosperous. Her industry was at full stretch, she was the world's biggest exporter of manufactured goods, and her ships carried a large proportion of the world's trade.

This economically powerful state was the capital of an Empire larger than any in the world's history. A quarter of the land surface and population of the world was controlled from London, and was guarded by a powerful navy and by an army strong enough to be successful against poorly armed and organised Africans and Asians. Much of this enormous area had been acquired in the last quarter of the nineteenth century, and 1900 was the heyday of an aggressive and truculent imperialism. Writers, such as R. L. Stevenson and Rudyard Kipling, who became a sort of unofficial spokesman for Britain's 'imperial destiny', were very popular. Kipling coined the phrase the 'White Man's Burden', and he tried to give a moral purpose to British imperialists who had a duty, he believed, to rule 'lesser breeds without the law'.

The appeal of imperialism was not universal. Between 1899 and 1902 the Boer War was fought (see chapter 8), and the new Labour Party and an important section of the Liberals regarded this war, in Lloyd George's words, as 'an outrage, perpetrated in the name of human freedom'. But critics were few, and public opinion, especially in London, was on the side of Cecil Rhodes.

At this time six states of the Empire enjoyed internal self-government: Australia, New Zealand, Canada, Newfoundland, Cape Colony and Natal. One other part of the Empire—Ireland—had been actively seeking this status for thirty years. Twice, in 1886 and 1893, Gladstone, the leader of the Liberal Party, had introduced Bills to give Home Rule to Ireland, but on both occasions he had been defeated by the Conservatives and a section of the Liberals who regarded Ireland as an integral part of the United Kingdom.

The head of this huge Empire was Queen Victoria, a dignified and popular constitutional monarch. She died in January 1901 after a reign of sixty-four years. Thus the Queen and the old century died together, and her death was widely thought to be the end of an epoch. She was succeeded by Edward VII, a widely travelled and broadminded man who was to have an important influence behind the scenes in politics. He came to symbolise the more emancipated Edwardian age—ostentatious, self-confident and opulent.

The relatively peaceful achievement of parliamentary democracy and a system of impartial justice are two of the outstanding features of British history. In 1900 Parliament consisted of the monarch, the House of Lords, in which sat all the peers of the realm, and the House of

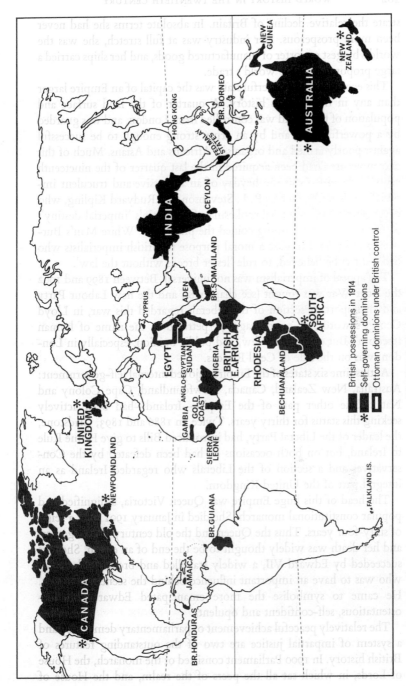

The British Empire in 1914

Commons which contained 670 members representing constituencies throughout the United Kingdom. About half the men of the country provided the electorate. The House of Lords was apparently powerful because it had to agree to all Bills before they could become law, but for over 300 years real power had rested with the House of Commons.

There were four main parties: Conservatives, Liberals, Irish National-ists and Socialists. The Conservatives received support from the landed and Church interest, half the middle class and from many of the work-ing class. Apart from a three-year break in the early 1890s they had provided the government since 1885. Lord Salisbury had been prime minister at the head of a strong cabinet since 1895. The Liberals were the other main party in the country, but they were weakened by a split over the issue of Home Rule for Ireland. Those who opposed Home Rule were known as the Unionists and had joined the Conservatives. There were about eighty Irish Nationalists in the House of Commons and they supported the Liberals.

The Labour Party was formed in February 1900. Socialist ideas spread rapidly towards the end of the nineteenth century. There was growing literacy and, with the development of the cheap press, interest in politics. Socialists in Germany and socialists on local councils in Britain had been successful. In addition, trade unionism had grown enormously in the 1890s following the success of the London Dock Strike in 1889. So the feeling grew that the working class could improve its conditions if it had stronger representation in Parliament. In 1900, therefore, three socialist societies and the Trades Union Congress met and set up the Labour Representation Committee. This had TUC financial support and its object was to send Labour MPs to Parliament. Its secretary was Ramsay MacDonald who became the dominant force in deciding the party's strategy, organisation and policy.

1900 to 1914

Conservative Government 1900 to 1905

The causes and events of the Boer War are dealt with in chapter 8. The Conservative government was criticised not only for the situation which produced the war, but also for the conduct of the war itself. Military planning was regarded as poor, the internment camps as unworthy of a civilised nation, and the cost of the war—over £200 million and 22,000 deaths, mainly from disease—as extremely heavy. After the war trade unionists particularly disliked what they called 'Chinese slavery'— the import of Chinese workers to run the mines in the Transvaal.

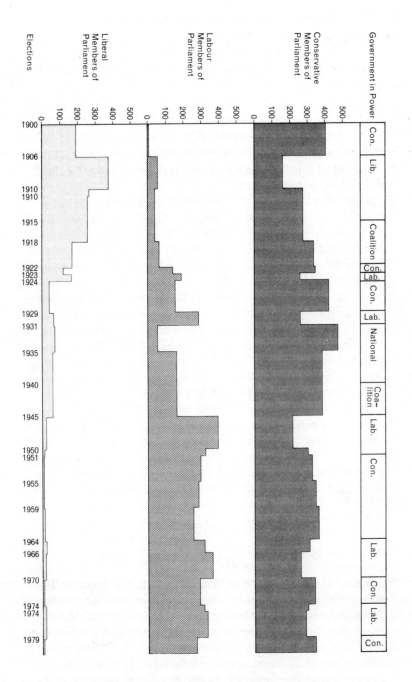

Governments and political parties in Britain: 1900–1979

Shortly after the Boer War ended (1902), Lord Salisbury resigned as prime minister. Churchill described him as 'an able and obstinate man, who joins the brain of a statesman to the delicate susceptibilities of a mule'. A calm and wise international statesman, he had no real domestic policy. He was succeeded by his nephew, A. J. Balfour. 'A languid, lazy, lackadaisical cynic', according to Churchill, Balfour was rather aloof and on the whole believed in the minimum of change.

Balfour was responsible, however, for one major constructive piece of domestic legislation which he pushed through Parliament at the cost of some unpopularity—the Education Act of 1902.

Board schools provided primary education and the universities were expanding, but state secondary education was badly needed. A test case had shown that secondary education in Board schools was illegal, and therefore Balfour decided to introduce a Bill not merely to legalise this form of education but to reform the complete system. School Boards were abolished, and county and borough councils through their education committees were to be responsible in their areas for education from infant school to university entrance level. Voluntary schools, often owned by religious groups, were to be partly financed from the rates and partly controlled by the local authorities. There was opposition from nonconformists who had the support of the Liberals in their dislike of Anglican and Roman Catholic schools receiving public money. Nevertheless, the Bill was passed and resulted in a big expansion of secondary education.

No other domestic Bills of importance were passed. The government refused to legislate on the powers of the trade unions. In 1900 the Taff Vale Railway Company had sued the Railway Union for damages (that is, loss of income) during a strike, and won its case. This virtually took away union power to strike by making it too damaging financially. Labour Party support grew enormously in the campaign to reverse the Taff Vale decision. There was an important change in foreign policy— the decision to abandon 'splendid isolation' and seek friends in an increasingly hostile Europe (see chapter 1).

The major controversy between 1903 and 1905 concerned Joseph Chamberlain's policy of Tariff Reform. Chamberlain (1836–1914) had entered Parliament as a radical Liberal, but he opposed Liberal policy of Home Rule for Ireland and together with other Liberal Unionists joined the Conservative Party. As Colonial Secretary after 1895, he believed it very important to unify the scattered empire. Since the prime ministers of the independent colonies refused to agree to any unified political organisation, the alternative was some form of economic unity. The colonies, who wanted to build up their own industries, opposed free trade within the Empire but agreed to British imperial preference. This meant lower or no duties on British imports from the colonies. However, since Britain was a free trade country, a policy of imperial preference would involve placing customs duties on foreign (that is, non-Empire) imports.

During 1903 Chamberlain spoke in opposition to free trade and in favour of imperial preference, and eventually resigned from the government in order to campaign for tariff reform. He argued that tariff reform would unify an Empire which provided a big market for British manufactured goods, that customs duties would end unemployment by reducing competition from foreign industry—this was very attractive to British industrialists—and tariffs would provide revenue which could be used for social reform. Opposition to tariff reform came from the Liberals and many Conservatives. They argued that free trade as the traditional policy was in itself good, and that tariffs on the import of foreign food would raise food prices.

The issue split the Conservative cabinet, but Balfour kept the party together longer than many thought possible. However, in December 1905 Balfour resigned, hoping the Liberals would split over personalities in forming a cabinet. But Campbell-Bannerman, the Liberal leader, immediately became Prime Minister and formed a strong government. In January 1906 an exciting general election campaign produced a sweeping victory for the Liberals who won 377 seats. The Conservatives were reduced in number to 157, two-thirds of whom were supporters of Chamberlain. The Irish Nationalists returned 83, but the particularly significant result was the election of 53 Labour MPs.

The Liberals, therefore, had a clear majority of 84. They had won for a number of reasons: the conduct of the Boer War, some of the terms of the Education Act, the lack of social reform, and particularly the failure to do anything about the Taff Vale judgment, the Liberal support for free trade with its emphasis on cheap food, and finally the general swing to the left in politics after ten years of Conservative government.

Liberal Government 1905 to 1914

Members of the Government   The Prime Minister from 1905 to 1908 was Campbell-Bannerman, a shrewd, patient and firm Scot. Sir Edward Grey was Foreign Secretary—British foreign policy is described in chapter 1—and H. H. Asquith was Chancellor of the Exchequer. Asquith (1852–1928) was the son of a Yorkshire wool manufacturer.

Educated at Oxford, he became a barrister and was elected to Parliament in 1886. A cool and rational man with a great belief in his own intellectual and social superiority, he was authoritative in the Commons and had a 'keen delving mind, with incisive powers of speech'.

The President of the Board of Trade in Campbell-Bannerman's cabinet was Lloyd George (1863–1945). His father was a schoolteacher who died when Lloyd George was a baby, and he was brought up by his mother and her brother, a shoemaker and an ardent Baptist. Lloyd George was educated at an elementary school in North Wales, and was always conscious of his humble beginnings. He trained as a solicitor and was elected to Parliament in 1890 for Caernarvon. He held the seat for 55 years. 'This fiery, mercurial, twisty, formidable little Celt',[1] with his quick mind and jaunty air, was a brilliant politician and an inspiring speaker whose speeches were a mixture of oratory and hard-hitting wit. It has been said that 'Lloyd George supplied Liberalism with driving force: Asquith kept it controlled and intelligent'.[2]

One of the other leading members of the government was Winston Churchill (1874–1965) who was to become one of the great statesmen of the twentieth century. The son of Lord Randolph Churchill, he was born at Blenheim Palace and was educated at Harrow where he was 'obstinate, rebellious and mischievous' and an indifferent scholar. He then went to Sandhurst and between 1895 and 1900 took part in fighting in Cuba, the north-west frontier of India, the Sudan and South Africa where, as a war correspondent, he was taken prisoner by the Boers only to escape soon after. In 1900 he was elected to Parliament as a Conservative, his policy being reform at home and imperialism abroad. In 1904 he joined the Liberals on the issue of free trade.

In 1908 Campbell-Bannerman resigned (he died soon after) and was succeeded as Prime Minister by Asquith. Lloyd George then became Chancellor of the Exchequer and Churchill became President of the Board of Trade (later Home Secretary and then First Lord of the Admiralty).

Social legislation The Liberal government was responsible for four pieces of social legislation which became foundations of the present welfare state. Two acts were passed which provided for the school meals service and the medical inspection of school children. In 1908 non-contributory old-age pensions were started: a pension of 5s per week was given to poor people over the age of 70. Then in 1911 the National Insurance Act was passed. Contributions from the employee

---

[1] *The Times*, 17 Jan. 1963.
[2] A. Briggs, *Edwardian England, 1901–14*, ed. S. Nowell-Smith.

(4*d*), the employer (3*d*) and the state (2*d*) provided for insurance against unemployment and sickness. There was intense opposition to this from the Conservatives.[1]

The House of Lords After 1906 the defeated Conservatives decided to use their majority in the House of Lords to block Liberal legislation. A series of important Bills were rejected by the Lords who were warned by Campbell-Bannerman in 1907 that their attitude would lead to a reduction in their powers. The Conservatives persisted in their policy, however, and a crisis was reached in 1909. In that year Lloyd George introduced his People's Budget which was designed to raise revenue for defence and the new social services. Income tax, death duties, and the tax on tobacco and spirits were raised, and supertax and petrol and motor licence taxation were introduced. In addition there was to be a tax on any increase in the value of property when it changed hands.

Encouraged by Harmsworth's newspapers (the *Daily Mail* and the *Daily Mirror*), the Conservatives opposed the Budget intensely. They regarded it as a deliberate attack on the upper classes and the thin end of a socialist wedge. In November 1909 the Budget was passed by the Commons but was rejected by the Lords. The long tradition that the Lords did not oppose finance Bills was broken, and the House of Commons condemned their action as 'a breach of the Constitution and a usurpation of the rights of the Commons'. Parliament was then dissolved and a general election held to test the opinion of the country. The election of January 1910 gave the Liberals a majority of two over the Conservatives (275–273), but this majority was increased by the support the Liberals received from the Irish (82) and Labour (40).

In April 1910 the House of Lords passed the Budget, and the Commons began consideration of the Parliament Bill to reduce the power of the Lords. The big issue during the rest of the year was whether and how the House of Lords should be reformed. A succession of meetings between the parties was held but with no agreement. Meanwhile Edward VII died and was succeeded by George V. Asquith obtained from the new king the promise that if a second general election produced similar support for the Liberals, then he would create sufficient Liberal peers to obtain a majority over the Conservatives in the Lords. In December 1910 a second general election produced an almost identical result and in the following May the House of Commons passed the Parliament Bill. There were three main terms: all money Bills were to

[1] For example, a meeting was held at the Albert Hall when duchesses exhorted servant girls not to 'lick stamps'.

be passed by the House of Lords within one month of receiving them; other Bills, if passed by the Commons in three successive sessions, must become law within two years of their first introduction in the Commons; general elections were to be held at least once every five years. Despite diehard opposition the Lords, in view of the threat to create Liberal peers, passed the Parliament Bill in August 1911.

Labour legislation　On the prompting of the Labour Party, the Liberal government passed the Trades Disputes Act in 1906. This reversed the Taff Vale decision by saying that a trade union was not liable to damages caused by a strike. Three years later, however, the position of the Labour Party itself seemed threatened by the Osborne Judgment. A railwayman named Osborne was upheld by the courts in his objection to the compulsory levy exacted by his union for Labour Party funds. Since voluntary payments were small, Labour Party funds were consequently greatly reduced and this particularly affected the salaries of Labour MPs. However, in 1911 an act was passed providing a salary of £400 a year for all MPs, and in 1913 another act was passed by which a trade union could set up a political fund so long as members were not forced to contribute to it. An additional piece of legislation was that establishing labour exchanges in 1909.

Strikes　There was intense labour unrest during the four years before the First World War. Between 1909 and 1913 the cost of living rose by 9 per cent while wages remained stationary, and the disparity between rich and poor was more obvious than ever. The feeling grew that Parliament was not representative of the nation, for, although the working class was strong in the country, it was weak in Parliament. The ideas of French syndicalism were influential: these were that direct and violent action by the trade unions was likely to be more effective than working through Parliament which was too slow. The trade unions had many examples of direct action before them at this time: the duchesses who threatened to disobey the law on national insurance; the House of Lords' undemocratic rejection of the budget; the suffragettes; the Conservative Party over Ireland.

　In consequence there were two years of major strikes between 1910 and 1912. Railwaymen, cotton workers, boilermakers and coalminers were on strike in 1910. The seamen and firemen won their case and strikes of lower paid workers, including the London dockers, continued. These strikes were often accompanied by rioting and violence. In 1914 a Triple Alliance was formed of miners, railwaymen and transport workers to oppose the employers, and the situation was ominous when, perhaps fortunately, the First World War intervened.

The suffragettes Another of the militant sectional groups of this period were the suffragettes who wanted women to have the vote. Women were now educated and they regarded the vote as a symbol of equality with men. In 1903 Mrs Emmeline Pankhurst founded the Women's Social and Political Union with the object of campaigning for women to be given the suffrage. The Liberal Government were divided on the issue, but decided that since the country did not yet show much interest in the subject and since they were planning other important legislation, the question should be postponed.

In 1907 Parliament did pass legislation allowing women to enter local government. However, this was not satisfactory to the suffragettes who began a campaign to win publicity for their views. Demonstrations, window breaking, women chaining themselves to railings, imprisonment and hunger strikes: these were the methods in the first phase of the suffragettes' campaign. During 1912 greater violence was used. Schools, empty houses, a railway station, a grandstand and pavilions were burned down; letters in letterboxes were set on fire; telephone wires were cut, pictures in public galleries slashed, the orchid-houses at Kew destroyed, the British Museum and the Tower of London were attacked; and the climax came when a suffragette was killed when she threw herself under the King's horse at the Derby.

The campaign certainly attracted public interest but not support, and women's suffrage which came in 1918 was based on the constructive work of women during the war rather than on these destructive tactics.

Ireland In 1912 the Liberal government decided that a third attempt should be made to give Home Rule to Ireland. The Parliament Act of 1911 meant that the House of Lords could now only hold up legislation for two years. In addition the Irish were now more prosperous and the Irish MPs at Westminster were much less extreme. In view of the success of events in South Africa (see chapter 8) the belief grew that Redmond, the Irish leader, would be an Irish Botha, moderate and pro-British.

In April 1912 therefore, a Bill was introduced in the Commons which provided for a federal system of government with a Parliament in Ireland and 42 Irish MPs continuing to attend Westminster. But opposition came from Ulster which included the six northern counties of Ireland. This area was the richest part of Ireland and also was largely Protestant in religion while the other three-quarters of the country was

Roman Catholic. Ulster refused to contemplate the idea of being ruled from Dublin by Redmond and intended to oppose Home Rule by force.

The leader of the Ulster MPs in the House of Commons was Sir Edward Carson In 1911 Carson addressed a huge rally in Ulster and said that if a Home Rule Bill was passed, then Ulster would set up a provisional government and defy Dublin. To back this threat up, Ulster began to organise a Volunteer Force in 1912 which numbered 80,000 when the Home Rule Bill was introduced. The government made no attempt to stop this. Ulster was supported by the Conservative Party which had, since the resignation of Balfour in 1911, been led by Bonar Law (1858–1923), a rich Scottish businessman who tried to keep control of the extremists in his party by supporting them. In July 1912 Law said, 'I can imagine no length of resistance to which Ulster will go, which I shall not be ready to support.' The Conservatives opposed this breakup of the United Kingdom, and when the Bill was passed by the House of Commons it was rejected by the Lords. It was clear, however, that the enactment of the Bill in two years' time would precipitate extremely serious trouble from Ulster.

In November 1913 Law appealed to the British army to disobey orders if it was told to force Ulster to accept rule from Dublin, and in the following March the officers in the army stationed at Curragh refused to move against Ulster. Again the government took no action against these officers. In April 1914 huge quantities of arms were landed on the Larne coast and were distributed to the Ulster Volunteers. In July similar gunrunning armed the Irish Volunteers who had been formed in southern Ireland. The threat of a violent civil war which might not be confined to Ireland was therefore very serious.

Possible compromises were suggested and rejected: that Ulster should be excluded from Ireland with possible inclusion later; that the Bill should be postponed from coming into force in Ulster for six years; that Ulster should exclude herself from Ireland by plebiscite. It was generally thought that Ireland without Ulster could not pay its way and therefore partition was ruled out. Various conferences were held including a final one at Buckingham Palace, but all failed. Then the First World War intervened, and in September 1914 the Irish Home Rule Bill was passed with an act suspending its operation until after the war.

Economic history 1900 to 1914

There were many indications of progress during this period. There was a considerable increase in trade which was carried by the biggest merchant fleet in the world. Coal production in 1913 was 287 million tons, the largest amount ever produced, and there was increased use of electrical power. Investment overseas was very large. There was great progress in public health, and it began to be assumed that poverty could be alleviated. There were many signs of a better standard of living; more holidays and more travel by car, bicycle or train.

Britain's industrial development, however, was slower than Germany's or the United States', as the following table shows:

Increases per cent, 1893–1913			
	UK	Germany	US
Population	20	32	46
Coal production	75	159	210
Pig iron	50	287	337
Crude steel	136	522	715
Exports of raw materials	238	243	196
Exports of manufactures	121	239	563

There were two main reasons for Britain's relatively poor performance: British industry tended to be old-fashioned and inefficient, and foreign tariffs reduced British markets. Unemployment fluctuated round 4 per cent, and was mainly in southern England. Large numbers of people emigrated. Compared with later years the state continued to interfere little in people's lives and to play a small part in the economy. 'Even in 1914, with the welfare state initiated and the demands of defence becoming daily more pressing, Britain was spending more on alcohol than on all the services of the central government combined.'[1]

First World War 1914 to 1918

Asquith—Prime Minister August 1914 to December 1916

For the first nine months of the war the Liberal government continued in office, the only major change being that Kitchener was brought in as Secretary for War. However, in May 1915 the Conservatives and Socialists entered the government to form a coalition. Asquith remained Prime Minister and Lloyd George became Minister of Munitions. Opposition in Parliament then vanished until almost the end of the war.

At first it was thought that the war would be brief and life continued much as usual. By 1915, however, as the Western Front relapsed into stalemate, the war began to dominate life. The power of the state increased enormously; food was rationed, some industries were closed, licensing hours were limited (so that less time could be spent away from

[1] A. L. Taylor, *Edwardian England, 1901–14*, ed. S. Nowell-Smith.

the production of munitions), the press was censored, there was virtual government control of railways and the coal industry, strikes were made illegal, and there was a big increase in income tax. Lloyd George at the Ministry of Munitions showed enormous energy and was given great powers to provide arms for the army of 4 million which Kitchener recruited.

The Irish problem was temporarily shelved. There was little support for the war effort from southern Ireland, and at Easter 1916 a group of Irish Volunteers seized the General Post Office in Dublin. In four days of fighting against the British army hundreds of people were killed.

As the war progressed, there was increasing opposition to Asquith as Prime Minister. The losses at Jutland and in the Battle of the Somme, the sinkings by German submarines, the inadequate control over the economy, the poor coordination between the government and the armed forces, all led to the feeling that Asquith was not a suitable war leader. The obvious alternative was Lloyd George who had wide backing from the press, the country as a whole and the leadership of the Conservative Party. Most of the Cabinet supported Asquith. In December 1916 Asquith resigned deliberately[1] in the hope of outmanoeuvring his critics. He failed, and Lloyd George became Prime Minister.

Lloyd George—Prime Minister
December 1916 to November 1918

Lloyd George formed a War Cabinet of five: himself, Law, Henderson (Labour), Curzon and Milner. Smuts of South Africa and Carson later became members. The cabinet met every day and proved very efficient. An observer wrote in 1918: 'The effects of the change in direction two years ago may be compared to the substitution of dynamite for a damp squib.' Generally a more vigorous and consistent policy was followed. It has recently been said of Lloyd George: 'Vitality was the foundation of his influence on men and events. His personality was electric.'[2] Four new ministries were set up, and new men brought into the government. In May 1917 Churchill, who had resigned earlier over the Dardanelles affair, became Minister of Munitions. Lloyd George was responsible for the convoy system which ended the submarine menace, and he also tried to set up a unified command in France although without success until 1918. Lloyd George was supported by the Conservatives, the Labour Party and most backbench Liberals. But the more prominent Liberals led by Asquith distrusted him and refused more than a

[1] This is a controversial subject. Some historians believe that Asquith was driven from office and did not resign as a tactical manoeuvre. [2] *The Times*, 17 Jan. 1963.

grudging acquiescence. On one occasion in 1918 they opposed the government.

In June 1918 Parliament passed the Reform Act which gave the vote to all men over twenty-one (except peers, lunatics and criminals) and all women over thirty, subject to a property qualification. This added 2 million men and over 8 million women to the electorate. In addition seats were redistributed to form constituencies of roughly equal size.

Effect of the war

About three-quarters of a million men from the United Kingdom were killed in the First World War, and 1½ million were permanently disabled. There were particularly high losses among the able young men who were junior officers. The civilian population suffered little; indeed, life improved in that welfare services increased and unemployment vanished.

Material losses were small, with the exception of the sinking of 40 per cent of the merchant fleet which was soon replaced. The war cost about £9,000 million. Thirty per cent of this was met from taxes and nearly all the rest from loans; in consequence there was a huge increase in the National Debt. About 10 per cent (£550 million) of British investments abroad were sold, but there was a large amount of new investment. Britain borrowed £1,340 million from abroad and lent £1,825 million to her allies. In three particular respects Britain suffered: prices and wages in 1918 were almost double those of 1914; there was too little investment in some industries (for example, railways), and too much in others (for example, shipbuilding); the war impoverished some of Britain's customers and enriched some of her competitors, for example, the United States and Japan.

Between the Wars 1918 to 1939
Coalition Government 1918 to 1922

Parliament was dissolved a fortnight after the Armistice. No election had been held since 1910 and the 1918 Reform Act had doubled the electorate. Lloyd George wanted fresh electoral support before the Paris Peace Conference. He had hoped to continue the wartime coalition, but Labour insisted on leaving and the followers of Asquith did likewise. On the whole the election was a quiet one, and was largely a plebiscite on whether the electorate wanted Lloyd George to continue as Prime Minister. The electorate did. The coalition of Conservatives

(339) and Liberals (136) had a vast majority over the Asquith Liberals (26) and Labour (59). All the leading Socialists and followers of Asquith were defeated. There were also the Irish MPs who are referred to below. During most of 1919, while Lloyd George was in Paris, the War Cabinet of five still functioned. In October, however, a new coalition started to operate headed by Lloyd George with Bonar Law as deputy prime minister.

From the end of the war to the middle of 1920 Britain enjoyed an economic boom. Demobilisation was accomplished quickly, prices increased rapidly, large numbers of houses were built and some industries over-expanded. In 1920 insurance against unemployment was extended to about 12 million workers on the assumption that unemployment would be about 4 per cent. Mass unemployment was not expected. The world economy had not yet recovered from the dislocation of war, however, and in 1920 the postwar boom ended. The ending of controls on prices after the war produced great inflation (1914—100; 1920—323), and government spending was suddenly reduced. In 1922 the Geddes committee recommended further economies. Taxation was increased and the bank rate was raised. The result of these deflationary measures was a big increase in unemployment which reached 2 million in June 1921. Throughout the 1920s there was a steady decline in prices and wages, and unemployment totals never fell below a million.

The economic problems provoked strikes. Early in 1919 the prewar Triple Alliance of miners, railwaymen and transport workers was reconstituted. Later in the same year a strike by railwaymen against a threatened reduction in wages was successful, and the Labour movement was confident. In 1921, however, the transport and railway workers refused to support a miners' strike, and the Alliance was split.

The problem of Ireland, in abeyance during the war, came to the forefront again in 1919. In the election of December 1918 every seat outside Ulster was won by Sinn Fein, an extremist Irish party led by De Valera (b. 1882) who had escaped from Lincoln gaol where he had been imprisoned after the Easter Rising. Redmond's Home Rule Party was eliminated. The Sinn Fein then proceeded to set up their own Parliament and administration, and in 1919 the Irish Republican Army (IRA) was formed from the Irish Volunteers. Guerrilla warfare then started between Sinn Fein and the IRA on the one side, and the British army and the Royal Irish Constabulary on the other. In 1920 the British brought in recruits for the RIC—well-paid ex-servicemen who became known as the Black and Tans, and who were expected to crush the rebellion by any means. The fighting then became brutal.

In 1920 the British Parliament passed the Government of Ireland

Act. This provided for two Parliaments, in Dublin and Belfast, and representatives of both at Westminster. There was provision for Irish unity to be later restored. Neither side accepted the terms, but nevertheless elections for the two Parliaments were held in May 1921: Sinn Fein won nearly all the seats in southern Ireland, and the Unionists did likewise in Ulster. A truce then ended the fighting and negotiations started. In December 1921 an agreement was reached which was accepted by a large majority of the British Parliament and in 1922 by a small majority of the Dublin Parliament. By this agreement southern Ireland was to be called the Irish Free State and was to be given dominion status, while Northern Ireland was still to be governed under the 1920 Act.

In 1922–23 De Valera opposed the settlement, and a further violent civil war was fought between the extreme and moderate nationalists, before the 1921 agreement was accepted. De Valera was Prime Minister between 1932 and 1948 and gradually separated the Free State from the United Kingdom. In 1937 Southern Ireland became an independent republic, henceforth known as Eire.

Meanwhile, opposition to the leadership of Lloyd George had grown. His government's handling of economic problems and events in Ireland was criticised. His foreign policy, especially his support for the Greeks against the Turkish nationalists (see pp. 35–6), was unpopular. He was criticised for lowering the tone of public life by selling honours in return for contributions to party funds. In 1921 Bonar Law had resigned for health reasons, and this weakened the coalition government. In addition there was the vague but real feeling that Lloyd George could not be trusted.

Therefore, in October 1922, when the government decided on a general election, the Conservatives resolved to leave the coalition and fight the election as a separate party. Lloyd George immediately resigned. He was not to hold office again. Churchill said of him: 'He was the greatest master of the art of getting things done and putting things through that I ever knew. When the English history of the first quarter of the twentieth century is written, it will be seen that the greater part of our fortunes in peace and war were staged by this man.' Brilliant and ruthless, he was, says A. J. P. Taylor, 'the most inspired and creative British statesman of the twentieth century'.[1]

Conservative Government 1922 to 1924

In October 1922 Bonar Law formed a Conservative government. In the following month the election was held in which the Conservatives

[1] A. J. P. Taylor, *English History, 1914–45.*

won 345 seats, Labour (now led by Ramsay MacDonald) 142, and the Liberals 117—roughly divided between the followers of Lloyd George and those of Asquith.

Bonar Law remained Prime Minister for only a few months. In May 1923 he resigned and died later in the year. On the advice of Law and Balfour, George V invited Baldwin to be the new Prime Minister. A wealthy industrialist as well as being a pig farmer, Baldwin (1867–1947) appeared an amateur in politics but in fact proved himself an astute politician, 'the most formidable antagonist whom I ever encountered', Lloyd George said. Baldwin's policy was usually to wait upon events and reach decisions slowly. With his appointment as Prime Minister a new period of British history began, more tranquil and more moderate. 'He preferred things to sort themselves out rather than be settled by him; and he was always prepared to await the event rather than forestall it.'[1]

Neville Chamberlain (1869–1940) and Ramsay MacDonald were the other two politicians who dominated the period between the wars. Neville was the son of Joseph and the half-brother of Austen Chamberlain. He was an extremely efficient, determined and practical administrator who showed great ability in the conduct of domestic affairs. During 1923 he was responsible for a Housing Act which encouraged the private building of small houses for sale.

In October Baldwin, for reasons which are not clear, suddenly decided that the only way to fight unemployment[2] was to end the policy of Free Trade and introduce Protection. This major change in policy required a general election which was held in December 1923. The result was a sharp drop in the number of Conservative seats and a corresponding rise for Labour and the Liberals. The figures were: Conservative 258, Labour 191, and Liberal 159. Baldwin's government continued for a few weeks, but in January it was defeated, and Ramsay MacDonald, as the leader of the Labour Party, formed a government.

Labour Government January to October 1924

The first Labour Government[3] was formed with Liberal support. It was in office but not in power in that Liberal opposition to any of its actions would bring automatic defeat. Therefore, fundamental changes were impossible. MacDonald accepted office because he wanted to

[1] D. Thomson, *England in the Twentieth Century*.

[2] 'Ain't We Got Fun' was the hit song of 1923. It complained of times getting harder with nothing in the larder, of the rich getting richer and the poor getting—children.

[3] George V wrote in his diary: 'Today 23 years ago dear Grandmama died. I wonder what she would have thought of a Labour government.'

show that Socialists, although inexperienced, could govern as competently as either of the other parties. On the whole British socialism was moderate and democratic; it believed in evolution, not revolution. Ramsay MacDonald (1866–1937), a self-educated man of fine appearance and strength of character, was typical of this moderate type of socialism.

The main domestic achievement of the government was a Housing Act which increased the state subsidy and gave the main responsibility for building houses to local authorities who built for rent. The programme laid down under this Act did not get rid of slums but did overcome the housing shortage. The financial policy followed was orthodox in that taxes were reduced and government expenditure lowered. Foreign affairs were left to MacDonald and his policy was both generally acceptable in Britain and successful. He persuaded France and Germany to accept the Dawes Plan, he recognised the Soviet government and he tried to make the League of Nations effective.

In the autumn, however, the government was defeated when it was suspected, on dubious evidence, of supporting communism. Another general election was held in October. Baldwin had by now renounced his policy of Protection until the public showed that it no longer wanted Free Trade, and the Conservatives with 419 seats won a massive majority over Labour (151) and the Liberals, who were reduced to forty seats.

Conservative Government 1924 to 1929

Baldwin became Prime Minister for the second time in November 1924. Apart from the excitement of the general strike, these were quiet years in which the government aimed at restoring 'normalcy' (see p. 173). In foreign affairs Austen Chamberlain, the Foreign Secretary, worked closely with France and Germany to produce the sense of security exemplified by the Locarno Pacts. Consequently, since Europe seemed peaceful, the government gradually cut down expenditure on defence.

In 1925 Winston Churchill, now back in the Conservative Party and Chancellor of the Exchequer, returned Britain to the gold standard. It was generally thought that gold was the only possible basis for a currency, and the return to this standard was 'a symbol of postwar restoration'. Although the move increased the cost of British exports, at the time it was approved by all except Keynes, the economist, who in the end was proved right. On the whole the standard of living during these years went up. Public housing proceeded well, the size of real wages went up and the size of families went down. Old age pensions were doubled, widows' and orphans' pensions were granted, and after 1928 unemployment benefits were given for an unlimited period to the genuinely unemployed. One million motor cars were registered by 1930.

In many respects, however, foreign as well as domestic, the Golden Age of the Twenties was illusory. The number of unemployed never dropped below one million. Imports increased and exports were 25 per cent down on the total for 1913. Fortunately, the large earnings from shipping, insurance and overseas investments prevented a balance of payments deficit. New industries, such as that of the motor car, were growing, but the old basic industries—cotton, iron and steel, ship-building and coal—were all declining. The cotton industry was losing its overseas markets and chaotic organisation was added to technical inferiority. The iron and steel industry suffered from foreign tariffs and could not compete with the more efficient methods of the large foreign firms. The shipbuilding industry was similarly outdated and inefficient, and was losing its markets at home and abroad. The decline of the coal industry was explained by bad organisation, inferior techniques, and the drop in demand because of improved output in Europe and alter-native sources of power.

Coal was the largest of these industries, employing over one million men. Discontent amongst its workers was intense. 'Between 1911 and 1945 the miners, who constituted little more than 6 per cent of the industrial workers, provided nearly 42 per cent of all strikers.'[1] The troubles of 1921 were followed by four years of peace, but in 1925 the owners decided that to maintain British sales abroad, prices would have to be reduced, and therefore wages would have to be lowered and hours increased. The miners refused to contemplate this, and trouble was only averted in 1925 when the government temporarily subsidised wages and appointed a Royal Commission to enquire into the industry.

The Samuel Commission reported in 1926. It recommended an immediate reduction in wages, the amalgamation of smaller pits and better working conditions. The owners rejected amalgamation, while the attitude of the miners was given by their leader: 'Not a penny off the pay, not a minute on the day.' At the end of April 1926 the miners came out on strike and received the support of the TUC. On 3 May the so-called General Strike began. It was intended in its early stages to be a partial, selective strike, and for nine days about 2 million men in trans-port, printing, some heavy industry and the building, gas and electricity industries stopped work. The government had prepared for such a

[1] D. Thomson, *England in the Twentieth Century.*

strike, however, and essential supplies were maintained. There was remarkably little violence, both the government and the TUC aiming at restraining the militants.

On 12 May the TUC, which had always lacked enthusiasm for the affair, called off the strike. The miners continued for another six months and were then forced back to work on the owners' terms. The general strike as a weapon had failed, union membership fell, and there were fewer strikes during the following years. In 1927 some of the good resulting from Baldwin's moderation during the strike was undone by the Trades Disputes Act: general strikes were made illegal, civil servants were not allowed to join a union affiliated to the TUC, and a scheme was evolved by which the unions' contributions to Labour Party funds were reduced.

The Conservative government was responsible for three other measures of importance. Legislation was passed which reformed local government and its relations with the Ministry of Health; this was the work of Neville Chamberlain. The 1928 Reform Act gave the vote to the 'flappers' by lowering the voting age for women from thirty to twenty-one. In 1926 the British Broadcasting Corporation was created by royal charter. It was run by a board of governors appointed by the Prime Minister. Reith, its first Governor-General, aimed to broadcast to every home 'all that was best in every department of human knowledge, endeavour and achievement'.

The period of Baldwin's government was one of change and development for the Commonwealth. The autonomy of the dominions, the term used to describe self-governing colonies, was recognised after the war, but it was considered that a more formal definition of the status of a dominion was required. At the 1926 Colonial Conference, therefore, Balfour put forward this definition: Great Britain and the dominions are 'autonomous communities within the British Empire, equal in status, in no way subordinate one to another in any aspect of their domestic or internal affairs, though united by a common allegiance to the Crown, and freely associated as members of the British Commonwealth of Nations'. This formula became law in the Statute of Westminster of 1931. It meant that, although Britain remained the most important member of the Commonwealth, the British Parliament was no longer sovereign over the dominions. Apart from the ties of sentiment and self-interest, only the monarchy united the members of the Commonwealth.

In May 1929 the general election was held. Labour emerged as the largest party with 288 seats, the Conservatives had 260 and the Liberals

59.

Labour Government 1929 to 1931

In June 1929 MacDonald formed his second government, again without real power. Before the world depression overwhelmed the government, it conducted a conciliatory foreign and colonial policy, and passed two important pieces of domestic legislation in 1930. The Coal Mines Act reduced hours of work, empowered the mine owners to fix output quotas and therefore prices, and appointed a commission to recommend ways to reorganise the industry. The Housing Act provided subsidies for slum clearance.

The world economic slump started in the United States in October 1929. Its immediate effect was to reduce British exports not only to the US, but also to other countries who were impoverished as a result of not being able to sell their export goods, both manufactured and raw materials. During the two years after October 1929 British exports halved. Consequently unemployment rose sharply. By July 1930 2 million were without work; two years later 3¾ million were unemployed. This represented over one-fifth of the working population.

North Britain and Wales had twice the unemployment level of southern England. In the north the old industries—shipbuilding, iron and steel, jute, coal, wool and cotton—suffered most, and the populations of whole districts were out of work with no hope of alternative jobs. The ancillary trades and local service trades suffered likewise. Unemployment in the new industries in the south—building, motor cars, electrical engineering, food industries—was relatively small. For the four-fifths of the population in employment, the standard of living rose because prices fell and wages remained stable. For the unemployed and their families, however, these were years of bitterness and poverty.

Lloyd George believed that the way to deal with the problem was through a major programme of public works—building, railways, roads—and the government should, if necessary, run up a deficit. Oswald Mosley,[1] a former Conservative, now in the Labour government, wanted expansion of the economy by the use of credit. Snowden, the Chancellor of the Exchequer, however, believed in rigidly orthodox methods of finance. In the 1930 budget he increased taxes in view of the expenditure on unemployment pay. In July 1931 a committee he had appointed to suggest economies recommended a 20 per cent cut in unemployment relief because it foresaw a deficit of £120 million in the budget. This led to a financial crisis, for foreign bankers began to withdraw their money fearing a devaluation of the pound. London bankers believed that only a balanced budget would restore confidence in the

[1] In 1932 Mosley left the Socialists and founded the British Fascist Party.

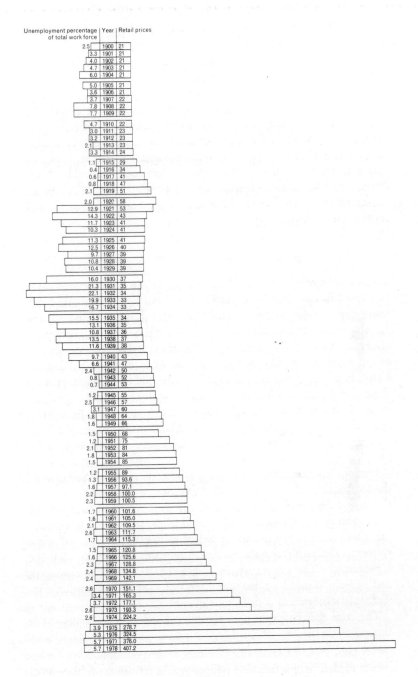

Unemployment percentage of total work force	Year	Retail prices
2.5	1900	21
3.3	1901	21
4.0	1902	21
4.7	1903	21
6.0	1904	21
5.0	1905	21
3.6	1906	21
3.7	1907	22
7.8	1908	22
7.7	1909	22
4.7	1910	22
3.0	1911	23
3.2	1912	23
2.1	1913	23
3.3	1914	24
1.1	1915	29
0.4	1916	34
0.6	1917	41
0.8	1918	47
2.1	1919	51
2.0	1920	58
12.9	1921	53
14.3	1922	43
11.7	1923	41
10.3	1924	41
11.3	1925	41
12.5	1926	40
9.7	1927	39
10.8	1928	39
10.4	1929	39
16.0	1930	37
21.3	1931	35
22.1	1932	34
19.9	1933	33
16.7	1934	33
15.5	1935	34
13.1	1936	35
10.8	1937	36
13.5	1938	37
11.6	1939	38
9.7	1940	43
6.6	1941	47
2.4	1942	50
0.8	1943	52
0.7	1944	53
1.2	1945	55
2.5	1946	57
3.1	1947	60
1.8	1948	64
1.6	1949	66
1.5	1950	68
1.2	1951	75
2.1	1952	81
1.8	1953	84
1.5	1954	85
1.2	1955	89
1.3	1956	93.6
1.6	1957	97.1
2.2	1958	100.0
2.3	1959	100.5
1.7	1960	101.6
1.6	1961	105.0
2.1	1962	109.5
2.6	1963	111.7
1.7	1964	115.3
1.5	1965	120.8
1.6	1966	125.6
2.3	1967	128.8
2.4	1968	134.8
2.4	1969	142.1
2.6	1970	151.1
3.4	1971	165.3
3.7	1972	177.1
2.6	1973	193.3
2.6	1974	224.2
3.9	1975	278.7
5.3	1976	324.5
5.7	1977	376.0
5.7	1978	407.2

Unemployment and retail prices: 1900–1978

pound, and they demanded a cut in unemployment relief in order to reduce government expenditure.

During August the cabinet failed to agree on the issue. Eleven, including MacDonald and Snowden, wanted to follow the advice of the bankers; nine refused to agree to reductions in unemployment pay. It was felt that the financial crisis was so severe that the delays and uncertainties of a general election would be dangerous. Therefore, the party leaders, MacDonald, Baldwin and Samuel (temporarily Liberal leader while Lloyd George was undergoing an operation) met and agreed to form a National Government. This was to be led by Mac-Donald in order to attract Labour support in the country. The National Government, believed at the time to be a temporary alignment, was formed on 24 August 1931.

National Government 1931 to 1939

MacDonald's cabinet consisted of four Socialists, four Conservatives and two Liberals. The Conservative Party and half the Liberal Party immediately endorsed the National Government, but the Labour Party and the remaining Liberals opposed it. At the time and for many years after MacDonald was regarded by Socialists as a traitor who was willing to cut relief for the unemployed and who had betrayed the Labour Party. In consequence, he was expelled from the party, together with those few Socialists who were associated with the National government. This action was probably unjustified. In 1966 Harold Wilson, the Labour Prime Minister, said that MacDonald 'sincerely felt he was putting the survival of his country above the survival of his party'.

During September 1931 Snowden, who continued as Chancellor of the Exchequer, carried out his policy of economies. All salaries paid by the state were cut by 10 per cent. In the same month Britain left the gold standard and the value of the pound fell by a quarter. The government then decided to call a general election to gain the approval of the country. The result was an overwhelming victory for the National Government. The Conservatives won 473 seats, National Labour 13 and National Liberal 35, making a total of 521. The opposition consisted of 33 Liberals and 52 Labour members.

The crisis therefore split both the Liberal and Labour Parties. After this point the decline of the Liberals set in. There were three main reasons for their continued loss of support since the First World War: the dispute over personalities between Asquith and Lloyd George weakened and confused the party; the failure to develop a clear policy which would show the Liberals to be an effective radical alternative to the rising Labour Party; the shortage of money for party funds.

In November 1931 the National government was reconstructed. The important change was that Neville Chamberlain became Chancellor of the Exchequer. Eleven of its twenty cabinet members were Conservatives, and this proportion increased during the following decade so that the 'National' government was such in name only—in policy and membership it was Conservative, although Ramsay MacDonald was still Prime Minister.

In 1932 the new government finally carried out Joseph Chamberlain's policy of tariffs and imperial preference. Most foreign imports were now subject to customs duties, while imperial goods were allowed in free of tariffs. This was decided at the Imperial Economic Conference held in Ottawa. This tariff wall helped to protect British industry while it recovered from the depression. In addition, credit for economic expansion was cheap: for nineteen years after 1932 the bank rate remained at 2 per cent. After 1934 income tax was lowered, unemployment benefits were restored, and the 10 per cent cut in salaries discontinued, thus producing more purchasing power. In 1934 legislation was passed to assist in the redevelopment of areas of high unemployment. Government grants were given to firms moving to certain areas and factories were provided at low rents. At the same time unemployed workers were encouraged to move to the new industries in the Midlands and the South. Despite the Special Areas Acts, however, the contrasts between the prosperous South and the depressed North grew more marked.

Agriculture was protected by import duties, and the government guaranteed prices by giving subsidies. Marketing Boards were established which regulated prices by restricting output. In shipbuilding and the cotton industry an attempt was made to reduce productive capacity. The government gave loans to ship owners to buy new ships to provide work for the remaining yards. The iron and steel industry gradually recovered after 1932 for various reasons: European competitors recovered more slowly and a $33\frac{1}{3}$ per cent tariff was placed on foreign imports; the British Iron and Steel Federation was formed in 1934 to assist the reorganisation of the industry, and generally techniques and location improved; the industry's customers recovered. The growth of new industries—chemicals, man-made fibres, cars, radios—and a boom in the building industry, all contributed to the gradual fall in unemployment. The index figures for production show the improvement: 1929—100; 1931—84; 1933—93; 1935—110; 1937—124.

In 1935 MacDonald, tired and overworked, resigned, and was

succeeded by Baldwin. In November 1935 a general election confirmed the National Government in power. It won 432 seats against Labour's 154 and the Liberals' 20.

In January 1936 George V died. By nature conservative, he was a conscientious, dignified and tolerant king, who through his tours and Christmas Day broadcasts made the Royal Family important and popular. His death produced a crisis for the British Monarchy for his eldest son and successor, Edward VIII, a bachelor of forty-one, wished to marry Mrs Simpson, an American lady who had divorced two husbands. Baldwin, the Archbishop of Canterbury and other leading figures opposed the marriage, and Baldwin, who regarded the public image of the monarchy as more important than this particular monarch, told Edward that he must either renounce Mrs Simpson, or abdicate. In December the affair became public when Edward decided to abdicate. He was given the title of Duke of Windsor, and was succeeded by his younger brother who became George VI.

The importance of economic affairs and then the abdication crisis of 1936 distracted public attention from the important events occurring in Europe (see chapter 2). Hitler came to power in 1933 and began to reassert German ambitions. But with a background of aggressive dictatorship and nationalism in Europe, Britain remained strongly pacifist[1] and in favour of disarmament in the first half of the 1930s. In 1935, however, a Defence White Paper announced a policy of limited rearmament, but before the Munich conference of 1938 Germany spent five times as much on her armed forces as Britain. After Munich there was much greater support in Britain for rapid rearmament.

In May 1937 Baldwin retired and was succeeded by Neville Chamberlain. The new prime minister was a precise and efficient man who unfortunately came to power at a time when foreign affairs, of which he had no experience, were far more important than domestic events. He is chiefly remembered for his policy of appeasement of Hitler, a subject which remains highly controversial and which is described in chapter 2. It can be said for this policy, however, that time was gained to unite Britain against Germany by showing that Hitler could only be stopped by war. Thus British entry into the Second World War in September 1939 received almost unanimous support from the country.

[1] In 1933 the Oxford Union passed the motion: 'This House will not fight for King and Country.'

Second World War 1939 to 1945

When the war started Chamberlain formed a War Cabinet and broadened the government by bringing in Churchill as First Lord of the Admiralty and Eden as Dominions Secretary. The Liberal and Labour Parties refused to join and therefore the National Government remained almost entirely Conservative.

The experience of the First World War stood the government in good stead. New ministries were formed, and the government was given wide powers. But Chamberlain's administration lacked decisive leadership. There was too much bureaucratic muddle, too little money for the new ministries, too much complacency. The phoney war on the western front resulted in a lack of urgency. Until May 1940 ordinary life was little affected by the war. Some school children were evacuated from the south-east, rationing was introduced, and precaution was taken against air attack, but in the spring of 1940 1 million people were still unemployed.

The abortive Norwegian campaign of April 1940 finally turned public opinion against Chamberlain. Lloyd George, in his last major speech in the Commons, asked Chamberlain to sacrifice his position and resign, and Amery quoted Cromwell's words to the Rump Parliament: 'Depart, I say, and let us have done with you. In the name of God, go!' About forty Conservatives supported the Labour censure motion, and on 10 May Chamberlain resigned. He was succeeded by Winston Churchill.

Churchill formed a War Cabinet of five which was later increased to eight or nine. Attlee, the leader of the Labour Party, was a member and presided over the cabinet in Churchill's absence. Bevin, the Secretary of the Transport and General Workers' Union, became Minister of Labour and National Service. Eden was in charge of foreign policy. Chamberlain was originally a member of the cabinet, but when he died later in 1940 his place was taken by Anderson who coordinated the work of the committees dealing with home policy. Beaverbrook, the owner of the *Daily Express* and the *Evening Standard*, held the important position of Minister of Aircraft Production, a post he occupied with great success.

Churchill kept the Ministry of Defence for himself. Not only was he a military historian, but he had seen active service himself in his youth, and had gained valuable departmental experience of the armed forces before and during the First World War. Now he was responsible for the military direction of the war as well as for the civil administration.

A. J. P. Taylor has written: 'Churchill carried the war on his shoulders
. . . Churchill provided political inspiration and leadership. He determined strategy and settled the disputed questions in home policy.'[1] He
was a war leader of the calibre of William Pitt, Earl of Chatham, two
hundred years before: a man of great energy and driving power,
imperious and defiant, a worldwide strategist, and an orator whose
language could inspire in time of crisis. Three days after becoming
prime minister, Churchill told the Commons:

> What is our aim? I can answer in one word: Victory . . . I have
> nothing to offer but blood, toil, tears and sweat.

And in the following month, after Dunkirk:

> We shall not flag or fail. We shall go on to the end . . . We shall
> defend our island whatever the cost may be. We shall fight on the
> beaches. We shall fight on the landing grounds. We shall fight in the
> fields and in the streets. We shall fight in the hills. We shall never
> surrender.

Churchill's government so enjoyed the confidence of the nation that
on only one occasion during the five years from 1940 to 1945 was it
challenged in the House of Commons—and then the vote of censure
only received 25 votes.

The government exercised a tight control over the economy. The
budget of 1941 introduced a policy of subsidies, price control and
increased taxes in order to keep the cost of living at 25 per cent above
prewar level. In 1942 the Ministry of Fuel and Power was created to
centralise the administration of the coal industry. Rationing was
extended to most articles. A national system of railways was started.
The government controlled and directed agriculture and, in order to
reduce the dependence on imported food, concentrated on arable farming and increased home production by 70 per cent. In addition there was
widespread direction and allocation of labour.

While the war was at its height the government made plans for postwar reconstruction in three particular fields: social security, employment and education. In 1942 Sir William Beveridge produced a plan
which suggested that in place of the various prewar methods of providing welfare, the social services should be united into a single system. In
return for insurance contributions, an individual should receive free
medical treatment, unemployment pay, assistance if very poor, family
allowances, pensions and other forms of help. The Beveridge Plan was

[1] A. J. P. Taylor, *English History, 1914-45.*

accepted by the government and arrangements were made to implement it. Then in 1944 appeared a White Paper on Employment Policy. Its contents owed much to the influence of Keynes. Although hedged with qualifications, it pledged the government to a deliberate policy of securing full employment by means of financial measures after the war. In the same year the Butler Education Act was passed. Education was to be in accordance with 'the age, ability and aptitude of the pupil', and was to be organised in three progressive stages, primary, secondary and further education. Three types of school were envisaged for the secondary stage—modern, technical and grammar—and all fees were to be abolished. The school leaving age was to be raised to fifteen (this came in 1947) and later to sixteen, and the teaching of religion and daily worship were made compulsory.

Although Britain was victorious in the Second World War, the economic and human cost was great. About 400,000 people lost their lives; three-quarters of these were in the armed forces, the remainder being civilians and merchant seamen. Overseas investments were halved, external debts had increased by over £3,000 million, and national wealth to the extent of £1,700 million was lost either by destruction or obsolescence.

On 8 May 1945 Churchill announced the victory over Germany. He then proposed that the coalition government continue until the end of the war against Japan, but when this was rejected he decided to hold a general election. The campaign was fought during June and July, and the election at the end of July resulted in a sweeping victory for the Socialists. Labour gained 393 seats, the Conservatives 213 and the Liberals 12. Churchill immediately resigned and Clement Attlee became Prime Minister.

'The electors cheered Churchill and voted against him.'[1] While Churchill was extremely popular, however, the Conservative Party was much less in favour. The Conservatives had been in power for most of the period between the wars, and consequently were connected in the public mind with unemployment at home and appeasement abroad. The planned economy had been successful in wartime, and Labour, whose electoral machine was better than that of the Conservatives, wanted limited nationalisation and the retention of government controls. This was attractive to a public who wanted the state to promote a more egalitarian society. There was mounting demand for a welfare state, and it was felt that Labour was more likely to introduce this. In addition, the Labour ministers in the coalition government were given considerable credit for the administration of the war.

[1] A. J. P. Taylor, *English History, 1914-45.*

Since 1945

Labour Government 1945 to 1951

Attlee, the new Prime Minister, was a rather remote and self-effacing leader, poor at public relations and not a good orator. However, he was a man of great integrity and determination who kept national unity during a trying period and who controlled the powerful individuals in his cabinet. The Deputy Prime Minister was Herbert Morrison who was responsible for economic planning and coordination until 1947 and after that for domestic legislation in general. The Foreign Secretary was Ernest Bevin, a tough and hard-headed trade union leader who was a master of detailed negotiations (although his grammar was often improvised—he never bothered much about the difference between singular and plural). Sir Stafford Cripps was President of the Board of Trade until 1947, and then Chancellor of the Exchequer until his retirement through ill-health in 1950. He was a man of powerful intellect and had a great sense of dedication and moral purpose. The other outstanding member of this government was Aneurin Bevan, the Minister of Health. He was one of ten children of a Welsh miner, and became a great platform orator and a self-confident individualist.

One of the major objectives of the Labour Government was the maintenance of high employment. In this it was successful, for unemployment was rarely higher than 3 per cent. There were three main reasons for this. Firstly demand for goods was high: this was because of destruction during the war, accumulated savings and the rise in wages which increased spending on consumer goods. Also, there was little foreign competition. Secondly, the methods of the economist Keynes were now used to control unemployment: public and private expenditure were increased to encourage greater buying and investment. Thirdly, the government now kept stricter control over the economy. One of the consequences of this policy of full employment was continual inflation. The labour shortage and trade union power forced up wages and, therefore, prices. In addition, world prices were rising which increased import prices, and government controls were gradually lifted.

The other important aim of the government was nationalisation. It was believed that state control of firms would lead to efficient planning and coordination in the public interest. In 1946 the Bank of England, the coal industry and civil aviation were nationalised, and in the following year the British Transport Commission was formed to run the railways, canals and road haulage, and the electricity and gas industries were brought under state control. The iron and steel industry was nationalised by 1951.

In 1945 the coal industry was in a sorry state: its equipment was obsolete, its manpower depleted and the best seams were worked out. The industry 'emerged from the war with an almost limitless demand but an utter inability to meet it'.[1] The Nationalisation Act set up the National Coal Board to run the industry, which was divided into eight divisions and given £150 million for re-equipment. Although there were severe coal shortages, especially early in 1947 when as a result several million industrial workers were made idle, output gradually increased. There was little opposition to the nationalisation of the coal industry, but determined resistance from the firms concerned and the Conservatives to the attempt to nationalise steel, which was a comparatively efficient industry. About a hundred steel firms were nationalised by an Act passed in 1949 which did not become operative until February 1951.

At the end of the war agriculture was enjoying greater prosperity than it had done for the last seventy years. It was pressed by the government to produce the maximum amount because of the world shortage of grain and the British shortage of foreign currency. In 1947 the Agriculture Act was passed. This aimed to promote 'a stable and efficient agricultural industry'. Stability was to be obtained by an annual reviewing and fixing of prices, and efficiency by the government supervision of farming methods and by continued mechanisation. The consequence was a 20 per cent increase in output between 1947 and 1952, and in the long run British farming became one of the most highly mechanised in the world.

One of the most serious economic problems facing the Labour Government concerned the balance of payments. This is the difference in value between all foreign payments (mainly for imports) and receipts (mainly for exports). If payments continue to be greater than receipts, there is a drain on reserves of gold and foreign currency. In 1947 the United Kingdom deficit was £450 million and in 1951 it was £400 million. There were a number of general reasons for this unfavourable balance: earnings on invisible account, especially from overseas investments, had dropped sharply; there were large interest payments to make on wartime loans; the terms of trade were unfavourable in that the price of British imports rose nearly twice as much as the price of exports; inflation impeded the expansion of exports and encouraged the growth of imports; the cost of maintaining defence forces overseas was high. There were, in addition, particular causes of the crises in 1947 and 1949.

[1] S. Pollard, *Development of the British Economy, 1914-50*.

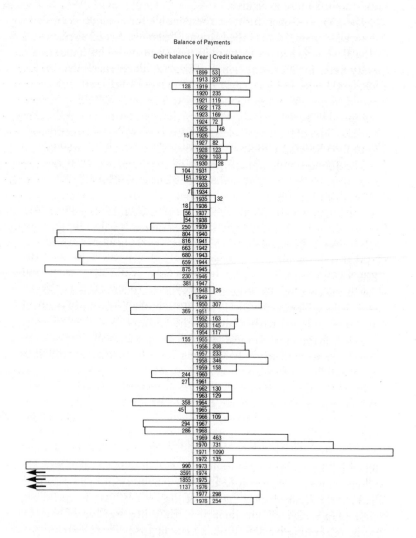

Balance of Payments

Debit balance	Year	Credit balance
	1899	53
	1913	237
128	1919	
	1920	235
	1921	119
	1922	173
	1923	169
	1924	72
	1925	46
15	1926	
	1927	82
	1928	123
	1929	103
	1930	28
104	1931	
51	1932	
	1933	
7	1934	
	1935	32
18	1936	
56	1937	
54	1938	
250	1939	
804	1940	
816	1941	
663	1942	
680	1943	
659	1944	
875	1945	
230	1946	
381	1947	
	1948	26
1	1949	
	1950	307
369	1951	
	1952	163
	1953	145
	1954	117
155	1955	
	1956	208
	1957	233
	1958	346
	1959	158
244	1960	
27	1961	
	1962	130
	1963	129
358	1964	
45	1965	
	1966	109
294	1967	
286	1968	
	1969	463
	1970	731
	1971	1090
	1972	135
990	1973	
3591	1974	
1855	1975	
1137	1976	
	1977	298
	1978	254

British Balance of Payments: 1900–1978

The latter was ended when Cripps took the drastic step of devaluing the pound so that only 2·80 American dollars could be obtained for one pound sterling instead of 4·03. This meant that exports were cheaper and imports more expensive.

The Labour Government was responsible for a major expansion of the welfare state. In 1946 the National Insurance Act implemented the ideas Beveridge had put forward in 1942. It provided insurance to meet every likely form of need—unemployment, illness, maternity, widowhood, old age. In 1946, also, the National Health Service Act was passed, although strongly opposed by the doctors. The Act provided a free medical service for all. The government also encouraged council house building but, nevertheless, an acute housing shortage remained—3½ million houses had been damaged or destroyed during the war.

The foreign and colonial policy of the government is described elsewhere.[1] In February 1950 there was a general election. Labour could claim that their rule had brought a higher standard of living; the Conservatives, however, emphasised the continued shortages, the rising prices, the balance of payments deficits. The result of the election was a fall in the Labour majority to six. Attlee continued in office for a further eighteen months. During this period there was little legislation. The Korean war led to further inflation because of rearmament and the rise in the costs of raw materials. In addition, there was a serious split within the government: Bevan and Wilson, the President of the Board of Trade, resigned when Gaitskell, the Chancellor of the Exchequer, imposed charges for National Health Service treatment. Bevin, Cripps and Attlee were all seriously ill during 1951. In September 1951 Attlee dissolved Parliament and in the subsequent election the Conservatives gained a majority of seventeen: the Conservatives won 321 seats, Labour 295, the Liberals 6 and there were 3 others.

Conservative Government 1951 to 1964

Churchill began his first peacetime government in October 1951. For Churchill personally it was rather a sad anticlimax since his capabilities had clearly declined since the end of the war. In 1953 he had a heart attack but recovered and remained Prime Minister for another two years, celebrating his 80th birthday late in 1954. There were no great changes in policy, economic or foreign. In view of the small majority, controversial legislation was kept to a minimum, although in 1953 steel was almost entirely denationalised. Rationing was gradually ended

---

[1] See the sections on Europe, the Middle East, the Indian subcontinent, Malaya and Korea.

during the first part of the 1950s. In 1952 George VI died and was succeeded by his young daughter as Elizabeth II.

The Labour Government had nationalised the steel industry in the belief that steel was too important to the economy to be left in private hands. It also claimed that the industry was inefficient, that productivity was low compared with foreign competitors, that it failed to provide for home needs and that price fixing was against the public interest. The Conservatives, however, argued that an Iron and Steel Board with strengthened powers could solve the industry's problems without the upheaval of nationalisation. Therefore, while one firm remained state-owned, the other steel firms were denationalised in 1953 and a Board was created to supervise the industry with the cooperation of the British Iron and Steel Federation. The government could issue directions to the Board on general policy. Up to 1960 demand for steel was high and the industry flourished; in the early 1960s there was a depression. Nevertheless, the production of steel in 1964 was 26 million tons compared with 12 million tons in 1945.

Three of Britain's older industries, coal, cotton and shipbuilding, continued to contract in the 1950s. The development of new sources of power reduced the demand for coal, and the Coal Board began the closing of mines and the reduction of the labour force. In the early 1960s the coal industry was more efficient but less important. The cotton industry declined in the 1950s because of increased competition from Japan and India, and the development of man-made fibres. The government encouraged the modernisation and integration of firms. Orders for the shipbuilding industry gradually declined in the fifteen years after 1950. Although since 1960 there has been considerable re-equipment, better research and the recruitment of newer and younger managers, the industry has continued to suffer from demarcation disputes between unions, the failure to create large firms and the extremely strong competition from Japan.

While these old industries continued to decline in the 1950s, there were big advances in the chemical, motor-car, metal-engineering, electrical goods and aircraft industries. In agriculture, too, there was a continued rise in output. In 1954 controls and government trading were ended and deficiency payments to farmers were introduced. These represented the difference between the price of goods on the free market and the official guaranteed price. Farmers' incomes trebled during the ten years after the war, and by the early 1960s various forms of government subsidy accounted for 80 per cent of farmers' incomes (1962: £350 million out of £430 million). Unemployment generally remained low but the cost of living continued to rise.

Meanwhile the divisions within the Labour Party continued. The general division was between the 'Bevanites' who included Wilson, and Attlee, Morrison and Gaitskell, and was based as much on personal jealousies as on policy differences. The dissension was public knowledge and weakened the party.

In April 1955 Churchill finally resigned as Prime Minister. This was the end of his active political life, although he remained a member of Parliament until his death in 1965. So ended the career of one of the great men of British history. He was succeeded by Sir Anthony Eden whose career had been almost wholly concerned with foreign affairs. A month later there was a general election resulting in a Conservative majority which was now increased to over sixty: the economy had recovered from the immediate postwar difficulties, and the Labour Party was divided, poorly organised and associated with strikes in the mind of the public. Later in 1955 Attlee resigned and Gaitskell was elected leader of the Labour Party.

The dominating event of Eden's short premiership was the Anglo-French-Israeli intervention in Egypt. A description of the events leading up to this, Eden's motives for opposing Nasser by force, and the consequences of the affair are given in chapter 7. The crisis split British public opinion in general and the Conservative Party in particular, with the resignation of opponents of Eden's Suez policy. During 1956 Eden's health worsened and deteriorated further under the strain of fierce criticism of his policies. In January 1957 a combination of illness and political failure led to his resignation.

The Prime Minister from 1957 to 1963 was Harold Macmillan. Born of well-to-do middle-class parents, he was educated at Eton and Oxford, and was severely wounded in the First World War. In 1924 he was elected to Parliament as the member for Stockton, and throughout the 1920s and 1930s he was on the progressive left wing of the Conservative Party and was increasingly opposed to the policy of appeasement. Since 1951 he had been Minister of Housing and Chancellor of the Exchequer. Macmillan gave the appearance of being slow and old, but in fact he was sharp, shrewd and ruthless, and had a detached self-assurance which acted as a steadying influence upon a Conservative Party and a country in disarray. The government's popularity had sunk and Labour was temporarily united, yet 2½ years later the Conservatives were to win their third successive general election.

During this period Macmillan calmed and united the Conservative Party, repaired Britain's damaged relations with the United States, and reconciled Britain to the idea of colonies becoming independent. Meanwhile the standard of living continued to rise: better housing, more consumer goods, shorter working hours, more foreign travel, an increase in car ownership. Macmillan's foreign policy appeared successful, but it is probable that the domestic prosperity was of greater consequence for the electors, 'You've never had it so good', they were told by Macmillan. Consequently, in the general election of October 1959 the Conservatives increased their majority to over 100.

During the election, Gaitskell, the leader of the Labour Party, had appeared as a man of great sincerity, intellectual eminence and warm humanity, but his party presented a poor image. Apart from its decade of personal quarrels, people associated the Labour Party with the working class, a group which was declining, and with inflexible nationalisation. Gaitskell now attempted to change this image by asking for the alteration of Clause 4 of the Party constitution which called for common ownership of the means of production, distribution and exchange. However, this only served to divide the Party once more, and in 1960–61 there was a further division over defence policy. The Party Conference rejected official policy on defence and declared for the unilateral renunciation of nuclear weapons. Gaitskell succeeded in reversing this decision in 1961.

The problem of defence provided one of the major controversies of the early 1960s. Large numbers of people, and for one year a majority of the Labour Party Conference, supported unilateral nuclear disarmament by Britain. The Conservative government, however, despite the cost of attempting to compete with the strength of America and Russia, insisted on maintaining an independent British nuclear force. But in 1960 the project to build a Blue Streak rocket which would fire a nuclear warhead from the ground was abandoned. In place of it, the government agreed to buy US Skybolt rockets which would be fired from aircraft. At the end of 1962, however, the US announced that it intended to stop the production of Skybolts and concentrate on Polaris missiles fired from submarines. At a meeting at Nassau in December, Macmillan and President Kennedy agreed that the US should supply Polaris missiles to Britain.

During the 1950s there was steady inflation which continued to weaken Britain's balance of payments position. In the early 1960s the government attempted two methods of ending this inflation and at the same time expanding the economy: it tried to stop wage increases and it set up two bodies to assist with the central planning of the economy, the National Economic Development Council and the National Incomes Commission. The attempt to establish a system of central economic planning was a considerable change in Conservative policy, but a change of much greater consequence was the government's decision in 1961 to open negotiations for British membership of the European Economic Community.

Both the Labour and Conservative governments had been lukewarm in their attitude to the European Movement (see chapter 3). Britain had the opportunity to join the Common Market in 1957, but for political and economic reasons she decided not to do so. Britain disliked the supranational authority involved in the EEC. This would mean a decline in Britain's sovereignty which would, it was believed, weaken her ties with the United States and with the Commonwealth. The system of Commonwealth preferences would have to be abolished if Britain entered the Common Market, and since economic preferences are the only material bonds linking Commonwealth countries, their removal might lead to the disintegration of the Commonwealth. The advantages of Commonwealth trade were stressed: imports from the Commonwealth were cheap, and the population of the Commonwealth was 850 million while that of the Common Market was only 170 million. In addition if Britain joined the EEC, the system whereby British agriculture was subsidised would have to be changed. Also, it was thought that greater international competition would not necessarily improve British industry.

However, the comparative stagnation of the British economy and the remarkable economic growth of the Common Market countries persuaded the Conservative government that a change in policy was required. Negotiations were started in November 1961 and were continued throughout 1962. Now the advantages of membership were stressed: the benefits of large-scale production for a rich market; the inducement to greater efficiency through increased competition; the small purchasing power of the Commonwealth countries and of EFTA. It was believed that satisfactory arrangements could be made for British agriculture and for Britain's partners in EFTA. In addition, it was said that a united Europe would have a stronger voice in world affairs, and that if she stayed out of Europe, Britain's stature in the world would diminish.

However, the negotiations came to an abrupt end in January 1963 when President de Gaulle of France vetoed Britain's application for membership. The failure of his Common Market policy was one of the reasons for the resignation of Macmillan in October 1963.

In addition, his government was shaken by an unsavoury scandal involving Profumo, the Secretary of State for War. In the autumn Macmillan himself was seriously ill. The Conservative Party schemed and struggled over the succession, and finally Sir Alec Douglas-Home emerged as the new Prime Minister. A year later, in October 1964, the general election was won by Labour with a very small majority. Harold Wilson, who became leader of the Labour Party following the death of Gaitskell in 1963, became Prime Minister, and the thirteen years of Conservative rule came to an end.

Labour Government 1964 to 1970

Labour had an overall majority of six in the new parliament. Harold Wilson formed a government which lasted for eighteen months. During this period the Conservatives elected Edward Heath as their new leader. A politician unconnected with the traditional Conservative governing class, a convinced European and on the reforming wing of the party. Heath nevertheless took a long time to impress his personality on his party and the nation. Wilson had a considerable personal following and in addition the public tended to blame the country's continued ills on the previous Conservative government. Consequently in the General Election of March 1966 the Labour majority was increased to 97.

Wilson was Prime Minister throughout the six years of the Labour government. An economist and former Oxford don, he was anxious to present an image of a modern technocrat. He was a very able political manager whose tactical skill kept the Labour Party united despite the pressure from the left wing for further nationalisation, sweeping defence cuts and opposition to American policy in Vietnam. Wilson's own account of his government gives a picture not only of a political tight-rope walker but of a man preoccupied with short-term manoeuvres and day-to-day crises. A new Department of Economic Affairs was created. George Brown, a man at once able, courageous and energetic but also erratic and volatile, was in charge from 1964 to 1966. He then became Foreign Secretary until, critical of the highly personal way Wilson ran his government, he resigned in 1968. James Callaghan was Chancellor of the Exchequer until 1967 when he was succeeded by Roy Jenkins who had previously been Home Secretary.

The period was dominated by economic problems. Despite the growth in world trade there was a balance of payments deficit from 1963 to 1968. The position in 1964 was particularly bad. From 1953 to 1964 the average annual increase in retail prices was 2.8 per cent; from 1965 to 1969 it was 4.1.[1] Economic growth throughout the 1960s was low compared with that of other industrial countries,[2] and

[1] Figures derived from *Economic Trends,* Central Statistical Office, HMSO, 1979.

[2] From 1964 to 1969 the average percentage increase in industrial production was: in Japan 17·3, United States 7·1, West Germany 5·7, France 5·7, Italy 7·9 and United Kingdom 3·0. (Figures derived from *Main Economic Indicators 1960–1975,* OECD, 1976.)

Winston Churchill and Clement Attlee

Edward Heath, Prime Minister, and Harold Wilson, Leader of the Opposition, leading members of the House of Commons to the House of Lords for the State Opening of Parliament, 1970

Britain's share in world exports of manufactured goods dropped substantially. There were damaging strikes, especially of an unofficial nature. The result was international lack of confidence in the British economy and fear that Britain would devalue sterling. Holders of sterling would sell to buy dollars or other currencies, and Britain's reserves were depleted in efforts to protect sterling.

There were three basic causes of Britain's relatively poor economic performance. Firstly, investment in new machinery and factories was low. The government's deflationary measures—high interest rates, high taxation, controls on prices—and the prospect of low profits meant a lack of incentive to invest. The result was not only that the costs of production were too high, but also that the quality of British goods could not compete with those produced elsewhere. Secondly, the British response to greater industrial competition at home and abroad was inadequate. Traditionally, the United Kingdom's foreign trade had been the exchange of manufactured goods for the import of foodstuffs and raw materials, and the bulk of trade was with the Commonwealth and overseas sterling countries. By the 1960s this was no longer the case: the proportion of trade with industrialised and urbanised countries, especially in Western Europe and particularly in the EEC, had steadily grown. Thus Britain's trade was increasingly dominated by the mutual exchange of manufactured goods, and the British manufacturing industry therefore experienced much greater foreign competition, especially as tariffs were reduced. Britain's response to this increased competition was insufficient: the application of research was inadequate, there was a failure to keep delivery dates, after-sales service was poor, salesmanship was not sufficiently aggressive. In addition Britain failed to produce and market the new commodities required; there was too much concentration on goods for which world demand was growing relatively slowly.

The third cause was poor industrial relations. Good communication between management and employees was often lacking, for example, in the discussion of future plans or the introduction of new machinery. Some attributed this to the social structure of British society, its class divisions and differences of outlook, manners and speech. Restrictive practices by trade unions harmed the economy: over-manning, the refusal to work new machinery, time-wasting, keeping capital equipment working well below capacity, demarcation disputes. Ninety per cent of factories were unaffected by strikes, and official strikes were few. Britain's strike record compared favourably with that of most Western countries. But unofficial strikes—often sudden, involving a small number of people but affecting many more—were damaging.

Between 1965 and 1967 95 per cent of disputes in industry were unofficial. Not only were shop-floor workers more militant, but union leaders seemed out of touch with members.

The Labour government's response to these problems was fourfold: reduction in consumer demand, trade union reform, help for industry, and a second attempt to enter the Common Market. The reduction in consumer demand aimed to contain inflation and reduce the demand for imports. A succession of budgets increased various taxes and imposed new ones. Unfortunately these extra taxes had the undesirable effect of putting up industrial costs and thus making Britain less competitive. Higher interest rates and controls on bank lending and hire purchase were also introduced. However, the stringent measures taken in the budgets of 1964 to 1967 to reduce demand were ineffective. The trade balance continued in deficit. Further deflation was not possible, while import controls would invite retaliation. Therefore in November 1967 the pound was devalued. It had been equivalent to $2.80, and was devalued by 14 per cent to $2.40. The result was that exports were cheaper and imports more expensive, and the balance of payments improved. However, the increased price of imports raised domestic prices, and therefore added to the demand for wage rises. The government tried to operate both a voluntary and a statutory policy of limiting incomes during its period in office. In 1965 the Prices and Incomes Board was established to examine particular cases. In 1966–67 a statutory freeze for six months on all prices and wages was followed by six months of severe restraint. In 1968–69 there was a ceiling on most wage increases. The aim of this policy was to keep wage increases in line with productivity increases, and thus help to control inflation. Nevertheless, prices did rise and the unions were increasingly resentful of what seemed to be a permanent policy of wage control. By 1970 there were ominous demands for large wage increases.

In 1968 the Donovan Report on Trade Unions was published. It recommended fewer and better organised unions, a move away from national wage agreements towards agreements between individual companies and unions, and the establishment of an independent Industrial Relations Commission to investigate problems. It also supported the principle of the closed shop. Six months later, in 1969, Barbara Castle, the Minister of Employment, introduced her White Paper *In Place of Strife*. This contained the government's proposals for reforming trade unions and reducing the number of unofficial strikes. There was to be a legal right to join a union, with protection against unfair dismissals. An Industrial Relations Commission would be set up.

The government could order a trade union to ballot its members before calling an official strike, and could order a 28-day conciliation pause on workers threatening an unofficial strike. An Industrial Board would be able to impose fines on workers or unions who failed to obey. These proposals were widely criticised. They were regarded as inadequate for dealing with unofficial strikes—how in practice were the penalties to be enforced—and unions considered that they were the first step towards restricting the right to strike. Indeed, the Labour Party threatened to break up over the proposals, and finally they were withdrawn, the TUC promising to try to prevent unofficial strikes. This was generally considered to be a defeat for the government and a victory for the unions.

In its attempt to help industry the Labour government extended public ownership: nationalisation of the fourteen largest steel companies brought 90 per cent of crude steel manufacture under public control. The Industrial Reorganisation Corporation was established to encourage the merger of firms (for example, Leyland and BMC). There were financial incentives for firms to move into areas of high unemployment.

In 1966–67 Britain again tried to join the Common Market. The reasons that had led Macmillan's government to attempt to join remained: Britain needed wider markets in Europe; the Commonwealth and sterling area markets were inadequate. But after a year of negotiations conducted by Wilson and Brown, de Gaulle again imposed his veto (see p. 128).

Britain's economic problems had consequences in a number of areas: social services, education, defence and foreign policy. In the social services there was an important change of principle. The Welfare State was based on Beveridge's view that services should be available to all equally and as of right—the idea of universality. But there was now a reaction against this: the total cost of welfare services was huge and increasing, while the services were not tackling the hard core of poverty but were being spread too thinly. Therefore the view gained ground that resources should be concentrated on those in greatest need—the idea of selectivity.[1]

The 1960s was a period of vast and ambitious expansion in education, especially higher education. In 1965 local authorities were requested to plan for comprehensive secondary schools. However, an example of the restrictions caused by the need to economise was the decision to postpone the raising of the school-leaving age from 15 to 16: this was

[1] This seemed to fit in with the socialist principle of 'To each according to his need, from each according to his means'.

now to be effective in 1973 instead of 1971.

The Conservatives had begun the policy of substantially reducing Britain's armed forces, but this was continued by Labour. Deliveries of the most recent strike aircraft, like the TSR 2 and F III, were cancelled. Aircraft carriers were to be phased out of service by 1971. The armed forces, which had numbered 626,000 in 1958, were down to 400,000 by 1968. Such a reduction could only be achieved by cutting commitments. Accordingly, in 1967 a plan was announced for the withdrawal of British forces from the Persian Gulf and the Far East. This was tantamount to saying that Britain was to be in future a European, not a world, power.

Diminished resources and reduced status modified foreign policy. Unlike France, Britain was reluctant to engage independently in any major initiatives. Negotiations with Ian Smith's Rhodesia failed (see p. 359) while relations with South Africa deteriorated after the decision not to sell arms to that country. In Nigeria the British government supported the federal side against Biafra. Despite protests from some students and the left wing of the Labour Party, the government supported American policy in Vietnam.

Although the period of the Labour government was one of major economic problems, the standard of living of most people rose. In 1964 3.3 million Britons went abroad for their holidays—in 1968 the number was 4.6 million. In 1963 7.3 million cars were licensed—in 1968 the number was 10.8 million. By 1968 90 per cent of households had television. The number of households owning refrigerators and washing machines similarly grew. Average earnings continued to rise steadily. 'Swinging' Britain, with its pop groups (the Beatles came on the scene in 1963) and boutiques, was in some respects the centre of international fashion. Although there were pockets of poverty, generally British people were living in an affluent society.

A number of social problems came to the fore during this period. One of the most difficult was race relations. Immigration of coloured people into Britain had increased during the 1950s. Britain was short of labour, especially for certain occupations, and few politicians considered that such immigration should be controlled, despite the race riots in Notting Hill in London in 1958. At the beginning of the 1960s the number of Commonwealth immigrants grew suddenly. From 1955 to 1960 the total averaged 39,000 per year; from 1961 to 1962 it rose to 122,000 per year. The immigrants settled in certain parts of London, the West Midlands and West Yorkshire. A high proportion were of working age, and many found employment on the railways and buses and in hospitals.

Pressure to control the flow of immigration grew, and in 1962 the Conservatives passed the Commonwealth Immigrants Act which introduced a voucher system in order to limit numbers. Consequently, from 1963 to 1968, the average number of immigrants dropped to 50,000 per year. In 1965 the Race Relations Act was passed by which it became a civil offence to discriminate on grounds of race in public places and to incite to racial hatred. The Race Relations Board was set up with a number of local conciliation committees: the emphasis was on conciliation rather than on legal action. At this point there were about 900,000 coloured immigrants in Britain, half from the West Indies, and most of the remainder from India and Pakistan.

In 1968 the stresses caused by large-scale immigration, concentrated into certain areas, became a tense and difficult national problem. The Kenya government began refusing work permits to about 100,000 Asians who were citizens of the United Kingdom and living in Kenya. This was caused by racial tensions within Kenya, and a mass exodus of Asians from Kenya resulted. Britain was unable to absorb them all. Enoch Powell, a leading right-wing Conservative MP, embarked on a series of speeches, using lurid and emotional language, in which he opposed continued immigration and favoured government-financed repatriation. This put the whole racial issue in the forefront of politics. The consequence was the 1968 Commonwealth Immigrants Act which effectively limited the immigration of Kenyan Asians to 7,000 per year. In theory about 2 million people were entitled to enter Britain on British passports, including many from Hong Kong and Singapore. There were in future to be controls on those who had 'no substantial connection with Britain'.

There were a variety of other social issues during these years, many of which can be described under the newly coined heading 'the permissive society'. Some said that this liberal society was more civilised than in the past, some that it was more disorderly. Certainly there was a disturbing rise in crimes of violence, although the abolition of the death penalty in 1965 probably had little to do with this. Legislation allowed easier divorce, and it also became easier to obtain a legal abortion. The censorship of plays was ended; the age of majority was reduced from 21 to 18; the rising number of illegitimate births, the problem of drug addiction, the new frankness of manner and speech, the demand for 'participation', the emphasis on youth, all of these caused concern and controversy.

Four constitutional issues became important during the Labour government's period in office. First, the Maud Commission recommended changes in the structure of local government. Second, the reform of the House of Lords was again proposed, and in 1969 a Parliament Bill was introduced with the intention of gradually replacing hereditary peers by life peers (the bill was not proceeded with). Third, Welsh and Scottish nationalism emerged as a political issue. This was caused by a number of factors: an ancient sense of national identity, disillusionment with the two main parties, higher unemployment than in England, a feeling of being neglected by government based in London, and, in the case of Scotland, the view that Scotland should particularly benefit from the discovery of large reserves of oil under the North Sea.

The fourth and most difficult issue was Northern Ireland. Since 1922 (see p. 217) Ireland had been divided. Northern Ireland remained part of the United Kingdom with its own MPs at Westminster but also with its own Parliament at Stormont in Belfast. The majority of the population was Protestant in religion and was represented by the Unionist Party. The electoral system was so constructed that the Stormont Parliament was always controlled by the Unionists, and the Roman Catholic minority had no share in political power in proportion to its size. Laws and government decisions appeared to discriminate against the Catholics, living conditions, especially in some parts of Belfast, were poor, unemployment was high: these genuine grievances were used by the IRA who wanted the British connection to end and Ireland to be reunited. In 1968 and 1969 there was violence when Protestant extremists and mainly Roman Catholic civil rights demonstrators clashed. After violence in Londonderry and Belfast, British troops were sent to guard public installations. In August 1969 a complete breakdown of law and order threatened, and British troops took over from the police in Catholic areas. Meanwhile Terence O'Neill, the Prime Minister, resigned and was succeeded by James Chichester-Clark.

For most of its period in office the Labour government was very unpopular. Nevertheless, there was a recovery of popularity during 1969 and early 1970, and the election campaign of June, 1970 was closer than expected. In the event the Conservatives won 330 seats with 46 per cent of the votes, Labour 287 with 43 per cent and the Liberals 6 seats with 7.4 per cent.

Conservative Government 1970 to 1974

Edward Heath was the Prime Minister during the Conservative administration. Greatly respected for his ability, frankness and principles, his style and leadership never really appealed to the mass of the electorate. Iain Macleod was appointed Chancellor of the Exchequer but died suddenly in July 1970. A formidable orator and experienced politician, his death was a major blow to the government. He was succeeded by Anthony Barber. Geoffrey Rippon was in charge of the Common Market negotiations, Alec Douglas Home became Foreign Secretary, while William Whitelaw was Leader of the House of Commons but was particularly important in 1972 and 1973 as Secretary of State for Northern Ireland. This period of Conservative government was dominated by three issues: British entry into the Common Market, the serious deterioration of the situation in Northern Ireland, and major problems concerning the economy and industrial relations.

Following the resignation of President de Gaulle of France, Britain reopened negotiations to join the Common Market. There were three main problems dealt with in the negotiations which lasted from June 1970 to June 1971: the role of sterling as an international currency, the size of Britain's contribution to the Common Agricultural Policy, and how to protect Caribbean sugar producers and New Zealand dairy farmers who sold 90 per cent of their butter to the UK. The turning point in negotiations was a successful meeting between Heath and President Pompidou in May 1971. Pompidou was convinced of the soundness of Britain's attitude to Europe, and Heath that France was not looking for excuses with which to justify another veto. A minority of the Labour Party considered that the terms for Britain's entry were satisfactory, but a majority led by Wilson opposed the terms and came close to rejecting British entry in principle. Nevertheless, the House of Commons by a majority of 112, and the House of Lords by an enormous majority, supported British entry, and in January 1972 Heath signed the Treaty of Accession. During 1972 the necessary legislation for Britain to join passed through Parliament, although the crucial second reading of the bill in the House of Commons was only passed by 309 to 301 votes. In January 1973 the United Kingdom formally joined the European Community.

The first year of membership was not a happy one (see p. 130). Old arguments over costs were given a new intensity. Critics said the increase in food and other prices was caused by British membership, and were particularly incensed when the Common Market sold surplus butter to Russia for 8 pence per lb. when the cost in shops in the UK was 28 pence per lb. The Labour Party boycotted the European Parliament and other Community institutions until the issue of British membership was submitted to the electorate either in a General Election or a referendum.

The history of Northern Ireland during the Conservative government divides into two parts: 1970 to March 1972, during which time the Stormont government continued to rule, and after March 1972 when there was direct rule from London. During 1970 there was an increase in IRA terrorist activities, and this was accompanied by counter-terrorism by extreme Protestants. The number of British troops increased. At first the Catholic minority welcomed British troops as a protection against the Protestants, but gradually lost confidence in the Army's impartiality. In March 1971 Chichester-Clark resigned to be succeeded by Brian Faulkner, who remained in office for a year and was to be the last Prime Minister of Northern Ireland. Faulkner was a man of political tenacity and moderation. He was committed to the union of Northern Ireland with Great Britain, but realised that the Unionists could not exclusively hold all important political positions. However, despite his attempts at conciliation, the gulf between the religious factions widened. In 1972 Faulkner introduced internment without trial of people suspected of violence or IRA activities. Several hundred people were arrested. The argument was that normal judicial proceedings would not work in a situation of civil disorder when witnesses would be threatened. However, internment proved counter-productive: there were allegations of illtreatment of internees by the security forces,[1] it antagonised the Catholic minority, and several political groups refused to negotiate with the government unless internment was ended.

Meanwhile, there was a horrifying escalation of violence. Some areas of Belfast and Londonderry were under IRA control with barricades preventing the police or army from entering. In January 1972 there occurred what became known as 'Bloody Sunday': thirteen people were killed when the Army opened fire on marchers in Londonderry. Relations with the Irish Republic worsened, especially after the burning down of the British Embassy in Dublin. With this situation the British government lost faith in Stormont's capacity to govern and in its ability ever to secure the confidence of the Catholic minority. In March 1972, therefore, it was decided to suspend the Stormont government and introduce direct rule of Northern Ireland from London. Faulkner resigned and Whitelaw became Secretary of State for Northern Ireland.

Whitelaw was a man of geniality and patience with a flair for personal relations. His aim was to re-establish law and order, and to

[1] Investigations by the Compton Committee showed that interrogation techniques were limited to, for example, keeping heads covered, continuous monotonous noise and deprivation of sleep.

secure all-party agreement to constitutional reforms. He decided to phase out internment, but the violence continued and spread to England with car-bombs in London and Birmingham. In Northern Ireland 467 people were killed in 1972 and 250 in 1973. One year after direct rule was introduced, the British government set out its proposals: Northern Ireland would remain part of the United Kingdom as long as the majority of the population wanted it, but a Council of Ireland should be established; there would be laws against discrimination on religious or political grounds; a new Assembly would be elected by proportional representation, with a nominated Executive; the control of security would remain with London.

Elections for the Assembly were held in June 1973 and during the autumn agreement was finally reached on the formation of an Executive containing both Protestants and Catholics, with Faulkner as Chief Executive. This was to start functioning in January 1974. In December representatives of the British, Irish and Northern Irish governments met at Sunningdale, near London. Ireland there conceded that the status of Northern Ireland could not be changed until the majority wished it, and the Northern Ireland Executive agreed to the establishment of a Council of Ireland with representatives from both south and north.

The Conservative government faced serious economic problems. The balance of payments was in surplus from 1969 to 1972 but then moved into deficit which by 1974 was over £3,500 million. The industrial problems of shortage of investment and lack of competitiveness remained. Unemployment steadily rose to a peak in 1972 when 3.7 per cent of the work force (over 1 million) were unemployed. Between 1970 and 1974 retail prices increased by 48 per cent.[1] This high rate of inflation was caused by a number of factors. From 1970 to 1972 the pent-up force of previous years of income restraint produced a wages explosion. This was followed by two years (1972–74) when Britain suffered from a massive increase in import prices because of a rise in world prices. This was the main factor in causing inflation after 1972. In June of that year the government decided there should be a floating exchange rate for sterling. This led to a steady depreciation in the value of the pound which also helped to raise import prices. There were other factors which contributed to inflation: an increase in the money supply; the policy of encouraging economic growth which increased demand; some considered that in 1971, when Britain changed to decimal currency, some retailers took the opportunity to raise prices.

[1] *Economic Trends,* Central Statistical Office, HMSO, 1978. (See also footnote on p. 110.)

From 1964 to 1969 the average number of working days lost per year by strikes was 3.6 million. From 1970 to 1972 the number had risen to 16.1 million.[1] In its first six months in office, the government twice declared a state of emergency. One of the most serious and damaging disputes was the coal-miners' strike of January–February 1972. It arose out of a pay claim which far exceeded the Coal Board's offer. At first it had little effect because of large coal stocks and a mild winter, but when the miners picketed power stations to prevent coal deliveries, and rail workers refused to move coal, the situation worsened. The miners' case was that they were only moderately paid in view of their job being difficult, dirty and dangerous, and their product important. The government considered that the Coal Board's offer was good and that other unions would not concede that the miners were a special case. Eventually a Committee of Enquiry under Lord Wilberforce reported that the miners were exceptional and this was reluctantly accepted by the government. The result was a blow not only to attempts to curb wage inflation but also to the authority of the government: in confrontation with a united and determined trade union the government had retreated.

When the Conservatives first took office they opposed state aid to both nationalised and private industry: they wanted more competition and economic self-reliance. They also opposed state direction or involvement, and therefore Labour's Industrial Reorganisation Corporation was wound up. In both these respects circumstances forced a change of attitude. Early in 1971 Rolls Royce, one of the world's biggest manufacturers of aircraft engines, went bankrupt, a huge shock to business confidence and public morale. To the surprise of the Conservative Party, its own government nationalised the aero engine division of Rolls-Royce. The government also decided to subsidise coalmining and continue the expensive development of Concorde, a supersonic airliner being jointly manufactured by Britain and France. In 1972 a Minister for Industrial Development was appointed with functions very similar to those of the Corporation ended two years before. Barber, the Chancellor of the Exchequer, introduced a series of budgets which reduced taxation, one aim of which was to encourage economic growth.

The Conservatives were committed to introduce legislation to regulate trade unions, and in 1971 the Industrial Relations Act was passed. The act conferred the right on an employee to join or not join a trade union, and gave safeguards against unfair dismissals. There was to be no closed shop, that is an employee had the right not to

[1] *Employment Gazette,* Department of Employment, HMSO, 1979.

join a trade union. Up to 1971 a contract between an employer and a union was not legally enforceable: if one side broke a contract, the other could not claim damages. Now, unless explicitly stated and agreed by both sides, a negotiated contract was legally enforceable. In an attempt to stop unofficial strikes, only registered unions would continue to be immune from claims for loss or hardship caused by a strike. A National Industrial Relations Court with the status of a High Court would enforce the act. It could in addition order a 60-day cooling-off period and/or a secret ballot before a strike.

From the start the TUC were bitterly hostile to the Act. It considered that the Court would be biased against unions, and that the law was not an appropriate means of dealing with industrial relations. During 1972 the effectiveness of the new Court was severely tested. An increasing proportion of goods traded between countries were being packed into standardised containers by firms sited outside the docks. Dockers considered that this development was threatening their livelihood, and therefore refused to allow containers to leave the docks. The main Liverpool transport firm concerned took the case to the Industrial Relations Court, who supported the firms. However, the dockers' action continued, so the Court fined the dockers' union (Transport and General Workers' Union). The view that the union was responsible for the actions of its members was upheld by the House of Lords. Meanwhile the dockers' 'blacking' continued, and the Industrial Court ordered the arrest of three dockers. At this point most dockers went on strike, the Appeal Court stopped the arrest, and the strike ended. A month later five dockers were imprisoned for 'blacking', and a second national dock strike resulted, together with sympathetic action by other workers. Four weeks later the strike ended when a new report on the problems of dock labour was accepted. The Industrial Relations Court was further involved in a dispute over the wages of railwaymen. It ordered a 14-day cooling-off period for further talks. When this was ineffective a strike ballot showed a large majority in favour of a strike.

The Conservatives had come into office opposed to the idea of an incomes policy: wage negotiations should be left to union–employer bargaining without government interference. However, by autumn 1972 the government was negotiating with the TUC and the CBI (Confederation of British Industry). When talks broke down, the government imposed its own policy. There were three phases: Phase One was a freeze on all price and wage increases; Phase Two limited wage increases to £1 per week plus 4 per cent of existing wages to a maximum of £250 per year, and set up the Pay Board and Price

Commission to investigate particular cases; Phase Three limited wage increases to 7 per cent, with extra payments for unsocial hours, increased productivity or price rises above 7 per cent. Phase Three operated from November 1973. In the previous month, as a result of the Middle East War, the Arabs had cut back oil production and quadrupled the price. There was a consequent shortage and increase in the price of petrol and other oil products. The supply of petrol steadily worsened, and rationing was planned.

Against this background the miners again asked for higher wages. They refused to accept a Phase Three offer and in November 1973 started an overtime ban which gradually reduced the stocks of coal at power stations. At the same time power engineers and train drivers were threatening strike action. The government declared a state of emergency in order to control the use of power, and decided that many areas of industry and commerce would go on a three-day working week from 1 January 1974. The miners seemed deliberately to want a confrontation with the government. A ballot showed a large majority for strike action, and the efforts of the government and the TUC to find a solution failed. The government then considered a number of alternative courses of action, all of which had their disadvantages. Heath decided to hold a General Election to find out whether opinion in the country supported a government wanting wage restraint by law or unions wanting free bargaining for wages. Therefore on 9 February, when the miners' strike began, Heath announced that an election would be held on 28 February.

The Conservatives stressed their moderation against militant trade unionism, and the need for strong government. For most of the campaign it seemed likely that they would win, but they were harmed by a number of factors: the unpopularity of the Common Market, the high rate of inflation, balance of payments deficits and the Industrial Relations Act. During the campaign the Director General of the CBI called for its repeal, and Labour stressed the need to 'get the British back to work'. The result was very close. Labour polled 11.6 million votes and obtained 301 seats, the Conservatives 11.9 million votes and 296 seats, and the Liberals 6 million votes and 14 seats. Heath resigned after unsuccessful attempts to form a coalition with the Liberals.

Labour Government 1974 to 1979

Wilson formed his third administration in March 1974. Despite about twenty defeats in parliament, the Labour minority government continued until October. Six days after the government came into office there was a settlement of the miners' dispute—on terms very close to the miners' claim in full. By August the Industrial Relations Act had been repealed, although protection was still provided against unfair dismissal.

During the summer the government and the TUC together produced what was called the Social Contract. The TUC would support wage restraint with 12-month intervals between wage claims, the lowest-paid workers being favoured in wage negotiations. The government in response would help to restrain rents, rates and prices, and would provide higher pensions and food subsidies. In October Labour then presented the Social Contract as an attractive alternative to the confrontation and three-day week policies of the previous Conservative government, and in the second General Election of 1974 Labour obtained 319 seats, the Conservative 276 and the Liberals 13. An unusual feature of this election was the strength of the nationalist vote: the Scottish Nationalists gained 11 seats, the Ulster Unionists 10 and the Welsh Nationalists 3. Labour continued in office with an overall majority of three. In 1975 Margaret Thatcher replaced Heath as leader of the Conservative Party, the first time a major British political party had been led by a woman.

Wilson remained Prime Minister until March 1976. This period of eighteen months divides into two parts: the first nine months, October 1974–June 1975, was a disastrous period for the economy; there was some improvement during the remainder of the time. Many industrial firms were obliged to receive government aid in return for an extension of public control. The best known of these was British Leyland—a team under Sir Don Ryder examined the state of the company, and its report recommended huge state financial aid, together with modernisation and managerial changes. Unemployment rose while wage increases were enormous. By June 1975 wage rates were 36 per cent higher than one year earlier. The wage restraint section of the Social Contract was largely ignored. The consequence was massive inflation. By the middle of 1975 prices were rising by 24 per cent per year, and there was danger that inflation was getting out of control. As a result of the recession in world trade, the rise in world commodity prices and this huge inflation, international confidence in the British economy fell. The value of the pound then declined, and this raised import prices.

During the period up to June 1975 two important events occurred. The Industry Act was passed which allowed large-scale government participation in private industry; and Britain's terms of membership of the Common Market were renegotiated. In the October election

Labour committed itself to a referendum on British membership. The question to be answered was 'Do you think the UK should stay in the European Community (Common Market)?' The government led by Wilson recommended a Yes vote, but a third of the cabinet campaigned for a No vote. The result showed that all four parts of the UK voted in favour, with 67 per cent of the electorate overall saying that Britain should remain a member.

There were only two ways of bringing the inflation under control: deflation of the economy which would have produced high unemployment, or a reduction in wage increases. Clearly the Social Contract was not working. By July 1975 a new method of wage control was agreed between the government and the unions. This agreement, largely the work of Jack Jones, Secretary of the TGWU, restricted increases to £6 per week, with all salaries frozen above £8,500. The restriction was voluntary, but the government could impose sanctions against a private firm which paid more than the guidelines allowed.

In March 1976 Harold Wilson resigned as Prime Minister. He was certainly a party manager of consummate ability, having kept the Labour Party together and having won four of the five elections he fought. Nevertheless, he had a reputation for deserting in opposition causes he supported in office—trade union reform, the Common Market, incomes policy. He was succeeded as Prime Minister by James Callaghan, a man of great experience, having held all the important posts in government. In May 1976 a new wage agreement was reached, by which wage increases were limited to 4½ per cent. However, the incomes policy was coming under increasing strain, particularly from those who disliked the erosion of differentials. In Autumn 1976 there was a major economic crisis. A seamen's strike, doubts about the pay policy, decline in industrial production, large public expenditure: these persuaded foreigners to sell sterling. The Bank of England stopped supporting the pound and let it find its market value. In December a large loan from the International Monetary Fund was given on condition that the government cut public spending.

In addition to this very serious economic position, the government now had no overall majority. Labour therefore negotiated with the Liberals, and the result was the so-called 'Lib-Lab' Pact which lasted from March 1977 to Autumn 1978. The thirteen Liberals would support the government in return for regular consultation on government policy and direct elections to the European Parliament.

During the next two years there was a dramatic change in Britain's financial fortunes. There was a large inflow of foreign funds, the

Balance of Payments moved into surplus, and interest rates fell. The value of the pound increased from $1.58 in October 1976 to $2.10 in April 1979. The rate of inflation fell to 16 per cent in 1976 and 1977, and to 8 per cent in 1978. There were three main causes of this improvement: production of North Sea oil had reached two-thirds of the country's requirements by early 1979 and this reduced the import bill for oil; there was stricter control over the money supply and public expenditure; and during 1977 and 1978 the government had relative success in restricting wage increases. After July 1977 the government tried to limit wage increases to a maximum of 10 per cent, and this figure was generally adhered to. For example, a firemen's strike was ended after the army (whose own pay was relatively low) took over firemen's duties. Miners accepted productivity agreements by which they received extra pay in return for increased output.

However, during the winter of 1978–79 the government's pay policy ran into serious opposition. Callaghan and Denis Healey, the Chancellor of the Exchequer, sought to limit pay increases to 5 per cent. The TUC opposed continued wage restraint, and in October the Labour Party Conference voted against the policy. The first major breach came after a strike lasting several weeks at Ford's carworks. Then, in December, the government was defeated in the House of Commons in its efforts to apply sanctions against firms who agreed to pay increases beyond the guidelines. Between January and March there were strikes by oil-tanker drivers, road-haulage workers, railwaymen, ambulance crews, dustmen and other local authority and health service workers. A standing Commission on Pay Comparability for public sector workers was established, and several groups of workers had their pay claims referred to this new body. In the meantime, however, pay awards averaged between 9 and 15 per cent.

Governments usually have four main economic objectives: adequate economic growth, full employment, a satisfactory balance of payments, and stable prices. It was clear that Callaghan's government after Spring 1977 was reasonably successful in the latter two objectives, although by Spring 1979 prices were beginning to rise again as a result of wage increases and oil shortages. But unemployment remained high—about 1.4 million, or 6 per cent, of the workforce—and economic growth was low. The trend over successive governments continued: productivity compared with similar industrial countries was poor. Three main reasons for this were now being stressed: first, overmanning, the refusal to operate new machinery and other restrictive practices by trade unions; second, government was placing too much emphasis on the preservation of low-productivity jobs and too little on the creation of high-productivity jobs; third, it was suggested, especially by the Conservatives, that very high direct taxation was removing the incentive to work hard, and that there should be a shift in the balance of taxation from income tax to indirect taxes. The consequences of this poor growth rate were low investment, low wages and low living standards compared with many other industrial countries.

Industrial trouble and the search for reasons for the United Kingdom's sluggish economy inevitably brought to the fore the question of union power. There was general agreement that over the previous decade the balance of power between unions and management had moved strongly in favour of the unions. It was felt that trade unionists, in pursuit of higher wages, paid too little attention to the effect on other workers or members of the public not involved in the dispute. An example was the picketing of firms not directly or even remotely involved in a dispute. It seemed that strike action was taken too easily and not as a last resort. The Conservatives considered that a secret ballot should be held before any strike was called, and that the payment of supplementary benefits to strikers was encouraging strike action. In addition, it was becoming clear that some trade unions, although powerful in relation to employers or the government, were unable to control their own members. The number of unofficial disputes showed that the authority of national executives and officials over local membership had weakened. Finally, there was increasing public support for the view that the whole system of collective wage negotiation required fundamental reform.

The issue of an industrial firm's right to conduct itself within the law as it saw best, and the employee's freedom to join or not to join a union was pinpointed in a dispute in 1976–77 involving a small London firm called Grunwick. Some workers, who wished to be represented by a union in negotiation with management, went on strike, and were dismissed. The company continued to operate with those of the workforce who did not wish to strike or join a union. There was general union support for the dismissed workers and mass picketing was organised. Amidst scenes of violence, the police tried to keep order and protect workers entering and leaving the factory.

Northern Ireland remained a continuing problem. For the first 5 months of 1974 the new Executive, headed by Faulkner, ruled Northern Ireland. It was opposed both by the IRA and hard-line Unionists. The latter disliked power-sharing, and also saw the agreement on an all-Ireland Council as the first step towards Irish unification. In May a general strike, organised by Protestant workers, stopped all essential services. The Army did not intervene, and the Executive resigned. For the next year Ulster was again placed under direct rule from London. Attempts to form a new Executive failed, and the policy of Sunningdale was scrapped. In 1975 a Convention was elected to form a new government, but this too failed to agree. Thereafter the British government brought forward no new proposals. The policy was the restoration of law and order, a temporary extinction of the provincial parliament, but no new political initiatives. Internment was ended but the terrorism continued. From 1976 to 1978 there was a drop in the level of violence, but a new outbreak in 1979, especially the assassination of the Conservative spokesman on Northern Ireland, Airey Neave, as he was leaving Parliament buildings at Westminster, was a sharp reminder that the basic problem remained unsolved.

In 1975 a White Paper was issued on the future government of Scotland and Wales. This was based on the Kilbrandon Report of 1973. Scotland was to have a legislative assembly with a cabinet and chief executive, Wales to have an executive assembly. These assemblies would receive block grants from the Westminster Parliament, and would have powers over local government, health, personal social services, schools, housing and roads. In 1976 a bill to enact these proposals was introduced. It was, however, widely criticised. Some felt the proposals went too far, others, especially the extreme nationalists, that they did not go far enough. Both main political parties were split over this issue.

After long debate the Scotland and Wales Acts were passed by Parliament in 1978, but were not to be implemented until an advisory referendum in the two countries showed that at least 40 per cent of the electorate supported them. It became clear that Welsh nationalism, based mainly on culture and language, had a dividing rather than a unifying effect, and was supported by only a small minority. In Scotland, however, the majority of the population had for many years wished to have a greater say in their own affairs. This was partly caused by discontent at the economic weakness of the United Kingdom, and was an example of the general swing in Western Europe towards regional and national loyalties. In many European countries the devolution of power to regional parliaments had reduced tension and increased stability. The problem was how to give Scotland a measure of self-government while preserving the economic unity of the United Kingdom and allowing efficient and workable government. There was little enthusiasm for the proposed Scottish Assembly, rather, there was a great deal of confusion and indifference. The Scottish Nationalist Party, whose support was declining, said that devolution was a first step towards an independent Scotland. The Labour leadership said the Assembly was good in its own right. The Conservative leadership opposed the Assembly, saying the proposals would bring more but not better government. The referendum was held in March 1979. Only 12 per cent of the Welsh electorate supported the proposals, a clear rejection of the Wales Act. In Scotland, however, 33 per cent supported and 31 per cent opposed the Scotland Act, and the situation was unresolved. The government refused to implement the Act immediately. Consequently, the Scottish Nationalist MPs, together with the Conservatives and Liberals, opposed the government in a vote of confidence. Labour lost by one vote, and Callaghan announced a General Election for May 1979.

Clear policy differences between the two major parties emerged during the election campaign. On wages the Conservatives wanted free, responsible collective bargaining, while Labour supported a voluntary incomes policy. Conservatives wanted some legislation to limit the power of trade unions, while Labour said this would produce confrontation. The Conservatives wished to reduce income tax and public expenditure and to increase indirect taxation; Labour said this would weaken essential services, raise prices and benefit only the better-off. Labour were critical of the cost of the Common Market's Common Agricultural Policy, the system of high and guaranteed prices paid to farmers irrespective of demand so that unwanted food surpluses were bought and stored at great expense; Conservatives were generally less critical of the European Community. The Conservatives put great stress on measures to promote law and order. Labour had attempted to compel Local Authorities to have comprehensive schools, and Conservatives opposed this. The Conservatives wanted greater defence spending to counter the build-up of Russian forces, and over Africa were inclined to take a more sympathetic view of the internal settlement in Rhodesia. In general, it appeared that Callaghan and Labour were offering more of what had gone before, while Mrs Thatcher and the Conservatives were preaching the need for change. The latter were more in line with the national mood, and the result was a sweeping Conservative victory. The Conservatives polled 13.6 million votes and gained 339 seats, Labour received 11.5 million votes and gained 268 seats, while the Liberals polled 4.3 million votes and only won 11 seats. Other parties had 17 seats between them. As leader of the Conservative Party Margaret Thatcher became in May 1979 the first British woman Prime Minister.

The Commonwealth

The character of the British Empire and Commonwealth has changed greatly since the Statute of Westminister in 1931 (see p. 221) defined the relationship of the dominions—Britain, Canada, South Africa, Australia, New Zealand, Newfoundland[1] and Eire. These originally constituted the Commonwealth. At this point Britain still directly ruled an Empire consisting of large numbers of colonies throughout the world. In 1932 the Ottawa Economic Conference introduced imperial preference, and the trading links between the dominions grew. But their political independence was real. When Britain declared war on Germany in 1939, Australia and New Zealand automatically did likewise. Canada and South Africa, however, only declared war after their parliaments had agreed to do so. In 1947–48 India, Pakistan, Ceylon and Burma became independent. All except Burma decided to join the Commonwealth. Soon after, India became a republic and continued to recognise the British monarch only as Head of the Commonwealth. India, too, remained uncommitted in the Cold War, thus indicating that the Commonwealth no longer attempted to follow a common foreign policy. In 1957 Ghana and Malaya attained independence. During the ten years from 1960 to 1969, nineteen other countries ruled by Britain obtained independence and all (except Sudan) became members of the Commonwealth. By 1977 there were thirty-six members. Thus the character of the Commonwealth has changed from an organisation consisting mainly of people of British descent to one including most races of the world.

In January 1978 the independent members of the Commonwealth were:

United Kingdom	—1931 (Statute of Westminster)
Canada	—1931 (Statute of Westminster)
Australia	—1931 (Statute of Westminster)
New Zealand	—1931 (Statute of Westminster)
India	—1947 (Date of independence)
Pakistan	—1947
Ceylon	—1948
Malaysia	—1957 (Malaya before 1963)
Ghana	—1957
Nigeria	—1960
Cyprus	—1961
Sierra Leone	—1961

[1] Newfoundland was incorporated into Canada in 1949.

Tanzania   —1961 (Tanganyika before 1964)
Uganda   —1962
Jamaica   —1962
Trinidad and Tobago —1962
Kenya   —1963
Malta   —1964
Malawi   —1964 (formerly Nyasaland)
Zambia   —1964 (formerly Northern Rhodesia)
Gambia   —1965
Singapore   —1965 (part of Malaysia, 1963–65)
Guyana   —1966
Lesotho   —1966 (formerly Basutoland)
Botswana   —1966 (formerly Bechuanaland)
Barbados   —1966
Nauru   —1968
Mauritius   —1968
Swaziland   —1968
Tonga   —1970
Western Samoa   —1970
Fiji   —1970
Bangladesh   —1972
The Bahamas   —1973
Grenada   —1974
Papua New Guinea —1975
The Seychelles   —1976

In addition there are 5 million people living in self-governing states and dependencies linked with member countries: these are mainly small islands.

Three countries have resigned from the Commonwealth: Eire in 1949; South Africa (because her racial policies were unacceptable in a multiracial Commonwealth) in 1961; and Pakistan in 1972 because Britain and other countries had recognised Bangladesh. The area covered by the Commonwealth in 1978 is about a quarter of the world's land surface, and the total membership is about 1,000 million people. All members recognise the British monarch as Head of the Commonwealth.

There are a number of links between the members of the Commonwealth which serve to give some sort of form to this nebulous organisation. Trade within the Commonwealth was once a very important factor. After the 1932 Ottawa conference the system of

Commonwealth preferences—that is, reduced or nil tariffs on goods imported from other Commonwealth countries—helped to develop mutual trade. In 1951 51 per cent of British exports were sent to the Commonwealth. However, after the early 1950s other industrial powers recovered from the war or emerged for the first time. In addition the developing countries of the Commonwealth (which before had taken British manufactured goods) now developed their own industries. Consequently, trade among the Commonwealth partners fell rapidly. During the 1960s Britain halved its exports to the Commonwealth, while the countries of the EEC became Britain's fastest-growing market. For most Commonwealth countries Britain became less and less important as a trading partner. When Britain entered the Common Market in 1973 arrangements were made to deal with Caribbean sugar exports and New Zealand dairy produce, but in other respects the loss of Commonwealth preference meant very little to most of the developing countries.

Nevertheless, one fifth of total trade by Commonwealth members is carried out with other members, and questions of finance, trade and economic relations are frequently discussed at Heads-of-Government meetings. The richer members of the Commonwealth provide the poorer members with economic and technical aid. Eighty per cent of Britain's overseas economic aid, for example, goes to the Commonwealth.

There are a large number of educational contacts between members of the Commonwealth, especially at university level. There is a vast network of exchanges, both of teachers and students, between member countries. The legal systems of many members are similar. Cooperation in health matters, possible because of broadly similar systems of medical schools and health services, has been increasing. There are in all about 250 Commonwealth organisations below inter-governmental level which promote contacts, and about 50 meetings are held each year. The Commonwealth Foundation was formed in 1965 to enable professional men and women in the member states to meet each other. In 1947 it was agreed that each Commonwealth country would recognise as British subjects its own citizens and citizens of other Commonwealth countries, but this agreement has since been radically changed. The question of immigration and the movement of Commonwealth citizens between member states has aroused considerable controversy, especially in Britain.

Since 1944 the Commonwealth Heads of Government have met in conference at intervals of about eighteen months. Twenty-one such meetings have been held so far. Before 1965 all the meetings were held in London; since then other capital cities have been the venue. Until about 1960 major international issues were discussed. The meetings were held in private, they took place in a frank and informal atmosphere, and provided an opportunity for personal contacts. During the 1960s, however, the membership grew, the number of officials present increased, and the meetings became more formal. African problems tended to dominate: after 1965 the problem of Rhodesia, and in 1970–71 the proposal of Heath's Conservative government in Britain to supply arms to South Africa to help in the defence of the sea routes round the Cape. On both issues Britain found herself bitterly attacked by African states: on Rhodesia they wanted tougher British action against Smith's regime, and in connection with South Africa they considered that no member of the Commonwealth should support a regime which practised racial discrimination with any assistance which could consolidate or strengthen it. The British, on the other hand, were not prepared to use force against Rhodesia, and said that there was no question of arms for South Africa being used to enforce the policy of apartheid. In addition the British considered that the Commonwealth could not be allowed to dictate the national policy of any member state.

After the Conference at Singapore in 1971 when the subject of arms for South Africa dominated, there was widespread pessimism about the future of the Commonwealth. The likelihood of British admission into the Common Market, together with the sharply reduced military presence east of Suez, seemed to indicate that Britain's world role and, indeed, interest, were ending. The British attitude to the Commonwealth changed during the 1960s. Before this point there was general pride in the organisation and the fact that nearly every country of the Empire remained in the Commonwealth softened the effect of loss of power in the world. But after about 1960 Britain's attitude became less enthusiastic; there was irritation at the Commonwealth's blunt criticism of British policy, for example, towards Rhodesia; some opinion was contemptuous of the Commonwealth mystique and lack of substance—it appeared to be a grin without a Cheshire cat—and there was the feeling that Britain should concentrate on Europe, its natural cultural home.

However, the Commonwealth appeared to revive during the 1970s. The atmosphere was constructive and optimistic at the Ottawa Meeting in 1973 which was presided over by Trudeau, the Prime Minister of Canada. He set the tone of lively informality. At this and subsequent conferences economic affairs were much in prominence, and subjects which would find no place on the agenda of other meetings (for example, comparative techniques of government) were discussed.

The Commonwealth remains a very nebulous organisation. The formal strands which hold it together hardly exist, and loyalty to the British monarch is much less than it used to be. It is no longer composed of like-minded countries: some are democracies, some are dictatorships; some belong to alliances, some are non-aligned. The larger it has grown, the greater has become the diversity of views within it. There are wide differences of living standards between wealthy countries like Australia and Canada and poverty-stricken countries like Malawi and Tanzania. It is possible for two countries to go to war against each other—as did India and Pakistan in 1965— and still remain members of the Commonwealth. Many of the benefits which derive from membership could be maintained if the organisation did not exist. 'Almost any adjective . . . can be applied to the Commonwealth as it has grown since 1947. It is shapeless, unorganised, anomalous, illogical. Equally, it is flexible, adaptable, pragmatic, useful.'[1]

The Commonwealth is held together by a number of factors: a common background in that all the members were once ruled from London; a common language—English; the contacts between governments and peoples that have been described above; the value which is attached to the Commonwealth as a multiracial organisation—'a pilot scheme for world cooperation'. The Commonwealth Secretariat, which was formed in 1965, has been the main agency for communications in recent years (Arnold Smith, a Canadian, was Secretary-General from 1965 to 1975, and was then succeeded by Shridath Ramphal from Guyana). The Commonwealth is valued by many as a forum for discussion and an instrument for understanding the nature of problems, a place for pooling experiences, sharing expertise and arguing viewpoints. It remains to be seen whether its members consider the Commonwealth sufficiently important to foster its growth in the years ahead.

[1] *The Times*, 7 July 1964.

7

North Africa and the Middle East

Beginning of the Twentieth Century

Over half of the territory described in this chapter is desert. Much of the remaining area is infertile and underpopulated, most people being crowded into small areas of relatively high population density. With the exception of Persia (Iran), southern Sudan and Israel, everybody speaks Arabic and is a member of one of the sects of Islam. Persia is separated from the Arab world by geography, language and religion. In 1900 much of this area, with its long history of civilisation, was under the control of the Turks, the British and the French. Weak and despotic governments ruled the rest.

North-west Africa was under the rule or influence of France. In 1830 the French captured Algiers from the Turks, and by 1850 the hostile native population of Algeria was conquered. About half a million Europeans—hard working, patriotic but narrow-minded—were living in Algeria at the beginning of the twentieth century. They regarded themselves as superior to the primitive, landless agricultural labourers who made up the mass of the Muslim population. The official French policy of assimilation was regarded as a joke by the Europeans who showed little concern for Muslim welfare. 'It is difficult to try and convince the European settler that there are rights other than his own in an Arab country and that the native is not a race to be taxed and exploited at his whim' (Jules Ferry, 1892).

East of Algeria was the small independent state of Tunisia. Italian influence was strong here, but in 1881 the French forced the Bey to recognise a French protectorate. French ambition was now directed towards Morocco. In 1894 the last strong and energetic Sultan died, and was succeeded by a boy of fourteen. Under his feeble rule, authority soon crumbled. The British consul-general described Morocco at the time as 'a loose agglomeration of turbulent tribes, corrupt governors, and general poverty and distress'. Clearly the current imperialist urge could not ignore this strategically-placed state. France wanted to round off her north-west African empire, and therefore encouraged French financiers to invest in Morocco in order to increase French influence. Spain also had ambitions but was too weak to fulfil them, while Britain's main concern was to neutralise the southern shore of the Mediterranean opposite Gibraltar. Germany's aims were not clear: an Atlantic port, commercial influence, a quarrel between Britain and France—all played some part in Germany's motives.

Britain ruled in Egypt and the Sudan at the beginning of the twentieth century although both states remained nominally part of the Turkish Empire until 1914. Egypt had been in practice an independent state since the reign of the great Mohammed Ali in the first half of the nineteenth century. With the big increase in European settlement in Asia, the Mediterranean–Red Sea route became very important, especially after the opening of the Suez Canal in 1869. Six years later the extravagant Khedive or sovereign of Egypt, who was heavily in debt, sold his 44 per cent share in the capital of the Suez Canal Company to the British Government. Following the bankruptcy of Egypt in 1876, there was joint Anglo-French control of Egyptian finances in order to protect European investments. This growing European interference in Egypt's internal affairs led to the beginnings of Egyptian nationalism among a small group of young men with modern western ideas. The killing of many Europeans in a nationalist revolt in 1881 resulted in the bombardment of Alexandria by the British fleet and a military occupation of the country.

Thus began the *de facto* British rule of Egypt. It was based on conquest and had no legal title. At first the British intended to withdraw, but eventually stayed, partly in order to protect and control the Suez Canal, so important on the line of imperial communications, and partly because of imperialist pride and the urge to acquire territory. The Khedive's government continued but acted on the direction of British advisers, headed by Lord Cromer. There were many good reforms—irrigation, education, health, finance, administration—but discontent among the Egyptian middle and upper classes produced a second surge of nationalism that was growing stronger by 1900.

Egypt governed—or rather misgoverned—the Sudan from 1820 to 1883. In 1881, however, the sincerely religious, the politically discontented and the nomads who disliked established government, gave their support to a Sudanese who said he was the expected Mahdi or Messiah. The Egyptians were defeated, and in 1885 the fearless, brilliant but perverse General Gordon, sent with instructions to withdraw the remaining Anglo-Egyptian troops, was killed. For thirteen years after 1885 the Mahdists ruled the Sudan but British occupation was inevitable: apart from the need to gain control of the upper waters of the Nile in order to protect Egypt (for other European Powers—France, Italy, Belgium—were casting ambitious eyes on the Sudan), the British public demanded revenge for the death of Gordon.

Consequently an Anglo-Egyptian army under Kitchener advanced up the Nile and in 1898 won the Battle of Omdurman.[1] Twenty-seven thousand Sudanese and about 400 Anglo-Egyptians were killed or wounded. The Mahdi's tomb (he had died some years before) was razed to the ground. There were even rumours that Kitchener intended to send the Mahdi's skull to the Royal College of Surgeons in London to be placed on exhibition alongside the intestines of Napoleon.

News of the expected French intervention in the Sudan reached Kitchener a few days after the battle. A small French party under the intrepid Captain Marchand occupied Fashoda in July 1898. Kitchener, wearing an Egyptian uniform and flying the Egyptian flag, arrived at Fashoda with a considerable force and warned Marchand that the French presence was an infringement of Anglo-Egyptian rights. For two months relations were tense, but finally in November the French government ordered Marchand to leave.

In 1899 the British and Egyptians agreed upon the government of the Sudan. The so-called Condominium Agreement provided for joint Anglo-Egyptian rule. This was an artificial agreement, without precedent in international law, and in fact the British ruled alone through a British-appointed governor-general.

The central part of the area described in this chapter was in 1900 part of the oppressive and inefficient Turkish Empire, and included the countries that were later known as Iraq, Syria, Lebanon, Palestine, Jordan, Saudi Arabia, the Yemen and Libya. Control of the outlying parts of this Empire was only nominal. There had been some reforms during the second half of the nineteenth century, but, nevertheless, the semi-educated officials who governed were not very interested in improving the backward state of their subjects.

---

[1] Churchill took part in one of the last great cavalry charges in history at Omdurman. Lord Cromer later wrote: 'The cannon which swept away the Dervish hordes at Omdurman proclaimed to the world that on England—or, to be more strictly correct, on Egypt under British guidance—had devolved the solemn and responsible duty of introducing the light of Western civilisation amongst the sorely tried people of the Sudan.'

The two most populated areas were Iraq and Syria. In both there was a small cultured intelligentsia living amongst poverty-stricken and illiterate peasants and tribesmen. There were few roads, no railways, and no modern industry. One British official has written of Iraq, 'The country passed from the nineteenth century little less wild and ignorant, as unfitted for self-government and not less corrupt, than it had entered the sixteenth century.'[1] In Syria the position was slightly better, partly because of the activities of French and American missionaries. Since the Crusades, the French had regarded themselves as protectors of the Christians in Syria. In 1900 half the number of children receiving education attended French schools. The result of this European educational influence was the fostering of Western political ideas and, since the Americans published school textbooks for them in Arabic, a revival of interest in Arab literature, history and civilisation. This, in turn, had produced by 1900 a tiny but significant group of nationalists.

British influence was strong in the coastal areas of Arabia. Aden had been occupied since about 1840 and British protectorates established over the twenty-five small and primitive states, mainly east of Aden. Similarly amongst the backward sheikhdoms of the Persian Gulf, the British presence was clear. In 1899 the Sheikh of Kuwait, believing that the Turks were threatening his independence, asked Britain to establish a protectorate.

East of Turkish Iraq and stretching as far as the borders of Afghanistan and British India was the mountainous land of Persia, the world's oldest kingdom. Separated from the Arab world by its mountains, its language and its religion (the Persians support a particular Muslim sect), Persia was medieval in its ways and open to Russian and British penetration.

1900 to 1914

Crises over Morocco 1905 to 1906, 1911

At the beginning of the century Morocco was one of the leading subjects of diplomatic negotiation between the great powers. France aimed at securing the formal acknowledgment from these powers of her special interests in the country. In 1900 Italian approval was obtained when in return for Italian recognition of Morocco as a French sphere of influence, France recognised Tripoli as an Italian sphere of influence. After 1902 when the Anglo-Japanese Alliance was formed the

[1] S. H. Longrigg, *Iraq 1900–1950*.

need for agreement with Britain became more urgent, for there was the danger that a war between Japan and Russia would involve their respective allies, Britain and France. Neither Britain nor France wanted such a war and therefore it was necessary to reach agreement over Morocco.

In 1904 the Anglo-French Agreement was negotiated. France recognised that Egypt, already under the secure rule of Lord Cromer, was to be a British sphere of influence. In return Britain recognised Morocco as a French sphere provided that Spain's interests were safe-guarded and the Mediterranean coastline opposite Gibraltar was not fortified. Later in the year a Franco-Spanish Agreement arranged that Spain was to receive a narrow strip of northern Morocco around Tangier.

Thus France had secured the approval of Italy, Britain and Spain for her imperial interests in Morocco. However, Germany's approval had not been gained, and this omission caused the crises of 1905–6 and 1911. In March 1905, Kaiser William II landed at Tangier. His precise aims were not clear, but he recognised the independence of the Sultan and demanded an international conference on the future of Morocco. This conference was held early in 1906 at Algeciras near Gibraltar. The independence of Morocco was formally declared, but there was to be international control of Moroccan finances, and France and Spain were to supervise the Moroccan police. In practice the Algeciras conference gave France a free hand to intervene if conditions deteriorated within Morocco.

During the next few years there was growing disorder, and in May 1911 the French occupied Fez in order to guard the Sultan and European interests. Since it was almost certain that a French protectorate would follow, the German government decided to press for compensation for themselves. In July the German gunboat *Panther* arrived at Agadir, theoretically with the object of guarding German subjects and property.[1] For several weeks tension was high. Lloyd George and the British government gave firm support to the French, and there seemed the strong possibility of war starting. However, by November Germany, in return for two strips of territory in the French Congo, agreed to a French protectorate over Morocco, and the crisis died down.

Early in 1912 the French established their protectorate, and a French Resident General was installed. Later in the year Spain received her promised territory around Tangier.

---

[1] A German citizen was hurriedly sent to Agadir in order to be protected.

Beginnings of Arab Nationalism

In the previous section it was seen that nationalism was developing secretly among the intellectuals and politically ambitious upper-class Arabs of Syria and Iraq. This tiny minority wanted religious and political reform, but had little concern for social problems. For about a year following the Young Turk Revolution of 1908 (see p. 5), the Arabs were hopeful of securing some of their aims, but the Sultan's attempted counterrevolution provided the excuse for the Young Turks to clamp down on Arab organisations, and nationalism was once again driven underground. Some temporary concessions, for example, the introduction of Arabic as an official language, were made by the Turks just before the First World War, when they agreed to the requests of the Young Arab Congress which had met in Paris.

In Egypt nationalism was more active and vocal. Lord Cromer retired in 1907 to be succeeded by Sir Eldon Gorst, a competent and conscientious man who, however, lacked personality and powers of leadership. Under the direction of the Liberal Government British control was relaxed. In 1907 the National Party was founded by the eloquent French-educated Mustafa Kemal, and an outburst of violent nationalist agitation followed. Four years later Gorst was replaced by Kitchener who had instructions to channel the energies of Egyptians away from nationalist activities. Kitchener created a Legislative Assembly which could delay legislation for a period, but otherwise he used his great prestige to provide strong and reforming government.

German influence in Turkey

German influence in the Turkish Empire was military and economic. The political implications of this influence were dealt with in chapter 1. From the 1880s German officers had been training the Turkish army. That this training had proved rather unsuccessful was seen by the ease with which Italy occupied Libya in 1911 and the Balkan League defeated Turkey in 1912–13. A high-ranking German general was therefore sent in 1913 to reorganise the Turkish army more vigorously.

German military assistance was probably more important, but until 1913 caused less concern, than German railway building in the Turkish Empire. In the early 1890s the Germans had built a railway from the Bosphorus to Ankara, and in 1899, following a visit by Kaiser William II to Constantinople and Damascus when he proclaimed himself the friend of all Muslims, a German company was given the right to continue the railway to Baghdad and the Persian Gulf. This railway would clearly be of considerable economic and military advantage to Turkey, and at first received British encouragement. After about 1903, however, Britain, fearing for the maintenance of British power in the Persian Gulf with an influential Germany also there, adopted a more hostile attitude. The controversy continued until 1913 when an agreement was finally made between Turkey, Germany and Britain: the Baghdad Railway was to be completed on condition that it went no farther than Basra.

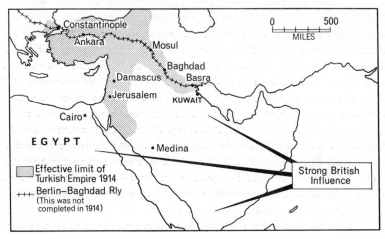

The Turkish Empire in 1914

Russo-British influence in Persia

Growing discontent with the government of the Shah led to a revolution in 1905. This culminated in the Shah's agreement to the creation of a representative assembly. This met in 1906. However, the disorders continued and Britain, fearing that Russian penetration would reach the borders of India, decided in 1907 to negotiate with Russia. It was finally agreed that Persia was to remain independent, but with the northern third of the country within the Russian sphere of influence, the south-eastern third within the British sphere and a neutral zone in between. In addition it was agreed that Afghanistan was to be within the British sphere of influence, and that Tibet was to remain a neutral buffer state.

This division was purely strategic. Oil was not involved, but the agreement was clearly to Britain's advantage when major discoveries of oil were made along the northern shore of the Persian Gulf. The Anglo-Persian Oil Company was formed in 1909, and after 1914 this was controlled by the British Government.

Zionist Movement

Mention should be made at this stage of the beginnings of a movement that was to be of crucial importance in Middle Eastern affairs from 1918 onwards. In 1900 there were, as there had been for centuries, only a few thousand Jews living in Palestine, the ancient home of the Jews, but some 15 million were scattered around Europe and North America. There had been illtreatment of these Jewish minorities for centuries, but in the late nineteenth century the persecution in Russia (where two-thirds of the world's Jews lived), France (for example the Dreyfus case), and Germany was particularly intense. A few Jews emigrated to Palestine; many more went to the United States or Britain, and the feeling grew that a country of their own would raise the status of Jews.

Then in 1896 Theodore Herzl, a Viennese journalist, published a pamphlet called *The Jewish State* in which he called for the creation of a Jewish national home. Next year the World Zionist Organisation was founded at Basle.[1] The British Government offered part of Kenya as Jewish territory, but the Zionists decided that their home could only be Palestine. Steady immigration took place so that by 1914 about 80,000 Jews were living in Palestine.

First World War 1914 to 1918

After some delay, in October 1914 Turkey entered the war on the side of the Central Powers. There were two main areas of fighting in the region covered by this chapter, Iraq and Palestine.

Following Turkey's declaration of war British forces occupied Basra and, by the middle of 1915, southern Iraq. This was primarily to protect the Persian Gulf and British oil interests in Persia. During the greater part of 1916 the Turks counterattacked and, after a long siege, reoccupied the city of Kut. But at the end of 1916 the British advance continued against only light opposition; Baghdad was captured and just before the armistice was signed Mosul was reached. Meanwhile British troops occupied the southern half of Persia during most of the war; Russian troops were in the north until the Bolshevik Revolution.

With the declaration of war, the British clarified their legal position

[1] Herzl wrote in his diary: 'At Basle I founded the Jewish state.' Fifty years later Herzl's dream became a reality.

in Egypt by proclaiming a protectorate. Large numbers of troops arrived and a Turkish attack in 1915 was easily repulsed. Meanwhile the British began negotiations with Hussein, ruler of Mecca and other Muslim holy cities in the Hejaz, with the object of stimulating an Arab revolt against the Turks. MacMahon the British High Commissioner in Egypt and Hussein continued these negotiations during 1915 and into 1916. This correspondence became very controversial since it appeared that the British (who were not certain of the extent to which Hussein, an ambitious man, spoke for the rest of the Arabs) agreed to the formation of independent Arab kingdoms in Arabia, Palestine, Iraq and Syria in return for Arab support against the Turks. Unfortunately for British and French relations with the Arabs it later became known that at about the same time in 1916 the Sykes-Picot Agreement arranged for the partition of Turkey's Arab Empire between Britain and France: France was to rule the Syrian coast and form a protectorate over the rest of Syria, while Britain was to govern central and south Iraq with a protectorate over the north.

However, the Sykes-Picot Agreement was not made public until the end of 1917. Meanwhile MacMahon's promises, together with harsh treatment from the Turks, persuaded the Arabs to revolt in June 1916. Arab forces led by Hussein's son, Feisal, and by the famous Lawrence of Arabia attacked the flank of the Turco-German line.[1] Judgment of the usefulness of the revolt varies widely, but it certainly had nuisance value, it meant that the British fought in friendly country, and it stimulated nationalism. At the end of 1917 British forces occupied Jerusalem, and a year later Feisal, Lawrence and the Arabs entered Damascus.

One final event of importance should be mentioned here. During the war the Zionist Movement became increasingly influential in Britain and the United States. Its leader in Britain was Dr Weizmann, a Russian-born lecturer in chemistry at Manchester University who made important discoveries in explosives. Weizmann converted Balfour, the British Foreign Secretary, to the idea of Palestine for the Jews, partly because a Jewish state would help in the defence of Suez. In November 1917 the Balfour Declaration was made:

HM's Government view with favour the establishment in Palestine of a National Home for the Jewish people, and will use their best endeavours to facilitate the achievement of this object, it being clearly understood that nothing shall be done which may prejudice the civil and religious rights of other non-Jewish communities in Palestine.

[1] See T. E. Lawrence, *The Seven Pillars of Wisdom*, an historical and imaginative commentary on the war.

Thus during 1916–17 the British Government had made three contradictory and incompatible pledges: that the Arabs should set up independent states, that the Jews should have Palestine as national territory, and that Britain and France should divide up Syria and Iraq between them.

1918 to 1939

Mandates established

When the war ended in November 1918, Feisal and the Arabs in Damascus were ruling Syria, Lebanon and Jordan, while the British had control of Iraq and Palestine. During 1919 the British handed over to the French the military occupation of the Syrian coast.

In June 1919 the Treaty of Versailles provided for mandates in Turkey's Arab Empire, but a decision on details was delayed until a treaty with Turkey had been arranged. Meanwhile Arab nationalism was growing, and in March 1920 the nationalists proclaimed Feisal as King of an independent Syria, Palestine and Lebanon, and his brother Abdullah as king of Iraq. But in the following month, at an Allied conference at San Remo, France was officially given the mandate for Syria and Lebanon, and Britain the mandate for Iraq, Palestine and Jordan.

France and Britain had four main motives: imperial strategy and communications; commercial interests; the genuine feeling that the peoples of the areas concerned needed training for self-government; and the hope that these countries, when eventually independent, would ally with them. But they underestimated the strength and feeling of Arab nationalism, and both the British and French were faced with constant unrest.

Iraq

The period of the British mandate divides into two clear sections, 1920–22 and 1922–32. Following the confirmation of the mandate the British were immediately faced with a nationalist rising, mainly in the countryside of central and southern Iraq. Considerable damage was done, but order was soon restored. In October 1920 the British announced that they intended to establish an Iraqi government whose independence would be at first limited by the presence of British advisers. A Provisional Government of Iraqi ministers, each with a British adviser, was then set up. In 1921 Feisal (who had been driven

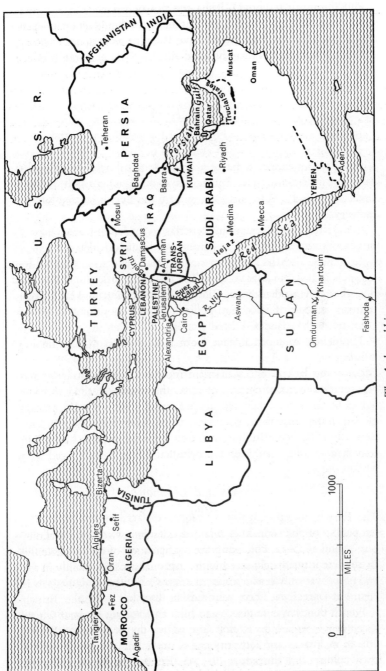

The Arab world in 1924

out of Syria) was accepted as King, and in 1922 the Anglo-Iraqi Treaty was signed. This gave legal effect to the existing situation in which British approval was necessary for the actions of the Iraqi Government.

During the next ten years British control worked reasonably well. In 1924 a Constituent Assembly ratified the 1922 treaty and drew up a constitution providing for an appointed Senate and an elected Chamber of Deputies. The parliamentary system suffered from frequent changes of government, but was greatly helped by the charm, political flair, good sense and personal authority of King Feisal who restrained the activities of a small number of ambitious politicians. The British contributed to the development of the new state by stabilising frontiers, creating an administration, a judicial system, a modern police force, a small army and a new currency, and by developing agriculture and industry.

In the late 1920s negotiations were started for full independence, and in 1930 the second Anglo-Iraqi Treaty was signed. Britain retained the right to have air bases and other military installations in Iraq, and Iraq was to help Britain in time of war. The British Ambassador was to have precedence over other ambassadors, and both countries were to avoid mutually embarrassing foreign policies. This treaty came into force in 1932, when the mandate officially ended.

The period of independence from 1932 to 1941 was marked by political weakness. Feisal died in 1933 and was succeeded by his son Ghazi—who lacked his father's experience and judgment. There were on average about five changes of government each year. These factors led to Iraq's first military *coup d'état* in 1936. For a year the younger officers in the army ruled with left-wing support, but soon lost public sympathy. The constitution was then restored, although the army remained an influential element in politics.

Syria and Lebanon

The French, like the British in Iraq, were faced at first with active nationalist opposition. This was temporarily ended by the French occupation of Damascus, but flared up again on two other occasions. In 1925-26 a well-organised and widespread rebellion cost many lives and peace was only restored after the French had twice bombarded the centre of Damascus. There were further disorders in 1936.

French policy was to divide and rule. By dividing the territory into seven provinces, and by exploiting religious divisions, the French were able to maintain their authority and to encourage the growth of their own culture and education. In 1928 negotiations for a constitution began between the French and moderate Syrian politicians. It was hoped that this would eventually be modelled on the Anglo-Iraqi Treaty of 1930, but no agreement was reached, and the French imposed their own constitution. In 1936, however, the Popular Front Government in France which was more sympathetic towards the nationalists, concluded a draft treaty with Syria and Lebanon. This was ratified by the Syrian Parliament, but in France concern for the maintenance of the French strategic position in the Eastern Mediterranean, combined with concern for the future of the Christian minorities, delayed ratification. Just before war broke out in Europe the French dissolved the extreme nationalist organisations and suspended the constitution.

Transjordan

In 1920 the British said that they intended to grant immediate self-government to this poverty-stricken and mainly desert state east of the Jordan. But in the following year Feisal's brother, Abdullah, and an Arab force, occupied Amman and were welcomed by the people. The British, whose mandate continued, did not oppose Abdullah who took over effective government. He ruled peacefully and securely with British military, financial and technical help.

Palestine

Between the wars Britain reaped in Palestine the consequences of conflicting promises given to Jews and Arabs in 1916–17. By 1920 the Arabs were feeling particularly bitter towards the British, firstly because of the establishment of the mandate when they had expected independence, and secondly because the British were allowing Jews to immigrate in growing numbers. Britain's self-imposed obligations under the Balfour Declaration—to build up a national home for the Jews, and to preserve the rights of the Arabs—were irreconcilable. It became clear that the Jews wanted not a home but a state. The bitterness of the Arabs showed itself in communal riots and violence, and was only partly appeased by the 1922 White Paper. This said that the Balfour Declaration did 'not contemplate that Palestine as a whole should be converted into a Jewish National Home, but that such a home should be founded in Palestine'.

The British hoped that Jews and Arabs would cooperate to form one country, but this hope became more and more unrealistic as the years passed. The number of Jews increased to 150,000 by 1928 and their agriculture, industry, health services and standard of living generally were far in advance of those of the Arab majority. The concessions given to Egypt, Iraq, Syria and Transjordan stimulated the Palestine Arabs to seek similar powers themselves. A second wave of rioting broke out in 1928–29. Hundreds of Jews were killed or injured and a Royal Commission was sent out to investigate the cause. The Commission's report pointed out the inconsistency contained in the two pledges in the Balfour Declaration and recommended a limitation on Jewish immigration. An expert enquiry into agriculture likewise recommended that there should be no more immigration until land had been developed.

A White Paper in 1930 was based on these two reports. There was an immediate outburst of furious Jewish opposition which influenced the British Prime Minister, Ramsay MacDonald, to such an extent that he restated British policy in what the Arabs called the 'Black Letter'. This stated that the British did not intend to limit either immigration or the acquisition of land by Jews.

Jews continued, therefore, to emigrate to Palestine, especially after the Nazis came to power in Germany. Before 1933 the average number of immigrants was 9,000 per year; in 1935 alone 62,000 arrived. A large proportion of the new arrivals were scientists, engineers, doctors and businessmen: the social and economic gap between Jews and Arabs widened while the numerical gap narrowed. By 1935 a quarter of the total population of Palestine was Jewish.

The Arabs grew more and more discontented and in 1935 demanded from the British High Commissioner democratic government, the prohibition of land transfers from Arabs to Jews and the immediate stopping of immigration. Widespread disturbances broke out during 1936: armed bands of Arabs took to the hills, and Jewish crops and property were destroyed. A Royal Commission was sent to Palestine in 1937 and decided that the mandate in its present form was unworkable and that partition was the only solution. Partition received only moderate support from the Jews and was totally rejected by the Arabs whose terrorism increased to such a pitch that the British lost control of parts of Palestine. The need to appease the Arabs, particularly with a second world war threatening, together with the economic difficulties of partition, eventually persuaded the British that a federation was preferable. The 1939 White Paper therefore abandoned the idea of partition and said that immigration and land transfer should be limited. This was the unsatisfactory and unsettled position when the Second World War intervened.

Saudi Arabia

The most powerful ruler in eastern Arabia after 1902 was Ibn Saud. From his capital at Riyadh, he gradually consolidated his grip on the desert people, and took no part in the Arab revolt. After the war Ibn Saud occupied the territory of his ancestral enemy to the north. This achieved, he then turned his eyes on Hussein's lands in the Hejaz. Husein was unpopular for a number of reasons. He had called himself King of the Arabs and then attempted to enhance his position further by declaring himself Caliph of the Muslims. This was too much for the puritanical Muslim sect to which Ibn Saud belonged, who regarded Mecca and Medina as centres of idolatry. In 1924 Hussein was foolish enough to quarrel with his two powerful supporters, Britain and Egypt. In the following year, Ibn Saud seized his opportunity and occupied the Hejaz.

In 1927 Britain recognised Ibn Saud as king of the territories that were later called Saudi Arabia. In return King Saud recognised Feisal and Abdullah, the sons of Hussein, as rulers of Iraq and Jordan respectively. Saudi Arabia, ten times the size of the United Kingdom, is nearly all desert, is sparsely populated, and was desperately poor until oil was discovered during the 1930s. Before the enormous income from this source began to pour in, the country's revenue came largely from the tourist and pilgrim trade in Mecca and Medina, and from customs duties and tithes.

Egypt

Egyptian nationalism, temporarily stifled first by Kitchener and then by the presence of a large British army, flared up once more when the war was over. The strongest party, the Wafd, was well organised and had the support of the rich landowners. At its head was Zaghlul, a tall, ungainly lawyer, with exceptional powers of leadership. In 1919 Zaghlul, who wished to present his case for complete independence at the Paris Conference, fomented strikes and disturbances. Eventually he was allowed to attend the Conference, but failed to make any impression. However, early in 1920 the British sent the Milner Commission to Egypt to consider a new form of government. The Commission recommended an independent Egypt ruled by a constitutional monarchy and a parliament, but with independence limited by an alliance with Great Britain and by the right of the British to keep an army in Egypt to defend the Suez Canal. During 1921 negotiations broke down over Egyptian insistence that the British Army should be confined to the Canal Zone. The British government then decided on a unilateral decision, and in February 1922 the protectorate was ended, and Egypt became independent. But it was independence with conditions: the British insisted on their right to defend the Suez Canal and Egypt, to protect foreign residents and to rule the Sudan.

So began in 1922 the very limited independence of Egypt. The first elections produced a Wafdist government and Zaghlul became Prime Minister. He again demanded that all British troops should leave Egyptian soil and that Sudan should be returned to Egypt. The British again refused and tension rose. When the British Commander-in-Chief of the Egyptian army was murdered in a Cairo street in 1924, the British response was determined and swift. The Wafdist government fell from power, and for two years King Fuad (1917-36) ruled without parliament.

From 1926 onwards there were constantly changing governments, usually dominated by the Wafdists who were unpopular both with the King and the British, but who had a nationwide organisation and nearly always won general elections despite frequent royal intervention. Periodic negotiations with the British had no positive result. Then in 1935 the Italians conquered Ethiopia. Both British and Egyptian interests appeared to be menaced by Fascism, and in 1936 a compromise agreement was reached through the Anglo-Egyptian Treaty. The British were to keep troops in the Canal Zone only—Egyptians were to be admitted to the Sudan on the same terms as the British—and Egypt was to be responsible for the protection of foreign minorities in Egypt. This treaty, which was to last for twenty years, was welcomed in both countries, and was a decisive step towards Egypt's genuine independence.

Sudan

By 1918 the pacification of the Sudan was complete except in the far south, and the frontiers were settled. An efficient administration had been formed with British in the higher ranks and Egyptians in the lower. The economy was developing: railways had been built, and cotton, experimentally planted in 1900, was soon to become a principal export.

It was inevitable that these developments, together with events over the border in Egypt, should foster Sudanese nationalism. From the start in about 1922, the nationalists were divided as to whether to form one state with Egypt or to remain separate. In 1924 there were demonstrations in Khartoum and a mutiny in part of the Sudanese army.

From this point onwards the British regarded the Sudanese middle classes and potential leaders with suspicion. Education was allowed to stagnate and the old tribalism was encouraged to counterbalance the modern educated politicians. All Egyptians were expelled and forbidden to re-enter until the signing of the Anglo-Egyptian Treaty of 1936.

North-west Africa

As in other parts of the Arab World, the French were faced with the first stages of nationalist movements in their three states in north-west Africa. In Tunisia in the early 1920s the first nationalist party was formed, but a second and more important group, led by Bourguiba, was founded in 1934. Similarly in Morocco the economic crisis of the 1930s stimulated disturbances by the nationalists. Both these states were protectorates; it was in the French colony of Algeria that the beginnings of events of much greater consequence took place.

The period from 1900 to 1940 was the heyday of the European settlers in Algeria. Attempts by the weak French government to encourage assimilation of Muslims with Europeans had minute effect. Only a few thousand Muslims responded to a law of 1919 which said that educated Algerians could obtain French citizenship if they abandoned their rights under Muslim civil law. Later in 1936 the Popular Front government in France wished to allow educated Muslims to become French citizens while keeping their rights under Muslim law, but the settlers, who felt that concessions would be the thin end of the wedge, objected vigorously and the proposal was rejected. So the status of the Algerians remained low.

Meanwhile nationalism was growing. In 1925 Messali Hadj, later called the 'Father of Algerian Nationalism', founded the North African Star, a party demanding complete independence. Messali was the son of a shoemaker; he married a French woman, had various jobs in France and eventually joined the Communist Party. However, although he maintained a communist form of organisation in his own party, he gradually moved away from communist beliefs.

A few years later the Religious Teachers Association was founded. Primarily a religious organisation, it aroused political feelings. Children in the Association's schools began each day chanting, 'Islam is my religion; Arabic is my language; Algeria is my country.' A more moderate party was formed by Ferhat Abbas just before the Second World War. Abbas, the son of an influential pro-French Algerian, became a qualified chemist. He was one of the few amongst Europeans and Algerians who sincerely wanted assimilation.

Persia

Persia, unlike the other states of the Middle East, remained genuinely free of European interference between the wars. This was partly because General Reza Khan and the army imitated Kemal Ataturk by setting up in Persia a strong reforming government. In 1921 Reza Khan occupied Teheran, the capital, and four years later deposed the Shah and assumed this office himself. The administration was modernised and centralised, the financial system overhauled, towns, roads and factories built, and after a new agreement in 1932 with the Anglo-Iranian Oil Company royalties from oil increased.

Second World War 1939 to 1945

The military events of the Second World War have been described in chapter 2. Here it remains to give a brief account of the effect of the war on the countries of the Middle East and North Africa.

During the most critical phases of the war, the Egyptian government cooperated with the British. But after El Alamein, and particularly after the Axis Powers had been driven from Africa, the absence of danger stimulated renewed opposition to the British whose troops were again in Egypt in large numbers. The attitude of the Jews in Palestine was rather similar. The White Paper of 1939, which prevented Jews from acquiring land and which restricted immigration, was the subject of a bitter attack from the Jews.[1] Nevertheless the Jews were determined to help the British win the war against Germany. 'We shall fight the war', they said, 'as if there were no White Paper, and the White Paper as if there were no war.' Therefore, while Jewish units served in the British Army and Jews provided supplies for the Allied cause, Jewish demonstrations, arson, bomb-throwing and general terrorism gradually increased.

In contrast to Egypt and Palestine pro-German tendencies were strong in Iraq and Persia. In 1941 an Iraqi attack on a British airbase was repulsed and was followed by the British occupation of Iraq and the establishment of a friendly government under Nuri-es-Said. The same year saw the Anglo-Russian occupation of Persia and the abdication of Shah Reza Khan.

Following the fall of France pro-Vichy governments were estab-

[1] One Jewish newspaper described it as 'a creature of funk spawned by a Government dominated by a passion for appeasement'.

lished in Syria and north-west Africa, but these were short-lived. The British and the Free French occupied Syria and Lebanon in 1941 and these two states were declared independent. During 1942–43 the Allies occupied Morocco, Algeria and Tunisia, and, although independence was not gained, nationalism was greatly strengthened. In 1943 Abbas, who became Algeria's most important nationalist, issued a manifesto demanding self-determination, racial equality and the use of Arabic as an official language. By 1944 Abbas was claiming half a million supporters for the view that Algeria should be an independent republic federated to France.

1945 to 1979

Arab League

In March 1945 the Arab League was formed in Cairo. It had seven foundation members—Egypt, Iraq, Syria, Lebanon, Saudi Arabia, Jordan and the Yemen. Most other Arab states joined in succeeding years. Its object was 'the strengthening of relations between the members, the organisation of political plans aiming at collaboration among them, the protection of their independence and integrity, and the general discussion of the affairs and interests of the Arab world'.

The creation of the Arab League is an indication of a tendency in Arab thinking away from purely national interests towards the unity of the Arab world. During the 1920s, '30s and '40s, Arab leaders were nationalists and socially conservative. But during this period communications were improved and an awareness of the social backwardness as well as the common interests of the Arab world developed, particularly among educated army officers. Erskine Childers puts it thus:

> Young people looked at the condition of the mass of the peasants; the disease and ignorance; the inefficiency and corruption of administration; the inefficacy of Parliaments apparently subject to the whims of palace, foreign embassy and conservative leadership. They became more and more convinced that the Arab world faced the necessity of two revolutions: one against imperialism, the other against what they called feudalism in their own society.[1]

Thus, amongst the new generation of Arab leaders who came to power during the 1950s, first of all in Egypt, the ideal was genuine independence, followed by a policy of Arab unity, social reform and neutrality in international affairs. The establishment of the Arab

[1] E. Childers, *Common Sense about the Arab World.*

League by the older generation of leaders showed the change of spirit that was taking place. That the many divergent interests made the League an almost powerless body also indicated that the change of spirit was as yet only superficial. The obvious disunity and defeat in Palestine in 1948–49 seemed to symbolise the weakness of the Arabs and this realisation was a blow from which the old national leaders never recovered.

Palestine and the Arab-Israeli Question 1945 to 1979

1945 to 1948   During 1945 to 1948 the last stage took place in the sad story of the British attempt to reconcile two groups whose objects were irreconcilable. Now the Jews were aided by the revelation of the appalling barbarities of Nazism and by the pity they evoked. With the election of a Labour Government in Britain in 1945 the Jews hoped that a policy more favourable to them would follow. But this was not to be. The British continued to limit immigrants. Many, coming from various parts of Europe, attempted to enter illegally by landing on lonely parts of the Palestine coast. Many were intercepted and taken to Cyprus or even returned to Germany.

At the end of October 1945 the Jewish underground organisation began terrorism on a large scale. Railways, bridges, airfields and government offices were blown up. It was with this background of constant terrorist activity that the final decisions on Palestine's future were taken. First in 1946 a joint Anglo-American Committee recommended a federal plan, but this was rejected by both Arabs and Jews. Then in 1947 the British Government submitted the dispute to the United Nations who set up a committee of investigation which finally decided in favour of partition on the lines of the 1937 Royal Commission Plan. In November 1947 this decision was accepted by the United Nations despite intense Arab opposition.

1948 to 1949: Creation of the State of Israel—First War   During the first months of 1948 British troops were gradually withdrawn. Finally in May 1948 the Jewish state of Israel, with a population of about 650,000, was proclaimed. It was immediately invaded by Arab armies from Lebanon, Syria, Jordan and Egypt, and for the rest of the year fought for survival with the strength of desperation. For a variety of reasons the Jewish armies were successful. They were well armed and administered, while the Arab armies were, with the exception of Glubb's Arab Legion, poorly equipped and disunited. Abdullah of Jordan welcomed partition since the Arab half of Palestine could then

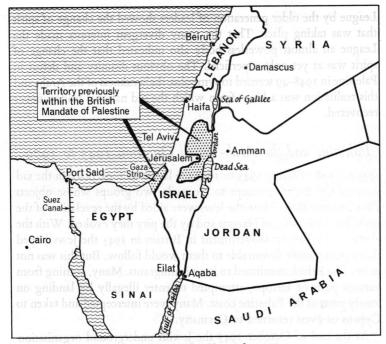

Israel and her Arab neighbours after 1948

be incorporated into his own kingdom. So, early in 1949, Egypt, followed by the other Arab states, signed an armistice with Israel. The result of the fighting was that Israel retained 23 per cent more land than under the original United Nations' plan. Jordan then annexed the West Bank, while Egypt assumed the government of the Gaza Strip. No peace treaties were signed.

1949 to 1956: Uneasy peace leading to Suez—Second War About three quarters of a million Arab refugees left Israel during the war to settle just beyond its new frontiers. Half of the refugees lived in the West Bank, a quarter in the Gaza Strip, and the remainder in Syria and southern Lebanon. Most were destitute. The United Nations Relief and Works Agency (UNRWA) began work in 1950, and provided minimum rations, shelter, medical services and education, but the aid was inadequate. Some refugees obtained jobs but most stayed in the camps, frustrated, bitter and hoping to return to their villages and land. Both Israel and the Arabs refused to compensate the refugees or to settle them. Israel could not afford to compensate, while the Arabs wished to keep the refugees as political pawns. They were therefore not integrated into their host countries.

Meanwhile the 1952 Revolution occurred in Egypt and Nasser came to power. The events involving the Suez Canal are described on p. 303. During 1954 to 1956 guerrilla raids on Israel increased, until finally in October 1956 there took place the invasion of Egypt by Britain, France and Israel (see p. 304). It appears that there was collusion between the three powers. By the end of 1956 Israel had withdrawn to its previous frontier.

The prestige of Nasser and Egypt had risen considerably. Nasser had emerged victorious diplomatically if not militarily. However, the Suez Crisis seemed to confirm for the Arabs that Israel was both created and supported by the West. In addition, the success of the Israeli invasion 'accentuated the Arabs' sense of shame and backwardness, incapacity and feebleness, which they experienced after the 1948 fighting'.[1] One important result of the war was the establishment of a UN force on the Israeli-Egyptian frontier.

1957 to 1963: Arabs divided—progressives and reactionaries During the six years after Suez the divisions among the Arab states became clear. Certain Arab states—Jordan, Lebanon, Saudi Arabia and the Gulf states, Libya and Morocco—tended to support the West. This was shown, for example, in 1958 when, in response to appeals for help, US marines landed in Lebanon and British paratroopers were flown to Jordan. Other Arab states, however, were opposed to the West because the West was connected with imperialism. Consequently they tended to support Russia because Russia had never colonised the Arab world, had never supported Israel and had no military bases or oil interests in the Middle East. When in 1957 the United States tried to form pacts with the Arab states there was violent opposition in some countries.

During these years a number of attempts were made to link Arab countries together, but these failed. The Syrian Government, under the influence of the socialist and nationalist Baath Party, favoured union with Egypt. Nasser was wary at first thinking it would create too many problems, but finally agreed. In 1958 Egypt and Syria joined to form the United Arab Republic. Three years later, however, a more conservative government in Syria ended the union.

Soon after the formation of the UAR, an Iraq-Jordan federation was formed. This link-up with Hussein, one of the main opponents of the new Arab nationalism symbolised by President Nasser, was too much for many Iraqis. The result was a revolution in July 1958. The new

[1] P. Calvocoressi, *The Listener*, 18 Aug. 1966.

government of Kassim, however, opposed the union of Iraq with the UAR, and gradually relations between Egypt and Iraq worsened. By the time Arif, who was more favourable to union, came to power in 1963, Nasser was too sceptical of the whole idea, partly because of events in the Yemen. In 1958 Yemen joined the UAR, but this union too did not last, and after 1962 a third of Egypt's army was in the Yemen supporting the republicans against the Imam.

1964 to 1967: Events leading to war   The three important factors during the period 1964 to 1967 were the establishment by the Palestinian Arabs of their own organisation, the massive rearming and increasing militancy of Syria and Egypt, and the radio propaganda against Israel.

In 1964 a conference of Arab heads of state was held in Cairo. It was decided to set up a body to represent the Palestinian Arabs, those who had lost their land as a result of the creation of Israel, and to entrust the organisation of this to a Cambridge-trained lawyer named Shukairy. Later in the year the Palestine Liberation Organisation (PLO) was formed. Almost from the start, however, the PLO was divided and became an umbrella organisation for a number of groups. One of these, a radical left-wing organisation formed in 1957 and called El Fateh, was led by Yasir Arafat[1] and soon became prominent. El Fateh believed in direct action. It received military training and arms from Syria, recruited young men from the refugee çamps for its guerrilla groups, and in 1965 began its first major raids on Israel. This guerrilla organisation effectively brought the Palestine question to the forefront of politics once more.

Meanwhile the Arabs were receiving large supplies of arms— aircraft, missiles, tanks, guns—from Russia. The Arabs had always had numerical superiority over Israel; now they considered they had military superiority as well. At the same time Syria was growing more left wing and more sympathetic to the revolutionary views and methods of Mao Tse-tung and Che Guevara. In November 1966 a Joint Defence Treaty was signed by Egypt and Syria. It provided for regular joint staff meetings and a joint command in war-time. This gave the Syrians added self-confidence and made war more likely in that if Israel seriously threatened Syria, Egypt would have to act.

An important element during these years was the effect of the inflammatory propaganda, hostile to Israel and the West, that came from Arab radio stations. For example, Cairo radio said of the Americans: 'Bloodsuckers of the people, the arch criminals of the twentieth

[1] Born in Jerusalem, he had been educated at Cairo University, and had fought in the 1956 War.

century, the savage barbarians. . . . Here we shall bury American gangsterism. Arabs, dig graves everywhere, dig them for every US presence. Dig up all the homeland. Dig it, Arabs. Dig it, Arabs.' Much of the propaganda was wishful thinking. For example, on 7 May 1967: 'The situation in Israel is deteriorating. Eshkol and his government are at their last gasp and are in a state of confusion and division.' This sort of propaganda both raised the expectations of ordinary people and made the leaders more extreme. At the same time the Arabs may well have underestimated Israel's strength.

From 1965 onwards, therefore, there were increasing guerrilla attacks on Israel. At first Israeli settlements near the border were the targets, but gradually the raids became more professional and more daring. Roads were mined, buildings blown up, and the infiltration into Israel became deeper. This produced the inevitable Israeli reprisals: on Jordanian villages closest to the point of the guerrilla attack; once a penetration as far as the suburbs of Damascus. The Israeli policy of replying in relative strength to minor attacks against her increased Arab anger and is an important cause of the war. Most of the guerrilla fighting was on Israel's northern and eastern frontiers. Egypt was criticised by other Arab states, especially Syria, for not attacking Israel, and this provoked Nasser into assuming a more militant anti-Israel position.

In May 1967 the crisis developed. It is probable that Egypt believed (incorrectly) that a big Israeli attack on Syria was imminent. Therefore, on 14 May, Egyptian forces were moved into Sinai. On 16 May Egypt asked the United Nations force of 3,000 observers to leave, and two days later, perhaps to Nasser's surprise, U Thant, the UN Secretary General, agreed to its withdrawal. The UN has been criticised for leaving and for leaving too quickly, although legally the United Nations Emergency Force could not stay against the wishes of the host country. The consequence of these Egyptian moves, together with the removal of the UN force, was that Israel mobilised.

Then on 22 May Egypt closed the Straits of Tiran. This prevented ships bringing oil and other supplies to the Israeli port of Eilat. Israel had said in the past that interference with the freedom of shipping in the Gulf of Aqaba would be a cause of war. During the following week there was a war of words between the leading Powers about the legality of Egypt's action, but it became clear that nobody was going to open the straits for Israel. Finally, on 30 May, Jordan, hitherto regarded as non-aggressive, signed a new defence agreement with Egypt. This was a decisive event for Israel.

On 1 June General Dayan became Minister of Defence in Israel.

Public opinion in Israel was now impatient with the government for not starting the war immediately. Prolonged mobilisation was very expensive; a pre-emptive strike was necessary against Arab air bases in order to stop Arab air raids on Israel and to give cover to Israeli ground forces. It was widely thought too, that war was inevitable and Israel must not be defeated, for while the Arabs could be defeated several times, Israel could only be defeated once.

June 1967: Six Day War—Third War On Sunday 3 June Dayan told foreign correspondents that nothing of great importance was likely to happen for several weeks. Two days later, at 7 a.m. on 5 June, Israeli planes took off and within hours the Egyptian air force was almost wiped out. Nearly two-thirds of Egypt's 400 aircraft were destroyed on the ground. At 8.15 a.m. the Israeli army attacked.

By 8 June the Israelis had reached the Suez Canal. Hundreds of Egyptian tanks and other weapons were destroyed in Sinai by an Israeli advance whose speed was astonishing. At the same time the Arab half of Jerusalem and a large part of the West Bank of Jordan had been occupied, and most of Jordan's army taken prisoner. By 10 June the Israelis had, in addition, completed the occupation of the West Bank and taken over the Golan Heights in Syria. The Israeli victory was complete. Israel had the advantage of surprise and the consequent control of the skies, but the victory was the result of careful planning combined with audacious generalship. The Israeli forces had technical skill and high quality weapons, but in addition superb morale and strong motivation.

Israel now occupied Sinai, the West Bank and the Golan Heights. A war which had started as a dispute over shipping rights and frontier security had ended with major realignments of frontiers. Israel had mopped up as much territory as possible in order to be in a strong bargaining position. But the cease-fire lines were attractive frontiers geographically and militarily, and the Israelis were soon divided over what could and what could not be returned to the Arabs in exchange for peace. All were united in saying that Jerusalem should remain Israeli. The West Bank was more important to Israel than Sinai. The Golan Heights were militarily important because they overlooked the Israeli settlements immediately to the south. Some right-wing politicians wanted to annex all the occupied territories, although this would increase the number of Arabs in Israel (400,000 before the war, 1·3 million after the war), and change the character of the Jewish state. In the following years there was a gradual reduction in the number of areas that Israel was prepared to return.

The Arabs for their part were incredulous, dejected and bitter. They had received a stunning blow. As far as Egypt was concerned, 80 per cent of the army's equipment was destroyed, the Suez Canal was out of action, the Sinai oil lost, production dislocated and Nasser's prestige and charisma damaged. Jordan had lost the West Bank and acquired 100,000 bitter and angry refugees. The Arabs refused peace negotiations until there was an unconditional Israeli withdrawal from all occupied territories. It soon became clear that, despite its overwhelming victory, Israel had won a battle but not the war, and that Israel's dominance would last as long as it took Egypt to acquire a new air force. Next time, too, Egypt might strike first.

1967 to 1973 In July, 1967 it was arranged to station a small number of United Nations' observers along the Suez Canal and on the Golan Heights. Although this may have prevented serious fighting, it did not stop innumerable incidents during the next three years so that on occasions the cease-fire lines became battle fronts.

In November 1967 the United Nations Security Council passed resolution 242. This called for: a just and lasting peace; the withdrawal of Israeli armed forces from the occupied territories; respect for the sovereignty of every state in the area and the right to live in peace within secure and recognised boundaries; freedom of navigation through international waterways in the area; a just settlement of the refugee problem; and demilitarised zones. This compromise statement was the basis for peace negotiations during the next ten years.

The resolution also called upon the Secretary General to send a Special Representative to the Middle East to seek an agreement in accordance with these terms. Dr Jarring, a Swedish diplomat, was appointed, and from 1968 to 1970 he attempted to persuade the two sides to agree. In 1970 the United States made a similar attempt, but all these negotiations failed. There was deadlock over whether Israeli withdrawal should precede or follow a negotiated settlement. Both sides became increasingly rigid in their attitudes. In addition time gradually converted *de facto* frontiers into *de jure* frontiers; this made a fourth war more likely as the only way to effect a change.

Meanwhile Egypt and Syria received massive Soviet technical, military and economic assistance. Airfields and bomb-proof underground bunkers were built, missiles, fighters, bombers and tanks, and other advanced weapons, provided. At the same time the United States reinforced Israel: for example in 1968 Phantoms, the finest strike aircraft in the world, were delivered.

President Nasser speaking at the ceremony marking the completion of the first stage of the Aswan High Dam in 1964. Khrushchev (right) is listening to an interpreter. Seated under the picture of Nasser is President Arif of Iraq

Sinai, 1967. Burnt out Egyptian tanks, lorries and troop carriers scattered along the road of Israel's advance from Gaza to Suez

Throughout these years the Palestinian Arabs, the original sufferers from the creation of the state of Israel in 1948, lived in their refugee camps. In 1968 their approximate numbers were: 260,000 in the Gaza Strip, 250,000 in the West Bank, 450,000 in the East Bank of Jordan, and 150,000 in south Lebanon. Many of these refugees had vegetated for twenty years, without a country or a job or much hope of ever obtaining either. They lived in poor conditions and on food provided by UNRWA. The militancy of the three years prior to the 1967 War was strengthened after that war. The Palestine Liberation Organisation came increasingly under the control of extreme left-wing elements. This trend was part of a world-wide movement favouring direct violent action whose supporters were inspired by Mao Tse-tung and Che Guevara. The Palestinians, led by Yasir Arafat and the more militant George Habbash, had supporters, especially among the young, in many Arab countries. The bitterness of the 1967 defeat and the deadlock in the diplomatic situation gave the movement support. Most of the guerrilla groups came from the refugee camps: these young men and women had nothing to lose but their lives. At the same time it became clear that an Arab neo-Zionism had also developed. For many Arabs, especially intellectuals, their emotional attachment to the land of Palestine was as strong as that of the Jews: they passionately wished to return to their homeland.

The consequence was regular sabotage raids from bases in Jordan or Lebanon into Israel or Israeli-occupied territory. The object was to provoke Israeli retaliation and thus to keep the whole problem before the attention of the world. Another important method of gaining publicity was the hijacking of civil aircraft. In July 1968 an El Al (Israeli) airliner was hijacked off the coast of Italy and taken to Algeria. The Israelis ransomed the airliner and passengers by releasing sixteen Arab terrorists. In December 1968 two Arabs attacked an El Al airliner with incendiary bombs and gunfire at Athens airport. In retaliation, two days later an Israeli commando unit using helicopters raided Beirut airport and destroyed thirteen Arab aircraft valued at £22 million. In September 1970 three airliners belonging to Britain, the USA and Switzerland were hijacked and flown to North Jordan. For six days 280 passengers were surrounded by Arab guerrillas who were themselves surrounded by Jordanian army units trying to release the passengers.

After 1970 two new terrorist groups became active. In May 1972 three Japanese terrorists of a group linked with the Palestinians killed 26 people and wounded 70 in an indiscriminate attack at Lod Airport in Israel. Then in September 1972 the Black September group of

Palestinians (called after the events in Jordan in September 1970) seized eleven of the Israeli Olympic team in Munich in West Germany. In a subsequent fight with the West German police, all the Israeli hostages were killed and five of the Palestinians. Then in March 1973 members of the Black September movement occupied the Saudi Arabian Embassy in Khartoum and murdered two US and one Belgian diplomat before surrendering.

There were many other terrorist incidents of this sort. All served to raise tension. The Israeli retaliation was usually greater than the original provocation, and the scale of the fighting mounted, with both sides growing more callous. The Israelis could not solve the problem of how to deal with guerrillas, and the governments which allowed them to operate, without damaging the process of negotiations.

The Arabs in the occupied territories suffered from this situation. If they collaborated with the Israelis they were threatened by the guerrillas; if they collaborated with the guerrillas their houses were blown up by the Israelis. On the other hand there was a dramatic improvement in the economy of the West Bank, with far more jobs available largely because of the building boom. Between 1967 and 1972 the standard of living improved by 50 per cent. This, however, led to the suspicion that Israeli occupation was only the preliminary to annexation, with the River Jordan as the natural frontier. New settlements, new buildings, new roads, with the Arabs providing a pool of cheap labour for Israeli industry—all pointed to a permanent occupation. The Gaza Strip was divided up and settled by colonists from Israel to make it easier to control.

If the refugees and the Palestinian Resistance Movement created a danger for Israel, they were a major problem for Jordan and Lebanon. By 1968 there were well over half a million refugees living in Jordan. They had their own organisation and leaders and extremist attitudes, and rapidly became a state within a state. In 1968 and again in early 1970 there was fighting between the guerrillas and the royal Jordanian army. The guerrillas virtually controlled Amman and King Hussein's authority was gradually whittled away. The crisis point came in September 1970 when the Jordanian army reoccupied Amman after severe fighting. Thousands of Palestinian Arabs were killed, and by 1971 the guerrillas in Jordan were no longer of political or military significance. The position in Lebanon was similar. A large number of refugees were living in the south of the country, and were using the camps as bases for sabotage attacks on Israel. These provoked Israeli reprisals in which inevitably Lebanese civilians also suffered. Lebanon was divided between those who supported freedom of action for

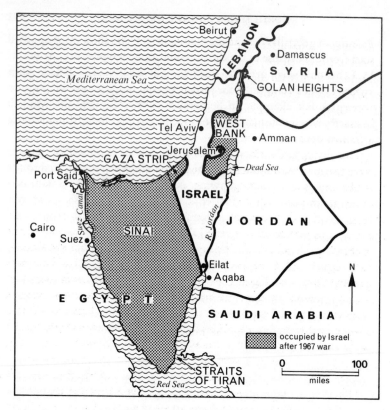

Israel's conquests in the 1967 war

If you look back at the map on page 283 you can see clearly how Israel more than doubled her size in the Six Day War, occupying Sinai, the West Bank and the Golan Heights. This was the Arab-Israeli situation which led to the Yom Kippur War of 1973.

Palestinian guerrillas despite the consequences, and those who opposed such freedom because of the threat to Lebanon's sovereignty. Attempts by Lebanon's small army to curb the guerrillas usually failed. After 1970-71, when refugees from Jordan arrived in Lebanon, the position worsened. For example, in September 1972, following the Munich massacre, Israeli commando troops spent two days in Lebanon leaving a trail of destruction.

Thus by 1973 the situation was tense. All the countries in the area were rearmed with modern, sophisticated weapons. It appeared to the Arabs that the Israelis, growing in number because of increased immigration, were intending to keep the gains from the 1967 war permanently. Negotiations through normal diplomatic means had failed. It seemed to all concerned that war was the only answer to the problem and for the Arabs the need to strike first was obvious. During 1973 Egypt and Syria prepared for war. This Arab build-up was known to Israeli intelligence. Perhaps the Israelis wanted to demonstrate Arab aggression and therefore Israel's need for secure frontiers. Perhaps Israel miscalculated the strength of the Arabs, as the Arabs had themselves miscalculated in 1967. On this occasion, however, the Arabs did strike first.

October 1973: Yom Kippur War—Fourth War   On 6 October, the Jewish Day of Atonement (Yom Kippur), the Egyptians crossed the Suez Canal. Simultaneously Syria attacked the Israelis on the Golan Heights. Egypt broke through the Israeli defences, occupied the east bank of Suez to a depth of several miles, consolidated and then advanced into Sinai. The Syrians made advances but on a smaller scale. The scale of the Arab attack showed it to be carefully prepared over a considerable period and successfully timed to secure maximum surprise. The new and sophisticated Russian weapons were particularly effective.

On the Golan Heights the Israelis began to push the Syrians back, and on the twelfth day of the war, a small Israeli tank force crossed the Suez Canal and threatened to cut off the Egyptian line of communications. However, the United Nations arranged a cease fire which became effective on 25 October. Compared with before the war, there was little change of frontiers on the Syrian front. On the Egyptian front, however, the Egyptians now had a foothold on the east side of the Suez Canal.

Clausewitz's doctrine that war is the continuation of policy by other means was strongly supported by both sides in the Middle East. The aim of this war was twofold: firstly, to create a political situation in which the Arabs could recover the occupied territories, and secondly to undermine Israel's military confidence. On the first point the Arabs had some success. World public opinion was shown to be very largely anti-Israel. The pressure of oil needs, Israel's occupation of land they were considered to have no right to, the military competence and courage of the Arabs, all helped to shape this opinion, and during the next two years there were disengagement treaties. On the second point the war shattered previously held assumptions: it showed that Arabs could fight well, could use sophisticated weapons with success and could coordinate their national military moves. One other result of this war was to show the importance of oil. King Feisal of Saudi Arabia mobilised the oil wealth of the Arabs in support of Egypt and Syria. There was an embargo on oil to the United States and the Netherlands, and a progressive cut-back in supplies to the West and Japan.

1973 to 1979 During the four years after the Yom Kippur War negotiations had some limited success. In December 1973 Egypt, Jordan and Israel met at the Geneva Conference. Syria refused to attend. After a short time, however, the conference was adjourned pending the Israeli General Election. It never resumed. However, as a result mainly of the 'shuttle' diplomacy of Dr Kissinger, the US Secretary of State, Israel and Egypt in Sinai and Israel and Syria on the Golan Heights, moved their forces back. Dr Kissinger sometimes travelled backwards and forwards almost daily between the capitals of the countries involved. This not only had some diplomatic success, but also helped to restore the American position in the Middle East. But on the basic issue of the occupied lands and the Palestinian Arabs, there was no real movement.

The Palestinian Arabs reached the height of their diplomatic prestige and power after the 1973 war. In 1974, at an Arab summit conference at Rabat, the PLO was recognised as the sole representative of the Palestinians. The United Nations by 105 votes to 4 recognised the PLO as 'the representative of the Palestinian people', and in November 1974 Yasir Arafat addressed the UN General Assembly. Meanwhile, some groups amongst the Palestinians continued to commit terrorist acts, and there was the inevitable retaliation by the Israelis. One event which gained world-wide attention was the Israeli raid on Entebbe Airport in Uganda in 1976 in order to release a hijacked airliner. In Lebanon clashes between the Palestinian guerrillas and the Lebanese authorities continued with a steady hardening of attitudes. This finally developed into a two-year civil war (1975–76) which ended with the Syrian army occupying most of Lebanon and crushing the guerrilla organisations. In March 1978 a Palestinian commando attack on Israel led to a full-scale Israeli invasion of southern Lebanon. A United Nations force was sent to the area, and the Security Council called for an Israeli withdrawal.

The issues at stake in this intractable problem have not changed since 1967, nor in essence since 1948. There were four main issues: Israel's right to exist, the rights of the Palestinian Arabs, Israel's need for secure frontiers, and Jerusalem. The Arabs had not recognised Israel's right to exist as a state. Hence, they refused to meet Israel at a conference table because this would be seen as tantamount to recognition of Israel. Similarly the Israelis refused to recognise the rights of the Palestinian Arabs who were dispossessed in 1948 and 1967. Should a new Palestinian state be formed, on the West Bank alone or linked with the Gaza Strip? Should such a state be independent or federated with Jordan? This question was connected with the third issue. If Israel was to exist, it should have security of frontiers. The 1949 frontiers were not secure. For example, the Golan Heights when occupied by Syria were a threat to northern Israel. On the other hand, when occupied by Israel, they were a threat to Damascus. The Israeli occupation of Sinai was an affront to Egypt, but its occupation by Egypt would be militarily alarming to Israel. In the same way, a new Palestinian state on the West Bank would be seen as a threat to Israel. The suggestion contained in the 1967 UN Resolution for demilitarised zones was important here. The last issue is the future position of Jerusalem, a city sacred to three religions—Judaism, Christianity and Islam. Because of its particular connections with these religions, the question was raised whether Jerusalem should be the exclusive property of one state connected with only one of these religions.

In November, 1977 President Sadat of Egypt tried to break this deadlock. He visited Jerusalem, spoke to the Israeli Parliament and presented the Arab case. In the following month Menachem Begin, the Israeli Prime Minister, visited Cairo. However, despite the optimism that these exchanges produced, negotiations broke down during the first half of 1978 and the gap between the two sides remained wide. The critical breakthrough occurred in September. Sadat and Begin met with President Carter at Camp David in the United States. Two agreements were reached: the terms of an Egyptian-Israeli Peace Treaty, and a Framework for Peace in the Middle East. Under the Egyptian-Israeli Treaty Israel would withdraw completely from Sinai over a three year period, Egyptian forces stationed in the area would be limited, United Nations' forces would remain and would only be removed with the unanimous agreement of the five permanent members of the Security Council, free passage of Israeli ships through the Suez Canal and the Gulf of Aqaba was agreed, and normal relations would be established between the two countries. The Framework for Peace stated that Israel, together with Egypt and Jordan, whose delegations could include Palestinians, would join in negotiating the establishment and powers of an elected authority for the West Bank and Gaza. This self-governing authority would be elected by the inhabitants of the area and would replace the existing Israeli military government. The authority would continue for five years during which time negotiations would be conducted to determine the final status of the area.

These arrangements received a hostile reception from the Arab world which united in opposition to Egypt. The basic criticism was that the treaty did nothing tangible to resolve the fundamental problem of the rights of the Palestinian Arabs. The signing of the Egyptian-Israeli Treaty was not conditional upon any changes in the West Bank and Gaza. Any such changes would follow negotiations which might or might not be successful. Indeed, Israel, in the weeks following the September agreements, seemed to suggest that a new Palestinian state would never be set up. In addition, there was no mention of Jerusalem. However, Sadat believed that the Israeli concessions over Sinai would create a momentum which would lead to complete Israeli withdrawal from Arab lands, and, despite the opposition, the Treaty was signed by Egypt and Israel in April, 1979. It remains to be seen whether successful negotiations concerning the West Bank take place.

Israel 1948 to 1977

When the first Arab–Israeli War ended in 1949, Israel was left as a small country with tortuous frontiers and great variations in climate and scenery. The population was about one million of whom one-fifth were Arabs and the rest were Jews. Half the total population lived in Tel Aviv and Haifa. Six thousand people had died in the war and there was considerable loss of civilian property. The economic problems were immense. In addition to huge defence costs, there were all the problems of establishing the economic life of a new state. Imports were greater than exports. There was the need to provide housing and employment for new immigrants. Natural resources were few and there were large infertile areas. It was necessary to establish an administration and government. The problems were many but there was also a determination to maintain and strengthen the new Jewish state despite the hostility of the surrounding Arabs.

Parliamentary democracy was established. Elections were to be held every four years for the Knesset or Assembly. There was to be universal suffrage and voting by proportional representation. The consequence was a large number of political parties so that governments were also rather unstable coalitions. From 1948 to 1977 the Labour Party was the basis of all these coalitions.

Except for a two-year period in the mid-1950s the Prime Minister from 1948 to 1963 was David Ben Gurion. Born in Russian-occupied Poland, he came to Palestine at the age of twenty in 1906 and worked as a farm labourer. A keen socialist, he played a big part in the formation in 1919 of the only important Jewish trade union organisation. Three quarters of Jewish workers belonged to it. The Labour Party, of which Ben Gurion was leader, was formed from this organisation.

Ben Gurion was a man of powerful personality. The great driving force of his life was the determination to establish an independent Jewish state. In May 1948 he formed a government on the basis of a broad coalition with the object of uniting the new state against the Arab invasion. When the immediate threat was over, elections were held in January 1949. The Labour Party emerged as the largest party, and Ben Gurion formed a coalition of Labour together with a number of small religious parties. He remained in office until the autumn of 1953 when, being 'spiritually weary', he retired to a kibbutz in the Negev desert in the south of Israel. This was part of a campaign to inspire young Israelis to settle in the desert areas.

Sharrett became Prime Minister. Fourteen months later, however, Ben Gurion was back in the government as Minister of Defence and, after the elections of 1955, he became Prime Minister again, this time the coalition being composed of Labour and left-wing parties. His second term of office was from 1955 to 1963. The major event at the start of this period was the Israeli invasion of Egypt. As a result of the frequent raids into Israel from the Gaza Strip and other places in Egyptian hands, the Israelis, acting in concert with Britain and France, invaded and occupied most of the Sinai peninsula (see p. 304). Israel eventually withdrew.

Ben Gurion's position had been strengthened by the Israeli success. However, in the early 1960s there was increasing opposition to his authoritarian ways. The reduced threat from the Arabs meant that more attention was given to internal affairs. Ben Gurion was inclined to antagonise his colleagues by impetuous actions or speech. The Foreign Minister would be offended at major foreign policy initiatives taken behind his back by Ben Gurion. In 1963 he resigned. Ben Gurion continued to be closely involved in politics although he never held office again. He died in 1973. A prophet and a statesman, more than any other man he was responsible for the creation and continued existence of Israel.

Levi Eshkol succeeded Ben Gurion as Prime Minister, and held this office until his death in February 1969. Eshkol came from the Ukraine in Russia, and arrived in Palestine in 1914. He landed at Jaffa 'wearing the tight fitting, brass-buttoned uniform of a Russian secondary school student, and his only possessions were a small valise and a pillow with a red pillow slip his mother had given him'. A farmer and then an official in the trade union movement, he held a high position in the Jewish underground organisation after the Second World War. He entered the government in 1951, and, because he was a man of charm and affability with considerable talents as a conciliator, he was often used by Ben Gurion as a political trouble-shooter. His conciliatory approach was shown by the decision to abolish the military administration of the Arab areas, and to allow Arabs to join the main trade union movement. It is ironic that the non-militant and easy-going Eshkol was Prime Minister during the 1967 war. When it became clear that war was inevitable, Eshkol brought his political opponent, Moshe Dayan, into the cabinet as Minister of Defence.

Eshkol died in office in February 1969. For the next five years the prime minister was Mrs Golda Meir. Like Eshkol she came from the Ukraine where her father was a carpenter. In 1910 she went with her parents to the United States. There she came under the influence of Zionism and in 1921 arrived in Palestine. After several years of hardship she eventually became secretary general of the trade union movement. She had been in the government since 1949, and was an experienced, influential and tough politician, obstinate, patient and courageous.[1] Golda Meir formed a broad coalition government until the autumn 1969 election when the shift to the right in politics was reflected in her new cabinet. Golda Meir was Prime Minister during the Yom Kippur War of October 1973 when the assumption that Israel could control events was shattered. She won the election held early in 1974 but her coalition government proved to be too unstable and she resigned in April 1974.

From 1974 to May 1977 Yitzhak Rabin, the former chief of staff in 1967, was Prime Minister. Although inexperienced as a politician, he was regarded as a moderate and reasonable leader. He resigned in 1977

---

[1] A political opponent once described Mrs Meir thus: 'She comes clumping along, looking like everybody's favourite elderly aunt, with that sad, suffering face, and that wonderful warm smile. You rush to help her to your seat, and she thanks you kindly. And the next thing you know—you're dead. She's the only lovable force of nature I have ever met.'

and in the elections in May the Labour Party was greatly reduced in strength. For the first time since Israel came into existence twenty-nine years before, a government was formed without the Labour Party being represented. The new Prime Minister was Menachem Begin, the leader of the Irgun, the Jewish terrorist organisation active against British and Arabs in 1945–48. Although his manner was mild, he was regarded as autocratic and inflexible and the prospects for an accommodation with the Arabs appeared to be diminished.

The population of Israel more than trebled during the first twenty-five years of its existence. By 1973 it had reached 3.2 million, of whom 2·7 million were Jewish. Hundreds of villages and nearly thirty new towns were built. From independence to the end of 1950, half a million immigrants arrived, including 70,000 survivors from Nazi concentration camps. Because of the need to increase the population and strengthen the country, Israel appealed to Jews everywhere to come and settle in Israel. The Law of Return in 1950 said that every Jew has the right to come to Israel, while the Law of Nationality in 1952 gave Israeli nationality to every Jew, whether or not he renounced his original nationality. It also gave Israeli nationality to every person, including Arabs, who were residing in Israel on the day the State was proclaimed.

During 1952–54 the flow of immigrants thinned considerably, but in 1954, 100,000 Jews arrived from north Africa. During the 1960s, when there was little anti-semitism, the average number of immigrants each year was 60,000. The provision of housing and employment for these immigrants was costly, but a greater problem was that of integration. There were considerable differences of culture and education between European and American immigrants on the one hand, and Jews from north Africa, the Middle East and Asia on the other. The newer immigrants tended to be less educated: for example, large numbers from Yemen, Libya and Iraq were illiterate.

An important factor in Israeli life is the Jewish religion. Many of the founders of Israel were sceptics or non-practising Jews, but 30 to 40 per cent of Israelis lead active religious lives and their influence is greater than their numbers warrant. In 1970 there was a controversy over whether a Jew could be defined by religion, race or way of life. This arose out of a court decision that a person could be Jewish by nationality and yet not be a believer in the Jewish religion. This was opposed by religious leaders and the decision was reversed by a new law, but the controversy showed the tension between the religious and secular conception of the state of Israel, an important issue in view of the large number of Arabs in Israel after the 1967 War.

Israel is overwhelmingly an urban country. Only 14 per cent of the population are engaged in agriculture, but they produce over three-quarters of Israel's food requirements. Half the rural population live in the kibbutzim or in cooperative farms. Although the economy of Israel is capitalist, many of the early settlers from Russia were influenced by the socialist ideas of Marx and Tolstoy, and 230 kibbutzim have been established. A kibbutz is a communal settlement. No wages are paid, and all work, property and amenities are shared. The guiding principle is: from each according to his ability; to each according to his needs. They are basically agricultural, but some kibbutzim have factories, workshops and hotels. Food and clothing are given to families according to their need; children live separately from their parents whom they visit only in the evenings. Cooperative farms are similar in their economic organisation, but their social structure is not as extreme as the kibbutzim. An important factor in Israeli agriculture is water. A scheme was completed in 1965 for diverting water from the Jordan to the Negev desert. In the twenty-five years since independence, the cultivated area in Israel has more than doubled.

The technological and productive skills and hard work of the people have resulted in very considerable economic growth. Israel has a mixed economy. By 1970 30 per cent of workers were employed in state-owned undertakings, mainly in heavy industry, building and agriculture, but the public sector produced half of the total national wealth. Israel has always been in a somewhat precarious financial position. Up to half the annual budget has been spent on defence, since it was essential for security to have both sufficient and superior weapons. Capital equipment and raw materials for building and industry, housing and social services for new immigrants, have all meant heavy expenditure. The closure of nearby Arab markets contributed to the balance of payments problem. The government's sources of income were taxation, large donations from overseas Jews especially from the United States, German reparations both to the state and to individual Jews (between 1952 and 1964), and in recent years tourism.

Despite all her problems, the standard of living in Israel is generally high compared with most countries, especially the neighbouring Arab states other than those wealthy because of oil. There is an intensive, well-organised and up-to-date economy; social security arrangements are extensive; education is free and compulsory. The Army is an important social factor in that all men and women serve in it for a period, which thus spreads education and the use of the Hebrew language. In the twenty-five years from 1948 to 1973 living standards rose by 250 per cent. Many people have two or three jobs; most wives work full-time. Israel in the mid-1970s presents a picture of an affluent, bustling and go-ahead society, confident and more self-critical than the previous generation and perhaps less idealistic.

Egypt

1945 to 1952   Four factors dominate the period from the end of the war until 1952. Firstly an extreme and militant nationalism erupted into open violence. Negotiations with the British over the Sudan and over the presence of the British Army in the Canal Zone failed, and finally in 1951 Egypt cancelled the 1936 Treaty. Civilian labour boycotted British military installations; there were frequent guerrilla attacks on British personnel: and the depths of bitterness were felt when British troops surrounded and killed forty-three Egyptian policemen.

The second factor was the growing opposition to the King and wealthy landlords. The pleasure-loving King Farouk (1936–52) was most unpopular, and failed to provide the strong leadership required to unite the political factions. The opposition was led by the Muslim Brotherhood, a large and well-organised religious-cum-political body. It particularly objected when Farouk in 1951 went on his honeymoon during the Muslim Feast of Ramadan.

The third factor was the desire for social reform. Lastly, the Arab failure in the Palestine war had a profound effect on Egypt. The radicals now felt that the government must be overthrown. A group of middle-ranking army officers, led by Colonel Nasser and with the respectable and popular General Neguib as figurehead, had been plotting such a coup for years. Finally, at midnight on 22 July 1952 they decided to act. Army units took up key positions in Cairo, a broadcast informed the Egyptian people of the revolution, and three days later King Farouk, after some hurried packing and to the accompaniment of a 21-gun salute, sailed out of Alexandria and into exile. He died, still in exile, in 1965.

Nasser 1952 to 1970   The army leaders followed a moderate policy while the revolution was consolidated: the monarchy was kept for a year, during which Farouk's young son reigned, and then a republic was proclaimed; Neguib remained the figurehead for two years until he was removed and Nasser concentrated all authority into his own hands. Gamal Nasser was thirty-four at the time of the revolution. He was the son of a minor official in the post office and, like most young men of his age in Egypt, was involved in student nationalist activities. He entered the army, served in the Sudan and eventually became an instructor at the Military Academy. Here he began to build up the secret organisation of younger nationalist officers. Both Nasser and Neguib were wounded in the fighting against the Israelis in 1948–49, and during the next three years the Free Officers, as the organisation was known, planned the coup while the civilian government crumbled.

(a) Government   During 1954 both the Muslim Brotherhood and the Communists were purged. The old political parties were ended and in 1956 a new constitution was issued. This provided for a presidential system of government and a National Assembly. Nominees for election to this assembly were selected and screened by the army officers, and in the plebiscite to elect the president Nasser received 99 per cent of the votes. In practice there was a military government. The National Assembly was completely under the control of the government. A second constitution came into operation in 1964. The President, nominated by the National Assembly and confirmed by plebiscite, lays down the general policy of the state and supervises its execution, but the Assembly was given rather more power, at least in theory. In 1962 the Arab Socialist Union was formed as the main political party whose function was to set out the broad principles of national policy. Nasser was re-elected President in 1965.

(b) Foreign policy   Throughout Nasser's period of government the Arab–Israeli question was the dominating factor in foreign affairs. In the early years, however, Egypt's relationship with Britain and the West was the main issue. Nasser's policy towards the Sudan had mixed success. In 1952 a Legislative Assembly with considerable power was elected in the Sudan. By the terms of an agreement with Britain in 1953 Egypt accepted this Assembly for a period of three years on condition that the Governor-General's powers were reduced. The elections at the end of 1953 were preceded by a vigorous propaganda campaign by Egypt, with the result that the party wanting union with Egypt won. This seemed a great success for Nasser, but during the next three years Egypt failed to maintain its popularity in the Sudan which became independent in 1956. Since this point relations have been dominated by the question of the Nile waters, which is dealt with below.

Nasser's policy towards the Suez Canal made him a figure of international importance. The first phase of the Anglo-Egyptian negotiations broke down over the conditions whereby the British could reoccupy the Canal Zone in case of war. In 1954, however, negotiations were reopened, and in October a treaty was signed. The British garrison was to withdraw from the Canal Zone by July 1956, but could reoccupy in the event of aggression against a member of the Arab League or Turkey.

This treaty appeared satisfactory to both sides. But Nasser's moderation was unpopular among extreme nationalists in Egypt, and there was even an attempt on his life. He therefore began to follow a more nationalist foreign policy which appeared at the same time to be anti-Western. During 1955 Egyptian propaganda in support of the Algerian nationalists, the Mau-Mau in Kenya and Eoka in Cyprus, poured out of Cairo, and attempts were made to undermine British influence in South Arabia. Iraq's membership of the Baghdad Pact (April 1955) was vigorously opposed, and Jordan was successfully persuaded not to join the Pact. In March 1956 Jordan dismissed the British commander of her Arab Legion. Raids and sabotage on Israel increased. Then in September 1955 Czechoslovakia agreed to provide aircraft and heavy armaments for Egypt (who had previously approached the West for arms), this agreement being accompanied by the offer of Communist help for other Arab countries.

In December the United States tried to increase Western influence by offering financial aid for the new High Dam to be built on the Nile at Aswan. Nasser delayed acceptance in the hope of a larger offer from Russia, and partly for this reason, when the Russian Foreign Minister was in Cairo in June 1956, Egypt announced recognition of Communist China. Events then began to move quickly. On 19 July, quite suddenly and with no previous warning, the United States withdrew its offer to finance the High Dam. Nasser was clearly very angry, and a week later announced the nationalisation of the Suez Canal, the revenues from which would be used to finance the Dam. Shareholders would be compensated and free passage guaranteed. The Canal Zone had already been evacuated by the British, and the premises of the Canal Company were now occupied by the Egyptian army.

This move both excited the Arab world and shocked the West. The British government said that nationalisation was illegal. Eden compared Nasser's nationalisation of the Suez Canal in 1956 with Hitler's occupation of Austria and the Sudetenland in 1938, and decided that the policy of appeasement which had not worked then, should not be tried this time. He believed that if nationalisation was allowed to stand, a similar nationalisation of western oil interests in the Persian Gulf would soon follow. Nasser appeared to be leading an anti-western movement which would eventually mean a communist Middle East, and Gaitskell, the British Labour Party leader, said that what was at issue was not just control of the canal, but the balance of power in the Middle East.[1]

[1] The Labour Party later opposed British policy over Suez.

On 16 August the twenty-two countries who used the Suez Canal most met in London. The majority of these, led by Britain and France, wanted a Suez Canal Board to provide international operation of the canal in cooperation with Egypt, and early in September this proposal was presented to Nasser who rejected it. On 5 October the British and French governments presented new proposals to the Security Council of the United Nations, but some of these were vetoed by Russia.

With the failure of diplomacy, the two Western nations concerned decided to resort to force. The British government, convinced that Nasser was a second Hitler, feared that Egyptian control of the canal would cut off British supplies of oil. France had similar fears, and also wished to stop the help Nasser was giving the Algerian nationalists. The other country involved was Israel, who believed that the current hostility of two major powers to Egypt was the opportunity to open the Gulf of Aqaba to Israeli shipping and put a stop to Egyptian border raids. Since the beginning of August there had been a build-up of British forces in the Eastern Mediterranean. On 29 October Israeli forces invaded Egypt. Whether or not this was with the encouragement and agreement of Britain and France remains a matter of dispute, although there seems to be growing evidence of collusion. However, Britain seized the opportunity to demand that her troops be allowed to occupy the Canal Zone to protect the canal. Egypt refused and on 31 October Britain and France bombed Egyptian airfields and other installations. Nasser immediately blocked the canal and Syria prevented oil from Iraq reaching the West. On 5 November British and French troops landed in Egypt, meeting little resistance. The invasion was condemned by an overwhelming majority of the United Nations, including the United States and Russia.

The pressure of world opinion, especially that of the United States, persuaded Britain and France on 6 November to end hostilities. During the following six weeks they withdrew to be replaced by United Nations forces, who later took up positions on the frontier between Egypt and Israel.

The Suez crisis aroused greater emotions than almost any event after 1945. Interpretations of its significance and the motives of all concerned are still subject to these emotions. However, the crisis revealed the crumbling of Britain's position in the Middle East, and it may have brought to a head Britain's sense of frustration at the loss of world power. On the other hand, President Nasser had now become a world figure with greatly enhanced prestige. The canal has remained Egyptian property, and has been run more competently than before 1956, taking ships half as large again as before that date.

(c) Economic policy   Nasser's economic policy was as important and influential in the Arab world as his foreign policy. The vast majority of Egypt's 20 million population in 1952 gained its precarious living from agriculture. Since only about 4 per cent of the total land area was cultivated, the rest being desert, land was in very short supply. The peasants were increasingly impoverished: in terms of income they were about six times worse off than the agricultural population of western Europe. The bulk of Egypt's foreign exchange came from sales of cotton, but while the Korean War had inflated cotton prices, in 1952 demand fell sharply. There was very little industry, and much of this was controlled by foreigners, there being only a very small Egyptian administrative and managerial class. Direct government control was limited to irrigation and the railways.

During the period 1952 to 1956 Nasser carried out one major change in agriculture but otherwise followed a cautious and moderate policy. Two months after the revolution the Agrarian Reform Law was passed. Farms were limited in size to 200 acres and the surplus land was distributed to the landless or those with very small holdings. Compensation was paid. The reform caused a sensation in the Arab world, but it was mainly a political measure and it effectively broke the power of the land-owning groups in central government. Only 10 per cent of cultivated land was redistributed, and less than 10 per cent of peasants benefited. The reform improved the living conditions of some of the poor, but it did not shift capital from agriculture to industry, and it did not raise agricultural output very much. There were improved yields, but production per head fell because of the rise in population. A start was made in the organisation of cooperatives. Apart from this measure, however, there were few developments of any importance in the economy. The regime was too involved with political issues.

After 1956 a much more radical policy was followed. Western capitalist countries were responsible for the Suez invasion and closer Egyptian ties with the Communist and neutral blocks followed. In addition, the free enterprise system seemed unable to stimulate the economy. Other underdeveloped countries, especially India, were using socialist economic methods. In July 1956 the Suez Canal Company was nationalised, and in November, following the Anglo-French withdrawal, a large number of British and French companies and banks were confiscated and 'Egyptianised'. In the early 1960s Egyptian-owned industry, transport, finance and trading companies were transferred to the state. Although the right to private property was maintained, free enterprise largely disappeared: 90 per cent of industry was now owned by the state. Central planning began in 1958. A major factor in this planning was the Aswan High Dam, on which work started in 1960. The first stage was completed in 1964 when Khrushchev (much of the cost was covered by Russian loans) visited Egypt, and the whole project was finished four years later. The dam created a 300-mile-long lake,[1] two-thirds in Egypt, the rest in Sudan. The purpose of the dam is twofold: firstly, to keep the level of the Nile constant throughout the year, and thus by controlled irrigation to increase the crop area of the country by 25 per cent; secondly, to provide cheap electric power.

In order both to solve the unemployment problem and to raise the standard of living a massive programme of planned industrialisation was followed. Many hundreds of new factories were built. Natural gas resources in the Delta were developed, and oil was discovered at El Alamein (where old Second World War mines had to be cleared before drilling could begin) and near the Red Sea. By 1969 production of oil was roughly double Egypt's domestic requirements. Other measures aimed at achieving greater economic equality. Land-holding was further limited in 1961 to 100 acres, there was a sharp rise in direct taxation, and the property of several hundred of Egypt's richest families was confiscated by the state. Partly as a result of these economic measures, partly as a result of the considerable expansion of education at all levels, the old Egyptian ruling class largely disappeared under Nasser, to be replaced by a new class of technocrats and young officers from the armed forces.

Much had been achieved. Nevertheless, during the last five years of Nasser's government, from 1965 to 1970, there was growing discontent. This was only partly caused by the Egyptian defeat in 1967 and the presence of the Israeli army on the eastern shore of the Suez Canal. Nasser announced his resignation, but distraught crowds swarmed through Cairo demanding that he continue in office. Indeed, Nasser became more indispensable in defeat than he would have been in victory, and his personal popularity was apparently undiminished. But the economic problems remained great.

The war in the Yemen, with a third of Egypt's army committed, was a heavy burden. There was a huge balance of payments deficit because of the purchase of arms and capital equipment from abroad. Population growth absorbed the growth rate in both industry and agriculture. The closure of the Suez Canal and the destruction caused by the fighting in the towns near the canal worsened the position. The consequence was that after 1967 Egypt was near bankruptcy and was

---

[1] Before the area was flooded, the colossal Ancient Egyptian statues at Abu Simbel were raised to higher ground.

over-dependent on Soviet aid. In 1965 many hundreds of critics of the regime from both left and right were imprisoned. Twice in 1968 there were serious riots by students. There was a general feeling that the bureaucracy was incompetent and unresponsive to the problems of the ordinary people, and that the new ruling class had lost its idealism and common touch.

In September 1970 Nasser died from a heart attack at the age of fifty-two. His health had deteriorated during the previous three years, but his death was sudden and left Egyptians stunned and unbelieving. Two days after his death *The Times* of London wrote: 'The only way to describe the past 18 years in the Middle East is the Nasser era'.[1] He was the one Arab with a world-wide reputation, and was undisputed leader, of the Arab world as well as Egypt, for most of this period. His reputation is based on both his economic and social reforms and his foreign policy. He gave dignity, self-confidence and national pride to Egypt. At the age of seventeen, in 1935, Nasser wrote to a friend: 'Where is the man to rebuild the country so that the weak and the humiliated Egyptian people can rise up again and live as free and independent men?' Nasser provided that man in himself. Cairo, the largest city in Africa and the Middle East, situated at the geographical point where the European, Asian and African worlds meet, is now an international capital. In the Arab world Nasser was a major force, a sort of 'secular caliph', encouraging the unity of Arabs under his leadership, standing for socialism and republicanism, setting the example of how to modernise a backward economy and how to obtain independence from imperialists.

Tom Little has said that Nasser 'in his early years was pragmatic, cautious, patient; he became more doctrinaire, impatient, reckless'.[2] Lord Trevelyan, the British Ambassador in Cairo 1955–56, has described Nasser's 'tendency to overplay his hand, to push too hard'. Compared with many of his contemporaries Nasser could be regarded as a moderate. It is said that he read *The Tale of Two Cities* while at school and this influenced him against revolutionary violence. Certainly his government was less repressive than many. Neutralism or non-alignment was a cardinal point in Egypt's foreign policy, and Nasser received aid from, and quarrelled with, both the United States and Russia. He was one of the outstanding rulers of Egypt, and one can look upon him with critical admiration.

Sadat: 1970 to the Present   In September 1970 Sadat became President of Egypt. Anwar Sadat was the young officer who announced the

[1] *The Times*, 30 Sept., 1970.   [2] T. Little, *The Observer*, 11 June, 1967.

overthrow of King Farouk on the morning of 24 July 1952. He was an ardent nationalist, devoted to Islam, and a friend of Nasser for many years.

For a year there was collective leadership. In reality this cloaked a struggle for power between Sadat, who wished to have the same power and influence as President that Nasser had enjoyed, and other ministers who, at least in the short term, wished to share power. By the end of 1971 Sadat had emerged as winner of this struggle. The army remained loyal to the President. The Arab Socialist Union, which had been used as the mouthpiece of some of Sadat's opponents, was now given a very subordinate role, although it remained as Egypt's only political organisation.

The presence of the Israelis on the east bank of the Suez Canal remained the major factor in Egypt's politics. The 'no peace, no war' policy seemed unlikely to succeed, and there was a deep sense of national humiliation and frustration.[1] The huge cost of arms meant less money for economic and social investment, high taxation and low living standards. Egypt was very dependent on Russia who, in a treaty signed in 1971, promised economic and military aid. The Russians, however, refused to provide Egypt with offensive weapons, the 20,000 Soviet advisers were unpopular, and in 1972 relations between Egypt and Russia deteriorated, and the advisers were sent home. There was also greater inclination to comply with the wish of Muammar Gadafi of Libya to unite the two countries. However, the theoretical union of Libya and Egypt in 1973 meant very little. Indeed, in 1977 there was a brief but bitter outbreak of fighting between them.

Criticism of the government produced student riots in 1972 and 1973, and consequently the spies and secret police increased their activities. Any policies of liberalisation were likely to be precarious so long as Egypt's external situation remained so parlous.

Sadat began secretly preparing for war from the start of 1973. Although the eighteen days of fighting in October ended in stalemate, the Egyptian successes in the early days fully restored Sadat's reputation with the Egyptians in particular and the Arab world in general. Previously he had been an underrated politician; afterwards he was almost canonised. His government was more secure and more confident thereafter, and Sadat took the place of Nasser as the national hero. The consequence was greater political freedom. Restrictions on the press were reduced, the Intelligence Service was cut down, and there were amnesties for political prisoners. In October 1976, in the elections for the People's Assembly, opponents of the government

[1] This frustration gave rise to some cynical jokes, for example: 'Egypt's victory will come on 32 December'.

were for the first time since 1952 allowed to present criticisms in the press and in public meetings. Relations with the United States, the West and the conservative oil-rich Arab states were good.

The economy, however, remained under considerable strain. The two greatest problems that Egypt's planners faced were the conflict with Israel and the rapid population increase. In 1952 the population of Egypt was 21 million; in 1977 it had reached 38 million and was expected to reach 70 million by the end of the century. Each year over 1 million children were born; these had to be fed, clothed, educated and eventually employed. There were shortages and serious inflation in the mid-1970s, and in January 1977 food price increases caused the worst rioting and anarchy since the 1952 revolution. The economy of Egypt was totally dependent on foreign credit. The need for the peace treaty with Israel in 1979 was crucial (see p. 295).

Jordan

In 1946 the British officially ended their mandate, and an independent Jordan came into existence. Following the partition of Palestine, the Arab part was annexed by Jordan which thus quadrupled its population.

In 1951 the long reign of King Abdullah was ended by his assassination. He had many enemies amongst Arab Nationalists who thought he was subservient to Great Britain and who disliked his expansionist ambitions. In the following year King Hussein, straight from Harrow, an English independent school, came to the throne. While successfully opposing those who wished for a stronger pro-Nasser policy he was forced to modify his links with the West. In 1956 General Sir John Glubb, the British commander of the Arab Legion, was dismissed, Jordan refused to join the Baghdad Pact, and the treaty giving Britain military bases was ended. Hussein's position was particularly critical in 1957, and in the following year British paratroopers came to support his regime.

The first half of the 1960s was relatively quiet, with the emphasis on economic development—agriculture the extraction of minerals, tourism. But in 1967 Hussein signed a defence agreement with Egypt and in the Six Day War of that year lost East Jerusalem and all the West Bank. A quarter of Jordan's fertile land and half her industry were lost, the tourist industry was temporarily ended, the major part of her army destroyed, and the port of Aqaba badly affected by the closure of the Suez Canal. In addition a large number of militant and bitter refugees from the West Bank moved to the East Bank near

Amman, the capital of Jordan. Relations with the guerrilla organisations that operated from the refugee camps gradually worsened and a
crisis was reached in 1970 when the Jordanian Army crushed the
guerrilla opposition (see p. 291).

The first half of the 1970s thus began with an uneasy calm imposed
by the army which was loyal to Hussein. Jordan played no part in the
Yom Kippur War of 1973, and thereafter there was modest but
increasing prosperity. The calm and courageous King Hussein was the
symbol of Jordan's will to survive. He had escaped many assassination
attempts and on several occasions the fierce hostility of the more
left-wing Arab states. Yet despite immense problems Jordan in 1977
had confidence and stability.

Syria

After some difficulties French and other foreign troops had withdrawn
from Syria and Lebanon by 1946. A succession of short-lived governments followed in Syria, with power alternating between civilian
politicians and the army. During the 1950s the Ba'ath Party, with the
typical ideals of the young Arab nationalists—Arab unity, neutralism,
socialism—gained in strength, and in 1958 an army *coup d'état* led to
the proclamation of union with Egypt. But this never worked smoothly,
and three years later a new army coup led to the withdrawal of Syria
from the UAR.

During the 1960s there was a succession of governments formed
mainly from different groups from the very divided Ba'ath Party.
Generally policies were socialist and anti-Israeli. In 1967 Israel occupied
the Golan Heights and the Syrian army was overwhelmed. In 1970
General Assad came to power and during the 1970s consolidated his
control. Both political and economic life became freer, and increased
oil production and aid from the oil-rich states helped the economy.
The army gave a better account of itself during the 1973 war, and in
1976 extended its influence into Lebanon.

Lebanon

From 1945 until 1956 government worked smoothly in Lebanon, a
small state with a population of 1½ million divided roughly equally
between Muslims and Christians. The two groups agreed that the
Christians would not seek for a pro-Western policy while the Muslims

would not press for a pro-Arab policy. But between 1956 and 1958 the Suez crisis and the government's decision to accept American aid produced strikes and civil war. Eventually a new President was found in the unambitious army leader, General Chehab, and after 1958 there was a return to peace and prosperity.

Until 1967 Lebanon managed to avoid being involved in the Arab–Israeli quarrel. Her political life was based on a delicate balance between Christians and Muslims, her economy depended on commerce and tourism, and the army was relatively weak; therefore Lebanon was very dependent on internal peace. But the arrival in 1967 and 1970 after 'black September' of large numbers of Palestinian refugees, many of whom supported guerrilla activities, produced a tension in Lebanon which eventually led to a two-year civil war in 1975 and 1976. Sabotage attacks on Israel by guerrillas based on the refugee camps in Lebanon resulted in massive Israeli retaliation in which Lebanese civilians inevitably suffered. The more militant groups in the PLO frustrated all attempts by the Lebanese authorities to control their activities. The Falange Party, who had the support of Christians, wanted the Palestinians put in their place as tolerated guests, not as a community with its own voice in Lebanese affairs. During 1975 there was intense civil strife, and thousands were killed during a year of repeated cease fires. The Palestinians were largely supported by the Muslim community. The situation gradually became more complicated, particularly when the Syrian army decided to intervene. Unexpectedly, the Syrians supported the Christian Right against the Palestinian and Muslim Left whose forces were crushed. Eventually the civil war ended, when Syria, Lebanon and the PLO signed the Rijadh Agreement (October 1976). The Israeli invasion of southern Lebanon in March 1978 caused further massive destruction.

Iraq

The history of Iraq after the Second World War is clearly divided into two parts by the military revolution in 1958. Before this date politics were similar to those of prewar days—constantly changing governments, manipulated elections, and political power limited to the conservative upper classes. There were two particular centres of political influence, the palace and Nuri-es-Said. The boy King Feisal (1939–58) was rather cut off from his people by his education at an English preparatory school and at Harrow. He came of age in 1953, but both before and after this, the Crown Prince who was Regent was most influential behind the scenes. Nuri-es-Said, a shrewd and experienced politician, was unsympathetic towards the nationalism of the younger generation. He believed that progress and stability depended on firm government and gradual reform, and aimed at leadership of the Arab world for Iraq, not Egypt.

This regime was supported by the landowners and upper classes and received the acquiescence of the uneducated. It was opposed by most educated Iraqis—students, teachers, members of the middle and lower branches of the civil service. This section of the community wanted genuine democracy, socialism and an anti-Western foreign policy. It believed, particularly after the events of 1941 and 1956, that Britain wished to continue its control of the Arab states.

The economic policy of the government was good, but did not satisfy its opponents. There was more emphasis on irrigation and drainage; an increasing number of agricultural specialists were trained; there was much greater industrialisation, and foreign development of the oil industry resulted in the export of 33 million tons in 1958.

But although economics were important, political events aroused most passion. In 1948, for example, the government negotiated a new treaty, more favourable to Iraq, to replace the 1930 Treaty with Britain, but demonstrations and strikes in opposition to the military concessions to Britain resulted in failure to ratify the treaty. The Arab failure in the Palestine war was a major source of dissatisfaction, as was Iraq's membership of the Baghdad Pact. In 1955 Iraq, Turkey, Persia, Pakistan (countries along Russia's southern frontier) and Britain signed a pact in Baghdad. Iraq was the only Arab country to join. Finally in 1958, a fortnight after the announcement of the creation of the UAR, the Iraqi-Jordan federation was formed.

This linkup with Hussein, one of the main opponents of the new Arab nationalism symbolised by President Nasser, was too much for the opposition politicians in Iraq, who wanted a policy of cooperation with Egypt, not rivalry with her. In July 1958 Brigadier-General Kassim and contingents of the army occupied Baghdad. King Feisal, the Crown Prince and Nuri were killed, and considerable damage was done by looting crowds. A republic was set up and the recent federation with Jordan ended.

Kassim ruled for nearly five years, largely through a civilian cabinet, although the power behind the regime was the army. The government, with the backing of Communists and Socialists, withdrew from the Baghdad Pact in 1959 but did not press for union with the UAR, and, in fact, Nasser did not encourage such a union as there were already considerable difficulties between Egypt and Syria.

However, pressure for a further step towards Arab unity came from the passionate and impetuous Colonel Arif, who in February 1963 led a new military revolt in which Kassim was killed. During the next five years first Arif and, after his death in an air crash, his brother, ruled Iraq. There were enthusiastic moves by the Arifs and cautious moves by Nasser towards an Iraqi–Egyptian union, but this was geographically difficult without the connecting link of Syria or Jordan or both. In 1968 Arif was deposed by General al-Bakr. During the following nine years the government was left-wing, pro-Russian, authoritarian (especially towards the Kurdish minority in the north), and increasingly isolated in the Arab world. Nevertheless, the production of oil meant considerable economic expansion in the 1970s.

Saudi Arabia

King Ibn Saud, the founder of Saudi Arabia, died in 1953, and was succeeded by one of his 33 sons. The new King Saud (1953–64), a tall, lean, shy man, a lover of ceremony and luxury and with a vast retinue in his many palaces, continued the absolute rule of his father. One of his advisers was his younger brother, Crown Prince Feisal, a widely travelled man who was more sympathetic to the ideals of Arab nationalism, and who gradually assumed power. Both Saud and Feisal disliked Nasser's variety of Arab nationalism, and were very suspicious of Yemen's federation with the UAR in 1958. Four years later Saudi Arabia supported the Imam of Yemen when the republican revolution broke out with Egyptian support. In November 1964 King Saud was deposed, apparently without resistance, and Feisal, who had ruled in fact for some years, then reigned over this oil-rich country.

The reign of King Feisal (1964–75) saw the transformation of Saudi Arabia into one of the world's richest and most influential nations. The source of this wealth is oil. Production gradually increased during the 1960s until in 1970 Saudi Arabia became the fifth largest producer in the world, and had enormous reserves. Thirty per cent of the non-Communist world's oil resources came from Saudi Arabia; 90 per cent of the country's revenue came from oil. During the six months following the October 1973 Arab–Israeli war, the price of oil increased fourfold. During 1974 the country's oil revenue was £11,000 million, or over £1 million per hour.

Apart from oil the country has few resources. Saudi Arabia is the size of Western Europe but has a population, 8 million in 1977, smaller than that of London. Nearly all the country is desert, and until recent years there has been almost no industry. However, there are two other factors which contribute to the country's strength: religion and the power of Arab tradition. Mecca and Medina are both in Saudi Arabia, and the king as protector of these holy places, is a principal figure in the world of Islam. Some 300,000 pilgrims visit the country annually. Indeed the Koran provides the basis of the constitution for the country.

King Feisal was an austere and astute ruler. A strong personality, he knew what he wanted, and could be described as a conservative reformer. He believed in evolution rather than revolution; internal change must be controlled and introduced cautiously. Nevertheless, in a relatively short period of time, Saudi Arabia changed dramatically. Most of the huge oil revenue was spent on bettering social conditions. Schools, hospitals, roads, ports and factories were built. There was a major need for educated manpower, and a third of the national income was spent on education. Modern buildings, communications, especially roads, were built as fast as the hard-pressed construction industry would allow.

The government remained a traditional feudalism. The king's authority is absolute, and power was rarely delegated beyond the large royal family. A plot to assassinate Feisal in 1969 was discovered but the monarchy appeared immensely strong compared with the insecurity of governments in more 'progressive' Arab states. The character of the government has meant that Saudi Arabia's influence in the Arab world has depended more on money than on ideas, and in many ways Feisal was not in tune with other leaders. He was a force for moderation. Relations with Britain and the United States were good; Feisal wanted stable government in the Persian Gulf; the Royalists in the Yemen were supported; relations with Iran were good as both countries had a common interest in maintaining stability. Almost throughout his reign Feisal gave financial backing to Egypt.

In 1975 Feisal was assassinated by a disgruntled nephew. King Khaled, Feisal's brother, succeeded him, but Prince Fahd, the dynamic Crown Prince, rules in effect.

Sudan

During the Second World War, political feeling increased in the Sudan. Two parties were formed, an extreme nationalist party wanting union with Egypt, and a moderate nationalist party wishing Sudan to become independent and remain separate from Egypt. In 1948 a Legislative Assembly was elected, in which the moderates had a big majority. Although the British Governor-General retained extensive powers, this was a step forward.

Then in 1952 an Anglo-Sudanese Commission recommended the creation of a parliament which would control internal affairs. This was accepted by the British Government, who also agreed with the Egyptians in the following year that the Governor-General's powers should be reduced, and that full independence should come by 1956. The elections for this new parliament were won by the party wishing for union with Egypt, but it soon became clear that only a small minority of people were in fact in favour of union. Accordingly, when on 1 January 1956 the British and Egyptian flags were officially hauled down, Sudan remained a separate state.

During the three years after independence the party system began to disintegrate—the parties were never more than groups attached to leaders—and the politicians were regarded, as elsewhere in the world, with cynicism and impatience. There was growing opposition from the non-Arab south, the leaders of which were demanding a federal constitution, and then in 1958 a world fall in the demand for cotton produced an economic crisis.

In November 1958, in a bloodless revolution, the army occupied Khartoum. For the next six years, the Supreme Council of the Armed Forces, led by President Abboud, ruled Sudan. Government was autocratic in that Parliament, political parties and trade unions were dissolved, but was also honest and well-intentioned. Agreement was reached on the question of the Nile waters: Sudan's share of the waters was to increase from 4 to 18½ billion cubic metres, and she was to receive compensation for the part of Sudan to be flooded by the new High Dam. But the problem of the south, different in race, religion, culture and geography, remained, with rebels taking to armed resistance in the three southern provinces.

In November 1964, as a result of growing opposition to the military government, President Abboud stepped down. For the following five years civilian governments ruled the Sudan. However, the problems of 1956–58 re-emerged: unstable government, three prime ministers in five years, and constant bickering and manoeuvring between party groups; an attempt at secession by the non-Arab southern Sudan which was crushed; the poverty and inequality of society in the Sudan. The consequence was a second military coup, in May 1969, which brought to power a group of junior officers led by Colonel Nimeiry.

At first the policies of the Nimeiry regime were similar to those of other left-wing governments in the Arab world. Nimeiry, who modelled himself on Nasser, was appalled by the inefficiency and corruption of successive civilian governments. He banned all political parties, limited the activities of the Mahdists, nationalised what remained of industry and trade which was under foreign control, and passed legislation making it a capital offence to impede the path of socialist revolution in any manner.

However, Nimeiry, a devout Muslim, with a strong following in rural areas, became more moderate and middle-of-the-way in his policies. In 1970 and 1971 there were attempted coups both by the right-wing Mahdists and by the Communists. At the same time the rebellion in the south became more active and better armed. Consequently Nimeiry started to broaden the base of political and popular support for his administration. In October 1971 he was elected President by referendum and then turned his attention to solving the problem of the south.

Sudan is an enormous country, the size of Britain, France, Spain, Portugal, Italy, Norway and Sweden combined. It is a member of both the Arab League and the Organisation of African Unity. This is both its strength and weakness, for its small population (17 million in 1976) is divided. The north is Arabic speaking and Muslim in religion; the south is African in culture, Christian or pagan in religion, and has a great variety of languages. Communications were quite inadequate and the country was generally very poor and undeveloped. In 1972 Nimeiry arranged a cease fire in the south, and a peace treaty was signed. This provided for the establishment of a semi-autonomous southern regional government, and for Africans to be promoted to high office. Hundreds of thousands of refugees could now return to their homes after years of hiding in the bush or in exile.

This fragile peace in the south held, but for it to work satisfactorily Nimeiry had to persuade all Sudanese that their country was not an Arab but an Afro-Arab state. Fanatics who wanted to arabise the south by force had to be stopped. Arabs who wanted the Sudan to play its part in the struggle against Israel were disillusioned for Nimeiry now adopted a 'Sudan first' policy, more pragmatic and less ideological, seeking aid from whatever source it would come, and playing little part in foreign affairs. Thus help from the United States and the West, as well as from Russia, was welcomed. In 1973 when a group of 'Black September' Palestinians seized and killed some Western diplomats at the Saudi Arabian Embassy in Khartoum, Nimeiry decided to try the terrorists, implying that terrorism should not be condoned. In 1975 Nimeiry said that the State of Israel must be accepted as a tangible reality.

Nimeiry's line has not been unopposed. Extremists of both left and right have shown their dislike both of the moderate approach in foreign affairs and the slow progress in the development of the

economy. In 1976 300 people were killed in Khartoum in fierce
fighting and another 100 were executed. Sudan has 200 million acres
of rich agricultural land. Only 10 per cent of this was under cultivation
in the mid-1970s. The oil-rich Arab states of the Persian Gulf have
given considerable aid in the belief that the Sudan could become a
major supplier of cereals and sugar to the rest of the Arab world. The
problems of development, however, are immense, and the continuation of stable government is essential.

North-west Africa

Morocco   In all three territories of north-west Africa the nationalist
movement was encouraged by the events of the war which had
demonstrated the weakness of France. Most politically articulate
Moroccans supported the Sultan in demanding the withdrawal of the
French, and in 1950 the Sultan refused to sign decrees of the French
administration, thus depriving them of legality. Although diehard
French settlers, with the support of the army, organised a rising
(1953–55) against the Sultan by the Berber chieftains in the south, the
mass of the population continued to regard him as their ruler. The
French government, more liberal than the settlers, restored him to the
throne with the title of King Mohammed V, and in March 1956 Morocco received its independence from the protecting powers, France
and Spain.

Mohammed V, a benevolent autocrat, died in 1961 and was succeeded
by King Hassan II, a pleasure-loving young man who was to become a
responsible and shrewd ruler. In 1963 he established a parliamentary
regime, but government instability, high unemployment and serious
student rioting in the big towns led him to proclaim a state of emergency in 1965 in which he appointed himself Prime Minister. Thereafter the King has been the ultimate source of power and for much of
the time has ruled without a parliament. He has governed firmly and
through a selected and frequently re-shuffled corps of advisers, party
politics have been tolerated, elections have been held, new constitutions
issued, but Hassan has remained an autocratic monarch who has seen
no need for the government to be responsible to an elected representative body.

Opposition to Hassan has often been violent. In 1971 and 1972 there
were attempts on his life. Senior army officers were responsible for an
attack on the royal palace in 1971, and in 1972 a civil aircraft bringing
the King back to Morocco from France was attacked over the sea by
airforce planes using rockets and machine guns. In addition there was

frequent trouble between the government and students of Rabat University, and in 1973 there was an abortive rising in the Atlas Mountains. In consequence, although political opposition is tolerated, its scope is increasingly circumscribed, and the regime is in many ways harsh and arbitrary.

Relations with France have remained reasonably good. Hassan's foreign policy is basically Western-inclined, but the King wished to have economic links with as many countries as possible—the United States and Russia as well as France. During the 1960s Morocco kept away from involvement in the Arab–Israeli conflict, but this policy changed in 1973 when Moroccan troops fought the Israelis on both the Golan Heights and in Sinai. There was now a more assertive Arab nationalism. In 1974 Hassan pressed claims for the Spanish Sahara, traditionally part of Morocco. Not only would this be a valuable economic acquisition, but it would create a diversion from internal problems and increase Moroccan prestige among Arab nationalists. In October 1975, Hassan marched 350,000 unarmed men a few miles— the Green March—into the Spanish Sahara. Early in 1976 Spain handed over the territory to Morocco.

Economic progress during the 1960s was steady with the government concentrating on projects to extend efficient agriculture through irrigation and mechanisation. Advance was more rapid in the early 1970s when Morocco became the world's largest exporter of phosphates, a basic ingredient of fertilisers. There was a sudden rise in the world price for phosphates, and the government was able to extend cultivable land and increase investment in industry.

Tunisia   In Tunisia there was similar opposition by the French settlers to any liberal reforms passed by the French Government. In consequence, the nationalists, led by Bourguiba, organised demonstrations and began to use force. Government through a puppet ruler, the Bey, was becoming impossible, when the French in 1954 decided to grant internal autonomy to Tunisia. Soon after agreement on self-government was reached, and in March 1956 Tunisia gained her independence.

Bourguiba has been Prime Minister since independence and President since 1974. His long rule has brought stability and security. He has been an outspoken and autocratic leader and very self-confident—he once told his ministers that Bourguibas do not grow on trees. There has only been one political party, the Destour Socialist Party, but this split in 1971 when one wing which favoured more democracy and liberalisation, separated from the group supporting Bourguiba. The only serious opposition to the government came from a trade union-organised general strike in January 1978.

Tunisia has stayed out of foreign involvements, preferring to take an independent line. Bourguiba was almost alone in denouncing Nasser for the Egyptian failures in the 1967 war, and he was quite prepared to criticise Gadafi's views on Arab unity, saying that unity on paper was worth nothing. Tunisia under Bourguiba has a reputation for being practical and disciplined. The economy is efficiently managed, and great emphasis is put on education.

Algeria   In Algeria the Second World War ended with the moderate nationalists in a relatively strong position. Ferhat Abbas issued a manifesto in 1943 calling for a democratic constitution giving equality to all the population regardless of race and language. Later he wanted Algeria to be an autonomous republic federated to France. But three factors in the years after 1945 led to a decline in the authority of the moderates: the Sétif riots, the conduct of elections, and the continued disparity in wealth between Europeans and Algerians.

In May 1945 a parade on VE Day in the town of Sétif turned into anti-European rioting. Bands of Muslims armed with clubs, axes and knives roamed through the town savagely attacking Europeans of whom about eighty were killed or wounded. The French retaliated savagely. Cruisers shelled coastal villages, bombers strafed settlements; officially 1,000 Algerians were killed, but it is possible that the actual figure was as high as 50,000. All expectation of a moderate settlement was now at an end, and the nationalists believed that an armed uprising was their only hope.

In 1946 French citizenship was given to the inhabitants of all overseas territories, and in the following year a new constitution provided for a National Assembly of 120 elected delegates, half French and half Algerian. (The population of Algeria at this point was 7·7 million Algerians and one million Europeans.) But in 1948 the first elections under this constitution were obviously rigged, and the moderate nationalists' faith in democracy destroyed.

Algiers and Oran were prosperous and modern cities surrounded by rich farmlands and with good communications, but the interior was desperately poor. In 1954 the annual income per head of rural Algerians was £16. Eighty per cent of Algerian children did not go to school. The great difference in wealth between Europeans and Algerians contributed to the sense of frustration which helped the nationalists.

So the younger, more extreme nationalists became more powerful, and preparations were made for revolt. The strongest personality among these nationalists was Ben Bella, who had fought for the French army in Italy, and who now headed the Secret Organisation. In 1949 he led a masked raid on the Central Post Office in Oran stealing over 3 million francs. In the following year the French police uncovered the Secret Organisation and imprisoned Ben Bella, who, however, escaped in 1952.

In November 1954 the Algerian nationalist rebellion started. The National Liberation Front (FLN) organised attacks on Europeans which quickly spread panic and disorder. In 1956 terrorism, often in the form of indiscriminate bomb attacks, moved to Algiers. The nationalists had the support of most of the Afro-Asian bloc of countries, and especially that of Egypt, Tunisia[1] and Morocco after 1956. But they underestimated the courage and obstinacy of the European settlers and the strength of the French army. By the end of 1956 the French, at huge financial cost, had 400,000 troops in Algeria; after events in Indo-China, French public opinion would not allow concessions. The army answered the terrorist tactics of the nationalists with similar excesses of their own. Villages were destroyed and suspects brutally interrogated. But although Ben Bella was captured, the rebellion continued.

The weak governments of the Fourth Republic gradually lost control over both the army and the European settlers. In 1956 Mollet, the Prime Minister, was pelted with cabbages and tomatoes in Algiers by a French crowd which disapproved of a new liberal governor-general. In May 1958 the frustrations of the Europeans and the army in Algiers produced the revolt which toppled the Fourth Republic. There had been no government in Paris for nearly a month, the Algerian nationalists appeared to be growing stronger, and there were signs that French politicians were willing to reach a settlement with Algeria as they had done with Tunisia and Morocco. Therefore Europeans seized government buildings in Algiers, and, in the belief that he would support 'L'Algérie française', demanded that de Gaulle be appointed to lead a new French government.

The revolt was successful (see page 98) and de Gaulle came to power at the head of the Fifth Republic. But the result for Algeria was not what the army officers and Europeans there had expected. While fighting continued in Algeria and FLN terrorism was extended to France itself, de Gaulle gave no hint of his Algerian policy. Then in 1959 the President broadcast an offer of 'self-determination' to Algeria within four years of the restoration of peace. It was clear that de Gaulle was moving towards a policy of independence for Algeria, and twice the European settlers and a section of the army tried to stop him. Early

[1] In February 1958 the French bombed the Tunisian border village of Sakhiet, suspecting that it was an FLN base. About seventy people were killed, half of whom were children.

in 1960 a second revolt in Algiers was crushed when the loyal section of the army besieged the city. A year later a rising led by a number of generals and with the support of a settler organisation called the OAS also failed.

Meanwhile a referendum in January 1961 gave de Gaulle wide powers to act on Algeria, and soon after negotiations started at Evian between the French government and the FLN. In March 1962 an agreement giving independence to Algeria was signed. Referendums in France and Algeria supported this, and in July 1962 French rule in Algeria came to an end.

The first Prime Minister of independent Algeria was Ben Bella. He remained in this post until his overthrow in an army coup led by Colonel Boumedienne in 1965. Algeria was then ruled by a military dictatorship. The FLN continued, but was more of a government department than a political movement. In contrast to the years before independence, Algerians generally became apathetic to political organisation. Elections were held and the government attempted to decentralise and involve the people in politics but with limited success. In 1967 the Army Chief of Staff led an attempted coup against Boumedienne. This failed and the government was then unchallenged with no organised opposition.

Boumedienne was a tough and austere man, cautious and realistic yet with a strong sense of Islamic tradition and Arab nationalism. His government gave stability and dynamism. It contained a group of young, dedicated and gifted administrators who were both realistic and determined. The consequence was that after 1965 Algerian policy swung away from the revolutionary idealism associated with Ben Bella to a hard-headed business approach. Algeria remained socialist, but pragmatic and moderate in its application of socialism. Economic development was the keynote of policy. In foreign affairs, while opposing imperialism and communism and maintaining radical postures over Israel or liberation movements, Algeria's image as one of the Third World's leading revolutionary countries slowly died. Algeria would, for example, be apparently hostile to the United States, but at the same time would sign immense natural gas deals with American companies. Other Arab states criticised Algeria's excessive preoccupation with its own affairs, but this, combined with political stability, sensitive and able government, and the wealth coming from oil and natural gas, transformed the economy.

In the early 1960s Algeria had little industry, backward agriculture, high unemployment and an economy dominated by France. In addition, there had been a mass exodus of French administrators, technicians, teachers and experts. The Boumedienne government believed that only by industrialisation could Algeria lift itself to a better economic level. After 1967 the income from oil and natural gas rose dramatically. A high proportion of this money went into big industrial projects. Algeria also encouraged foreign capital for industrial development carried out in partnership with the state. The climate of political stability was attractive to foreign investors, and industrial development was impressive.

Much of this industrial development, however, was capital-intensive. It has not required a great deal of manpower and unemployment was not much affected. In the early 1970s as much as half the potential work force in Algeria was either unemployed or seriously underemployed. There was a great number of landless and workless peasants. After 1972, therefore, the government gave more money and attention to agriculture. In view of the high birthrate and growing population, it was necessary to increase the production of food. Large estates were taken over by the state and the land given to peasants who were then formed into cooperatives so that economies of scale were not lost. This may have reduced rural unemployment, but the immediate result was not to increase food production.

In December 1978 Boumedienne died at the age of 51. He could be described as a benevolent despot, and was certainly an able, respected and pragmatic leader. His successor was Chedli Benjedid.

Libya

Libya ceased to be an Italian colony in 1942. From that point until 1951 there was a British Military Administration, which came to an end when the British handed over power to Mohammed Idris, the head of the Senussi tribe and the most respected local leader. Idris was King of Libya from 1951 to 1969.

Theoretically Libya was a democratic state, but there were no political parties, the deputies represented tribal or business interests, and the King kept authority in his own hands. King Idris was a man of dignity and understanding. He had a retiring disposition and was revered by many of his people, but at the same time he was a resolute and skilful politician. The problems he faced in the 1950s were immense. Libya is a country half the size of India, yet with a population of only 1·5 million, mainly living along the coast. Industry was almost non-existent, and agriculture did not provide enough funds for development. There were tensions between the three main provinces of the country, and between the young and progressive on the one hand and the old and traditional on the other. In 1953 the Anglo-Libyan Treaty was signed: it was supposed to last twenty years; each side would aid the other in war, Britain would supply arms to the Libyan forces and would give Libya financial aid; in return Britain would have bases in the country. (In the 1960s the United States had a large air-base in Libya.)

All was changed, however, with the discovery of oil deposits in vast quantities in the late 1950s. This caused a dramatic economic upheaval. In 1961 production totalled less than 1 million tons; by 1968 the total was 130 million tons, and government revenue was £200 million per year. Apart from the new oil industry, service industries grew up. Large sums were devoted to public works, agriculture, communications, education and public health.

The rapid social and economic change far outstripped political growth. The regime of King Idris was conservative, traditional in outlook, pro-western and only reluctantly democratic. The King provided continuity and stability and there were great achievements in his reign, but he was autocratic, his government was accused of corruption, and Libya was too isolated from the rest of the Arab world. The British connection was unpopular. The army and the younger generation in the towns wanted change. In September 1969 the frail and partly blind 79-year-old King, who was convalescing in Turkey, was deposed. In a bloodless coup, a group of young officers led by Colonel Gadafi took control of the government.

Libya was now under a very different ruler. Oil production continued to expand rapidly so that in 1970 the country became the world's fourth largest producer. By 1972 the government's income from oil was £1,000 m. and this rose with the huge increase in world prices during the next two years. With these vast financial reserves, there were ambitious plans for new industrial projects—expansion of ports, public housing, two new oil refineries, petro-chemical plants, cement works and smaller industries. Foreign firms were nationalised and as far as possible the country's commerce and industry was to be run by Libyans.

In foreign affairs Gadafi supported the radicals in the Arab World and elsewhere. During 1970 both the British and Americans evacuated their bases in Libya. France provided Mirage jets for Libya, but most military help now came from Russia. The cause of the Palestinian Arabs was enthusiastically supported, and the more right-wing Arab governments were publicly condemned. Gadafi gave his support to a wide variety of terrorist groups: for example, the surviving members of the 'Black September' group involved in the Munich Olympic

Games shooting were given a heroes' welcome in Tripoli.

Gadafi was a fervent admirer of Nasser. His relations with Sadat have been less happy. In 1971 an agreement was signed in Benghazi by Egypt (30 million population), Syria (5 million) and Libya (2 million) setting up a Federation of Arab Republics. In the following year Libya and Egypt signed a charter of union, and, indeed, in 1973 a unified state was declared. Egypt was very glad to get a share of Libya's oil revenues, but less keen to repeat the sad experience of union with Syria. The Libya–Egypt union was no more than a paper deal. Egypt regarded Gadafi with scepticism and distrust. Gadafi thought Sadat's views were too bourgeois.

Gadafi has a complicated and contrasting character. He is a political radical, more interested in the ideological direction and mass organisation of the Libyan people than in the details of government. But he is also an Islamic fundamentalist, puritan in his views, and anti-communist. Austere, outspoken, unpredictable and impetuous, he arouses either fervent support or great hostility. There is no organised opposition to him in Libya, but many distrust his eccentric idealism.

Iran (Persia)

In 1941 Mohammed Reza, aged twenty-one, pleasure-loving and supposedly harmless, became Shah of Persia. Until 1953 his part in the government was relatively small. After the war Iran, though not strictly part of the Arab world, was subject to the same influences that were felt in other parts of the Middle East. When the Second World War ended the Russians were occupying the northern part of Persia and encouraging both a strong Persian Communist Party and separatist movements in the Caucasus where oil was important. The Russians finally left in 1946 after United Nations pressure.

A succession of weak governments in Persia culminated in the assassination of the prime minister in 1951. The emotional and unrealistic Dr Moussadek then headed the government. He immediately proclaimed the nationalisation of the Anglo-Iranian Oil Company, but great difficulty in finding markets for the oil caused a financial crisis. Moussadek's general support waned, and he had to rely on the Communists. The Shah attempted to dismiss him, failed and fled the country. But after a few days, and following mass demonstrations in his favour and the announcement of American financial help, the Shah returned. From 1953 onwards the Shah personally controlled the government of Iran, and democracy withered.

The Shah's personal government was autocratic. Persia was described

President Carter (USA), President Sadat (Egypt) and Prime Minister Begin (Israel) in the United States, September 1978

Iran, 1979. Demonstrators in Teheran demanding the return of Ayatollah Khomeini

as a benevolent police state. Government was 'a pyramid with the Shah on top. Everything flows down from him'.[1] He oversaw every decision of state, large or small. Parliament met but it was uncritical and unrepresentative. Its principal task was to rubber-stamp the decisions of a Shah who had many times voiced his contempt for Western democracy and the freedoms it allows. There was no important opposition until early in 1978. The Shah's supreme autocracy was enforced by Savak, the security police who had an unsavoury reputation for the use of torture on a large scale.

There are several reasons why the Shah's dictatorial government was so long-lasting and successful. Economic and social policy, especially since the 'White Revolution' of 1963, was effective. Foreign policy, based on ever more powerful armed forces, was independent. The old and conservative groups in society—the clergy, the landowners, the tribal groups—who may have wished to retain their traditional powers, were weakened, and the army, the newly educated and the businessmen increased in influence. These new groups saw the Shah as a guarantor or their continued prosperity.

The monarchy, too, was seen as a unifying force in a fiercely nationalistic society. In 1971 there was a celebration to mark the 2,500th anniversary of the Persian monarchy. The emphasis was on the original dynasty founded 2,500 years ago and the present dynasty of the Shah and his father. In each major town a stone plinth was erected, one side bearing a copy of the charter of Cyrus the Great, the other the twelve points of the Shah's 'White Revolution'. Shah Mohammed Reza was a very able ruler, determined, well-informed, patient and hard-working. A ruthless politician, at the same time his handsome appearance, his marriages and his sporting recreational interests presented an attractive image. The experience of 1941 when Britain and Russia occupied his country made him determined to make modern Iran strong and self-reliant.

The basis of Iran's power is oil. In 1954 an agreement was reached with the Anglo-Iranian Oil Company, now renamed the British Petroleum Company, for the refining and marketing of the oil, through an international group. Half the profits in future were to go to the Iranian government. Thereafter production, and Iran's income, steadily increased. Between 1972 and 1974 there was an eight-fold increase in oil prices. Iran for the first time set the price of Iranian oil and in return gave an assurance to the consortium that they could extract oil until 1993.

The wealth from oil was enormous. In addition, particularly during

[1] G. de Villiers, *The Imperial Shah*, Weidenfeld and Nicolson, 1977.

the 1950s, Iran received considerable aid from the United States. This money was used in the central planning of the economy. The first Seven-Year Plan (1949–55) gave direction to the economy but little was achieved. The second Plan (1956–62), however, brought rapid economic advance: irrigation, large-scale industrial development, support for private investment in light industry, building of roads and other communications. The third Seven-Year Plan (1963–69) was very successful. Political stability encouraged domestic and foreign investment, and progress was rapid.

Land reform, which started in 1962, was regarded by the government as an act of revolutionary significance. Despite the importance of oil, agriculture was the real basis of the economy, with three-quarters of the population dependent on farming. There is great variety of land and climate in Iran: barren mountains and vast, arid deserts make up most of the country, only one-tenth of which was cultivated. Land was owned by a relatively small number of landlords before 1962. The peasants, who lived near subsistence level with no prospect of improving their lot, provided labour and were not far removed from serfdom.

In 1962 the redistribution of land started. Gradually over a period of time the size of holdings was reduced. Peasants who received land had to become members of the local cooperative which was under government supervision. Farmers were provided with seed and fertilisers, and the government financed irrigation schemes. These changes have yet to result in any substantial increase in agricultural production, partly because it takes time to change farming methods, and partly because land reform was a huge and complicated operation. In effect it was a social revolution, for the power of the old landowners was broken and a large number of small peasant landowners was created who naturally gave their political support to the Shah.

Out of a population of 20 million in 1959 only 300,000 people were employed in industry, and they were mainly small craftsmen. During the 1960s, however, there was rapid industrialisation with factories and industrial plants producing a wide variety of goods. In 1962 the Shah's scheme for profit-sharing for industrial workers was introduced: as an incentive to increase production, 20 per cent of the profits would go to the workers. A substantial industrial base had been established by 1970. These agricultural and industrial changes ensured that during the twenty-five years between 1953 and 1978 the standard of living of the mass of Iranians rose. Health services and education improved, and despite opposition from religious groups there were important moves to emancipate women.

From 1953 to the mid-1960s Iran followed a pro-Western foreign policy. The oil crisis was settled, the Shah was fearful of Communist subversion, American financial aid was considerable, and in consequence Iran was a member of the Baghdad Pact (1955) and remained a member in 1959 when Iraq withdrew and it was renamed the Central Treaty Organisation (CENTO).

After about 1965 Iran developed a more confident and independent line. The armed forces were built up so that Iran became the most powerful country in the Middle East. The regime remained Western-oriented, but relations with Russia and eastern Europe improved. In the summer of 1965 the Shah visited Moscow, and thereafter there was considerable Russian investment in Iran. Relations with Iraq remained tense. The extremism of the Iraqi government and its general support for Nasser and the cause of Arab nationalism were not favoured by the Shah, partly because of Iran's wish to counter-balance, if not undermine, Egypt's influence in the Arab world.

In the mid-1970s Iran appeared to be a rich, stable and well-led nation occupying a key strategic area of the world, and therefore acquiring power and influence. The Shah had transformed a backward domain into a modern imperial state, wealthy, powerful and strong. Beneath the surface, however, there were serious problems and tensions. After the increase in oil prices in 1973 the government doubled its investment in large, prestigious projects. But the essential planning was inadequate, the skilled labour was lacking, and the consequence was waste, inflation and failure to achieve the unrealistically high targets. Agriculture was neglected and this accelerated the already rapid urbanisation of Iran. There was great resentment at the ostentatious wealth of the few and social divisions widened.

Religion provided a rallying point for the opposition. In many parts of Africa, the Middle East and the Indian subcontinent, it was clear in the late 1970s that Islam was still a potent political force. The mosque in Iranian towns and villages was an important social centre, and the right-wing mullahs led the opposition to the government's imposition, as they saw it, of an alien Western culture in Iran. They disliked the growing disregard of Koranic law and the emergence of women into full participation in the life of the country, and they wished to reassert traditional Islamic values.

At the same time that these economic, social and religious tensions developed, the Shah took the first tentative steps in the relaxation of his autocratic control. Dictatorships are usually most in peril when they begin to relax. There is no liberal tradition in Iran, the people were unaccustomed to freedom of political expression, and there was immediate pressure for increased freedom in all aspects of life. In January

1978 there were religious demonstrations in the holy city of Qom, and during 1978 the opposition became more and more intense. The conservative-religious groups joined with liberal-nationalist and left-wing groups in massive demonstrations and strikes. The oil industry almost came to a stand-still in the autumn, and exports of oil ceased. Concessions made by the Shah—the removal of the Head of Savak, the arrest of ex-ministers, the promise of free elections, an amnesty for political prisoners—were unavailing, and only served to demonstrate that his authority was crumbling. The extent of personal hostility to the Shah became clear.

The symbol and focus of the revolt was the Ayatollah Khomeini, a revered religious leader who had lived in exile in Iraq for many years after taking part in religious demonstrations in the early 1960s. Now aged 76, and living in France, this tall, stooping man with a craggy face and a white beard showed total and intransigent opposition to the Shah, whose government he wished to replace with an Islamic republic. After months of rioting and increasing disorder, the Shah finally left Iran in January 1979, leaving behind a liberal politician, Dr Bakhtiar, as Prime Minister. Early in February the Ayatollah returned to Iran. Within a few days the army, the last support of the Shah's government, changed its allegiance, Dr Bakhtiar lost control, and the Shah's regime came to an end.

8

Africa

Late Nineteenth Century

Until the last quarter of the nineteenth century Africa south of the Sahara was almost unknown to the outside world. The coastline had been explored in the sixteenth century, and by 1875 there were a few tiny European settlements in west Africa and larger colonies in the south. But apart from the reports of a few intrepid explorers, the interior of Africa was unknown. Here, secluded from the rest of the world by the absence of good communications and by a difficult natural environment, lived innumerable Negro tribes. With few exceptions they had made no technical progress and had little spirit of enquiry. The time-hallowed customs of the tribe were accepted. 'Alongside the joys of the dance, the drum, the hunt, the beer-drink, the picture is dark with poverty, ignorance, hunger, disease, isolation, cruelty, even cannibalism.'[1]

This was the Africa which confronted the white man when, after about 1875, European penetration and colonisation began on a large scale. There is controversy among historians about the motives for this colonisation. Some stress the economic motive: exploration having provided the necessary information, Europeans wished to expand their trade with Africa by importing raw materials in return for manufactured goods. It was then necessary to protect this trade by establishing an administration. Other historians say that the supreme motive was to achieve power and prestige. In addition the excess population from overcrowded European states could emigrate to the colonies and still be connected with the mother country. To some extent the colonists, who were often preceded and accompanied by missionaries, went for philanthropic reasons.

[1] M. Perham, *The Colonial Reckoning.*

The European colonisation was accomplished with only sporadic opposition from the African population, and although relations between the rival European powers were often bitter (for example, the Fashoda incident in the Sudan), the penetration and forming of frontiers were achieved with only one major war between the rivals. This was partly because of the vast size of Africa, and partly because at the Berlin Colonial Conference of 1884–85 the powers concerned had arranged that Africa should be divided into spheres of influence. The war between the British and Dutch settlers in South Africa was the one exception.

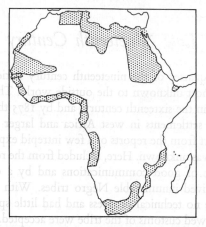

Africa in 1880, showing the extent of European and Turkish influence

South Africa to 1910

In 1900 a bitter war was being fought between the two British colonies of Natal and Cape Colony and the two independent Dutch or Boer states of Transvaal and the Orange Free State. Relations between the British and Boers had long been unfriendly. In 1886 the discovery of gold in Transvaal led to large numbers of British miners settling in and around Johannesburg. The Boers under their extremely conservative and anti-British President, Kruger, both feared and hated these Uitlanders (foreigners), as they called the miners. The Uitlanders, about half the population, were taxed heavily, were given no political rights, and soon began to plot rebellion.

In 1890 Cecil Rhodes became prime minister of Cape Colony. The studious son of a Hertfordshire parson, he had come to South Africa in

1870 and soon became extremely wealthy as a result of diamond mining at Kimberley. His encouragement of British expansion to the north of the Transvaal worried the Boers, whose suspicions of British aggressive ambitions seemed confirmed in 1895. In that year a friend of Rhodes, an impetuous Scottish surgeon named Dr Jameson, invaded the Transvaal in the hope that the Uitlanders would rise in rebellion. They did not, and Jameson's force was defeated. The raid had far-reaching consequences. Rhodes was blamed for the invasion because he had been involved in its planning, and resigned as prime minister. The British Colonial Secretary, Joseph Chamberlain, was suspected of implication, and thereafter relations between the Boers and British deteriorated. Negotiations over the political rights of the Uitlanders produced no agreement, but behind the Uitlanders' franchise problem was the deeper question of whether the British or the Boers were to be supreme in South Africa. The Boers armed themselves and decided to attack while they had the advantage of the element of surprise.

The Boer War lasted three years, from 1899 to 1902. During the first three months the Boers were successful, but instead of heading for the Cape, they made the strategical mistake of besieging the comparatively unimportant towns of Kimberley, Mafeking (defended by Baden-Powell) and Ladysmith. The self-confident but ill-prepared British relieving forces were all defeated. Then Lord Roberts was appointed commander-in-chief of the British forces with Kitchener as his chief of staff. During the first half of 1900 the besieged towns were relieved, the main Boer army was defeated and Pretoria was occupied.

Believing the war to be virtually over, Roberts then returned to England leaving Kitchener in command. But two years of guerrilla fighting were to follow, however. The Boers made isolated but effective attacks on British positions, and the British retaliated by dividing the country into compartments surrounded by barbed wire and blockhouses, clearing one compartment of Boers at a time. Farms and crops were destroyed and internment camps set up for Boer women and children. Here shortage of food, beds, medical and sanitary facilities caused the death of 26,000 people. It has been said that these camps 'form the last and most terrible item in the indictment against England that remains indelibly printed on many Afrikaner minds'.[1]

Peace was finally made at Vereeniging in 1902. The British annexed the two Boer states, but the Boers were given £3 million to repair the damage caused by the war, and were promised self-government in due course. Although this was a wise and generous[2] peace treaty, the

[1] A. Keppel-Jones, *South Africa*.
[2] It has been frequently said that the Boers lost the war but won the peace.

British victory was a costly one: the Boers never forgave the manner of their defeat and Anglo–Boer relations were at a low ebb.

After the war Milner, the British High Commissioner, very ably restored the administration. Agriculture was revived and the mines restarted (with the help of workers brought from China). In 1907 full responsible government was given to the Transvaal and the Orange Free State, as the Boers had been promised. During the next two years

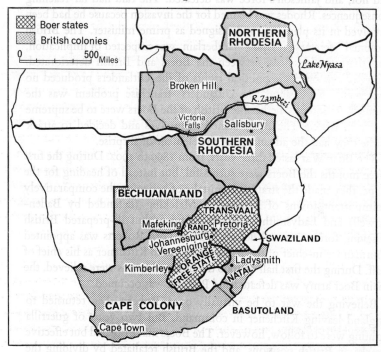

Southern Africa in 1900

discussions took place between political leaders about the formation of a union or federation between the four states of South Africa. The economic arguments for a larger grouping were powerful, and in addition some leading Boers (for example, Smuts) believed that this would help reconciliation between the two peoples.

The four states finally decided to form a union, and in 1909 the South Africa Act was passed by the British Parliament. This provided for a Union Parliament consisting of a Senate and a House of Assembly. The government in Pretoria was to be responsible to Parliament which sat at Cape Town. The Afrikaans and English languages were to have equal status. In May 1910 the Union of South Africa came into being.

The Establishment of Colonies

British West Africa

The two small colonies of Sierra Leone and Gambia had been established by Britain at the beginning of the nineteenth century. Farther east the larger colonies of the Gold Coast and Nigeria were not formed until 1900. The coastal states of the Gold Coast became a British colony in 1874. During the last five years of the century the British, after two attempts, forced the submission of the proud and hostile Ashantis to the north, and a protectorate was set up in the territories farther inland.

In Nigeria, as in the Gold Coast, European contacts were for long confined to the slave trading posts on the coast. British efforts to stop the slave trade after 1807 were largely responsible for the increase in her influence. A colony was established at Lagos in 1861, and the whole country was occupied between 1885 and 1900. First, protectorates were formed in the southern areas in order to help trade and to prevent slavery and human sacrifice. In 1886 the Royal Niger Company was formed, and extended its control over central-south Nigeria.[1] In 1900 the British Government took over the administration from the company, by which time the present western and northern boundaries of Nigeria had been decided.

French West and Equatorial Africa

Senegal had been a French base in West Africa since the seventeenth century. From this base between 1880 and 1900 the French took possession of the whole of the area south of the Sahara not already occupied by Liberia or other European states. Thus her colonies in Guinea, Ivory Coast and Dahomey were linked up, and a vast empire in West and Equatorial Africa was created.

The Congo

The decisive journey in opening up the Congo to European influence was that of H. M. Stanley who arrived at the mouth of the Congo River in 1877 having travelled 7,000 miles from the Indian Ocean in 1,000 days. Only Leopold II, King of the Belgians (1865–1909) was sufficiently interested to finance a further expedition. After great difficulties, the site of Leopoldville was reached and building started in 1882. Two

---

[1] The Africans in the south lost trade. Therefore in 1895 they attacked the Company's post on the coast, eating forty-three of the sixty men captured.

years later the Berlin Conference agreed that Leopold should rule the Congo Free State, and this was approved by the Belgian Parliament. So an area the size of India passed to the rule of one man.

By 1895 all the essential features of the country were known, the frontiers had been fixed and Arab slave traders in the east driven out.[1] Having established an administration, Leopold, an ambitious and talented king, quickly built up a huge commercial empire. The state was given a monopoly of the trade in ivory and rubber, the two most valuable products of the Congo. These products were harshly collected: Africans were subjected to forced labour, each village was given a quota, and flogging and mutilation followed if the quotas were not reached. It was estimated that Africans received under £3 for rubber which would sell for £52. Stories of this exploitation of the Congo came mainly from missionaries, and were publicised and confirmed by the report of Casement, a British consul in the Congo. Leopold's government had ended the slave trade, cannibalism, human sacrifices, intertribal warfare and had brought security. Nevertheless public outcry over the economic exploitation of Africans persuaded the Belgian government to intervene. In 1908 sovereignty over the Congo passed formally from Leopold to Belgium.

The British and Germans in East Africa

In 1886 the Sultan of Zanzibar's mainland possessions were divided into British and German spheres of influence. For the first few years the British sphere was administered by the British East Africa Company, but in 1895 the British government assumed authority and formed the East Africa Protectorate which covered what is now Kenya, Uganda and Zanzibar. After some fighting against the Arabs and Africans on the coast, the British extended their influence inland along the line of the railway. This was built from the coast, reaching a Masai kraal named Nairobi[2] in 1899 and Lake Victoria in 1903. A large part of what is now Uganda was made up of Buganda, a kingdom ruled by a Kabaka. During the last fifteen years of the nineteenth century the ruler was weak, and the whole area was in a state of confusion when the British arrived. An agreement in 1900 provided for indirect British rule in Buganda and direct rule elsewhere in Uganda.

[1] One young Belgian in a campaign in 1893 wrote: 'Certainly 1,000 people were killed in a few hours. Happily Gongo's men, cannibals par excellence, ate them up at the same rate. It's horrible but exceedingly useful and hygienic.'

[2] Nairobi in 1902 was a town 'inhabited mainly by railway employees. The only shop was a tin hut selling everything from cartridges to beer, sardines, jam and paraffin, and the only hotel was a structure of wood and tin.' K. Ingham, *History of East Africa*.

Meanwhile German rule was established in what became known as German East Africa. By 1903 the whole of the area was conquered, and considerable capital investment had already taken place. The Germans, like King Leopold in the Congo, exploited the Africans economically both in East and South-West Africa. This led to a series of unsuccessful rebellions, of which the most serious was the Maji-Maji rising, so called because its supporters swallowed medicine said to make them immune to bullets.

Angola and Mozambique

The Portuguese had ruled these two colonies on the west and east coasts of southern Africa, together with Portuguese Guinea, since the sixteenth century. There was very little settlement before the mid-nineteenth century, but after about 1870 the Portuguese began to expand inland. However, attempts to link up their two colonies were frustrated in 1890 by Cecil Rhodes's expedition to Salisbury. During the next thirty years Portugal concentrated on pacifying the area she already ruled. A number of tough and dedicated men arrived, organised the administration, and forced the Africans to work, often in conditions of slavery, for their Portuguese masters.

The Rhodesias and Nyasaland

Cecil Rhodes once said, indicating the area between the Transvaal and the central African lakes: 'I want to see all that red, British red; that is my dream.' In addition he wanted to surround the Boers on three sides, and therefore he persuaded the British government in 1885 to establish South Bechuanaland as a colony, and the rest of Bechuanaland up to the Zambezi as a protectorate. In 1889 the British South Africa Company was founded to govern and trade in the regions north of Bechuanaland and west of Mozambique. In the following year the Company organised an expedition of 600 men, each promised a 3,000 acre farm. The local African king[1] was tricked into believing that all the Europeans wanted was gold, and the expedition arrived safely and founded Fort Salisbury. During the next ten years African opposition was crushed, native reserves were set up, farms for an increasing number of white immigrants laid out, and railways and a telegraph system developed. It was decided to call the colony Rhodesia.

---

[1] Lobengula—'this six-foot-four, twenty stone, Rider Haggard kind of Chief, who received his European visitors in his kraal—naked except for a sporran of leopard skins'. M. Perham, *The Listener*, 16 June 1966.

At the same time British occupation of the area west and south of Lake Nyasa was proceeding. This was the work of the British government, the African Lakes Company and Scottish missionaries. By 1891 frontiers had been fixed with Portuguese and German territories, and a British Protectorate set up.

African Rule in Liberia and Ethiopia

Only two countries managed to evade European colonialism, Liberia and Ethiopia. Liberia was formed in the early nineteenth century as a home for American Negroes, while Ethiopia has a history stretching back for probably 3,000 years. In 1900 the country was ruled by the Emperor Menelik, head of a royal family which claimed descent from King Solomon and the Queen of Sheba. Menelik was important in two ways: firstly, under him Ethiopia defeated the Italians at the Battle of Adowa in 1896 and thus preserved their independence from European colonialism; secondly, he attempted to modernise the country by the introduction of, for example, railways and electricity.

Consolidation of Rule and Economic Development by Europeans 1900 to 1945

Gold Coast and Nigeria

There were few political changes in the Gold Coast before the end of the Second World War. The usual type of British colonial government —a governor and executive and legislative councils—ruled the coastal states and Ashanti directly, and the northern territories indirectly through local rulers. There was little enthusiastic support from the Africans but no great opposition. Meanwhile, roads, railways and a port were built; cocoa, the farming of which was begun in the 1880s, soon became by far the most valuable crop; and minerals, such as gold, manganese and diamonds, were mined. Because of this economic development, more was spent on education, medicine and other social services, so that the Gold Coast became the richest country in West Africa.

In Nigeria in 1906 there were two separate British territories, Southern and Northern Nigeria. The dominating figure in the early history of Nigeria was Lugard, who was British high commissioner in Northern Nigeria between 1900 and 1906, and governor-general of Nigeria between 1912 and 1918. In Northern Nigeria, having first

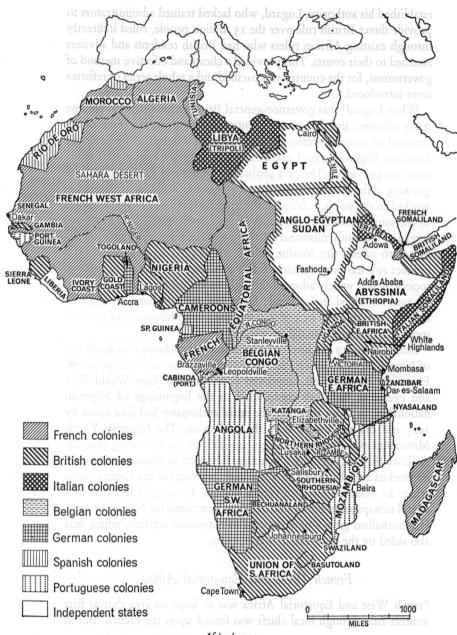

Africa in 1914

French colonies

British colonies

Italian colonies

Belgian colonies

German colonies

Spanish colonies

Portuguese colonies

Independent states

0   1000
MILES

established his authority, Lugard, who lacked trained administrators to provide direct British rule over the 15 million people, ruled indirectly through existing African rulers who had British residents and advisers attached to their courts. This provided a cheap and effective method of government, for the country was pacified and a whole series of reforms were introduced.

When Lugard[1] was governor-general British administration became really effective, and the volume of internal trade grew as a result of the removal of customs duties between areas of Nigeria. Northern and Southern Nigeria formed one territory in 1914 but remained divided into two provinces. This was probably a mistake as it encouraged the growing differences between the two regions. Whereas indirect rule worked in the north, it failed in the south as there were no local rulers of the same standing as the emirs of the north. Whereas Christianity spread in the south, missionary activity was excluded from the north so as not to offend the Muslim rulers. Although Lugard's practice of indirect rule has been criticised for maintaining a traditionalist form of society, it was widely adopted throughout British territories in Africa. 'Lugard ennobled indirect rule from just an expedient in times of financial hardship and lack of staff to a complete philosophy of government for Britain's colonial peoples.'[2]

Internal security and improved communications helped the economy of Nigeria. Cocoa, ground nuts and palm oil were the main products. Economic development, improved education, the First World War and events in India, all contributed to the beginnings of Nigerian nationalism in about 1918. But the initial enthusiasm had died down by 1923 and did not restart until the mid-1930s. The Nigerian Youth Movement was founded in Lagos in 1936. In the following year Dr Azikiwe (b. 1904) became a member. Educated in missionary schools, he worked as a clerk for four years, and then went to the United States where he obtained three university degrees. From 1934 he ran a successful newspaper in the Gold Coast until he returned to Nigeria in 1937. His journalism gave a new impetus to nationalist activity, which was also aided by the outbreak of war in 1939.

French West and Equatorial Africa

French West and Equatorial Africa was so huge an area that at first indirect rule through local chiefs was forced upon the French. But as

---

[1] 'This taut, smallish man, with the square cut of a soldier, the imperious eyes under a domed forehead, could work all night on a mountain of files and ride all day with fever.' M. Perham.　　　　　　　　　　　　　　[2] M. Crowder, *The Story of Nigeria.*

soon as possible French administrators arrived, and a hierarchy of government was established. The African headman in each village was responsible to a District Officer, who was in turn responsible to a Provincial Officer. The latter was answerable to the Governor of the Colony. The eight colonial Governors of West Africa were subordinate to a Governor-General whose headquarters were at Dakar in Senegal, while the four colonial Governors in Equatorial Africa were responsible to Brazzaville on the River Congo. If he fulfilled certain conditions any African could become a French citizen, which gave him various economic and political privileges. But in 1937, out of 15 million Africans in French West Africa, only 80,000 were French citizens.

Economic exploitation of the area was difficult for various reasons. The population was small, scattered and poverty-stricken; the ground was generally infertile, and there were no important minerals; communications were poor, and the French had little capital available. In general, the nearer the colony was to the coast, the more it prospered.

Belgian Congo

The centralised form of government started by King Leopold in the Congo was continued by the Belgian government. The important developments that occurred before 1945 were economic rather than political.

Agriculture benefited from government aid, and the First World War stimulated the production of rubber and palm-nut oil. In 1917 a law was passed obliging each tribal community to grow cash crops which could be marketed. The copper mining industry of Katanga was particularly important. In 1910 the railway between Elisabethville and Rhodesia was opened, and this was followed by a big influx of white immigrants into Katanga, whose climate was suitable for Europeans. There was unemployment at first, but the First World War stimulated the demand for copper, and by 1921 Katanga became the biggest producer of copper in the world. The building of towns, schools, churches, subsidiary industries and power stations followed fast. Elsewhere, diamonds, gold and tin were discovered, and railways and other forms of communication were built. In 1918 there were 2,000 business firms in the Congo.

The work of missionaries was very important in developing the country. Mission stations were small centres of civilisation. There is little doubt that all these changes resulted in a higher standard of living for the Africans.

Kenya, Uganda and Tanganyika

The most fertile land in Kenya is the region later known as the White Highlands. This was almost unpopulated until a growing number of white settlers arrived and farmed the area. African settlement was then limited to Native Reserves, where farming methods remained backward, and where part of the population provided labour for the big European estates. The question of land was the main source of bitterness between Europeans and Africans. The latter believed that the land in the White Highlands was stolen from them. They had sometimes been deprived of essential grazing grounds for their cattle, and since the African population was growing rapidly with the establishment of law and order in the country, there was increasing pressure on the land available within the Native Reserves.

In 1920 the country became known as Kenya Colony and Protectorate. White immigration increased after the war, and the settlers, led by Lord Delamere, demanded self-government for Kenya. The British government refused (cf. Rhodesia), but the attitude of the settlers, together with the land question, helped to stimulate nationalism amongst the Kikuyu, the largest African tribe in Kenya. In 1921 Harry Thuku formed the Young Kikuyu Association. Its membership, which grew into thousands, was largely made up of young, educated Africans, and large public meetings were held. The movement collapsed when Thuku was arrested. Other organisations were formed, but were inclined to be pressure groups rather than political parties, and there were the usual divisions between moderates and extremists.

There were only a handful of Europeans in Uganda and they took little interest in politics as they did not expect to settle permanently. Good communications and the maintenance of law and order helped the steady economic progress of the country. Cotton was introduced in 1904 and ten years later became the leading export.

Allied forces attacked German East Africa in 1914, but the German defence, which was very ably conducted, was not overcome until 1916 when a British administration was set up. After the war Germany's four African colonies became mandated territories of the League of Nations. The government of Tanganyika, as it was now called, was given to Britain.

In practice there was little difference between Britain's rule in Tanganyika and that in her other African colonies, except that white immigrants did not feel that the future was sufficiently secure to encourage permanent settlement. Partly for this reason the economy developed slowly. Sisal became the most valuable product. Sir Donald

Cameron was Governor after 1925. A man of bold ideas and great energy, he sincerely wished to promote the well-being of the country. He had previously been in Northern Nigeria and he introduced into Tanganyika Lugard's system of indirect rule. The African rulers had certain responsibilities but the British administration had ultimate power.

Angola and Mozambique

The Portuguese government of Angola and Mozambique was similar to that of the French colonies in that there was a hierarchy of administrators stretching from each small district official to the Governor-General. Although the economies of both colonies rested largely on the supply of cheap forced labour, there was little development. Educational facilities were inadequate, the number of white settlers was relatively small, there were few important mineral deposits, and Portugal, one of the poorest countries in Europe, did not possess the capital for economic development.

The Rhodesias and Nyasaland

Although the British government had final responsibility, the administration of Northern and Southern Rhodesia before 1923 was by the British South Africa Company. In 1898 a Legislative Council was set up for Southern Rhodesia. There were two separate administrations in Northern Rhodesia, one in the north-west and one in the north-east; these combined in 1911. Throughout the period before 1953 Nyasaland was directly under the authority of the British Government, and remained politically and economically a separate unit.

In Southern Rhodesia a variety of mineral deposits were found, but very little gold. Therefore agriculture was encouraged and experiments were successfully made with the growing of cotton and tobacco. The best land was occupied by Europeans, the African population being limited to Native Reserves. In Northern Rhodesia, although copper-mining was begun at Broken Hill in 1904, the European population remained very small.

When the South Africa Company's charter to administer the two Rhodesias expired, a referendum was held in Southern Rhodesia in which the white population were asked whether they wished to unite with South Africa or remain separate but with responsible government. By a three-two majority they chose the latter alternative. Therefore in 1923 a new constitution came into effect in Southern Rhodesia. The colony received the right to internal self-government, except that the British Government had the power (never exercised) to veto legislation affecting African interests. In Northern Rhodesia it was considered that the territory was not self-supporting since the European population was so small. Therefore in 1924 the British government assumed full power, with the usual crown colony form of government.

For the next ten years the Rhodesia Party ruled Southern Rhodesia. After 1933 the United Party led by Sir Godfrey Huggins was in control, and the more moderate Rhodesia Party gradually disappeared. The United Party believed in keeping the white and black races apart. To this end Africans were stopped from obtaining permanent land rights in European areas, Africans were not allowed to form trade unions, and the free movement of Africans was limited.

Legislation said that no African over fourteen years could move outside his reserve without a visiting pass, a permit to seek employment in a town or a current certificate of service. White immigration was encouraged. 'The Europeans in this country', said Huggins, 'can be likened to an island in a sea of black.' This policy of segregation and white supremacy was not adopted in Northern Rhodesia. Here the white population remained smaller and agriculture was of less importance than to her southern neighbour. The white settlers would have liked to see Huggins's policy carried out in Northern Rhodesia, but the British Government refused.

Meanwhile the Africans benefited on the whole from the peace and security that the white rulers brought. The population grew and an increasing number of Africans were educated. However, the standard of living in the rural areas declined because of the shortage of land. Able-bodied men moved to the towns, thus creating an atmosphere of decay in the neglected villages.

South Africa

When South Africa became an independent state in 1910, the British minority of the white population was dominant. The highest posts in most fields were held by Britons, who controlled industry, commerce and finance. The English language and culture were uppermost. There were two main political parties in 1910: the Unionist Party which was mainly British, and the South Africa Party which had largely Afrikaans (or Boer) support. At the first election the South Africa Party won conclusively, and Botha became the first Prime Minister. Botha, a magnanimous leader who stood for cooperation with the British, however, was not typical of his fellow Boers, and in 1912 an extremist section of the South Africa Party led by Herzog separated and formed the National Party. The Nationalists wanted a twin policy of supremacy of white over black, and Afrikaner over British. 'The Afrikaner', said Hertzog, 'must be master in South Africa.'

When Botha agreed in 1914 to the British request to invade German South-West Africa, the Afrikaner nationalists rebelled. The rebellion was ill-coordinated and soon put down, and South Africa played an important part on the Allied side during the First World War. In the 1920 elections, however, the Nationalists gained forty-four seats to the forty-one of the South Africa Party now led by Smuts. But at this point the British-dominated Unionist Party merged with the moderate South Africa Party which gave Smuts a majority over the militant Afrikaner Nationalists.

The attitude of the British and Afrikaners towards the coloured population of South Africa differed only in emphasis. On the whole the Afrikaners favoured a harsher policy towards the Africans and the small number of Indians. Various laws were passed. A coloured man who wished to travel from his home or work had to carry a pass. The object of this law was to control the movement of native labour so that it was available where the white employers most wanted it, while preventing unemployed Africans from staying in the towns. Two Acts were passed (1911, 1924) which prevented Africans from striking and from joining trade unions. The object of these laws was to protect semiskilled white industrial workers from African competition. In 1913 a law segregated black and white farmers by making it impossible for Africans to acquire land in most parts of the country, and ten years later an Act was passed restricting native residence to certain parts of towns. Most of these laws did not apply in Cape Province where educated coloured people had the vote.

The 1924 elections were won by the Nationalists with the support of the Labour movement. The latter was mainly composed of white miners from the Rand who were opposed, not only to employers, but also to cheap native labour. Hertzog became Prime Minister. There were two main aspects of his government's policy, firstly to ensure white supremacy, and secondly to remove all evidence of former British domination in South Africa.

The basis of Hertzog's racial policy was segregation: the white and the coloured races were to be kept separate. In the Cape the African franchise was abolished (other coloured voters finally lost the vote in 1955), and in South Africa as a whole a complicated system of indirect election was arranged for natives, by which they returned four members to the Senate. A Native Land Trust was set up to hold a large amount of land available for native settlement. In practice, only a small proportion of this land was given to Africans. An Act was passed preventing coloured workers from holding skilled positions in mines and other industries. In addition the government put pressure on employers to engage poor white workers rather than natives.

A whole series of relatively small regulations were passed to reduce the role played by Britain in South Africa. The King was prevented from conferring any titles on South Africans; postage stamps appeared without the King's head; equality between the English and Afrikaans languages was enforced; the national anthem was changed from 'God save the King' to 'God save South Africa'. After the statute of Westminster of 1931 (see p. 221), South Africa had full control over her foreign policy.

The world economic depression brought unemployment and bankruptcy to South Africa. Labour withdrew its support from the Nationalists, and it seemed certain that Smuts would win the next election. Smuts believed, however, that a coalition government was required to solve the country's economic problems. Therefore in 1933 the South Africa Party and the Nationalists formed a coalition which won the election easily. Hertzog remained Prime Minister with Smuts as his deputy. In the following year the two parties united to form the United South Africa National Party or United Party for short.

In spite of misunderstandings and disagreements, the Smuts-Hertzog alliance lasted six years until 1939. But the British and Boer extremists opposed the alliance. The British formed the Dominion Party, but this never attracted much support. The Boer extremists maintained the Nationalist Party, and were led by Dr Malan (1874–1959), an ex-minister of the Dutch Reformed Church who became a journalist and politician. His party was helped by a strong Afrikaner nationalist movement which swept through South Africa during the late 1930s. The centenary of the Great Trek[1] was celebrated by an ox-wagon procession from Cape Town to Pretoria. In this emotional atmosphere, Afrikaners formed their own organisations in every sphere from business and banking to sport and Boy Scouts. In addition, some of the extreme Afrikaners were attracted by Nazi racial theories.

The United Party, always an uneasy coalition, split in 1939 over the issue of South African support for Britain in the war against Germany. Smuts opposed Nazism and wanted South Africa to help Britain. Hertzog, much more sympathetic towards Hitler, favoured a policy of neutrality. However, Parliament decided in favour of war, and Hertzog resigned.

[1] Between 1835 and 1838 about 12,000 Boers trekked north from Cape Colony to Natal and the Orange Free State to escape from British rule.

From 1939 to 1948 the prime minister was Smuts, one of the few South Africans who have won international renown. The government coalition consisted of the pro-war section of the United Party, and the Labour and Dominion parties. The anti-war section of the United Party, led by Hertzog until his death in 1942, eventually linked up again with the Nationalists. There were large numbers of volunteers for the South African armed forces who fought in Ethiopia, North Africa and Italy. In the 1943 elections, with the Allies winning the war, the government coalition won a large majority.

The Growth of African Nationalism 1945 to Independence

European rule in Africa brought three major benefits: peace from tribal wars, the reduction of famine and disease, and the introduction of education and technical knowledge. But 'the ruling powers had hardly begun their work of bringing Africa into the mainstream of western civilisation when the Second World War, and all the subsequent changes it released, brought their power to an end.'[1]

There were various reasons for the rapid spread of African nationalism after 1945. The education provided abroad in Europe and America and that given by Christian missions in Africa, had produced a new generation of educated Africans. In addition, the development of the economy had led to the growth of towns where a new African working class grew up. These two groups were very receptive to new ideas and influences. India, a major non-white country, received its independence from the colonial power in 1947. Ethiopia and Liberia were two African states that successfully ruled themselves. What was the difference, the educated Africans asked, between the peoples of Ethiopia and Kenya, or between those of Liberia and the Gold Coast?

Then there was the influence of communism. Russia not only criticised the imperialists' economic exploitation of Africa, but also seemed to provide an example in herself of how communism can develop a country. But the particularly strong influence was that of race. Africans who travelled abroad found that black men were everywhere exploited and often despised, and they gained a dangerous sense of humiliation. Not only did the Africans demand equality with white men, but an end to the equal humiliation of colonialism. 'Nationalism, or Africanism, was born, a resolve to force the unwilling world to give Africans social equality through political independence.'[2]

[1] M. Perham, The Listener, 16 June 1966.   [2] M. Perham, The Listener, 4 April 1963.

After 1945 the Africans believed they could succeed. The colonial powers had been weakened by the war, the two major world powers, the US and the USSR were hostile to colonialism, and public opinion in Britain, especially within the Labour Party, was opposed to maintaining colonial administrations where they were not wanted. Therefore, during the twenty years after 1945 African leaders, using the mass party and the mass meeting, awakened their docile peoples to press for independence.

The Gold Coast

In 1946 there was an elected African majority in the Legislative Council of the Gold Coast for the first time. African politics therefore became more important, and in 1947 Dr Danquah formed the United Gold Coast Convention. Its general secretary was Kwame Nkrumah.

Nkrumah was born in 1909 near the Ivory Coast border, the son of a goldsmith. He was educated at Roman Catholic mission schools and trained as a teacher. Having taught for five years, he went to the United States where, after graduating in economics and sociology, he became a lecturer in political science. In 1945 he came to London to take a doctorate in law. 'These years in America and England', he wrote, 'were years of sorrow and loneliness, poverty and hard work. But I have never regretted them, because the background that they provided has helped me to formulate my philosophy of life and politics.'

On his return to the Gold Coast, Nkrumah helped to organise the UGCC into a mass party. A few months later there was severe rioting in Accra. The government blamed the UGCC and Nkrumah spent a short period in prison. However, an official enquiry into the disorders said that the cause was African political frustration, and that a new constitution was required. An all-African committee was appointed to work out the details of such a constitution, but Nkrumah and other extremists refused to take part. In 1949 he formed a new party, the Convention People's Party, which wanted 'Self-government Now'. After further disturbances, Nkrumah was again imprisoned.

Meanwhile a new constitution had been worked out in which the Executive Council could contain a majority of African ministers. In the elections of 1951 the Convention People's Party won easily, and Nkrumah was released from prison to become a minister in the government. In 1952 he became Prime Minister. During the next five years there were no major changes while the African ministers were learning the rules of representative parliamentary practice with the colonial administration as umpire. The Convention People's Party maintained its popularity in the south, but in view of opposition to it in Ashanti and the cities of the north, Nkrumah agreed that the regional assemblies should have considerable powers. Finally in 1957 came independence.

Nigeria

In 1944 Azikiwe formed a new party in Nigeria, the National Council of Nigeria and the Cameroons (NCNC). 'Zik', as he was commonly known, became immensely popular, especially after he led the successful general stike in 1945.

In 1946 a new constitution introduced two major changes. Firstly there was to be an African majority on the Legislative Council, and secondly three regional councils were to be set up in the north, east and west of Nigeria. The constitution was criticised on three counts. Firstly, Northern Nigeria, containing 75 per cent of the area and 60 per cent of the population of the whole of Nigeria, was much bigger than either of the other two regions. Secondly, while the constitution aimed to promote unity while allowing for diversity, it encouraged the growth of regional nationalism. And thirdly, Africans had no real power since the Executive Council still consisted of Europeans.

Nevertheless when, after long discussion, a new constitution was worked out in 1951, it again provided for three regional assemblies, although now these were to elect the Central Legislature and were to be controlled by Africans. Power was to be divided between the regions and the centre. In the elections which followed a different party won in each region. Azikiwe's NCNC controlled the eastern region; the Action Group led by a rich lawyer named Awolowo controlled the western region; and the Northern People's Congress (NPC) led by Bello, the Sardauno of Sokoto, a genial and powerful character, won the northern region. As a result central government almost broke down. A further series of constitutional conferences were held which in 1954 finally decided on a federation for Nigeria, with Lagos as the federal capital. There would be separate elections for the regional and federal assemblies.

Between 1957 and 1959 the three regions achieved self-government, and finally in 1960 Nigeria itself became an independent state.

French West and Equatorial Africa

In 1944 General de Gaulle, in a speech at Brazzaville, promised constitutional progress in the colonies of France. Consequently, in 1946 each French territory in Africa had its own general council, and a larger number of African deputies were sent to the French Parliament. Many African nationalists were disappointed with this constitution, and formed a party called the African Democratic Convention (RDA). This was led by Houphouet-Boigny, a doctor from the Ivory Coast. The RDA, which became closely linked with French Communists, demanded independence, and was opposed by the authorities, who, in an atmosphere of growing disorders, eventually suppressed it. In the mid-1950s the RDA emerged again, having broken its links with Communism. Houphouet decided that a policy of conciliation was wiser, and in 1956 he became a member of the French Cabinet.

France made an abrupt change of policy in 1956. Up to this point she had followed a policy of 'no change' in black Africa. Now she issued a law by which each territory in French West and Equatorial Africa was to have universal suffrage and its own Executive Council in which Africans would have some power. Each colony was to have more direct links with France and the two Governors-General at Dakar and Brazzaville were to have less authority. Africans were satisfied with the power this gave them, but some feared that the law would lead to the balkanisation of French Africa, and that each colony would be too small and weak to stand up against France. Sedar Senghor of Senegal and Sekou Touré, the radical leader from Guinea, were of this opinion. During the next two years political leaders debated whether French West and Equatorial Africa should be organised as two federations which would be linked with France, or whether each territory should become an independent sovereign state with its own direct links with France.

In September 1958 de Gaulle, now President of the Fifth Republic and again speaking at Brazzaville, announced a referendum in the French African colonies. They had to choose between immediate independence and full internal self-government within the new French Community, the member states of which would have a common defence, foreign and overall economic policy. All the colonies except Guinea decided to join the Community. Four days after the referendum Guinea became an independent state with Sekou Touré as President. The French administration was withdrawn and all French aid to Guinea was immediately stopped.

During 1959 all the other states decided to become independent while remaining within the Community, and by 1961 all had become independent. There were now fourteen states where three years earlier there had been the two apparently solid federations of French West and Equatorial Africa.

The Congo

The Congo continued to advance economically in the postwar period. There were large increases in industrial and agricultural production, and the Congo became the leading African producer of cobalt, diamonds, zinc, tin, silver and tungsten, and the second biggest producer of copper after Northern Rhodesia. The value of exports trebled during the ten years after 1945. As a result of this economic development, the Africans' standard of living improved. By 1960 nearly all children of primary school age attended school. Secondary and higher education were neglected, however. About a quarter of the population of 13 million lived in towns; Leopoldville doubled its size to 300,000 between 1951 and 1955.

Africans continued to take no part in the colonial government. Indeed, a nationalist movement was almost non-existent before 1958, and the Congo was regarded by other colonial states as an oasis of stability in an otherwise increasingly disturbed continent. Communications in such a vast state were too poor for nationalist movements to spread easily, and anyway, most Africans were reasonably contented with their lot. Any discontent was soon crushed by the Force Publique, a strong and well-trained security force.

However, the Congo could not be isolated for ever from the effect of nationalist movements elsewhere in Africa. In 1956 the French granted a large measure of internal self-government to their colonies; in 1957 the Gold Coast became independent as Ghana, and in 1958 de Gaulle offered complete independence to any French colony that wanted it. In consequence, a number of political movements grew up in the larger towns of the Congo, most of them based on regional rather than national loyalties. The conference of African independence movements in Accra was attended by three Congolese politicians one of whom was Patrice Lumumba, the leader of the largest political party and one standing for the unity of the Congo.

Meanwhile the Belgians decided that the Congo must advance more quickly towards self-government. In 1957 they allowed democratic elections to be held for the larger urban councils, and in January 1959 it was announced that communal and provincial councils would be elected by universal suffrage. However, violent rioting in Leopoldville in January, and in Stanleyville in October 1959, together with tribal fighting elsewhere, persuaded the Belgians that an even more rapid advance towards independence was necessary.

Therefore at the beginning of 1960 a Round Table Conference was held in Brussels. There the Belgian government agreed to independence, hoping by so doing to keep the goodwill of the Congolese. It was agreed that Belgians should continue to operate the administration and public services, although Congolese would be in political control. This, it was thought, would help to maintain order and progress in the country. There was one important conflict between the Congolese political parties. Most of them represented regions and were in favour of federal government. Lumumba believed that a strongly centralised state was essential, and in this he was supported by the Belgians. Lumumba won his case, although provincial governments were to continue.

On 30 June 1960 the Congo became independent, with Lumumba as head of a coalition government and Kasavubu as president. The country had been brought from full colonial dependence to complete self-government within three years and the consequences were soon to be felt.

Tanganyika, Uganda and Kenya

Tanganyika After 1945 Britain governed Tanganyika under the United Nations Trusteeship Council. In 1951 a report on future constitutional progress put forward the principle that political power should be shared equally between all three races: Africans (8 million), Asians (70,000) and Europeans (20,000). This was opposed by the African nationalist organisation, the Tanganyika African National Union. TANU was refounded in 1954, and was based on a much older organisation. Its leader was Julius Nyerere, a graduate of Edinburgh University and a man of great ability and sincerity. TANU wanted eventual independence for a Tanganyika in which Africans dominated politically.

In 1958 and early 1959 elections were held in which the electors voted for three candidates, one African, one Asian and one European. Nevertheless, TANU had candidates from all three races, and swept the board. The party was now very powerful and there were some disorders.

The new governor, Sir Richard Turnbull, realistically accepted TANU's view that a future Tanganyikan government must be African, and accelerated the advance towards independence. This was helped by the growing friendship between Turnbull and Nyerere. In 1959 a Council of Ministers which included Africans replaced the Executive Council, and in 1960, when TANU again won a crushing victory in the general election, Nyerere became chief minister. In December 1961 Tanganyika became independent.[1]

[1] In 1964 Tanganyika linked up with Zanzibar to form Tanzania.

Uganda Apart from the construction of the great Owen Falls dam on the Nile, there was little industrial progress in Uganda, which remained almost entirely an agricultural state. British attempts to introduce elements of democracy were opposed by the conservative rulers of Buganda. This, together with the possibility of forming an East African Federation comprising Kenya, Tanganyika and Uganda, led to critical relations between the British administration and Buganda, whose Kabaka was exiled to Britain between 1953 and 1955. Nevertheless, during the 1950s an increasing number of Africans entered the Legislative and Executive Councils, and political parties were formed, the two largest combining in 1960 to form the Uganda People's Congress led by Obote. During 1961 conferences were held in which it was decided that in the following year Uganda should become an independent federal state, Buganda being part of the federation.

Kenya In Kenya, as in all African states, there was great inequality of income between the races. A United Nations survey in 1953 showed that the average annual income of Europeans in Kenya was £660, of Asians £280 and of Africans £27. This economic inequality acted as a spur to the growing political discontent of the African nationalists. In 1946 the Kenya African Union was founded and Thuku became chairman. But Thuku was now too moderate, and in the following year he was replaced by Jomo Kenyatta.

Kenyatta had been an early supporter of African nationalism, having joined Thuku's Young Kikuyu Association. He twice visited London to present Kikuyu grievances to the British government. The second visit[1] was extended so that he could take a Diploma in Anthropology at the London School of Economics. During the Second World War he worked on a farm in Sussex, and in 1946, after about seventeen years in Europe, he returned to Kenya. A big, tall, imposing man and a born leader, under him the Kenya African Union grew in strength. Amongst other things it wanted more Africans on the Legislative Council and in the higher posts of the civil service. The response of the British administration in 1951 was to nominate six Africans to a Legislative Council of fifty-four members, and one African to the twelve-man Executive Council.

At this point attention was diverted from constitutional development to an outbreak of primitive violence led by a group called the Mau Mau. The object of the Mau Mau was to drive out the Europeans who had taken African land and made Africans into mere labourers. At midnight

[1] In London he shared a flat with Paul Robeson, the famous American Negro singer.

meetings in the forests, members took elaborate oaths to kill Europeans and all Africans who collaborated with them.

Until 1952 the government showed little concern about the Mau Mau, despite occasional violence. But in 1952 the new governor, Sir Evelyn Baring, declared a state of emergency. African political parties were banned, Kenyatta and 200 other African nationalists were arrested and imprisoned on charges of managing Mau Mau,[1] and British troops were flown in. Nevertheless, sporadic raids by the Mau Mau on isolated European farms gave way to large-scale attacks. Early in 1953 occurred the Lari massacre when the inhabitants of several villages were hacked and burned to death by a large gang. But this was the height of the crisis, and in subsequent years the number of incidents was reduced because of the activities of the security forces and the loyalty of most of the Kikuyu. In 1960 the Emergency was ended. It has been estimated that the suppression of the Mau Mau revolution cost £50 million. Altogether 13,000 people were killed of whom only 100 were European.

The Mau Mau emergency did not prevent, indeed, it probably encouraged, constitutional changes which led eventually to African control of the government. African parties had been banned during the first part of the emergency, and after 1955 were allowed at district level only. This encouraged the development of parties based on tribes which was not good for future national unity. In 1956 African representation on the Legislative Council was raised to eight. But in the elections which followed, the eight Africans elected all refused office in the government unless they were given more seats in the Legislative Council. The Africans were, therefore, given fourteen seats, the same number as the Europeans and Asians, and learned from this episode that their pressure could force changes.

The turning point in the Kenya Africans' struggle for self-government came in 1960. A conference held at Lancaster House in London in that year finally agreed on a new constitution, despite the opposition of the right-wing Europeans. Africans were to be given four positions on the Council of Ministers, and it was probable that Africans would control the Legislative Council. It was also agreed that independence was the ultimate objective. Thus the period of European political control was at an end, and some of the settlers left the country, particularly when Africans were allowed to buy land in the hitherto exclusively white Highlands.

Thereafter events moved quickly. National parties were now allowed, and two were formed: the Kenya African National Union (KANU) which was dominated by the Kikuyu, and the Kenya African Demo-

---

[1] The connection between Kenyatta and the Mau Mau remains uncertain.

cratic Union (KADU), which was rather more moderate and which represented the smaller tribes. The general election of 1961 was won by KANU, but it refused to form a government until Kenyatta was released from prison. The administration gave way, and soon after his release Kenyatta joined KANU.

In 1962 a second conference in London divided Kenya into six regions based on the main tribal areas, each having a government with local powers. Kenyatta opposed this reduction in the authority of the central government, and a further conference reduced the powers of the regional governments. KANU continued to command a big majority in Kenya, and in June 1963 Kenyatta became prime minister, choosing his ministers, however, from different tribes. In December 1963 Kenya became independent.

Angola and Mozambique

After 1951 Portuguese colonies became overseas territories, and therefore integral parts, of Portugal. About one per cent of the African population reached the required level of Portuguese culture, and therefore become assimilated and, in theory, of equal status with white Portuguese citizens. Government remained totally in the hands of the Portuguese and, despite considerable economic advance during the 1950s, there was widespread discontent. This produced a serious rising in the northern part of Angola in 1961 which was harshly repressed by the Portuguese. World opinion as expressed in the United Nations and elsewhere became increasingly hostile to the African policy of Portugal, who after 1961 received firm support only from Spain, South Africa and Rhodesia.

From 1961 to 1973 Portugal spent large sums of money on education and new industries in an attempt to keep African support. Politically, there was no change until the death of Dr Salazar in 1968. His successor, Dr Caetano, was a little more conciliatory, and in 1973 new Legislative Assemblies were elected in both colonies. But this move was too limited and came too late. Throughout the period the Portuguese maintained large armies to combat the growing threat from African guerrilla groups. In Mozambique there was only one such organisation, the Front for the Liberation of Mozambique, known as Frelimo. In Angola there were rival nationalist organisations. The guerrillas operated at first from the African states on the frontiers and then eventually moved into the countryside subverting the African population. They were well-armed and trained by Cuban or Algerian exponents of guerrilla warfare. The Portuguese, although spending 35

WORLD HISTORY IN THE TWENTIETH CENTURY

per cent of the national budget on defence, could not eliminate them, nor could the guerrillas defeat the Portuguese army.

This military deadlock was broken by political events in Portugal. In February 1974 General Spinola, the Deputy Chief of Staff of the Armed Forces, published a book in which he said there was no likelihood of a Portuguese victory over the guerrillas, and that Portugal should recognise the right of the people of the colonies to determine their own future. Gomes, the Chief of Staff, endorsed this view. The book gave authoritative backing to widely held suspicions, and for the first time public opinion against overseas military involvement showed itself. The war was very costly, the Roman Catholic Church brought to light stories of atrocities committed by Portuguese troops, and Portugal was now less dependent economically on her African empire. These factors, together with purely domestic ones, led to the Army coup in April 1974 when Dr Caetano's government was overthrown and General Spinola became President (see p. 115). The new regime was increasingly controlled by the left wing, and it became clear that Portugal was going to withdraw from its colonies.

Events then moved rapidly and Portugal was unable to control the speed or direction of the decolonisation movement. The nationalists refused to consider anything short of independence. In Mozambique Frelimo gained the military initiative and in September a ceasefire was negotiated, a new Frelimo government was officially installed, and independence was arranged for the following June. Preceded by a mass exodus of Europeans, Mozambique duly became independent in June 1975. In Angola the position was more complicated, partly because the white settler community was larger, and partly because of a struggle between three separate African nationalist organisations. Throughout 1974 and 1975 there were clashes between these three groups with the Portuguese playing a very small part. Finally, in November 1975, the Portuguese declared independence without handing over to any new government. During the following months the MPLA, the most left-wing group, with the vital help of Cuban soldiers, came to power.

The Rhodesias and Nyasaland

In the 1930s the white settlers in Southern Rhodesia, Northern Rhodesia and Nyasaland began to press for a union or federation of the three territories. They believed that a larger political unit would be beneficial economically and would lead to a higher standard of living. In addition it would be easier to maintain white rule in the two northern territories if they were linked with Southern Rhodesia where the number of white settlers was far greater. But the report of a Royal Commission in 1939 pointed out difficulties about the proposal: the constitutional status and native policies of Southern Rhodesia differed from those of the other two territories whose African population opposed the scheme. The Commission recommended one government for Northern Rhodesia and Nyasaland, and more economic coordination between the three territories.

The war then intervened, but the idea was renewed after 1945 by Huggins, prime minister of Southern Rhodesia, and Welensky, leader of the white settlers on the Legislative Council in Northern Rhodesia. Welensky came from a poverty-stricken white family in Salisbury. He had a succession of jobs, was heavyweight boxing champion of Rhodesia, and then became an engine driver and moved to Northern Rhodesia where he was eventually elected to the Legislative Council. The Labour Government and the Conservative opposition in Britain, however, opposed the linking of the territories until the Africans showed that they wanted it. But the British settlers were alarmed at the growth of both Afrikaner nationalism to the south and African nationalism to the north of them, and were attracted by the booming economy of Northern Rhodesia. They therefore stressed the undoubted economic advantages of federation while suggesting that control of native affairs could remain with each territorial government.

Between 1949 and 1953 a series of conferences were held in London and at Victoria Falls when the British government (Conservative after 1951) agreed to a federation. The limited electorate of Southern Rhodesia and the assemblies of Northern Rhodesia and Nyasaland all favoured the scheme. Therefore in October 1953 the Federation of Rhodesia and Nyasaland was officially born. It had a cabinet responsible to a federal parliament which dealt with defence, trade, finance, industry and communications. All other matters which affected Africans most closely were to be dealt with by the territorial governments. The federal capital was Salisbury. It was assumed that the Federation, which had a population of 8 million Africans and 300,000 Europeans, would eventually become a self-governing dominion.

So the Federation came into being, despite the views of those who pointed out that African opposition was widespread and deep-seated, and that imposition of federation would inevitably lead to political trouble. From the start Africans opposed the Federation. At all the conferences before 1953, Africans had either not been present or, if they had, had opposed the scheme. They feared, firstly, that Southern Rhodesian native policy would be extended to the other two territories, and secondly, that the Federation would become an independent state before Africans had at least reached equality with Europeans. They 'regarded Federation as a disguised step towards amalgamation for the sole purpose of maintaining white supremacy as they saw it existing in Southern Rhodesia'.[1]

The federal elections of 1954 and 1958 were won by the United Federal Party which defeated the extreme right-wing parties. Lord Malvern (previously Sir Godfrey Huggins) was Prime Minister from 1953 to 1956. He was then succeeded by Sir Roy Welensky, who began to campaign for the independence of the Federation. But by 1958 African hostility to a Federation, whose leaders preached partnership but seemed to practise segregation, was growing increasingly militant.

In 1958 Dr Hastings Banda returned to Nyasaland to become leader of the African Congress, the main nationalist party. Banda, a graduate of American universities in history as well as medicine, had lived in Britain from 1937 to 1953, practising as a doctor in London after the war. He had then set up a medical practice in the Gold Coast before returning to Nyasaland. Early in 1959 disorders and violence led to the governor declaring a state of emergency in which Banda and 600 Africans were imprisoned. In Northern Rhodesia in 1958 Kenneth Kaunda criticised the leadership of the African Congress, and formed the Zambia African National Congress which demanded secession from the Federation. Early in 1959 it was proscribed and Kaunda was imprisoned. In Southern Rhodesia opposition was led by Joshua Nkomo. Early in 1959 Sir Edgar Whitehead, the prime minister, declared a state of emergency, banned the Congress Party and arrested 500 Africans. Nkomo, who was out of the country at the time, remained in exile.

In view of this African opposition to a Federation whose leaders wanted independence, the British government appointed in 1960 a Royal Commission under the chairmanship of Lord Monckton to investigate. The Monckton Commission said that dissolution was undesirable on economic grounds, but that the Federation could only continue if drastic changes were made. It made four main recommendations: the franchise should be extended and Africans should have more seats in the federal parliament; the federal government should be responsible for defence and economic policy only; legislation discriminating against Africans should be repealed; and territories should have the right to secede.

The report was the beginning of the end of the Federation which gradually disintegrated over the next three years. Banda and Kaunda were released, and new and better organised African parties replaced those that had been proscribed. In 1961 Africans were given a majority

[1] A. J. Wills, *Introduction to History of Central Africa*.

on the Legislative Council and seats on the Executive Council of Nyasaland. In the elections which followed Banda's Malawi Congress Party won an overwhelming victory. The result was regarded as a virtual referendum on secession from the Federation. In Northern Rhodesia, after passionate opposition from the European minority, a new constitution in 1962 provided for the possibility of an African majority on the Legislative Council. In the subsequent elections the two African parties won a majority and formed a government.

In Southern Rhodesia, on the other hand, the European right-wing group became stronger. The Europeans kept a two-thirds majority on the Legislative Council, and African nationalist parties were banned. In the election of 1962 the right-wing Rhodesian Front defeated Sir Edgar Whitehead's United Federal Party. The new prime minister was a tobacco farmer named Winston Field, and his government was very unenthusiastic towards the Federation, wanting independence for Southern Rhodesia.

By 1963 it was clear that the Federation was at an end. All three territories possessed internal self-government and the right to secede from the Federation. It was clear that the Conservative government of Macmillan in Britain intended to support the African majority. Not even the Southern Rhodesian government now supported the Federation. After a conference at Victoria Falls had arranged for its dismemberment, the Federation of Rhodesia and Nyasaland officially ended on the last day of 1963.

In 1964 Nyasaland and Northern Rhodesia became independent and were renamed Malawi and Zambia respectively. It was natural that Southern Rhodesia should demand a similar independence. In April 1964 Field was succeeded as prime minister by Ian Smith, a farmer and ex-fighter pilot of the Second World War. Smith began a vigorous campaign to persuade the British government, but Wilson, the British Prime Minister, insisted on certain conditions being satisfied: there should be unimpeded progress towards majority rule, guarantees that this would continue after independence, an improvement in the political status of Africans, and progress towards ending racial discrimination. Long drawn out negotiations took place but without success, and in November 1965 by a unilateral declaration of independence (UDI), Southern Rhodesia severed her links with Britain.

The immediate response of Britain was twofold: to declare the Smith action illegal and his government unconstitutional, and to impose economic sanctions and thus stop all commercial contact between Britain and Rhodesia. With the exception of Portugal and South Africa, the rest of the world was hostile to UDI and did not recognise the Smith regime. Independent African states were clearly opposed to Smith, while the leaders of African opinion within Rhodesia were in prison.

During the next ten years there was a succession of attempts to reach a political settlement. In December 1966 Wilson met Smith for talks aboard *HMS Tiger* in the Mediterranean. Britain proposed a referendum to see whether there was majority support for independence for Rhodesia before majority rule, but this was rejected by Smith. In October 1968 the two leaders met again, this time on board *HMS Fearless* at Gibraltar, but disagreement on fundamental issues remained. In 1970 the Conservatives returned to office in Britain and the Foreign Secretary, Sir Alec Douglas Home, attempted to find a settlement based on the five principles or conditions set out in 1965. The fifth principle was that any new agreement must be acceptable to Rhodesians 'as a whole'.

After lengthy negotiations, in November 1971, Britain and Rhodesia issued agreed proposals for a settlement. A new African electoral roll would be created, with income, property and educational qualifications. As the number on this roll increased, so there would be additional seats for Africans in Parliament, and eventually majority rule would be accomplished. But there were doubts about these proposals. In the absence of external safeguards, could the white Rhodesians be trusted to implement them? The franchise would be very difficult for Africans to achieve: it would be the end of the century at least before there would be majority rule. In addition there was the failure to reverse any of the recent moves towards apartheid. In December a broadly based African National Council under Bishop Muzorewa was formed to fight these proposals. In accordance with the fifth principle, the Pearce Commission was sent by Britain to Rhodesia to test the acceptability of the proposals, and reported in May 1972 that Africans were almost unanimously against them. So the proposals lapsed and there were no further important negotiations to reach a settlement until 1976.

There were two ways of putting pressure on the white Rhodesian regime: the use of economic sanctions and of armed force. In November 1965 Britain had imposed sanctions. In December 1966, following the breakdown of the *Tiger* talks, the United Nations Security Council voted for sanctions on Rhodesian exports and on the export of oil to Rhodesia. In May 1968 the UN imposed comprehensive sanctions on all trade with Rhodesia. In many ways the Rhodesian economy suffered. The export of tobacco was badly hit; it was difficult to trade in other goods, and there was unemployment especially among the

Ian Smith, Prime Minister of the illegal regime in Rhodesia. On the right is his successor, Bishop Muzorewa.

Mugabe's supporters celebrate his election victory in Salisbury, Rhodesia, March 1980

expanding African population. However, some important countries did not cooperate with the United Nations. New customers and sources of supply, especially France, West Germany and Japan, were found, and Mozambique and South Africa acted as commercial go-betweens. Rhodesians showed skill and resource in combatting the sanctions: farming had always been efficient; light industry was developed to provide goods unobtainable through sanctions.

Britain refused, because of the cost and the opposition of public opinion, to use armed force, despite pressure from the African states. International action was not seriously considered. Therefore African guerrilla groups acted on their own. By 1966, through acts of sabotage and attacks on isolated European farms, they began to make themselves felt. But terrorist activities were on a relatively small scale until 1973. Then, using bases in Mozambique as well as Zambia, they conducted bigger and more effective campaigns. The Rhodesian government established protected villages and spent large sums on defence.

Meanwhile the personal position of Smith was almost unchallenged, and the white minority were united. In 1968 Rhodesian judges ruled that the Smith government was a *de facto* government since it was in effective control of the country. A new constitution establishing a republic came into effect in 1970. White supremacy was entrenched, the number of African MPs being dependent on the sum total of income tax paid by all Africans. Only 1 per cent of income tax revenues was contrbuted by Africans. At the same time the Land Tenure Act was passed. This divided the country into white and black areas. Although Europeans (240,000) were only one-twentieth of the total population, they received one-half of the land.

Most of the leaders of African opinion were in prison until December 1974. They were then released to enable them to attend talks in Lusaka, in Zambia, with representatives of the Smith government. The talks broke down because the nationalists wanted immediate majority rule. There were four main leaders of the Rhodesian Africans: Bishop Muzorewa and the Reverend Sithole who were the more moderate, Nkomo, a veteran leader who steadily became more extreme, and Mugabe who was committed to armed struggle. There were personal rivalries between them as well as political divisions. Their relative strength had never been tested in an election and was therefore unclear.

During 1975 and 1976 the pressure on the Smith regime increased. As a result of the independence of Mozambique and Angola in 1975, Rhodesian communications with the outside world were weakened and these two countries could be used as bases for guerrilla bands attacking Rhodesia. The guerrilla war escalated in 1976: guerrillas operated in large groups and were more daring in their attacks, despite big Rhodesian raids on camps in Mozambique. The war increased tension, with white Rhodesians leaving the country at the rate of 800 per month. But the attitude of the United States and South Africa was the crucial factor in 1976. In April Dr Kissinger, the American Secretary of State, said, 'We support majority rule for all the peoples of southern Africa'. It was clear, after their experience in Vietnam, that the United States was not prepared to support regimes it regarded as doomed. So the weight of American power and influence was now against Smith. During 1976 there were meetings between Kissinger and Vorster, the South African Prime Minister. Both feared that Rhodesia could go the way of Angola, and Vorster told Smith that Rhodesia could no longer rely on support from South Africa.

Therefore, in September 1976, there came what appeared to be a major break-through. Smith agreed to the Anglo-American proposals put to him by Dr Kissinger. Firstly an interim government would be formed with an African Prime Minister and African majority, although the ministers for defence and law and order would be European. Secondly, within two years of the setting up of this interim regime there would be majority rule. Thirdly, there would be an immediate lifting of sanctions and an end to the guerrilla war. This appeared to be a major step towards reaching a settlement, but doubts appeared almost immediately. In particular, it was not clear whether Africans inside or outside Rhodesia had agreed to the proposals. Disagreements and deep distrust became clear when the African nationalist leaders and Smith met at the Geneva Conference during the autumn of 1976. Smith considered that the conference was to implement the Anglo-American proposals; the Africans, who were very divided, put forward their own demands and wished for independence within the 2-year period. Neither side showed a willingness to compromise.

Thus at the start of 1977 there was once again stalemate, except that Smith had now publicly accepted the principle of majority rule. During 1977 Dr Owen, the British Foreign Secretary, put forward new proposals: British rule in Rhodesia, a United Nations force to help maintain security, a development fund to assist the Rhodesian economy, elections based on universal adult suffrage, and independence during 1978. These proposals, however, were unacceptable both to Smith and the African nationalist leaders in Rhodesia, and to Nkomo and Mugabe, the guerrilla leaders outside Rhodesia.

With the guerrilla war worsening and the majority of the white population apparently willing to live under a moderate black government, Smith opened negotiations with the nationalist leaders in

Rhodesia, Bishop Muzorewa, the Reverend Sithole and Chief Chirau. The talks took place between December 1977 and February 1978 and made substantial progress. In March 1978 Smith and the three black leaders signed the following agreement: the four men would form an Executive Council to control government for the remainder of 1978; this Council would appoint a Ministerial Council with both an African and European minister for each department of government; the new constitution would establish a parliament of 100 members, 72 of whom would be black and 28 white; elections based on universal suffrage would be held during 1978 and the new regime would come into operation at the end of the year. Clearly, this was a major step towards a multi-racial state of Zimbabwe. During the following months political detainees were released and racial discrimination in law was abolished. However, despite these advances, the internal settlement failed to obtain international recognition—African and Western governments remained hostile—and sanctions were not lifted. The guerrilla war continued and worsened. In addition to guerrilla incursions from Zambia and Mozambique, Muzorewa and Sithole had their own armed supporters. The numbers killed rose dramatically, and by the end of 1978 three quarters of Rhodesia was under martial law.

The fighting led to the postponement of elections. In a referendum in January 1979 85 per cent of the white population accepted majority rule. Elections for the new parliament were eventually held in April 1979. Sixty-four per cent of black Rhodesians voted, a higher number than expected, and Muzorewa's United African National Party won a clear majority. However, the new black government remained unrecognised by the international community. The economy continued to be badly affected, not only by sanctions, but by the intensifying war– 7,000 people were killed in Rhodesia during 1979. At the same time the economies of Zambia and Mozambique were suffering similarly. There was no prospect of an end to war. Indeed, a typical stalemate position seemed to have been reached, with the Patriotic Front (the forces of Nkomo and Mugabe) unable to defeat the Rhodesian security forces, who themselves were unable to prevent guerrilla activity.

At the Commonwealth Conference at Lusaka in August 1979 it was decided that Britain should convene a new conference in London. This met from September to December 1979. Muzorewa, Nkomo and Mugabe were under considerable pressure to reach a settlement, while it was clear that Smith's influence had declined. After lengthy negotiations agreement was finally reached, both on a new constitution with reduced white powers and a ceasefire. Lord Soames arrived in Salisbury in December 1979 as the new British Governor and the illegal regime, begun in 1965, finally came to an end. In March 1980 elections were held. Of the 100 seats in the new Parliament, Mugabe's ZANU party won 57, Nkomo's Patriotic Front won 20, Smith's white Rhodesian Front won 20 and Muzorewa's UANC party won only 3. The first actions of Mugabe, the new Prime Minister, seemed conciliatory as the new independent African state of Zimbabwe, faced with great problems of reconciliation and reconstruction, was born.

Africa since Independence

Between 1957 and 1977 thirty-nine states south of the Sahara became independent. The process was started by the British and accelerated by General de Gaulle. The African states so formed were faced with many problems. They were all, to a greater or lesser extent, economically weak. For example, 'by the time Malawi attained independence there were only two secondary schools for its 3 million Africans, no roads to speak of, only one railway line, and not a single industrial plant. A primitive and low yield agriculture was based almost entirely on growing mealies.'[1]

The new governments were inexperienced and lacked trained administrators. Their rulers were faced with the question of whether or not to continue to rule democratically in view of the limited experience of democracy, the lack of non-tribal opposition parties, and an ill-educated population. There was the danger, too, that the unity previously imposed by the European authorities would now weaken. The nationalism created in opposition to these European rulers could decline now that they had gone, and there was the possibility of a resurgence of tribalism. Many African rulers believed that a one-party state was the answer to these dangers. In many states, after a period of civilian rule, the army has intervened to establish military government. Whereas in the Arab states military regimes have tended to be radical, African military governments have tended to be conservative in their policies.

There was also the problem of the relations these new states should have with each other. The states form a mosaic of different languages, cultures and religions, and on many issues have little in common with each other. They have, however, a common experience of colonialism and of obtaining independence, though often in very different circumstances. At meetings of the OAU the principle of African brotherhood is often invoked. The Organisation for African Unity held its first

[1] J. Listowel, *The Listener*, 5 May 1966.

meeting in 1963 at its headquarters in Addis Ababa. It has been useful in mediating between states to ease personality conflicts and to solve boundary disputes. It has played no significant role in southern Africa other than condemning continued white rule. The rift between moderate and extremist governments prevented a common approach to many topics. In the 1970s there has been a further complication with the involvement of other non-African states in affairs of Africa. Immediately after independence, western European states continued to be most influential, although supporting the view that African solutions should be found to African problems. But in the late 1960s and first half of the 1970s Russia, Cuba, China and the Arab states established themselves in Africa: Russia and Cuba as the principal allies and suppliers of weapons to liberation movements, China by the skilful use of aid programmes—for example, the construction of the railway linking the Zambian copper belt with the port of Dar-es-Salaam—and the Arabs through their oil 'weapon'. The United States remained on the sidelines until the mid-1970s. An example of conflicting interests and ideologies is the situation involving Ethiopia and Somalia in 1976–77.

A brief outline of the history of Ghana, Nigeria and the Congo since their independence will serve to illustrate some of the problems faced by the new African states. The problems of Ethiopia are similar, while those of South Africa, whose racial policies have aroused the hostile reactions of the rest of the continent, are entirely different.

Ghana (Gold Coast)

Ghana was launched into independence with good qualifications for future success: an impartial civil service and police, a flourishing economy, a prime minister who had already five years of experience in this office, and a strong ruling party. Nkrumah ruled Ghana from 1957 to 1966. During this period he came to symbolise for the world the new Africa, and thus influenced feelings towards Africa throughout the world. There were three major aspects of his policy: his support for the Pan African movement, the development of a dictatorship in Ghana, and an over-rapid expansion of the economy.

In 1959 Ghana and Guinea formed a union, and in the following year they were joined by Mali. However, no close cooperation resulted, and it was dissolved 'in the interests of wider unity' after the Addis Ababa conference in 1963.

During the nine years of his government, Nkrumah steadily retreated from parliamentary government and concentrated authority into his own hands. Apart from the wish to maintain and extend his own power, Nkrumah distrusted democracy in a country containing several tribes, regional differences and few common traditions. Therefore, he gave himself powers to deport opponents and critics[1] and to imprison for up to five years without trial. The police were given greater authority, the judiciary was controlled, the regional assemblies were abolished, the parliamentary opposition was ended, and Nkrumah's own party was purged. Free speech disappeared. In these circumstances the only form of opposition left was violence. In 1962 a bomb attack on the President (Ghana became a republic in 1960) led to a state of emergency. Nkrumah's powers and the measures he took to defend himself prevented any further opposition from showing itself until 1966.

The economy at first expanded rapidly under Nkrumah. Industry was built up so that there should be less dependence on the sale of cocoa. In 1959 work started on the Volta River project. This was a huge regional scheme involving the construction of a dam which would be used for irrigation and for providing hydroelectric power. During the second half of Nkrumah's period in power, the economy ran into difficulties, partly because of balance of payments deficits caused by heavy imports and a decline in the market for Ghana's products, and partly because of government extravagance.

The combination of economic difficulties and discontent with an increasingly harsh dictatorship, led to Nkrumah's fall in February 1966. While the president was on a visit to China, the army and police staged a successful *coup d'état*.

Nkrumah lived in exile until his death in 1972. His achievements were considerable: the new harbour at Tema and the completion of the Volta River Project, the building of good communications, a tremendous advance in education. In particular, he led Africa on to the world stage, and set in motion the rapid progress to independence in black Africa. On the other hand, he became a harsh dictator, detaining political opponents and ending the rule of law. His prestige construction projects and badly run state farms and industries had brought Ghana to the edge of bankruptcy by 1966. He was an example of the corrupting influence of absolute power.

During the next three years there was a military government led for most of the time by General Ankrah. From the start it planned to restore democracy in Ghana. Political parties were at first banned, but in 1969 were allowed on condition that they were not based on tribal or religious groups. Constitutional commissions produced plans for a return to civilian rule and in 1969 a well-ordered, fair and free election

---

[1] For example, an Anglican bishop was deported for criticising the chanting of slogans such as 'Nkrumah is our Messiah, Nkrumah never dies.'

was held and won by the Progress Party led by Dr Busia. The military then withdrew from power.

From 1969 to 1972 Ghana was again ruled by civilians. Busia was a quiet, reflective man who slowly increased in stature. The style of his government was calm rather than showy. However, the economic and political problems of Ghana in the 1960s gradually worsened. Foreign debts grew, the production of cocoa, the main export, declined and its price went down, while other prices continued to rise. Population was increasing and reached 8·5 million by 1970; food production did not keep pace. By 1971 the economy had seriously deteriorated and discontent mounted. In addition, party politics degenerated into divisive tribal strife. The result was that the army intervened for the second time, and civilian government again came to an end.

The new military government was led by Colonel Acheampong. The son of an Ashanti cocoa farmer, he had received his military training in France and the United States. Acheampong had no driving ideology and prided himself on being a simple soldier who was intent on reconciling the main interest groups in Ghana. The constitution was abrogated, political parties again banned, and government has been by decree. On the fifth anniversary of the coup, in January 1977, the Military Government said in an advertisement in the London *Times,* that it hoped a future regime 'will avoid a return to party politics which, in the past, encouraged rivalry, tribalism, corruption and other social vices among Ghanaians'. Later in 1977, however, a strike by a group of professional people—lawyers, engineers, doctors— led to a promise by Acheampong that civilian rule would be restored. However, in 1978 Acheampong in his turn was deposed, and a new government led by General Akuffo was formed. One year later, in June 1979, Akuffo in his turn was removed in a further military coup, led by a Fl. Lt Rawlings and junior ranks of the armed forces.

Nigeria

The history of Nigeria since independence has been dominated by the question of unity. There are several races and languages in the four regions of the federation,[1] and while Christianity is strong in the south, Islam is the religion of the north. As a result political parties were based on tribal and regional loyalties, not national interests. The basic division was between the authoritarian and conservative Northern Region with its 30 million population, and the more progressive southern regions with their combined population of about 25 million.

Disputes between parties intensified tribalism and frustrated efficient

[1] The Mid-West Region was carved out of the West Region.

rule by the federal government. Until 1964 the latter was based on a coalition of the NPC and the NCNC, that is the parties of the Northern and Eastern Regions. The federal prime minister, Sir Abubakar Tafawa Balewa, a wise and moderate statesman and a firm supporter of unity, managed, with the help of Dr Azikiwe, the president since Nigeria became a republic in 1963, to keep the coalition together. But the strains and jealousies increased, particularly during the general election of 1964. Finally in January 1966 the army intervened, and both Balewa and the Sardauno of Sokoto were killed.

The rising had been carried out by young army officers who were mainly from the Eastern Region. The civilian regime was ended and a new military government, led by General Ironsi, was formed. During the next few months the army purged the administration of corrupt officials and arrested many ex-politicians. Then it decided to maintain the unity of Nigeria by changing from a federal to a unitary form of government. This was seen by Northerners as a way of spreading the power and influence of Ibos from the Eastern Region, and immediately provoked several days of violence in which Northerners attacked and killed many hundred Ibos who lived in the north. Then Northern soldiers mutinied and killed Eastern officers and soldiers. In the course of this fighting in July Ironsi was killed.

Ironsi was succeeded by Lt Col. Gowon, a Northerner, who was to rule Nigeria until 1975. Gowon was educated at Sandhurst, and was an unassuming, humane and (as events were to show) magnanimous man. He was to become a popular and respected ruler, partly because of his humble background and simple life style, and partly because of his considerable political maturity and judgment. Gowon spent his first year attempting by peaceful means to maintain the unity of Nigeria. On the one hand were soldiers from the Northern Region who were demanding the secession of the North from the Federation. On the other hand, the Eastern Region, led by its governor, Lt Col. Ojukwu, had assumed a *de facto* independence. In September there were more anti-Eastern riots in the North. By the end of 1966 about 20,000 Easterners had been killed, and millions of refugees were crowded into the Eastern Region.

Against the background of this slaughter, Gowon tried to reach agreement with Ojukwu. They debated whether there should be a strong or a weak federal government and whether to retain the existing four regions or create more. The decree to establish a unitary state had been withdrawn by Gowon who now decided to divide Nigeria into twelve states. This was designed to prevent any one group from dominating the others. But the demand from the Ibos for a separate

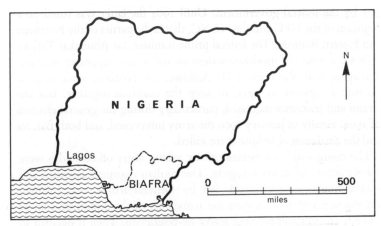

Nigeria showing Biafra

state was overwhelming. Both sides were active in re-equipping their armed forces, Ojukwu declared the independence of the Eastern Region (called Biafra), and in July 1967 fighting began.

The Nigerian Civil War, in which Biafra attempted to make itself an independent state, lasted for two and a half years. Although relatively small in area, there were 12 million people in Biafra when the fighting started. The war took the form of Gowon's Federal forces imposing a gradually tightening military and economic blockade of Biafra. By the end of 1967 Biafra was surrounded. During 1968 the Federal army made huge gains, and by the end of the year Biafra held only 10 per cent of its original territory. Despite some successful Biafran counter-attacks, in 1969 there was a massive onslaught by encircling Federal troops with the result that in January 1970 the Biafran forces surrendered. As the war proceeded, the civilian population of Biafra suffered enormously. They faced famine and disease as well as war and up to one million people died. Outside agencies provided relief, but this humanitarian policy could well have prolonged the war. Similarly, the provision of weapons for Biafra, probably from France, encouraged Biafra to pursue a military struggle and not make peace. The Biafrans fought bravely and well, and with desperation from the belief that surrender would mean mass genocide by the Federal forces.

There were in fact very few atrocities after the war ended. Starvation and malnutrition accounted for most deaths. Gowon set the tone both for the conduct of the war and the peace that followed. He was intent on the unity of Nigeria and therefore Biafra must be defeated. But having won the war he then followed a policy of the three Rs: reconciliation, rehabilitation and reconstruction.

The Nigerian economy managed to stand the strain of civil war and even to expand. Economic growth depended heavily on oil. Production rose, especially after fresh oil discoveries. In 1971 Nigeria joined OPEC, and in 1974 she replaced Libya as Africa's largest oil producer. There was substantial Nigerian participation in the oil companies and a gradual reduction in foreign control. The revenue from oil increased, especially after the price increases of 1974, and the government pressed for the reinvestment of this revenue in other sectors of the economy. The population of Nigeria in 1974 reached 80 million, an increase of 25 million since the census of 1963. Despite considerable industrial development, 70 per cent of the population was in the early 1970s employed in agriculture. Farming methods were old-fashioned and inefficient and in 1971 the average income of a farmer was only £30 per year. Agriculture remained backward; money for capital investment was not the problem; rather it was the lack of a substantial managerial class to implement the ambitious programme of agricultural development.

In the 1970s Nigeria became a major force in African affairs because of its size and wealth and because of strong government. In 1968 the federal system of twelve states began functioning. Government remained under the control of the multi-tribal army of a quarter of a million. In 1970 Gowon outlined the problems that would need to be settled before the end of military government: an accurate census, the end of corruption, a new constitution, and national political parties. In 1972 he promised a return to civilian rule by 1976 but announced in 1974 that this would not happen. In the early 1970s there was general satisfaction with the government, but by the middle of the decade there were signs of unrest. Gowon was at the OAU Conference in Uganda in July 1975 when middle-ranking officers in the army organised a *coup*. Another northerner, Brigadier Mohammed, became Head of State.

Zaire (The Congo)

On 5 July 1960, six days after independence, the Force Publique mutinied against its Belgian officers. Anti-white violence broke out, and Belgian troops were flown to the Congo. Six days later the provincial president of Katanga, Tshombe, with the vigorous support of the Belgians in Elisabethville, declared Katanga independent. Thus the huge tax revenue from Katanga's copper mines was cut off from the central government. Then in September 1960 President Kasavubu and the army dismissed and imprisoned Lumumba, the prime minister. A few months later Lumumba was killed. A further complication was that one of Lumumba's supporters, Gizenga, established himself in Stanleyville and declared that he represented the legitimate government of the Congo.

After this disastrous start to independence, United Nations troops arrived at the request of the Congolese government in Leopoldville. Their object was first to prevent civil war and remove all foreign military and political personnel from the Congo, and later to end the secession of Katanga. At the end of 1961 there was fierce but indecisive fighting between the United Nations[1] and Katanga forces. In 1962 the situation improved. The central government under the new prime minister Adoula, established more effective control over the Congo: the Gizenga regime in Stanleyville was ended, and at the end of the year the United Nations defeated Tshombe's government in Katanga.

However, civil disorders continued. A rebellion in the eastern provinces persisted. At the same time there were divisions in the central government. The economy was in chaos. In consequence the Army decided to intervene. In a bloodless coup in November 1965 President Kasavubu was deposed, and General Mobutu, the Commander in Chief, assumed the presidency with the power to legislate by decree. He has remained in power since that time.

General Mobutu is an ambitious man of iron will. Impulsive and abrupt but with shrewd political intuition, he continues the tradition of great African paramount chiefs. He did not believe that power was to be shared. Congo is an enormous country with regions that have markedly different climates, economic bases and traditional cultures and languages. National unity was fragile. After the strains of civil war during most of the first six years of independence, Mobutu was intent on providing strong, centralised government. The rebels were defeated and the ex-politicians were executed, imprisoned or exiled. In 1967 a constitution providing for a more powerful central government was issued. Mobutu's own party, the People's Revolutionary Movement, was reorganised and strengthened, and only government approved candidates were allowed to stand for parliament. Censorship was tightened. The Roman Catholic Church—an important unifying force since over half the population of 21 million (1976) are members—was also compelled to support the government in every way.

Mobutu followed a policy of Congolese nationalism. As a result for three years, 1965–68, relations with Belgium were strained. Mobutu was determined to end Belgian control of the economy. In 1967 the

[1] The United Nations Secretary-General, Dag Hammarskjöld, was killed in an air crash during a visit to the Congo (see pp. 543–4).

government seized all the assets of the Union Miniere, and for a time the Belgians withdrew many of their personnel from the Congo bringing chaos to schools and to the economy. After 1968, however, relations improved, and a large number of Belgian specialists and technicians returned to the Congo. Another aspect of Mobutu's policy of encouraging national consciousness was the replacement of European with African names. Hence in 1971 Congo was renamed Zaire; Leopoldville had previously become Kinshasa. Streets were renamed, and people were given African names. For example, any man called Raphael was known after 1971 as Komi Botokei, and any woman called Marie-Celeste was renamed Mbasi Moi. Music, art, laws, fashion had to be authentically African. In some areas Beethoven, Chopin and Bach were banned.

Until 1971 the economic position improved. Currency reforms, sound finances, greater efficiency of government and a rising price for copper, produced an unprecedented growth and expansion. But in 1971 there was a sharp fall in copper prices, and during the next few years imports, wages and prices increased at a rate the economy could not stand. The change of government in Angola in 1975 threatened the security of the copper-producing areas of the south. Twice, in 1977 and 1978, Angolan-based troops attacked and were repelled by French and Belgian soldiers who came to the aid of Mobutu.

Ethiopia

In 1913 the Emperor Menelik died. The next ruler was deposed three years later and Menelik's daughter became Empress with his cousin, Ras Tafari as Regent. When the Empress died in 1930 Ras Tafari was crowned Emperor with the title of Haile Selassie ('Might of the Trinity'). Therefore, Haile Selassie ruled in effect from 1916, with a break of five years (1936–41) during the Italian occupation (see chapter 2) when he lived in exile in Bath in England.

During Haile Selassie's long reign, Ethiopia made considerable material progress. Health, educational and judicial reforms were introduced, although social services tended to deteriorate away from the vicinity of the capital, Addis Ababa. The economy is primarily agricultural and in many ways is still backward.

Haile Selassie retained complete power throughout this period. In 1931 a constitution established a Senate and Chamber of Deputies chosen from among the chiefs and other dignitaries. Both could only advise the Emperor. In 1955 a new constitution provided for a legislative assembly, partly elected, partly nominated, but again its function was only advisory and executive power remained with the Emperor. While Haile Selassie was in Brazil in 1960, there was a shortlived revolt of the Imperial Guard. This, together with the presence of a newly educated middle class, a powerful army, discontented minorities and the influence of other African states, may have convinced the conservative elements in Ethiopia that further steps towards democracy were necessary. After 1960 young ministers were given more responsibility and the Legislature more power, but the dignified Haile Selassie, surrounded by the magical aura of monarchy, still retained ultimate power.

From the mid-1960s, however, the problems facing the aging emperor steadily grew. There were disputes with Somalia and the Sudan, and there was an increasingly active secessionist movement in Eritrea. In 1963 Eritrea, with its mainly Muslim population, had been incorporated into the Ethiopian empire. From that point onwards the Eritrean Liberation Front supported a rebel army that the Ethiopian forces could not crush. The insurgents received aid from the Arab states, and their guerrilla tactics were a constant trouble to the government. In addition, students became politically active, at first demanding more money for education, but later criticising many aspects of government policy. The year 1973 was a disastrous period of drought. Despite help from world relief organisations, many tens of thousands died from famine.

In 1974 the Army intervened. At first the Army was loyal to the Emperor, but as the strikes and demonstrations by students and trade unionists continued, the military arrested former ministers, members of the current government and relations of Haile Selassie. Finally, in September 1974, the Emperor was deposed after fifty-eight years of power. There then followed a confusing period of successive military governments, each more left-wing than its predecessor. Moderates, and eventually Marxists, both civilian and military, were arrested and killed. As policies within Ethiopia steadily became more extreme, so the external threat from Eritrean rebels and a Somali invasion increased. At the end of 1977 the Somalis invaded eastern Ethiopia, land they had for long claimed as their own. However, the Communist military government of Ethiopia was now receiving massive Russian and Cuban military help, and early in 1978 the Somalis were driven out.

South Africa

The 1948 election gave the reunified National Party a majority of five over the United Party. Dr Malan therefore became Prime Minister.

President Nkrumah

Dr Verwoerd

African leaders meet in Nairobi. From left to right (front row): Obote (Uganda), Nyerere (Tanzania), Mobutu (Congo), Kenyatta (Kenya), Haile Selassie (Ethiopia)

The Nationalist Party gradually grew stronger. In the 1953, 1958, 1961 and 1966 elections they increased their majority, while the United Party, their chief opponent, has grown progressively weaker. Malan resigned in 1954 and was succeeded by Strydom, an anti-British republican from the Transvaal. Strydom died in 1958 and his place was taken by Dr Verwoerd (1901–66).

Verwoerd, whose father was a missionary, arrived in South Africa at the age of two. He rejected a scholarship to Oxford and attended German universities instead. Between 1927 and 1937 he was professor of applied psychology and then of sociology at the University of Stellenbosch. For the next eleven years he was editor of a Johannesburg newspaper, and had opportunity to show his anti-Jewish and anti-British views. He hoped Hitler would win the war, and during the visit of the British King and Queen to South Africa in 1947, his paper only reported traffic congestion caused by the presence of some overseas visitors. Verwoerd entered the Senate in 1948 and in 1950 he became Minister of Native Affairs. In this office, and later as Prime Minister between 1958 and 1966, he became the leading champion and exponent of the policy of apartheid.

Verwoerd was assassinated by a white man in Parliament in September 1966. He was succeeded as Prime Minister by Vorster, the Minister of Justice, a strong and determined leader, although perhaps a little more pragmatic. Vorster was Prime Minister for twelve years. He retired in 1978, and was succeeded by Pieter Botha, the Defence Minister, a man with a reputation for tough and authoritarian policies.

Apartheid, which means separateness, first became the racial policy of the Nationalist Party in 1947. It is based on the belief that the political equality of white and black in South Africa would mean black rule because two-thirds of the population is African. Since this would supposedly imperil European society, the Africans must be kept in permanent subjection by keeping them separate from Europeans. In practice, therefore, apartheid is a means of enforcing white minority rule.

Verwoerd, more than any other man, was the brain behind the apartheid policy. From 1950 onwards a whole series of laws aimed at its achievement. Marriage between white and non-white was forbidden. A population register was drawn up and identity cards were issued so that every person could be given a racial classification. With this information apartheid could be implemented. Nearly all schools were brought under government control so that an education separate and different from that of white children could be enforced for Africans.[1]

[1] Dr Verwoerd said in the debate on this subject in 1953: 'When I have control of native education I will reform it so that natives will be taught from childhood to realise that equality with Europeans is not for them.'

University education was also segregated.

In 1950 the whole country was divided into separate areas for the different races. This obviously presented great difficulties involving movements of population and was enforced very slowly. Then in 1959 the Bantu (that is the African) Self-Government Act was passed. The native reserves were to be consolidated into seven units called Bantustans. These would be separate states where the Bantus could develop freely in their own way under their own governments. They would eventually become independent states. Those Africans who lived outside the Bantustans would have no political rights, and the small native representation by Europeans in Parliament was abolished.

The basic aim of apartheid is, therefore, to separate the areas where whites live and work from the areas where non-whites live and work. But this has proved very difficult for two reasons. Firstly, the Bantustans cover only 13 per cent of the area of the country. This 13 per cent cannot adequately support the existing native population, regardless of the natives who live outside the reserves. Secondly, over half the non-white population is economically integrated with the white population. White farming, mining, industry and commerce, domestic services, all rely on the labour of those Africans who do not live in the reserves. To force all the non-whites to live together in the reserves and stop them working in white areas would mean the virtual collapse of the economy.

Therefore, the emphasis in racial policy has been on the further segregation of white and non-white in the white areas. Segregation in hospitals, railway stations, buses, beaches, churches, sport and all forms of entertainment has been enforced. Non-whites are forced to live in separate areas often outside but near towns. Any African who walks outside his residential area without a police permit can be sent to prison for two weeks, and any African who leaves his house without his pass can be imprisoned or fined.

During the first half of the 1970s there was some relaxation of petty apartheid, that is the less important laws separating the races. In international sport, a New Zealand rugby team containing Maoris was allowed to tour South Africa. Evonne Goolagong, a part Australian Aborigine, was allowed to compete in the South African Open Tennis Tournament. In 1973 a racially mixed South African Games was held. Natal decided in 1974 that black nurses could tend white patients in private hospitals, and there were moves to allow racially integrated libraries, parks, public seats and queues. A major theatre and opera house in Cape Town, and first-class hotels, admitted all races.

The policy of apartheid has been opposed in South Africa and in the world at large. In the South African Parliament the opposition has been weak because the main opposition party also wants to maintain white supremacy but has no clear-cut alternative to apartheid. Other political parties have been formed, for example, the Liberal Party wanting a policy of non-racialism, but these have not become important numerically. In the 1974 election the Progressive Party won 6 seats (United Party—41; National Party—122), and this minor success pushed the United Party into more positive policies. The UP announced that it wanted full citizenship for Coloureds, black trade unions and integrated sport. However, in the 1977 election the National Party increased its number of seats to 134, the Progressive Party to 17, while the United Party was almost destroyed.

Outside parliament white businessmen have criticised apartheid on economic grounds. Although the economy has been most successful, they consider that further expansion is being restricted. There is a serious shortage of skilled labour, which can only be overcome if non-whites are trained for skilled jobs. Further industrial expansion can only be achieved by increasing the proportion of non-whites working in industry. Differences of educational and then job opportunity are depriving South Africa of potential skills. For promotion to be normally dictated by colour rather than efficiency or aptitude is bad for whatever concern is involved. In addition to these arguments, economists point out the inefficiency of non-whites spending long hours travelling between their place of work and the township or Bantustan where they live. The result, too, of migratory labour is a high turnover. It is very obvious that the income level of non-whites is far below that of whites. While 80 per cent of the population have very low wages, domestic consumer demand is kept low. A further argument is that the widespread condemnation of apartheid abroad has led to some boycott of South African goods.

The non-whites of South Africa have intermittently shown their opposition. In 1952 the African National Congress led by Chief Luthuli and the South African Indian Congress organised a passive resistance campaign. Non-whites would, for example, enter European waiting-rooms and cafés. Many thousands were imprisoned and the campaign was ended by the Criminal Law Amendment Act which provided severe punishment for anyone protesting against a law by breaking it. In 1956 an increase in fares on the bus route from Johannesburg to an African township ten miles away produced an African boycott of buses for three months. Thousands of Africans walked the ten miles to and from work until finally they succeeded in reducing the fares.

In 1957 an attempt to impose the pass system on women as well as men was resisted violently. In the same year 150 people of all races were arrested and accused of treason. The trial dragged on for four years before all were eventually acquitted. In March 1960 at Sharpeville, near Johannesburg, about seventy Africans were shot and many more wounded during a demonstration against the pass laws. This was followed by rioting and a wave of protest across the world. A state of emergency was declared, hundreds were arrested and African political parties were banned. The atmosphere became even more tense when a white man shot and badly wounded Dr Verwoerd. In the early 1960s underground movements committed acts of sabotage, but these groups were soon broken up.

1973 and 1974 brought to a head a rising tide of black labour unrest. There are different wage rates according to colour, and the majority of African workers have been paid very low wages. Yet African labour is essential to the economy. This was shown by about 500 strikes during these two years, mainly in the heavy industries. For a time the port of Durban was brought to a halt. In 1973 eleven rioting African miners were shot by police. The result was not only a rise in wages of between 30 per cent and 60 per cent but also a realisation that skilled and unskilled black manpower was vital to industry. During the 1970s. there developed what became known as the Black Consciousness movement: manifest by the withdrawal from orthodox Christianity and the formation of specifically black separatist churches and the giving of African rather than European names to children. This movement gained mass support from the African townships, that is the areas on the outskirts of towns and cities where non-whites live. One of the largest of these townships is Soweto, about ten miles from Johannesburg. About one million Africans live there in 100,000 small, hut-like, almost identical buildings, with a few dilapidated shops. There are some fine amenities but these are inadequate for the area. A survey in 1969 said that 'the minimum needs for a household of 5 persons, allowing for no expenditure on household goods, drink, recreation, tobacco, books, luxuries or for assistance to relatives, were defined as £450 per annum. Even on this desperately low threshold of poverty, 68 per cent of Soweto families were found to be living below the breadline.' The frustrations eventually produced an explosion. In June 1976 students in Soweto protested against the use of the Afrikaan language in schools. There were other educational grievances, and the students were supported by adult groups. The protests became riots which spread to black townships in other parts of South Africa. The rising young black generation were clearly in a militant and violent mood. 174 people were killed, and many more wounded, in the riots.

The leaders of the Bantustans have also shown their dislike of the

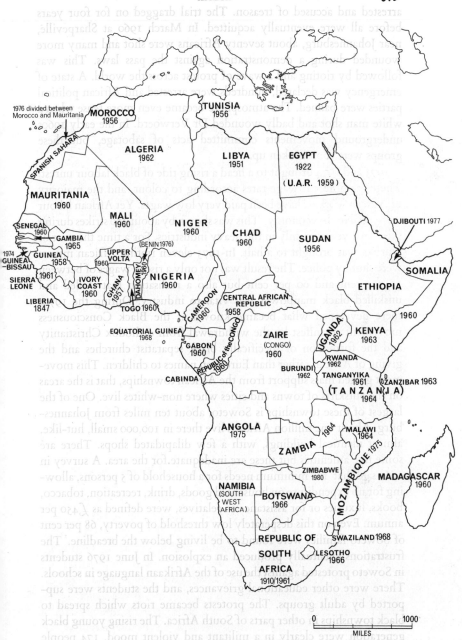

Africa in 1980

practice of apartheid. All Africans are assigned citizenship in one of the eight homelands to which theoretically they will eventually move. In 1970 47 per cent (that is 7 million) of Africans lived in the Bantustans, depending on subsistence agriculture and remittances sent home by the 8 million living 'temporarily' in white areas. The Bantustans contain the poorest agricultural land, they are unsuitable for industry being remote from good communications and power, and their territories are scattered. Zululand, for example, has 29 separate pieces of territory. By 1973 six of the eight homelands had been given self-government. This meant that they had Legislative Assemblies which controlled education, health, welfare, minor roads, agriculture and water; the white central government controlled everything else. In 1976 one of the Bantustans, the Transkei, became an independent state. Other countries, however, have regarded this as an elaborate fiction, and have not recognised the Transkei. In 1970 its leader bluntly asked for greater power, more land, more investment and a coastline with a port. In 1975 the leaders of the eight Bantustans expressed their dissatisfaction with their scattered lands and their wish to consolidate their territories. In 1977 a second tribal homeland, Bophuthatswana, became independent.

All the non-white and a large part of the white peoples of the world have condemned apartheid as morally wrong[1] and economically and politically impracticable. There have been long discussions in the United Nations and elsewhere about the possibility of imposing economic sanctions on South Africa to force her to change her policies. In 1960 Macmillan, the British Prime Minister, after a tour of Africa, reminded the South African Parliament of the strength of African national consciousness: 'In different places it may take different forms, but it is happening everywhere. The wind of change is blowing through the continent.'

In 1960 a referendum was held amongst the white population on whether they wished South Africa to become a republic. Fifty-two per cent voted in favour. On becoming a republic, a dominion has to apply for readmission to the Commonwealth, but at the Commonwealth Conference in March 1961 the opposition to South Africa was so intense that Verwoerd decided to withdraw South Africa's application for renewal of Commonwealth membership. It was generally felt among members that the presence in a multiracial Commonwealth of a state practising apartheid would lead to the disintegration of the

[1] Two well-known books critical of apartheid are Trevor Huddleston's *Naught for your Comfort* and Alan Paton's *Cry, the Beloved Country*.

organisation. Therefore in May 1961 South Africa became a republic outside the Commonwealth, and proceeded yet another step towards diplomatic isolation in the world.

South Africa has remained a member of the United Nations, although in 1974 the General Assembly voted to suspend her from the current session. Throughout the period of the Rhodesian rebellion, apart from a few months in 1976, South Africa supported the Smith government and refused to apply economic sanctions. Despite United Nations opposition, the Vorster government continued to rule South-West Africa (Namibia), originally given to South Africa as a mandate under the League of Nations in 1920. With the United Nations replacing the League of Nations, the legal position of the mandate was unclear. In 1966 the International Court of Justice said that the UN could not 'invigilate' over South Africa's administration of the territory. Consequently the UN General Assembly decided to end the mandate, but South Africa said that this was illegal, and continued to assimilate the territory into South Africa. In a fresh judgment in 1971 the International Court found that the continued presence of South Africa in Namibia was illegal, and during the 1970s there have been various moves to persuade South Africa, reluctant because of the new-found mineral wealth in the area, to grant genuine self-government to the country. In 1978 South Africa finally accepted a plan for the independence of Namibia.

The policy of apartheid, together with attitudes to Rhodesia and South West Africa, and support for Portugal, have produced very strained relations with most other African countries despite South Africa's offers of aid and technical assistance. In 1971 Dr Banda, the President of Malawi, paid a successful state visit to South Africa, but his example has not been followed. On the other hand, Mr Vorster has visited the Ivory Coast and Liberia, and held talks with President Kaunda of Zambia at Victoria Falls. The independence of Angola and Mozambique in 1975 presents a potential threat to South Africa, particularly as South African troops supported the unsuccessful moderate leader in the Angolan civil war that followed independence. The countries of the world have discovered that international sport can be used to express political views. There have been a number of moves to isolate South Africa from international sporting activities. For example, in 1968 South Africa was excluded from the Olympic Games in Mexico, and the MCC cancelled a cricket tour of South Africa because Basil D'Oliveira, a coloured man from Cape Town who had emigrated to England, was in the team and the Vorster government said he could not come. South Africa is a country of sports enthusiasts, and this type of action was found to be an effective way of striking at white morale.

Yet South Africa has managed to maintain her policies and her prosperity. There are four main reasons for this. Firstly, there has been strong government. Dr Verwoerd and Mr Vorster, self-assured and powerful men, have provided tough and inspiring leadership. Secondly, isolation has led to the unity of the white population—'a drawing together in a common fear', as the United Party leader has said. White South Africans tend to dismiss foreign criticism of apartheid as ignorant and misguided; inside the country, it is difficult for whites to get to know the attitudes and views of non-whites. Thirdly, South Africa's efficient industry and flourishing commerce have led to economic prosperity. The country is rich in minerals: gold, iron ore, chrome ore and many others. Some of these are found only, or in large proportion, in South Africa. It is the world's largest producer of platinum and diamonds. During the 1960s there were boom conditions with new capital flowing in and industry developing rapidly. Only Japan had a higher growth rate. Agriculture is less efficient but South Africa produces nearly all its food requirements. Indeed, oil is the only major import for which the country is dependent on the outside world. This economic prosperity and independence is an important factor in the continuation of apartheid.

Fourthly, the government has been successful in keeping the non-white population quiescent. Any expression of opposition is soon crushed. The Suppression of Communism Act provided a broad definition of communism, enabling the government to suppress any organisation and to imprison any individual it regarded as being dangerously critical of its policies. For two years in the early 1960s the police could seize any person on suspicion of subversion and keep him or her in solitary confinement for renewable periods of ninety days. The 1967 Terrorism Act gave the police broad and sweeping powers to arrest, detain incommunicado, and to interrogate without limit prior to charge or trial. During the following ten years the police have increasingly used techniques of fear little different from those employed by their counterparts in other authoritarian and police states. Deaths of suspects in detention—that of Steve Biko in 1977 aroused considerable world-wide anger—have increased.

9

The Indian Subcontinent

Beginning of the Twentieth Century

The Indian subcontinent, mainly hilly and for most of the year very hot, had a population of nearly 300 million in 1900. This huge area and population was conquered by Britain between about 1750 and 1850. India was an economically backward country. On average there was less than one acre of cultivated ground per person, since the system whereby land was divided equally between the members of the family and not left to the eldest child had led to small holdings. The chief crops were rice, wheat and cotton, but farming methods were antiquated. Industry was negligible. The standard of living was, therefore, very low; most people were undernourished; diseases such as smallpox, tuberculosis, cholera and leprosy were widespread, and the death rate was high.

Religion was (and still is) a very important factor in the lives of the people. About two-thirds of the population were followers of Hinduism, a complicated religion which has covered India with temples and places of pilgrimage. Hinduism affected the life of Indians in two main ways. Firstly, as we have seen, it insisted that land was shared amongst the family. Secondly, there was the caste system. There were four main castes: about 15 million Brahmins (the priestly or learned class), about 10 million Rajputs (the fighting class), traders and cultivators, and the remainder. But each caste was subdivided, and there were about 3,000 subcastes. These were hereditary and generally connected with occupation. Various customary laws or taboos restricted contact between members of different castes; for example, a Hindu must marry within his caste. Outside the caste system altogether, however, were the outcastes or untouchables. Their life, especially in south India, was a miserable one; they were, for example, excluded from most occupations, and were forbidden to use roads, wells and schools. At the beginning of the twentieth century the caste system was better organised than it had been fifty years earlier, but Western influence was gradually working against it.

The other important religion of India, Islam, was strongest in the north-west and in Bengal. The differences between Muslims and Hindus were to be of vital importance during the twentieth century. Islam, believing in one God, is a much simpler religion than Hinduism, and its followers regard Hindus as idolators. Muslims tend to be more evangelical than the more tolerant Hindu. Islam tends to be democratic, whereas Hinduism has no idea of equality. Disputes between Hindus and Muslims usually occurred for apparently quite trivial reasons: Muslims would eat cows which Hindus believed to be sacred; Hindus would play music outside Muslim mosques.

There were other religions in India, which were unimportant in comparison with Hinduism and Islam. Three had broken away from Hinduism during the centuries: the Buddhists, mainly in Ceylon, the proud and aggressive Sikhs of the Punjab, and the Jains. In addition there were a small number of Christians.

One reason for the poor standard of living of most Indians was lack of education. Over 90 per cent of the population were illiterate despite the considerable progress of education during the previous 100 years. For the fortunate few, elementary education was given in the native language, while higher education was in English. Most schools were privately owned but received government grants. By 1900 there were five universities in India. This Western education received by Indians had very important results. Firstly, it created an educated Indian middle class. Secondly, this middle class learned of Western liberal ideas, of Rousseau and John Stuart Mill, of the revolt of the American colonies against Britain, of the French Revolution, of the struggle to obtain democracy in Britain in the nineteenth century, and of the granting of self-government to Canada and Australia. Why, the Indian intellectuals were beginning to ask, should democratic self-government not be given to Indians also? Thirdly, the ideas of Western socialism were studied, and the belief grew that the British were in India purely for economic profit. Fourthly, Indian history was discovered, and national pride grew with the knowledge that India possessed a long history of rich civilisation. And lastly, because this education was received in one language, English, and because India was administered as a single country under one code of laws, the rising nationalism had an all-India character.

Nevertheless 1900 seemed the zenith of British imperialism, and the West generally seemed dominant in the world. British rule in India had been unquestioned since the Mutiny fifty years before. Sixty per cent of the area and three-quarters of the population were ruled directly by Britain. The remaining territory, scattered all over the subcontinent, was divided between over 500 states, some very large like Hyderabad, some very small. (One state was so small that its prince was supposed to rule only a well.) In these princely states Britain was responsible for defence and internal order only. The whole country was administered by the Indian Civil Service (ICS).

At the beginning of the twentieth century, Lord Curzon, the Viceroy, was ruling with a benevolent but masterful hand. He, like nearly all Englishmen, did not foresee any possibility that India would or could ever rule herself. However, Indians were allowed freedom of the press and public meeting, and in 1885 the Indian National Congress was formed with the approval of the government. It was started with the help of two retired English civil servants, and was valued by the government as a convenient way in which public opinion could be expressed. Its members were mainly middle-class intellectuals, lawyers, landlords, university teachers, newspaper editors, and it was very moderate for the first twenty years of its existence, asking only for a larger share of the government for Indians.

So in 1900 there were few outward signs of the changes that were to take place during the next fifty years, but the seeds of these changes had been sown. In 1900 Curzon said 'My own belief is that Congress is tottering to its fall, and one of my great ambitions while in India is to assist it to a peaceful demise.' But Curzon was to assist in doing the exact opposite.

Start of the Nationalist Movement 1905 to 1916

In 1905 came the first major disorders of the twentieth century. Apart from the new nationalism already mentioned, these were caused by inflation, agrarian grievances in the Punjab, Curzon's reform of universities by which Indians lost positions of authority, and, most important, Curzon's decision to partition Bengal. For sound administrative reasons, it was decided that East Bengal and Assam, a largely Muslim area, should become a separate province. This immediately produced rioting and terrorism in Bengal and the Punjab. Extremists, led by Tilak, gained temporary control of the National Congress, enormous meetings were held, and there were the usual communal disorders.

The extremist leaders were imprisoned and the disturbances gradually died down. By 1907 Congress was again controlled by the moderates.

However, there were two important consequences of these disorders. Firstly, the new Liberal Government in Britain after 1905 decided to extend Indian representation in the Legislative Councils. Secondly, leading Muslims believed that Congress was likely to favour only Hindus, and therefore decided in 1906 to form the Muslim League. This new party would aim to protect Muslims by securing for them separate representation on the Legislative Councils.

Curzon resigned in 1905 after a disagreement with Kitchener over army reforms. The new Viceroy was Lord Minto and the Secretary of State for India was Morley. In 1909 these two drew up the third Indian Councils Act, generally known as the Morley-Minto Reforms. For the first time Indians were represented on the central and provincial Executive Councils. The Central Legislative Council was trebled but a small majority of non-elected officials was retained. The Provincial Legislative Councils were doubled in size and elected members were now in a majority. Thus Indians were given a much greater chance to both advise and criticise the government, but no opportunity to control it. Morley did not believe that a democratic parliamentary system would work in India. The act of 1909 contained an important decision of principle; believing that as wide a representation of interest as possible was desirable, the British Government gave separate representation to Muslims and Sikhs. Hindus believed that this was an example of the British policy of 'divide and rule'. One historian has said that Muslims were now bound to think of themselves as Muslims rather than Indians, and in this sense the origin of Pakistan can be traced to the decision.

The years from 1910 to 1916 marked the peak of British authority. The partition of Bengal was annulled. Great satisfaction was given to national opinion by the transfer of the capital from Calcutta to Delhi. Amidst great pomp and ceremony, George V visited India. Congress was loyal. Nehru, describing the delegates dressed in morning coats and immaculate trousers, said it had more the appearance of a social gathering than a political assembly. The Viceroy, Hardinge, became a national hero by publicly supporting the rights of Indians who were suffering from racial laws in South Africa. In 1914, when war broke out in Europe, the British Government received enthusiastic support from Indian public opinion. Well over a million men were recruited, £100 million was given to the government, and Indian soldiers served in France, the Middle East and East Africa. But by 1916 this enthusiastic loyalty was waning.

Gandhi and Civil Disobedience 1916 to 1922

Several events had occurred in the world during the first two decades of the twentieth century which had an important influence on the development of Indian nationalist opinion. In 1905 Japan had soundly defeated a European country, Russia, and the First World War showed the West to be divided and Britain weaker than had been thought. In 1908 the Young Turks and in 1911 the Chinese Nationalists, both using Western methods and ideas, had overthrown their governments, and in 1918 President Wilson of the United States had publicised the idea of self-determination. These events provide the background to Indian nationalism.

In 1916 the extremists, again led by Tilak, regained control of Congress. Soon the two important leaders of modern India, Mahatma Gandhi and Jawaharlal Nehru, came to the forefront. Gandhi (1869–1948) was born in Gujerat in Western India, a member of a subcaste connected with trade. At the age of thirteen he was married, and six years later came to London to study law. Returning to India in 1891, he practised as a lawyer in Bombay for two years, and then went to South Africa on behalf of an Indian business firm. There Gandhi was soon involved in the struggle against South African racial laws. He organised demonstrations, was often arrested and imprisoned, and developed the technique of non-violent non-cooperation. During the Boer War he organised an Indian ambulance corps. After twenty years in South Africa, Gandhi returned to India, where he began a campaign that he continued for the rest of his life to improve the lot of the untouchables.

Nehru's background was very different. His father, Motilal Nehru, a Kashmiri Brahmin and a strong and commanding character with liberal views, was a leading lawyer of Allahabad, a city on the Ganges. Jawaharlal spoke of his father as being 'something like a Renaissance prince'. Jawaharlal Nehru (1889–1964) was an only child for several years and lived in a palatial home with every material comfort. As a boy his tutors were English, and at the age of fifteen he came to England, first to Harrow and then to Cambridge, where he studied Natural Sciences. After Cambridge Nehru studied law in London, and in 1912 returned to India, where he practised law under his father. He was in no way outstanding at this point in his career, but in 1917 his interest in Indian nationalism was aroused, and he began his life's work.

The strength of Indian nationalism was increased by the temporary agreement of Hindus and Muslims. The latter had been alienated by the Allied campaign against Turkey, and were more offended later by the severe terms of the peace treaty imposed on Turkey. In 1916 the Lucknow Pact was signed: led by M. A. Jinnah, a barrister from Bombay, the Muslims agreed to support the Congress campaign for self-government in return for separate representation for Muslims. This unlikely Muslim-Hindu alliance, coupled with the economic discontent caused by the war, persuaded the British Government that a change of policy was required. In 1917 an important statement promised 'increasing association of Indians in every branch of the administration and the gradual development of self-governing institutions with a view to the progressive realisation of responsible government in India as an integral part of the British Empire'.

The following year, the Viceroy, Lord Chelmsford, and the Secretary of State for India, Montagu, announced details of how this policy was to be carried out. The Montagu-Chelmsford Reforms, as they are generally known, formed the basis of the Government of India Act of 1919. The Act retained complete British control of the central government. The Central Legislature had now a majority of elected members, but ministers were not responsible to it. In the provincial government, a system called dyarchy was introduced. There were already majorities of elected members in the Provincial Legislatures. Now some provincial ministers, in charge of, for example, public works, forests and education, were responsible to the Legislatures, and were therefore likely to be Indians. But provincial ministers in charge of law and order and defence would continue to be responsible only to the Governor. The Act also provided for a commission to visit India ten years later to consider the possibility of extending responsible government.

Although this Act was a big advance on that of 1909, Indian nationalist opinion was disappointed. In view of the 1917 statement and India's wartime sacrifices, Indians expected much greater concessions. During 1918 disorders increased, and grew worse as demobilisation took place. The result was that the government decided to pass the Rowlatt Act which retained the wartime emergency powers. This was the signal for Gandhi to start his first mass movement of civil disobedience. Disturbances, some violent, broke out all over India early in 1919. The government arrested Gandhi and banned all meetings and processions. But the disorders continued and reached a climax in April 1919, at Amritsar, a large city in the Punjab, where, after several days of anti-European rioting, British troops fired on a dense and milling crowd of Indians, killing 379 and wounding about 1,000. The Amritsar massacre, as it was soon called, became a symbol of British cruelty, and although order was gradually restored during the rest of 1919 the situation was now changed.

In 1920 Tilak died. Gandhi's magnetic personality and his ideas of non-cooperation now dominated Congress, which, instead of being exclusively middle class, was now becoming a mass party. Indians stopped paying taxes, resigned from government offices, refused to attend government schools, and boycotted the elections for the Legislatures. Thousands of Congress workers were imprisoned. But two incidents convinced Gandhi that the people were not yet ready for the methods of non-violent non-cooperation. In 1921 the visit of the Prince of Wales was accompanied by rioting in which fifty people were killed, and in 1922, at a village called Chauri Chaura in north India, twenty-two policemen were burned alive in the police station by the villagers. Gandhi decided to call off the campaign, but with its leaders in prison, the non-cooperation movement had by 1922 passed its peak.

The Simon Commission and the Round Table Conference 1922 to 1935

From 1922 to 1928 there was little political activity. Congress was weakened by internal dissension over non-violent political methods and over whether or not to cooperate in working the 1919 constitution. Eventually one section of Congress, led by Motilal Nehru, decided to fight the elections, and entered the Legislatures. The constitution worked quite well, and the provincial ministers did good work, but were faced with great difficulties after the world economic depression in 1929. The central government under Lord Reading (1921–26) and Lord Irwin (1926–31) showed itself to be tactful and sensitive to public opinion. The alliance of Hindus and Muslims of 1916 had ended by 1924, and communal disturbances broke out once more.

Meanwhile British rule continued to be stately and impressive. Earl Winterton has thus described an official dinner party at the Viceroy's palace:

> As the Viceroy and his wife walked slowly into the dining room preceded by two aides-de-camp marching in step, the band crashed into the National Anthem and the brilliantly attired Indian servants to the number of a dozen or more standing behind chairs buried their heads in their hands as a mark of respect.

Another description of British rule is given by E. M. Forster in his novel, *A Passage to India*. Ronny Heaslop, a young City Magistrate, is speaking to his mother:

'We're not out here for the purpose of behaving pleasantly.'

'What do you mean?'

'What I say. We're out here to do justice and keep the peace. Them's my sentiments. India isn't a drawing-room.' ·

'Your sentiments are those of a god,' she said quietly . . .

'There's no point (said Heaslop) in all this. Here we are, and we're going to stop, and the country's got to put up with us, gods or no gods . . . I am out here to work, mind, to hold this wretched country by force. I'm not a missionary or a Labour Member or a vague sentimental sympathetic literary man. I'm just a servant of the Government; it's the profession you wanted me to choose myself, and that's that. We're not pleasant in India, and we don't intend to be pleasant. We've something more important to do.'

In 1928 the British Government decided to hold the enquiry envisaged by the 1919 Act. The Chairman of the Commission was Sir John Simon. Indians, however, boycotted the Commission,[1] partly because it contained no Indians, and partly because they regarded it as insulting to have a commission to enquire whether they were fit for self-government. Motilal Nehru said the British were treating Indians as schoolboys who, if good, would be promoted to a higher form. However, the Simon Commission produced a valuable report which recommended self-government in the provinces. Responsible government in the centre should follow the setting up of a federation joined by the princes of India, and the solving of the problem of minorities. A Round Table Conference was to meet in London in 1930 to discuss these two points.

But Congress demanded immediate self-government and dominion status, and in 1930, under the presidency of Jawaharlal Nehru and backed by Gandhi, it decided to start the civil disobedience campaign again. This was formally opened by Gandhi. If the nationalist movement was to succeed, it had to be based on support from the whole population. Gandhi realised this, and therefore chose to break the law that only the government could make salt. Breaking this simple law would be understood by the masses. Now aged sixty-one, Gandhi walked 240 miles down to the Arabian Sea coast, and there obtained salt by distilling seawater. The march turned into a religious pilgrimage which aroused huge publicity. This was followed by the breaking of the salt law on a large scale and a boycott of all foreign manufactured

---

[1] Lord Attlee, who was a member of the Commission, described in his autobiography, *As it Happened*, their arrival in Bombay: 'No untoward incident occurred though a bomb had been prepared for us. Its custodian, however, dropped it from the rack of a railway carriage with unfortunate results for himself.'

cloth. Gandhi, the Nehrus and thousands of Congress supporters were arrested.

When the first session of the Round Table Conference began, therefore, Congress representatives were absent. However, progress was made. as the princes agreed to enter an Indian federation. For the discussion of the problem of minorities, though, it was necessary to have Congress present. In January 1931, the respected and patient Lord Irwin released Congress leaders, and persuaded Gandhi[1] to go to London, where he attended the second session of the Conference. For three months Gandhi lived with friends in the East End of London, meeting a whole range of people from Charlie Chaplin to Bernard Shaw. Sir Samuel Hoare, the Secretary of State for India, has described his meetings with this thin, bent little man, with sharp, penetrating eyes, bony knees and toothless mouth. Although King George V rather objected to Gandhi attending a reception at Buckingham Palace 'with no proper clothes on, and bare knees', the meeting between them passed off with no incidents. The King's parting remark was: 'Remember, Mr Gandhi, I won't have any attacks on my Empire.'

However, the Round Table Conference reached deadlock on the question of minority representation. Congress was not represented at the third session of the Conference in 1932, because the new Viceroy decided to adopt a tougher policy towards Indian nationalism. Congress leaders were again imprisoned and Congress itself and all public meetings were banned. By 1934 the enthusiasm of the nationalists had died down, and Gandhi officially called off civil disobedience.

The Muslims demand Pakistan 1935 to 1945

The findings of the Simon Commission and the Round Table Conference provided the basis for the Government of India Act of 1935. India was to be a federation. In the Central Legislature, the Indian states were to be represented as well as the rest of India. The system of dyarchy which had operated in the provinces since 1919 was now to be transferred to the centre. Ministers in charge of defence and foreign affairs were to be responsible only to the Viceroy, but other ministers

---

[1] Churchill, who adopted a very conservative position towards Indian nationalism, said of this meeting: 'It is alarming and nauseating to see Mr Gandhi, a seditious Middle Temple lawyer, now posing as a fakir of a type well known in the East, striding half naked up the steps of the Viceregal Palace, while he is still organising and conducting a defiant campaign of civil disobedience, to parley on equal terms with the representative of the King-Emperor.'

were to be responsible to the Central Legislature. In all eleven provincial governments there was now to be full responsible government. Burma was now separated from India.

In 1937 the first elections were held under the new constitution. Nehru conducted an energetic and extensive campaign in which he addressed about 10 million people, and Congress did well, winning 715 out of 1,585 seats. In five provinces Congress gained a clear majority and in three it was the largest party. But since Congress had at first opposed the 1935 Act, there was some delay before the new governments in the provinces could be formed. Eventually, however, Congress ministries took office in eight of the eleven provinces. There were no Muslims in these eight ministries unless they were Congress members. Congress was fully within its rights in not offering positions in the ministries to members of the Muslim League, but the decision not to do so proved, as we shall see, to be politically tactless. The Muslim League did badly in the elections, and coalition governments were set up in the other three provinces. The central part of the 1935 Act was never implemented, because the princes could not at the last moment be persuaded to join, and therefore the British continued to control the central government.

The fairly smooth functioning of the provincial governments was brought to an abrupt halt soon after the outbreak of the Second World War. In September 1939, the Viceroy, Lord Linlithgow, without consulting the Central Legislature, proclaimed India at war. This action was legal, but tactless. Congress, in return for support for the war, demanded complete independence for India as soon as the war was over, and meanwhile a share in the central government. The Viceroy replied that steps would be taken to achieve dominion status after the war provided that the problem of minorities could be solved. This did not satisfy Congress, and in November their eight provincial ministries resigned. In 1940 Congress called on the people not to support the war, and as a result many thousands of Congress leaders were imprisoned.

These events from 1937 to 1940 had an important effect on Muslim opinion. It had long been feared that democracy in India meant rule by Hindus, but until 1930 the Muslim League had never considered the possibility of the Muslims of India forming a separate independent state. In 1930, however, this idea was presented by the philosopher-poet Iqbal at a meeting of the League. It was repeated three years later by some Muslim students at Cambridge, and the idea gradually took shape. It developed rapidly after the 1937 elections, for it now seemed apparent that under democratic conditions India must be ruled by Hindus, and, except for a few areas, Muslims would be in a perpetual minority. The Congress ministries made changes which seemed un-favourable to Muslims. The result was that Jinnah, the leader of the League, was fully converted to the Pakistan[1] plan, that is that the Muslim areas of north-west and north-east India should separate from the predominantly Hindu remainder. The cry, 'Islam is in danger', went out. 'Muslims can expect neither justice nor fair play under Congress,' said Jinnah. 'There are in India two nations.' This seemed to be confirmed by Congress's attitude to the British Government's attempts to settle the communal problem before handing over power. Finally a meeting in 1940 of the Muslim League, now vastly stronger, passed a resolution officially demanding the formation of Pakistan.

The political deadlock continued throughout 1941, but after Japan's rapid victories in South-East Asia, the position in 1942 was critical. To try to reach a settlement, the British Cabinet sent Sir Stafford Cripps to India. He proposed that India should be independent as soon as possible after the war, that the constitution should be decided by Indians, and any state or province should have the right to secede. This would clearly allow Pakistan to be formed, and Congress therefore rejected the proposals. Apart from this, Congress believed that time was on their side; the Japanese were winning the war so it did not matter what Britain offered. In the middle of 1942, Gandhi began his 'Quit India' campaign, and Congress threatened to start the non-cooperation struggle again. The government now acted swiftly. The Congress leaders were again imprisoned, this time for the duration of the war. Countrywide disturbances—destruction of railway stations, post-offices and government buildings—were stopped quickly and effectively. Congress was removed as a political force.

Meanwhile, the Indian army had been increased to $2\frac{1}{2}$ million, and played an important part in the defence of Assam. With the unfortunate exception of the famine in Bengal in 1943 when 2 million people died, the government machine worked smoothly and efficiently.

The Last Stage to Independence 1945 to 1947

The last and most critical stage in the long history of British rule in India was reached with the end of fighting in 1945. The imprisoned members of Congress were released and elections were held. The result showed Congress control of eight of the eleven provinces, and

[1] The name Pakistan is derived from the initial letters of Punjab, Afghans (i.e. North-west Frontier Province), Kashmir and Sind, with the suffix 'tan' meaning country. The whole word conveniently means 'Land of the Pure'.

League control of the other three. In 1946 the new British Labour Government under Attlee made a final attempt to solve the problem of the Muslim minority without partition. A Cabinet Mission proposed an all-India government dealing only with foreign affairs, defence and communications. Remaining matters would be dealt with by provincial governments which, if they wished, could form groups. But this scheme, too, was rejected. Congress wanted weak provincial governments and a strong central government; the League wanted the reverse. The distrust between the two sides was now so great that an agreement on details could not be reached.

In August 1946, the events of a year later were rehearsed. In Calcutta Muslims attacked Hindus, and therefore in neighbouring Bihar Hindus attacked Muslims. Thousands were killed, often in a revolting way. 'There seems', said Nehru, 'to be a competition in murder and brutality.' By the end of the year, both Congress and League had acceded to the request of the Viceroy, Lord Wavell, to enter the central government, but the attempt to get the two parties to cooperate failed. By the beginning of 1947 Congress was realising that unless it agreed to partition civil war would result, and any hopes of developing the subcontinent economically or politically would be dashed.

With this feeling developing Attlee announced in February 1947 that the British would transfer power not later than June 1948. The next month Wavell was replaced by Lord Mountbatten of Burma, the head of South-East Asia Command during the war, and an energetic and dynamic leader of men, with a flair for personal relations and a capacity for rapid decisions. Mountbatten's arrival coincided with serious rioting in the Punjab and a big decline in the morale of the Civil Service. He soon realised that the date for independence must be advanced, and that partition was the only answer. The outline plan for partition was agreed to by the League, Congress and the British Government. Pakistan was to consist of North-West Frontier Province, Baluchistan, Sind, West Punjab, East Bengal and part of Assam. India would consist of the rest. The 560 princes were to decide which of the two states they would join. And so on 15 August 1947, two new states came into existence, and British rule in India came to an end.

But the enthusiastic celebrations of independence were terribly marred by savage civil war in Bengal and especially in the Punjab where about 200,000 people were killed. Millions of pathetic, terror-stricken refugees moved—Muslims to Pakistan, Hindus to India. There were large-scale train massacres. Penderel Moon, a British member of the Civil Service, has described the disorders in East Punjab. 'Murderous-looking Sikhs armed with large kirpans prowled about the platforms of railway stations sniffing for blood, and when a train halted, searched the carriages for Muslim travellers, and, if they discovered any, stabbed them to death.'[1]

That the disorders were not worse in Bengal was largely due to Gandhi's activities in easing tension between Hindus and Muslims. This earned for him the hatred of the orthodox Hindu extremists, and the sequel came in January 1948, when Gandhi was assassinated in Delhi by a fanatical Brahmin.

Mahatma Gandhi was one of the great men of the twentieth century. From 1920 to 1947 he guided and restrained the Indian nationalist movement, and it was his great achievement that generally speaking the movement was peaceful. Sir Ivor Jennings has described him as a 'fighting politician who scorned to fight',[2] and Mrs Pandit, Nehru's sister says that 'Gandhi fought a mighty empire without arms and without hatred'. Probably his repudiation of violence would not have worked against a Nazi or Communist regime, and in many ways Gandhi was unrealistic. His revolt against the age of machinery was not suited for the India of the future. Gandhi lacked Nehru's international outlook and emphasis on modern economic planning, but Gandhi understood the Indian masses, and they revered him as a saint. Nehru, on the evening of the assassination, said, 'The light has gone out of our lives . . . the Father of the Nation is no more.'

India after 1947

Nehru 1947 to 1964

Political From 1947 to 1950, while the constitution was being drafted, India was ruled under the 1935 Act. During these years there was considerable danger that the princes of India would try to remain independent, but a great deal of pressure was put on the states by Sardar Patel, who was in charge of the negotiations, and by 1949 they were merged completely into India. Some were consolidated into unions; the rest were merged into neighbouring provinces. The rulers kept their titles and personal privileges. Two states, however, provided greater difficulty—Hyderabad and Kashmir. Hyderabad was the largest of the states, and its ruler, a Muslim, was supposed to be the richest man in the world. But the great majority of his subjects were Hindus. The prince tried to remain independent, negotiations broke down, and eventually

[1] P. Moon, *Divide and Quit.*   [2] I. Jennings, *British Commonwealth of Nations.*

his state was occupied by the Indian army. Kashmir was to provide much more serious and lasting trouble, and will be dealt with under foreign policy.

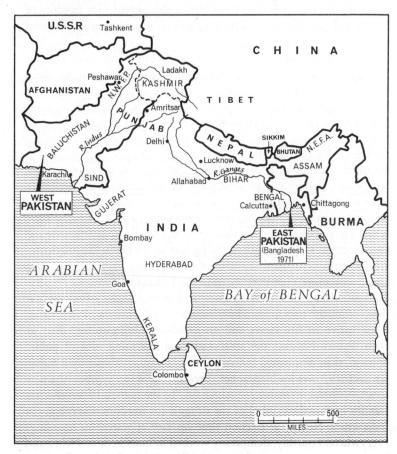

The Indian subcontinent after 1947

In 1950 the Constitution of India, a long, elaborate and complicated document, was drawn up. There is a Federal Parliament consisting of a Lower House of 500 members directly elected by the people, and a Council of States consisting of 250 members elected by the state legislatures. The Federal government deals mainly with foreign affairs, defence, communications and tariffs, and has power to intervene in certain circumstances in state affairs. In fact, the constitution is heavily weighted in favour of the centre. In 1962 there were fifteen states in

India, including Kashmir, and each has a Governor and a Legislature. The State Governments deal mainly with public order, health, agriculture and education. India has a President who is elected for five years by the central and state legislatures. He is in many ways the equivalent of a constitutional monarch. The Constitution also provides for freedom of speech and equality of opportunity, and sets out a number of social ideals, such as free education.

Three general elections were held while Nehru was premier. Despite a huge and largely illiterate electorate of over 170 million, these elections were conducted smoothly. Indeed, one of the outstanding features about India compared with other newly independent countries has been the smooth functioning of democracy. For this there were four main reasons. Firstly, there was the influence of British parliamentary institutions and the gradual training during the first half of the twentieth century in how to work them. Secondly, Indian politics were dominated by a single large party, the Indian National Congress, with a nationwide organisation. In all three elections Congress won about 360 seats, although receiving only about 45 per cent of the total votes. The opposition parties were weak and small, the strongest being the Communist Party, with its strength in south India. Although the Communists controlled the state of Kerala from 1957 to 1959, they never won more than thirty seats in the Federal Legislature. Thirdly, India was ruled after 1947 by good and trusted leaders. For the first three years, the two outstanding leaders were Nehru and Patel. Patel, conservative in his views and an excellent administrator, died in 1950. Pandit Nehru,[1] the aristocratic and charming idol of public opinion, then dominated Indian politics. 'To most Westernised Indian intellectuals,' says his biographer, Brecher, 'he was a symbol of a new society—liberal, humanist, equalitarian.' To the masses, however, after Gandhi he was the symbol of the struggle for freedom. Everybody in India knew Nehru; at election time his face appeared on hoardings everywhere. Fourthly, democracy worked in India because Nehru and his government were sensitive to public opinion. Freedom from the British, the government believed, must lead to freedom from hunger and other economic weaknesses and from social evils.

However, there have been weaknesses in Indian democracy. The big majority of the electorate was illiterate and had little idea of political responsibility, and the caste system continued to separate society into

---

[1] Each morning Nehru devoted an hour to reading the newspapers and to yoga exercises. 'Only under severe pressure of work does he forgo the pleasure of standing on his head. Among other benefits, he has remarked, one cannot take problems too seriously from that position.' M. Brecher, *Nehru*.

groups. There was considerable doubt expressed as to whether democracy was suited to these conditions. The Congress party, after so many years in power, tended to become stale and complacent, and new men and new policies, and particularly an obvious successor to Nehru, were slow in coming forward. And because Congress was the dominating party, decisions made by Congress tended to be more important than decisions made by Parliament. Finally, there has been fairly widespread corruption and inefficiency in administration.

The other outstanding political feature about India since 1947 has been her unity. A sense of nationalism amongst people is usually based on a common language and religion, and many feared that with so many languages and religions the Indian Federation would weaken and go the same way as Austria-Hungary. That this has not occurred is partly due to the strength of the nationalism created under the British, partly to the fact that political parties have been national and not regional, and that Congress remained united under Nehru, and partly to the unifying influence of Hinduism. India, since Pakistan separated in 1947, has been far more homogeneous. Two issues, however, have raised doubts in the minds of the pessimists. The first is the question of a national language. Apart from providing a medium for contact with the West both in diplomacy and in science, the knowledge of English amongst the educated has helped to unite India. But English has helped to create another barrier between the educated minority and the uneducated masses, and the Constitution therefore provides for English to be replaced by Hindi as the national language after 1965. Hindi, however, is the language of the Ganges Valley people, and south India especially objected to its imposition. In 1958 it was agreed as a compromise that Hindi should be gradually introduced all over India after 1965, but English would still be used.

The second issue which it was thought would weaken Indian unity was the move during the late 1950s and early 1960s to reorganise the states on the basis of language. In 1956 the States Reorganisation Act was passed, which provided for states to be formed on linguistic lines. The Sikhs of the Punjab, however, did not obtain a Punjabi-speaking state, and in 1961 a Sikh leader, Master Tara Singh, probably helped by a little glucose or fruit juice, fasted for forty-seven days in the Golden Temple at Amritsar to try to persuade Nehru to agree to this. He broke his fast, but did not get his way.

Economic and social policy   The stability of India depended a great deal on economic progress, particularly after China began to develop so rapidly under a Communist regime. But the problems facing India were immense. Agriculture was backward, antiquated methods were used, and productivity was low. For example, in 1950 Japan produced 4,293 lb of rice per acre and India only 1,140. The uneconomic system of landholding was described at the beginning of the chapter. The food position was worse after 1947 because of the loss of the wheat-growing areas of the Punjab to Pakistan. In addition most of the jute-growing regions of Bengal were in East Pakistan. The need for an increased food supply was apparent, not just because of the malnutrition in the existing population, but because of the huge rate of population growth. In 1951 the population of India was 356 million, and, despite the fact that the average age of death was twenty-seven in 1947, it was growing at the rate of about half a million a month. In the years immediately after partition, too, about 7 million refugees from Pakistan had to be fed and housed.

Living conditions were also very poor. There were terrible slums in the big cities, especially Calcutta. Very simple mud huts were usually the homes of the country people. Only a tiny percentage of villages had electricity.

Industry had greatly expanded since the beginning of the century, and provided a good foundation for further development. But in 1950 there were only 2½ million factory workers, and India was dependent on foreign machinery and foreign capital for further advance. Also required was far more extensive education to provide skilled workers for industry and agriculture. In 1950 only about 15 per cent of the population were literate. One indication of the poverty of underdeveloped India was that the average income per person in Britain in 1958 was about £350 per year, whereas in India it was only £25 per year.

It was clear to the economic planners that the immediate priority must go to agriculture, since, unless food production went up, foreign food would have to be imported in return for valuable foreign exchange. Therefore the First Five Year Plan (1951–56) concentrated a third of expenditure on agriculture, on artificial fertilisers, irrigation and hydroelectric projects. The target figures were largely achieved: food production went up by 20 per cent, about 16 million additional acres were irrigated, the generation of electric power was doubled, and industrial production went up by 20 per cent. Part of the Plan was the Community Development Project started in 1952. Under this scheme villages were grouped into what are called Development Blocks, and trained workers were sent to guide the villagers into helping themselves. The aim was better education, sanitation, agricultural methods, communications and amenities generally. It was hoped, too, that the responsible functioning of the village councils would help to develop local democracy. By 1962 the scheme covered nearly 200 million people living in about 400,000 villages.

There was slow progress in land reform, despite the activities of Vinoba Bhave, a disciple of Gandhi, who, after 1951, with no money or organisation, tramped through rural India, persuading the rich to give land to the landless, and eventually whole villages to the people. This collectivisation of land by non-violent means was helped by the government's policy after 1959 of cooperative farming on a large scale.

Probably influenced by China, the Second Five Year Plan (1956–61) concentrated on heavy industry—iron and steel, coal, heavy chemicals, cement. It was hoped to reduce dependence on foreign machinery, and create more opportunities for employment. However, the plan soon ran into difficulties because of poor harvests and resulting inflation and drain on foreign exchange. Despite considerable aid from the United States, Britain, Germany, and Russia, the plan had to be pruned. It was generally thought that agriculture received too little attention in this plan, and this was rectified by the Third Five Year Plan (1961–66).

Meanwhile there was considerable scientific and educational advance, although science and technology were not given the highest priority as in China. In 1947 about 1,000 students graduated in science and technology; in 1957 the figure was 24,000. In 1961 there were forty-one universities, but they were very crowded and standards were not high. In the same year 60 per cent of children aged six to eleven were being educated.

More extensive education, greater movement about the country, the influx of refugees, the Community Projects, and the determination of the government, all contributed to some easing of the rigidity of Indian society. In 1947 there were over 40 million untouchables in India. The Constitution abolished untouchability, and in 1955 an act was passed which provided punishments for those who discriminated against people who had been untouchables. Nevertheless, this act took a long time to be effective. There have also been moves to obtain equality for women.

Foreign policy   India's foreign policy from 1947 to 1964 was controlled by one man, Nehru. He alone of Indian nationalist leaders had taken an interest in, and had a detailed knowledge of, international affairs, and until the 1960s his leadership in this field was almost unquestioned. Nehru's foreign policy was dominated by four issues: the wish to keep neutral in the Cold War, opposition to colonialism and racialism, relations with Pakistan, and lastly, relations with China.

Nehru refused to join either of the two sides in the Cold War. He felt that if India remained neutral it was more likely that her international status would increase and that she would receive economic aid from both sides. India was, therefore, one of the important leaders of the uncommitted or non-aligned powers, most of which are Afro-Asian. After the 1955 Bandung Conference, it seemed probable that a third force would emerge in the world, but this did not materialise. Because of Nehru's Socialist views and the effect of the struggle against British rule, there seemed to be a slight bias in India's policy towards the Communist bloc in that the Western bloc was associated with colonialism. India opposed the regional military alliances involving Asian powers (SEATO in 1954, and the Baghdad Pact in 1955) because this seemed to her an indirect way for the old imperialist nations to re-establish control. In 1956 India condemned the Suez campaign of Britain and France, but withheld judgment when the Russians crushed the Hungarian rebellion.

However, relations between India and both the United States and Russia were cool until the late 1950s, and India seemed genuinely neutral. She used her moral influence as a mediator to help bring about a ceasefire in Korea in 1951 and in Indo-China in 1954. India has been prominent in providing civil and military personnel for United Nations Forces in the Gaza strip, the Congo and Cyprus. In general Nehru, under the continuing influence of Gandhi's ideas, emphasised peaceful, non-violent methods for settling international disputes. Because of this, India's invasion of the little Portuguese colony of Goa, south of Bombay, in 1961 was somewhat out of character.

One feature of Nehru's policy that was much criticised by the extremists in India was his decision in 1949, at a meeting of Commonwealth Prime Ministers, that India, though a republic after 1950, would remain in the Commonwealth. The Indian historian, K. M. Panikkar, has given four reasons for this decision. Firstly, membership of the Commonwealth gives India a greater position in the world; secondly, India's parliamentary and legal system is largely British; thirdly, the British were helping to train and equip Indian armed forces; and fourthly, since the Commonwealth is multiracial, it would help to create better understanding between Asia and Europe.

Relations between India and Pakistan have been a continual cause of bitterness and suspicion in the subcontinent since 1947. Apart from the circumstances of partition, the continued movement of refugees across the frontiers, and disputes about refugee property, there were before 1964 two main subjects of disagreement.

The first and more important concerns Kashmir. The Maharajah of Kashmir was both unpopular and a Hindu. Eighty per cent of his 4 million subjects were Muslim, mostly living in the beautiful vale of

Kashmir. At the time of partition, the Maharajah, like the ruler of Hyderabad, hoped to remain independent, but the Muslim League wanted Kashmir to join Pakistan. In October 1947, Muslim tribesmen invaded Kashmir. Whether they were encouraged by Pakistan or not is not clear. The Maharajah then asked for Indian assistance in return for joining India. The Indian army soon arrived, and rapidly occupied about two-thirds of Kashmir. The other third was occupied by Kashmiri Muslims with the support of the Pakistan army. Since India now regarded Kashmir as part of her territory, early in 1948 she accused Pakistan of aggression before the United Nations. During 1948 the United Nations negotiated for a ceasefire, and this took effect in January 1949. The military war had now been ended, but the diplomatic war began. Various proposals were put forward by both the United Nations and Commonwealth countries for the withdrawal of the armed forces of both sides and the holding of a plebiscite. But deadlock was reached on the details of how the plebiscite was to be held and who was to control Kashmir while it was held.

Meanwhile from 1948 to 1955 the Indian-controlled part of Kashmir was ruled by the popular Sheikh Abdullah, a supporter of Congress. By 1953, however, he had decided in favour of independence for Kashmir, and he was therefore removed with the connivance of the central government and replaced by Bakshi Ghulam Mohammed who ruled until 1963. Apart from a short interval in 1958, Sheikh Abdullah remained in prison from 1953 to 1964. There has been considerable Indian economic aid for Kashmir, and the state has been administered in the same way as any other Indian state. While Pakistan continued to press for a plebiscite, believing that this would show a big majority in favour of joining her, India felt that for Kashmir to leave India on religious grounds would be dangerous in view of the many Muslims (over 40 million) still in India. Prestige was an important factor which hindered a settlement.

The second main subject of disagreement between the two countries concerned the head waters of the five rivers of the Punjab which flow into the Indus. Much of the irrigation of West Pakistan was dependent on canals connected to these rivers. But the source of these rivers was in India or in Indian-held Kashmir, and therefore, if India chose to cut off water supplies, the position of Pakistani farming would rapidly become desperate. Indeed, when there was a natural water shortage, India would divert the waters into her own canals. Apart from this, India intended to build a canal which would bring the waters from these rivers to a desert south-west of Delhi. When this canal was completed, no more water would flow into Pakistan.

Naturally Pakistan objected to this scheme. Between 1951 and 1960 long negotiations took place between India, Pakistan and the World Bank, and in 1960 an agreement was reached. India was to provide

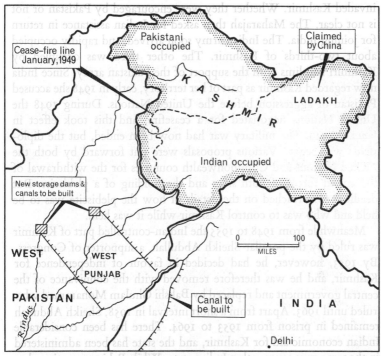

Kashmir and the Indus River

Pakistan with a fixed amount of water for ten years. During this period, Pakistan, with foreign financial assistance amounting to £375 million, would build two huge storage dams on the other rivers of the Indus system. Canals would be built from these dams to the area in west Punjab previously watered by the five rivers. Thus some of the Indus waters which pour into the Arabian Sea will be stored at the time of flood, and there will be enough water for both Pakistan and India.

India's relations with Communist China passed from friendship to strain to open war. India was one of the first countries to recognise Communist China in 1949. She was not greatly disturbed when in the next year the Chinese conquered and occupied Tibet, and in 1954 India recognised China's sovereignty over Tibet. But during the 1950s Tibetan resistance grew and eventually a guerrilla revolt broke out which was severely crushed. In 1959 the Tibetan religious leader, the Dalai Lama, fled to India.

Meanwhile the Peking government published maps which showed mountainous parts of Bhutan, Nepal and north-west and north-east India inside Chinese territory. In 1958 it was discovered that the Chinese had built a road in the Ladakh area of Kashmir, and the next year there was fighting there and in the North-East Frontier Agency between Indian and Chinese troops. Both sides produced a vast amount of historical evidence to show that the disputed territory was theirs, but could reach no agreement. During 1962 relations deteriorated. Nehru refused to consider any further negotiations until the Chinese withdrew their troops. During the summer there were frequent clashes, and in October, the Chinese 'frontier guards' attacked in force in the North-East Frontier Agency. The Indian army was routed. Then, quite suddenly, after four weeks of fighting, with the Western powers and Russia hurrying military aid to India, the Chinese withdrew their forces north of the McMahon Line, the old frontier of British India. India was both defeated and humiliated, and, since she now strengthened her forces with mainly Western help, the short war forced India away from her policy of non-alignment. Relations with China have since remained tense and unsettled.

The death of Nehru   Nehru died in May 1964 at the age of 74. During the last two years, as his strength began to flag, a sense of drift and stagnation was felt in India. The Chinese invasion was a blow to Nehru's prestige. The Third Five Year Plan was clearly failing; resources were diverted to defence, and despite considerable foreign help, production was static. Corruption in the administration was growing, Congress was losing direction, and Nehru himself was beginning to lose the authority he once enjoyed without question.

Nevertheless, his death was the occasion for worldwide mourning. For seventeen years he had ruled India, and he was certainly one of the great figures of history. As the President of the Philippines said: 'Asia has lost its most eloquent advocate for reason, moderation and peace.'

Shastri 1964 to 1966

Nehru, the world-statesman, was succeeded as prime minister by Lal Shastri, a man who had never travelled outside India. A tiny, sparrow-like figure, with an apparently gentle and self-effacing character, Shastri had started from humble beginnings and had risen gradually in the Congress Party hierarchy, where he had shown quiet effectiveness as an administrator. The problems facing him were immense—

food supplies, rising prices, Kashmir, the threat of renewed Chinese invasion, a Congress Party riven with disputes, and a decline in the authority of the central government.

During his first year in office, Shastri seemed to lack the firmness, even ruthlessness, which many thought necessary to cure India's economic problems. Early in 1965 there was a desperate food shortage and only huge imports of American and Australian grain prevented widespread starvation. But during the last six months of his government, Shastri showed a firmness in dealing with Pakistan which restored his declining reputation.

Pakistan was soon disappointed in the hope that Shastri would be more flexible than Nehru over the Kashmir problem, and consequently decided that force must replace negotiation. Border disputes in Sind early in 1965 were followed by the infiltration of guerrilla troops into Indian-held Kashmir. In August 1965, their troops invaded on a large scale, and this provoked a counterattack by the Indian Army across the ceasefire line. This soon developed into war on a limited scale between the Pakistani and Indian armies. However, the pressure of world opinion expressed through the United Nations brought a ceasefire in September. Four months later, in January 1966, Kosygin, the Russian Prime Minister, negotiated an agreement between Shastri and Ayub Khan which was signed at Tashkent in southern Russia. The agreement provided for the withdrawal of armed forces to positions held before August 1965, for the restoration of diplomatic, trade and cultural relations between India and Pakistan who agreed in future not to use force to settle their differences. A few hours after signing the agreement, Shastri died from a heart attack.

Mrs Gandhi 1966 to 1977

Shastri was succeeded as premier by Indira Gandhi,[1] the daughter of Nehru. She was a compromise choice as Prime Minister: the main object of the Congress 'kingmakers', as in 1964, was to keep out Desai. Mrs Gandhi had been the constant companion and confidante of her father, especially in his later years. She was cosmopolitan in attitude, had long mixed in government circles, and shared with him his secularism and impatience with oppression and inefficiency in the name of tradition. Indeed, she was seen as representing progressive and modern India. During her eleven years in office Mrs Gandhi showed a highly developed political instinct, a confident and independent will, and a capacity for acting promptly.

[1] Her husband was no relation of Mahatma Gandhi.

Gandhi in London during the Round
Table Conference, 1931

Nehru

Mrs Indira Gandhi addresses a crowd outside government buildings in
New Delhi during the State of Emergency in 1975

Mrs Gandhi became Prime Minister in January 1966. During her first year she made various political mistakes, and gave an impression of uncertainty and lack of personal authority. In February 1967 there was a General Election. Congress Party lost 90 seats in the Federal Parliament but nevertheless kept a small majority. In the state parliaments Congress did badly, losing control of nine states. The non-Congress governments that were formed were often coalitions which frequently fell apart, with the result that there was no continuity of administration. The growth of opposition was caused mainly by the divisions, disloyalties and factionalism within the ranks of Congress itself. Many commentators spoke of the general irresponsibility and opportunism of the politicians. For too many the dominant purpose of politics was just the attainment of office and its powers. With the exception of the Communist Party, political parties did not reproduce western ideologies. Jan Singh, for example, which was very strong in North India in 1967, wanted a Hindu social order and Hindi as a national language. In addition, caste and kinship were powerful associatons in Indian society and worked against a sense of common purpose.

During the four years from 1967 to 1971 there was a general feeling of political instability and doubt about India's future. Relations between the central and state governments were uneasy. It was difficult for local politicians to take a national view when this conflicted with the state attitude. Many politicians, mainly from the Congress Party, who had dominated Indian public life for years, had been rejected by the electorate in 1967 and replaced by younger men with local influence only. Not one of the opposition parties to Congress offered itself as a party througout the country. The language issue, which dominated politics in 1967, showed the strength of regionalism. There was widespread opposition to the imposition of Hindi as an official language in non-Hindi-speaking areas. Eventually, in December 1967, a law was passed which retained English as the official language as long as it was desired by states where Hindi was not the language of the majority. The twenty years since independence had seen a steady drain of authority from the centre to state level. Indeed, many believed that the weakness of the centre had gone too far to be reversed even by a strong Prime Minister.

In the late 1960s there was an increase in various forms of agitation: by university students who feared unemployment; communal disturbances; a Communist campaign of violent peasant revolts against landlords; unrest in the border areas. This agitation, the political divisions and lack of real economic progress, all produced serious doubts about the future of India as a democratic state and united country. The problem of a huge electorate with a high proportion of illiterate peasants making an informed judgment on national personalities and issues, seemed too great. There was talk of military intervention. The army had rapidly expanded and reorganised after its defeat by China in 1962, and its prestige had increased after the 1965 war with Pakistan. It had on several occasions been called in to maintain internal security. Thus there was a feeling that democracy was not producing strong and effective government.

In the autumn of 1969 there was a major split in the Congress Party. Mrs Gandhi wanted a mixed economy but with a higher degree of state control. 'The Communists', she said, 'have already established a foothold in the country, and if a progressive economic policy is not followed, they will gain in strength.' Mrs Gandhi wanted, for example, the nationalisation of banks. She was supported by most Congress MPs and public opinion, but opposed by the right wing of Congress who controlled the party organisation. In December 1969 she was expelled from the Congress Party. The result was two Congress Parties, each claiming to represent the true party.

Mrs Gandhi was now dependent on support from left-wing parties, including Communists. A year later she decided to dissolve Parliament and hold an election in March 1971. Mrs Gandhi herself seemed popular in the country, there were fears that the economic situation would deteriorate, and the Supreme Court had recently stopped a government measure which would have abolished certain privileges of the Indian princes. Mrs Gandhi fought the election on personal appeal rather than policies. Her blend of aristocratic personality and left-wing ideas was very successful, with the result that her section of the Congress Party won 350 of the 523 seats. She was now in complete control and her opponents were in disarray.

Economic Policy   From independence to 1965 the economy had made considerable progress. National income had increased by 70 per cent, and in all sorts of ways there had been growth: for example, electricity generating had increased four-fold, and railway freight-carrying capacity was up three-fold. In many areas of the economy progress continued during the decade 1965–75. India started to manufacture a wide variety of consumer goods—TV sets, transistor radios, electrical goods and watches. In agriculture there was a dramatic increase in production as a result of using high-yielding seeds, chemical fertilizers and developing an ample and regulated supply of water. The Green Revolution, as this is called, started in 1966–67. It was especially successful in north-west India where production increased 2½ times between 1966 and 1971. The new methods were put into practice by educated and profit-conscious farmers, often retired professional people, and very different from the illiterate peasants who were chronically short of capital and wedded to traditional methods. Throughout India in the three years 1969–71 there were bumper crops, so that India was virtually self-sufficient in food grain.

Despite these advances the overall position of the Indian economy was worrying. Economic conditions varied: in the north-west they were good, in the east bad, elsewhere they were mixed; and even in the north-west the benefits of the Green Revolution were limited to a small proportion of the population. The Fourth Five Year Plan, due to begin in 1967, was postponed because of the disruption caused by two minor wars and two bad monsoons, and the political situation from 1967 to 1971 made all-India planning very difficult. India was unable to overcome the problems caused by bad weather: for example, the drought in 1972 led to the failure of hydro-electric power. Foreign exchange earnings were inadequate, and therefore foreign debts grew. After the Chinese invasion in 1962 money and resources were diverted to defence, so that by 1972 India had the fourth largest army and the fifth largest air force in the world. In addition there was the expenditure on refugees in 1971. But the major problem was population growth. In 1951 the population was 356 million; in 1972 it had reached 548 million, and was increasing by 13 million per year. This enormous rise was due to people living longer rather than to a higher birth-rate. In 1947 the average expectation of life was 27 years, in 1968 it was 50. The consequence was rural unemployment, a drift to the towns, and a very low standard of living. It was estimated in 1975 that half the population was living below an austere poverty line. It was clear, therefore, that economic take-off had not been reached.

Foreign Policy The military threat from China continued in that the Chinese armies along the border were strengthened and that China also conducted nuclear weapon tests. In 1967 there was fighting between Chinese and Indian troops in Sikkim, and the Cultural Revolution made Chinese intentions very uncertain. Thereafter relations did not improve but nor did they worsen.

Despite the hopes expressed at the time of the Tashkent Agreement in 1966, there was no substantial improvement in relations with Pakistan. No progress was made in settling the Kashmir dispute, although in 1968 Sheikh Abdullah was released. India watched the events in East Pakistan carefully (see p. 417). Her sympathies were with the separatist movement but Mrs Gandhi, despite appeals from many of her people, refused to intervene. But from March to December 1971 there was a massive flow of mainly Hindu refugees into India. It seemed that this problem and the military stalemate in East Pakistan could only be solved by Indian intervention. During the autumn of 1971 there were a number of incidents which escalated into full-scale war between India and Pakistan in December. The war had lasted thirteen days when Pakistan surrendered. During 1972 the refugees returned to what was now Bangladesh, and India now had a weak and friendly state on her eastern border. In addition India was occupying 3,000 square miles of Pakistani territory and holding 90,000 prisoners of war.

Mrs Gandhi and Bhutto, the new Pakistani Prime Minister, met at Simla in July, 1972. Each country promised to end the conflict and confrontation that had hitherto marred their relations. There would be a resumption of communications, travel, trade, scientific and cultural links, and the withdrawal of forces, except in Kashmir over which there would be separate talks. In December 1972 an agreement on a new border line dividing Kashmir was made. The higher hopes raised by the Simla Agreement were not quickly fulfilled. The Delhi Agreement of 1973 arranged for the return of the prisoners of war, and in 1974 postal communications were resumed. Pakistan, however, was now no longer in the same league as India militarily, and relations remained strained. When, for example, India successfully exploded a nuclear device underground, and thus became the world's sixth nuclear power, Bhutto said that the explosion was meant to dominate the sub-continent.

During the 1960s public opinion gradually moved away from the view that India must follow a policy of positive non-alignment to the view that India should be attached to both sides, Russia and the United States, in order to derive as much benefit as possible for India. Thus while remaining on reasonably friendly terms with the United States, India signed an agreement with Russia in 1971.

Mrs Gandhi was at the height of her popularity and success in the years 1971 and 1972. Following the election victory in March 1971 and the military victory in December, a heady atmosphere of confidence and optimism pervaded India. In the state elections in 1972 Congress swept the polls, winning 70 per cent of the seats. In the two years from the middle of 1973 to June 1975, however, a number of serious economic and political problems emerged. Failure of the rains led to a drop in food production and famine in several parts of India.

Inflation increased to about 25 per cent—lentils, for example, the main dish at meals in most homes, shot up in price beyond the reach of the average wage-earner—and this caused widespread discontent. Industrial growth declined, and the number of unemployed reached 25 million. The Fifth Five Year Plan, due to begin in 1974, did not start because inflation made the target figures meaningless. In addition there were strikes, especially on the airlines and railways.

Politically the divisions and factionalism that had affected the Congress Party in the second half of the 1960s reappeared, and in elections the party lost seats. Then in 1974 Narayan, a supporter of Mahatma Gandhi who had not been involved in politics for twenty years, asked for the dissolution of the Bihar Assembly, where Congress was in the majority, because it had ceased to represent the electorate and was corrupt. Mrs Gandhi refused, but Narayan's action was supported by opposition parties from a large number of states and regions of India. He came to represent a movement of dissent, and toured the country to link together areas of discontent and frustration. By early 1975 India had the same feeling of doubt and instability that had been widespread from 1967 to 1971. One writer in January 1975 spoke of a sense of 'looming calamity'. The climax came in June 1975: the Allahabad High Court held that the election of Mrs Gandhi to Congress in 1971 was void, and that she was disqualified from holding elective office for six years on grounds of corrupt practices.

A fortnight after this decision, the President of India proclaimed a State of Emergency as 'the security of India is threatened by internal disorder'. Mrs Gandhi in a broadcast said the action was taken to safeguard the country's unity and stability. There then followed the arrest of many thousands of political opponents, and a number of political groups were banned. The press was censored, and elections were put off for one year. Parliament approved the State of Emergency, then proceeded to give the Prime Minister immunity from criminal proceedings and to change the constitution in order to give the Prime Minister much greater power and prohibit a wide range of political activities. Mrs Gandhi announced a detailed economic programme which aimed to bring down prices, economise on government expenditure and improve agriculture.

Mrs Gandhi's personal rule lasted from June 1975 to March 1977. In January 1977 she announced that the twice-postponed elections would be held in March, and lifted the ban on political parties to allow them to take part. The result of the election was a shattering blow to Mrs Gandhi and her party. She was defeated in her own constituency and the number of Congress MPs dropped from 350 to 152, while those of the Janata Alliance increased from 39 to 297. Morarji Desai, at the age of 82, became Prime Minister, and the Congress Party, after ruling India since independence, was out of office.

It is too early to form any judgment on the State of Emergency. Mrs Gandhi said she declared the emergency to maintain unity and give stability. Her opponents said this action was taken to maintain her own rule and that of the Congress Party. There was certainly a need for strong central government, but whether the benefits gained in practice outweighed the loss of political and judicial freedoms is a matter of controversy. Mrs Gandhi was defeated for a number of reasons—one was the protest against the compulsory sterilisation programme—but it was quite clear that India at that time was repudiating her personal rule.

Desai remained Prime Minister until July 1979 when he was succeeded by Charan Singh, but the Janata Alliance, always a precarious coalition, disintegrated. Politicans quarrelled with each other, and were generally unresponsive to the problems facing India. Another general election was held in January 1980. The majority of the electorate of 350 million was clearly disillusioned with the personal ambitions and petty rivalries of politicians whose government had been incompetent and ineffective. Issues were not debated during the campaign. Mrs Gandhi was the only national politician, and again she offered discipline and strong government. The result was a land-slide victory for Congress who gained 351 seats out of 542, and Mrs Gandhi, now aged 62, became Prime Minister once more.

Pakistan after 1947

Pakistan faced the first years of independence with even greater problems than India. Like India, Pakistan received an influx of refugees. It was estimated in 1947 that one in every five persons in West Pakistan was a refugee; in all about 8 million Muslims fled from India. Like India, too, Pakistan was faced with the problems of Kashmir and the head waters of the Indus river system.

But unlike India, Pakistan was a country divided by 950 miles of a foreign and hostile state. The physical separation of West and East Pakistan remained a constant difficulty. Moreover, the language of the former is Urdu and that of the latter is Bengali. East Pakistan began to feel that the favours of government went to West Pakistan, and the rift between the two gradually widened. Unlike India, too, Pakistan in August 1947 had to organise a civil service almost from scratch. The Hindus who left Pakistan were generally the educated middle class. Not only did the Pakistan government lack experienced and educated men, but government buildings and equipment were totally inadequate. Pakistan faced the same problems as most under-developed countries. About 85 per cent of her population of 75 million (1951) were illiterate. Agriculture was backward, and only a few thousand people were employed in industry. But partition added to the problems. For example, 70 per cent of the world's jute was produced in Pakistan, but in 1947 there were no jute mills; they were all in India. There were very few cotton mills, and the two ports, Karachi and Chittagong, were poor. However the position gradually improved by the early 1960s. By that time Pakistan had the largest group of jute mills in the world. Exports of raw materials, such as jute, cotton, wool, tea and hides, increased. There was a big development of light industry. Two huge dams have been constructed with foreign aid, one near Peshawar, and the other near Chittagong. In 1953 the Village Agricultural and Industrial Development (Village AID) Project was started. This is part of the Community Development movement. Workers are trained to go to the villages to teach the people how to improve agricultural methods, education and sanitation; in other words, how to improve standards of living. Unlike in India, Village AID developed very slowly in Pakistan. In 1959 only just over one million people were affected by it.

India, as we have seen, was fortunate in that she was ruled for many years after independence by one strong political party under trusted leadership. She therefore enjoyed political stability. Pakistan was ruled in 1947 by the strong Muslim League which was dominated by Jinnah, who became Governor-General. But Jinnah died in 1948 and the Muslim League was soon dominated by landlords and lawyers and lost the support of the masses. After 1948 Pakistan lacked a leader of the stature of Nehru or Sukarno. The Prime Minister from 1947 to 1951 was Liaquat Ali Khan, an able, experienced and patriotic man, but lacking a personality strong enough to lead and control the politicians in his cabinet. In 1951 he was assassinated, and from that point to 1958 there was a succession of six weak and ineffective prime ministers. During this period, some measure of stability was provided by the two Governors-General. The first was Ghulam Mohammed, an impetuous and impatient man who believed in strong government. In 1954 he dismissed the Constituent Assembly and appointed a cabinet which was controlled by Major-General Iskander Mirza, and included General Ayub Khan. A year later Ghulam Mohammed, who was ill, resigned, and Iskander Mirza became Governor-General.

During all this time, Pakistan had been ruled under the terms of the 1935 Act. A Constituent Assembly had been trying to agree on a constitution and in 1956 finally did so. Pakistan, like India, became a republic within the Commonwealth. But the new constitution had hardly begun to function when an army revolution swept it away. There had been growing economic discontent. The First Five Year Plan was failing. Higher prices, shortages of basic commodities and extensive smuggling had led to labour unrest and food riots. Urban refugees still lived in miserable conditions. But the basic discontent was political. Politicians were corrupt; there were constant disputes between the executive and the legislature, and between East and West Pakistan; stable government seemed an impossibility. In this situation, in October 1958, President Iskander Mirza suspended the Constitution, dissolved all political parties and declared martial law. There was no bloodshed. General Ayub Khan was appointed Chief Martial Law Administrator. Before the end of the month, Mirza had resigned, and Ayub Khan, a bluff, genial product of Peshawar and Sandhurst, became Head of State. Now Pakistan was to be ruled by a sound administrator and a man of action.

Ayub Khan 1958 to 1969

The first action of the new military government was the removal of all civil servants and politicians who were considered to be corrupt. Land reform was the next subject dealt with. The size of individual holdings of land was restricted, the former owners being compensated. This had three results: it removed unrest in the countryside, created a class of small proprietors, and helped to break the power of the big landlords.

The Second Five Year Plan (1960–65) was a great success, the growth in production over this period being 28 per cent, double the rate of population increase. Progress of the Third Plan (1965–70) was hindered by difficulties. The consequence of the 1965 war with India was a higher proportion of national income devoted to defence. Foreign aid, especially from the United States, was reduced. Nevertheless, industrial production continued to increase, and there was a big upsurge in agricultural production after 1967 as a result of better seed, more fertilisers, improved machinery and (crucial for this sub-continent) improved irrigation. Pakistan was near self-sufficiency in food production. As far as the standard of living is concerned, however, it is probable that disparities in income and wealth increased, with the poor remaining much the same and the rich becoming richer.

Pakistan's foreign policy has been similar to that of India only in her membership of the Commonwealth. Whereas India's relations with

Communist China gradually worsened, Pakistan and China have remained on friendly terms. Pakistan, too, did not consider that a policy of neutralism was practical. In 1954 she formed an alliance with Turkey which was enlarged in the following year into the Baghdad Pact. After Iraq withdrew from the Pact in 1959, it was renamed the Central Treaty Organisation (CENTO). In 1955 Pakistan joined SEATO. In view of her support for the West in the Cold War, Pakistan received military aid from the United States. Despite a statement that this was to be used purely for defensive purposes, it aroused fear in India, just as the military aid for India during her war with China in 1962 aroused fear in Pakistan.

Pakistan's relations with Afghanistan remained poor. The turbulent, warlike Pathan tribesmen formed a large section of the population of both countries. The Afghan Government, by propaganda and subversion, hoped to gain control of the Pathan areas of Pakistan, but with little success. The Pakistan Government's policy of friendship and trust towards the tribesmen worked, resulting in improved law and order and economic progress.

Ayub Khan said, when he first took over power, 'Our ultimate aim is to restore democracy.' The ordinary people of Pakistan, like those of most Afro-Asian countries, were unused to the working of democracy, so Ayub Khan decided that before national democracy would work efficiently, local democracy must be developed. In 1959 his method of doing this was announced. The country was divided into constituencies, each of about 10,000 population. Each constituency was called a Basic Democracy. Councils elected by each Basic Democracy would deal with local affairs and would combine local government institutions with machinery for rural development. After Ayub Khan had toured the country, gathering the people together and explaining the scheme, the first elections were held, and about 80,000 candidates, called Basic Democrats, were elected. Early in 1960, 96 per cent of the Basic Democrats, in a secret ballot, approved of Ayub Khan as President.

Next came the discussion of a new central constitution. There were two main problems: firstly, how to link the Basic Democracies with the central government, and secondly, how to have a strong central executive and still keep democracy. In 1962 the new Constitution was adopted. The Central Legislature was to be elected, not directly by the people, but by the Basic Democrats. All Bills passed by the Central Legislature need the President's assent, although this can be overridden by a two-thirds majority of the Legislature. The president, who appoints ministers, can be removed by a three-quarter majority of the Legislature, but members who attempt this and fail risk losing their seats. The President, therefore, had great power, the regime being essentially authoritarian with some ingredients of popular consultation.

By 1965 political parties were allowed to re-emerge, and martial law was lifted. In the presidential election of that year the opposition parties managed to agree on a single candidate, Miss Jinnah, the sister of the founder of the country. The theme of her campaign was 'restore democracy'. In the event Ayub was supported by two-thirds of the Basic Democrats and remained in power, but the election showed the strength of the opposition to the regime from two quarters: the East Pakistanis and the educated middle classes.

The people of East Pakistan differed from the West in language, culture and standard of living. Economically, they had always considered that they had suffered in comparison with the other half of the country. The main political party in Bengal was the Awami League, which wanted considerable autonomy for East Pakistan, while some of its members wanted complete independence. The educated middle classes disliked the Basic Democracy system. They regarded it as a gimmick to keep Ayub's regime in power. They objected also to the government's tight control on press criticism. In 1967 two new political groups were formed: several opposition parties joined to create the Pakistan Democratic Movement, and the People's Party was formed by Bhutto. Educated at Oxford and California Universities, Bhutto was a lawyer who came from an aristocratic background. From 1958 to 1966 he served in Ayub Khan's government, the last three years as Foreign Minister. However, he opposed the end of the war with India in 1965 and disliked the Tashkent Agreement (see p. 405). He resigned soon after this, and began his opposition to Ayub, attacking the regime as 'dictatorship under the label of democracy'. Bhutto was an emotional speaker. Very rich himself, he appeared left-wing and at the same time nationalist.

Later in 1968 the opposition increased. There were demonstrations and disorders during which Bhutto was arrested. The middle-class politicians were demanding greater political freedom against a background of agitation by industrial workers whose wages had remained low. Early in 1969 there was a general breakdown of law and order, and signs that the armed forces were turning against Ayub Khan. In March 1969 Ayub Khan resigned and handed over power to General Yahya Khan, the Commander-in-Chief of the forces.

Yahya Khan 1969 to 1971

The first task of Yahya Khan was to restore order. Martial law was again imposed, and there were heavy penalties for offences against public order and for strikes and corruption. Yahya Khan said that he wanted an orderly transfer of power to democratically elected government, and in the meantime appointed civilian ministers. In November 1969 he announced plans for a new constitution. West Pakistan was to be divided into four provinces (Punjab, Baluchistan, North-West Frontier and Sind) instead of the undivided whole which had existed under Ayub. The Assembly would be elected by universal suffrage which would give East Pakistan with its 70 million population a majority over the 50 million of West Pakistan. Yahya Khan seemed quite genuinely to be trying to ensure a fairer deal for the East. He did not anticipate that any one party would win decisively in one part of Pakistan. There were, after all, fifteen political parties or groupings in East Pakistan, and the rivalry between them was sharp and fierce. If the Awami League were to win most seats in the East, it would still have to enter into an alliance with other parties.

The election for the Assembly was due to take place in December, 1970. It was preceded in November by the biggest natural calamity of the century. A devastating cyclone and tidal wave swept over the coastal areas of East Pakistan. A quarter of a million people died, and huge areas of land were flooded. The central government's organisation of relief was slow and cumbersome, and the Awami League, led by Sheikh Mujibur Rahman, exploited this emotional situation. This helped to explain the result of the election: the Awami League won 167 out of 169 seats in East Pakistan, while Bhutto's People's Party won 82 out of 138 seats in West Pakistan.

Between the election and March 1971 there were negotiations between Yahya Khan, Bhutto and Sheikh Mujibur Rahman. The Awami League had enough seats to control the new Assembly without support, and therefore was in a strong position. It is probable that Sheikh Mujibur Rahman did not want secession but rather Pakistan to be a loose federation of five states, with a large measure of autonomy for East Pakistan, especially control over its finance and economy. Bhutto, however, wanted strong central government with as much power as possible for West Pakistan, while Yahya, who was no politician, was surrounded by generals who opposed concessions to East Pakistan. Consequently, Yahya Khan postponed the meeting of the Assembly, with the result that extremists within the Awami League began to demand independence. There were strikes and rioting, and a campaign of civil disobedience.

In March 1971 Yahya ordered the army to restore order. Sheikh Mujibur Rahman was seized and imprisoned in West Pakistan. There then began a reign of terror. The Pakistan army, composed mainly of Moslems from the Punjab, attacked, with hysterical cruelty, Awami League officials, together with students, intellectuals, university staff, police, any who may have expressed support for greater autonomy for East Pakistan. In addition, the army seemed to think that the Hindu minority—about 12 per cent of the population—were behind the secessionist movement. Hindus became the victims of indiscriminate and unrestrained brutality. The result was an enormous movement of refugees to India. Eventually about 10 million had arrived by the end of the year, and lived in overcrowded and disease-ridden camps. The East Pakistanis organised guerrilla activity against the army. Communications in this land of waterways, always bad, were now almost completely disrupted. There was great bitterness against West Pakistan, and it was clear that only a prolonged military occupation would now keep the two parts of the country united.

However, the civil war ended because of Indian intervention. The danger of another war between India and Pakistan gradually increased during the year. The persecution of the Hindus, the Pakistani army's chase of guerrillas producing skirmishes along the frontiers, the increasing refugee problem, which seemed likely to continue as long as the civil war lasted—all produced a potential war situation. Finally, in December 1971, Mrs Gandhi decided on quick action. The Indians had superiority of numbers, air supremacy, and an imaginative strategy. After thirteen days there was a cease fire and a Pakistani defeat.

The West Pakistan army returned to its homeland, and East Pakistan became in practice an independent state with the name of Bangladesh (the state of Bengal). A few days later Yahya Khan resigned. Bhutto took charge of the government of a country now limited to what was previously called West Pakistan.

Pakistan since 1971

Bhutto became President on the resignation of Yahya Khan on 20 December 1971. The problems he faced were daunting: a people demoralised by overwhelming and rapid military defeat, industry at a standstill and no constitution. West Pakistan itself was divided, for Sind, Baluchistan and the North-West Frontier provinces have always looked to Bengal as a political counterweight to Punjabi dominance in the West.

Mr Bhutto's government lasted from December 1971 to July 1977.

He began with the advantage of being an elected leader, but nevertheless could use the shock of defeat without having been involved in its shame. In 1973 a new constitution established a federal government based on universal suffrage. The government would be responsible to the National Assembly. Economic progress was variable. Agriculture was dependent as before on factors beyond Pakistan's control: the weather and world price levels. When these were favourable, then farming prospered. Industry recovered from the war and the loss of the Bengal market, but the world recession of the mid-1970s, together with the policy of nationalisation which reduced private investment in the economy, meant an eventual fall in production. Pakistan's relations with India are described on p. 410. In 1972 Pakistan left the Commonwealth in protest at its members' recognition of Bangladesh. However, two years later Pakistan herself officially recognised Bangladesh, and Bhutto paid a successful visit to Dacca to discuss matters resulting from the secession.

In March 1977 Bhutto decided to hold a General Election. He sought to strengthen his position as the saviour who had rescued Pakistan from the debacle of 1971, and his Pakistan People's Party was widely expected to win. Nevertheless, the opposition was stronger than he had anticipated. The Pakistan National Alliance, a combination of nine mainly right-wing opposition groups, disliked Bhutto and what they regarded as his autocratic style of government. They pointed out the large rise in prices, the heavy foreign debts, the problems of industry and Bhutto's harsh treatment of political opponents. The election result was a convincing win for the People's Party—155 seats out of 200. However, as soon as the result was announced, there were accusations of vote rigging and demands that the election be annulled. From March to July there were demonstrations and riots in which over 300 people died. Eventually Bhutto was driven to concede fresh elections, but in July 1977 the army again intervened, and General Zia ul-Haq imposed martial law. Bhutto was imprisoned and then condemned to death on a charge of conspiracy to murder. Despite world-wide appeals for clemency, he was executed in April 1979.

Bangladesh after 1971

The problems facing the new state of Bangladesh in December 1971 were colossal. Bengal had always been the poorer wing of Pakistan, with an underdeveloped economy and poverty-stricken people. There was no industry to speak of, apart from the production of jute, but what little existed was now without its West Pakistan management. In November 1970 the country had suffered a devastating natural disaster, and for nine months in 1971 a bitter civil war had been fought in which nationalist guerrillas particularly aimed to disrupt the economy by, for example, destroying communications. The population, only 20 per cent of which was literate, stood at 75 million and was increasing at about $2\frac{1}{2}$ milllon per year. It was estimated that by the year 2000 it would reach 160 million in a country the area of England and Wales. In addition, there was no constitution and the legal basis for the country was not yet settled.

In January 1972 Sheikh Mujibur Rahman returned to Bangladesh and became Prime Minister. He was to rule until August 1975. Born in 1920 into a fairly humble, rural background, he was educated at Calcutta and Dacca Universities, and helped to found the Awami League in 1949. The Sheikh was a shrewd politician who mixed demagoguery with appeals for discipline and hard work. Soon after his return a committee was appointed from among those elected in December 1970, and this group produced a constitution by the end of the year. In March 1973 there were elections. The Awami League completely swept the board and the Sheikh continued as Prime Minister.

By 1973, however, the enthusiasm for independence had evaporated. During the next two years the economic and political problems facing Bangladesh worsened. Prolonged drought followed by flooding helped to cause a grave shortage of food grains. The world price for raw jute fell, while the cost of imports rose so that foreign exchange reserves fell. Inflation increased to about 40 per cent, unemployment was growing, and there was a general sense of hopelessness. In addition to this economic failure, there was widespread disorder, corruption and administrative inefficiency. Political murders by former guerrillas of the 1971 war were frequent, an underground opposition to the government gained strength, and the Awami League itself, held together only by the strong personality of the Sheikh, was riddled with factions.

In December 1974 Sheikh Mujibur Rahman declared a state of emergency, and in the following month he became President with virtually dictatorial powers. In August 1975, however, the Sheikh was brutally murdered by four majors in the army, and a former minister was installed in his place. During the next two months there was a struggle for power within the army which culminated in November 1975 with the emergence of General Zia-ur-Rahman, who rapidly asserted his authority. As in West Pakistan, democracy seemed unable to produce the necessary political leadership.

10

China

Beginning of the Twentieth Century

If in 1900 the people of China had been placed in single file, the line would have stretched about fifteen times round the Equator. The population was over 400 million, yet 90 per cent of these people lived in about one-sixth of the country: for well over half the vast country of China consists of mountains or semi-deserts, and most people lived in the fertile eastern plains, particularly in the Yangtze delta.

The mountains and deserts of the west and north and the sub-tropical rain forests of the south helped to produce a civilisation which owed little to foreign influence. At many stages in its long history, Chinese civilisation was more advanced than that of Europe, but by 1900 the government, society in general and the economic system had petrified and become archaic. The Manchus, who were the ruling dynasty, had governed China since about 1650. They had originated in Manchuria, and although they became Chinese in culture, they ruled China as would any foreign imperialist power. The central administrative system and the provincial government were entirely in the hands of a bureaucracy of scholar-officials called mandarins. The only way of entering this public service was by a public examination. About 2 million candidates took the examination annually, but only about 2 per cent passed. The syllabus for these examinations, however, had been laid down in about AD 600, and consisted entirely of Chinese classics, especially the works of Confucius. As a result, the members of the administration were very conservative and totally opposed to the introduction of necessary reforms. One historian has described the mandarin system as 'completely fossilised, a gigantic, inhuman and inefficient machine corroded with dust'.

The landed gentry, from whom the scholar-officials came, were a

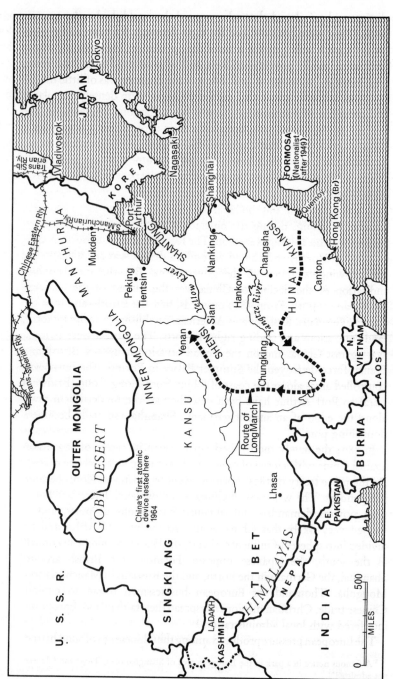

China in the twentieth century

distinct and privileged class who wanted the established order to continue. They were both disliked for their demands for taxes and respected for their learning by the mass of the population, the peasants, whose lives were usually poverty-stricken, and who suffered from high rents, high taxes and shortage of land. Most of the country was of little use for farming, with the result that cultivated areas were densely populated and consisted of lots of small farms. Near Canton, for example, the average size of a farm was three-fifths of an acre. There was very little industry, although China possesses big reserves of coal and iron ore. Towards the end of the nineteenth century, some railways and engineering works were built, but in general industrial development was very superficial.

Discontent with this political and economic system produced a number of risings during the nineteenth century, of which the most serious was the Taiping Rebellion. The fact that this took fourteen years to crush (1850–64) and caused 20 million deaths was an indication of the growing weakness of the government. But the most obvious indication of the decline of China was the success of the growing European pressure. From 1840 onwards, first the British, and then the French, Germans, Russians and Americans established, usually by force, land concessions and trading rights at ports. The British were twice at war against China, and on the second occasion in 1860 a British and French force destroyed the Summer Palace in Peking. The European-controlled areas along the coast of China from Hong Kong (British in 1842) to Port Arthur have been described as 'the modern hem sewn along the edge of an ancient garment'. Shanghai especially became a flourishing port.

In 1894 the newly modernised Japan began its career of aggression against China with a series of rapid and devastating victories (see p. 461). By the peace treaty of 1895, Formosa went to Japan and Korea became independent. The weakness of China was now clear. Thereafter European powers demanded and obtained concessions of ports, and it seemed very likely that China would go the way of Africa and be divided into spheres of influence, that is, the French would be in control in the south, the Japanese opposite Formosa, the British around Shanghai, the Germans in the north, and the Russians in Manchuria and Mongolia. Thousands of European businessmen began to exploit Chinese trade. Christian missionaries spread their faith inland. Europeans interfered with local administration.[1]

The European pressure produced among the Chinese a profound hatred

---

[1] A famous notice in a park in the European area of Shanghai read, 'Dogs and Chinese not admitted'.

of foreigners. This, combined with military defeat, led to more pressing demands for reforms from the small Western-educated minority of intellectuals. In 1898 the young Emperor, under the influence of this minority, produced a sudden flood of reforms known as the Hundred Days of Reform. But these aroused tremendous opposition from the powerful conservatives, and the Dowager-Empress Tz'u Hsi, who had been the clever and unscrupulous power behind the throne since 1861, imprisoned the Emperor, and the reforms were reversed. This was the last chance the monarchy had of leading a reforming government.

The low point in the fortunes of the Manchus was reached two years later. On top of the discontent resulting from the infiltration of foreigners, especially missionaries, there came a number of natural disasters: two successive harvests failed, and the Yellow River flooded huge areas. This produced an explosive situation which was exploited by a secret society called the Boxers. In the summer of 1900 the Boxers began a series of murderous attacks on European missionaries and their Chinese converts, and in Peking the foreign legations were besieged. For several sweltering weeks the foreigners held out, until finally relieved by an Allied Expeditionary Force which seized Peking as the Empress and her court fled westwards. Order was restored, and in the following year China was forced to agree to punish those involved in the Boxer Rising and to pay a large indemnity. The Manchus had reached the point of no return.

The End of the Manchus 1900 to 1912

Despite its incompetence and weakness, the Manchu government lasted until two years before the First World War began in Europe. In 1905 it attempted to stop the rising tide of dissatisfaction by reintroducing many of the abortive reforms of 1898: the army was modernised, provincial assemblies were elected, and the old syllabus for public examinations was abolished. But the moment a weak government begins reforming is always a dangerous one for it, and these changes served only to encourage the wish for revolution, not to appease it.

The middle class, from whom revolutionary leaders usually come, was growing stronger, particularly in the south of China. Literature advocating revolution was spread among students and intellectuals. Sun Yat-sen was one of these. He was born near Canton in 1866. His family was poor, but he was educated from the age of twelve at a mission school in Honolulu and became a Christian. He was then trained as a doctor of medicine in Hong Kong. Becoming interested in politics, he wanted radical reforms, and took part in a rising against the Manchus in 1895 to enforce these. The rising failed, and Sun Yat-sen spent the next sixteen years in exile.[1] Most of his time was occupied with spreading amongst Chinese students and others living overseas his revolutionary ideas for Western reforms in politics, economics and society. In 1905 he founded in Tokyo the political party which in 1912 became the Kuomintang. One of its early supporters was a Chinese military cadet named Chiang Kai-shek (b. 1887) who was undergoing training in Japan.

The disintegration of the government began with the death of the Dowager-Empress in 1908.[2] Her nephew, the Emperor, died a few hours earlier, possibly killed by Yuan Shih-kai, the leading minister from 1898 to 1908, who had opposed the Hundred Days of Reform in 1898 which the Emperor had instigated. The new Emperor was two years old, and the provincial governors soon began ruling independently of the central government.

The revolution began almost by accident. An explosion in a house in Hankow in October 1911, led to the police finding a collection of arms and a list of names of conspirators. The latter decided that an immediate rising was their only chance. The local army mutinied and the revolt spread. Governors of provinces removed the Manchu garrisons and proclaimed their independence. Sun Yat-sen first read of the rising in a newspaper in the United States. He arrived in Shanghai in December, and was immediately elected provisional President of the new Chinese Republic.

But the situation was not yet clear, for while most provinces supported the republic, the three northern ones did not. Yuan Shih-kai had full control of the small modern army in the north. His attitude would decide the situation. In February 1912, Yuan Shih-kai persuaded those responsible for the young Emperor that he should abdicate.[3] A republic was then set up. In the following month Sun Yat-sen, in the interests of unity, resigned the presidency in Yuan's favour, and China seemed united.

[1] In 1896 Sun Yat-sen was kidnapped by the Chinese in London, and would almost certainly have been executed had not his old medical professor informed the British government who successfully demanded his release.

[2] She is supposed to have said as she died, 'Never again let the affairs of an Empire be managed by a woman.'

[3] ' "THE SON OF HEAVEN" HAS ABDICATED' was the headline in *The Times*. The revolution marked the end of 2,132 years of imperial rule in China.

The period of the War Lords 1912 to 1928

The unity of China under Yuan Shih-kai lasted for four years. Even during this period, however, the Peking government exercised little power in the provinces, and from 1916 to 1928 there was complete anarchy.

It soon became clear that Yuan was opposed to both democracy and republicanism, although he was not against modernisation. Sun Yat-sen realised the danger to his political hopes for China, but his new party, the Kuomintang, or National People's Party, formed in 1912, was crushed by Yuan. This was followed by the ending of the constitution, and the appointment of Yuan as President for life. In these and other activities Yuan was given financial aid by the European powers. He now had the authority of the old regime, and his next step in 1915 was to persuade a specially elected Assembly to offer him the title of Emperor. It was announced that he would assume the imperial title in the following year, and Yuan began to worship at the Temple of Heaven, the prerogative of the Emperors.

But the announcement met with bitter opposition, both within China and from Japan. Yuan had lost prestige in the eyes of nationalists when he had virtually agreed in 1915 to all of Japan's Twenty-One Demands. These provided for Japanese economic control of Manchuria and Shantung. Nationalist was thus added to republican sentiment in opposing Yuan, while both Chinese provincial rulers and the Japanese feared the prospect of a strong, centralised Chinese government. There were, consequently, provincial revolts, which led Yuan to renounce his intentions. His career ended in 1916 when he died from a stroke.

On the death of Yuan a new President was appointed, but for the next twelve years the government was central in name only. The western areas of Mongolia, Sinkiang and Tibet declared their independence, while the rest of China was controlled by a small number of rival war lords[1] and an indefinite number of robber bands of varying size. Private armies totalling about 1½ million men, and financed by extortionate taxes, caused chaos and suffering in the countryside. The hoped-for reforms, especially of land ownership, failed to materialise. Throughout China, the peasants wished above all else for the creation of a strong, stable and reforming government. This accounts for the support they gave in the short run to the Kuomintang and in the long run to the Communists.

[1] One such war lord, a Christian, is supposed to have baptised the soldiers of his army with a hosepipe.

The Kuomintang and the Communists

During this period of anarchy in China, Sun Yat-sen endeavoured to maintain the organisation of his outlawed party, the Kuomintang. His activities were mainly concentrated on the coastal cities between Shanghai and Canton. Often he was forced to flee to Japan because of the opposition of a local war lord. Yet he persevered, and this persistence in the face of constant frustration is part of his importance.

Meanwhile in the north of China Marxist ideas were developing, particularly amongst students. Accompanying the political anarchy of the times was a ferment of ideas among intellectuals known as 'The New Tide'. With the Revolution and the breakup of the old society, Confucian thought was generally disregarded, and after the Russian Revolution of 1917, the writings and speeches of Marx and Lenin became popular amongst the intellectuals. In 1918 a 'Society for the Study of Marxism' was formed in Peking University, and was attended by crowds of students including a young assistant librarian named Mao Tse-tung. Three years later, at a girls' school in Shanghai, the Chinese Communist Party was formed.

Mao Tse-tung was one of the official delegates at this first meeting of the Communist Party in 1921. Mao was born in 1893 in Hunan in south-east China. His father, a well-to-do peasant, and a firm supporter of the Manchus, was a man of stormy temper, and there were constant clashes between father and son. Mao, who was very fond of reading,[1] soon showed his ability, and in the spring of 1911 he entered the Junior College at Changsha. Within a few months the revolution broke out, and he immediately joined the revolutionary army. A year later, however, he left the army, and entered the Teachers' Training College in Changsha. Here he remained until 1918, spending long days in the public library and becoming a confirmed radical. He then moved to Peking, and for a year occupied a humble position in the university library. In 1919 Mao began his political activities in earnest, and it was as an organiser of trade union activities in Hunan and as a convinced communist that he was present at the Shanghai meeting in 1921.

Meanwhile Sun Yat-sen, who had received little support from the West, was also influenced by the successful Russian Revolution, and decided that the Kuomintang must be reorganised on the lines of a Communist party. Accordingly Chiang Kai-shek was sent to Moscow

[1] Before the age of ten, Mao had read the great Chinese novel *All Men are Brothers*, a sort of Robin Hood story of peasants attacking landlords. Mao's later military tactics were much influenced by this novel.

Dowager Empress Tz'u Hsi with ladies of her court in 1903

Chiang Kai-shek and Sun Yat-sen in 1923

Mao Tse-tung

to study Russian government and party organisation, and in 1923 the Russians sent Michael Borodin to China. A Communist with wide experience and great diplomatic skill, Borodin's aim was to reorganise the Kuomintang as a centralised mass party, and to build up a revolutionary army. This was achieved with great efficiency. The Whampoa Military Academy was founded near Canton with the assistance of Russian officers. Its first director was Chiang Kai-shek. On the staff, in charge of political activities, was the Communist Chou En-lai, for the Kuomintang, influenced by its Russian contacts, decided in 1923 to form an alliance with the Chinese Communist Party as the only hope of creating a strong enough group to oppose the war lords. Communists, therefore, were allowed to join the Kuomintang as individuals.

But the alliance of the Kuomintang and the Communists remained an uneasy one. The Kuomintang was now organised on Communist lines, but it did not adopt Communist policies. In 1924 Sun Yat-sen gave a series of lectures in which he described 'Three Principles of the People' as the aims of the Kuomintang. Firstly, Nationalism—the Chinese people must unite and develop a spirit of nationhood in order to withstand foreign oppression; secondly, Democracy—the ultimate aim was to be parliamentary democracy, but, since the idea of democracy was foreign to the Chinese, a period of dictatorship under the Kuomintang was necessary first so that the people could be taught how to rule themselves; and thirdly, the People's Livelihood—moderate land reform was necessary, with socialism as the ultimate object. This rather vague system became the official policy of the Kuomintang.

In March 1925 Sun Yat-sen died. He was not a leader of personality and originality as Lenin was or Mao Tse-tung was to become, but as a sincere and persistent revolutionary leader, he became the symbol of opposition, first to the Manchus and then to the war lords. His actual achievement was small, apart from the reconstruction of the Kuomintang, but after his death he was idolised by both the Kuomintang and the Communists. His rather unimpressive features appeared monotonously on postage stamps, and a huge memorial was built to him in Nanking.

Sun Yat-sen's successor as leader of the Kuomintang was Chiang Kai-shek. From the start he had been suspicious of the Communist alliance, and exactly a year after Sun Yat-sen's death, he removed all Communists from important positions in the party, although the alliance was maintained and Borodin remained. A few months later, in the summer of 1926, Chiang considered his strength sufficient to begin the conquest of China. Starting from Canton he moved north with an ever-increasing army. By the end of the year Hankow had been captured, and early in 1927 Shanghai and Nanking were besieged. One major reason for the Kuomintang success was that their allies, the Communists, won the support of the peasants by offering radical land reform. Behind Chiang Kai-shek's armies, Communist-inspired Peasant Associations were set up. In April 1927 Chiang decided that Communist power and influence had become too dangerous. While engaged in the siege of Shanghai, the financiers there offered him their support if he crushed communism. Quite suddenly, therefore, all Communists within the Kuomintang were removed and many executed.[1] Diplomatic relations with Russia were broken off, and Soviet advisers, including Borodin, fled back to Russia.

Chiang Kai-shek's conquest of China continued. By various methods—force, secret diplomacy, intrigue, poison—the northern war lords were brought under control, and in 1928 Peking was occupied. Once again there was in China a central government with some power.

1928 to 1937

Extermination Campaigns and the Long March

With the sudden and violent end to the alliance between the Communist Party and the Kuomintang, the members of the former party were in almost complete disarray. Some semblance of an organisation remained in Shanghai, but this rapidly became ineffective largely because it insisted, with the encouragement of Russia, on concentrating its propaganda upon the working class in the towns and on infiltrating the Kuomintang. Mao Tse-tung and the younger element in the Communist Party opposed this policy. Mao believed that the Kuomintang grip on the towns was too strong, and that the peasants were the really revolutionary group in China. Consequently, he concentrated his energies on organising the peasantry,[2] and was largely responsible for the Peasant Associations created after Chiang Kai-shek's successful march north.

When the break with the Kuomintang came in 1927 Mao and a few hundred Communists retreated into the wild mountains on the border between the provinces of Kiangsi and Hunan. Here they stayed for

---

[1] 'Chou En-lai was captured and was ordered to be shot. By accident, the officer in charge of the execution was one of his former pupils at the Whampoa Military Academy. He allowed Chou to escape. Many other Communist cadres were not so fortunate.' Guy Wint, *Common Sense about China.*

[2] 'Instead of a decisive *coup d'état* in the capital of China, he had to wage protracted guerrilla warfare in the countryside.' V. Dedijer, *The Times,* 18 Nov. 1963.

the next seven years. Their position at the beginning was desperate, for they possessed few weapons, little food and unsuitable clothing for the foggy pine forests and rugged mountains in which they lived. Moreover they were constantly attacked by the Kuomintang. Chiang Kai-shek organised five 'extermination campaigns' against the Communists. But the numbers in Mao's army gradually grew, and the Kuomintang was never able to penetrate the mountains successfully. The Communists were more mobile and more daring, and they were skilfully controlled by Mao and Chu Teh, a former war lord and professional soldier who had joined the Communist Party when it was formed. It was during this time that Mao developed his famous four principles of guerrilla warfare:

When the enemy advances, we retreat.

When the enemy halts and encamps, we trouble them.

When the enemy seeks to avoid a battle, we attack.

When the enemy retreats, we pursue.

Constant propaganda at a time when landlords were raising rents meant that the Communists could always count on the support of the peasants and were kept informed of Kuomintang army movements. The Communists were, in addition, aided by the fact that Chiang Kai-shek's armies had also to fight the war lords, and after 1931 there was a constant threat from Japan as well.

By 1933 Mao Tse-tung was in full control of Chinese Communism. But, despite its success during the previous few years, the pressure on his regime was becoming more severe. Chiang had a million troops round the Communists, and early in 1934 he built a circle of fortified posts round their positions. With the situation becoming increasingly serious, Mao decided to break out and leave Hunan for safer territory. Therefore, in October 1934 the Communist army of about 100,000 set out on the Long March.

The original aim of the march was to move the Communist head-quarters to a point a few hundred miles to the west where the threat from the Kuomintang armies would be less intense. However, in face of superior armies, the Communists were forced to continue westwards to the desolate regions on the borders of Tibet, and then move north-wards (see map). This march was to become legendary. The marchers were continually harassed by Kuomintang forces, by local war lords and by unfriendly tribesmen. But the worst enemy was the country through which they passed: mountain ranges of up to 16,000 feet, flooded rivers, precipitous gorges and treacherous swamps. On one occasion the Red Army had to capture a bridge consisting of iron chains and a few wooden planks which spanned a gorge. Beneath came the deafening roar of the river and beyond came machine-gun fire from Kuomintang contingents. As they proceeded on their 6,000 mile journey through eleven provinces, the Communists gathered new recruits and organised soviets (workers' and peasants' councils). Nevertheless, of the 100,000 who set out, only 20,000 finally arrived in northern Shensi late in 1935.

The survivors of the Long March were in a very battered condition, but were temporarily out of reach of the Kuomintang forces. They were soon joined by other Communist armies, and by 1937 Mao Tse-tung was the ruler of over 10 million people. Soviets were set up in the villages of Shensi and Kansu. The base for the eventual Communist conquest of China had been established.[1]

The Kuomintang Government

The establishment of the Kuomintang Government with its capital at Nanking put an end to the prevailing anarchy in China. The possibility of China being partitioned amongst European powers or war lords or both was now remote. But, while Chiang Kai-shek's hold on the central areas was strong, it was precarious in the outlying provinces. Manchuria in the north, and Sinkiang and Kansu in the west were virtually independent, and in some areas local war lords still exercised power. Chiang Kai-shek now had the opportunity to carry out Sun Yat-sen's Three Principles. In the sense that the Kuomintang government in theory ruled all China, the first principle, that of Nationalism, was realised. Moreover, the unequal treaties with foreigners were ended, and the Chinese gained control of customs duties. Eventually in 1943 the British and Americans gave up their territories on the coast of China. But as will be seen in the next section, in his policy towards the Japanese, Chiang Kai-shek hardly put nation before party.

The second principle, Democracy, was not attempted. The dictatorship of the Kuomintang, which Sun Yat-sen regarded as a temporary measure, became rigid and fixed. It was based on the support of the middle classes and the conservative elements in the country, and all opposition was crushed by the secret police. The government was, in fact, controlled by the landlords and became increasingly reactionary.

The third principle, the People's Livelihood, was put into practice with remarkably little enthusiasm. Communications were extended, education was improved, the currency was reformed, irrigation was

[1] An excellent account of the Long March and life among the Communists in Shensi is given in *Red Star over China*, written in 1937 by an American journalist named Edgar Snow.

restored and industry developed (although the latter was largely owned by foreigners). But nothing was done about land reform, except in one province where a League of Nations scheme was adopted. Indeed, in former Communist-controlled parts of south China, land was taken from peasants and given back to the landlords. It was their failure to reform the system of landholding which, above all else, lost for the Kuomintang the support of the peasants.

The Kuomintang and Japan

Since 1895 China had been vitally affected by Japanese expansion. First Formosa and Korea were occupied, and then Japanese ambitions were focused on Manchuria. The legal position of Manchuria was doubtful. Although it was generally regarded by the outside world as part of China, Russia considered the northern part and Japan the southern part of Manchuria as their spheres of influence, and Japan especially was increasing her economic as well as political control of the area. When the Manchurian war lord began to oppose Japanese interests in 1928, he was murdered. He was succeeded by his son, who, however, handed over Manchuria to the Kuomintang government whose nationalist propaganda soon began to undermine the Japanese position.

This was the background to the events of 1931. In that year the Japanese army staged an incident near Mukden. Within a very short time they gained control of all the main cities in southern Manchuria and, by the end of the year, the northern part as well. Chiang Kai-shek offered very little resistance, partly because he was not strong enough and was too busy enforcing his rule over other parts of China, and perhaps also because he preferred Japanese to Russian occupation of Manchuria. There was some fighting early in 1932, especially in Shanghai, but otherwise the Japanese conquest was unopposed. A League of Nations' Commission was sent to Manchuria, but its suggestions (see p. 533) were ignored and Japan resigned from the League.

Manchuria was renamed Manchukuo, and the ex-Emperor of China, who had abdicated in 1912, was made its puppet ruler. Early in 1933 the Japanese continued their expansion south of Manchuria. In May a truce was signed, but it was a truce in name only, for the Japanese continued to occupy north Chinese provinces while developing Manchuria as a military base.

Chiang Kai-shek's attitude throughout was one of appeasement. He believed that the Kuomintang must first establish its power over the Chinese, and especially over the Communists, before it could risk a full-scale war against Japan. Therefore, while nationalist feeling was building up, anti-Japanese demonstrators were punished. In 1936 came one of the most extraordinary events of recent Chinese history. Chiang Kai-shek went to Sian in southern Shensi in order to arrange for his armies there to make a massive attack on Mao Tse-tung's stronghold farther north. But the army, which mostly contained men from Manchuria and was much influenced by Communist infiltrators, was far more intent on attacking the Japanese than the Communists, and mutinied. Chiang was kidnapped by his own troops and threatened with execution unless he ceased the attacks on the Communists and concentrated his forces on the Japanese. He refused and his execution seemed imminent. But Mao, when he heard of the situation, sent his very able foreign affairs expert, Chou En-lai, to Sian. Chou had three conferences with Chiang, who eventually gave way and was released. So the Communists forfeited their chance of removing their archenemy, for Mao believed that Chiang Kai-shek was temporarily necessary to hold together the Kuomintang to fight the Japanese. Without the Kuomintang armies to bear the brunt of the Japanese attacks, the Communists themselves might be exterminated. In addition, too, the Communists appeared to be the really patriotic element in the country, and so gained the support of the strongly nationalist and influential middle classes.

When Chiang returned to Nanking, he publicly repudiated the Sian agreement. Nevertheless, the attacks on the Communists gradually ceased, and a stronger line was adopted towards Japanese expansion.

War against Japan 1937 to 1945

The war began with the Marco Polo Bridge incident in July 1937. A clash between Japanese and Chinese troops occurred at a railway junction a few miles from Peking, and this developed into the long-expected war. By the end of the month, the Japanese had occupied Peking and Tientsin, and by the end of the year the north-east of China, as far south as Nanking, was in their hands. The Kuomintang armies were easily and quickly defeated, and eighteen months after the war started the Japanese had occupied the whole of the eastern half of China. Chiang Kai-shek's capital was removed to Chungking, where it remained for the rest of the war.

The Kuomintang armies played only a minor part in the war thereafter. They received supplies from the Western powers and from Russia, who continued to support Chiang Kai-shek rather than the

Chinese Communists in the north. Eventually the Burma road, which connected Chungking with the outside world, was cut by the Japanese, and supplies, which, after Pearl Harbour, had come in massive quantities from the United States, were flown over the Himalayas. But little effective use was made of these supplies. For this there were two main reasons. Firstly, the Kuomintang Government became increasingly inefficient and corrupt. Cut off from the coastal capitalists, more and more power was placed in the hands of the conservative landlord class, and the Kuomintang became isolated from the people. Secondly, Chiang Kai-shek's military aims were divided, and it seems probable that he regarded his constant attempts to stop the Communists from strengthening their hold on northern China as more important than fighting the Japanese. Despite the Sian agreement, the Kuomintang armies frequently attacked the Communists.

Meanwhile the Communist hold on the north was extended. Mao Tse-tung's headquarters were moved at the end of 1936 to the town of Yenan. Here life was primitive for the town itself was soon flattened by Japanese bombs, and an intricate network of homes was established in caves in the hillside. Here Mao spent much of his time in the study of Marxist-Leninist principles and in long-term planning for what he regarded as his inevitable victory. From his cave, outside which he grew his own tomatoes and tobacco, Mao ruled an ever-widening area. In 1937 10 million people lived under Communist rule; in 1945 the figure was 100 million.

The Communists rarely attempted large-scale fighting against the Japanese, but concentrated instead on guerrilla warfare at which they were seasoned experts. The Japanese controlled the important towns and railways, but their hold on the countryside was weak. This was exploited by the Communists, who taught the peasants how to make bombs and mines, and at the same time spread their propaganda on land reform.

So it was clear when the Japanese war ended in August 1945 that the war between the Kuomintang and the Communists was about to begin in earnest.

The Communist Victory 1945 to 1949

With the announcement of the Japanese surrender, both groups in China took immediate steps to occupy the Japanese areas. In this race for territory, the Kuomintang appeared to be mainly successful, for the cities and railways soon fell into their hands. Even north China, the area around Peking, was soon controlled by Chiang Kai-shek's forces, largely because of the aid given by American naval and air transport.

Manchuria, however, was occupied by the Russians. Russia had declared war on Japan on the same day that the atomic bomb was dropped on Nagasaki. When the Japanese surrendered, a Russian army entered Manchuria, and remained in control until it was withdrawn in May 1946. There is controversy about the significance of this. Some historians take the view that Mao Tse-tung greatly benefited, believing that the Russians handed over captured military equipment to his forces and that when they eventually withdrew Mao's Communist guerrillas were allowed to establish themselves in the countryside. Other commentators, however, stress the unfriendliness of relations between Stalin and Mao Tse-tung, because the latter refused to obey directives from Moscow. They emphasise four points: that the Russians gave no assistance to Mao during the war; that in August 1945, an agreement was signed between Russia and the Kuomintang government, in which Stalin said he would support the latter and would not interfere in China's internal affairs; that Moscow-trained Chinese Communists, opposed to Mao, accompanied the Russian forces in Manchuria; and that the Russians removed valuable goods from Manchuria and took them to Russia, not to Yenan.

Meanwhile the United States was trying to prevent the spread of the civil war by persuading the two sides to negotiate. This policy was temporarily successful, for in September 1945, Mao Tse-tung flew to Chungking to meet Chiang Kai-shek. The talks lasted over a month, but with no result, for within a few days of Mao's departure fighting was renewed. During 1946 General George Marshall twice negotiated ceasefires, but both were short-lived. Disillusioned with the rigid attitudes of both Chiang and Mao, he encouraged a third group, the Democratic League. This had the support of the intellectuals and middle classes and wanted parliamentary government. It seemed the only possible non-Communist alternative to the Kuomintang. But the Democratic League was crushed by Chiang Kai-shek's secret police, and its supporters terrorised and imprisoned. By the beginning of 1947, everybody had given up hope of a ceasefire and peaceful negotiation for a coalition government. A decision had to be reached by force.

It seemed to the outside observer in 1947 that the Kuomintang must win this struggle. Its forces controlled the administration, ports and communications, and were receiving massive aid from the United States. Moreover, they had occupied Yenan, the Communist capital. But this picture of success was superficial. The Kuomintang soldiers, mainly drawn from the peasants, were disillusioned and discontented, and often deserted in large numbers taking their modern American equipment with them. The Kuomintang government was corrupt and put increasing reliance on terrorist methods to maintain its authority. Little attempt was made at reconstruction after the devastation of the Japanese occupation, and only a fraction of the vast amount of American aid reached the people. Moreover, there was rapid inflation[1] which ruined many middle-class people who would normally have supported the Kuomintang. Communist propaganda was ever present, and Mao gained the support of the middle class by moderating the declared Communist aims. What Communists wanted, Mao said, was the rule of the people, not the proletariat, the end of exploitation, not absolute equality.

Early in 1948 the Communists controlled the northern half of China except for the cities. Stalin, who appeared to fear the rapid emergence of a strong Communist China, advised the continued use of guerrilla tactics by the Communists. But Mao now ordered large-scale military movements, and one by one the cities were captured. In autumn 1948 the Kuomintang lost the decisive battle for control of the Yangtze valley. In January 1949 Peking fell to the Communists, and Chiang Kai-shek's armies began to disintegrate rapidly. Whole divisions joined the Communist forces. Chiang's final moves—the meeting of a national assembly and his personal resignation—failed to stop the Communist advance. In the summer of 1949, he and his armies fled to the island of Formosa, ninety miles from the coast, leaving the mainland under Communist control.[2] On 1 October an impressive ceremony was held in Peking. An immense crowd thundered, 'Mao Tse-tung live ten thousand years', as the Communist leader, dressed in drab cloth cap and worn clothes, announced, 'The Central Governing Council of the People's Government of China today assumes power in Peking.'

China under Communism

Government

In September 1949, before fighting had ended in the south of China, the People's Political Consultative Conference met in Peking. This conference, which consisted of over 650 delegates from the Communist

---

[1] Victor Purcell describes in his book *China* the effect of the inflation. In May 1947, his hotel bill in Shanghai was $120,000 a night; later in the year it was $800,000 a night. A suitcase of banknotes was required to pay for a meal—the shopkeeper did not count these notes, he weighed them.

[2] The Kuomintang is henceforth referred to as the Nationalist Government.

Party and other left-wing organisations, elected the Central Governing Council with Mao Tse-tung as its Chairman. This Council ruled China for the next five years. Having established its authority, it arranged for a system of local and national elections which produced the National People's Congress.

The Congress met in Peking in September 1954, and the constitution of China, which was then officially adopted, has since remained unchanged. The sole legislative authority in the state is the National People's Congress (the equivalent of the Supreme Soviet in Russia), which consists of deputies elected by local assemblies, the armed forces and the national minorities. It is elected for four years and meets at least once a year. The National People's Congress elects the Chairman of the Republic and the members of the State Council, the supreme executive and administrative body. The State Council is headed by a premier who is nominated by the Chairman of the Republic. The Constitution, which says that the aim of the state is to build up a socialist system, also contains a list of fundamental rights which are to be safeguarded. These include equality before the law, the right to vote for all men and women over the age of eighteen, freedom of religious belief, of association and of speech. From 1954 to 1958 Mao was the Chairman of the Republic; from 1954 to 1976 the premier was Chou En-lai.

Superficially this constitution is not very different from that of a Western democracy. In practice the difference is immense, for the controlling factor in the state is the highly organised and all-powerful Communist Party. The Communists control the elections to the National People's Congress, and all the important members of the government are also members of the Communist Party. Other left-wing parties are allowed to function, and some of their members are represented in the government, but they have little power in practice. The Communist Party has a similar structure to that of the state. It has a National Congress which is elected for five years, and this chooses the Central Committee, which in turn elects the twenty-man political bureau headed by the chairman who was Mao Tse-tung. Apart from these central bodies, the Communist Party has a well-organised local network spreading throughout the country. Its function is not only to diffuse propaganda and to see that party wishes are carried out, but also to keep the national leaders in touch with local public opinion. The membership of the party steadily grew: it was 1 million in 1945, 6 million in 1950, and over 17 million in 1964. This out of a population of nearly 700 million in 1965 was small, but nevertheless Communists make up for small numbers by fanatical enthusiasm and hard work.

These qualities also help to explain the success of the national leadership. The primary need of China in 1949 was peace and unity, and this could only be achieved by a strong central government. This the Communist Party provided,[1] for the first time in China in the twentieth century, partly because, above all else, the mass of the people demanded it, and partly because of the dedicated leadership of the Communist Party. Mao Tse-tung and his colleagues were and indeed still are ambitious and ruthless men, intent on concentrating power into their own hands. But from many years of practical experience of government in Kiangsi and Yenan, they understood the problems of the masses, and in the early years were tactful in making policies acceptable to the people. The emphasis was on persuasion rather than force in achieving unity, although force was used if necessary. The prestige of Mao was enormous, but within the political bureau it would seem that discussion was open and frank.

From the beginning Communists aimed at what they called 'democracy for the people and dictatorship for the reactionaries'. The latter included all supporters of the Kuomintang, together with landlords and the larger capitalists. Many of these lost their lives during the civil war, but many more remained and the Communist Party believed that they provided a potential danger to the Revolution. During its first year the Communist government followed a policy of moderation while its authority was established. But in 1951 the government was engaged in two major activities, the redistribution of land and the Korean War. Believing that the upheaval caused by these events would encourage reactionary forces to attempt a counterrevolution, and wishing to stress the power and authority of the government, the Communists began a reign of terror in which possibly two million people were killed. People's Courts,[2] a primitive and biased system by Western standards, gave little chance of acquittal to the accused who were usually sentenced to execution or forced labour. Executions were often broadcast on the radio; crowds could be heard shouting 'Shoot! Shoot! Shoot!' this being followed by the sound of rifles. Children were encouraged to denounce their parents.

Having shown its hand the government allowed the terror to die down. Until the mid-1960s, with one exception, there were no important signs of opposition to the Communist regime. The exception came in 1957. One of the reasons for the defeat of the Kuomintang in 1949 was their failure to retain the support of the intellectuals, who saw

[1] There was one important threat to unity in 1954 when the Communist leader in Manchuria, backed by Russia, aimed at independence. He committed suicide.

[2] 'The main duty of the court is not to distinguish right from wrong. It is to further the cause of the revolution.' Guy Wint, *Common Sense about China*.

in Communism, if not the ideal government, at least an opportunity to secure peace and stability in China. Although the Communist government regarded these people with suspicion, their expert knowledge in education and industry was needed, especially in the early days. But the intellectuals, in common with everybody else, were not allowed to criticise the government or its policies. In 1957, however, there was a temporary lifting of this restriction on free speech. The government, confident of its strength and possibly influenced by the relaxations in Russia (see pp. 157–8), decided to allow candid and free expression of opinion. The episode, which lasted just over a month, is known as 'The Hundred Flowers', because in the previous year Mao had put forward as the slogan for the experiment, 'Let a hundred flowers bloom, let diverse schools of thought contend'. Prominent intellectuals began with criticisms of faults in the Communist system—the purges, the arrogance of Communist officials—but as the movement gathered momentum, the system itself was attacked. A university lecturer said that the people hated Communist leadership and he attacked Communist economic policy. Similar opinions were widely reported in the official Communist press, which also gave news of student riots.

The government then began its counterattack. By various methods, the critics were persuaded to confess their mistakes. In the newspapers which had previously contained their criticisms, there now appeared articles under such headings as, 'I Admit Guilt to the People' and 'A Review of My Mistakes and Crimes'. The freedom to criticise continues in theory, but in practice no such freedom exists.

The episode of 'The Hundred Flowers' has been variously interpreted in the West. Some believe that it was a genuine attempt by the Communist government to invite criticism, but that it got out of hand. Others believe that it was a cunning method of persuading reactionary elements to make themselves known so that they could be dealt with accordingly.

In the mid-1960s China was convulsed by a movement known as the Cultural Revolution. Cultural only in the broadest sense, it was in fact a ruthless and complicated struggle between moderates and young revolutionary extremists which almost produced civil war. Perhaps the evidence of the discontent of the intellectuals and the example of the changes in post-Stalinist Russia persuaded Mao that a campaign against 'bourgeois revisionists' was required. Mao believed in continuous revolution, in perpetual struggle. Revolution needs to be continually renewed, or it becomes stagnant. Old customs and habits must continually be eradicated, or capitalist ideas will creep back into the system: the traditional, revisionist and pragmatic must be opposed.

Young Red Guards in Canton preparing for a rally during the Cultural Revolution of the 1960s

The years from 1963 to 1965 saw the beginnings of the campaign against the 'revisionists'. Heretics were purged, and all ranks in the Army were abolished. However, there was growing disagreement between Mao, the aging visionary, and the practical men in the government, the army and the party. Consequently, Mao organised the Red Guard movement in order to eliminate the opposition. The Cultural Revolution was at its height from autumn 1965 to summer 1967. Hundreds of thousands of young, hysterical and fanatical Red Guards demonstrated and paraded in Peking and other big cities in order to mobilise mass feeling against anyone suspected of bourgeois sympathies. For a whole year high schools and universities were closed to revise the curriculum, and students were thus free to demonstrate. Free transport, food and accommodation encouraged mammoth rallies in which the teenage Red Guards would wave a small, red plastic-covered book, *Quotations from Chairman Mao Tse-tung*. The Chairman was eulogised as the central source of all wisdom and leadership, the infallible superman,[1] the philosopher and poet whose works, together with those of Marx and Lenin, were quoted as gospel. The *Thoughts of Mao* provided the essential guidance in all activities. For example, an article in a party journal by one of China's world table-tennis champions claimed that the *Thoughts of Mao* were a vital study for the better playing of table tennis. An engine drivers' manual recommended the study of Mao's works for the steadier driving of engines, even though the locomotives, bought in Russia, were 'rotten pieces of goods sold us by the revisionists'. The Red Guards opposed the whole Communist Party structure which ruled the country, and party officials and intellectuals were publicly criticised and terrorised. Mao hoped his young rebels would take over the factories, offices, newspapers and radio stations in which they worked, and gradually new ruling authorities would emerge. Mao was clearly rebelling against his own party, and appealing to youth to destroy the old before building the new, but the precise aims of the movement were vague.

The Red Guards were opposed in their turn. When they attacked party officials in the provinces, the victims summoned local workers to their defence. In the outlying provinces Communist war lords emerged who opposed the obstreperous Red Guards, and hundreds were killed in clashes in Tibet and Inner Mongolia. All over China there were battles in factories, and demonstrations and counter-demonstrations. There was considerable danger that China would break up in civil war. Eventually the position became very complicated

[1] In July 1966, Mao, at the age of seventy-three, swam nine miles (with the current) in sixty-five minutes in the Yangtze River.

with the young revolutionary Maoists divided among themselves. However, by the end of the summer of 1967 the moderates, often with radical titles, were in the ascendant. The Army under Lin Piao, despite the prompting of Mao and his wife, Chiang Ching, would not aid the Red Guards and eventually opposed them. The excesses of the students antagonised large sections of the population, especially in the industrial cities and in the west and south. With the danger of chaos from inexperienced government, there was opposition from the previous leaders of the Communist Party at a local level. There was no massive popular support for the revolution because the basic motives of the Cultural Revolution ran counter to what most Chinese wanted, peace and order and a rise in living standards. Moreover, the Prime Minister, Chou En-lai, China's chief executive and indispensable to Mao, wanted order. Probably most government ministers were alarmed at the damage the Cultural Revolution had done to the economy and to national discipline.

The struggle between moderates and radicals continued from 1968 to 1976, but the disorder and chaos of the Cultural Revolution were not repeated. New Revolutionary Committees were set up in 1968, but they were not paragons of revolutionary virtue: they were very like the old order with the previous bureaucrats reappointed under a new name. The main shopping street in Peking was named 'Revolution Street'; this led to the 'Street of the Permanent Revolution' which bisects 'Anti-Imperialism Street'. Nevertheless, the moderates were now in control, the radical element was weakened, and the Army increasingly exercised a moderating influence. Party Congresses pressed the theme of unity and concentration on dealing with problems of practical organisation.

In the first half of the 1970s the indefatigable Chou En-lai controlled the government. Mao Tse-tung became increasingly senile and incapable of controlling events. In 1976 both these great leaders died, and China came to the end of an era.

Economic policy

The economic problems facing the Chinese Communist government in 1949 were immense. Industry had suffered greatly from the long years of war, and unemployment was high. Inflation was out of control. Agriculture was backward and inefficient and farms were small. It seemed clear that if the Communists were to consolidate their hold on China, they must greatly improve the living standards of the mass of the people. It was the failure to do this which partly accounted for the downfall of the Kuomintang.

Since the middle of the 1920s, Mao Tse-tung had insisted that land reform was essential if the support of the peasantry was to be gained. Therefore, first in Kiangsi, and then in an ever-growing area around Yenan, the Communists took land from the rich and distributed it amongst the mainly landless peasants. The technique was usually to hold village meetings, to charge the rich with tax evasion and exploitation, and then to divide up their land between the people of the village. This method, used in a limited area before 1949, was applied throughout China in 1950–52. In June 1950 the Agrarian Reform Law was passed, and during the next two years land was distributed among about 300 million peasants. This was a huge operation. It was carried out by obedient and fanatical Communist cadres, who would first investigate the local situation and would then arouse resentment against landlords and rich peasants. Public meetings were then held to be followed often by harsh sentences imposed by the People's Courts. No uniform rules were followed; each village decided its own methods. There is some controversy about the ease with which the transfer was accomplished. Some say it was carried out with far less bloodshed than occurred in Russia in the early 1930s; some say that there were mass executions. When the land was redistributed, a large number of factors had to be taken into consideration—the quality of the land, the size of the families, the availability of water. By the end of 1952, however, the agrarian reform had been completed in the whole country, except those parts inhabited by some of the national minorities.

The effect of this revolution in the countryside was to end completely the power of the landlords and to win the support of the peasants. But land reform in itself was not sufficient to raise food production. If the peasants kept the land they had just been given, the result would probably be to create a huge new class of society, conservative, and devoted to free enterprise. Also, the average size of each peasant's plot was under half an acre—too small to be economically efficient. The next step, therefore, was to organise methods of cooperation between peasants. For the supply and marketing of goods it was relatively easy to organise cooperatives. By 1954 170 million peasants were members of such cooperatives, and these expanded trade between town and country. But the formation of cooperatives for the production of goods was much more difficult, for in these the individual peasant would merely be a member of a team and would play a very small part in making the decision as to what should be grown on his own land.

In order to introduce the peasant gradually to the idea of cooperation in farming, mutual aid teams were organised. With these, each peasant would decide what he would grow, but at busy times peasants would pool their tools and help each other, thus allowing a more effective division of labour. This cooperation gradually spread to other aspects of farming, especially as it was discovered that the greater the degree of cooperation, the higher the rate of production. During 1956 the drive to form cooperative or collective farms was intensified, so that by the end of the year practically all peasant holdings were included. At first twenty to fifty farms would be linked together into a cooperative; later it would be a 100 to 300, according to the geography of the land. The pace of this advance towards cooperative farming seems to indicate that the peasantry welcomed it. For this there are three possible reasons. Firstly, peasants could keep for personal use up to 5 per cent of their original holdings, and could theoretically withdraw all their holdings from the cooperative at any time. Secondly, there was no long tradition of land ownership amongst Chinese peasants as there was in Russia. Thirdly, the government approached the problem tactfully and persuasively, showing how great were the economic advantages of the new system.

Having in the space of six years (1950-56) redistributed land, organised mutual aid teams and then cooperative farms, it was widely thought that the government would call a halt to the rapid changes in the Chinese countryside in order to give the people time to become accustomed to them. But this was not to be so, for in two months, August and September 1958, 90 per cent of the peasant population of China were organised into 26,000 communes, averaging about 5,000 families in each.[1] A commune is different from a cooperative farm in that it includes not just farmers but everybody in an area. It is, in fact, a unit of local government. Apart from the peasants engaged in farming, it contains small industrialists, traders, school-teachers, administrators, soldiers, all, in fact, who have a function in a small section of society. This merging of farming and industry into one unit was first suggested by Marx and Engels in 1848, and the whole idea of communes carried Communism in China further than anywhere else in the world, including Russia. Each commune has its own schools, nurseries, clinics, hospitals, theatres, libraries and shops, all collectively owned. The establishment of public dining-halls and nurseries means that women can be released from domestic work and can take part in production. It is widely believed that this will weaken the family as a social unit. Life in a commune can be very regimented, with set hours of work, military training and political and cultural study. Meals and other services are free, and wages therefore low, being paid in accordance to work done. The commune guarantees to its members food, clothing, medical care,

[1] The first commune to be organised experimentally in April 1958 was called 'sputnik'.

shelter and funeral expenses. The sense of security this brings is new in China, and, indeed, in Asia. One major advantage of the communes is that it is easier to organise labour for big projects, such as irrigation and water conservation; also, labour can be switched from one task to another quite easily.

The system operates chiefly in country areas, but is spreading gradually to the towns. At the start there would appear to have been some opposition from the peasants who objected to the regimentation, and organisational difficulties led to food shortages. After differences of opinion within the political bureau of the Communist Party, the spread of the communes on a large scale in the cities was slowed down at the end of 1958. But in the years since 1958 there has been little indication that the peasants are greatly dissatisfied with the commune system. Foreign visitors have been impressed, especially by the willing sacrifices made by the Chinese in order to achieve future prosperity.

The economic results of all these changes as far as production of grain is concerned have been good. In 1936, the last year of peace before the Japanese invasion, the grain crop totalled 150 million tons; in 1949 it was 113 million tons. There was a steady increase under the Communist regime; in 1955 the total was 184 million tons. Hard work, combined with better agricultural implements and methods, more thorough irrigation and greater use of fertilisers, explain the improved output. In all fields of the economy, 1958 was to be the year of the Great Leap Forward when great pressure was put on workers to produce even more. Early in 1959 it was announced that 375 million tons of grain had been harvested but a few months later the government admitted that the totals had been gravely over-estimated, and that the actual total was 250 million tons. Although a big reduction, this still represents a major increase since 1949. During the winter of 1959–60, however, a series of natural calamities, the worst of the century, caused serious damage to agriculture. Droughts, floods and typhoons so reduced the grain crop that China was forced to buy large quantities of grain from Canada and Australia, and famine was only avoided by rationing. Since 1960 the position has improved.

While these important changes were taking place in agricultural organisation and production, there were equally important achievements in industry. Before there could be any progress, the government had to restore some measure of stability to the economy. This was achieved during the first two years after 1949. Inflation was controlled, unemployment reduced, and communications and industrial production restored. Just as in agriculture the Communist Party believed that state control of the means of production was necessary if output was to be increased, so it considered that industrial progress depended on state ownership. By 1955 85 per cent of heavy industry and about half of light industry had been nationalised. Thus for the first few years of the Communist regime, some firms were owned by the state, some were owned by private capitalists, and some were run by joint state-private management. Gradually all were brought under state control.

In 1951 the State Planning Commission began drawing up the First Five Year Plan, which came into operation in 1953. From the beginning the Communist aim was industrialisation in a very short period, and in the First Five Year Plan (1953–57) the emphasis was on heavy industry, such as coal, iron and steel, chemicals and machine tools, with less expenditure devoted to light industry and communications. The problem for all countries that wish to expand their industry is where to find the necessary capital. China received a small amount of financial aid and considerable technical assistance from Russia, but nearly all the capital that was required was raised by increased production combined with austerity.[1]

The government claimed that the Five Year Plan had been very successful. In the five years production of capital goods increased three times, and the production of consumer goods doubled. All industries showed increases in output. For example, 150,000 tons of steel were produced in 1949, 1,340,000 tons in 1952 and 5,240,000 tons in 1957. In 1958, the year of the Great Leap Forward, the output of steel was more than twice that of 1957, and there was a similar increase in coal production. The second Five Year Plan (1958–62) again set ambitious targets in all fields of the economy, there being rather less emphasis this time on heavy industry and more on medium and small enterprises. Nevertheless, the production of, for example, steel continued to rise fast: in 1960 18·4 million tons were produced.[2] But on the whole the four years, 1959–62, were bleak years for the economy. Natural disasters, the lack of foreign aid, and the dogmatic amateurism of the regime, were mainly to blame.

The Cultural Revolution of the 1960s disrupted the economy. Leadership and planning were lacking, the uncertainties and dislocation reduced production, and there were consequent shortages. China recovered during the first half of the 1970s. There were growing purchases of plant and machinery from abroad, and heavy industry was modernised and expanded. At the same time, light industry and

[1] Chou En-lai has said, 'It is better to bear certain hardships and inconveniences in order that in the long run we shall live in prosperity and happiness' than 'to seek petty benefits now and thus never be able to shake off poverty and backwardness'.
[2] In 1960 Britain produced 24 million tons and Russia 67 million tons.

the production of consumer articles were increased. Agriculture, which employed 80 per cent of the work force, steadily expanded.

Social conditions

There seems to be little doubt that the Communist Government has raised the standard of living of the mass of the people. Visitors to China who are aware of the conditions that existed before 1949 are impressed by what they see today: modern buildings, well-fed and healthier people, the absence of beggars, full employment, steady prices, and a new and more determined spirit in the people. Some commentators say that political, economic and social advance has been achieved by increasingly ruthless control and regimentation. Nevertheless, the people now see hope in the future, something that was almost totally absent before 1949 and something for which they give the Communists the credit.

Four aspects of the life of the people in Communist China stand out for particular comment: the improved position of women in society, the spread of education, the rise in population and the policy towards religion. In Imperial China women occupied a very inferior position, and for those who lived away from the coastal fringe this continued until 1949. In 1931 the Kuomintang government had passed a law providing for the equality of women, but this remained a dead letter. The Communists, however, have always advocated the emancipation of women and the end of the strict authority of the father in the family. They believe that the traditional loyalty of the Chinese to the family is harmful to the building up of loyalty to the socialist state. In 1950 a Marriage Law was passed which provided for equal rights for women. Women now work at all levels in government, industry, agriculture, education and medicine. The killing of girl babies, fairly common before 1949, has been ended. Particularly since the communes were organised in 1958, and public nurseries, laundries and restaurants were started on a large scale, women have been freed from household work and have provided a large new source of labour for industry and farming.

A large majority of the population of China had always been illiterate. There were few schools, especially in the country districts, and the education provided in them was limited. The Communist Government has gradually expanded educational services aiming at universal compulsory education. In 1949 there were 25 million children over the age of six in primary schools; in 1958 there were over 90 million. This, combined with similar increases in secondary education and a vast system of adult education, has now confined illiteracy to the very old.

Education was strictly related to politics: reading and writing were taught through texts with a clear political message favouring the policies of Chairman Mao; primary school children, for example, could be taught Mathematics by calculating the number of American casualties in Vietnam. The curriculum was very vocational; all schools ran productive workshops, and children would spend several weeks of the year working in factories or on communes. The emphasis was on practical knowledge—how, for example, to keep commune accounts.

The number of university students multiplied five times during the 1950s, and in 1958 was about 800,000. The emphasis is on engineering and science. Cultural activity is flourishing, although rather dull and monotonous. One of the difficulties facing educationalists is the large number of complicated characters in the classical Chinese language, all of which have to be learned before reading is possible. During the twentieth century, the vernacular has gradually replaced classical Chinese, and an attempt has been made to reduce the number of dialects. In 1956 the government approved the 26-letter Latin alphabet, but this is being introduced very cautiously.

Thirdly, there is the problem that the fast-growing population will upset all China's plans for the future. Before 1954 it was estimated that the population was about 475 million but a census held during the elections for the National People's Congress revealed a population of 583 million, excluding those Chinese who lived on Formosa or abroad. By the mid-1960s the population had reached about 700 million, and was increasing at the rate of 15 to 17 million per year. This is not as fast as the increase in food production, but it seems that the time must come when agricultural production will reach a limit and the result will eventually be widespread starvation. The government's attitude to this problem has not remained the same. From 1954 to early 1957 the Ministry of Health publicised knowledge about and the need for birth control; and then quite suddenly, the campaign was stopped. Chinese experts say that the problem is not as great as foreigners seem to think. Chou En-lai in 1960 pointed out three factors: firstly, the density of population in China is low; secondly, the cultivated area can be doubled; and thirdly, population growth is not so large when compared with China's natural resources and the labour required to develop them. In addition there is considerable scope for improvements in agricultural techniques. By the 1970s, however, the government was again supporting birth control. Nevertheless, the population was increasing by 10 to 15 million a year, or 40,000 per day, with the consequent problems of unemployment as well as pressure on food supplies.

Although the constitution of 1954 guaranteed religious toleration, Communism officially condemns religion. The prospect, therefore, for the various religions of China was not a happy one, especially since their disunity led to weakness in opposing Communist propaganda. Confucianism had been declining amongst intellectuals since the beginning of the century, and has disappeared in Communist China. Buddhism, too, has lost temples, lands and clergy, although it still continues to exist. Christianity has been greatly weakened; Protestants, who lacked the united organisation of the Roman Catholics, especially declined. Schools and hospitals run by the churches have been taken over by the state, and foreign missionaries have left. Islam has probably fared better than the others, possibly in order that China could gain the friendship of the Arab world.

National minorities

About 40 million of the people of China are not Chinese. These include Tibetans, Mongolians, Tartars, Manchus, Koreans and many others, a large number of whom have their own languages, customs and religions. The Kuomintang continued the policy of the emperors in repressing these minority races; massacres of Muslims, for example, were frequent. The policy of the Communists is hard to determine, for, while it is difficult enough for the foreigner to visit the more densely populated areas of eastern China, it is almost impossible to visit some of the more inaccessible areas of western China where most of the minority peoples live. Therefore, there are few first-hand reports of conditions amongst these peoples.

But it would seem that up to about 1957 the policy towards local nationalism was tolerant, especially in view of the potential value of these areas as sources of raw materials and space to which surplus population could emigrate. The constitution of 1954 said that 'the national autonomous areas are inalienable parts of the People's Republic of China'. The people of these areas, which cover 60 per cent of the area of China, were allowed to keep their own languages and religions and were represented in the National People's Congress, but it is not clear whether the Communist government puts the stress on 'national autonomous areas' or on 'inalienable parts of China'. The example of Tibet, about which most is known, would seem to indicate that the government does not interfere as long as its basic wishes are being carried out, but that the people resent the strict control of their affairs and the radical and sweeping changes that are being made to their ways of life.

Tibet, the mountainous country north of India, was extremely backward. The government, monasteries and nobles, representing 5 per cent of the population, owned all the land, and the peasants were serfs. In 1951 a treaty was signed by the Dalai Lama of Tibet and the Chinese Communist government in which the former officially recognised Tibet as part of China. (At the beginning of the century Tibet had been in the Manchu empire, but not under direct Chinese rule. Her effective independence after 1912 had never been internationally recognised.) Thereafter the Chinese attempted to modernise through the existing government. This proved unsuccessful and anti-Chinese revolts broke out which culminated in a full-scale rebellion in 1959. This was crushed by military action and the Dalai Lama fled to India (see p. 403).

Foreign policy

Many of the ideas which dominate Communist foreign policy were formed before 1949. The United States had provided massive aid to the Kuomintang in its struggle against Mao Tse-tung. This, combined with its vigorous anti-Communist attitudes after about 1946, led to the United States being branded as the supreme example of a capitalist and imperialist power. Britain, France, Holland and Belgium were likewise regarded as enemies in view of their capitalist societies and records of colonial expansion. Japan, Germany and Italy were clearly aggressive, Fascist powers. The Communists, indeed all Chinese, felt strongly about the humiliations and insults that China had suffered during the past century of weakness, and they aimed at restoring Chinese authority.

The attitude to the USSR was somewhat mixed. On the one hand, Russia was until 1945 the only Communist country in the world, and was therefore to be looked up to as the great example and guide. On the other hand, Stalin had never been friendly towards Mao. Before 1932 Russia wished the Chinese Communist Party to work with, and attempt to infiltrate, the Kuomintang rather than oppose it, and therefore Mao's armies in Kiangsi were frowned upon. After about 1932 and up to about 1946 Russia officially supported the Kuomintang in order that China should be united and strong to oppose Japan who represented a threat to Russia's eastern flank. Considerable Russian aid was given to Chiang Kai-shek and nothing to Mao Tse-tung. Even after 1946 when an ultimate Communist victory seemed more likely, the Russian support for Chinese Communism seemed half-hearted.

Two other important factors need to be mentioned. One is the lack of knowledge Chinese Communists had of the outside world. Of the twenty leading Communists after 1949, nearly all originated in rural areas of west-central China. Few had ever travelled abroad; with the exception of his visit to Moscow in 1950, Mao had never left China. China has traditionally never developed any sense of international relations, and this national tendency towards a proud and self-centred isolation was reinforced for the Communists by the geographical setting of their headquarters, first in the mountains of Kiangsi, surrounded by Kuomintang troops, and secondly in Yenan, with the Gobi desert on one side and the Kuomintang on the other. The other factor is the distinction Chinese Communists make between governments and peoples. Whereas governments very often are to be condemned for their actions, the peoples are rarely to blame, for it is thought that they have no say in the running of their countries.

The government of Mao Tse-tung had been in office less than a year when the Korean War broke out. Korea, ruled by Japan since 1910, was divided by the 38th parallel into two zones in 1945. The northern zone, containing a third of the population and most of the industry, was occupied by Russia, and the southern zone containing two-thirds of the population and most of the farming areas, was controlled by the United States. It was not intended that this division should be permanent, but as in Germany the occupying forces failed to agree on a unified government acceptable to both sides. In 1947 the United Nations sent a commission to try to reach a settlement but without success. In 1948, therefore, elections, supervised by the United Nations, were held in South Korea, and Syngman Rhee became president. In North Korea the Russians set up the People's Democratic Republic headed by a Communist government. Soon after the Russians and Americans withdrew their forces.

In June 1950, however, North Korea invaded South Korea. Communist motives for the Korean War are not known with any certainty. It is not clear whether China knew about the proposed North Korean attack, whether China wanted war, or whether Stalin was solely responsible. During the spring and summer of 1950 Chinese Communist forces were built up along the coast opposite Formosa. It seemed that an invasion of Chiang Kai-shek's Nationalist stronghold was imminent, and was, perhaps, to coincide with the attack on South Korea. However, almost immediately after the Korean War began, the United States sent their Seventh Fleet to patrol the straits between Formosa and the mainland, and this effectively prevented any invasion.

A few hours after the Korean War started, the United Nations

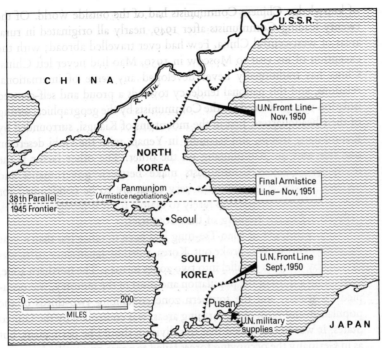

U.S.S.R.

C H I N A

R. Yalu

U.N. Front Line–
Nov, 1950

NORTH
KOREA

Final Armistice
Line– Nov, 1951

Panmunjom
(Armistice negotiations)

38th Parallel
1945 Frontier

• Seoul

SOUTH
KOREA

U.N. Front Line
Sept, 1950

0   200

MILES

Pusan

U.N. military
supplies   J A P A N

The Korean War

Security Council met, and in the absence of Russia (who was boycotting the Council in protest against the failure to let Peking represent China) called for the withdrawal of North Korean forces. When this resolution was ignored the Security Council asked members of the United Nations to send contingents to help South Korea. Sixteen countries responded, but the United Nations army so formed was dominated by the United States, and General MacArthur, then in charge of the American occupation of Japan, was put in command (see chapter 14).

The fighting lasted a year. When United Nations forces arrived in September 1950, only a small area around Pusan was not occupied by the Communists. However, in three weeks the whole of South Korea was recaptured by the United Nations. The decision was then made to continue the counterattack into North Korea, and by mid-November United Nations forces had reached the Yalu River on the frontier between Korea and China. At this point China sent her 'volunteers' into the war, and such was the strength of the Chinese armies that the United Nations were driven back south of the 38th parallel. Between January and June 1951 the United Nations counterattacked for the second time, and when fighting ended in June, the two sides were facing each other roughly along the 38th parallel.

Armistice talks then began, and continued for two years. Much of the negotiation was concerned with whether Communist prisoners should be repatriated against their wishes. Finally in July 1953 an armistice was signed. No agreement has since been reached on a peace treaty.

Twelve months of savage and destructive conflict had devastated Korea, leaving 200,000 dead and 5 million homeless. Communism had been contained, the authority of the United Nations vindicated, and the war had been kept localised. But Korea remained divided and unsettled. North Korea remained Communist, and South Korea continued until 1960 under the repressive regime of Syngman Rhee. In that year riots forced him to resign, and in 1961 the army took over the government.

After the Korean War, Communist China gave increasing support to the Viet Minh, the Communist forces fighting against the French in Indo-China. At the Geneva Conference on Indo-China in 1954, Communist China was represented. This was the first time she had taken part in an international conference, and it marks the beginning of a new phase in her foreign policy. Trying to emphasise the contrast between the rigidity and aggression of United States' foreign policy under Dulles and her own reasonableness and toleration, China attempted to win the support of the underdeveloped countries of Asia, Africa and Latin America. For example, in April 1954 an agreement was reached with India on the question of Tibet. The two countries promised to adhere to five basic principles of peaceful coexistence in their relations with each other. A similar agreement was made with Burma.

A possible result of Communist China's diplomacy was seen later in 1954 in the lukewarm Asian response to the Manila Pact which established SEATO. Only three Asian countries—Pakistan, Thailand, and the Philippines—joined. In the following year, 29 of the uncommitted nations attended the Bandung Conference.[1] Chou En-lai, the skilful, subtle and flexible Chinese premier, continued the attempt to create trust in China, but was faced with attacks on both Communism and power blocs. The uncommitted countries seemed intent on remaining uncommitted. Nevertheless, Chinese diplomats continued to be active. In 1956 diplomatic relations were established with Egypt, who received the wholehearted support of China at the time of the Anglo-French Suez landings. Chinese prestige among the Arab nations rose. Support, both moral and material, was given to the Algerian nationalists in their

[1] At this conference, an agreement was made with Indonesia by which all Chinese living in Indonesia had to choose in two years whether they wished for Chinese or Indonesian nationality. Previously they had claimed both.

struggle against France. A steady stream of visitors from the under-developed countries came to Peking.

Meanwhile in 1955, after the Bandung Conference, Communist China decided upon less hostile relations with the United States. Some American airmen, who had been captured during the Korean War, were released, and talks with the object of settling outstanding differences and of reducing tension, began at ambassadorial level in Geneva and Warsaw. But China refused to renounce the use of force towards Formosa, and the United States refused to end her protection of Chiang Kai-shek. Therefore, no progress was made. In 1958, in fact, relations with the United States took a sudden turn for the worse. In August China began a military bombardment of Quemoy, the small island a few miles from the Chinese mainland belonging to the Nationalist regime. The United States warned China of a possible attack on the mainland. Russia supported China, saying that if the United States attacked China with atomic weapons, Russia would retaliate using the same weapons. The crisis died down, however, when Dulles visited Formosa in October, and reached an agreement with Chiang Kai-shek not to use force to reconquer the mainland. Thereafter, the United States and Communist China continued to regard each other with hostility, each having a highly distorted view of the other.

The trust in her intentions and policies which Communist China was attempting to create in Asia received a heavy blow from events in Tibet and from her frontier dispute with India (see p. 404). Despite the much-needed reforms that China introduced in Tibet, Asian opinion was offended by the methods used to crush Tibetan independence, especially after the flight of the Dalai Lama in 1959, and by the invasion of India in 1962.

Meanwhile China's relations with Russia went through four main phases. The first was from 1949 to the death of Stalin in 1953. It was dominated by Mao's visit to Moscow during the winter of 1949–50 when a treaty of Friendship and Mutual Assistance was signed, by the Korean War and by the slowness of Russian economic aid to China. However, the outside world saw only the monolithic unity of the Communist camp, and this seemed to be reinforced during the second phase, from 1953 to 1956, when Russo-Chinese relations improved. This was typified by more economic aid to China, and the visit of Khrushchev, Bulganin and Mikoyan to Peking in 1954. From 1956 to 1960 relations worsened. Chinese intervention in eastern Europe, differences of attitude towards the Cold War, ideological divisions, and Russian fear of Chinese expansionist ambitions, all served to weaken relations. But this remained unknown to the outside world, although some people did suspect that disagreement on these lines existed. After 1960, however, the Russo-Chinese dispute became public, the Russians withdrew their economic and military advisers and the two countries have since engaged in open and bitter quarrelling.

The causes of this quarrel can partly be found in past history. During the nineteenth century Tsarist Russia acquired large tracts of Chinese territory north of Vladivostok and the Amur River, and in north-west Sinkiang. Since 1963 China has laid claim to these territories. Secondly, the Chinese have traditionally disliked Russia, and during the Stalinist era the Chinese Communists particularly distrusted the Russian dictator. After 1953 the Chinese dislike of Khrushchev helped to embitter relations. And thirdly, since 1949 China has suggested to developing countries that the model to be followed should be the Chinese revolution based on peasant support rather than the Russian revolution based on the urban worker.

But the main cause of the quarrel is probably ideological. Russia under Khrushchev believed in peaceful coexistence with capitalist systems which could eventually be crushed without war. China, on the other hand, believed in the need for force and violent revolution. Russia emphasised the dangers of nuclear war; China minimised these dangers. Russia said that it was possible to achieve Communism by different methods; China believed that only Marx and Lenin show the correct method. Much of this was, and is, a difference of emphasis.

Between 1965 and 1969, the period of the Cultural Revolution, China's relations with Russia, as with all other countries, deteriorated. There was a series of skirmishes along the borders in Manchuria and the dust-blown deserts of Sinkiang, with the constant danger that if these skirmishes escalated, it would be difficult for either side to pull back. Each country had about 50 divisions facing the other across the frontier. In addition to the border dispute, China seemed intent on undermining Russia's influence in various parts of the world. Russia was accused, for example, of supplying obsolete weapons to North Vietnam. In the early 1970s China supported the expansion and strengthening of the European Economic Community as a counterbalance to the strength of Russia in Europe. There were an increasing number of contacts with European countries. For her part, Russia regarded with suspicion the improvement in China's relations with the United States after 1971.

During the 1960s China's reputation and influence declined. The Cultural Revolution whipped up China's latent xenophobia. Foreign embassies in Peking, even that of neutral Switzerland, were attacked.

China's ambassadors abroad were recalled for 're-education'. Revolutionary movements in the Middle East, Asia, Africa and Latin America were supported which obviously aroused the hostility of the governments of the countries concerned, who complained of attempts to export the Cultural Revolution. Suharto of Indonesia was typical of other leaders in saying in 1968 that China was in 'the first rank of those who try to meddle in other nations' affairs'. At the same time the failure of China's economy to grow during the 1960s reduced her influence with developing countries who looked less favourably on the Chinese economic model.

China's relations with the United States remained tense throughout the 1960s. In addition to the constant irritation of the US presence in Taiwan (Formosa), there was the increasing American involvement in Vietnam, historically an area which China has regarded as her sphere of influence. China had to support North Vietnam for both ideological and security reasons: North Vietnam was Communist; the US air force were bombing only a few miles from the Chinese border. China was, too, suspicious of the growth of Japanese economic power, and was fearful of a rearmed and expansionist Japan. In addition, China's own nuclear power increased tension. In 1964 and 1967 she exploded her first atomic and hydrogen bombs respectively. In 1970 China's first satellite was launched.

However, there was an apparently dramatic improvement in relations with the United States in the early 1970s. The Cultural Revolution had died down, and the Americans had begun to withdraw from Vietnam. In 1971 President Nixon talked of the need to start a dialogue with China. Soon after, an American table-tennis team toured China, and twice in that year Dr Kissinger, the US Secretary of State, visited Peking. The United Nations finally agreed to accept China as a member and expelled Taiwan from the Security Council. In February 1972 President Nixon himself visited China. He met Chairman Mao and there were optimistic speeches. During the following few years Sino-American contacts increased, and it became clear that only the problem of Taiwan (Chiang Kai-shek died in 1975) was stopping the resumption of full diplomatic ties. Japan recognised the Peking government in 1972. A succession of other western visitors came to Peking.

China in the mid-1970s

In September 1976 Mao Tse-tung died at the age of eighty-two. In his last years there was a solid majority against the continual revolution conducted by the small minority of radicals who had his support. He was succeeded by Hua Kuo-feng as Chairman of the Chinese Communist Party, and the radicals led by Chiang Ching, Mao's widow, were gradually removed from power.

Mao Tse-tung had ruled China for twenty-seven years. One of the great revolutionaries of history, Mao is clearly one of the most important figures of the twentieth century. *The Times* of London in a leading article on the day of his death said: 'few men in the world's history have driven forward so great a change in so large a country'. He gave China the leadership and strength and doctrine that restored its pride and self-confidence, put an end to backwardness and inspired the country's regeneration.

It has been estimated that 100 million people died as a result of droughts, floods, civil wars and foreign invasions in the century before 1949. The Communist regime has given peace and strong government, with Mao as the unchallenged leader. Foreign imperialism in China has almost ended, and the Chinese can feel fully independent and confident of their power. The central government reaches into every village. Although China is no country for the individualist or liberal intellectual, and there is nothing approaching the democratic freedoms of a western society, yet there is still a strong element of popular consultation.

Agriculture, industry, health services and education have all developed rapidly. China does not match the world's advanced economies but great progress has been made. The country is well down the world league table of income per head but, while there are no rich men, there is very little want either.

Mao broke down the sharp distinction between the rulers and the ruled of old China. While on the one hand he was a distant and awe-inspiring figure as ruler of China, and was the subject of an extravagant personality cult, on the other hand he was an earthy and understanding father-figure in the eyes of the masses. His was a complex and contradictory personality: an intense nationalist, he was traditionally Chinese in many ways, yet his views on continuous revolution struck against the ideals of harmony and compromise that are strong in the Chinese mind. He was an untiring revolutionary and thinker, a skilled strategist both in war and politics, and a brilliant tactician. Mao Tse-tung was to China what both Lenin and Stalin were to Russia.

II

Japan

Beginning of the Twentieth Century

Japan in 1900 occupied an almost unique position in the world, for, with the exception of the United States, she was the only non-European power to have achieved a developed industrial economy. On the basis of this economic strength, Japan had built up considerable military power, and this had given her an increasingly influential voice in foreign affairs.

This flourishing situation was in marked contrast to that fifty years before. For over 200 years before 1850 Japan had successfully cut herself off from the West. During this time, in contrast to the West, there was little industrial or social development, and, although there was a semidivine Emperor, political power was in the hands of one aristocratic and conservative family. During the 1850s, however, pressure from the United States and European countries forced Japan to trade with them. Treaties were signed with the United States, Britain, Russia and France which Japan regarded as 'unequal' since the terms for trade were unfavourable to her. The success of this foreign intervention, together with growing political and economic discontent in Japan, made the government very unpopular. In 1868 a brief and successful revolution ended the power of the ruling family, and political power was restored to the Emperor, then a young boy named Meiji.

Government, however, remained in the hands of a small group of men, who, while they wanted industry and agriculture to be modernised, believed that strong, efficient and authoritarian government was essential. This was reflected in the Constitution issued in 1889. This provided for a Diet or Parliament consisting of two houses: the House of Representatives elected by about one per cent of the population who owned a certain amount of property, and a House of Peers. The powers

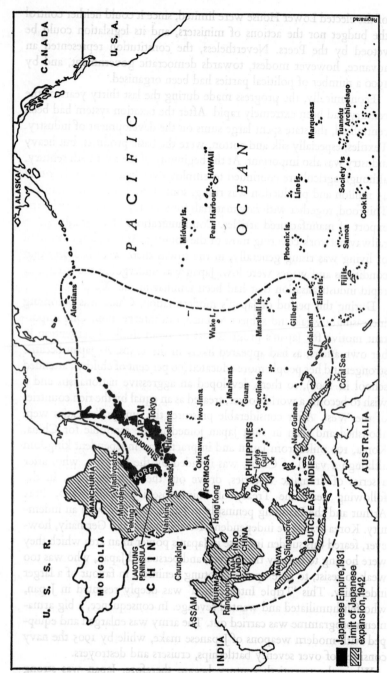

Japanese expansion, 1895–1942

of the elected Lower House were limited, since it could neither control the budget nor the actions of ministers, and its legislation could be vetoed by the Peers. Nevertheless, the constitution represented an advance, however modest, towards democratic government, and by 1900 a number of political parties had been organised.

Economically, the progress made during the last thirty years of the century had been extremely rapid. After the taxation system had been centralised, the state spent large sums on the development of industry. Textiles, especially silk and cotton, were the basic products, but heavy industry was also important. At the beginning of the twentieth century, although agriculture continued to employ over half the population of 45 million and production was rising, some food had to be imported. This food, together with raw materials for industry, was paid for by the export of manufactured articles. Communications were good, with a railway network covering most of the country. Although the standard of living was rising generally, in the towns there were bad working conditions and wages were low. Japan was undergoing the stresses of rapid industrialisation that had been familiar in the West.

During this period of Japan's modernisation, China was becoming increasingly weak and subject to European intervention. One important motive for Japan's progress was to avoid similar intervention in her own affairs, as had appeared likely in the 1850s. As Japan became stronger and her people more educated (90 per cent of children attended school in 1900), so there developed an aggressive nationalism and a wish to become a world power, treated as an equal by the rich countries of the West. After considerable pressure, the 'unequal' treaties were abolished and then in 1894 Japan joined in the scramble for China. Korea, 100 miles from Japan and in practice an independent kingdom although a vassal of China, was invaded by the Japanese, who, after a series of dramatic victories, drove out the Chinese army. In the following year, the Treaty of Shimonoseki gave Formosa, Port Arthur and the Liaotung peninsula to Japan, together with an indemnity. Korea was to be independent. Russia, France and Germany, however, feared this sudden increase in Japan's power in an area which they were hoping to occupy themselves, and persuaded Japan, who was too weak to resist, to give up the Liaotung peninsula in favour of a larger indemnity. This 'Triple Intervention' was deeply resented in Japan, who felt humiliated and wanted revenge. In consequence, a big armaments programme was carried out. The army was enlarged and equipped with modern weapons of Japanese make, while by 1905 the navy consisted of over seventy battleships, cruisers and destroyers.

When the twentieth century began, therefore, Japan was strong politically and economically, and had already made a successful start to her fifty-year period of military aggression in east and south-east Asia.

1900 to 1918

Foreign affairs

An important factor influencing Japanese foreign policy at the turn of the century was her feeling that the advanced countries of Europe still regarded her as inferior. Events between 1900 and 1905, however, soon dispelled any such attitude that the West may have had. In 1900 the Japanese provided over half the troops who raised the siege of the foreign legations in Peking during the Boxer Rising (see p. 424). Less than two years later, Japan formed an alliance with Great Britain. Both powers wished to break their diplomatic isolation; both wished to stop Russian expansion. The agreement said that each country would remain neutral if the other went to war against one power; if either country was involved in a war against two powers, then the other would help. The terms of this Anglo-Japanese Alliance of 1902 were important, but, as far as Japan was concerned, an actual agreement on equal terms with one of the major world powers was even more important. It helped to restore her self-esteem.

Even more significant was the overwhelming Japanese defeat of Russia in 1904-5. Following the Triple Intervention of 1895, the Russians had spread into south Manchuria and seemed to be threatening Korea. Both these areas were regarded by Japan as her sphere of influence, and were the subject of negotiations between Russia and Japan in 1903. Early in 1904 Japan broke off negotiations, and war began immediately. On land there were two main areas of fighting: around Port Arthur, which after bitter fighting fell to the Japanese in December, and along a seventy-mile front near the town of Mukden, where three-quarters of a million men fought a battle in February and March 1905, which ended in defeat for the Russians. At sea the Russian performance was equally disastrous. In the first weeks of the war, the Russian Pacific Fleet was put out of action, and in May 1905 the Baltic Fleet was destroyed, after a voyage lasting over seven months half way round the world.

Japan then asked the United States to mediate, and later in 1905 the Treaty of Portsmouth (US) was signed. South Manchuria, the Liaotung peninsula and Korea came within Japan's sphere of influence. The Japanese public felt that Russia should have paid an indemnity, but

Japan was too exhausted militarily and financially to press for this. Even without an indemnity, victory in the war brought tremendous prestige to Japan, especially in Asia. It was the first occasion in modern times that an Asian country had defeated a European one.

During the years after 1905 a confident Japan exploited its new spheres of influence. South Manchuria was developed economically, and the Japanese soon had control of Korean domestic and foreign policy. The assassination by a Korean of a prominent Japanese diplomat provided the excuse in 1910 for Japan's annexation of Korea. As soon as the First World War broke out, Japan seized Germany's Pacific islands north of the Equator and occupied Shantung.

The confusion in China following the downfall of the Manchu dynasty in 1912 seemed to Japan an excellent opportunity for expansion. Accordingly in 1915 Japan presented Twenty-One Demands to Yuan Shih-kai, the President of the new Chinese Republic. The demands not only asked for the transfer of German rights in Shantung to Japan and the extension of Japanese privileges in Manchuria, but also required the Chinese government to employ Japanese advisers. This strong-arm diplomacy aroused the hostility of both China and the European Powers who had interests in the Far East. However, none was in a position to resist, and, although the harsher points were omitted, later in 1915 the Chinese agreed to the Japanese demands.

Domestic affairs

Japanese successes abroad were accompanied by continuing modernisation at home. Industry expanded rapidly. Raw materials and food had to be imported in large quantities, and this produced an unfavourable balance of trade before 1914. When the World War broke out, however, ships and munitions were wanted by Western Europe, and Japan supplied the markets in Asia previously the province of Britain, France and Germany. This trade boom resulted not only in a favourable trade balance, but also in a sharp rise in the cost of living which was exploited by war profiteers.

In addition to her imperial and economic progress, Japan began to look like European countries in other ways. If the rickshaws had been missing, Tokyo would have resembled most western cities. Tourist hotels, visiting cards, cigarettes, western hairstyles, these and a great variety of other European innovations were becoming common.

Politically there were two developments of future importance, although few at the time realised their potential significance. The first was a decision in 1900 that only a serving general and admiral could be minister of War and the Navy respectively. The threat of resignation gave the armed forces great control over the cabinet. The second point was connected with this: no strong political parties developed, and governments, which were subjected to strong pressures from various influences, especially the army, were short-lived.

1918 to 1931
Domestic affairs

Economic depression, political weakness and the growth of Fascism in the army are the three important features of Japanese domestic history during this period. The boom conditions of wartime continued until 1921, although most sections of the community suffered from inflation, especially the rise in the price of rice. In 1921, however, the economic depression began. This was accompanied by a fall in silk and rice prices which benefited the town but hit the country workers. Left-wing movements, although strongly opposed by the government, made headway. 'Big Business' was very unpopular, especially after a banking crisis in 1927 led to the liquidation of many small firms.

But the real crisis came in 1930, and was the result of the worldwide economic depression which had such dire effects in Germany. Foreign countries increased tariffs to exclude Japanese goods. To make matters worse, a bumper rice harvest led to a fall in price which resulted in poverty in the countryside.

It was unfortunate that these economic troubles coincided with a time of political weakness. In 1921, the Prime Minister, an able politician who had built up his party to a strong position, was assassinated. Two elder statesmen, Okuma and Yamagata, died in the following year. Their successors, with the possible exception of Kato, did not have the same ability. Kato was Prime Minister from 1924 until his death two years later. During his premiership government was both strong (for example, he reduced the size of the army) and apparently liberal: male suffrage was granted to all over twenty-five, thus increasing the electorate from 3 to 13 million. But in general Japanese political life deteriorated. No strong leader emerged and parties were small, disunited, destructive in their criticism of the government and disorderly in their day-to-day conduct of parliamentary affairs. There was corruption on a large scale, and big middle-class capitalists were very influential.

The economic and political weakness combined with various social developments[1] to produce the seeds of Fascism. Fascist ideas were popular amongst junior army officers, most of whom were lower middle-class in origin. During the 1920s secret societies of junior officers were formed. These men were not precise in their objectives, but in general they wished to crush the power and influence of political parties and big business, and to establish 'state socialism administered by military dictatorship'.[2] A military government would create a strong and purposeful Japan, anti-foreign in its attitudes and following a policy of expansion abroad.[3] Many conservative elements in Japan found these ideas attractive.

Foreign affairs

Japan's policy of expansion on the mainland of Asia seemed to be helped by the Communist Revolution in Russia in 1917. The European Allied governments wanted Japan to assist primarily in the crushing of the Russian Communists, and secondly in the rescue of some Czech troops along the Trans-Siberian Railway. Accordingly, in 1918, Japanese troops were sent to Siberia and remained there until 1922. They achieved their secondary purpose, but made no impression on the power of the Russian Communists.

Since Japan had taken part in the First World War, although in a minor capacity, she was invited to the Conference at Paris in 1919. Two developments were of importance to her. Firstly, although Japan was given a permanent seat on the Council of the League of Nations, she failed to get a declaration on the principle of racial equality inserted into the Covenant of the League. This was the result of Australian and American pressure, and it hurt Japanese pride. Secondly, Japan received the mandate for the former German islands in the Pacific, and was also given the German rights in Shantung. The Americans, who both preached self-determination and regarded themselves as the protectors of the Chinese, agreed very reluctantly to this point about Shantung. Consequently relations between the United States and Japan deteriorated.

A further cause of tension between the two powers was naval building, and this was the subject of the Washington Conference between Great Britain, the United States and Japan in 1921. At this conference two naval agreements were made. Firstly, the ratio between the tonnage

[1] For example, the popularity of modern western fashions and ideas amongst the *mogas* and *mobas* (modern girls and modern boys).

[2] R. Storry, *History of Modern Japan*.

[3] Many of these ideas were contained in a book published by Kita Ikki just after the First World War.

of capital ships of Britain, United States and Japan should be 5:5:3 respectively. Secondly, with the exception of Hawaii and Singapore, naval bases and fortifications in the Pacific area should not be extended. This meant that Japan would have naval control of the Chinese coast. In addition to the naval agreements, two other decisions were taken at the Washington Conference. Firstly, the Anglo-Japanese Alliance of 1902 was terminated, and was replaced by a Four Power Treaty (Britain, United States, Japan, France) providing for mutual consultation. This was a much weaker agreement than the one it replaced, and British influence on Japanese policy was consequently reduced. Secondly, the Japanese agreed to withdraw from Shantung. This improved her relations with both China and the United States.[1]

Japan's aggressive policy towards China had been greatly helped during the period after 1894 by Chinese weakness and disunity. About 1928, however, it appeared that Chiang Kai-shek was going to end this situation and establish strong government. Many Japanese army officers believed that China must be exploited while the opportunity lasted. In 1928, therefore, the Chinese war lord of Manchuria was assassinated by Japanese officers at Mukden. If the officers had been united this should have been followed by a military *coup d'état*, but nothing was attempted. It was significant for the future that the General Staff opposed the disciplinary action against those concerned which the Emperor and Prime Minister wanted. The demand that the government should take strong action in Manchuria continued to grow. Late in 1930 the Prime Minister was shot and wounded, and in March 1931 a second military *coup d'état* was planned, this time for Tokyo, but was not carried out. On this occasion senior officers were implicated. Six months later the army effectively showed its independence of civil control.

1931 to 1937

This period, which marks the growing independence of the army from civilian control, began in September 1931 with the Mukden coup. Since 1928 the Kuomintang had increased its nationalist propaganda in Manchuria, and the Japanese army felt that Japan's economic and political position there was threatened. During the summer of 1931 junior officers, with the possible connivance of their seniors, drew up a plan for the military occupation of Mukden and other towns. Early in September the Japanese government heard of the plot, but its protests

[1] Relations worsened in 1924, when the American government stopped Asian immigration into the United States.

arrived too late. For in mid-September, on the pretext that the Chinese were sabotaging the Japanese-owned South Manchurian railway, Japanese troops suddenly attacked Chinese troops near Mukden. Although the Japanese government attempted to limit the fighting, the army insisted that military necessity forced it to extend control, so that by the end of the year the whole of Manchuria was in Japanese hands.

Early in 1932 there was fighting in Shanghai, together with a naval bombardment of Nanking. In February Manchuria was renamed Manchukuo, and the Japanese made the ex-Emperor of China its puppet ruler. In the following year the Commission (see p. 533) appointed by the League of Nations condemned Japanese aggression and refused to recognise Manchukuo. Thereupon Japan withdrew from the League, while the army continued its expansion south of Manchuria. In May a truce was signed with the Kuomintang government, and a large demilitarised zone was created between Peking and Manchuria.

To most foreign observers at this time, it seemed that the Japanese government was being thoroughly two-faced, on the one hand protesting that Japan had no imperial ambitions and was only conducting a limited war of self-defence, while on the other hand allowing and encouraging aggressive militarism. It is now clear, however, that responsible civilian members of the government were unable to exercise control over the army. Emotional nationalism was growing rapidly which made any attempt to oppose military action appear unpatriotic. In 1932 the Prime Minister was assassinated by ultra-nationalists, and this was by no means the only murder at this time. Most politicians felt that any attempt to discipline the army would result in military revolution and civil war. No leader had the personality and determination to risk this possible outcome.

In February 1936 the radical element in the army attempted a military *coup d'état*. About 1,500 officers and men murdered members of the government and gained control of the centre of Tokyo. The Emperor, however, with the support of the more conservative section of the army, took strong action, and the mutiny was crushed after four days, and its leaders executed. But thereafter, despite popular revulsion against the army, civilian government was controlled by the right-wing nationalist officers in the armed services. No cabinet could be formed without a Minister of War, and the army said who this was to be.

Meanwhile the army had failed to respect the truce formed with the Kuomintang in 1933, and had continued to infiltrate the provinces of north China. By the beginning of 1937, however, following the Sian agreement (see p. 434), Chiang Kai-shek was adopting a tougher attitude towards the Japanese. In view of this, and believing that a strong foreign policy could ease political tensions at home, Japan began to make big preparations for war. The large-scale fighting which began in China in the summer of 1937 was eventually to lead, via Pearl Harbour, to the atomic holocaust of Hiroshima and Nagasaki.

1937 to 1945

War against China 1937 to 1941

In July 1937 there was a clash between some Japanese and Chinese troops near Peking. The fighting soon spread, and by the end of August Peking and Tientsin were occupied. The Prime Minister, Prince Konoye, wished to limit the fighting, but the Minister of War insisted on reinforcements. By the end of the year the north-east of China was in Japanese hands. Following the capture of Nanking in December 1937 military discipline broke down and terrible atrocities were committed by Japanese troops. This, together with an attack on a United States ship in the Yangtze River, removed all remaining American goodwill towards Japan.

The war continued during 1938. In the autumn Hankow and Canton were captured. From the end of 1938 until 1945 the Japanese controlled the main cities and communications of eastern China, but their hold on the countryside remained weak. Chiang Kai-shek refused to surrender and his capital was moved to Chungking. Thereafter, large-scale fighting in China ceased.

Meanwhile the Japanese government extended its control at home. State control of fuel distribution, civil airlines, labour movement, and prices was accompanied by strict censorship of the press, radio and books. Political parties were ended and Prince Konoye organised a national party. A totalitarian state made any expression of discontent or opposition dangerous.

With a virtually Fascist government now in power in Japan, it was likely that closer relations with Italy and Germany would follow. In 1936 the Anti-Comintern Pact was signed with Germany, and during the summer of 1939 there was fighting against the Russians on the border between Manchukuo and Outer Mongolia. Somewhat cooler relations with Germany followed the signing of the Nazi-Soviet Pact in August 1939, and Japan adopted a policy of neutrality when war broke out in Europe. Following the fall of France, however, it seemed that

Germany and Italy were in complete control of Europe, and Japan deemed it wiser to ally with the stronger side. Therefore, in September 1940 the Tripartite Axis Pact was signed.

Now Japan felt herself politically and militarily in a very strong position. The rapid conquest of eastern China showed the strength of her armies. She was allied to the country dominating Europe. In South-East Asia the colonial territories of France, Britain and Holland seemed almost defenceless. This seemed an excellent opportunity for Japan to occupy these territories, secure the grateful support of the native populations freed from their European rulers, and establish an empire looking to Japan as its head. In addition there was the economic motive. Japan depended on imports of certain vital raw materials—oil, rubber, bauxite, tin—from South-East Asia. The creation of a huge area controlled politically and economically by Japan would solve many economic problems.

Clearly any Japanese military move south of China would be opposed by the European colonial powers, but more important to Japan was the opposition of the United States, the only power which could effectively prevent Japanese expansion. During the autumn of 1941 there were talks between the United States and Japan in Washington on the question of the Japanese in China. Deadlock was reached, and those in control in Japan decided that if their plans in South-East Asia were to be realised, the United States must be opposed by force. Since the American Pacific Fleet was concentrated at Hawaii, an attack on it would cripple the United States for a sufficiently long period for Japanese plans to be carried out. Therefore in December 1941, Japanese carrier-based planes attacked and virtually destroyed the American fleet in Pearl Harbour. The Pacific War had begun.

The Pacific War 1941 to 1945

Simultaneously with the sudden attack on Pearl Harbour, the Japanese struck at the Philippines, Hong Kong and Singapore. During the first few months of 1942, South-East Asia was overrun. Fine soldiers, combined with air and sea superiority, carried all before them.

In the summer of 1942, however, the first setbacks were experienced. Two inconclusive naval battles were fought, in the Coral Sea and near Midway Island. These marked the turning point in the war. The Australians stopped the Japanese advance in New Guinea, and the Americans gradually recaptured small islands in the Pacific. The Japanese soon lost the support of the native populations (see chapter 12), who found that much harsher Asian imperialists had replaced the Europeans.

After the Casablanca Conference in January 1943, the Allies agreed to devote more resources to the war against Japan. During 1944 the Japanese were gradually pushed back. The British advanced in Assam and Burma, and in October the Americans under MacArthur landed in the Philippines. Japanese naval power was destroyed in the Battle of Leyte Gulf. During the last twelve months of the war, massive air attacks devastated the big cities of Japan. Despite the fanatical fighting of the Japanese forces[1] it was clear that eventual defeat was now almost certain.

Towards the end of July 1945, with the end of fighting in Europe and the invasion of Japan itself now probable, the Potsdam Declaration called on Japan to surrender unconditionally. The Japanese made no response. Since the Japanese still had large land forces, it was likely that an invasion and the continuation of the war by conventional methods would be very costly. In order, therefore, to bring the war to a quick end, the Allies took the momentous decision to use nuclear weapons. On 6 August 1945 an atomic bomb was dropped on Hiroshima, completely destroying the whole city.[2] Although over 160,000 people were killed or seriously wounded, the Japanese Supreme Command remained unwilling to surrender unconditionally. However, the Russian attack on Japan, together with the dropping of the second atomic bomb on Nagasaki, made it quite apparent that Japan could not continue. On 15 August Emperor Hirohito said that Japan must 'endure the unendurable', and called upon the armed forces to surrender.[3]

Occupation 1945 to 1952

Japan formally surrendered in September 1945 to General MacArthur, Supreme Commander for the Allied Powers (SCAP), on the deck of the battleship *Missouri*. From this point until April 1952 the country was occupied, theoretically by the Allied Powers who had defeated her, in practice by the Americans only. For all but the last year of this period MacArthur was in charge of the occupation.[4] A self-confident soldier, MacArthur ruled efficiently and humanely.[5]

---

[1] For example, the suicide pilots, the Kamikaze.

[2] In this connection two books by Robert Jungk, a journalist, should be read. One, *Brighter than a Thousand Suns*, is an absorbing account of nuclear scientists. The other, *Children of the Ashes*, gives a graphic description of survivors of Hiroshima.

[3] The reason given was a slight understatement: 'the war situation has developed not necessarily to Japan's advantage'.

[4] He was dismissed by President Truman during the Korean War. (See p. 182).

[5] MacArthur was rather aloof and never toured Japan. 'The irreverent were heard to

Hiroshima, 1945

Young women assembling radios for Sony, Japan, during the 1970s

The first 2½ years of the occupation were devoted to the demilitarisation and political reconstruction of Japan. All military installations were destroyed and the Japanese armed services demobilised. War criminals were tried, and seven were executed. In addition about 900 minor war criminals were executed in South-East Asia. During 1946 a series of purges removed from positions of responsibility all who were believed to have supported Japan's militarist policies.

There then followed various measures to liberalise Japan's political life. Legislation allowed trade unions to be formed, and they were given the right to strike. Political prisoners were freed, and a new Japanese Communist Party was formed which attracted 3 million votes in 1949. The educational system was decentralised and reorganised on American lines. The semidivine position of the Emperor was ended.[1]

In October 1946 a new Constitution was promulgated. This provided for a Legislature of two houses. The House of Councillors is elected for six years, half of its membership being elected every three years. A general election is held every four years for the House of Representatives, and the members of the cabinet are responsible to this body. Sovereignty is formally vested in the people, not the Emperor. Article 9 of the constitution says that Japan should not have any armed forces.

From 1948 onwards the international situation led to a change in American policy. The emphasis was now on the creation of a strong Japan that would oppose Communism in Russia and China. The economic recovery of Japan had been slow because of war damage, loss of markets and shortages of raw materials. The United States now provided large quantities of aid and new plant. The big economic units were kept together, the power to strike was limited and Communists were purged. The outbreak of the Korean War in 1950 stimulated industry. Much less popular in a now strongly pacifist Japan was the decision in 1950 to create a National Police Reserve of 70,000 men. This was soon enlarged, and it seemed to Japanese, especially the Socialists, to be in blatant disregard of Article 9 of the constitution.

It was intended that the occupation should end much earlier than it did, but disagreement between Russia and the West prevented a settlement. In September, 1951, however, the Japanese Peace Treaty was signed in San Francisco. By this treaty, which Russia refused to sign, Japan renounced all her acquisitions of the previous ninety years. On

say that if a man rose early in the morning and was very lucky he might catch a glimpse of the Supreme Commander walking on the waters of the palace moat.' R. Storry, *History of Modern Japan.*

[1] Throughout the period described in this chapter, the Emperor, although theoretically possessing great power, in practice always acted on the advice of the Cabinet or armed services.

the same day at San Francisco the United States and Japan signed a Security Pact by which American forces were to remain in Japan for defence purposes. The Peace Treaty came into force in April 1952, and the occupation was officially at an end.

1952 to mid-1970s

Throughout the period since 1945 the conservatives have dominated Japanese politics. During the 1950s they never had less than 65 per cent of the seats in the House of Representatives. This is partly to be explained by MacArthur's land reform which created a large number of peasant land owners who tended to be conservative, and partly by the extremism of the Socialists. The first day after the occupation ended was marked by fighting between left-wing demonstrators and police, and there was serious rioting in 1960.

Japan wished to follow an independent and neutral policy in world affairs. Despite the government's dislike of Communism, it wished for economic as well as political reasons to improve relations with Russia and China. In South-East Asia the government genuinely wished to build up an image of a new peace-loving, democratic Japan. In 1955 Japan took part in the Bandung Conference. For these reasons the Security Pact with the United States was not very popular, especially with the left wing. American soldiers remained in large numbers in Japan, and the country still seemed to be occupied. In 1954 the Bikini Incident aroused intense feeling. The Americans tested a hydrogen bomb on Bikini Atoll in the Pacific and part of the fallout contaminated a Japanese fishing ship and its catch, causing radiation sickness amongst the crew.

In 1960 the anti-American feeling reached a climax. Agreement on a revision of the Security Pact was reached in January, but was strongly opposed by the Socialists. During May there were mass demonstrations by students outside Parliament, and in the following month a visit by President Eisenhower had to be postponed because of the disorders. Nevertheless, although the Prime Minister, Kishi, resigned, the conservatives again had a large majority in the next general election. For the next four years Ikeda was Prime Minister. The left wing was pacified, and economic growth became the uncontroversial goal of policy.

From 1964 to 1972 Sato, the younger brother of Kishi, was Prime Minister. A conservative bureaucrat and a shrewd politician, the eight years of his government was a period of political stability and unprecedented economic growth. The Liberal Democratic Party, supported by big business and the rural vote, remained unchallenged. One writer has said that the economic performance of Japan at this time has made the so-called German economic miracle look almost dilettante. By 1968 Japan's Gross National Product was the third highest in the world, the annual growth rate was very high, and there were big trade surpluses. Car manufacturing, shipbuilding, textiles, radio and TV were the main industries. The reasons for this economic success were many: hard work and, for a time, wages lower than those in the West; research and heavy investment resulting in a very advanced technology; protectionism; all stages of manufacture being together in one plant, with a single trade union per plant; few overseas responsibilities and relatively small social service expenses, thus enabling money to be spent on the domestic economy. Expo 70, a big trade fair, was visited by 64 million people, and seemed a tangible symbol of Japan's economic achievements.

Sato's policies were based on close economic and political links with the United States. Politically the factor which attracted most attention was the island of Okinawa which was under US administration and where there was a huge American military base. There was strong emotional support for the return of the island to Japan and the removal of nuclear weapons from Japanese soil. Left-wing students demonstrated, and there were serious anti-American riots in 1968 and 1969. In November 1969 Sato visited Washington, and it was announced that in 1972 Okinawa would revert to Japan.

Throughout the period there were demands for a more active foreign policy. The conservatives were content to cooperate with the United States; the radicals wanted a neutral approach and improved relations with China. In 1971 two events disturbed Japan's reliance on the United States: President Nixon imposed a 10 per cent surcharge on Japanese imports in order to improve America's trade balance, and later in the year announced that he was going to visit Peking.

During the first half of the 1970s this sense of uncertainty in foreign affairs was extended to political, economic and social matters. The Liberal Democratic Party continued to rule. There were two Prime Ministers after 1972, Tanaka and Miki, but in the General Election held at the end of 1976, the party for the first time lost its outright majority over all other parties. It was internally divided, and had lost popularity because it was associated in the public's mind with the policy of economic growth at all costs. There was an extensive national debate on the issue of whether to go all out for high economic growth or establish a genuine welfare state. Increasingly, it was accepted that growth must slow down and investment be directed away from productive industry to social provision and environmental control. The standard of living of the rapidly growing population had risen in consequence of economic prosperity, but there was increasing criticism of materialism. At the same time, the 1973 Arab oil embargo and other factors resulted in high inflation. Japan was dependent on the Arabs for 85 per cent of its oil supplies, and this was a disturbing reminder of her dependence on the outside world for supplies of raw materials.

Thus there was an increasing feeling of uncertainty and isolation. In most outward respects Japan is part of the western world—in its system of government, economic organisation, finance and trade, ways of life—yet by virtue of its geography, history and culture, it is not western. 'Japan is a remote country psychologically from Asia and geographically from the West'.[1]

[1] M. Kosaka, in an article on Japan in *The Times Supplement*, 24 Sept. 1969.

12

South-East Asia

Beginning of the Twentieth Century

The term 'South-East Asia' has only been used since the Second World War. It describes the area covered (in 1900) by the Dutch East Indies, Malaya, Siam, Burma, French Indo-China and the Philippines. Although this area is a fairly distinct geographical unit, there are many different races, languages and cultures, and the inhabitants have never thought of themselves as South-East Asians. With the exception of Siam, which remained independent, and the Philippines, which was a recently acquired colony of the United States, the area was divided between the Dutch, the British and the French.

East Indies

The Dutch had occupied Java and Sumatra since about 1640, but it was not until the second half of the nineteenth century that they conquered the outer islands of the East Indies. While engaged in doing this, the Dutch encountered strong opposition from fanatical Muslims in western Sumatra who were not finally crushed until 1908. By that time the East Indies were united under the Dutch, with the exception of the British possessions of North Borneo, Brunei and Sarawak, and the Australian occupation of half of New Guinea. Their administration was efficient, but in 1900 hardly extended beyond the towns.

In Holland, as in Britain in about 1900, the belief grew that the European colonising Power should rule for the benefit of the native population. In Britain this idea was summed up in Kipling's phrase, the 'White Man's Burden'. The Dutch during the nineteenth century had been mainly interested in economic, not political, control, and had exploited Indonesia very successfully. But at the beginning of the twentieth century the Dutch followed what they called their 'ethical policy', and rather more emphasis was put on the social and economic advance of the subject people. Most Indonesians were fishermen or small peasants, and many worked on European sugar, tobacco, tea and coffee plantations. Heavy investment in these plantations and other concerns, the discovery of oil in about 1900, and the big expansion of exports and imports, all made Indonesia (as this area was later to be known) a valuable colony for the Dutch.

Malaya

At the southern tip of the mainland of South-East Asia was the British possession of Malaya. As with the Dutch, the British interest was originally economic. The East India Company first acquired the island of Penang at the end of the eighteenth century. By 1826 Singapore and Malacca had been linked with Penang to form the Straits Settlements, which was later given Crown Colony status. Between 1874 and 1895 there was civil war between the remaining five Malay states. This hampered economic development by the British, who also feared intervention by other European Powers. Therefore, the British government increased its influence by signing agreements with each of the Sultans. British residents or advisers were appointed to the courts of the Sultans who acted in accordance with the advice received. In 1896 four of the states—Perak, Selangor, Negri Sembilan and Pahang—were formed into the Federated Malay States. This was, in fact, less a federation than a union necessary to coordinate administration.

Thus, in 1900 there were three political entities in Malaya: the Straits Settlements, the four Federated Malay States, and Johore. The population was about 2 million, of whom half were Malay and most of the remainder Chinese. The aristocracy of the states, the small rice farmers and the fishermen were Malays. Most of the merchants, planters and workers in the ports and big plantations were Chinese. The comparative size and wealth of these two groups was to be very important in the future.

Economically Malaya was a prosperous area. Apart from the sugar and coffee plantations, half the world's tin was mined here. In 1900 the rubber industry was in its infancy. It was in 1876 that an English botanist, having obtained seeds of the rubber tree in Brazil, cultivated about 3,000 trees in Kew Gardens in London. Some of these trees were eventually brought to Malaya, and early in the twentieth century the first Malayan rubber was produced.

Indo-China

The relatively easy British occupation of Malaya and Burma was in marked contrast to the French conquest of Indo-China. This took place between 1858 and the end of the century. In 1887 the Indo-Chinese Union consisting of Annam, Tongking, Cambodia and Cochin-China was formed under French control. Six years later Laos was added. Cochin-China was a French colony. The remaining four states of Indo-China were protectorates; thus the local rulers remained, but they governed under the instructions of French Residents. The capital of the French government and civil service was Hanoi, not very far from the Chinese frontier. But discontent with French rule showed itself from the very beginning, and when the twentieth century opened there were constant threats of rebellion.

Nevertheless the economic development of Indo-China was rapid. Most of the population lived along the coast or in the deltas of the Red and Mekong Rivers. In these areas communications were extended, and agriculture began to prosper. Rice, rubber and wheat were the main exports, but there was industrial potential in the north and some coal went overseas. One area, Laos, remained undeveloped and, indeed, almost unexplored.

1900 to 1942

Foreign imperialism was mainly responsible for the creation and development of nationalism. Roads and railways, centralised governments and administrations, western education and ideas, all helped to foster opposition to foreign rule.

East Indies

In the East Indies Dutch rule was highly paternalistic.[1] In 1903 a Decentralisation Law was passed, by which powers were delegated from Holland to the government in Batavia, and from Batavia to the local areas. In the following year local councils were started. Little was done to implement this law, and Indonesians played virtually no part in the government. Consequently in 1908 the first nationalist organisation was founded. This was called Budi Utomo or High Endeavour. It was a cultural body, consisting mainly of civil servants and students from Java, and wanting both better education and a bigger part for Indonesians in the government. But the Budi Utomo was of short-lived importance and was never a mass movement.

Four years later, however, the Sarekat Islam or Muslim Union was founded. This was originally a Muslim and Indonesian organisation formed to fight against the economic power of the Chinese. But it

[1] Some Dutch critics said that if a native wished to scratch his head, he had first to get a Dutch official's permission, and then get another Dutch official to show him how to do it. V. Purcell, *Revolution in South-East Asia*.

gradually became a socialist and nationalist body which in 1916 passed a resolution demanding self-government. Its membership then was 350,000; by 1918 this had risen to 2½ million, many of whom were Communist sympathisers. Encouraged by the events of 1917 in Russia, the Communists within Sarekat Islam attempted to gain control of the movement. In this, however, they failed, and in 1919 left to form the Indonesian Communist Party.

During the First World War Holland was neutral and therefore the East Indies was not disturbed. Indeed the increased demand for goods benefited the colony. In view of the growing nationalist agitation, however, the Dutch government decided in 1917 to create a People's Parliament. This continued to function until 1942, but it had very little power. Until 1927 its purpose was purely advisory. After that date the membership increased and it had an elected majority, a third of whom were Indonesians. But, although the parliament could influence policy, the governor-general and his ministers were not responsible to it.

During the 1920s the Communists and Sarekat Islam were rivals for the leadership of the nationalist movement. In general the Communists were more successful because the more moderate Sarekat Islam concentrated on education and economic and local government reforms and so lost the support of the extreme nationalists. The Communists promoted strikes, especially in the towns, and in 1926–27 began a rebellion in western Java and Sumatra. This was quickly crushed; thousands were arrested and imprisoned; the Communist Party was declared illegal and the party temporarily declined.

In 1927 a third party was formed. A young engineer named Sukarno organised the Indonesian Nationalist Party. It was supported by the small westernised and secular middle class, and by 1929 had 10,000 members. But in that year the police raided the headquarters of the party; Sukarno was arrested and imprisoned, and in 1931 the party was dissolved.

During the 1930s government repression and press censorship checked nationalism. Sukarno, Hatta, Sjahrir and other nationalist leaders, after a short period of freedom, were imprisoned until 1942. And despite the economic depression, resulting in unemployment, reduced wages and increased agitation, political parties remained divided and weak.

Malaya

Compared with the other countries of South-East Asia, nationalism in Malaya was almost non-existent until 1945. There are a number of possible reasons for this. The population was quite small and was divided into three different races, Malay, Chinese and Indian. These tended to oppose each other rather than unite against the British. Also, apart from the Straits Settlements, the British were not the direct rulers of the Malay States. The division of the country into small states hindered the creation of national feeling, and the relatively high standard of living, combined with the fact that Malays could reach high positions in government service, discouraged the formation of political parties. Therefore, apart from the development of Communism amongst the Chinese and a few strikes in the late 1930s, Malaya remained quiet and peaceful.

In 1909, by treaty with Siam, the four Malay states of Perlis, Kedah, Kelantan and Trengganu, were separated from Siam and brought under British protection. These four, like Johore, remained unfederated. In the same year a Federal Council for the Federated States was created. This consisted of the four Sultans and Residents and four unofficial members.

This system of indirect rule worked smoothly and allowed Malaya to develop economically. Singapore, a focal point of trade routes, became one of the world's great harbours. The rubber and tin industries were the basis of Malaya's prosperity. In 1905 200 tons of rubber were produced and the industry first became profitable. During the next fifteen years the demand for rubber increased enormously; investment kept pace with this demand, and in 1920 200,000 tons of rubber, half the world's supply, was exported. During the next twenty years, however, the economic depression in the world's major industrial countries, reduced the demand for rubber, and prices fell. The tin industry, likewise, had expanded, and, especially during the great depression of 1929–33, suffered from over-production. Both industries, therefore, voluntarily restricted output in order to raise prices.

Despite these economic difficulties, the standard of living was high compared with the rest of Asia. This attracted Chinese and Indian immigrants in such large numbers that by 1941 the Chinese were in a slight majority, for while Malays predominated on the mainland, three-quarters of the large population of Singapore were Chinese. Because of Malay fears, a quota on Chinese male immigration was imposed from 1930. Women continued to arrive, however, and the Chinese immigrants, instead of remaining for a few years only, now began permanent settlement.

Indo-China, Malaya and Indonesia

Indo-China

Discontent with foreign rule had shown itself in Indo-China from the beginning of the French occupation. During the first twenty years of the twentieth century, various factors stimulated the discontent. In 1905 Japan, an Asiatic power, had secured a crushing victory over Russia; in 1912 the Manchu dynasty was finally ended by the Chinese Nationalists. And while the Indo-Chinese objected to the imposition of the French language and culture, they learned from this culture useful ideas from France's own revolutionary past. During the First World War, about 100,000 Indo-Chinese fought in France, and returned with first-hand knowledge of what they regarded as a European civil war in which the French had suffered greatly. Communism, too, was spreading from China, and many believed that the considerable wealth of Indo-China was largely benefiting the colonial power.

The growing nationalism led to occasional violent outbursts. In 1916 there was a major revolt which was crushed with great severity. Guerrilla activity in Tongking was always troublesome. But the most serious rising against the French came in 1930, and the man largely responsible for this was Ho Chi Minh. Ho was born in Tongking in 1890, his father being a minor and often drunken official who joined the rebel movement. When Ho was twenty-one years old, he came to Europe, serving as a galleyhand on a French steamship. After working for six years as a cook in a London hotel, he went to Paris where he soon became known as a Vietnamese nationalist, lobbying the Paris Peace Conference to grant independence to Vietnam, contributing articles for newspapers, and writing the pamphlet *French Colonialism on Trial*. In 1921 Ho was a founder-member of the French Communist Party, and two years later he went to Moscow to learn both the Russian language and revolutionary techniques. Early in 1925 he joined Borodin in Canton (see p. 429) as an interpreter. While in Canton Ho founded the Revolutionary Youth Movement, an organisation for the training and indoctrination of Vietnamese nationalists. In April 1927, following the Kuomintang-Communist split, Ho returned to Moscow, but eventually moved to Siam. Early in 1930 in Hong Kong, Ho Chi Minh united the Revolutionary Youth Movement with two other groups to form the Indo-Chinese Communist Party.

Meanwhile the Vietnam Nationalist Party, similar to the Kuomintang in that it attracted mainly the wealthy and middle class sections of the population, had been founded. In 1929 there was an attempt to assassinate the French Governor-General, and in February 1930, at Yen Bay, a fortress on the Red River north of Hanoi, the Vietnamese soldiers mutinied, killing their French officers. This was followed by a large-scale peasant revolt led by the Communists. Several soviets were set up in Annam. But the French were at this point too strong. The revolt was crushed in the so-called 'White Terror', and thousands of rebels were killed.

During the next ten years Indo-China was relatively peaceful. But in 1940 the French colonial administration was clearly weakened by the defeat of France by Germany. This weakness, together with the Fascist tendencies of the Vichy regime, accounted for the decision in 1941 to allow the Japanese to build three airfields in Tongking.

Japanese Occupation 1942 to 1945

The Japanese occupation of the countries of South-East Asia was completed by May 1942. The ease and rapidity with which this conquest was achieved surprised both the colonial powers and the native peoples. The former had tended to underestimate the strength and mobility of the Japanese forces and had inadequately prepared for the attack, whilst the latter had considered that their colonial rulers were stronger than was actually the case.

There was no French opposition to the Japanese occupation of Indo-China; in fact, French soldiers, officials and civilians remained free and continued to administer the country. Similarly in Thailand (as Siam was called after 1939) Pibul Songgram put up only token resistance in order to save his country from devastation. British naval and military resistance was soon crushed by the Japanese, and Singapore was captured in February 1942. In the following month came the surrender of the Dutch who had obviously been weakened by the German occupation of Holland nearly two years earlier. Opposition by the British in Burma and the Americans in the Philippines had been finally crushed by May. Thus, early in 1942, the Western colonial empires, built up steadily over the previous century, were devastatingly destroyed in the short space of six months. Their prestige never recovered from this blow, more particularly since it was followed by intense anti-western propaganda.

With the exception of Malaya, which was ruled as a colony, the Japanese formed governments in the occupied countries that were willing to collaborate with them. In all six countries, however, there were resistance movements which gradually gained in strength as the Japanese weakened towards the end of the war.

Malaya, especially, was exploited economically. Labour was conscripted for working the ports and military installations, the export of rubber and tin declined, food imports were much reduced and the standard of living fell rapidly. Meanwhile, about six or seven thousand Chinese Communists fled to the jungle and hills, where, helped by military aid from the British, they provided the nucleus of guerrilla resistance to the Japanese.

When the Dutch surrendered in the East Indies, the attitude of the Indonesians was divided. Some opposed the Japanese and formed secret resistance organisations. Some, however, led by Sukarno and Hatta, believed that the best method of achieving independence would be to support the Japanese. In March 1943 the latter group was allowed by the Japanese to form the People's Strength Concentration, an all-inclusive nationalist organisation. In addition, a defence force with Indonesian officers was created. In the last few days of the war the Japanese decided to follow in the East Indies the policy already adopted in Burma, the Philippines and Indo-China. Accordingly, they negotiated the terms of independence with the Indonesian leaders who on 16 August 1945 declared that Indonesia was an independent state.

The situation in Indo-China was similar to that in other South-East Asian countries with the important exception that the collaborating government was that of the colonial power, the French. This position continued until March 1945 when the Japanese interned the French and declared Vietnam independent, with the emperor of Annam, Bao Dai, as the new head of state. But this move came too late, both for the French and the Japanese, for by 1945 popular support had been given to the Viet Minh. Four years earlier this organisation, otherwise known as the Independence League of Vietnam, was founded in South China. It was led by Ho Chi Minh, and received support from a wide variety of people, from businessmen to peasants. A few months after its foundation, however, Ho was arrested by the Chinese Nationalists, then more intent, so it appeared, on opposing the Communists than the Japanese. He was eventually released in 1943 and began organising his guerrilla forces which were commanded by Vo Nguyen Giap, who had earlier studied guerrilla tactics under Mao Tse-tung. These forces were moved into the mountains of Tongking in 1944, and were so successful that by August 1945, when the Japanese war ended, the Viet Minh controlled what was later to be North Vietnam.

The 3½ years of the Japanese occupation were, therefore, of the greatest importance for the nationalists of South-East Asia. The colonial powers lost a great deal of their prestige, while the national movements, again with the exception of Malaya, had secured such a powerful grip on their respective countries that the authority of Britain, France and Holland was permanently weakened.

Independence 1945 to the Present

Indonesia

In accordance with the terms of the Potsdam Conference, British troops landed in the East Indies at the end of September 1945 as a temporary army of occupation. They immediately released about 200,000 prisoners of war, mainly Dutch. At the end of the year Dutch officials arrived from Holland, and by the summer of 1946 they had reoccupied nearly all the East Indian islands except Java and Sumatra. In these two islands the newly independent Indonesian government led by President Sukarno continued to function. Although not recognised by the Dutch, it claimed to rule the whole of Indonesia—that is, the islands making up the former Dutch East Indies.

Eventually, in November 1946 the British occupying forces arranged negotiations which led to a Dutch-Indonesian Agreement. The Republic of Java and Sumatra was recognised *de facto* by the Dutch, and was to join the rest of the Indonesian islands to form a federation known as the United States of Indonesia. This federal state was to be joined to Holland by a Dutch-Indonesian Union in 1949. Following this agreement, which was ratified in the following March, the British withdrew.

But unfortunately for future Dutch-Indonesian relations, this was an agreement on paper only: neither side intended to carry it out. The Indonesian government in Java and Sumatra wished to extend its rule to all the islands, while the Dutch intended to crush this government as soon as possible. Therefore, on two occasions, the Dutch attempted what they called 'police action'. In July 1947 Dutch forces attacked Java and Sumatra, and occupied the main cities and lines of communication. This led to immediate worldwide protests, especially from Asian countries, and in August the Security Council of the United Nations demanded a ceasefire. The Dutch, therefore, signed a truce. The second occasion was in December 1948. During the previous three months the Indonesian government had been fighting a guerrilla war against the Communists. In view of this disorder, the Dutch again occupied Java and Sumatra, this time imprisoning Sukarno and Hatta. But the Indonesian army was still intact and a long guerrilla war seemed likely. However, the Security Council again demanded a ceasefire and the release of prisoners. Pressure from world opinion, led by Nehru, demanded a settlement favourable to the Indonesians, and at the end of 1949 this settlement came.

Sukarno and Hatta were released in May 1949, and between August and November a Round Table Conference met at The Hague. This conference adopted a constitution for an independent state of Indonesia, which was to include all the Dutch East Indies except West New Guinea. Indonesia was to be a federal state, partly because Holland believed that she would be more likely to retain influence in a federal than a unitary state. In accordance with the 1946 agreement, there was to be a Netherlands-Indonesian Union, both countries being under one Crown. In December 1949 Indonesia became an independent state.

The circumstances in which independence was achieved were not likely to produce good relations between Indonesia and Holland. Within a year of independence, Indonesia had changed her constitution to provide for a more powerful executive and for a unitary rather than a federal state, and in 1954 the Netherlands-Indonesian Union was dissolved. Two years later Indonesia, partly because of her economic difficulties, repudiated her debts to Holland, saying that most of these debts represented the cost of the Dutch war against Indonesia between 1946 and 1949. This was followed by the nationalisation of Dutch estates and companies, and most Dutch residents were forced to leave by 1960. Throughout this period West New Guinea (i.e. West Irian) was a source of dispute. Indonesia claimed it as a part of the East Indies, while Holland said that its population was racially different. Probably using the dispute as a means of diverting attention from internal grievances, Sukarno ordered Indonesian troops to land in the territory in 1962. Eventually Holland transferred West Irian to United Nations administration, and in May 1963 it became part of Indonesia.

One of the major difficulties facing President Sukarno was the threat that Indonesia with its 3,000 islands would disintegrate. There have been four major rebellions since independence, twice in the Moluccas, Macassar and Amboina, and twice between 1956 and 1960 in Sumatra. In 1956 a Decentralisation Law allowing for greater local autonomy was passed, but the threat remained.

The constitution of 1950 provided for democratic government. This, however, did not prove to be successful. Until 1955 the members of the provisional Parliament were appointed, and a number of small parties were formed. The 1955 elections resulted in the four main parties—the Nationalists (of 1927), the progressive Muslims (or Sarekat Islam), the orthodox Muslims and the Communists—being of roughly equal size. This meant a continuation of weak and short-lived coalition governments. The one unifying influence was President Sukarno who was becoming more and more disillusioned with the working of democracy.

During 1956–57 tension mounted between Java and the other islands, and between the right wing and the Communists. In this situation

Sukarno said that Western democracy was not suitable for Indonesia; what was required was 'democracy with leadership' or 'guided democracy'. Thereafter parliamentary government became a mere facade until in 1960 the House of Representatives was dismissed altogether. A National Front was organised consisting of a People's Consultative Congress and a Supreme Advisory Council, but decisions were made primarily by President Sukarno. These moves towards dictatorship were supported by the Nationalists and Communists, but many important groups opposed.

Apart from lack of experience and too many political parties, democracy failed because of the immense difficulties facing Indonesia. Economic problems were not least among these difficulties. Although Indonesia has a wealth of raw materials, the standard of living failed to improve, and probably declined. This was mainly because of the rapid growth of population which in 1964 was just over 100 million. Well over half of this population lived in the small island of Java which often suffered from shortage of food. Although harvests have increased by one-third since 1945, rice has to be imported, and foreign exchange reserves have dwindled. Throughout this period, too, there has been sharp inflation, which has produced widespread discontent.[1]

It is probable that one motive for Sukarno's opposition to Malaysia was to divert attention from Indonesia's internal problems (see p. 491). In 1964 Indonesia began a series of minor attacks on Borneo and the Malay coast, and in January 1965 withdrew from the United Nations because Malaysia became a member of the Security Council. This move received the full backing of Communist China, and during the next few months it seemed that Sukarno, whose health was deteriorating, was leaning more and more on the powerful Indonesian Communist Party.

In October 1965 an attempted Communist *coup* aiming at the overthrow of the government was crushed by the army. Six generals were murdered by the rebels before order was restored. The circumstances surrounding this *coup* remain obscure, but China and the Communist Party were held responsible, and during the following weeks there was violent anti-Communist rioting accompanied by mass killings. Sukarno himself said that 87,000 people were killed. The embassy and other property of China were attacked, and relations between Indonesia and China deteriorated. During the next eighteen months Sukarno's position was gradually eroded, and his policies abandoned or reversed.

---

[1] In 1966, when he was criticised for failing to stop the inflation, Sukarno offered a cabinet post to anyone who could bring down prices within three months—with the proviso that the volunteer would be imprisoned for ten years or shot if he failed.

Early in 1966 there was a long period of student rioting directed against his retention of alleged pro-Communists in his cabinet. The army under General Suharto took over effective power. The Communist Party was banned, the civil service and other organisations were purged of left-wingers, and there were widespread killings of Communists. Sukarno came under increasingly heavy pressure to resign, and finally in February 1967 he signed away all his powers.

Thereafter Sukarno lived virtually under house arrest, until his death in 1970. He was 'flamboyant, conceited, erratic, amoral, devoted to what he saw as his own supernatural qualities, a direct link with the ancient god-kings of Java'.[1] A colourful and charismatic personality, he had given Indonesia a sense of identity. He saw himself as the epitome of Asian nationalism and anti-colonialism. Unfortunately, he lacked interest and ability in economics, finance and administration, and the economic situation, following years of mismanagement, was disastrous. Inflation in 1966 was at the rate of 600 per cent, exports had fallen, and there was hardly the money to pay the interest on foreign debts. This dreadful economic position, and his sympathies with Chinese communism, led to Sukarno's fall from power.

Suharto 1967 to the present   A military junta now ruled in Indonesia, but the leading general, Suharto, was soon to acquire a pre-eminent position. From a peasant background, Suharto joined the Dutch Army in 1940 and eventually fought as a guerrilla leader against the Dutch after the war. After independence he rose in the ranks of the army, and during the last years of Sukarno commanded the Malaysian confrontation campaign. Very different from Sukarno, Suharto is calm and unassuming, diligent and hard-working, and a determined traditionalist. He has shown considerable political skill during the ten years from 1967 to 1977.

The military government has remained, but has gradually become less obvious. In 1968 a People's Congress gave Suharto full presidential powers for five years. In 1971 elections, only the second since independence, were held, and the government party gained three-quarters of the votes. In 1973 Suharto was re-elected President. Gradually, greater freedom of discussion has been allowed, and more civilians, especially economists, have been brought into the government.

The economic problems were enormous: high inflation, low production, few exports and therefore lack of foreign exchange. However, Suharto's policies have generally been successful: by 1969 the rate of inflation was reduced to 4 per cent, production has increased, revenue

[1] H. Mabbett, in an article on Indonesia in *The Times Supplement*, 17 Aug. 1971.

from oil has gone up and the balance of payments improved. In addition there have been vigorous attempts to reduce corruption in the civil service. However, the growth in population remains a major problem, Indonesia having the fifth largest population in the world (1977: 132 m.). Indonesia's relations with her neighbours, including Malaysia, have also improved. She has followed a general policy of neutrality in world affairs but, because of her hostility towards China and communism, Indonesia has tended to be friendlier towards the West.

Malaysia

The British returned to Malaya in 1945 to be faced with big problems of reconstruction. While dealing with these, the British government began planning a change in the constitution which would both help to unite the country and give more political power to the people of Malaya. In January 1946 the arrangements for a Malayan Union were announced. The nine Malay States, together with Malacca and Penang, were to be members of the union, while Singapore remained a separate Crown Colony. The Sultans remained but were to possess very little power.

But there was immediate opposition to the scheme. The Sultans, fearing possibly that they would be accused of collaboration with the Japanese, had given their consent to the plan, but now regretted having done so. The Malay population supported them, and particularly objected to the political privileges given to the Chinese and Indians. Within two months the United Malay National Organisation (UMNO), the first Malay political party, was formed. This opposition was supported by many British civil servants and MPs. The British government bent before this storm of protest and the Malayan Union was never formed. Instead the provisional government continued until February 1948 when the Federation of Malaya, a more acceptable arrangement, was formed.

The Federation was similar to the Union in that it consisted of the nine Malay States together with the two Settlements, while Singapore remained a Crown Colony. Each state and settlement had an executive and legislature, and the Sultans retained considerable powers. The Federal government likewise had an executive council and a legislature which contained an unofficial but not an elected majority. The British High Commissioner could disregard the advice of the council and could veto bills. The activities of government were divided between the centre and the states, but power was weighted in favour of the centre. The franchise, being given to all born in federal territory or who had lived there for fifteen years, benefited the Malays.

The Federation had hardly begun to function when the Communist Emergency began. The nucleus of the opposition to the British government came from the Chinese Communist guerrillas who had resisted the Japanese during the war. In the three years after the war the Communists had organised several hundred strikes, but during 1948 this industrial action was replaced by a wave of violence. Ambushing, sniping, attacks on rubber plantations and police stations led in June 1948 to a declaration of a State of Emergency. The British and Malay police and troops were hampered both by the dense jungle from which the insurgents operated and by the help with manpower and food which the scattered Chinese squatters gave to the Communists. By 1951, when the High Commissioner was ambushed and killed, there was danger of law and order breaking down completely. Three factors prevented this from happening. Firstly, beginning in 1950, the half million Chinese squatters were brought into about 500 closely guarded villages. Secondly, the High Commissioner between 1952 and 1954, General Templar, introduced strong and determined security measures[1] which gradually weakened the terrorists who never numbered more than about 5,000 at any one time. And thirdly the Malays gave little or no support to the Communists, partly because the latter were largely Chinese, and partly because the British were prepared to allow moves towards self-government.

In 1949 the Malayan Chinese Association (MCA) was formed. Four years later this Chinese party had linked up with the UMNO, led since 1951 by Tunku Abdul Rahman, to form the Alliance Party in order to press for an elected majority in the legislatures. After some opposition this was agreed to. By July 1955, when the first elections were held under the new system, the Alliance Party had been joined by the Malayan Indian Congress (MIC), and the combined party won fifty-one out of the fifty-two seats. With this decisive majority, Tunku Abdul Rahman, the Chief Minister, pressed for full independence. Early in 1956 negotiations were held in London, and in August 1957 Malaya became an independent state within the Commonwealth.

Malaya remained a Federation, with a bicameral Legislature in the centre consisting of a Senate and a House of Representatives. Elections are held every five years for the 104 seats. Since the Alliance Party won seventy-four in 1959 and eighty-nine in 1964, there has been

---

[1] For example, rewards were given for the capture of rebels. 'One case is on record where a terrorist emerged from the jungle, took a taxi to the nearest police station, and on giving himself up, successfully claimed the reward for his own apprehension.' L. A. Mills, *Malaya*.

political stability. The strong government of Tunku Abdul Rahman, who appeared as both a moderniser and a nationalist, together with the natural wealth of the country, has brought economic prosperity. Apart from Brunei, Malaya had the highest national income per head in South-East Asia. The main products remained rubber and tin, but a wide variety of other goods were exported.

Singapore, an island about the size of the Isle of Man and less than a mile from the mainland, was separated from Malaya for three reasons. Firstly, three-quarters of the population are Chinese; if Singapore was linked with Malaya, the combined Chinese population would reduce the Malays to a minority. Secondly, while Malaya maintained tariffs, Singapore wished to keep free trade in order to encourage the use of her port. And thirdly, the British wished to retain the island as a military base in the Far East. Singapore therefore followed a parallel though less smooth constitutional development to that of Malaya, and in 1959 became independent. Since then Lee Kuan Yew, a Cambridge educated lawyer and leader of the radical People's Action Party, has been Prime Minister.

Malaya and Singapore were, however, economically interdependent, and for geographical reasons it was considered that they should be linked together politically. In the same area were the three under-developed British colonies of North Borneo, Brunei and Sarawak. If these three colonies joined in a federation with Malaya and Singapore, then the latter two countries could be linked together, and the Malays could keep their majority over the Chinese. Therefore, in 1961 Malaya proposed the creation of a federation of Malaysia. Talks in London in the following year reached agreement in principle on the proposal, and a British commission of enquiry decided that the peoples of the area were in favour. A referendum in Singapore supported the plan, and pro-Malaysia parties won local elections in North Borneo and Sarawak. The Sultan of Brunei at first agreed to join the new federation, but faced with a revolt in December 1962, he later changed his mind, probably not wishing to lose his oil revenues.

But opposition came from two quarters: the Philippines, who claimed North Borneo; and, more important, Indonesia. The reasons for Indonesia's opposition to Malaysia are not yet known with certainty. Sukarno, a fervent anti-colonialist, believed that Malaysia, because of the presence of British troops and capital, was a creation of British neo-colonialism, and was not supported by the population. In addition, he probably hoped that at least North Borneo and Sara-wak, and possibly even Malaya and Singapore, would in time become part of Indonesia, since the people of Indonesia and Malaya share the same basic language and ethnic origin. This new large state, to which the Philippines might also be added eventually,[1] would form a strong unit against possible Chinese expansion. Another suggested motive is that Malaysia, like West Irian, diverted attention away from the internal difficulties of Indonesia.

In answer to Indonesia's criticisms, a United Nations Mission visited the area during 1963 and decided that the population supported the creation of the new federation. In September 1963, therefore, Malaysia came into being strengthened by a defence agreement with Britain.

The next three years were a dangerous period for the new federation. Firstly, relations between Malaya and Singapore, never very good, deteriorated. Communal rioting in the island led eventually to Singapore's secession from the federation in August 1965. Secondly, Indonesia began a policy of 'confrontation' towards Malaysia—a policy of propaganda, subversion and guerrilla attacks which stopped short of open war. Small, seaborne parties landed on the Malay coast, there was one large-scale parachute drop inland, and there were frequent incursions across the jungle frontier in Borneo. A powerful buildup of Commonwealth (mainly British) troops, warships and aircraft came to Malaysia's aid, and the UN Security Council passed a resolution (vetoed by Russia) condemning Indonesia's 'blatant and inexcusable aggression'. However, the political changes in Indonesia reduced the power of the opponents of Malaysia, and in June 1966 an agreement to end confrontation was signed in Bangkok by Indonesia and Malaysia.

Relations with the Philippines were also uneasy and deteriorated in 1968. The cause of dispute was the Philippines' claim to Sabah, formerly North Borneo. Negotiations to settle the issue failed.

The most dangerous continuing problem facing the Malayan part of the federation concerned relations between the Malays and the Chinese. The Malays were in a majority and held the leading positions in the state. The Chinese, however, were richer and economically more powerful. Realising this situation, government policy was designed deliberately to favour the Malays to raise their opportunities and therefore their standard of living to the level of the Chinese. In 1967, for example, an act made Malay the sole official national language in western Malaysia. In 1969 the first all-Malaysian general election was held in an atmosphere of mounting antipathy between the major

---

[1] A wider confederation of Indonesia, Malaysia and the Philippines—Maphilindo—has been accepted in principle by all three countries.

racial communities. After the election was over, anti-Malay processions sparked off five days of serious rioting and arson in Kuala Lumpur when 200 people, mainly Chinese, were killed. The predominantly Malay army appeared unconcerned. The government proclaimed a state of emergency and for the rest of the year ruled by decree. Since that point, the racial tension has eased.

Malaysia, like other south-east Asian countries, has had to contend with Communist insurgents. Small groups of guerrillas operated in the jungles of Sarawak and along the Thailand frontier. The general threat of Communist expansion, together with the obvious wish of Britain to accelerate its military withdrawal from the area, led to cooperation between Malaysia and her neighbours, Singapore, Thailand, the Philippines, Indonesia, Australia and New Zealand to coordinate their defence of the region.

Despite these various problems, Malaysia has continued in being. Much of the credit for its success must go to Tunku Abdul Rahman the Prime Minister from 1963 to 1970, an extrovert and man of great charm who had the trust and respect of all the different communities. He resigned in 1970 and was succeeded by Tun Abdul Razak, who had been closely involved with the government for some years. Tun Abdul Razak died in 1976.

Indo-China

Vietnam In August 1945 it was clear that the Viet Minh controlled the northern half of Vietnam. Bao Dai, the ex-Emperor of Annam, who had been made Head of State of an independent Vietnam a few months earlier by the Japanese, resigned, and when the Viet Minh formed a government led by Ho Chi Minh in Hanoi, he joined it as 'Supreme Political Adviser'. This Viet Minh government rapidly occupied the southern half of Vietnam, which was early in September declared an independent state, for the second time in the year.

In the previous July, however, the Allied Powers decided at Potsdam that the British in the south and the Chinese in the north should assume the government of Indo-China from the Japanese. Late in September, therefore, British troops arrived at Saigon to find the Viet Minh in control, although not as strongly as in the north. They immediately released the French, who soon took over the government of the country. In the north, on the other hand, the Chinese Nationalist troops, who spent a great deal of time looting, did nothing to stop the Viet Minh who rapidly consolidated their hold. By the end of 1945 People's Committees had been set up at every level, and successful reforms carried out with the support of the Roman Catholic Church. Early in 1946 the British and Chinese troops withdrew, and the French and Viet Minh confronted each other. In March the two governments made an agreement by which North Vietnam was to be a free state within an Indo-Chinese Federation. But during the summer negotiations in France on the details of the Federation broke down. The new French constitution drawn up in October included all overseas colonies in a French Union which seemed to preclude all hope of real independence. Both sides prepared for war.

The start of eight years of most bitter and costly fighting came in November 1946. Widespread incidents were followed by a French naval bombardment of Haiphong from close range in which 6,000 were killed. During most of the fighting that followed, the French were in control of the towns and main lines of communications, while the Viet Minh ruled the country areas. In 1949 the French attempted to obtain the support of the population by declaring Vietnam (with Bao Dai again Head of State), Laos and Cambodia independent within the French Union, only foreign affairs and defence remaining under French control. But this move came too late and had little effect. During 1950 the problem of Indo-China became involved in the Cold War: China, Russia and the East European countries recognised the Viet Minh government, while the Western powers recognised the new Vietnam government of Bao Dai.

Meanwhile the military situation, almost a stalemate for the first half of the war, was becoming increasingly unfavourable to the French. While the French were receiving considerable American financial aid, the Viet Minh were being helped by the new Chinese Communist government, and were able to take the offensive. In November 1953 French troops arrived by air at the mountain village of Dien Bien Phu, north of Hanoi. The struggle over this village was the climax to the final phase of the war. During the next four months the Viet Minh built up their forces around the stronghold until they were in overwhelming strength. The French defeat was inevitable, and in May 1954 resistance was ended.

In April, before the fall of Dien Bien Phu, the Geneva Conference on Korea and Indo-China had opened. It was attended by representatives of Britain, France, the United States, Russia, Communist China, the Viet Minh, Vietnam, Cambodia and Laos. Britain and Russia supplied the joint chairmen. The French military collapse contributed a sense of urgency, and the Conference reached its decisions by July 1954. Vietnam was to be an independent state temporarily divided near the 17th Parallel; the Viet Minh were to control the north and Bao Dai's

Dien Bien Phu – a French soldier killed in battle is carried away

Ho Chi Minh in 1954

President Sukarno in 1964

government the south. Within two years a general election was to be held throughout Vietnam. Cambodia and Laos were to be independent. All these states were to remain neutral in the Cold War. Finally, an International Commission consisting of Poland, Canada and India was to supervise the implementation of these decisions.

The intention that the two parts of Vietnam should unite to form one country in 1956 was not realised. After 1954 French Indo-China became four quite separate countries. North Vietnam, with a population of about 16 million mainly in the Red River delta and along the coast, became a Communist state with Ho Chi Minh as President. From this base Communist guerrillas were sent to subvert the populations of the other three, South Vietnam, Laos and Cambodia.

South Vietnam was approximately the same size in both area and population as North Vietnam. From 1954 to 1963 the country was ruled by Ngo Dinh Diem, a staunch Roman Catholic and a member of one of the great Vietnamese families. The problems facing his government were immense. In the eight years of fighting against the French, the economy had been totally disrupted and communications destroyed. When the French administrators left, there was real danger that the country would decline into utter chaos. This was prevented by the decisive action of Diem who became in effect dictator. But thereafter the government of Diem, his brother Nhu, and the latter's wife[1], became oppressive, corrupt and inefficient.

Diem, with US backing, refused to hold the elections which were intended to precede a united Vietnam. Consequently, the Vietcong (the name given to the South Vietnamese Communists) began guerrilla attacks on government officials and installations. The Vietcong received support and supplies from the north. Led by their guerrilla war expert, General Giap, the North Vietnamese sent supplies down the Ho Chi Minh Trail, a long series of paths through the jungles of eastern Laos. Communist bases were established in Laos along the 1,000 mile border with South Vietnam and in the empty jungle of north-east Cambodia. From these bases the North Vietnamese infiltrated into South Vietnam in support of the Vietcong. They were increasingly effective: by 1962 it is probable that three-quarters of the population, voluntarily or through fear, supported the Vietcong.

The South Vietnamese government tried to raise the standard of living by building roads and railways, and through agricultural reforms. Strategic hamlets were constructed to combat the Communists. These were fortified villages into which the population of the

---

[1] 'Like the rest of the family, she became drunk with power. "Power is wonderful", she used to say. "Total power is totally wonderful".' D. Warner, *The Last Confucian*—a vivid account of the war in Indo-China.

surrounding countryside was moved. It was a sound policy militarily, but very unpopular because it involved movement of population and separation of farmers from their land. The failure of Diem to provide strong and efficient government led to mounting discontent. In 1960 an attempted army *coup* failed. During 1963 tension began to rise because Buddhist monks complained of religious discrimination on the part of the Diem government.[1] This discontent finally led to an army *coup d'état* in November 1963 when Diem and Nhu were killed.

At the beginning of the Diem regime the United States hoped to establish a strong, non-Communist government in South Vietnam as a bulwark against the spread of Communism in South-East Asia. The Americans did not wish to become militarily involved in any fighting, and when the guerrilla war started they were willing to provide only help and advice to the South Vietnamese army similar to that which had been given earlier to the French. In 1955 the first US advisers arrived; there were 1,300 by 1961. By 1962, however, it was clear that Diem's government was incapable of controlling the situation, and the United States began to increase her own military strength in the area. There was a total of 16,000 US military advisers in South Vietnam by 1963.

During the first half of 1964 the American government under its new president, Lyndon Johnson, prepared secret contingency plans to increase greatly the pressure on both the Vietcong and the North Vietnamese. Johnson at this point appeared less aggressive than Goldwater, who had been his rival in the presidential election (see p. 188). In August 1964 the Tongking Gulf incident provided the opportunity to implement these plans. Two United States destroyers were fired on by North Vietnamese gunboats. Whether or not they were in international waters was unclear, but a few days later the US Senate passed a resolution giving the President authority to resist armed attack, and to use armed force to assist any country requesting help in defence of its freedom. This allowed Johnson to increase massively the number of American troops in South Vietnam, and to bomb North Vietnam. In March 1965 the first ground combat unit of US marines landed. By the end of the year 150,000 American troops were in Vietnam. In February 1965 the bombing of the North began.

The years from 1965 to 1969 saw the height of United States involvement in Vietnam. The number of American troops rose to half a million. In 1965–66 there was heavy fighting by large formations from both sides. The Communists attacked communications, military targets

[1] Buddhist monks would draw attention to their grievances by committing suicide in public—having soaked their clothing in petrol, they would burn themselves to death.

and district towns, but suffered heavy casualties in the process. The South Vietnamese army purged, occupied and tried to protect villages, while American combat units chased and tried to destroy Communist forces, generally successfully. Consequently, in 1967 the Communists concentrated mainly on guerrilla attacks and avoided pitched battles. A Vietcong battalion going into action would break up into many groups of two or three men who would take different routes to their destination. They had no aircraft, tanks or artillery, but had excellent personal weapons, mortars, rockets and anti-aircraft guns. The Americans made considerable use of helicopters, both as gunships and for transporting men. Civilians suffered horribly. As is often the case in guerrilla war, both sides were indifferent to human suffering. The Americans and South Vietnamese often found it difficult or impossible to distinguish Vietcong from South Vietnamese civilians. The My Lai massacre of March 1968 is an example not only of the difficulty of distinguishing the enemy, but also of the strains induced by this war. During a search and destroy mission on the hamlet of My Lai, a Lt Calley is alleged to have killed 109 unarmed men, women and children begging for mercy and cowering in a ditch. The incident was described in horrifying detail in newspapers and television interviews. It is one of many atrocities committed by both sides in the war in Vietnam.

The Americans had almost complete control of the skies over Vietnam, being unopposed except towards the end of the war. A vast weight of bombs was dropped. In South Vietnam aircraft were used in support of ground forces: for example, the bombing of an area prior to an attack by ground forces, or the use of chemicals to strip foliage from the jungle. The Ho Chi Minh Trail was bombed to prevent the movement of supplies. Selected targets in North Vietnam—power stations, bridges, roads, railways, supply bases, factories—were attacked with the object of destroying the North Vietnamese means of making war, and to prevent the sending of Russian or Chinese supplies to the south. The Americans said many times that the bombing would stop as soon as the Communist infiltration of South Vietnam stopped. A further objective was to force North Vietnam to negotiate a peace treaty, not only by destroying the means of waging war, but also by undermining civilian morale. The bombing seems to have been ineffective.[1] It did not prevent production; far from demoralising the North Vietnamese, it probably had the opposite effect in increasing hatred of the United States and determination to resist; and it forced Russia and China to provide further supplies.

[1] Compare the Allied bombing of Germany during the Second World War (p. 66)

On the first day of the Vietnamese New Year, Tet, 31 January 1968, there was a sudden major offensive by the Communists. The American Embassy in Saigon was occupied by the Vietcong, all United States and South Vietnamese army bases were attacked, and major cities besieged. The attack was a complete surprise and at first was very successful. However, by March the Americans and South Vietnamese had regained the initiative and the Communists were beaten back, but only after 160,000 civilians had been killed, 2 million refugees made homeless, and massive destruction. The Communists were temporarily exhausted, and in May 1968 agreed to negotiations with the United States in Paris.

The negotiations in Paris continued for nearly five years, but little progress was made until autumn 1972. During this long period, while the war continued, the motives and aims of the two sides were closely examined. It was not clear whether Communism or North Vietnamese nationalism was the dominant motive behind the Communists' actions. Ho Chi Minh's movement had considered itself cheated by the French in 1946 and by the Americans in 1954–56. It was therefore not prepared to stop fighting until it was quite certain that the Americans would withdraw and leave Hanoi to deal solely with Saigon. Thus the Communists wanted to liberate Vietnam from foreign domination and unify a divided country. It is not easy to estimate Ho Chi Minh's direct part in policy-making in the 1960s, but his death in 1969 did not seem to alter North Vietnam's aims. Ho Chi Minh was one of the elder statesmen of international communism. His mild exterior concealed a shrewd, calculating and ruthless political brain.[1] He was determined to win justice for the non-white peoples of the world, and constantly emphasised the anti-colonial character of the communist movement.

In the 1950s the actions of the United States were based on the view that if South Vietnam fell to the Communists, the other states of South-East Asia would also fall 'like a row of dominoes'. However, in the 1960s and early 1970s it was not clear whether this domino theory was valid. It was clear by then that world communism was not united and monolithic: there were as many rivalries between Communist states as between Communist and non-Communist states. In addition, it was clear that a united Communist Vietnam would greatly affect Laos and Cambodia, but not necessarily other states in the area. The basic motive of the Americans was to stop South Vietnam from falling under Communist control: it was simply a war against Communism. It became

[1] 'He shuffled into the room in his rubber shoes and his reach-me-down tunic and slacks, a brittle matchstick of a man with out-turned feet and a threadbare beard, but before his appearance could raise a laugh his presence took the breath away.' *The Observer*, 7 September, 1969.

increasingly doubtful whether this objective was worth the cost in terms of deaths, destruction of property and social disintegration in Vietnam, and economic cost and political discontent in the United States. The last stage of American involvement in the war was from 1969 to 1973. President Nixon aimed to reduce the number of American troops: in December 1970 they numbered 350,000; by September 1972 they had been reduced to 40,000. As the Americans gradually withdrew from ground fighting so the forces of South Vietnam were built up. In the years 1969–71 the tempo of fighting was reduced, and the only major action took place along the borders of South Vietnam or inside Cambodia and Laos, in which the object was to disrupt or destroy Communist supply lines and bases. In March 1972 there was a sudden change of tactics by the Communist forces. Virtually the entire North Vietnamese army launched a full-scale conventional offensive across the 17th Parallel, with subsidiary attacks in central and southern areas of South Vietnam. American troops were now comparatively few, and it was necessary for the North Vietnamese to attack before South Vietnam's forces grew too strong. As with the Tet offensive in 1968, the Communists were at first very successful and occupied large areas of South Vietnam. They showed themselves to be as effectively armed as the South Vietnamese and more skilled and resolute. Indeed it was only the enormous weight of American air power which prevented a South Vietnamese defeat. President Thieu's forces were divided, badly led and showed little or no enthusiasm for resistance. The cost as usual was enormous in terms of casualties, civilian and military, and destruction. By September the offensive had ended.

In the following month negotiations in Paris between Dr Kissinger, the American Secretary of State, and Le Duc Tho, North Vietnam's chief negotiator, suddenly became more hopeful. Opposition from Thieu, president of South Vietnam since 1967, delayed a settlement, but in January 1973 the United States, North Vietnam, South Vietnam and the Vietcong, signed a cease-fire agreement. The South Vietnamese and Vietcong were to remain in the positions they occupied at the time of the cease fire; all United States troops were to withdraw within sixty days, by which time all prisoners of war would be released; the neutrality of Laos and Cambodia was to be respected, and military activity in both countries was to be ended; Vietnam was to be reunited eventually; finally, an International Commission and Joint Military Commission were to supervise the release of prisoners, troop withdrawals and elections.

So ended the direct American involvement in the war, which had started eighteen years before in 1955. The United States had apparently secured its object in that a non-Communist government was in power in South Vietnam. However, no mention was made in the agreement of the North Vietnamese troops in South Vietnam—the North never admitted that it had troops in the South. Events were to show that the South Vietnamese, without American military support, were no match for the North Vietnamese and the Vietcong.

The ceasefire was not observed. Indeed, fighting was almost continuous from the day the agreement was signed, and the International Commissions were ignored. The South Vietnamese Government was increasingly unpopular because of its corruption and military inefficiency. Meanwhile, the North Vietnamese began to expand their forces, equipment and supply network in the border areas. In March 1975 came the final Communist offensive. The South Vietnamese army collapsed: there were massive desertions and in some areas no resistance at all. In an atmosphere of chaos, as refugees tried to escape the oncoming Communist armies, President Thieu resigned. Before the end of April 1975, Communist forces had occupied Saigon.

So ended a war which had begun in 1946. The inhabitants of Vietnam had known no peace since before the Japanese occupation in 1941. An indication of their suffering is given by the comparative extent of the bombing: during the Second World War, 80,000 tons of bombs were dropped on Britain; during the period 1965–73, 7 million tons were dropped on Vietnam, nearly ninety times more, or the equivalent to three hundred atom bombs of the size of those dropped on Japan. In fact the war was a military stalemate. As long as the Americans had the political will to stay, they could not be driven out. Equally, the Americans could not by force of arms defeat the Vietcong and their North Vietnamese allies. Political success was essential, and the South Vietnamese government never gained the political support of the majority of South Vietnam's people. The effect on the United States was one of disillusionment and the strengthening of support for isolation and a policy of non-intervention.

Laos Communist infiltration into Laos from North Vietnam was equally successful. There can hardly be a country in the world more undeveloped than Laos, which consists of mountains and dense forests with virtually no communications other than narrow jungle tracks. This country of about 3 million people was given its independence within the French Union in 1949. In the following year the pro-Communist Pathet Lao (Free Laos) organisation was set up by Prince Souphannouvong, and, helped by North Vietnam, the Communists conducted a guerrilla war against the Royal Laotian government of

Prince Souvanna Phouma, which received aid from the United States.

The 1954 Geneva Agreement provided for the withdrawal of all foreign forces and the unification of the Pathet Lao and Royal armies. From this point up to 1959 there was an uneasy truce: the armies were never united, and the Pathet Lao continued to hold the north, while the government consisted of a precarious coalition of the three main rivals—the Communist Prince Souphannouvong, the neutralist Prince Souvanna Phouma and the right-wing Prince Boun Oom. This coalition finally collapsed in 1959 when the Communists were imprisoned and the right wing controlled the government. Civil war began again and, accompanied by confused political events, continued until 1962, by which time two-thirds of Laos was controlled by the Pathet Lao. In 1962 a second Geneva Conference attempted to restore the position to that of 1954 by re-establishing the coalition government under Prince Souvanna Phouma, and by agreeing on the neutrality of Laos in the Cold War.

Although this neutralist government remained in office, personal and political rivalries have been great and fighting has been renewed. However, the main cause of continued fighting has been North Vietnam's anxiety to keep open its line of communication down the east side of Laos from Hanoi into South Vietnam. In 1971 the Laotian Prime Minister said, 'If Hanoi lost the Ho Chi Minh Trail, it could lose the war in a few weeks.' Throughout the period of the Vietnam war, the east side of Laos remained under Communist control. Elsewhere there was fluctuating and sometimes heavy fighting between government forces and the Pathet Lao who were aided by North Vietnamese regulars.

Cambodia Like Laos and Vietnam, Cambodia became independent within the French Union in 1949 and fully independent in 1954. This low-lying agricultural state of about 5 million people was ruled by Prince Sihanouk, who in 1955 abdicated in order to lead his own political party. An ebullient, magnetic, impulsive yet shrewd ruler, he provided strong and popular government, managing to keep his country united and at peace by stimulating nationalism and democracy, and by following a neutral foreign policy.

Sihanouk ruled Cambodia until 1970. During the 1960s his main problem was how to maintain Cambodia's independence and neutrality in view of the fighting in Laos and South Vietnam. Until 1963 Sihanouk received economic aid from both China and the United States. From 1963 to 1967 he appeared to incline towards the Communist camp: the receipt of American aid was stopped and diplomatic relations with the United States were broken off. However, in 1967 relations with China, then involved in the Cultural Revolution, cooled, and the Cambodian Ambassador in Peking was withdrawn. In addition the Vietnam war threatened to engulf Cambodia: the North Vietnamese and Vietcong used the empty areas of north-east Cambodia as a sanctuary and supply base, Cambodian ports were used for Communist supplies and in 1969 Sihanouk admitted that the Vietnamese Communists controlled large areas of his country. At the same time the Cambodian Communists, the Khmer Rouge, were increasingly active in several provinces. Consequently Sihanouk moved towards the United States, diplomatic relations were resumed in 1969, and Sihanouk said that the independence of Cambodia depended entirely on the Americans remaining in south-east Asia to provide counter-pressure to that of the Communists.

However, in March 1970 there was a right-wing coup against Sihanouk led by General Lon Nol, caused, it would appear, more by irritation at Sihanouk's personal dominance than by his recent change of policy. Sihanouk went into exile in Peking. For the next five years there was civil war between the right-wing forces of General Lon Nol and a variety of Khmer rebel groups supported by the Vietnamese. During most of this time the major towns and the majority of the population were under government control while the insurgents controlled three-quarters of the countryside. Eventually much of the fighting was concentrated along the highways into Phnom Penh, the capital, as the Communists tried to cut the supply routes into the city. Phnom Penh finally fell in April 1975, about a fortnight before the Vietnamese Communists captured Saigon. Thereafter an extreme Communist regime under Pol Pot imposed its authority by widespread massacres. This was removed in its turn, however, when the Vietnamese invaded and occupied most of Cambodia during 1979.

In 1967 five of the countries in the area—Indonesia, Malaysia, the Philippines, Singapore and Thailand—formed the Association of South-East Asian Nations (ASEAN). Its object was regional, especially economic, cooperation. At first it achieved little of substance and made only a slight impression. However, after the communist victories in Vietnam and Cambodia in 1975 it was also seen as an organisation of states opposed to the expansion of communism.

13

Central and South America

Beginning of the Twentieth Century

Central and South America stretch 7,000 miles from the US frontier to Cape Horn, and in area are $2\frac{1}{2}$ times the size of Europe. The mountains which cover much of the region cut off the main centres of population from each other, and make internal communications very difficult. Most of the scattered population are Europeans (mainly of Spanish and Portuguese descent), Indians, Mestizos (or half-breeds) and Negroes. With the exception of Brazil (Portuguese) and Haiti (French), Spanish is the common language of all Latin America, and in all the states Roman Catholicism is the dominant religion.

In 1900 the region contained nineteen republics that used to be part of the Spanish or Portuguese empires. In South America there were nine Spanish-speaking republics, and Brazil which was formerly ruled by Portugal. In Central America was Mexico and five small states sometimes impolitely described as 'banana republics'. In the Caribbean were Cuba and Dominica, and the ex-French Negro colony of Haiti. This chapter is largely concerned with Latin America, but in 1900 the region also contained the colonies of three European countries. Britain ruled· British Guiana, British Honduras, the Falkland Islands, and various islands in the Caribbean of which the leading ones were Jamaica and Trinidad. The French used French Guiana (Cayenne) as a penal settlement, and also owned Guadeloupe and Martinique. The Dutch ruled Dutch Guiana (Surinam).

Cuba and Puerto Rico remained Spanish colonies until 1898. All the other states of Latin America became independent republics in about

1820. During the nineteenth century anarchy alternated with dictatorship. In a long succession of coups, often bloodless and of little significance, the 'ins' were replaced by the 'outs'. It was not surprising that dictatorship based on a small class of landowners should be the normal form of government. There had been no training in self-government under the Spanish and Portuguese and most of the population regarded government as the prerogative of a small ruling class. And as Blakemore says: 'When anarchy was the alternative, even dictatorship had its merits, and the tradition of the caudillo, the autocratic military leader, was thus strongly established. It is far from dead today.'[1] Since dictatorship was usual, revolution became accepted as the normal means of acquiring power.[2]

However, government was effective in most states in 1900, and was supported by landowners, the army, and commercial and foreign elements who wanted stability. There was a tiny but important minority of radicals who wanted economic and political changes. In general they disliked foreign economic control, and wanted a freer political system and the introduction of social reforms.

All the states, with the possible exception of Argentina, were economically underdeveloped. There was some exploitation of a few raw materials and agricultural products, but very little development of manufacturing industry. The area lacked capital and technical skill. Britain, who could provide both, had invested heavily in Latin America in the nineteenth century because, like other European countries, she needed raw materials and cheap food. As a result towns and ports grew. Nevertheless, there was over-dependence on a limited range of exports and much greater capital investment was required. The weak economy meant that in 1900 the vast majority of the population was extremely poor.

The Monroe Doctrine of 1823 said that the United States would not allow any intervention by Europe in the affairs of Latin America. Despite this, British power dominated the area during the nineteenth century. After about 1890, however, the situation changed. The United States became increasingly assertive abroad when expansion within her own frontiers ended. Moreover, she had a sense of power and considerable wealth, and in consequence began to challenge Britain's position politically and economically. One method of doing this was through the Pan-American movement. The secretariat was started in 1890 and the first Pan-American conference was held in Washington in 1899. On the whole, however, this was regarded with suspicion in Latin America where it was considered an instrument of US domination.

[1] H. Blakemore, *Since 1945, Aspects of Contemporary World History*. Ed. J. L. Henderson.
[2] Ecuador has experienced over 50 *coups* in 155 years of independence.

The leading states of Latin America at the beginning of the twentieth century were Argentina, Brazil, Chile and Mexico.

Argentina

Until 1916 the government of Argentina was in the hands of an oligarchy of rich landowning families. This conservative government was good in that it provided stability and encouraged economic development. British capital was responsible for much of this development. Britain financed and built the 10,000 miles of railways in Argentina in 1900. British pedigree stock, British barbed-wire fencing and the introduction of meat freezing so developed the cattle industry on the pampas that by 1900 278 refrigerator ships were in service between Argentina and Britain. Arable farming also expanded so that in 1904 the value of grain exports was greater than that of beef.

The population grew fast. During the thirty years before the First World War, 3 million immigrants, mainly Italians and Spaniards, went to the Argentine. Buenos Aires, the capital, expanded, and the urban middle class prospered. 'As a result of her extraordinary economic development, by 1900 Argentina was pre-eminent among the republics of Latin America.'[1]

Brazil

Brazil, the fourth largest country in the world, is vast and comparatively empty with a whole variety of racial groups. She had become independent of Portugal in 1822 and had benefited from nearly fifty years of internal peace and stability during the reign of Emperor Pedro II. However, in 1889 the army with the backing of landowners and the Church forced the abdication of Pedro after he had agreed to a law abolishing slavery. Two years later a new constitution established a federal republic. The leading families ruled ably and the nation, although always in danger of disintegrating, held together.

At the beginning of the twentieth century the economy was based first on coffee and then on rubber. In 1900 Brazil was supplying three-quarters of the world's coffee and almost all the world's rubber. Rubber was in tremendous demand, and many speculators became extremely wealthy. But by 1912 the Far East, where the rubber trees were grown on plantations, had replaced Brazil as the world's chief supplier, and poverty replaced the great wealth of many in the Amazon area.

[1] G. Pendle, History of Latin America.

Central and South America

Chile

Chile was the leading power on the Pacific coast. The government, as elsewhere in Latin America, was in the hands of the landowning aristocracy who provided autocratic but capable rule.

In 1900 most people lived by farming, but techniques were so backward that food had to be imported. Most of the wealth of Chile came from the mining of nitrate and copper. Between 1879 and 1883 a successful war was fought against Peru and Bolivia to obtain control of the nitrate areas that are now in the north of Chile. Using British capital, the nitrate boom lasted from 1883 to the First World War, and Chile enjoyed considerable wealth. But during the war Germany produced a synthetic substitute for nitrate which other countries copied. The boom ended abruptly, and Chile then depended almost wholly on United States-owned copper mines for her foreign exchange.

Mexico

Between 1876 and 1910 Mexico was ruled by the efficient and ruthless Porfirio Diaz. After a long series of revolts and wars, Diaz provided order by a mixture of brute force and bribery. This security and stability meant a golden age for the great landowners and foreign investors. Diaz paid Mexico's debts, he was friendly towards the United States[1] and foreign capital poured in. American and British investors owned and exploited mines and oilfields. In 1901 Mexico's first successful oil well was drilled, and until 1910 Mexico was the world's chief exporter of petroleum. But this economic growth flourished at the expense of the masses. Three-quarters of the people lived by agriculture, yet 95 per cent of them were landless. This, together with the xenophobia created by the foreign investors, produced the revolution which led to the downfall of Diaz.

1900 to the Present

For the greater part of the period from 1900 to about 1960, life for most people in Latin America continued with little change. Levels of income, standards of housing, education and general amenities all remained very low by European or North American standards. On the other hand, big cities like Rio de Janeiro, São Paulo, Buenos Aires and

[1] 'Poor Mexico, so far from God, and so near to the United States' (Diaz).

Mexico City enjoyed the latest advantages of modern civilisation. The contrast between urban and rural life became greater, and led to the migration from country to towns with the consequent problem of shanty towns round the big cities.

The introduction of democracy was fraught with many difficulties: the widespread illiteracy and poverty, the feeling amongst the masses that politics was not for them, the tradition of authoritarianism and the general wish for government which was effective although possibly undemocratic. Military intervention and revolution remained relatively common. 'The problem that has baffled many democratic Latin American leaders [is]: how can social reforms be effected by parliamentary methods when the armed forces disapprove.'[1] Two changes have, however, taken place. With the growth in the size of towns there has emerged since about 1930 a new type of dictatorship with power based on the urban workers rather than on the landowners. Secondly, since the Second World War, while army intervention in politics has by no means declined, there have been many indications that the armed forces have acquired a new sense of responsibility and have acted in the national interest rather than merely for the sake of obtaining power.

Until the late 1950s Latin America remained on the periphery of world affairs. The region played little or no part in either of the two world wars, although most states were anti-German. Both wars were of importance, however, in that Latin America was cut off from European capital and manufactures. This had two consequences: firstly, a great increase in imports from the United States, and secondly, a stimulus to greater industrial diversification in order to be less dependent on foreign imports of manufactured goods.

The other major world event affecting Latin America was the economic depression starting in 1929. This resulted in a big decline in exports from the region and consequent cuts in expenditure by governments. Unemployment, accompanied by labour unrest and rioting, resulted and in 1930 and 1931 there were revolutions in eleven states. During the 1930s dictatorship with strong nationalist leanings was common.

Probably the most important point about Latin America in the late 1960s and early 1970s was the population explosion. Between 1945 and 1962 the population of Latin America rose from 130 to 216 million. The 3 per cent annual increase in the 1960s was the highest in the world. In

[1] G. Pendle, *History of Latin America.*

1970 half the population in many countries was under the age of twenty, and further large growth seems inevitable. A common factor throughout the area is the inefficiency of methods of farming. A consequence of population growth and rural backwardness was a drift to the shanty towns round the big cities. But employment in the towns was also difficult to find. A combination of inflation (in some countries at certain times, on a colossal scale), reduced US aid, investment in industries which require less labour, and in many cases weak administrations, has resulted in high unemployment. This in its turn has contributed to another factor common throughout the continent: the vast extremes of wealth and poverty. A United Nations' report in 1970 said: 'Those at the top of the social pyramid have conspicuously prospered but the benefits of development have hardly touched the broad masses relegated to the lower income strata. Instead of growing narrower, the gap has been gradually widening.'

This situation would seem to present the basic ingredients for revolution. Indeed, it is just when things are improving and the social order is changing that revolutions begin. During the 1960s there were left-wing movements in most Latin American countries. On the whole, however, they were ineffective. There was a basic split between the orthodox communists who sought power through political activity, and the guerrilla fighters who believed in armed struggle. This reflected the Moscow–Peking conflict, and prevented the emergence of a cohesive revolutionary force. In addition, the guerrillas tried to apply to the rest of Latin America methods which were effective in Cuba because of the particular conditions there. They concentrated on the countryside and found little popular support from the conservative peasants. National security forces, trained by the US in counter-insurgency methods, were increasingly effective.

One Latin American guerrilla leader achieved a world-wide reputation in the 1960s. Che Guevara was born in Argentina, qualified as a doctor, and in 1956 joined Castro. He was one of the twelve survivors of Castro's landing in Cuba in December 1956, and became his chief lieutenant and tactician. As a result of his experiences, Guevara wrote a much-quoted book called *Guerrilla Warfare,* part revolutionary programme and part do-it-yourself handbook on how to be an effective guerrilla soldier. After Castro took over the government of Cuba, Guevara became eventually the Minister for Industry. However, he was a professional and dedicated revolutionary with a Maoist belief in peasant armies. He became increasingly restless with the prosaic job of running Cuba's industry, and in April 1965 suddenly disappeared. For the next two years nobody knew where he was, but later it was learnt that he had gone to Bolivia, disguised as a balding Uruguayan businessman. He then proceeded to attempt to light the fires of revolution, but the expedition was a misconceived and badly executed fiasco and Guevara was killed in a skirmish in Bolivia in October 1967. Che Guevara aroused deep passions and became a fascinating legend. He was an inspiration not only to those who actively promoted revolution, but to those who vaguely yearned for a renewal of politics and society, and to young radicals who wanted improvisation, excitement and permanent revolution.

In the late 1960s the guerrilla movement concentrated increasingly on the towns. Its aim was to undermine the authority of governments, to make people conscious that they were being oppressed and exploited, and to change the political system. The middle-class intellectuals, who often made up the guerrilla groups, were difficult to identify, and for a time the movement prospered.

One consequence of the urban guerrilla movement was the growing involvement of the armed forces in the governments of several Latin American countries and the steady erosion of democratic institutions. Soldiers came to power because politicians had failed to solve national problems, including terrorism. The characteristics of the military regimes were all different. Some aimed merely to maintain security and the existing order; others wanted thoroughgoing reforms.

One example of military intervention which aroused world-wide interest and concern was Chile. For the six years from 1964 to 1970 a reforming Christian Democrat government had ruled in Chile. Then in 1970 Salvador Allende, a Communist, was elected President having obtained 36 per cent of the vote in the elections. He formed a coalition government of Communist and radical parties. Allende, a medical doctor with a professional knowledge of the state of the poor, had a genuine popular touch. He had a reputation for caution and compromise, for being a pragmatic politician who preferred evolution to revolution. His government attracted world-wide attention in that a Communist had come to power by democratic means. It seemed a test case to determine if it was possible to combine Communism and democracy. Allende carried out a policy of land reform and nationalisation of industries, especially the big copper mines previously owned by the United States. This inevitably caused some disruption, but in addition there were shortages, gross inflation which by 1973 had reached nearly 300 per cent, and a fall in the world price for copper. Industrial production fell catastrophically, there were crippling strikes and a wave of street violence. Allende had not the political strength to control the situation, and in September 1973 there was a military *coup*. Allende himself was killed when the presidential palace was bombed. During the next four years the military junta led by General Pinochet became a byword for repression in which thousands who were suspected of left-wing sympathies were arrested and tortured.

Five countries—Mexico, Argentina, Uruguay, Brazil and Vene-zuela—will serve to show the progress that has been made in parts of Latin America during the twentieth century, and the problems that have faced the continent.

Mexico

The rising against the dictator Diaz in 1910 was basically a social revolu-tion. Its aim was to distribute land amongst the people and to reduce foreign control over the economy. It was encouraged by crop failure and by the government's brutality in dealing with strikers. The down-fall of Diaz was followed, however, by ten years of virtually continu-ous and savage civil war in which the land-hungry peasants led by Zapata fought against the army and the central government. There was enormous destruction in towns and countryside, and a quarter of a million people died.

However, during an interval in 1917 caused by exhaustion, the present-day constitution of Mexico was drawn up. It included some striking innovations. The ownership of all land, minerals and waters was vested in the nation; the Church was forbidden to hold land and to take part in public education, and the activities of priests were limited; and there was a most generous and advanced labour code.

For some years the ruling oligarchy took little notice of this consti-tution, but gradually during the 1920s a one-party state emerged whose object was economic and social reform. Between 1920 and 1924[1] Mexico was ruled by President Obregón. Some land was redistributed, trade unions were encouraged, and schools were built on a large scale.

The politics of the ten years after 1924 were dominated by President Calles. During the first part of this period land distribution continued, and in 1925 American and British oil companies had to exchange their titles for fifty-year leases. Between 1926 and 1929 the government was engaged in a bitter quarrel with the Church. Calles closed all clerical primary schools and the Church in retaliation stopped all its services. Calles was also responsible for the formation of the official party, the Party of Revolutionary Institutions (PRI) in 1929. It incorporated most shades of opinion, except the extreme left and right, and has helped to

---

[1] It was at this point that Diego Rivera, the most famous of Mexico's artists, painted some of his wall frescoes.

provide political stability.

During the early 1930s there was little economic or social progress, but in 1934 the left wing of PRI forced the choice of General Cárdenas as president. A man of humble beginnings and a supporter of the revolution, he proved a strong ruler who enjoyed the firm support of the urban and rural working classes and the army. His government was notable in two particular ways. Firstly, 50 million acres of land were redistributed to the peasants (compared with 20 million during the previous twenty years) and large cooperative farms were formed which received state financial and technical aid. Secondly, the largely foreign-owned railways were nationalised in 1937, and in the following year the oil companies were seized by the state with virtually no compensation to their owners. Cárdenas, an energetic and sincere man, is the outstanding figure in the Mexican Revolution.

His successors since 1940 have on the whole been less radical, but the outstanding feature of Mexico compared with many Latin American countries has been its political stability. The PRI has dominated political life, always gaining a very big majority of votes in elections. Presidents, elected for six-year periods, have all come from the ruling party, tending to alternate between slightly left and right of centre. For example, from 1964 to 1970 President Ordaz tended to be conservative, while his successor, President Echeverria (1970–76) was more leftist and spoke of the need for fundamental reforms. The PRI has the support of the business community, the powerful and independent trade unions, the conservative element in the Roman Catholic Church, and the peasantry. The political scene has remained relatively quiet and there is a great deal of political apathy. The military play scarcely any political role, and the police similarly have a low profile. Again in contrast to other states in Latin America, there is freedom of association and of expression. Relations with the United States have been good.

This political stability has been the cause and the effect of very rapid economic expansion in the 1960s and early 1970s. Mexico has a fortunate economy: there is varied agriculture and mining, industry is advanced, and the income from tourists is important. Certainly, there has been steady progress in industrialisation, financial stability has been maintained with (except in 1976–77) low rates of inflation, and overall economic growth has outstripped even the big rise in population. In the late 1970s the income from oil became increasingly important. The government continued the policy of Mexican ownership of foreign firms, but nevertheless stability attracted foreign investment. Mexico was generally regarded as the most successful country in Latin America, having now reached a point at which the economy can sustain its own growth. 'As an example of a successful, non-communist social and economic revolution in an undeveloped country, it is without parallel in our time—perhaps Atatürk's transformation of Turkey is the nearest thing to it.'[1]

However, the development of the 1960s was uneven. There was excessive concentration on the nation's income, industry and finance, leaving vast pockets of poverty in rural areas. The great disparities between wealth and poverty have grown in recent years. The majority of Mexicans continue to live at subsistence level, ill-fed, ill-housed and often illiterate. Indeed, Mexico is a land of contrasts: modern concrete blocks of flats and the cave homes of some Indian tribes; the Spanish business talk of the cities and the fifty tribal languages of the hills. Mexico City is a bustling, modern metropolis with 6 million population, but it is surrounded by squalid poverty in the shanty towns.[2]

In 1968 the first major opposition to the existing order was expressed The Olympic Games were held in Mexico City. Just prior to the opening of the Games, and in the glare of world publicity, there were serious student disorders in which several people were killed. The students had academic grievances but more basically there was general dissatisfaction with the regime. The disorders could be regarded as part of a world-wide movement, students being 'the critical consciences of their countries', but more particularly the Mexican students were attempting to shake up the political system, revitalise the PRI and reduce corruption. The liberal wing of the Church was also critical of government policies, asking whether economic progress had been purchased at too high a social price.

Argentina

About the turn of the century the middle class created by Argentina's economic development began to demand honest elections and a greater share in the government. In 1892 a Radical Party was founded which achieved one of its objects twenty years later when electoral reforms providing for universal male suffrage and secret and compulsory voting were passed. This changed the face of politics, and in 1916 the Radical leader, Irigoyen, was elected president.

Irigoyen was president with the support of the lower and middle classes on two occasions between 1916 and 1930. There were some social

---

[1] J. Joll, The Listener, 9 April, 1959.

[2] See Oscar Lewis's two fascinating books on life in Mexico City slums (The Children of Sanchez) and in a Mexican village (Pedro Martínez). Part of the latter book describes fighting during the Civil War, 1910–20.

reforms and the standard of living generally increased. For example, in 1928 there were more cars per head of population in Argentina than in Britain. But Irigoyen's supposed radical government proved inept. The administration eventually became chaotic and corrupt. This, combined with the onset of the depression in 1930, provoked a bloodless coup d'état by the army. From 1930 to 1943 the conservative landowners again ruled until they in turn were overthrown by a fresh military rising.

During the 1930s some sections of the army developed strong nationalist and radical views. They had visions of a strong, modern Argentina, dominating South America, with a government based on the growing number of industrial workers. The army ruled for three years, from 1943 to 1946. One member of the government was Colonel Juan Perón who became head of the insignificant Secretariat of Labour and Welfare. Previously a military attaché in the Italy of Mussolini, he believed in a dictatorship based on the working classes. Perón assiduously fostered his public image, both by his ostentatious friendship with famous people such as footballers and racing motorists, and by his reforms. He built up a powerful trade union movement and, as Secretary of Labour, supervised collective bargaining in which the workers usually benefited. Flats were built for the working class and all wage earners received compulsory holidays with pay. Perón also urged free elections.

All this was done with the utmost publicity so that in 1945 the military government, fearing Perón's popularity, arrested him. Immediately there were huge demonstrations organised by Perón's future wife, Eva, which led to his release. Soon after, in February 1946, free elections supervised by the army resulted in sweeping successes for Perón's Labour Party and made him president.

Perón was President of Argentina from 1946 until 1955. His government was autocratic: opposition was suppressed and the press was censored. It was based on the support of the urban working class who were organised into strong trade unions. The government encouraged the growth of industry and attempted to control the economy. But, although the British-owned railways were nationalised, no attempt was made to nationalise Argentina's big estates, and in general the countryside was neglected.

After 1952 opposition began to grow. In that year Eva Perón, who was one of the driving forces of the regime, died at the age of thirty-three. Inflation and the neglect of agriculture reduced the volume of exports, thus producing a foreign exchange crisis. And not only did the administration become more and more bureaucratic and corrupt, but

Perón's autocratic methods annoyed the Church and the army. This opposition led to more moderate and less nationalist policies. For example, foreigners, who had been frightened by Perón's earlier policies, were now encouraged to invest their capital in Argentina (this was disliked by the nationalists in the army). Events came to a head in 1955. Rumours that Perón intended to distribute weapons to his trade union supporters led to a successful army and navy revolt, and Perón went into exile.

For the next three years the army again ruled Argentina, dismissing all Peronists from important posts. The 1958 elections, in which the still powerful Peronists were not allowed to put forward candidates, resulted in a radical, Frondizi, becoming president. Four years later Frondizi allowed the Peronists to vote in further elections and they won big successes. In consequence, the army again stepped in, deposed and imprisoned Frondizi, and ruled for the following year. From 1963 to 1966 there was a civilian government before the army again intervened. Social and economic difficulties were not resolved, there was a resurgence of support for the exiled Perón in Spain, and the army considered that a doctrinaire approach was creating new problems.

However, despite military control of the government from 1966 to 1973 problems were not reduced. General Onganía was President for the first four years of this period. Political parties were disbanded and for a time there was stability. But policies of austerity which particularly affected the provinces produced strikes and general unrest. Onganía was replaced, but the army generals were clearly floundering and had lost authority. The inflation rate reached 60 per cent in 1972 and there was high unemployment. In about 1970 two left-wing terrorist groups began their activities: the People's Revolutionary Army, which was Communist, and the Montoneros, which was a Peronist guerrilla group. The support from the working classes for Perón grew. His reputation for removing foreign control, for promoting industry and helping the exploited working man, was combined with popular adulation for the memory of his second wife Eva ('Evita') who, apart from being young and beautiful, loved, it was thought, the poor and hated the rich. Eva transformed Peronism, already a strange mixture of fascism, national-ism and socialism, into a religion. Towards the end of 1972 Perón returned to Argentina. He did not immediately stand for president, but in September 1973 was elected with 62 per cent of the votes cast.

Perón was elected on a wave of nostalgia for the period of his first government. In addition, the record of the military was poor, and Perón's party and his personality were a magnet for a wide variety of dissident groups. But Perón was 78 and ill with a heart condition.

Perón, a photograph taken a few months after his exile from Argentina in 1955

Fidel Castro

A shanty town on the outskirts of Brasilia

Most of the campaigning in the election was done by Isabel Perón, his third wife and candidate for Vice-President. There was little time for Perón to produce any effect before he died. He was succeeded in 1974 by his widow. Isabel Perón was both unpopular and unqualified for office, opposed by left and right, and before long there was political anarchy with violence, strikes, and economic chaos with inflation running at 900 per cent in 1975. Inevitably the army intervened, and in March 1976 a military junta led by General Videla overthrew the Peronist government. There was clearly a need to restore law and order, but in the process the army and the notorious para-military police groups instituted a reign of terror in which thousands of people who were suspected of left-wing sympathies disappeared.

Argentina is a country as big as India with a population in 1967 of 22 million. It has lavish natural resources—cattle, grain, oil, minerals—and its people are relatively well educated, the country is substantially industrialised and there is little hopeless poverty. Yet there has been economic stagnation since the Second World War, with frequent labour unrest and a sense of drift. For much of the time the rate of inflation has been high, with a consequent lack of incentives to work, manage or invest. Gunther wrote in 1967 of Argentina's 'severe intellectual, moral and spiritual crisis. The country gives a sense not merely of lack of direction but of outright lostness; it seems spiritless, bereft, forlorn.'[1] Argentina has failed to produce an able and responsible ruling class, capable of understanding and keeping the support of a volatile and restless people who are quick to express resentment and frustration.

Uruguay

Uruguay is a small, compact country, 90 per cent of whose population of 3 million (1960) are of European descent. There was the usual political chaos in the nineteenth century, and in 1880 one military dictator resigned saying that the people were ungovernable. Shortly before this, however, universal free education had been introduced, so that when the twentieth century began half the population were literate.

The one individual who has dominated Uruguay's history in the twentieth century is José Batlle y Ordóñez, a great man and a remarkable statesman. He was a political journalist who became leader of the main political party and was elected President twice between 1903 and 1915. His first presidency was mainly taken up with imposing the authority of the central government. During his second term of office he introduced a large number of progressive reforms. Old age pensions

[1] J. Gunther, *Inside South America*, Hamish Hamilton, 1967.

were brought in, and the working day was reduced to eight hours. Capital punishment was abolished (as was bullfighting). Education was reformed and the press was given freedom. He also advocated a policy of nationalisation and a reduction in the power of the presidency.

Batlle died in 1929 but his influence continued. A large number of industrial concerns in Uruguay were eventually nationalised, and in 1952 a new constitution was introduced in which the office of president was abolished. The country was then ruled by a national council of nine members, six of whom came from the largest party. During the 1950s Uruguay seemed a stable and progressive state, something of a model republic. There had been no revolutions for over sixty years, and the army was small. The revenue from wool and meat brought financial prosperity.

During the early 1960s, however, this economic prosperity declined, and the national council was divided. By 1965 there was economic stagnation, massive inflation and growing unemployment which produced frequent strikes. It was therefore decided to return to presidential government, and in a peaceful and orderly way the constitution was changed and a President took office in 1967. The economy did not improve though. Violent street demonstrations and the terrorist activities of the Tupamaros, an increasingly bold urban guerrilla movement, produced acute political and social tension. Eventually in 1973 the constitution was suspended, and the President ruled by decree with army support. There was an obsession with security and political repression, but the economy continued to deteriorate and skilled people emigrated on a large scale.

Brazil

After the collapse of the rubber industry before the First World War, Brazil's economy depended on the production of coffee and cotton. When the world economic depression began, demand for these exports slumped, and huge stocks of unsold coffee were burned. The consequent unrest produced the revolt of 1930 when the army gave the office of president to Vargas, the governor of one of the southern provinces.

Vargas, a skilful and tactful statesman, ruled Brazil for fifteen years, from 1930 to 1945. His government was autocratic but not repressive. Trade unions were encouraged and measures taken to improve the lot of urban workers. Education and medical services were improved. Vargas tried to diversify the economy by providing state aid for the expansion of new industries, such as textiles, chemicals and steel. On the other hand agriculture was neglected and impoverished rural workers flocked to the towns. In 1945 Vargas was forced to resign. From 1945 to 1964 Brazil attempted to develop democracy. Vargas was elected president again in 1950, but in general his government was now incompetent and in 1954 he committed suicide. During the 1950s there were big industrial developments and the major decision was taken to move the capital from Rio de Janeiro to a new city, Brasilia, 600 miles from the coast. Brasilia, the capital since 1960, was the particular enthusiasm of President Kubitschek. Its position was chosen with the intention of encouraging the development of the thinly populated interior of Brazil—three-quarters of Brazil's 75 million population lived within 100 miles of the coast. Brasilia is remarkable for the vigour and unconventional forms of its architecture, much of which is the work of Oscar Niemeyer.

The political situation in Brazil deteriorated during the three years before 1964, partly because of economic difficulties and in particular a very sharp inflation. A left-wing president, Goulart, after two years of moderate compromise with the right wing, decided to support a policy of enfranchising illiterates (about half the population), of nationalisation and of legalising the Communist Party. This provoked an army coup in 1964 and the experiment with democracy was ended.

For the next four years the military government allowed some political rights. There was a great deal of public support for the action of the army in 1964, but by 1968 there were signs of opposition. There was a lack of positive enthusiasm for the regime rather than a desire for change, but students and the more liberal element in the Church showed concern for the social inequalities of Brazil. The dissatisfaction of various groups in society was increasingly vocal and violent. Consequently, in December 1968 President Silva assumed complete dictatorial powers, suspended Congress, imposed press censorship and disposed of what civil liberties remained. There was thus a reversion to completely authoritarian government.

In the late 1960s a well-organised urban guerrilla movement became active. However, it attracted little support, partly because the government pursued intelligent development programmes and partly because military action against the terrorists was effective. For the decade following 1968 the army provided stable and strong government. Politics took second place to economic development. Only towards the end of the decade did there arise a general wish on the part of businessmen, the church and sections of the army for the restoration of civil liberties and a return to the rule of law.

Authoritarian government was accepted because of the success of economic policies since the mid-1960s. It has been said that 'the one thing that matches Brazil's size is Brazil's potential'; during this period the potential began to be realised. The founding of Brasilia in the wilds of the jungle led to the opening of the interior and symbolised new forms of development away from the heavily populated coastal strip in the south. Brazil is the fifth largest country in the world in size and the seventh in population. The region of Amazonia is rather larger than Europe, yet it supports an estimated Indian population of about 120,000. It is known to have large reserves of minerals, but remains a land of mystery. To develop this vast area it was necessary to improve communications. The Trans-Amazonian Highway was built in the 1970s. In 1964 there were 12,000 km of paved roads in Brazil, by 1976 the figure had risen to 45,000 km. Industry and agriculture were developed by technocrats who had great authority and freedom of action and who were very able. Ideology was unimportant—there was faith only in the profit motive. The result was an unprecedented expansion by a confident nation of over 100 million (1973) people.

This economic success was achieved at the cost of political repression and continuing social inequalities. After 1974 the government of President Geisel aimed to combat illiteracy, improve public health and seek a better distribution of wealth. But the problems were huge. In 1976 the average Brazilian earned one eighth of his British equivalent. Most Brazilians spent 80 per cent of their wages on food, yet three-quarters of the population is undernourished. Housing conditions, especially in the shanty towns round the big cities, are very bad.

Venezuela

Venezuela could be regarded as a typical Latin American state at the beginning of the twentieth century. Chaos and dictatorship had alternated during the previous century, and in 1908 another caudillo, Juan Gómez, seized power. He was to rule until 1935, however, and during his government oil, the source of Venezuela's great wealth, was discovered.

Gómez, an uneducated mestizo, ran a brutal but efficient dictatorship in which the secret police, through terrorism and censorship, prevented the emergence of any opposition. Gómez, 'the Tyrant of the Andes', was greatly helped by the discovery of huge oil fields in 1913. Production on a large scale by the American, British and Dutch companies, began in the early 1920s. By 1938 Venezuela was the third largest oil-producing country in the world. The foreign countries exploiting this oil paid high taxes to the Venezuelan government who paid off all foreign debts and became very wealthy. But this wealth was not reflected in the country as a whole. Other branches of the economy declined and living standards remained very low.

Gómez died in 1935 but his system of government continued for another ten years. In 1945, however, junior officers in the army overthrew the government and placed in office a civilian government led by Betancourt. Betancourt attempted revolutionary changes too quickly. Plans were made to distribute uncultivated land to the peasants, to increase the taxation of the foreign oil companies in order to pay for welfare legislation, and eventually to exclude the army from politics. This provoked a second coup by the army, and a military government led by a ruthless dictator, Pérez Jiménez, ruled from 1948 to 1958. During this period foreign investment increased, particularly by the United States. This, together with government expenditure, did diversify the economy, and in some ways the standard of living improved; for example, large blocks of workers' flats were built.

In 1958 a new group of young officers opposed to military dictatorship intervened, and civilian government with Betancourt as president was again attempted. There now began a period of uninterrupted democratic growth. During the 150 years prior to 1958 not one legally elected President had lasted out his term of office. In the twenty years since 1958 a stable, multi-party democracy has developed. Betancourt was one of the few effective democratic leaders in Latin America in this century, and his successors have continued to provide good government. Nevertheless, the great contrast in Venezuela is still between the modern technology of the foreign firms and the immemorial poverty of the peasants. Oil has brought riches to some, but there are pressing problems of poverty and envy.

Growth of United States' Influence

American power and wealth, referred to earlier, came to dominate Central and South America and the Caribbean during the twentieth century. When the century opened, the United States had just occupied the two islands of Cuba and Puerto Rico which she had conquered by defeating the Spanish in 1898. Cuba and Puerto Rico were the two remaining fragments of Spain's vast American empire. During the nineteenth century there were frequent revolts by Cubans against Spanish control and in 1895 a further revolt started which was still smouldering three years later. The US not only was sympathetic towards the rebels but also wished to increase her influence in the Caribbean. Therefore, when a US warship blew up in Havana harbour in 1898 (whether by accident or not is unknown), the US declared war on Spain, and in three months the Spanish fleet and army were defeated. The Spanish evacuated both islands. From 1898 to 1902 Cuba was under US military rule, and when the Americans finally left they retained naval stations in Cuba and the right to intervene in certain circumstances in Cuban internal affairs. Puerto Rico became an American possession, its inhabitants being granted US citizenship in 1917.

It had long been obvious to maritime nations that a canal was required across Central America to link the Atlantic and Pacific Oceans. De Lesseps and the French had tried to build such a canal in about 1890 and had failed. President Theodore Roosevelt (see p. 169) decided that the US must build and own the canal. The isthmus of Panama is the narrowest point across Central America and this belonged to Colombia. Roosevelt therefore asked Colombia in 1903 for the lease of land to build a canal, but he was refused. However, soon after there was a suspiciously convenient revolt in Panama against Colombia, and the independent republic then proclaimed was protected by US forces. Panama immediately agreed to lease to the US a ten-mile strip of land from coast to coast. Work on the canal then started, and the first ship passed through on 3 August 1914.

Roosevelt's attitude to Colombia (who received $25 million in compensation from the United States in 1921) and to other Latin American countries was summed up in his words: 'Speak softly and carry a big stick.' Since the Monroe Doctrine forbade European interference in the affairs of the American continent, Roosevelt made an important amendment to the doctrine in 1904. The Roosevelt Corollary said that the US would intervene in Latin America in order to maintain order. This North American police action was largely to prevent any European intervention. Until the 1930s when this policy was finally repudiated, the United States intervened directly in five countries, Cuba, Mexico, the Dominican Republic, Haiti and Nicaragua. In the case of the last three, the Americans occupied the country for many years and trained local forces to take over the government after they had left. In all three cases repressive dictatorships followed the withdrawal of US forces. President Wilson, who intervened briefly in Mexico, said the US would not recognise governments that had come to power by unconstitutional methods.

The Monroe Doctrine and the Roosevelt Corollary were regarded by Latin Americans as a cover for American intervention. The countries of the region had a kind of love-hate attitude towards their powerful neighbour, a relationship compounded of both admiration for American wealth, standards of living and democratic government, and dislike born of fear and jealousy. The US became the dominant influence not only politically but also economically. The following figures demonstrate the increase in American investment relative to British between 1913 and 1929:

	GB	US
1913	$4983m.	$1242m.
1929	$5889m.	$5587m.

Latin America needed, but disliked, this 'dollar imperialism'. Pendle has described US relations with Latin America, and especially with Cuba, as 'a story, on the US side, of good intentions and self-righteousness, idealism and self-interest, jingoism and exuberant commercialism; and on the other side of inexperience, poverty and corruption, the desire to have US aid, and the fear of US domination'.[1]

The opposition to political intervention produced a change in US policy after 1933. Franklin Roosevelt, in his 'Good Neighbour' policy, agreed that the US would not intervene in the internal affairs of any state, and would give economic and technical assistance to Latin America. After the Second World War, Presidents Truman and Eisenhower followed a similar policy, except that their dominant motive was now to keep Communism out of the American continent. For this reason they tended to support old-style dictatorships because they provided stable anti-Communist governments. American policy can be illustrated by its dealings with four countries, Guatemala, Bolivia, Cuba and the Dominican Republic.

Guatemala Guatemala was ruled by dictators until 1944. Its economy was dominated by powerful United States firms, and nearly the whole of the population, Indian or mestizo, was landless. A revolutionary movement then began which aimed at social and political reforms and the distribution of land to the peasants. In 1950 Colonel Arbenz became President. His regime depended on the army, organised labour and the Communist Party organisation. Uncultivated land was appropriated for distribution to the landless, and workers for foreign firms went on strike for higher wages and better conditions. Opposition to his policy meant that Arbenz was forced to rely heavily on the Communists, and the United States became alarmed at the possibility of a Communist state so close to their frontiers. Therefore, in 1954 the US gave support to Guatemalan refugees who invaded Guatemala and overthrew Arbenz. A new right-wing dictatorship (which was not against reform) was established, and the Communists were purged.

[1] G. Pendle, *History of Latin America*.

Bolivia In Guatemala US policy was to overthrow a government supported mainly by Communists. In Bolivia, on the other hand, the policy was to support and aid a left-wing government which included Communists. Bolivia is a landlocked state whose 3 million population is mainly engaged in agriculture. The one important industry is tin mining. In 1940 a revolutionary party was formed by an ex-professor of economics named Paz Estenssoro. In 1951 this party won the elections but was stopped from taking office by the army. In the following year, however, a successful revolution led by the mine workers made Paz Estenssoro President. He immediately began a series of reforms which included the nationalisation of the tin mines and the splitting up of the big estates among landless peasants. But this produced difficulties in that production of tin and agricultural goods began to decline. The US then decided to shore up the regime by providing very considerable economic aid for Paz, who remained the virtual ruler of Bolivia until 1964.

Cuba When US military rule in Cuba ended in 1902 American political and economic domination continued and was the crucial factor in Cuban history in the twentieth century. The likelihood of US military intervention in the event of disorder meant that Cuban leaders could shift ultimate responsibility for the conduct of affairs on to their powerful neighbour a hundred miles to the north. The US felt that she had to support dictators because the instability of Cuban politics was such that the alternative would lead to chaos and suffering.

The economy of Cuba was controlled by the US who owned most of the best land, which was used for the growing of sugar, half the railways and most of the electricity and telephone services. In the 1950s US investment totalled about $1,000 million. By the usual standards of comparison—for example, income per head—Cuba is one of the richest Latin American countries. In the 1950s half the national income came from industry. But there was an extremely wide gulf between the rich and the poor, and considerable seasonal unemployment in the sugar industry which, the mainstay of Cuba's economy, was itself stagnating in the 1950s. Left-wing groups demanded reform, but during the brutal dictatorship of Batista from 1933 to 1958, confidence in the idea of a peaceful social revolution was lost.[1]

Fidel Castro was one of those who believed that force was necessary. Coming from an upper-class background, he studied law at Havana

[1] 'Revolutions (by which I mean a profound social upheaval) usually occur not when countries are poor, though they may be: they are usually inspired by stagnant economies and made acute by the weakness of institutions.' Hugh Thomas, *The Listener*, 9 Jan. 1964.

University, and made his first attempt against Batista's government in 1953. It failed and he was sentenced to fifteen years' imprisonment. Released after two years as the result of an amnesty, Castro began a guerrilla war in the hills of eastern Cuba in 1956. A sort of bearded Robin Hood figure, his followers never numbered more than 300, and were at one point down to twelve. He was at this stage a radical nationalist who wanted to end US economic power in Cuba and to distribute land to the peasants. Gradually Batista's regime disintegrated as public opinion turned against the terrorist methods he used to combat Castro's guerrillas. At the end of December 1958 Batista fled to the Dominican Republic, and on 1 January 1959 Castro, then aged thirty-two, became ruler of Cuba.

Before long relations with the US deteriorated. In 1959 many estates and factories were nationalised. Since many of these were American-owned and only long-term compensation was promised, the US retaliated by not buying sugar from Cuba. By the end of 1960, however, all US property in Cuba had been appropriated by the government. Gradually the moderates in Castro's government were replaced by Communists, partly because of the latters' power, partly because their organisation was the best one available for carrying out Castro's policies, and partly because of his sympathies with them. In 1961 he declared himself a Communist and was by this point receiving considerable aid, economic and military, from the Soviet bloc.

Many supporters of Batista, and those harmed by Castro's measures, had sought refuge in the US. With the connivance of the American government, they attempted to invade Cuba in April 1961, hoping for a popular rising in their favour. No such rising occurred and the invaders were soundly defeated. Not only had Castro a gift of leadership and a good sense of public relations, but his social policy of higher wages and cheap housing was gaining support for him. During 1962 Cuba became the centre of a major world crisis when the Americans discovered that the Russians had built missile bases in the island (see p. 83). After 1962 Castro still continued in power, tolerated by the Americans, and gradually losing the world publicity which surrounded the first years of his government. In many areas of government during the 1960s and 1970s Castro did more than any other Latin American leader. There were considerable advances in public health, education and land reform. Corruption in government was ended, and the coloured one-third of the population had more opportunities. There is certainly more social freedom. The army is Latin America's largest and best equipped. On the other hand, the performance of the economy has been poor, there have been major shortages of food and other consumer goods, and living standards have remained low. There is no political freedom and there are many thousands of political prisoners. Castro remains an overwhelming personality, a caudillo figure, a man with great charisma and personal magnetism and with great gifts of oratory.

Dominican Republic The fourth example of recent US policy towards left-wing regimes is found in America's dealings with the Dominican Republic. Here in 1961 President Trujillo was assassinated after thirty-one years of corrupt and tyrannical dictatorship. A democratic government was then established and the US seemed determined to help by sending generous economic aid. Early in 1963 President Bosch took office after receiving 64 per cent of the votes of the electorate. With the support of the peasants, urban labour and the lower middle classes, he tried to implement a social reform movement. But business and other property interests accused the President of communism, and in September 1963 the army intervened. Bosch was exiled, and the army installed a new civilian government more to their liking. Support for Bosch grew, however, particularly amongst the younger army officers. Finally, fearing another Castro-like communist movement, the US sent 20,000 troops to Dominica and this support was crushed.

By the beginning of the 1960s the general economic position in Latin America was worsening, partly because the prices of the region's products were declining, and partly because of the huge population growth (see p. 509). Therefore, in 1961 President Kennedy formed the Alliance for Progress in which the US promised massive economic and technical aid to those Latin American states who followed a policy of progressive reform. This aid was promised at a time when the threat of communism spreading from Cuba seemed very great.

In the first half of the 1960s the Alliance for Progress seemed to be successful. By the end of the decade, however, it had become a dead letter. Social reform had not taken place on any extensive scale, and US financial aid was reduced. For example, the Frei government in Chile from 1964 to 1970 was regarded as the show piece of the Alliance: a constitutional government aiming to carry out radical reforms. But the problems were too great, and the election of Dr Allende, a Communist, in 1970 and the subsequent nationalisation of the American owned copper mines, was a major blow to United States' prestige.

Until 1970 regional organisation was dominated by the United States. Pan-Americanism was replaced in 1948 by the Organisation of American States (OAS). This is an association of governments which have promised to resist jointly any outside attacks, and who have agreed to attempt to settle any interstate quarrels between themselves without recourse to the United Nations. In 1961 the Latin American Free Trade Association (LAFTA) was formed with the aim of reducing tariffs, and plans were made for the development of a common market in the area in the 1970s. But the early 1970s saw a sharp decline in United States' influence in Latin America. American ideological and political control seemed to be coming to an end.

14

World Organisations

Growth of World Organisations

Over the past hundred years there have grown up over 1,200 international organisations, most of which have nothing to do with governments. One of the first was the International Telecommunications Union formed in 1868 for the regulation of telegraph, telephone and radio services. Others followed before the end of the nineteenth century: for example, the Universal Postal Union in 1874, the World Meteorological Organisation in 1878 and the Inter-Parliamentary Union in 1889. At the turn of the century virtually all states could attend the two conferences held at The Hague to discuss general political questions, in particular disarmament. During the twentieth century the number of international organisations has grown enormously and covers almost every human activity. 'The world is already enmeshed in a spider's web of international associations, federations, organisations.'[1]

Better communications had made possible more contacts between the peoples of the world, and strong social and economic reasons for greater coordination and cooperation encouraged the growth of international organisations. Nations, especially in the twentieth century, were growing more interdependent and found organisation of activities on a world scale to be necessary. As the number of these groups increased, so the habit of international cooperation developed. However, at the same time a vigorous and aggressive nationalism grew, and this finally helped to produce the First World War. The slaughter and destruction of this war persuaded a number of leading statesmen to support the idea of a peacekeeping organisation which all the nations of the world could join. Consequently, the League of Nations was born.

[1] H. Nicholas, *The Listener*, 14 Dec. 1961.

The League of Nations

The most eminent of the supporters of the League of Nations was President Wilson of the United States. It was largely as a result of pressure from Wilson that the Covenant of the League was worked out at the Paris Peace Conference and included in each of the treaties that were signed after the First World War. This had disadvantages, but it did mean that the League of Nations was given responsibility for carrying out many of the provisions of these treaties, and therefore could not be ignored. On the whole, British and American ideas dominated in drawing up the constitution.

Organs of the League

The League contained five bodies: the Assembly, the Council, the Secretariat, the Permanent Court of International Justice and the International Labour Organisation. Each member of the League—fifty in 1924—was represented in the Assembly. It discussed general policy, and any decisions taken had usually to be unanimous. The Council was the executive of the League. It was originally intended that the five Great Powers—Britain, France, Italy, Japan and the United States—would be permanent members of the Council, and that four lesser Powers would sit for short periods. In fact, the United States did not

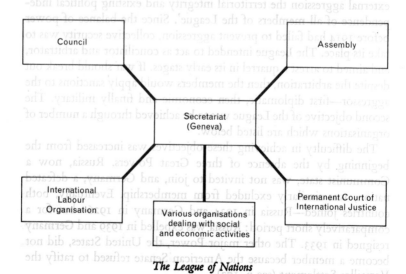

The League of Nations

become a member of the League, and the number of lesser Powers on the Council was increased to six in 1922 and nine in 1926. Each member had one vote, and since decisions had to be unanimous, even the small nations possessed the right of veto.

The Secretariat provided the machinery which carried out the decisions of the League. Its small and efficient staff of international civil servants was headed by a secretary-general. The first person to hold this post was Sir Eric Drummond from Britain. The headquarters of the League were at Geneva, but the Permanent Court of International Justice was set up at The Hague. The court contained fifteen judges; it could not compel states to appear before it, nor enforce its verdicts.

The International Labour Organisation consisted of a secretariat and a general conference which included four representatives from each country—two from the government, one from the employers and one from the employees. Its purpose was to collect information on conditions of labour throughout the world, and if necessary to persuade governments to pass laws to improve these conditions.

Purpose of the League

The League had two main objectives: to maintain peace and security through collective action, and to promote international cooperation in economic and social affairs. According to Article 10 of the Covenant of the League, members undertook 'to respect and preserve as against external aggression the territorial integrity and existing political independence of all members of the League'. Since the balance of power before 1914 had failed to prevent aggression, collective security was to take its place. The League intended to act as conciliator and arbitrator, and aimed to arrest a quarrel in its early stages. If war should break out despite the arbitration, then the members would apply sanctions to the aggressor—first diplomatic, then economic and finally military. The second objective of the League was to be achieved through a number of organisations which are listed below.

The difficulty in achieving these objectives was increased from the beginning by the absence of three Great Powers. Russia, now a Communist state, was not invited to join, and Germany, a defeated nation, was similarly excluded from membership. Eventually, both countries joined—Russia in 1934 and Germany in 1926—but for a comparatively short period: Russia was expelled in 1939 and Germany resigned in 1933. The other major Power, the United States, did not become a member because the American Senate refused to ratify the Versailles Settlement (see p. 172).

Political activities

Between 1920 and 1925 the League was called in to settle a number of disputes between European countries. In three of these the League was successful. In 1920 a dispute arose between Sweden and Finland over the sovereignty of the Aaland Islands in the Gulf of Bothnia. The League sent a committee of enquiry which concluded that the islands should go to Finland on certain conditions. In the following year the League was asked to settle the frontier between Poland and Germany in Upper Silesia. This was an area of mixed population and an important economic centre. A committee of the League decided that the frontier should go through Upper Silesia, but that the area should be an economic unit supervised by the League for fifteen years. The third dispute was between Greece and Bulgaria in 1925. Greece invaded Bulgaria, the League ordered a ceasefire and after investigating, decided that Greece was to blame and fixed reparations.

In two disputes during these years the League was overruled by the Conference of Ambassadors. This was a body set up in Paris by the Great Powers to deal with any matters not settled by the Peace Treaties. The first question involved the claim by Poland and Lithuania to the territory of Vilna. The League believed that Vilna should go to Lithuania, but the Ambassadors intervened on the side of Poland. The dispute between Mussolini's Italy and Greece in 1923 is described on page 33. Italy occupied Corfu and demanded a large indemnity from Greece. Although the League acted with vigour, the Conference of Ambassadors ordered Greece to pay the indemnity.

By the mid-1920s, therefore, the League had been successful in some of the problems brought before it. Furthermore, its government of Danzig and the Saar was effective. In other cases, however, it had been overruled by a rival organisation. During the second half of the 1920s, however, the League became the centre of European diplomacy. After the Treaty of Locarno was signed Germany joined the League and was given a permanent seat on the Council. Briand, Stresemann, Chamberlain and many other foreign ministers were regular attenders at the meetings of the Assembly and the Council. In about 1927, too, the United States and Russia began to join in the non-political activities of the League.

One of the major problems of this period was how to achieve disarmament. Under the auspices of the League, various approaches were made, but all failed. In 1923 a treaty of Mutual Assistance was drawn up, by which nations willing to disarm would have their security guaranteed by the League whose members would be obliged to come to the help of such nations if they were attacked. In the following year the Geneva Protocol provided for automatic arbitration in any dispute. Both the treaty and the protocol were rejected. In 1925 the Council of the League set up a commission to prepare for a Disarmament Conference. It was not until 1930 that the commission managed to draft a statement of principles based on limitation of expenditure and the size of forces as a basis for a conference.

Despite the problems arising from the economic depression, the Disarmament Conference finally met in February 1932. It was immediately faced with a demand from Germany for equality of arms with France. When this was rejected Germany withdrew from the conference until December when the principle of German equality was conceded. However, France wished to delay this equality for a further eight years, and in October 1933 Hitler withdrew Germany from the conference and from the League.

Germany's resignation from the League followed a few months after a similar step by Japan. A description of Japan's attack on Manchuria in September 1931 is given in chapter 11. China appealed to the League who asked Japan to withdraw. When the latter refused, the League then sent a commission under the chairmanship of Lord Lytton to investigate, and in September 1932 the Lytton Report was received. The report condemned Japan while admitting that the situation in Manchuria had been anomalous, and recommended the setting up of an autonomous regime in the province under League auspices. When the report was accepted in February 1933 Japan resigned from the League. The question of sanctions to compel Japan to respect the wishes of the League was never raised. The European Powers had enough problems of their own without attempting to apply sanctions to a strong naval power like Japan. The League had been successfully defied.

Two years then elapsed before the event which finally ended the authority of the League of Nations: the details of Italy's attack on Ethiopia are given on pages 33-5. In October 1935 the Council and the Assembly of the League condemned Italy and applied sanctions: imports from, and loans to, Italy were banned; some exports to Italy were also stopped, but these did not include oil, coal and steel. Although the United States and Germany were not subject to the League's ban it is possible that the sanctions applied would have been effective if Ethiopia could have held out longer but in May 1936 her resistance ended. Soon after sanctions were lifted. The damage had been done, however. Not only did Italy resign from the League in 1937, but the whole idea of sanctions was discredited, although these had been only partially applied.

Thereafter the League was a passive witness of events, taking no part in the crises over the Rhineland, Austria, Czechoslovakia and Poland. Its last spark of life was in December 1939 when Russia was expelled for her attack on Finland. The Assembly did not meet again, and the League of Nations was finally dissolved in 1946.

Social and economic activities

On the whole the League's social and economic activities were more successful than its operations in the political field. The Mandates Commission received annual reports from those Powers governing ex-German and ex-Turkish colonies, the Powers concerned undertaking specific obligations towards the inhabitants of these territories. The League supervised those states that had agreed to give rights to their racial, religious or linguistic minorities. Two world economic conferences were held by the League but with no results. More successful was the League's negotiation of loans for the reconstruction of the Austrian economy after the war. The Health Organisation dealt with outbreaks of cholera and typhus in war-devastated Europe, and collected information on a world scale on diseases, drugs and standards of nutrition. Work was done by other specialist agencies to stop the traffic in dangerous drugs and in slaves. Dr Nansen, the explorer, became the League's commissioner for refugees, and many thousands of prisoners of war were repatriated and stateless people given passports.

Reasons for failure of League

There are a number of reasons why the League of Nations as a political organisation failed to keep the peace. In some respects the structure and rules of the League were weak. For example, every state, however powerful or weak, had equal representation and voting rights, and the unanimity of members was required for most decisions. In addition, the League had no military power available and therefore lacked the backing of a compelling force. The United States never became a member of the League, and Russia only joined when the organisation was clearly in decline. Although the League had a worldwide membership, it appeared to be too much centred on Europe. In addition, since the Covenant was part of the treaties which ended the First World War, the League appeared to be an organisation of those who were victorious in this war.

The basic reason for the failure of the League, however, was that the members failed to support it. The League's founders underrated the power of nationalism. While they had the power, Italy, Japan and Germany refused to be bound by the limitations imposed on them by the Covenant of the League. Britain and France were the only major Powers left, and they were not enthusiastic supporters of the League. Cecil, one of the British founders of the League, has written: 'Influential officials in the Foreign Office did not conceal their suspicion of the League . . . The League was officially tolerated. It was never liked.'[1] As Thomson has said, the League 'existed to facilitate and to encourage cooperation among states. It could not make them cooperate if they did not want to.'[2]

United Nations Organisation

The United Nations Organisation was planned during the four years from 1941 to 1945. In June 1941 the nations fighting against Hitler stressed the need for future international cooperation to achieve world peace, and twenty-six nations signed the Washington Declaration of January 1942 which endorsed the Atlantic Charter and stressed the need for mutual cooperation in the war against the Axis Powers. In October 1943 representatives of Britain, China, the United States and Russia met in Moscow and decided to make detailed plans for an international organisation to replace the League of Nations. The plans that were drawn up during the next few months formed the basis for the discussions at the Dumbarton Oaks Conference in Washington in the late summer of 1944. The Great Powers agreed on the main structure of the organisation, although leaving undecided some questions such as voting procedures. These questions were then settled at the Yalta Conference in February 1945. It was also decided at Yalta that all countries that had declared war on the Axis by 1 March 1945 should be eligible to join.

The final conference which established the United Nations Organisation was held in San Francisco in April 1945. Fifty nations were present to draft the Charter of the Organisation, which set out its aims, rules and structure. The peoples of the United Nations, it said, were determined 'to save succeeding generations from the scourge of war which twice in our lifetime has brought untold sorrow to mankind', and aimed to uphold human rights, establish justice and promote social and economic progress. In June the Charter was signed, and on 24 October 1945 the United Nations Organisation formally came into being.

---

[1] Q. Cecil, *A Great Experiment.*   [2] D. Thomson, *Europe since Napoleon.*

Organs of the United Nations

There are six parts to the structure of the United Nations Organisation: the General Assembly, the Security Council, the Secretariat, the Economic and Social Council, the Trusteeship Council and the International Court of Justice. Basically the structure is the same as that of the League of Nations, but there are important differences in detail.

The General Assembly contains all the members of the United Nations. It meets in regular session every September, but holds emergency meetings, whenever required. Its function is to debate and pass resolutions on political problems. All states whatever their population have equal voting rights, but resolutions need not be passed unanimously as in the Assembly of the League. It was intended by the Great Powers in 1945 that all important questions would be discussed and settled in the Security Council, not the General Assembly. But the latter has gradually become more important, partly because of the stalemate in the Security Council which led to the Uniting for Peace resolution[1] in 1950, and partly because of the huge increase in the membership of the Assembly. There were fifty members in 1945 but 122 in

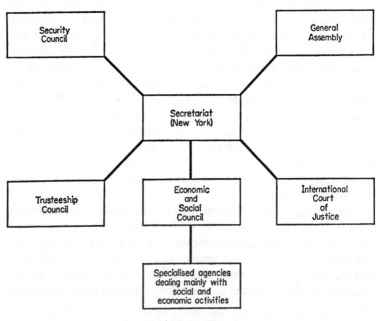

The United Nations Organisation

[1] See p. 540

December 1966.[1] This increase had made it more difficult for the Great Powers to control the voting in the General Assembly. Countries with a common ideological or geographical interest—the Communists, the Arabs, the Africans, the Asians, the Latin Americans, the West Europeans and North Americans—tend to make collective decisions on how to vote.

Up to 1965 the Security Council contained eleven members, five permanent (China, France, Russia, Britain and United States) and six non-permanent; these were elected by the General Assembly for two-year terms, three each year. Decisions required at least seven votes, including those of all five permanent members who therefore had a veto. Since August 1965 the number of non-permanent members has been increased to ten, and decisions now require nine votes. The Great Power right of veto means a reduction in the power of small countries compared to that they enjoyed in the League of Nations. But the innovation is a realistic step for powerful states cannot be forced to act in a way they do not like. It is probable that the United States and Russia would not have joined the United Nations if they had no right of veto.

The Security Council meets more frequently than the Assembly, and was originally intended to deal with emergencies as they occurred. The members of the United Nations agree to accept and carry out the decisions of the Security Council. It was assumed in the planning of the United Nations that the five permanent members would act together to crush any violation of the world's peace. The Cold War intervened, however, and Russia, nearly always in a minority on the Security Council, has used her veto frequently to prevent the Council from acting. The result has been that the Assembly has become more important than originally intended, and that members have sought security from regional organisations like NATO rather than from the United Nations. The Security Council set up a Military Staff Committee in 1946 to plan for any future collective military action by the United Nations, but it could not agree on the contributions member states should make to the policing force, and the Committee has not functioned since 1948.

The Secretariat operates from the United Nations headquarters in New York and has about 4,000 members. It is the civil service of the Organisation, and its functions include translation, drafting, minuting and other clerical tasks, the provision of information for delegates, and the execution of United Nations decisions. It is headed by the Secretary-General, the chief administrative officer of the Organisation,

---

[1] Absentees included Communist China, West and East Germany, Switzerland, North and South Vietnam, North and South Korea.

who is elected for five-year terms of office by the Security Council and the General Assembly. Four men have held the post so far: Trygve Lie of Norway (1946–53), Dag Hammarskjöld of Sweden (1953–61), U Thant of Burma (1961–71) and Kurt Waldheim of Austria (since 1971). The Secretary-General has greater power and responsibility than his predecessor in the League of Nations. Article 99 of the Charter says that he may 'bring to the attention of the Security Council any matter which in his opinion may threaten the maintenance of international peace and security'. The past twenty years have seen a considerable growth in the authority of the Secretary-General.

The Economic and Social Council (ECOSOC) contains twenty-seven members elected by the General Assembly (eighteen until August 1965) and meets twice a year. It is a coordinating body responsible for a number of commissions—on population, human rights, the status of women, narcotic drugs, regional economic development—and linking the activities of a whole range of specialised agencies. The International Labour Organisation is the sole survivor of the League of Nations agencies. It had flourished as the League declined, and has now widened its activities to include economic planning, full employment and social security. There are four financial agencies. For example, the International Monetary Fund was set up in 1946 to improve the stability of international currencies and make available currencies that were needed for trade. The International Development Corporation was set up in 1956 to stimulate private investment in underdeveloped countries.

The Food and Agriculture Organisation, from its headquarters in Rome, aims to improve food production and distribution by providing technical assistance and information. The World Health Organisation concentrates on the prevention and cure of widespread diseases. The International Atomic Energy Agency was set up in 1957 in Vienna to encourage research into the peaceful uses of atomic energy. The United Nations Educational, Scientific and Cultural Organisation (UNESCO) is responsible for a vast array of projects, but particularly in the field of literacy and popular education. The United Nations Children's Emergency Fund (UNICEF) originally dealt with children suffering from the effects of the Second World War, and since about 1950 has given assistance to governments for children's welfare.

The Trusteeship Council is another of the main organs of the United Nations. In 1945 it was responsible for eleven trust territories most of which had been mandates of the League of Nations. These territories gradually became independent so that by 1966 only three were left: New Guinea and Nauru (administered by Australia) and some Pacific

Islands (administered by the US). The Council has the right to submit questionnaires and receive reports from the administering powers, and to visit the territories concerned.

The International Court of Justice is almost identical to the Permanent Court of Justice established by the League of Nations. It meets at The Hague in the same buildings, and also contains fifteen judges. Decisions are by majority vote, and states are not obliged to accept the jurisdiction of the Court. On the whole it has been less busy than its predecessor. One of the most important cases brought before it concerned South Africa's administration of the ex-German colony of South-West Africa which was given to South Africa as a mandated territory after the First World War. In 1960 Ethiopia and Liberia, representing the African countries which dislike South Africa's racial policies, brought the case of that country's administration of its mandate before the court. In 1962 the Court decided it had the right to hear the case but four years later appeared to reverse this judgment. This and other cases support the view of those who hold that the Court is not suitable for arbitration in a changing world in that law tends to uphold the *status quo*.

1945 to 1978

Much of the first year of the United Nations history was taken up with discussion of rules of procedure, setting up committees and commissions, and deciding on the location of a permanent headquarters. The Organisation was first housed in a women's college in New York, then a converted skating rink on Long Island, before the present buildings were finished in 1952 on land in Manhattan bought by Rockefeller, the American millionaire. During 1946 Trygve Lie, the Foreign Minister of Norway, was elected Secretary-General, and the Security Council discussed its first complaints, against Russia over Persia (see p. 324), and against Britain over Greece (see p. 72).

The years from 1947 to 1950 marked the height of the Cold War, and Russia made frequent use of her veto in the Security Council. In 1947 Britain brought the problem of Palestine to the United Nations which decided on partition of that country between the Arabs and the Jews (see p. 282). In 1949 the Communists drove Chiang Kai-shek's Nationalist government from the mainland of China to the island of Formosa where it has since remained. Russia then proposed that a representative of Communist China should replace the representative of Nationalist China on the Security Council. This was defeated, however, and China continued to be represented by the government of

Formosa. In protest at the exclusion of Communist China, Russia then decided to boycott the Security Council and all other United Nations organs.

On 25 June 1950 the United Nations Commission in Korea informed the Security Council that South Korea had been invaded by North Korea (see pp. 451–4). The Council met immediately and, in the absence of Russia, passed a resolution calling for an end to the fighting and asking all members of the United Nations to help in this. Two days later the United States said that she had sent troops to help South Korea, and the United Nations recommended other members to do the same. Eventually sixteen countries contributed forces, and forty-five countries gave some sort of aid. The United States dominated, however, and the American General MacArthur commanded the United Nations forces.

In August 1950 Russia returned to the Security Council. It was realised that the UN was able to give aid to South Korea only because of the temporary absence of Russia, and consequently the West tried to devise an alternative procedure for the United Nations to act in future when the Security Council could not reach a decision because of the veto by one of the five permanent members. Therefore, in November 1950 the General Assembly passed the 'Uniting for Peace' resolution. This said that if the Security Council could not reach agreement to intervene in a crisis, then the General Assembly should meet in emergency session and could recommend the use of armed force if necessary. Russia regarded this resolution as illegal.

In July 1953 the signing of an armistice ended the fighting in Korea. The war had increased the importance of the General Assembly and the authority of the United Nations as a whole. It also increased the support for the American case against allowing Communist China to join the United Nations. Although Lie, the Secretary-General, had favoured giving the seat in the Security Council to Peking, he had also taken a strong line against North Korea's aggression. Consequently, he was now accused by the Russians of being the tool of the United States and Britain, and in February 1951 Russia vetoed the renomination of Lie, the Secretary-General. Since the United States said she would veto any other candidate, deadlock was reached, until it was agreed that Lie should 'continue in office' for another three years. Russia continued to boycott him, however, and in November 1952 Lie announced his intention to retire. Dag Hammarskjöld, the Director-General of the Swedish Foreign Ministry, was elected to succeed him in April 1953.

Apart from Indo-China, in which the United Nations was not involved, there were no major crises in the period from 1953 to 1956. Hammarskjöld was able to use these relatively quiet years to establish

The United Nations Security Council

United Nations soldiers inspect the ceasefire lines between the Turks and Greek Cypriots in Nicosia, Cyprus, 1974

confidence in himself. Nicholas has said of Trygve Lie that 'he used his political powers with more exuberance than discretion'.[1] Hammarskjöld, an inscrutable and rather remote man, whose career had been connected with both economics and foreign policy, believed that diplomacy should be carried out with the minimum of publicity. Meanwhile, the membership of the Organisation increased: between 1946 and 1954 it grew from fifty-two to sixty-three and in 1955 sixteen additional states joined. 'The United Nations was at this time essentially a conference organisation. It could debate, exhort, recommend, promote a modest level of good works in the social and economic fields, but it was not, politically speaking, an operational agency. Its presence was moral rather than visible.'[2] This was the position when the Suez affair increased the power and influence of the United Nations.

Up to October 1956 the United Nations had played little or no part in the Suez Canal problem (see chapter 7). On 13 October the Security Council's six unexceptionable principles for the settlement of the problem were vetoed by Russia. Then on 29 October Israel invaded Egypt. On the following day the United States proposed in the Security Council a resolution calling on all United Nations members to refrain from force. This, however, was vetoed by Britain and France, and the question was then transferred to the General Assembly under the Uniting for Peace resolution of 1950. On 2 November the General Assembly passed a resolution urging a ceasefire and the withdrawal of attacking forces. Despite this resolution, Britain and France invaded Egypt three days later, but said that they would withdraw if a United Nations force could keep the peace between the Arabs and Israelis and make satisfactory arrangements for the canal. Hammarskjöld then drew up a plan for a United Nations Emergency Force (UNEF), and on 15 November the first contingents arrived in Egypt. Eventually 5,000 men from ten neutral countries made up the force. The British, French and Israelis gradually left, and UNEF remained as a buffer between the Israelis and the Egyptians until 1967.

The Suez operation increased the stature of the United Nations. The Organisation had enabled the weight of international opinion to be concentrated on the four states concerned, and had shown that it had a role to play in pulling back nations from full-scale war. UNEF was a precedent for the Congo operation of 1960. The Suez crisis also led to an increase in the power of the Secretary-General. In an extremely delicate situation, Hammarskjöld had acted with careful but vigorous diplomacy. 'His initiative as well as his negotiating skill and administrative efficiency were vital to the functioning of the Organisation in this

[1] H. Nicholas, *The United Nations as a Political Institution*.
[2] H. Nicholas, *The Listener*, 11 Aug. 1966.

crisis.'[1] The Assembly showed great confidence in Hammarskjöld and the feeling developed that countries could 'leave it to Dag'.

The Hungarian revolution against Russian control occurred simultaneously with the Suez affair. On 28 October the West brought the question of the Russian threat to Hungarian independence before the Security Council, and on 2 November Nagy appealed for help from the United Nations. Two days later Russia vetoed the Security Council resolution demanding the immediate withdrawal of Russian forces from Hungary. The same resolution was passed by the Assembly, but nothing was done except that Russia was condemned for 'violation of the Charter'. The failure of the United Nations to influence Russia's actions towards Hungary showed that if a Great Power was determined to defy the United Nations and had the power to do it, the Organisation was helpless.

The period from 1957 to 1960 was again relatively quiet for the United Nations. Hammarskjöld was elected to a second term of office. In 1958 the Security Council sent an observation group to the Lebanon when that country complained of intervention in her internal affairs by Syria. In 1960 seventeen new countries, mainly African, joined the Organisation. It was in Africa that the next crisis involving the United Nations occurred.

At the end of June 1960 Belgium granted independence to the Congo (see p. 370). A few days later the Congolese army mutinied and Belgian troops returned. On 13 July Hammarskjöld took the initiative and requested a meeting of the Security Council which passed a resolution recommending the creation of a United Nations force. This was known from the French initials as ONUC, and it was intended to help in restoring order so that Belgian and any other foreign troops could leave. Four days later over 3,000 United Nations troops arrived, and the Belgians then gradually left. In August Lumumba, the Congolese Prime Minister, asked the United Nations force to attack the breakaway state of Katanga. Hammarskjöld would not recognise the right of Katanga to break away, but refused to allow the United Nations troops to attack the province. Lumumba then looked for help from other sources, including Russia.

At this point the United Nations action in the Congo lost the support of Russia whose representatives began a personal attack on the Secretary-General. In September Khrushchev himself visited New York and demanded the resignation of Hammarskjöld and his replacement by a three-man directorate—the 'troika' proposal.[2] But Hammarskjöld

---

[1] H. Nicholas, *The United Nations as a Political Institution.*

[2] 'There may be neutral nations but there are no neutral men' (Khrushchev).

refused to resign. 'By resigning', he said, 'I would . . . throw the Organisation to the winds. . . . It is not the Soviet Union or indeed any big Powers who need the United Nations for their protection; it is all the others.' The small countries supported Hammarskjöld and the Russians withdrew their demand.

Meanwhile the United Nations force grew to about 20,000 men, widely scattered and lacking good communications in this enormous country. In addition, about 500 experts were assembled to distribute food, look after sanitation and water, and provide general administration. Hammarskjöld believed that the Congo was a potential battleground between East and West as well as between different groups of Africans, and in February 1961 he was given greater authority by the United Nations to prevent an outbreak of civil war in the country. In July the Organisation helped to arrange a meeting between the various political leaders of the Congo, and in September 1961 United Nations forces entered Katanga. At this point the Secretary-General himself was in the Congo. While on his way to a meeting with Tshombe, the president of Katanga, his plane crashed and Hammarskjöld was killed. U Thant of Burma succeeded him as Secretary-General in November 1961. By the end of 1962 United Nations operations against Katanga were finally successful, and two years later the UN military forces finally left the Congo.

Since 1962 the United Nations has played an important role in a number of disputes. Indonesia's quarrel with the Netherlands in 1962 over West Irian is described on page 486. This was quickly settled by the UN, and the territory at issue was transferred to Indonesia. The recurrence of fighting between the Greek and Turkish communities of Cyprus at the end of 1963 (see p. 120) led to the creation of a United Nations force in 1964 to preserve the peace. In this it succeeded for ten years, but failed to prevent the 1974 crisis in the island.

In 1965 war broke out between India and Pakistan over Kashmir (see p. 405). The United Nations had been successful in its supervision of the cease fire in Kashmir since 1949, but was not successful in arranging a plebiscite in the territory. In 1965 Pakistan decided to use force to press her claim, and in September war broke out with India. The Security Council, in which the Great Powers were for once unanimous, called for a cease fire, sent missions to both countries, and thus brought the fighting to an end. The cease fire functioned successfully until the Tashkent Agreement was signed.

In the Middle East the United Nations Emergency Force maintained relative tranquility on the borders of Egypt and Israel for ten years. However, tension in the area gradually increased (see pp. 285–7) and in May 1967 Egypt asked for the UNEF to be withdrawn. U Thant had no legal grounds for refusing Nasser's request: Israel refused to allow UNEF to be stationed on her side of the border, and consequently the force was withdrawn. About two weeks later the Six Day War between the Israelis and the Arabs was fought. In July 1967 a small number of UN observers were stationed along the Suez Canal and on the Golan Heights, and in November the Security Council passed resolution 242 (see p. 288) on the Middle East. Dr Jarring was appointed as UN mediator to seek an agreement on the basis of the resolution between the parties concerned. However, the negotiations made little progress. In 1973 the Middle East again erupted in war, and again the United Nations arranged a cease fire with a United Nations Emergency Force deployed on the Egyptian–Israeli front.

The other important area of United Nations' concern was southern Africa. Following the breakdown of negotiations between Britain and the illegal minority government of Rhodesia, the United Nations imposed economic sanctions on Rhodesia (see p. 359). However, for a variety of reasons the UN has failed to solve the Rhodesian issue. Similarly the UN has on frequent occasions condemned South Africa both for its policy of apartheid and its government of South-West Africa, but these resolutions have proved ineffective.

The prestige and influence of the United Nations has declined since the mid-1960s despite, and in some cases because of, the Organisation's involvement in these disputes. In addition the UN has not been concerned to any great extent in a number of major international disputes: Berlin, Cuba, the Sino-Indian frontier, Czechoslovakia, Nigeria and Biafra, India and Pakistan in 1971, Angola and Mozambique, and Ethiopia. The absence of UN involvement in Vietnam, because neither North Vietnam nor Communist China were members, was particularly marked. The United Nations has failed to coordinate attempts to deal with international terrorism, especially the hijacking of civil aircraft. Important international negotiations over, for example, disarmament or the Middle East, have tended not to be held under UN auspices. Consequently, when the twenty-fifth anniversary of the United Nations was celebrated in 1970, the Organisation was widely criticised for its irrelevance and ineffectiveness.

A number of reasons are suggested for this ineffectiveness. Firstly, all international affairs must take account of the realities of rivalries between the Great Powers. The United Nations can, for the most part, only act when the interests of the Great Powers coincide or when they are not greatly concerned about an issue. Vietnam is an example of the inability of the United Nations to act when the interests of the super powers clash. Another source of weakness has been the absence until 1971 of Communist China, with nearly a quarter of the world's population. In that year Taiwan was expelled from the Security Council and its place taken by mainland China. Having corrected this weakness, however, there then followed a series of clashes between China and Russia. East and West Germany were only admitted to membership in 1973.

In 1964–65 the United Nations was almost bankrupt, for the Congo operation had been very expensive. Russia, the Communist states, Belgium, France and South Africa all said that the United Nations force there was not properly authorised, and they refused to pay their contribution to its cost. The dispute was basically about what the UN should or should not do, rather than who should pay for it.

Some commentators have considered that the permanent officials of the Organisation have failed to give constructive leadership. Hammarskjöld was an outstanding world figure whose reputation has grown with time. He was an initiator who deliberately and consistently stretched the authority of the Secretary-General and put strains on the United Nations. Nevertheless he made the post of Secretary-General an international power in its own right. His two successors have been quite different. U Thant (1961–71) was a patient, moderate and cautious conciliator, a non-political public servant. He helped the United Nations to survive after the Congo crisis, but perhaps at the cost of ineffectiveness. Waldheim, who has been Secretary-General since 1971, is again patient, industrious and diplomatic, but not an activist. Some have considered that more drive and the taking of initiatives are required if the United Nations is to be more vigorous and creative.

During the 1960s there was a widespread view that the United Nations should create a standing international police force, always ready to repel aggression and encourage peaceful settlements. However, no such force has been created. In addition it is suggested that the United Nations lacks the right machinery for dealing with disputes in their early stages before they become military conflicts. When the UN does prevent fighting, mere peacekeeping tends to 'freeze' a situation rather than solve it.

The rapid increase in membership during the 1960s and 1970s has changed the character of the General Assembly. By 1976 there were 147 member states. Each state, however small[1], has one vote and is given a world stage upon which to act. Many of the new countries regard the United Nations as a forum for conducting their struggle

[1] The Seychelles has a population of 60,000 and has one vote. China with a population of 900 million also has one vote.

against colonialism and racialism. The resolutions passed reflect this and are often unrealistic. The United Nations has been brought into disrepute and its weakness underlined when resolutions are passed which cannot be enforced. The support of some countries for the United Nations has become lukewarm as the Organisation is seen as a platform for propaganda.

However, the United Nations has clearly become an important and, compared with the League of Nations, relatively successful organisation. It has prevented minor disputes from becoming major ones; it has acted as a safety valve for the expression of views[1]; and it has become a forum for world opinion. The United Nations work in coordinating and directing social and economic activities has become increasingly important. The UN has no power in itself. It merely reflects the balance of forces among the member states, and its virtues and faults mirror those of the world. The United Nations, it has been said, is 'only as strong and as effective as its members wish it to be'.[2]

World development and population

In May 1966 U Thant, the Secretary-General of the United Nations, made the following two statements in a broadcast interview:

Since the end of the Second World War there is general agreement that the rich countries are getting richer and the poor countries are getting poorer. This widening gulf between the haves and the have-nots constitutes a more serious threat to international peace and security than any other rifts, either ideological or racial.

In my view, the tension generated by racial discrimination or disparity of treatment between the white and the black is much more explosive than the division of the world on ideological grounds.[3]

These two statements are connected in that, on the whole, the rich countries contain white people and the poor countries contain coloured people. The widening economic division could well lead to an explosive racial tension. In the developed countries of Europe and North America agriculture is efficient and industrial production is high. whereas in the underdeveloped countries of Asia, Africa and Latin America farming is often inefficient and production is low.

[1] Conor Cruise O'Brien, the Irish diplomat who served with the UN in the Congo, has said that United Nations debates are a ritual substitute for destructive human activities.

[2] Robert Rhodes James, *Britain's role in the United Nations,* United Nations Association of Great Britain and Northern Ireland, 1970.

[3] U Thant, *The Listener,* 12 May 1966.

This disparity in wealth between the developed and underdeveloped countries of the world became very obvious in the early 1960s. At the same time the remarkable rise in the world's population, particularly in the underdeveloped countries, also became clear. At the time of Christ the population of the world was probably about 250 million. This number had doubled to 500 million by the seventeenth century, and had doubled again by 1850. During the next seventy-five years the total reached 2,000 million. Fifty years later (1975) the population of the world was nearly 4,000 million, and it is estimated that it will reach 7,000 million by the end of the century. The more optimistic demographers consider that the population will stabilise at that figure, while the more pessimistic believe it will eventually rise to about 11,000 million.

The cause of this enormous rise in population during the twentieth century is the advance of medical science. Various drugs and insecticides have greatly reduced the traditional killing diseases such as malaria, typhus, typhoid, smallpox, and cholera. Consequently, life expectancy is increased. For example, an Indian girl born in 1947 could expect to live to the age of 27 years; for one born in 1971 life expectancy was 50 years. Therefore an average Indian woman would now live through the whole of her reproductive life span, and more of her children would survive the infections of childhood to grow up.

During the 1950s the United Nations did much to establish the nature and extent of the problem, and the specialised agencies gradually came to a clearer understanding of the implications of population increase for health, education, employment and agriculture. The combination in the underdeveloped countries of rapid population growth and slow economic growth widened the gulf between them and the developed countries. It was necessary, therefore, not only to develop the economies of many countries, but also to reduce their population growth. In 1966 the United Nations established its Fund for Population Activities, which provided financial aid and coordinated and supported the efforts of United Nations agencies in this area. In 1974 the World Population Conference convened by the United Nations in Bucharest drew attention to the urgency of the problem.

The United Nations designated the 1960s as its first Development Decade. Its object was to help a number of countries to achieve self-sustaining growth. Agricultural production was increased by a variety of methods: by the provision of better seeds, more fertilisers, cheap pesticides, improved stock and mechanical tools; by drainage and irrigation and the conservation of water; by providing storage and marketing facilities, better communications and cheap credit; by the

Population and income per person: 1967, 1975-76

The following table gives the population and the annual income per person for thirty-five countries. Of the seven countries with over 100 million population in 1978, four are Asian and one is Latin American. Notice, on the other hand (a) the positions of these five countries in the income table, and (b) the number of European and North American countries with an annual income per person in 1975 of over £750. Notice, too, those countries where the population and income have grown most rapidly.

Country	Population in millions		Country	Annual average income per person in £ sterling[1]	
	1967	1978		1967	1975
China	716	933	Kuwait	1175	5713
India	514	638	USA	1078	3147
USSR	233	262	Sweden	729	3780
USA	200	219	Switzerland	725	3910
Pakistan	120	77	Canada	692	3161
Bangladesh (Part of Pakistan in 1967)	—	85	Australia	618	3139
Indonesia	105	145	France	550	2855
Japan	98	115	Great Britain	536	1832
Brazil	85	115	Netherlands	450	2745
Great Britain	54	56	Israel	382	1616
France	48	53	Puerto Rico	350	1606
Mexico	40	67	USSR	318	993[2]
Spain	32	37	Romania	254	N.A.
Egypt	31	40	Japan	236	1928
Burma	25	32	Argentina	232	927
Iran	23	35	South Africa	210	585
Argentina	22	26	Spain	189	1325
Ethiopia	22	30	Chile	161	312
Canada	20	24	Mexico	154	595
Romania	19	22	Cuba	129	480[2]
South Africa	18	28	Iraq	86	579
Congo (Zaire)	16	28	Algeria	82	396[2]
Algeria	13	19	Brazil	79	547
Netherlands	12	14	Iran	75	800
Australia	12	14	Ghana	74	231
Chile	9	11	Egypt	54	156
Iraq	8	12	China	34	N.A.
Ghana	8	11	Congo	30	63
Sweden	8	8	Pakistan	27	87
Cuba	8	10	Bangladesh	—	54[2]
Switzerland	6	6	Indonesia	25	100
Malawi	4	6	Burma	23	45
Puerto Rico	2·6	3·3	Laos	21	N.A.
Laos	2·6	3·5	India	18	68
Israel	2·4	3·7	Malawi	17	62
Kuwait	0·5	1·2	Ethiopia	15	45

Sources: *Population and Income per person*, 1967; *Monthly Bulletin of Statistics, United Nations.*

[1] Figures for annual income per person are based on a standard exchange rate of $2 to £1. They are not inflation adjusted and do not take into account the falling value of sterling.

[2] These figures are calculated on a different basis from the rest and are not strictly comparable.

reform of land ownership and by voluntary cooperative ventures. This 'green revolution' in many areas of the world seemed promising. Development projects in agriculture and industry require money. Much of the capital came from the underdeveloped countries themselves, but they also received considerable aid, both financial and technical, from the richer nations, either directly or through international agencies. During the second UN Development Decade in the 1970s there was greater concentration on smaller projects, rural rather than urban development, on agriculture and small industry rather than heavy industry. The United Nations Conference on Trade and Development (UNCTAD), with its headquarters in Geneva, was established in 1964 to discuss ways in which trade between the rich and poor countries of the world can be increased. The three meetings held in 1968 (Delhi), 1972 (Santiago) and 1976 (Nairobi) unfortunately failed to reach any real agreement on the issues involved.

The difficulties facing the underdeveloped countries were considerable: if modern machinery was introduced, it often resulted in unemployment; if production was increased, prices paid for their goods could go down; when the price of oil was quadrupled in 1973, poor countries had less money with which to buy other goods. Ghana in 1972 had to export five tons of cocoa to pay for one tractor; this was five times more than in 1960. Interest on earlier borrowing could take up a substantial part of new aid. Indeed there was criticism of the usefulness of aid from outside: some felt that it inculcated too great a spirit of dependence. There seemed to be no correlation between the flow of economic aid and success in economic development. One of the main problems, however, was the continued population growth which swept away all the benefits of development. There was a terrifying increase in big urban conglomerations which produced enormous strains on transport, housing, education and all the usual urban social services.

It was some time before the governments of some countries considered that a reduction in population growth was necessary. Roman Catholic countries in Europe and Latin America disliked most methods of limiting family size; some countries in Africa and South America considered that they were underpopulated. In all the underdeveloped countries, however, it is not easy to find methods of birth control which are cheap, acceptable and easily understood by uneducated people. Although family planning is spreading, the view gained ground in the 1970s that the most effective way to reduce population growth is to change the social conditions which influence the choice parents make about family size. The discouragement of early marriage, the availability of health services, the standard of living, the provision for old age, social status and the size of family, all these are important factors determining the number of children born. One particularly important need is to raise the social, economic and political status of women in the underdeveloped countries, and therefore traditional masculine attitudes and influence must be changed. The education of women is an essential element in solving the population problem. According to this argument, these factors will set the trend towards smaller families which family planning will only accelerate.

In the 1960s population growth was seen as a cause of poverty. In the 1970s population growth was also seen as a consequence of poverty. Clearly, positive development and control of population growth must go together. In 1972 another element in the situation was given prominence when the United Nations Conference on the Human Environment was held in Stockholm. Extravagant consumption by the developed countries meant that various world resources were rapidly becoming depleted. It was widely felt that if present trends in population growth, industrialisation, pollution, food production and resource depletion continued, limits to growth on this planet will be reached within one hundred years. Although technology could increase resources, the time needed to move from theoretical possibilities to practical realisation on a world scale would be insufficient.

Bibliography

General

BOYD, A. *Atlas of World Affairs*, 6th edn, Methuen, 1970.

CALVOCORESSI, P. *World Politics since 1945*, Longman, 1977.

CROWLEY, D. W. *Background to Current Affairs*, new edn, Macmillan, 1970.

ELLIOTT, F. *A Dictionary of Politics*, Penguin, 1973.

GILBERT, M. *Recent History, Atlas*, Weidenfeld & Nicolson, 1966.

HENDERSON, J. L. ed. *Since 1945: Aspects of Contemporary World History*, Methuen, 1966.

HOWARTH, T. *Twentieth-Century History: The World Since 1900*, Longman, 1979.

THOMSON, D. *World History from 1914 to 1968*, new edn, Opus Books, Oxford University Press, 1969.

WATT, D. C., F. SPENCER and N. BROWN. *History of the World in the Twentieth Century*, Hodder & Stoughton, 1967.

——*History of the 20th Century* (Many eminent authors. Originally published in weekly parts. Profusely illustrated), Phoebus, 1976.

Europe

BULLOCK, A. *Hitler, a Study in Tyranny*, Odhams Press, 1952, Penguin, 1969.

COBBAN, A. *History of Modern France, Vol. 3, 1871–1962*, Penguin, 1970.

CRAWLEY, A. *De Gaulle*, Collins, 1969.

CROUZET, M. *The European Renaissance since 1945*, Thames and Hudson, 1970.

EYCK, E. *A History of the Weimar Republic*, Harvard University Press, 1964.

FALLS, C. *The First World War*, Longman, 1960.

GRUNBERGER, R. *Germany, 1918–1945*, Batsford, 1964.

HIBBERT, C. *Benito Mussolini*, Longman, 1962, Penguin, 1975.

JAMES, L., ed. *Europe* (Vol. 1 of *World Affairs since 1939*), Blackwell, 1965.

KINROSS, LORD. *Atatürk: The rebirth of a Nation*, Weidenfeld & Nicolson, 1964.

LAQUEUR, W. *Europe since Hitler*, Penguin, 1972.

MOWAT, R. C. *Ruin and Resurgence, 1939–65*, Blandford Press, 1966.

POUNDS, N. J. G. and R. C. KINGSBURY. *Atlas of European Affairs*, Methuen, 1964.

ROBERTS, J. M. *Europe, 1880–1945*, new edn, Longman, 1972.

SHIRER, W. *The Rise and Fall of the Third Reich*, Secker & Warburg, 1960, Pan Books, 1968.

SMITH, MACK. *Italy*, University of Michigan Press.

TAYLOR, A. J. P. *The First World War: an Illustrated History*, Hamish Hamilton, 1963, Penguin, 1970.

——*Origins of the Second World War*, Hamish Hamilton, 1963, Penguin.

——*Struggle for mastery in Europe, 1848–1918*, new edn, Oxford University Press, 1971.

THOMAS, H. *The Spanish Civil War*, Eyre & Spottiswoode, 1961, 2nd edn, Hamish Hamilton, 1977.

THOMSON, D. *Europe since Napoleon*, Longman, 1963, Penguin, 1970.

THOMSON, D., ed. *Era of Violence 1898–1945* (New Cambridge Modern History), Cambridge University Press, 1960.

WESTERN, J. R. *End of European Primacy, 1871–1945*, Blandford Press, 1965.

WISKEMANN, E. *Europe of the Dictators 1919–45*, Collins, 1967, Fontana (Harvester Press), 1970.

Russia

CHARQUES, R. *The Twilight of Imperial Russia*, new edn, Galaxy Books, Oxford University Press (N.Y.), 1974.

CRANKSHAW, E. *Khrushchev*, Collins, 1966, new edn, Sphere, 1968.

DEUTSCHER, I. *Stalin*, new edn, Penguin, 1970.

DJILAS, M. *Conversations with Stalin*, Hart-Davis, 1962, Penguin, 1969.

FRANKLAND, M. *Khrushchev*, Penguin, 1966.

KOCHAN, L. *Making of Modern Russia*, Cape, 1962, Penguin, 1970.

MOOREHEAD, A. *The Russian Revolution*, Collins, 1958.

REED, J. *Ten Days That Shook the World*, Penguin, 1966.

SHUB, D. *Lenin*, Penguin, 1966.

SMITH, H. *The Russians*, Sphere, 1976.

WESTWOOD, J. N. *Russia, 1917–1964*, Batsford, 1966.

United States

FAULKNER, H. U. *From Versailles to the New Deal*, Oxford University Press.

FREIDEL, F. *America in the Twentieth Century*, new edn, Knopf, 1965.

NEVINS, A. and H. S. COMMAGER. *The Story of a Free People*, Oxford University Press.

NYE, R. B. and J. E. MORPURGO. *History of the United States*, Vol. 2, Penguin, 1965.

Great Britain

ENSOR, R. C. K. *England, 1870–1914*, Oxford University Press, 1936.

JENNINGS, I. *The British Commonwealth of Nations*, Hutchinson, 1961.

MARWICK, A. *The Explosion of British Society, 1914–70*, Macmillan, 1971.

MEDLICOTT, W. N. *Contemporary England, 1914–1964*, Longman, 1967.

MONK, L. A. *Britain, 1945–1970*, G. Bell and Sons, 1976.

MOWAT, C. L. *Britain between the wars, 1918–1940*, Methuen (University publications), 1968.

PELLING, H. *Modern Britain, 1885–1955*, Nelson, 1960.

POLLARD, S. *Development of the British economy 1914–50*, Arnold, 1962.

TAYLOR, A. J. P. *English History 1914–1945*, Oxford University Press, 1965, Penguin, 1970.

THOMSON, D. *England in the Twentieth Century*, Cape, 1964, Penguin, 1970.

North Africa and the Middle East

AMIN, S. *The Maghreb in the Modern World*, Penguin, 1970.

BULLARD, R. *The Middle East*, Royal Institute of International Affairs, Oxford University Press, 1958.

CHILDERS, E. *Common Sense about the Arab World*, Gollancz, 1960.

GABRIELI, F. *The Arab Revival*, Thames & Hudson, 1961.

KINGSBURY, R. C. and N. J. G. POUNDS. *An Atlas of Middle Eastern Affairs*, Methuen, 1966.

KIRK, G. E. *Short History of the Middle East*, Methuen, 1964.

LITTLE, T. *Egypt*, Benn, 1958.

LONGRIGG, S. H. *Iraq, 1900–1950*, International Book Centre (U.S.) 1968.

MANSFIELD, P. *Nasser*, Methuen, 1969.

Africa

BOYD, A. and P. VAN RENSBURG. *An Atlas of African Affairs*, Methuen, 1965.

CROWDER, M. *The Story of Nigeria*, 3rd edn, Faber, 1973.

FAGE, J. D. *An Introduction to the History of West Africa*, Cambridge University Press, 1962.

HEPPLE, A. *Verwoerd*, Penguin, 1967.

HODDER, B. W. *Africa Today*, Methuen, 1978.

INGHAM, K. *A History of East Africa*, Longman, 1965.

KEPPEL-JONES, A. *South Africa*, 5th edn, Hutchinson, 1975.

OLIVER, R. and J. D. FAGE. *A Short History of Africa*, Penguin, 1962.

PERHAM, M. *The Colonial Reckoning*, Fontana, 1963.

SAMPSON, A. *Common Sense about Africa*, Gollancz, 1960.

SLADE, R. *The Belgian Congo*, Oxford University Press, 1961.

WILLS, A. J. *An introduction to the History of Central Africa*, 3rd edn, Oxford University Press, 1974.

India and Pakistan

BRECHER, M. *Nehru*, Oxford University Press, 1959.

PANIKKAR, K. M. *Common Sense about India*, Gollancz, 1960.

SPEAR, P. *A History of India, Vol. 2*, Penguin, 1970.

STEPHENS, I. *Pakistan*, 3rd edn, Benn, 1967.

TINKER, H. *India and Pakistan*, Praeger, 1962.

China

FITZGERALD, C. P. *The Birth of Communist China*, Penguin, 1970.

PURCELL, V. *China*, Benn, 1962.

SCHRAM, S. *Mao Tse-tung*, Penguin, 1970.

WILSON, D. *A Quarter of Mankind*, Weidenfeld & Nicolson, 1966.

WINT, GUY. *Common Sense about China*, Macmillan, 1960.

Japan

BEASLEY, W. G. *The Modern History of Japan*, 2nd edn, Weidenfeld & Nicolson, 1973.

STORRY, R. *A History of Modern Japan*, Cassell, 1962, Penguin, 1969.

South-East Asia

BUTWELL, R. *South East Asia Today and Tomorrow*, Praeger, 1965.

HALL, D. G. E. *A History of South-East Asia*, Macmillan, 1964.

MILLS, L. A. *Malaya*, new edn, Greenwood Press (U.S.), 1973.

PURCELL, V. *Revolution in South-East Asia*, Thames & Hudson, 1962.
SHAW, A. G. L. *The Story of Australia*, Faber, 1962.

Latin America

GUNTHER, J. *Inside South America*, Hamish Hamilton, 1967.
HUMPHREYS, R. A. *Evolution of Modern Latin America*, Oxford University Press.
PENDLE, G. *A History of Latin America*, Penguin, 1963.
Volumes on each country produced by the Royal Institute of International Affairs, Oxford University Press.

World Organisations

CECIL, Q. *A Great Experiment*, Cape.
NICHOLAS, H. G. *The United Nations as a Political Institution*, 5th edn, Oxford University Press, 1976.
WALTERS, F. P. *History of the League of Nations*, Oxford University Press. 1960.

Index